The Three Dangerous Magi

Osho, Gurdjieff, Crowley

p.65 book suggestions

The Three Dangerous Magi

Osho, Gurdjieff, Crowley

P.T. Mistlberger

BOOKS

Winchester, UK
Washington, USA

First published by O-Books, 2010
O Books is an imprint of John Hunt Publishing Ltd., The Bothy, Deershot Lodge, Park Lane, Ropley,
Hants, SO24 0BE, UK
office1@o-books.net
www.o-books.com

Distribution in:

UK and Europe
Orca Book Services Ltd

Home trade orders
tradeorders@orcabookservices.co.uk
Tel: 01235 465521 Fax: 01235 465555

Export orders
exportorders@orcabookservices.co.uk
Tel: 01235 465516 or 01235 465517
Fax: 01235 465555

USA and Canada
NBN
custserv@nbnbooks.com
Tel: 1 800 462 6420 Fax: 1 800 338 4550

Australia and New Zealand
Brumby Books
sales@brumbybooks.com.au
Tel: 61 3 9761 5535 Fax: 61 3 9761 7095

Far East (offices in Singapore, Thailand,
Hong Kong, Taiwan)
Pansing Distribution Pte Ltd
kemal@pansing.com
Tel: 65 6319 9939 Fax: 65 6462 5761

South Africa
Stephan Phillips (pty) Ltd
Email: orders@stephanphillips.com
Tel: 27 21 4489839 Telefax: 27 21 4479879

Text copyright P.T. Mistlberger 2009

ISBN: 978 1 84694 435 2

Design: Tom Davies

A CIP catalogue record for this book is
available from the British Library.

Printed in the UK by CPI Antony Rowe

Disclaimer: A number of meditations and related psycho-spiritual exercises are offered in Part
Four of this book. None of these are intended to replace the services of qualified medical or
mental health professionals. Always consult first a physician or mental health practitioner if
you have doubt about your ability to undertake active or passive meditations and related
psycho-spiritual exercises.

We operates a distinctive and ethical publishing philosophy in all
areas of its business, from its global network of authors to
production and worldwide distribution.

CONTENTS

Part Four: The Inner Work

Part Five: Historical Influences

Dedication: For Madame DeJean.

Osho, G.I. Gurdjieff and Aleister Crowley are 'dangerous Magi' because their teachings were provocative and confrontational and require discerning interpretation. As metaphysical guru-figures, all three were capable of damaging their followers as well as providing them with profound spiritual insights. P.T. Mistlberger has personal experiential knowledge of the three esoteric paths pioneered by these Magi. In this excellent book he explains why all three have contributed to the perennial wisdom tradition despite the controversy associated with their teachings. The Three Dangerous Magi is thoroughly researched and accessibly written and I recommend it unreservedly. **Nevill Drury**, Ph.D, author of *The New Age: the History of a Movement* and *Stealing Fire from Heaven: the Rise of Modern Western Magic*

An astoundingly comprehensive analysis of three of the most influential spiritual leaders of the last 100 years. It not only compares and contrasts their personalities and practices, but puts them into the context of their predecessors, milieus, and eras, resulting in astute and literate realizations that make this book both intriguing and a delight, transcending the individuals and leaving true insight into the ultimate meaning of their work. **Donald Michael Kraig**, author of *Modern Magick*

If you want a wonderfully readable book about the sensational lives of these charismatic teachers, then this is clearly the book for you. But there is far more here than simple biography. There is history and social background, psychology, religion and mysticism. It is an in-depth study of what it means to be a seeker on a spiritual path, the conflicts that this entails in respect of society and everyday life. And, from the complementary viewpoint, it examines how some teachers defy accepted conventions of morality and conduct in order to break down the conditioning which obstructs progress. It also explodes the myth that enlightenment somehow catapults one to superhuman status. Gaining Self-knowledge, and having the skill and wish to pass this on to others, unfortunately does not always mean that one is no longer prone to human failings! If you are a seeker of truth, you will inevitably be interested in all of these aspects. With the background of his own search with Osho and other teachers, his meticulously researched investigation and his intelligent appraisal of both facts and myth, P.T. Mistlberger presents a veritable feast for your enjoyment and instruction! **Dennis Waite**, author of *The Book of One* and *Back to the Truth*

Mistlberger's work is a fascinating (and at times painfully candid) examination of three of the twentieth century's most under-appreciated, maligned, and misunderstood holy men. **Lon Milo DuQuette**, author of *The Magick of Aleister Crowley*

Mistlberger has written a VERY interesting book on three extraordinary people most people would not think to link up. He has certainly done his homework. **John Anthony West**, author of *Serpent in the Sky: The High Wisdom of Ancient Egypt.*

The Three Dangerous Magi is a must read/devour for those who have a penchant for Crazy Wisdom's top unframers! Mistlberger unravels and makes the three rascal awakeners come alive in all their unconventional glory. This book itself is dangerous for those who find shelter in the known, the safe and the road well worn. It is also a call for safety in the unknowable. Be ready to be stirred to the core, turned upside down and fit together again in new ways. **Satyen Raja**, author of *Living Ecstasy* and founder of WarriorSage Trainings.

An accurate, insightful, and fascinating discussion of three of the strangest spiritual teachers ever to have come to the public eye. **Richard Smoley**, author of *The Dice Game of Shiva* and *Inner Christianity*

A fascinating book about three hugely intriguing, larger-than-life, spiritual rascals. **Timothy Freke**, author of *The Jesus Mysteries* and *How Long Is Now?*

G.I. Gurdjieff

Magi: *Plural of Magus: one who is wise in the things of God and serves the divine.*
Porphyry, *On Abstinence*

The Holy Longing

Tell a wise person, or else keep silent,
because the mass man will mock it right away.
I praise what is truly alive,
what longs to be burned to death.

In the calm water of the love-nights,
where you were begotten, and where you have begotten,
a strange feeling comes over you,
when you see the silent candle burning.

Now you are no longer caught
in the obsession with darkness,
and a desire for higher love-making
sweeps you upward.

Distance does not make you falter.
Now, arriving in magic, flying,
and finally, insane for the light,
you are the butterfly and you are gone.

And so long as you haven't experienced
this: to die and so to grow,
you are only a troubled guest
on the dark Earth.
Goethe

Preface

I should, off the top, state the extent of my direct personal experience with the ideas and work of the three subjects of this book. I discovered Aleister Crowley in 1975 as a high school senior while exploring Nietzsche, Jung, and Castaneda. This first connection was primarily through his Thoth Tarot deck. I was soon trying to make sense of his magnum opus, *Book Four: Magick* and his *777: And Other Qabalistic Writings*. Most of his other significant works, including his massive autobiography, *Confessions*, fell into my hands over the years, as well most of the significant biographies about him by such authors as John Symonds, Gerald Suster, Israel Regardie, Lawrence Sutin, Martin Booth, and Richard Kaczynski. I've retained a lifelong interest in his life and work and have practiced some of his teachings and the teachings of mystery schools he was connected to such as the Hermetic Order of the Golden Dawn and the Ordo Templi Orientis.

Back in the early 1980s I was involved in the Gurdjieff Work, participating in a group that was run by a student of John G. Bennett (himself one of Gurdjieff's more prominent pupils). After a year or so in the Work I felt inclined to explore some of the alternative therapies that had grown out of the human potential movement of the 1960s, Primal and Reichian therapy in particular. After going through the work of the Primal/Reichian therapy community I then connected with Osho's work (at the time, Bhagwan Shree Rajneesh). In early 1983 I was initiated as a *sannyasin* (his term for his disciples) and subsequently spent close to a decade involved in Osho's teachings and worldwide community in North America, India, and

1

Nepal. Shortly after Osho's death in 1990 I drifted away from his movement, and explored other traditions such as Tibetan and Zen Buddhism, Advaita Vedanta, and the Western esoteric tradition.

I endeavor to approach the work of the three seminal spiritual figures highlighted in this book not with mere journalistic cynicism, nor with the wide-eyed credulity of one who has not explored a number of paths, but from the vantage point of a seeker of truth and practitioner of transformational work. Because of that, in many ways I believe the most important section of this book is Part Four in which some practical exercises are offered. Ultimately, for one interested in deep self-inquiry it's necessary to go beyond being a mere observer of, or commentator on, the lives of extraordinary spiritual figures, and taste directly what it was they were pointing toward. For it is all too often—especially in the case of highly charismatic men like Osho, Gurdjieff, and Crowley and their dramatic lives—that we lose sight of the contents for the cover.

Much of this book is written in an impartial fashion and most of it I believe accurately reported, as best as my research allowed for. In places I delve into both interpretation and judgment of the lives and work of these teachers and of certain people associated with them. This is acting in the spirit of the very same self-confirmation of truths that these teachers (for the most part) strongly encouraged in others. As Gurdjieff had posted at his center in Fontainebleau,

If you have not by nature a critical mind your staying here is useless.

There could perhaps be no better summation of the core truth that all three stood for—the need for independent self-verification of what one learns—and in particular when learning from a powerful and notorious magus.

Introduction

Osho, Gurdjieff, Crowley. Three names that strike fear into the hearts of many, in particular those with only a tepid interest or involvement in matters of personal transformation, spirituality and the perennial wisdom traditions. And for good reason: these were men who didn't just upset apple carts and disturb sacred cows, who didn't just challenge spiritual status quos and offend accepted canons of belief, they rather demolished them wholesale. They were the three chief *enfant terrible* of 20th century spirituality, for the prime reason that they were not only concerned with the uncompromised truth needed to bring about inner transformation, they were also deeply provocative personalities who behaved in ways that seemed at times impossible to reconcile with the wise men they otherwise presented themselves as. They were thoroughly uncontrollable and the very definition of the spiritual *avant-garde*. On the way, each was branded as sinister, even evil, by many who could not understand them, and each was a prime example of the antinomian crazy-wisdom master who defies moral codes en route to establishing and enacting their spiritual work. All were thoroughly dangerous to established religious doctrine—two in particular (Osho and Crowley) accordingly paid a heavy price. And contrary to views put forth by some of their most devoted followers, none was exactly a 'perfect master of the universe.' Each had significant human limitations—at times crudely apparent as in the case of Crowley and Gurdjieff, at other times far more subtle and complex as in the case of Osho.

Crowley's closest followers believe that he was the Prophet of the

3

new Aeon, and some even used the term 'Crowleyanity' to describe the religion he founded. Some of Gurdjieff's disciples have viewed him as a 'solar god,' or an emissary from a secret global brotherhood from a higher world, a man who came with an enormously important mission to link Eastern wisdom with Western civilization, and to re-introduce an ancient spiritual system to humanity. Osho was seen in a similar grandiose light by many—a good example being one Osho disciple I knew, an intelligent and mature adult and a professional therapist, who once stated to me with all sincerity and solemnity that Osho was 'the Lord of the World' and that it was 'extraordinary' that he had even been born. (Osho's famous epitaph at his ashram in Pune, 'Never born, never died, just visited this Earth from 1931-1990' represents as well as anything does the special light many of his followers see him in). Others found 'evidence' that Osho was the world teacher predicted in Nostradamus's quatrains. More prosaically, he was described by the *Sunday Mid-Day* in India as one of the ten people, along with Gandhi, Nehru, and Buddha, who have changed India. Both Osho and Crowley were listed by the *Sunday Times* in London as one of the '1,000 Makers of the 20th Century'.

At the more hysterical other end of the spectrum, Crowley is notorious for drawing to him numerous popular condemnations from some of the English intelligentsia of his time, but particularly from the English press—the most widely known being the headline printed in 1924 by the *John Bull* tabloid, 'The Wickedest Man in the World', or at another time, 'The Man We'd Love to Hang'. Another lurid headline, 'The King of Depravity', hints at the real reason for these attacks on his character, which almost always were triggered by rumor connected to his 'sex magick' practices. Gurdjieff was accused of being a Russian spy, confidence trickster, hypnotist, or black magician by more than one, and was compared by some to Rasputin as well as to Crowley himself. D.H. Lawrence famously disparaged Gurdjieff, referring to his center outside of Paris as a place where people were 'playing a sickly stunt'. Osho, especially following the debacle at his commune in Oregon in the mid-1980s, was severely maligned and expelled from twenty-one countries during his infamous 'world tour' in 1986. The attorney general of Oregon at the time, Dave Frohnmayer, later described Osho as 'evil' with a 'sinister light emanating from his eyes'. Some Christian fundamentalists saw him as an antichrist figure. In Oregon during the years in which he'd located his commune there, certain locals issued a T-shirt that depicted Osho's face in the middle of rifle cross hairs, along with such slogans as 'bag a Bhagwan' (his name then being Bhagwan Shree Rajneesh) or 'better dead than red' (a reference to the red clothes worn by Osho's followers at that time).

For the record, I don't subscribe to any of these dramatic, polarized views—the messianic or the diabolic. Gurus who are thought to be some sort of emissary from the higher worlds, or even 'lord' of the world, or the next messiah, or *the* messiah, etc., are a dime a dozen. Spiritual or religious leaders who get mired in scandal and are subsequently accused of being corrupt, depraved, or evil, are equally common. Were this to be a book about such gurus it would have to be a ten volume encyclopedia. No, the public notoriety of Osho, Gurdjieff, and Crowley does not constitute their uniqueness. However, for different reasons that I will lay out in this book, I believe that these three men in one respect *were* the three most significant (and coincidentally amongst the most notorious) spiritual teachers of the turbulent 20th century. I also maintain that all three were largely unheralded and even now, long after their deaths are still generally unrecognized or deeply misunderstood. That is perhaps in keeping with the nature of the times in which they lived, the powerfully wild 20th century, in which human civilization underwent giant spasms of growth as it desperately attempted (with questionable success) to throw off the shackles of centuries of deep unconsciousness amongst extraordinary natural disasters, famine and disease, environmental and political upheaval, overpopulation, unprecedented revolutions, and the most terrible wars in history.

Aside from a critical yet sympathetic look into the lives and teachings of these three men, the main thesis of this book is that all three were crucial links in the transmission of a timeless knowledge, what Aldous Huxley called the 'perennial wisdom'. The order I discuss the three in, in Parts I and II of this book—Crowley first, followed by Gurdjieff and then Osho—is intentional and shows what I believe to be the order of the transmission of their work as it reflects part of the cutting edge evolution of spirituality. That is, Crowley, although a contemporary of Gurdjieff, represented a transition point from archaic forms of esoteric knowledge—in particular the traditions of the legendary Merlin and of the Renaissance magus, best embodied in the important 15th-16th century German occultist Cornelius Agrippa and in the mysterious 16th century figure of Queen Elizabeth I's court advisor John Dee—into the form of the 20th century mystic, someone shaped by both the old ways of high magic and the modern reality of science. One of the names he had for his work was 'scientific illuminism'; he recognized the need to modernize the old occult ways, and this he largely accomplished. Like all true rascal sages he was a universal figure also embracing Eastern pathways (in particular, Raja Yoga and Taoism). Significantly, he strove to integrate the sexual force into his teachings, in so doing anticipating the general movement beyond the repressive sexual protocols of pre-1960s society.

Gurdjieff was of Crowley's generation—while the latter was being initiated by Samuel Liddell 'MacGregor' Mathers as an adept in the Hermetic Order of the Golden Dawn in 1900, and producing his key *The Book of the Law* in 1904, the former was wandering throughout central Asia and Tibet, staying variously in esoteric communities when he wasn't busy taking Tibetan wives or getting accidentally shot. Gurdjieff was unknown in the West until around 1912 when he appeared in Moscow. Both men, however, produced much of their most important work in the 1920s-30s, in their middle age. Gurdjieff's work follows a different line from Crowley's and at first appearances seems incompatible with Crowley's Thelemic teachings. But what he held in common with Crowley was his interest in *modernizing*. Gurdjieff had a fascination with the United States, once announcing in his old age, 'bravo to America!' He made a point of traveling to the U.S. a number of times, in an age before the commercial airplane, an era when it took about a week to sail from Europe to America—about thirty times longer than today's average jet flight across the Atlantic. Gurdjieff's intense interest in the evolution of the human race was matched by Crowley's passion in providing a teaching that would usher in a new Aeon. I believe that both men—along with other seminal figures like William James, Freud, Jung, Reich, Rudolf Steiner and Ernest Holmes—were instrumental in catalyzing a new 'octave' (to use Gurdjieff's term) of spiritual development. But where Crowley and Gurdjieff stand out is in their sheer charisma, in the conflicting forces of light and dark that clearly moved through them. They were nothing less than alchemy in action. Peter Ouspensky, the well known Russian philosopher and writer, spent several years as a close student of Gurdjieff. Eventually, he left his master for complex reasons but which ultimately had to do with his conclusion that Gurdjieff's ideas, which he considered to be of the highest value, needed to be separated from Gurdjieff the man. He said, 'in most people, a crowd of selves exist inside of them. In Gurdjieff's case, there are only two. However, one is very good, the other is very bad.' This notion of opposites, of black and white duality, and in particular of the tendency of modern men and women to be inwardly divided, is one of the key themes of this book.

Osho is of a different era, born over half a century after Crowley and Gurdjieff, and as such he may seem at first glance an unlikely character to include in this study. But he in fact had a great deal in common with both (and in particular with Crowley—despite the fact that he spoke frequently about Gurdjieff, and about Crowley, not at all). Osho, along with Nisargadatta Maharaj, Chogyam Trungpa, Shunryu Suzuki, Swami Muktananda, J. Krishnamurti, Harilal Poonja, and the strange anti-guru guru U.G. Krishnamurti, was one of the chief Eastern gurus guiding seekers from the so-called Baby Boomer generation. He was a right fit for many seekers of that generation, being an excellent representative of the rebellious mindset that typified so many hippies and Boomers. Crucially, he also integrated many of the modern ideas of Western psychotherapy that emerged during the incredible cultural and psycho-spiritual ferment of the 1960s. For example, he had a strong grasp of the concept of *repression,* and more importantly, how to work with it. He was above all concerned with the balanced development of the person, and the importance of addressing all dimensions of a human. He was a guru of the integral path. And it was in this regard precisely that he was, knowingly or not, carrying on the seminal work of Crowley and Gurdjieff.

Of course, philosophers and psychologists have long taught about the integral path—Sri Aurobindo and the more modern day example of Ken Wilber being two excellent representatives—but few have attempted to both teach it and live it out within themselves and the drama of their lives. Osho, Gurdjieff, and Crowley were all exceptionally vivid examples of this.

The issue of reconciling the light and the dark, and in particular how it plays out via the polarities of self and selflessness, is a topic we will turn to in this book but at this point one thing can be stated with confidence: amongst 20th century 'rascal sages' few had the intensity of contrast—arguably, of excellent balance—between light and dark qualities as did Osho, Gurdjieff, and Crowley. It is not hard to find at least some gurus in whom pure light clearly predominates with scarcely a trace of shadow—Ramana Maharshi perhaps being a demonstration of that—or in whom darkness reigns utterly (their number is legion, but two good 20th century examples being the madmen Reverend Jim Jones and Soko Asahara). However, there are few in whom the balance of light and dark—the basic material of what the depth psychologist C.G. Jung called the *mysterium coniunctionis*—are in such vivid and fascinating interplay as in the three subjects of this book. And because the 20th century, more than any known century in history was also an extraordinarily vivid amalgam of light and dark, of heroism and scandal, of adventure and bravery and disease and death, of good and evil, conscious and unconscious, creation and destruction and the attempt to see beyond both—it renders Osho, Gurdjieff, and Crowley as perfectly representative: heralds of the coming Zeitgeist and the dominant Magi of a dark and dangerous time.

(Note to the reader: In this book are occasional references to Crowley, Gurdjieff, and Osho as 'Magi' or as the singular 'magus.' Crowley had claimed a level ('Ipsissimus') that in his system is beyond 'Magus.' In using the terms Magi and magus in this book I am referring to the more generalized usage of the word, denoting an advanced sage of perennial wisdom).

Part One

Biographical Outlines

Chapter 1
Aleister Crowley: Wicked Magus

Crowley: Pronounced with a ~~crow so it rhymes with holy:~~ Edward Alexander Crowley, b. 1875 d. 1947, known as Aleister Crowley, known also as Sir Aleister Crowley, Saint Aleister Crowley (of the Gnostic Catholic Church), Frater Perdurabo, Frater Ou Mh, To Mega Therion, Count McGregor, Count Vladimir Svareff, Chao Khan, Mahatma Guru Sri Paramahansa Shivaji, Baphomet, and Ipsissimus; obviously, a case of the ontological fidgets—couldn't make up his mind who he really was; chiefly known as The Beast 666 or The Great Beast; friends and disciples celebrated his funeral with a Black Mass: or so the newspapers said. Actually it was a Gnostic Catholic Mass (even John Symonds, Crowley's most hostile biographer, admits that at most it could be called a Grey Mass, not a Black Mass—observe the racist and Christian-chauvinist implications in this terminology), but it was certainly not an orthodox R.C. or Anglican mass, I mean, cripes, the priestess took off her clothes in one part of it, buck naked, and they call that a Mass, gloriosky!

Robert Anton Wilson

I expect men to be rational, courageous, and to applaud initiative, though an elementary reading of history tells one, with appalling reiteration, how every pioneer has been persecuted, whether it's Galileo, Harvey, Gaugin, or Shelley; there is a universal outcry against any attempt to destroy the superstitions which hamper or foster the progress which helps the development of the race. Why should I escape the excom-

munication of Darwin, or the ostracism of Swinburne? As a matter of fact, I am consoled in my moments of weakness and depression by the knowledge that I am so bitterly abused and hated. It proves to me that my work, whether mistaken or not, is at least worthwhile.[1]

King Lamus, from Crowley's novel, *Diary of a Drug Fiend*

If you look up Aleister Crowley on YouTube, that early 21st century bastion of free entertainment that perhaps as much as anything reveals the average person's view of things, you receive a revealing glimpse into a public perception of a man that after all these years still remains murky and full of innuendo. Crowley inspired rumor (even if most of it turned out to be false); everything about him, at casual glance, suggested something sinister. But for one who bothers to look further into his life, it soon becomes clear that beyond all the bluster was a remarkable man of extraordinary depth, and one equally difficult to define.

A certain litmus test I have long had for metaphysically inclined people is their opinion of Crowley. He's the kind of guy who tends to frighten off anyone who still harbors significant religious conditioning or sexual inhibitions. But he also baffles the dabblers because once you actually read his writings you see his intellectual depth and breadth of learning. Crowley perhaps more than any other tends to provoke opinions from people who have not actually read even a page of his writings. It's something I've noted for several decades.

Of the three subjects of this book, Aleister Crowley leaves both Gurdjieff and Osho far behind when it comes to the sheer number of biographies and commentaries written on his life in the latter decade of the 20th century. That is a telling feature, one that speaks to a particular quality of Crowley, that may roughly be characterized as—perversely as this may sound to some—his very *humanity*.

Of the three, Crowley registers the most readily apparent human flaws and this, along with his obvious brilliance, sincerity, and accomplishments as a seeker, researcher, practitioner and writer of higher truths, makes him a compelling figure. He holds within him all human dimensions—or most, at any rate—and while Gurdjieff and Osho lived extraordinary lives and may have discoursed at length about both the multidimensional nature and limitations of the human being, it was Crowley who *thoroughly* lived it all, at times scaling sublime heights (literally), more often stumbling about in sheer human muck. Also, it is very clear that of the three, Crowley was by far the most isolated. Not that he did not have many people in his life—he did—but he did not garner anywhere near the support for his ideas and work that Gurdjieff, and certainly Osho, did. He had a far greater tendency to alienate people. This greater degree of isolation renders him a more tragic and human figure. Despite the outlandishness of much of his life, he is, quite simply, easier to relate to and ultimately a more accessible figure than Gurdjieff or Osho.

Like many 'spiritual bad boys', Crowley inspired deeply polarized opinions of what exactly he was. Witness these wildly disparate views of Crowley, first this from Israel Regardie:

He was one of the greatest mystics of all time, although a very complicated and controversial person.[2]

And this from Robert Anton Wilson:

Aleister Crowley was, in my opinion, one of the most original and important thinkers of this era—right up there with such titans as Einstein and Joyce. Indeed, what Einstein did for physics and Joyce for the novel (and Picasso for painting, and Pound for poetry, and Wright for architecture), Crowley did for the mystic tradition. He swept aside all 19th Century barnacles and incrustations, redefined every concept, and created something that is totally contemporary with our existence as 20th Century persons.[3]

And now this from Christopher Isherwood:

The truly awful thing about Crowley is that one suspects that he didn't believe in anything. Even his wickedness. Perhaps the only thing that wasn't fake was his addiction to heroin and cocaine.[4]

Or this from Maurice Richardson (in his review of Crowley's autobiography):

His great gas-bag of an ego which, like a true mystic he thought he had annihilated, must have been a fearful inconvenience.[5]

I will say it at the outset: I feign no disinterested balance of these polarized views of the man. I am more in Regardie's and Wilson's camp than in Isherwood's or Richardson's. That said, Crowley had a dark side, or more accurately, a *dangerous* side. To associate closely with him was to risk getting burnt. This was certainly true of Gurdjieff and Osho as well, but more so in Crowley's case.

As a thinker and writer of mystical matters, Robert Anton Wilson was right: he was brilliant, and, to boot, *prolific*. Osho never wrote; all his books are transcriptions of his talks. Gurdjieff wrote four books, one of which was very long. But Crowley's literary output was immense, and in many fields. He authored over twenty major works on esoteric matters alone, in addition to other works of fiction and poetry, and a massive autobiography. He was one of the most literate mystics ever. (To be honest I marvel how writers did it back in those days, pounding it all out on cumbersome typewriters, or in Gurdjieff's case, scrawling it all out with pencils in cheap notebooks. I am old enough to have written on typewriters, before the word processing era, and I remember the sheer frustration of dealing with typographical errors. The 'back key' back then consisted of white-out and a Bic pen).

Before covering Crowley's biographical story it will be helpful to clarify a few popular ideas about him that unfairly contribute toward his notoriety. Amongst the most common public negative views of him was that he was a Satanist, a black magician, childsacrificer, bisexual, drug addict, and even—hold for it—a cannibal (something like an esoteric version of Hannibal Lector, I imagine). To cut to the chase, two of those accusations are correct—he was openly bisexual and he did end up addicted to heroin for prolonged periods of time. The other charges are all false as any small effort at researching will quickly attest to.[6] Owing to considerations of space I will address only one of them here, the issue of Satanism.

Crowley was not a Satanist, plain and simple. The belief that he was is probably the most stubborn myth about him, and one that is still put forth to this day in poorly researched press articles or hysterical website commentaries written by people who have clearly not actually read him. Crowley rejected Christianity wholesale as well as the deities of its underworld. He denied the existence of the Christian devil altogether. The confusion in this area seems to stem in part from the loose connection between Crowley and such figures as Gerald Gardiner (the 20th century 'father' of modern Witchcraft— which also has nothing to do with Satanism), and Anton Sandor LeVay, the 20th century founder of the Church of Satan and author of *The Satanic Bible*. LeVay never met Crowley but he did begin studying some of his work in the early 1950s, a few years after Crowley had died; although he concluded that Crowley's teachings were 'too complicated'. LeVay also had an interest in the 16th century Angel magic of John Dee ('Enochian magic'), as did Crowley, but that's about as far as their connection went.

However, the most common reasons for linking Crowley to Satanism consist in his calling himself 'The Beast 666' as well as his inclusion of the pagan deity Baphomet in his Gnostic Mass. As to the first: Crowley's mother took to calling him the 'Beast' in his childhood, as he was a rambunctious and rebellious child (and she a committed Christian fundamentalist). Crowley enjoyed the designation and later added the 'number of the Beast'—666—from the Book of Revelation. In further research into Qabalistic gematria (number mysticism) he discovered that the number was connected to the symbolism of the Sun and the heart *chakra* of Hindu yoga. He also identified it as a powerful symbol for the 'new Aeon' that he taught we are now in (see Chapter 4 for more on this). But above and beyond the esoteric symbolism, it seems clear that Crowley simply delighted in disturbing others, particularly in the area of religious conditioning. He was, to use modern jargon, a 'button-pusher,' and even though this trait brought him much grief it also brought him publicity, which was something he clearly sought for much of his life. If he can be accused of anything it would be strutting like a peacock. He was no 'devil-worshipper' though. His intellectual sophistication and grasp of perennial wisdom traditions was so far beyond that of the people who would have liked to have burned him at the stake that he often did not bother to defend himself at all.

His usage of the deity Baphomet was as an alchemical symbol for the union of opposites. He had some classic Gnostic views, such as that the serpent of the Book of Genesis was an important esoteric symbol that had been misrepresented. There is a clear parallel for all that in the Eastern yogic teachings of *kundalini*, the so-called 'serpent force' that is thought to be the latent spiritual energy within a human being, symbolic of an evolutionary potential, but wholly devoid of anything 'bad.'

Early Years

Aleister Crowley was born Edward Alexander Crowley on October 12th, 1875, at 30 Clarendon Square, Leamington Spa, England. Via the magic of Google Earth I punch this address into the search field, and the planet below me starts moving. A few seconds later, I am zoomed right to Crowley's birthplace, hovering a few hundred feet above the home he grew up in. The cyber version of astral traveling may not satisfy in some ways, but the mere fact that Crowley's exact birthplace and time is available is a testament to the precision of the man—he kept copious notes and diaries wherever he went.

Crowley was raised in a family of Plymouth Brethren, an evangelical Christian sect originating in Ireland in the late 1820s. Any form of evangelicalism begins first and foremost with the importance of personal conversion, or what is traditionally called being 'born again.' The 'born again' experience has an element of mysticism in it, in that it generally involves a type of altered state of consciousness in some ways similar to certain effects brought about by Eastern Yoga austerities, particularly where there is devotion to a deity (like Krishna) or a living guru. This type of experience, if not backed by significant understanding of subtle states of consciousness, is ripe material for the basis of fundamentalism and even extremism.

Crowley, raised in an evangelical household, would have been exposed from the beginning to the tight controls of such a philosophy, a condition that usually compels children in such a family to do one of two things: either become very much like their parents, or rebel and become very much *unlike* them. Crowley's path was apparently clear from a young age, so much so that, as mentioned, his mother took to calling him the 'Beast', an appellation with sinister overtones that stuck with him the rest of his life. Crowley enjoyed the appellation and it became part of a life-long pattern of what appeared to be deliberately cultivated notoriety. As one of his close students, Grady McMurtry, once said,

> There is no sense in trying to whitewash Crowley's reputation. Aleister spent most of his life systematically blackening it.[7]

Looking at the sweep of Crowley's life, it can be seen that one clear characteristic of his was a certain aloofness, a tendency to avoid sustained intimacy—in essence, to never let anyone get too close to him. He refers to the possible roots of this (in 3rd person format, when at the time he was known as Alick) in a passage in his *Confessions*:

> On February 29th, 1880, Alick was taken to see the dead body of his sister, Grace Mary Elizabeth, who had only lived five hours. The incident made a curious impression on him. He did not see

why he should be disturbed so uselessly. He couldn't do any good; the child was dead; it was none of his business. This attitude continued through his life. He has never attended any funeral but that of his father, which he did not mind doing, as he felt himself to be the real centre of interest. But when others have died, though in two cases at least his heart was torn as if by a wild beast, and his life actually blighted for months and years by the catastrophe, he has always turned away from the necrological facts and the customary orgies. It may be that he has a deep-seated innate conviction that the connection of a person with his body is purely symbolic. But there is also the feeling that the fact of death destroys all possible interest; the disaster is irreparable, it should be forgotten as soon as possible.[8]

To remember such an event from four years of age is significant. The passage interests because it reveals a core trait of Crowley the man, that being a guarded heart. (A parallel event of striking similarity can be found from Osho's early years when at five years of age he too witnessed the death of a younger sister; he later lost his grandfather, with whom he had been very close, at the age of seven, and made a subsequent decision to never be so attached to anyone again). Crowley also had a discordant relationship with his mother, referring to her once as a 'brainless bigot'. His mother was a rigid Christian fundamentalist and by all accounts Crowley resented the ways she tried to control him.

The religious conditions of Crowley's early upbringing were strict—for example, he was only allowed to play with children from the same Plymouth Brethren sect as he. But overall he reports no serious traumas in his boyhood years, regarding it as a conventionally happy time. However, his father, a preacher whom he idolized, died when he was only eleven. His father had also been very successful in the brewery business and Crowley ended up inheriting a sizeable fortune in his university years. He would live off this money until it ran out in his thirties, using much of it for travel and the self-publishing of much of his prolific writings.

Crowley and Poetry

Crowley attended Trinity College, Cambridge, for three years, stopping just short of acquiring his degree, accompanied by his usual dismissive attitude—he wrote that appending 'B.A.' after his name would have been a 'waste of ink'. He was clear from that young age that he had no interest in an academic career. He was, as he put it, 'white hot for three things—poetry, magic, and mountain climbing'.[9] His poetry remained a recurrent and significant work in his life; he considered himself a real poet and he indeed wrote reams of it. Two of his poems are included in the Oxford Book of English Mystical Verse.

In his comprehensive biography of Crowley, *Do What Thou Wilt*, Lawrence Sutin writes:

Crowley was a prolific poet who displayed, intermittently, a pure and genuine talent. This was acknowledged by otherwise unadmiring contemporaries as G. K. Chesterton and William Butler Yeats (for whose famous poem 'The Second Coming', with its 'rough beast, its hour come round at last,' Crowley may have been a source of influence).[10]

Intrigued by Sutin's remark I looked again at Yeats' famous poem. It is one of those poems immediately recognizable by most—especially for a few lines in it that have been quoted probably as much as anything written by Shakespeare ('things fall apart, the centre cannot hold', and 'the best lack all conviction, while the worst are full of passionate intensity').

The Second Coming

Turning and turning in the widening gyre
The falcon cannot hear the falconer;
Things fall apart; the centre cannot hold;

Mere anarchy is loosed upon the world,
The blood-dimmed tide is loosed, and everywhere
The ceremony of innocence is drowned;
The best lack all conviction, while the worst
Are full of passionate intensity.

Surely some revelation is at hand;
Surely the Second Coming is at hand.
The Second Coming! Hardly are those words out
When a vast image out of Spiritus Mund
Troubles my sight: a waste of desert sand;
A shape with lion body and the head of a man,
A gaze blank and pitiless as the sun,
Is moving its slow thighs, while all about it
Wind shadows of the indignant desert birds.
The darkness drops again but now I know
That twenty centuries of stony sleep
Were vexed to nightmare by a rocking cradle,
And what rough beast, its hour come round at last,
Slouches towards Bethlehem to be born?

Contemplating this poem, a couple of things seem reasonably clear: 1. Yeats was a masterful poet, and 2. It is doubtful that he was referring to Aleister Crowley at any point or that Crowley had any influence on this poem. The latter conclusion I arrive at in part because the poem was written in 1919, on the heels of the greatest calamity civilization had known up to that point (the Great War). Such an event would provide more than sufficient influence.

In addition, there were Yeats' known views of Crowley. Both men had been initiates of the famous esoteric fellowship known as the Hermetic Order of the Golden Dawn. Yeats, born in 1865, was ten years older than Crowley. He joined the Golden Dawn in 1890, about eight years before Crowley. When Crowley joined he passed rapidly through the early grades and soon was applying for more elevated initiations. Yeats, who had a personal dislike of Crowley that was based on several issues—Crowley's sexual adventures being one, his precocious experimentation with specific elements of ritual magic, aided by esteemed Golden Dawn member Allan Bennett, being another—was part of the body of senior members who turned Crowley down.

Yeats was an authentic seeker of spiritual truths. In addition to his study and practice of the Western esoteric tradition, he was also a student of Eastern traditions. He once wrote,

> The mystical life is the centre of all that I do and all that I think and all that I write.[11]

Unfortunately, this sort of interest is often disparaged by the intelligentsia. The Anglo-American writer W.H. Auden once dismissed Yeats' mystical studies as the 'deplorable spectacle of a grown man occupied with the mumbo-jumbo of magic and the nonsense of India'. These short-sighted views are not uncommon amongst the literati. Many artists and writers, driven by vanity, seem more concerned with expression, form, and appearance, than they are with substance, and as a result many back away from the deeper spiritual inquiry (or vehemently condemn it—D.H. Lawrence's derogatory remarks on Gurdjieff and his spiritual school being a prime example). The artist is often very close to the path of inner transformation (if not already walking it) but commonly settles for the slighter slope of working with symbols (words, images) rather than treading the steeper path of intentional ego-deconstruction and self-realization. And therein lays a fundamental difference between an artist, poet, or visionary, and a mystic, philosopher, and bringer of a new spiritual paradigm. The former transmits his ideas about transformation via artistic imagery and symbol, and more or less leaves it at that. The latter attempts to go further by providing a practical means for people to actively participate in their personal transformation.

Yeats was a mystic and a teacher of inner transformation, but he was first and foremost a poet and artist. Crowley was a poet and artist (and other things), but he was first and foremost a mystic and teacher of inner transformation as well as a bringer of a new spiritual paradigm. So while I suspect that Yeats' famous poem bears no influence by Crowley, I also note that Crowley, at the end of the day, arguably did much more for the inner illumination of the human being than Yeats did.

Crowley had some sort of weird rivalry with Yeats when it came to poetry—as mentioned, he was prolific and fancied himself a significant poet. While some of Crowley's poetry seems competent and interesting and even on occasion striking, there seems little question that in this realm he was not up to the genius of Yeats. But when it came to mystical, spiritual, and philosophic prose, the reverse was true. Yeats did not come close to Crowley's sweeping depth of insight and comprehensive wisdom.

Crowley was also a strong chess player and at one point, in his early twenties, briefly considered dedicating himself wholly to the game—only to soon find out that that idea was severely misguided. (See Appendix II for more on Crowley and chess.) But his primary passion in his early adult years, outside of poetry, chess and the occult, was mountain climbing. While climbing in the Alps when he was twenty-three, Crowley met Julian Baker, a chemist who was associated with occult circles in London. Baker connected Crowley to the Hermetic Order of the Golden Dawn and at this point the young man's life began to take off.

The Golden Dawn

The Hermetic Order of the Golden Dawn was founded in 1888 in London by three Freemasons, William Woodman, William Wynn Wescott, and Samuel Liddell 'MacGregor' Mathers. All three men were also members of the Societia Rosicruciana in Anglia (Rosicrucian Society of England), an esoteric brotherhood of Masonic Christians founded between 1865 and 1867 in England.

This fraternity claimed a direct descent from the original Rosicrucian Society allegedly begun in the early 1400s in Germany by the legendary figure Christian Rosenkreuz. The earlier roots of Rosicrucianism are regarded mostly as mythic or allegorical, but the basic idea, that of esoteric Christianity, has very old roots going back to the original Gnostics around the time of Christ. The legend of Rosenkreuz took hold in the early 1600s when a number of documents appeared, heralding the supposed existence of a secret brotherhood of enlightened individuals who were preparing to transform the social and political landscape of Europe (an idea now known by some historians as the 'Rosicrucian Enlightenment').[12]

The Rosicrucian Society used a grade structure that derived originally from the Order of the Golden and Rosy Cross, an esoteric group founded in Germany in the 1750s. The essential grade structure looked like this:

First Order
Grade I: Zelator
Grade II: Theoricus
Grade III: Philosophus
Grade IV: Practicus
Second Order
Grade V: Adeptus Minor
Grade VI: Adeptus Major
Grade VII: Adeptus Exemptus
Third Order
Grade VIII: Magister Templi
Grade IX: Magus

This basic grade system with slight modifications was used by the Golden Dawn and has been highly influential in the many Orders found within the Western esoteric tradition since the late 19th century.

What differentiated the Golden Dawn from Freemasonry and the

Rosicrucian Society of that time was allowing non-Christians, non-Freemasons, and women to join. These were all significant steps, but the breaking of the gender barrier was unquestionably the most notable. At its height in the late 1890s the Golden Dawn had upwards of 35% female membership, remarkable for an esoteric fellowship of those times.

Crowley joined the Order in 1898, taking the Latin name *Perdurabo* ('I shall endure to the end.') Being exceptionally bright and eager, he advanced rapidly through the early grade levels. At that time he formed a close friendship with another member of the Order, Allan Bennett, who also became Crowley's private mentor in the magical arts (Bennett being an 'elder brother' in the Order, although he was only three years older than Crowley). By that time, however, problems were brewing in the fellowship, mostly centered on the leadership of 'MacGregor' Mathers. Mathers had made the questionable decision to move to Paris with his wife and live there, while still attempting to retain authority over the London temple. During those times communication was slow and cumbersome— there were no airplanes, teleconferences, or text messaging. This decline in communication between the leader and his Order had predictable consequences, and by 1900 a revolt had occurred. Crowley got caught in the middle of it, and soon had his own falling out with Mathers, concluding that his mentor was no longer in contact with the invisible spiritual guidance— the 'Secret Chiefs'— that he'd always claimed were the authority and force behind the Golden Dawn.

Just prior to this, in 1899, Crowley purchased a large manor named Boleskine house on the shores of Loch Ness in Scotland (known now as the home of the legendary 'Loch Ness monster'). He acquired this house for a very specific reason, intending to carry out a six-month retreat and detailed exercise in ceremonial magic called the Abramelin Operation. The specifics of this process can be found in the book, *The Sacred Magic of Abramelin the Mage*, a manuscript that allegedly hails from the year 1458 (although some argue it was written not before the 17th century), by 'Abraham the Jew' and purporting to describe the esoteric practices of an Egyptian sage named Abramelin. The book is considered a classic of modern occultism and was originally published in English in the late 19th century.

Crowley moved into this house and began the Abramelin Operation, but was unable to complete it as he was called away to London by Mathers on some urgent business. The collapse of the Golden Dawn that followed shortly thereafter ultimately led to it fracturing into several offshoot societies. Crowley decided to leave the whole scene and in a significant way too—he decided to travel the world. Having the means to do so (his inheritance was far from being exhausted at that time) he indulged his passions of mountain climbing in Mexico and the Himalayas. Prior to leaving England, Crowley had become known for some of his mountaineering feats, even setting some records in the Alps and in Wales. Stephenson in *The Legend of Aleister Crowley* remarks, 'A sinister interpretation was placed even upon these feats of agility and daring. Aleister Crowley was climbing unclimbable places. Obviously by supernatural aid.' (One is reminded there of the comical legend about Madame Blavatsky as reported in John Symonds' biography of her, that she once 'levitated her entire 17 stone body up to the ceiling toward a chandelier to light a cigarette'.)

Crowley, ever the adventurer, even tried big game hunting in southern Asia. In Ceylon (present day Sri Lanka) he met up with his old friend Allan Bennett, who'd left the Golden Dawn and ordained as one of the first Western Buddhist monks, and studied yoga and Buddhism with him there. This association with Bennett was very important to Crowley, not just because Bennett was one of his very few life-long friends, but also because yogic practices and disciplines became an important part of his personal practice and later spiritual system that he evolved.

The Book of the Law and the Kangchenjunga Disaster

The next—and what would prove to be crucial—pivotal event of Crowley's life was a strange experience he had in Cairo, Egypt in 1904, where, aided by his young wife at the time (Rose Kelly) he received a highly unconventional teaching allegedly originating from an entity named 'Aiwass'. Crowley over the years variously saw Aiwass as a distinct entity, or as his Holy Guardian Angel or higher self. The teaching was eventually put into book form and called *Liber AL vel Legis*, or *The Book of the Law*. It professed to be a radical new spiritual dispensation for humanity, propounding a philosophy of life based very much on honoring the individual—in effect, an opposite approach to the self-sacrificing ideals of Christian doctrine. (See Chapter 4 for more on this book.)

Crowley was actually not greatly inspired by the small book at that time, and being only twenty-eight years old then, he temporarily discarded it and plunged back into more physical, testosterone-based pursuits—in this case, putting together an expedition to climb Kangchenjunga in the Himalayas, the third highest mountain on Earth and, as of that time, unconquered. Up to that point Crowley already had extensive mountaineering experience but this was his first time leading an expedition. The climb proved disastrous, with Crowley's autocratic approach as a leader causing dissention amongst his team and an open revolt in which the climbing team fractured. While attempting to turn back and descend from a route deemed too dangerous by them, a group of the 'mutineers' slipped, triggering a small avalanche which killed four of them. Crowley—far away and falling asleep in his tent at the time—failed to assist in recovery of the bodies, apparently deeming it a futile waste of energy in a very precarious condition, and for that his reputation in the mountain climbing community was irreparably damaged. The Kangchenjunga fiasco proved to be his last climb.

Crowley devotes several pages in his *Confessions* to this climb, explaining his vantage point. In the following passage he describes his reaction (and his apparent prediction of the death of one of them) to the fateful decision of several climbers to descend before reaching the top and then his decision to not immediately seek to rescue them:

> To my horror, I found that Pache wanted to go down with them. The blackguards had not even had the decency to bring up his valise. I implored him to wait till the morning...I explained the situation, but I suppose he could not believe that I was telling the literal truth when I said that Guillarmod was at the best of times a dangerous imbecile on mountains, and that now he had developed into a dangerous maniac. I shook hands with him with a breaking heart, for I had got very fond of the man, and my last words were, 'Don't go: I shall never see you again. You'll be a dead man in ten minutes.' I had miscalculated once more; a quarter of an hour later he was still alive.
>
> Less than half an hour later, Reymond and I heard frantic cries. No words could be distinguished, but the voices were those of Tartarin and Righi. Reymond proposed going to the rescue at once, but it was now nearly dark and there was nobody to send, owing to Righi's having stripped us of men. There was, furthermore, no indication as to why they were yelling. They had been yelling all day. Reymond had not yet taken his boots off. He said he would go and see if he could see what the matter was and call me if my assistance were required. He went off and did not return or call. So I went to sleep and rose the next morning at earliest dawn and went to investigate.[13]

This passage, and the section of his autobiography where he describes the disastrous expedition is revealing of elements of Crowley's character in many ways. Crowley's biographer, Richard Kaczynski, sums up the enigma of the event:

Whether he bitterly felt the mutineers got what they deserved, or whether he didn't realize exactly what happened until morning, is unclear from Crowley's account.[14]

However, Lawrence Sutin, drawing from letters written by Crowley and published in major newspapers of that time, presents a less flattering view of Crowley's thoughts during the crisis as he remained in his tent preparing to sleep:

> As it was I could do nothing more than send out Reymond on the forlorn hope. Not that I was over-anxious in the circumstances to render help. A mountain 'accident' of this sort is one of the things for which I have no sympathy whatsoever.

Sutin concludes,

> Crowley was fond of invoking the standards of honor of the English gentleman. His behavior on this night flaunted those standards.[15]

There was a war of words between Crowley and some of his co-climbers in the press following the debacle and Crowley appears to have decisively lost the battle for public opinion. This sort of thing was typical in his life—my own suspicion about it is that it revealed something in Crowley's core-beliefs about himself, namely, that he ultimately has to do everything on his own—to struggle and endure (which is after all what *Perdurabo*, his Golden Dawn initiate name meant). Such a core-belief tends to lead to involvement in situations in which one generally ends up isolated and unsupported. Partly as a defense it then becomes necessary to pinpoint the failures of others (rather than face the core-belief within oneself). This seems to bear out in Crowley's concluding words about the matter:

I have very much minimized what I felt. If ever I am summoned before Almighty God to give an account of my deeds, my one great shame will be that I did not shoot down these mutinous dogs who murdered Pache and my porters.[16]

The irony of Crowley citing the Judeo-Christian God in his words has been noted by more than one. But more to the point we see his strident defense of the deeply vulnerable state he must have been in, recognizing that his leadership had been rejected and he isolated and effectively abandoned (all at the rarefied height of 21,000 feet). It was to prove to be a powerful metaphor for the overall sweep of his life.

The Equinox, The Order of the Silver Star, and the Ordo Tempi Orientis

In 1906 Crowley, along with his wife Rose and their infant daughter, journeyed across China. On this trip he claimed to have completed the Abramelin Operation inwardly in his mind via visualization. He also conferred upon himself the next level grade initiation, that of Exempt Adept. It's possible that at this point in his life a difficult element of Crowley's ego began to manifest, as any sort of self-initiation, or independent conferral upon oneself of an exalted grade is deeply problematic. The very basis of initiation is to be *confirmed* in some way by another person—symbolically, by a consciousness that is outside of one's ego-system. It may seem paradoxical, as the foundation of the mystical quest is to realize one's innate, sovereign association with the divine within—and yet the reason seekers have historically been mentored by elders within their spiritual community is precisely so that ego-delusion, and in particular grandiosity, can be averted. That noted, Crowley's sheer tenacity and focus in performing complex visualization practices while walking through China with his wife and baby is also indicative of that single-minded intensity and energy level that was so representative of him.

After departing China, Crowley decided on a different travel route than his wife. He would head back to England via the Pacific Ocean and North America, she (along with their little girl) via India and Europe. Not long after this the girl died after contracting typhoid and Rose descended into drink. Crowley himself also fell ill at that time; it was clearly a major period of deconstruction for him. He blamed the event on the 'gods' being unhappy with him for not following his higher destiny, but another way of looking at it is that he was confronting the outer adversity—what in the East would be called 'karmic seeds ripening'—that ultimately was a reflection of his stubborn character structure. At any rate, the next year, in 1907, along with George Cecil Jones, a former elder brother from the Golden Dawn, he set up his own mystery school called the Argenteum Astrum (Silver Star) or as it is traditionally designated, the A.˙.A.˙. An important phase of writing work began for him shortly after as he launched a bi-annual publication called *The Equinox*, ten editions of which were put out between 1909 and 1913.

Some of the teachings of the celebrated 16th century Elizabethan magus John Dee, who amongst other things was Queen Elizabeth I's court astrologer, were incorporated into the curriculum of the Golden Dawn—specifically, Dee's work with Edward Kelly in contacting and communicating with angels via a complex system of glyphs and letters that have come to be known as Enochian magick. Crowley, trained in the Golden Dawn, was exposed to this system and took a particular interest in it. In late 1909 he went, along with his student Victor Neuberg (who was also a lover) to Algeria, where together they took desert treks and practiced Enochian magick, using the method of the 'calls,' mantra-like chanting in the Enochian language designed to attune one's consciousness to the angelic realms. Here Crowley underwent an intense confrontation with elements of his ego, emerging from it as a Magister Templi ('Master of the Temple'). In Crowley's understanding this represents a crucial level of development in which the 'abyss' is crossed and the illusion of the separate personal self is fully recognized.

Part of this ordeal involved Crowley, in night time desert rituals aided by Neuberg that utilized the magician's circle and triangle of Solomonic ceremonial magick, invoking and confronting the terrible onslaughts of the Enochian demon Choronzon. The process proved to be intense and at one point involved Neuberg literally 'wrestling in the dark' with the demon—although in all likelihood the 'demon' was Crowley caught in an altered state of consciousness. Even so, the idea of encountering an adversarial force in the wilds is a legitimate part of shamanic lore; in the Christian myth even Jesus had to deal with Satan in the desert. The idea has long been an essential element in the drama of initiation, wherein the hero seeking to master himself must face directly into the most viciously resistant aspects of both human nature and his own psyche.

Crowley came to regard this figure of Choronzon as symbolic of the last barrier between an adept and full enlightenment. An analogous figure would be Mara of Buddhism, who according to Buddhist legend harassed and tempted the Buddha just prior to his final enlightenment under the Banyen tree. Crowley's interpretation of Choronzon ultimately proved to be rather Jungian: he regarded the demon as the 'destroyer of ego' who proves to be a key ally on the journey to self-realization—provided the aspirant is sufficiently prepared and worthy. Crowley wrote a book about his two months in the North African desert with Neuberg and the Enochian spirits called *The Vision and the Voice*. Many have been impressed by the passion, drama, and insights found in the narrative of the book.

The year 1910 proved to be a relatively auspicious one for Crowley. He won a celebrated court case against his former teacher Mathers, in which Mathers had filed an injunction attempting to block Crowley from publishing Golden Dawn rituals in his *Equinox*. The court case proved to be something of a farce, with the presiding lawyers and judges deriving much humor out of the proceedings, especially at Mathers' expense. Although occult organizations were commonplace at that time (and had been since the mid-1800s), it was all still mostly a cause for mockery by the general public. There were some particularly funny exchanges in this trial. Regardie and

Stephenson, writing in *The Legend of Aleister Crowley*, described it as an event that 'would...take first place among the comic trials of English history,' adding that the 'evidence of both parties was continuously punctured by laughter.' Here is one small example:

(Mathers cross-examined)

Counsel: Is it not a fact that your name is Samuel Liddell Mathers?

Mathers: Yes, or Macgregor Mathers.

C: Your original name was Samuel Liddell Mathers?

M: Undoubtedly.

C: Did you subsequently assume the name of Macgregor?

M: The name of Macgregor dates from 1603.

C: Your name was Macgregor in 1603? (Much laughter.)

M: Yes; if you like to put it that way.

C: You have called yourself Count Macgregor of Glenstae?

M: Oh yes.

C: You have called yourself the Chevalier Macgregor?

M: No, you are confusing me with some of Crowley's aliases.

C: Have you ever suggested to anybody that you had any connection with King James IV of Scotland?

M: Every Scotchman who dates from an ancient family must have had some connection with King James IV.

C: Have you ever stated that King James IV of Scotland never died?

M: Yes; that is a matter of common tradition among all occult bodies.

C: Do you assert that James IV of Scotland is in existence today?

M: I refuse to answer your question.

C: And that his existence today is embodied in yourself?

M: Certainly not. You are confusing me with Crowley's aliases. (Laughter.)

C: You believe in the traditions?

M: That is my private business.

C: His Lordship (to counsel): The 'Flying Dutchman' is another if
you want to pursue the subject. (Laughter.)

M: And, again, 'The Wandering Jew.' (Laughter.)

C: Have you any occupation?

M: That is as you like to take it. For a man of no occupation I am
probably the most industrious man living. (Laughter.)[17]

The trial brought Crowley a certain level of fame, and his *Equinox*
publications for a time sold very well. He also attracted some
students; his Argenteum Astrum had a few dozen members at that
point.

In 1912, an important event occurred during which a German
occultist named Theodore Reuss confronted Crowley about
publishing secrets held within Reuss's German mystical order, called
the Ordo Templi Orientis (or 'O.T.O.' as it's more commonly referred
to). Crowley denied the charge; it turns out what he'd written had
been produced innocently by him even though it did bear close
symbolic similarity to the secrets Reuss referred to. Through this odd
encounter, Reuss and Crowley became friends, and Reuss
empowered him to set up a branch of the O.T.O in England. In 1913,
Crowley traveled to Moscow and while there he composed his
Gnostic Mass, a ceremony that is still conducted today by members
of the existing O.T.O. branches.

Crowley spent the First World War (1914-1918) in America, where
he wrote what appeared to be pro-German propaganda. The
strangeness of these writings has led many occult historians to
strongly suspect that Crowley had been employed by the British
government to do espionage and collect intelligence on the German
agenda. His pro-Germans rants were seen, in that view, to be a cover
for his spy work. (Less sympathetic views have tended to simply
brand him a traitor to his homeland.) Entire books have been written
on this matter—the best attempt being Richard Spense's *Secret Agent
666* (2008)—but nothing has ever been definitively proved and, much
as with Gurdjieff's suspected espionage activities, it ultimately

remains conjecture. Crowley himself, in his *Confessions*, claimed that he was always loyal to England, and that his pro-German articles were both ironic and intended to aid in bringing America into the War against Germany.

In 1915, aged forty, Crowley claimed the grade of Magus, traditionally the highest level in various occult fraternities (although significantly, the Golden Dawn claimed that this level could only be attained after death). In 1918, Crowley made a 'magical retirement' on an island on the Hudson River in New York State. There he claimed to do considerable research into his past lives, recalling many in detail. He said he was able to procure these memories via the use of the 'magical memory', a spiritual technique for past life recall. (See Appendix I, the 'Crowley-Osho' link, for more on Crowley's claimed past lives.)

The Abbey of Thelema

In 1920, at forty-five years of age, Crowley traveled to the Italian island of Sicily and there founded what was to become the infamous Abbey of Thelema. This was a spiritual commune based on Crowley's Thelemic teachings, including practice of meditations, rituals, and study of select writings. A number of people visited the place, some stayed for lengthy periods of practice, and some were deeply and positively transformed by the event.

In 1923, a disastrous episode occurred at the Abbey when a young and promising disciple of Crowley's, Raoul Loveday, contracted enteritis after drinking tainted spring water, and died shortly after at the age of only twenty-three. Crowley's already maligned reputation was further ruined with the British tabloids calling him 'The Wickedest Man in the World'. (It was even claimed by one of the tabloids that Crowley had 'killed and eaten' two porters on a previous mountain climbing expedition in the Himalayas.) Not long after, the new fascist premier of Italy, Benito Mussolini, being informed of the Loveday incident and related fantastic rumors, expelled Crowley from his country. The Abbey of

Thelema remained open for another year run by a few students of Crowley, but without its Magus the commune had lost its animating force. (See Chapter 9 for a more detailed look at Crowley's Abbey of Thelema.)

After being expelled from Italy, Crowley departed with Leah Hirsig, his current 'Scarlet Woman' (Crowley's term for his magickal/tantric partner) for Tunis, Morocco, where he completed the writing of his *Confessions* (which renders this massive book only a partial autobiography, missing as it does the last twenty-four years of Crowley's life). The following year, in 1924, he claimed the supreme magical grade of Ipsissimus—a level beyond that of Magus in his system and so exalted as to allegedly be beyond all comprehension. That is, at least, the traditional spiritual definition of the level. (The matter of self-initiation has always been problematic, and is touched on elsewhere in this book.)

Theodore Reuss had died in 1923. Two years later, Crowley, at age fifty, became the new head of the O.T.O. It is interesting to note of Crowley that, in spite of his numerous interpersonal conflicts, the key points in his career involved close and complicated connections with others. Specifically, it was often Crowley's destiny to inherit something (beginning with his father's substantial fortune) and then upgrade it, as he did with the O.T.O. (though not with his father's fortune!), revising and developing its rituals and bringing new and needed energy to the whole Order. But he was less a pure innovator than Gurdjieff, for example. Two of Crowley's core rituals, the 'Star Ruby' and 'Star Sapphire', are modifications based on the template of existing rituals that were designed (likely by Mathers) in the Golden Dawn. Crowley's brilliant Thoth Tarot deck was co-created with Frieda Lady Harris (in the years shortly before his death). And thus an interesting paradox of Crowley's life is that despite his apparent antisocial nature, most of his work was born out of his *intense relationships* with others—both within mystery schools and with key individuals in his life.

In 1928, Crowley, living in Paris, was joined by Israel Regardie, then but twenty years old, who became the Beast's secretary. Regardie wrote extensively about this period in his biography of Crowley, *The Eye in the Triangle*. Regardie, like many others, had a difficult relationship with his mentor and eventually had a falling out with him over a remarkably petulant issue. Unlike those many others, however, Regardie had a change of heart a couple of decades after Crowley's death and decided to write his book on Crowley, which was largely sympathetic and corrected many falsehoods about his former master and friend.

Important Publications and Last Years

In 1930, Crowley published what is generally considered his magnum opus, *Liber ABA, Magick: Book Four*. The book received some positive reviews and, encouraged by this, Crowley signed a contract with Mandrake Press in London, which then put out several other books of his including his novel *Moonchild* and the first part of his *Confessions*.

In the early 1930s, Crowley traveled about Europe but the Mandrake publishing house failed and the sales of his books stalled. By 1935, he was bankrupt. Two year later, he managed to publish his *Equinox of the Gods*, as well as *Eight Lectures on Yoga*, a work that is considered by many to be amongst the best and most concise writings on the subject. That Crowley, a Westerner, could write with such comprehension about an Eastern spiritual path was testament to both his intelligence and his authenticity as a seeker and scholar of perennial wisdom.

In the World War II years of the early 1940s, Crowley formed something of an offbeat friendship with the English artist Frieda Harris—one of his few quality associations with a woman that appears to have not been sexualized. Together with Harris, they collaborated on the creation of what many today consider to be the finest Tarot deck ever designed, called the Thoth Tarot (named after the Egyptian god of writing and magic). Harris, under Crowley's strict and often difficult guidance, painted the deck, which Crowley accompanied with a written text, *The Book of Thoth*. Both the deck and the book were published in 1944 but it wasn't until a few decades later that they attained the recognition and popularity that they deserved with a higher quality printing. *The Book of Thoth* is far and away the most substantial and profound book ever written on the Tarot. Crowley shows in his writings a facility with understanding interlocking themes of symbolism that rivals C.G. Jung and Joseph Campbell.

In 1945, Crowley retired to a boarding house in Hastings where he completed and published *Magick Without Tears*, which is essentially a collection of correspondence between him and a female student (her identity is unknown; some have speculated that the Q & A was merely Crowley's literary device for the book). This book, as with his Thoth Tarot book, is considered some of his most lucid and mature work and shows without question that despite his extensive drug usage and age he retained clarity of mind till the end.

Crowley was in touch with a relatively small circle of students and other contacts during these last years. One of the more noteworthy ones was Gerald Gardner, the main inspiration behind the 20th century development of Witchcraft, or 'Wicca' as it is now more commonly known. Gardner, himself past sixty at the time, visited the elderly magus in May of 1947. What exactly transpired between them is not known, but what is clear is that Gardner used some of Crowley's ideas and writings in formulating the basis for a modern pagan faith. The tradition launched largely by Gardner via his 1954 book *Witchcraft Today* has grown rapidly in recent decades, dwarfing in size the Thelemic organizations originally overseen by Crowley. As demonstrated by Crowley scholar Jerry Cornelius, Gardner simply lifted some of Crowley's writings and used them verbatim in his Wiccan degree initiations and other Wiccan writings.[18]

Crowley passed away at the boarding house in Hastings on December 1, 1947, at seventy-two years of age. There are several legends attached to his death, all different. According to one of Crowley's earlier biographers, Gerald Suster, the most credible of them came from the manager of the Hastings boarding house who told

Suster that Crowley collapsed while pacing in his room—it was heart failure aggravated by his bronchial condition—and that he was alone at the time. This same manager also relayed an amusing tale to Suster about a Hastings bookseller who said he saw a magick symbol drawn by Crowley on one of the buildings at his boarding house. Disturbed by it, the man wiped it off with a dish-cloth and the next day Crowley died. Suster, with tongue-in-cheek, remarks, 'Now we know the truth at last; the Great Beast was rubbed out by a dish-cloth.'[19]

The common view is that Crowley 'died poor, addicted to heroin, and with a tarnished reputation.' The latter two of those are correct, but he was not actually in poverty; he died with a box of cash under his bed—£400 according to some (a value of about £10,000 or $17,000 USD in equivalent 2010 currency). The money was intended for the publishing of his most recent writings.

For the next twenty years, his reputation—and the memory of Crowley—largely faded from the public eye. (Two biographies on his life were published in the 1950s—John Symonds' *The Great Beast* and Daniel Mannix's lurid *The Beast*—but both were unsympathetic and neither served to incite significant interest in the man and in particular his ideas). It was only on June 1, 1967, when the Beatles put out their iconic *Sergeant Pepper's Lonely Hearts Club Band* album, the cover of which featured dozens of their 'people we like' amongst which was included Crowley's face (sandwiched between Paramanhansa Yogananda's guru Sri Yukteswar, and Mae West), that Crowley, like Lazarus, was magically revived and a deep—and deserved— interest in his life work renewed. In commenting on the Beatles' album montage, the October 23, 1969 edition of *The Evening News* of London wrote:

Glowering from between Mae West and an India guru in that spoof photograph on the Sgt. Pepper's Lonely Hearts Club Band LP is a face with lard-like jowls and hot staring eyes. He looks furious at being there—the Great Beast cut down to Beatle size.[20]

Of course the reviewer could not have been more mistaken. Crowley would almost certainly have been delighted at the publicity, and all the more so if he could possibly have known how that one act by a wildly popular music band would rescue him from oblivion, inject new life into his legend, and bring to the awareness of many sincere seekers of esoteric wisdom his vast literary offerings.

Crowley has been called a 'Victorian hippie' by some, and by others that phrase has been rejected as too suggestive of peace and love for a man of his character. But were all hippies children of peace and love? Not exactly. Many (if not most) were rebels, and for many so-called hippies their 'peace and love' was liberally mixed with a hostile undertone for the establishment and a volatile expression of anarchic thinking assisted by all sorts of consciousness-altering adventures. Crowley was indeed no flower-power child. But much of his thought and even more of his personality foreshadowed the psychological revolution of the 1960s. His rampant explorations of sex and drugs, his mocking of the British cultural establishment of his time, his travels in the East and deep study of Yoga, Buddhism, and Taoism, as well as the entire Western esoteric tradition, and his dedication to higher states of consciousness would (and did) indeed make him a patron-saint of many of the hippies of the extraordinarily transformative decade of the 1960s.

But ultimately he was more than any of that. He was a key link in the transmission from Renaissance magus to 20th century mystic, and one of the important initiators of a new psycho-spiritual current. He was a modern day Renaissance man with difficult and unsavory traits, a strange cross between John Dee and John Donne, magician and poet, artist and adventurer, scholar and mystic and prophet of a new religion, chess expert, mountaineer, big game hunter, drug addict and bisexual debauchee. Of him it can truly be said, he was anything but dull.

Chapter 2
G. I. Gurdjieff: The Black Devil
of Ashkhabad

Till Gurdjieff raised up his head, one could think he is only a great scientist, or something like that. But when he looks at you, you can no more see his face, neither know if he has great or little eyes; you see only two immense wells of black light.
Rene Daumal

Gurdjieff exercises on those who go to him a kind of grip of a psychic order which is quite astonishing and from which few have the strength to escape.
Rene Guenon

Gurdjieff is a kind of walking god…a planetary or even solar god.
A.R. Orage

Back around the year 2000, I received a mysterious phone call from a man in California who said he'd looked at a website of mine at the time, in particular an article that I'd written about Gurdjieff, and that he had some questions. While he wasn't exactly breathing heavily into the phone or using a voice modifier, he was rather evasive about his identity, preferring to tell me only that he'd been part of a group for a long time that had been on a mission to locate the Sarmoung Brotherhood (the mysterious Central Asian organization that Gurdjieff claimed to have been an initiate of). He said they'd

41

organized journeys and, during a rare lull between Afghan wars, they followed some tips and traveled to the Khyber Pass region. As is usually the case with such stories, he said the 'trail went cold' while in northern Afghanistan. I half-heartedly wondered to myself whether he'd bothered to consult *Fielding's Guide to the World's Most Dangerous Places* before setting off to the land of poppies and burkhas. Doubt as I might, however, he sounded legitimate and sincere—and no longer young—and he really wanted to know what I thought about the Sarmoung legend.

I told him about my own wanderings in that part of the world years before, particularly through Kashmir and up into Ladakh where I'd stayed for a while in a Tibetan monastery. I'd had a series of exotic and interesting experiences but I did not find any 'Sarmoung Brotherhood' either. In the end, I'd concluded that the value of the Sarmoung myth was very similar to the Tibetan idea of Shambhala (or Shangri-la)—that is, it was primarily allegorical—and perhaps might even be sourcing from the same story. This was tantalizingly hinted at by William Patrick Patterson in his book, *Eating the 'I'*, in which Patterson (then a student of Lord John Pentland, himself a direct disciple of Gurdjieff) recounts his meeting with the radical Tibetan Buddhist master Chogyam Trungpa in the early 1970s. Trungpa, who had fled Tibet in the 1960s, had been raised as the incarnate abbot of a group of monasteries in eastern Tibet known as 'Surmang'. Patterson noted the close similarity of the terms Sarmoung and Surmang—something made all the more interesting by the fact that Gurdjieff actually did claim that he spent a couple of years in Tibet around the period 1900-1903, studying their traditions, picking up some of the language, and even, he claimed, taking a Tibetan wife.[1]

As with so much of Gurdjieff's story, allegory blends easily with fact, as does fiction with teaching. Like Crowley, he was a man extraordinarily difficult to pin down, one given to changing on a moment's notice depending entirely upon which angle you were viewing him.

My familiarity with Gurdjieff went back further than the time of my phone call from the intrepid Californian. Sometime back around 1980, while living in Montreal, the janitor of my apartment building had me up to his room for tea one evening. While falling into a rather intense conversation with him and his girlfriend about altered states of consciousness and related matters, he asked me whether I'd heard of Peter Ouspensky, a Russian journalist who lived in the first half of the 20th century. I had, but only vaguely. I'd remembered his mention in Colin Wilson's book, *The Occult*[2], that I'd read back in high school in the mid 1970s.

Ouspensky, an intellectual, philosopher, and journalist well known in Moscow in the early 1900s, had also been a great seeker of wisdom and had traveled far and wide throughout Asia in a fruitless search for a teacher or teaching that could truly help him. He had discovered nothing substantial. Disappointed, he returned to St. Petersburg where shortly after he happened upon an ad for an upcoming ballet in a Moscow newspaper, cryptically entitled *The Struggle of the Magicians*. Ouspensky attended this performance, which consisted of finely choreographed dance sequences and mysterious demonstrations of psychic abilities by a group of Russians garbed in the robes of Eastern mystics. The whole performance was overseen by a dark, enigmatic, shaven-headed man named Gurdjieff, who seemed to hold a remarkable spell over his dancers. Intrigued, Ouspensky later attended an introductory meeting with the master and his students. Though unimpressed with the students who for the most part Ouspensky dismissed as young and gullible, he was unable to shake the fascination he felt for Gurdjieff, with his intense eyes, the magnetic self-assurance of his presence, and the depth of knowledge on esoteric matters he seemed to possess. Though a formidable intelligence himself (Ouspensky had already authored some well-known material on mathematics, philosophy, and mysticism), he soon apprenticed himself to Gurdjieff.

All of this is detailed in Ouspensky's now famous book, *In Search*

of the Miraculous[3], which my friend Peter the janitor recommended to me at the time. I read this work several times over, and all these years later I still consider it one of the best pieces of writing available on an extraordinary character and his esoteric teachings, rarely surpassed, remarkable considering it was published in 1949 and concerns events that for the most part occurred between 1915 and 1924.

Not long after reading the book, I found and was accepted into a Gurdjieff group in my city. It was led by a man who had studied at J.G. Bennett's center, one of Gurdjieff's more prominent direct disciples. I spent close to a year in this group. I eventually left and sought out more self-expressive forms of inner work (such as primal therapy and Reichian bodywork) and ended up in Osho's movement. However, years later, I would take up my study of Gurdjieff again, readier this time to grasp more deeply his ideas and more properly utilize some of his practices.

I recall one incident from my time in the Work (as Gurdjieff's system is known as) that revealed much of what it was all about. My teacher had asked me to report to his house one day for an assignment. Hoping that perhaps I was going to be the recipient of some special knowledge, I discovered at his door a simple note directing me to enter and proceed to one of the rooms. Once there, I was confronted with an unopened box; it appeared to be some shelving from Walmart or something. There was a note on it as well. It read, 'Please construct this steel shelf'.

That was my great assignment. Frustrated, I flashed back in my memory to a time two years earlier when a man I'd been having discussions with, a member of the Eckankar (an occult fraternity), was passing on some information to myself and another younger fellow we both worked with at the time. The younger guy was restless and irritated about something. After he left I asked my friend, the Eckankar initiate, what was wrong with the young man. He replied in his thick French accent, 'He want to become God in one day', and then burst out laughing.

Impatience is a problem of the young, yet in the middle of assembling my teacher's steel shelf I began to realize that the whole point lay in how I attended to the matter at hand. My mind was annoyed; I wanted personal attention and preferably some profound knowledge as well. And yet here I was with this silly shelf. What was spiritual about that? Everything, of course—and the practice of being mindful, staying alert, in the midst of the most mundane of things always remained the heart of Gurdjieff's teaching, I managed to remain quite 'present' while putting the shelf together and by the time I'd left, even without any contact with my teacher, I felt very good—balanced, clear, relaxed.

It is, however, of the greatest irony and interest that despite the core simplicity of Gurdjieff's practical work (the complexities of his theory notwithstanding), his life and what led him to his teachings was anything but simple. In keeping with the other two subjects of this book, his life was full of mystery and danger, of courage and adventure, and of extraordinary accomplishments.

George Ivanovitch Gurdjieff was born in Alexandropol (today known as Gyumri), in the Caucasus region of Armenia, near the Turkish border, of a Greek father and an Armenian mother. Anyone who is aware of the legend of Gurdjieff is aware that the year of his birth has long been a mystery that has never been conclusively solved. One of his passports listed 1877, but he used several passports with different dates, and 1877 has been shown by many to be in error. His two chief biographers of more recent times, James Moore and William Patrick Patterson, argue for different dates, the former for 1866, the latter for 1872. My own estimate is closer to 1872.[4]

The uncertainty of his year of birth is an excellent metaphor for the deeply enigmatic nature of the man himself. The main problem with the history of Gurdjieff's early years—reflected in the mystery of his age—is that, objectively speaking, there *is* none. The sole source of information for his life up till around 1912 is his own writing, most notably one book, *Meetings with Remarkable Men*.[5] The book is putatively about factual events but could easily be partial fabrication or even outright allegory. Carlos Castaneda, the controversial author of a number of influential books based on his (probably fabricated) apprenticeship to an old Mexican Indian shaman, used to talk about the idea of 'erasing personal history' as a means of preventing oneself from being trapped by the views and judgments of others. I know of no other important recent figure in world spiritual tradition to have more effectively erased—or perhaps more accurately *blurred*—his personal history than Gurdjieff. (Interestingly, Castaneda's date of birth was long controversial as well.)[6]

One argument presented as to the reasons behind all these discrepantly dated passports is that Gurdjieff may have been working in espionage. However, as with Crowley's alleged spy activities, nothing has ever been conclusively established in that area.

He grew up in Kars, in northeast Turkey, a town situated in the cultural melting pot region between the Black and Caspian Seas. This area was awash with a rich mixture of different races and traditions, being a migratory meeting ground for Asian and European peoples. Exposure to such variety was ideal to stimulate and fire the imagination of a bright young boy destined to become one of the most innovative and unique spiritual forces of the 20th century. As a youth, Gurdjieff made contact with many hermetic organizations, of political, occult, philosophical, religious, and mystical natures. Though he witnessed and experienced much that fascinated him, including a broad range of occult powers and altered states of consciousness, he was fundamentally dissatisfied owing to a failure to make contact with an authentic school of spiritual growth. At that point, he resolved to find such a school, as well as to search for ancient, lost knowledge.

The Unverifiable History
The following information is entirely gleaned from Gurdjieff's semi-

autobiographical *Meetings with Remarkable Men* and has never been independently corroborated by anyone, so its veracity remains uncertain. (My own sense is that much of *Meetings* rings true, reading like typical travel stories. If anything was embellished it is likely connected to some of the key characters in the book, who may or may not have existed, and to the Sarmoung problem—see below.) The book is, nevertheless, highly interesting, depicting as it does the archetypal hero's quest to find the Grail of true wisdom.

To facilitate his search for lost knowledge, Gurdjieff claimed that he and several others formed a loose organization of approximately twenty people called the 'Seekers of Truth'. All the individuals of this group had in common a deep desire to make contact with bona fide spiritual sources, and as such the purity of their combined intention enabled them to accomplish much. They traveled far and wide, from the Holy Lands and Egypt (where Gurdjieff worked for a while as a tour guide) through Central Asia, up into Tibet, Mongolia, and Siberia. They combed archaeological ruins and eventually made contact with the Naqshbandi Dervishes, an authentic lineage of Sufi mystics.

Sometime in his early twenties, Gurdjieff traveled with the Seekers of Truth to Ani, in eastern Turkey near the Armenian border. Back around 1000 AD, Ani had been a major urban center rivaling Baghdad or Cairo, but after being sacked by the Mongols and other invaders over the centuries it gradually fell into ruin. By the time Gurdjieff and his group were there it had been a ghost town for over a hundred years.

While there Gurdjieff claimed that he and his friend, Sarkis Pogossian, digging in the ruins of a decrepit church, found some crumbling old parchments. They had writing on them that was an archaic form of Armenian that neither Gurdjieff nor Pogossian could decipher. One parchment in particular grabbed their attention. It was a monk's brief recounting of a 'Sarmoung Brotherhood'. Gurdjieff and Pogossian recalled that they'd come across this name before in an Armenian book titled *Merkhavat*, and that it was the name of a 'famous esoteric school' that had its roots in Babylon some twenty-five centuries before Christ. Gurdjieff further claimed that the Brotherhood could be traced up till the 600s AD, around the time of Mohammad, but after that all traces of it disappear. He and Pogossian then did considerable detective work, eventually concluding that the key link were the Aisors, descendents of the Assyrians, and that the Sarmoung Brotherhood was likely still based somewhere near the border region between Turkey and north-western Iran.[7]

This is, of course, all very romantic. One has always to bear in mind the area Gurdjieff lived in. The ruins of Ani were a mere thirty miles from Alexandropol in northwestern Armenia, which served as a base for Gurdjieff and his band of seekers. The entire area was a fascinating playground for adventurous young men and women, and in his days many ruins were open and unattended. Archaeology was still a primitive science and the idea of historical preservation was only haphazardly recognized. So the idea that he and his friends could wander into the ruins of an ancient church, dig around, and find things is entirely believable. Whether the parchment story is true, however, is less certain; that part may be the embellishment that happens so commonly in stories involving a personal quest, so as to inject flavor—and in this case, that are designed to be a teaching allegory.

Gurdjieff said that what caught his attention about the Sarmoung legend was the claim that it was a custodian of great knowledge and secret mysteries. This, of course, was what he was looking for. Shortly after, he and Pogossian went on a journey to a valley that the old parchments had indicated the Sarmoung had travelled toward. Gurdjieff later claimed that these parchments were written over a thousand years before, so the idea that he thought that the Sarmoung would still *be* in that valley after all that time indicates just how driven he was to find answers.

On the way there, Pogossian was bitten by a venomous insect and, in order to recover, the two took refuge in the house of an

Armenian priest. It was here that Gurdjieff discovered another old parchment belonging to the priest that had on it a map. The priest claimed that he was once offered a large sum of money for it that he refused, but that he subsequently accepted in exchange for a mere copy of the map. Gurdjieff then asked to see it and upon viewing it reacted strongly—'seized with violent trembling'[8]—because what he saw was what he'd spent long months thinking about. He said it was a map of 'pre-sand Egypt'—Egypt as it was thousands of years ago, before the earliest period of recorded Egyptian history (that is, before 3500 BC). One day, when the priest was out and about, Gurdjieff stole into his room and furtively made a copy of the map.

This map resulted in Gurdjieff temporarily abandoning his search for the Sarmoung in eastern Turkey and diverted him to Egypt. On the way, he parted company with Pogossian. While in Egypt working as a tour guide, he met the Russian Prince Yuri Lubovedsky. (It is very amusing to read Gurdjieff's description of being a guide: 'In a few days I had learned everything that a guide needs to know and began, along with slick young Arabs, to confuse naïve tourists.'[9] I was in Egypt in 1998, a century after Gurdjieff had been there, and the sacred sites were still run by slick young Arabs who were still busy confusing naïve tourists). Gurdjieff recounts a tale where Lubovedsky—a wealthy aristocrat driven to a relentless spiritual search by the death in childbirth of his young wife— becomes excited when he sees Gurdjieff's special map. The significance of this map and of Egypt in general would surface years later when Gurdjieff would claim the following regarding the roots of esoteric Christianity, and of his own teaching:

The Christian form of worship was not invented by the fathers of the church. It was all taken in a ready-made form from Egypt, only not from the Egypt that we know but from one which we do not know. This Egypt was in the same place as the other but it existed much earlier...It may seem strange to people when I say that this prehistoric Egypt was Christian many thousands of years before the birth of Christ, that is to say, that its religion was composed of the same principles and ideas that constitute true Christianity.[10]

Egypt, of course, no longer practices the religion of its ancient ancestors, be those prehistoric or even of the Pharaonic ages. Egypt, for many centuries, has been a Muslim nation and as such the prime esoteric tradition found now within its borders is Sufism. The Sufi tradition (the mystical undercurrent of Islam) unquestionably had a most profound impact on the consciousness of the young Gurdjieff and from it he likely derived some of the ritual dances, meditation techniques, and sacred symbols (such as the enneagram) that he would employ in his later teaching years.

After leaving Egypt, Gurdjieff wandered throughout the region— including visits to Medina and Mecca in disguise—before eventually drifting east again toward central Asia and finally, he claimed, being led to the Sarmoung monastery that was somewhere in or near Afghanistan. The exact location of the monastery remained a mystery even to Gurdjieff, as he said he was taken there blindfolded for a journey that lasted several days. Some of his main teachers resided in this school and he found, to his great surprise, that his old friend Prince Lubovedsky was there also. This was around the year 1899. And so in an interesting parallel with Crowley, as one young seeker is entering the esoteric order (the Golden Dawn) in England that will train him, at the same time the other is entering a mysterious monastery in a geographic null zone that will train him.

However, as mentioned earlier, no one has ever been able to locate this monastery or Brotherhood, and it seems very possible that Gurdjieff fabricated this part of his past. If so, he will not be the first or last to do so. High profile examples of this found in the 20th century include T. Lobsang Rampa and Carlos Castaneda—both enormously influential writers who claimed they'd spent time in far off remote places apprenticed to advanced spiritual masters (Tibetan masters in Rampa's case, and a Mexican Indian shaman in

Castaneda's case). Both were subsequently proved to be almost beyond doubt frauds who had made their stories up, though some believe that there is a chance that at least part of Castaneda's story was authentic—Rampa, however, was shown to be an outright imposter.

Real or allegorical, after Gurdjieff left the Sarmoung monastery, he was not done exercising his wanderlust and headed off to Tibet where he claimed to absorb some of the Tibetan Tantric teachings and observe the sacred dances. He was not, however, the famous Buryat Mongol Aghwan Dorjieff, a prominent Tibetan official, as some writers have mistakenly assumed.

The problem of mistaken identity and other enigmas seemed to follow Gurdjieff around. From an early age, he acquired a reputation for being something of an opportunist, and at times even an outright confidence trickster. This was usually connected to money issues and his lifelong struggle to generate funds to keep his travel, research and later work going. In his twenties, he was a true jack of all trades doing whatever he could—carpet mender, tour guide, hypnotist, etc.—to finance his travels. He once captured some small birds, painted them, and then sold them (for a costly fee) as 'exotic American canaries'. The next day, it rained and Gurdjieff hastily fled town before his creativity was unmasked.

There is some evidence that in his thirties Gurdjieff functioned as a covert political agent and spy for the Russian government, though his motivation for doing so would most likely have been to attain the funds and travel capacity to continue his search for knowledge. He lived in a time of great political upheaval and religious foment. Much of his teaching work took place in times (the Russian Revolution and the two World Wars) and places that made travel and even survival difficult, let alone having the leisure time to do spiritual practices. However, Gurdjieff was a master of situations and could use even the most arduous conditions as a vehicle for intensifying work upon self. This is consistent with what all the masters have taught, that growth happens more effectively in the soil of insecurity. When things are too stable and safe we tend to go to sleep, as when it is dark and quiet at night.

By approximately 1900, the Seekers of Truth had disbanded. Gurdjieff's life around that time continued to be full of adventure: he spent some time in Persia where he studied magic with some magi; he met the Russian Tsar Nicholas II; and on three separate occasions during those years he claimed he was accidentally shot by warring soldiers, narrowly escaping death. The worst of these misadventures occurred in Tibet where he spent several months hovering between life and death as he slowly healed from a bullet wound.

After his Tibetan adventure, he spent two years participating in an unknown Sufi community, although it may well have been one of the Naqshbandi Order, some of whose teachings resemble his later system. While the Sarmoung story may be myth, his association with this latter Sufi community has the ring of truth. The Naqshbandi Sufi Order is well known.

After completing his time in the Sufi community, he was, essentially, a fully qualified spiritual teacher in his own right. The year was around 1907 and he was around thirty-five years old. He had already lived an extraordinary life full of adventure and character-building hardships. He had the ability to capture and direct the attention of others, as well as possessing a great depth of esoteric knowledge and teaching methods acquired from his many years of travels and contacts with extraordinary people. But more crucially, he had embodied what he had been taught, attaining, through his own fierce efforts, an internal unity that clearly marked him apart from the sleeping, 'mechanical' man.

At this point Gurdjieff settled in Tashkent, in Russian Turkestan (present day Uzbekistan, a few hundred miles north of Afghanistan—or as a wandering friend of mine once called it, 'far away-istan'). Here he set himself up as a kind of teacher-magician-healer, often slipping into deliberate roguery so as, as he claimed it, to further his study of human mechanical behavior and reactivity, but doubtless also to make a buck in order to fund his survival and travel. He was also successful in business, trading in several commodities. By around 1910, Gurdjieff began to develop and formulate the teaching system that would eventually be his legacy to the world. This period marks an important and interesting juncture in his life. In his short (and eventually self-repudiated) work, *The Herald of Coming Good*, written in 1932, Gurdjieff claimed that 'twenty-one years ago'—that is, in 1911— he bound himself to live 'an artificial life' that involved renouncing his capacity to manipulate others via charisma and knowledge of hypnosis, allegedly for the purpose of further self-purification. This is an important topic to consider, touching as it does on the role and legitimacy of a rogue-type guru. The main point here is that Gurdjieff was saying, basically, that he was dedicating his life to the 'Bodhisattva spirit'— that is, to help others wake up, rather than to only serve himself.

Beginning of Verifiable History

From here on in, we are on solid historical ground, knowing more or less without question that the following events in Gurdjieff's life, in fact, occurred.

After a few years in Tashkent, Gurdjieff drifted west toward the big cities of Russia. In 1912, at approximately age forty, he arrived in Moscow and shortly after in St. Petersburg married a beautiful young Polish woman, Julia Ostrowska. Her background is unclear— in some accounts she is described as a lady of the Tsar's court, and in other cases as a penniless woman from a destitute family whom Gurdjieff rescued. Occam's razor suggests the latter version is the more likely of the two. At any rate, she remained his wife until her death from cancer in 1926. She was described once by Katherine Mansfield, who was with her at the Prieure briefly in late 1922, as having the 'bearing of a queen'. But otherwise she retained a very low profile. There are few photographs of her. By all accounts she was both a loyal partner and a devoted student of Gurdjieff at the same time. It was said that she retained her last name in order to make it clear that she was merely another of Gurdjieff's students.

Despite this humility, Gurdjieff once stated that she was a 'very old soul'.[11]

At this time, he also attracted his first Western students. In 1914, he staged his famous ballet, _The Struggle of the Magicians_, which was attended by Peter Ouspensky. This meeting was pivotal for both men. As mentioned, Ouspensky was not the typical seeker as he had already traveled extensively, experimented with consciousness, and was the author of _Tertium Organum_[12], a philosophical work that came to achieve world-wide acclaim. On Ouspensky's return from his travels, he lectured in Moscow to audiences of over a thousand people, and yet such attention did not unduly swell his head. He was a man of true intelligence and thus was able to recognize his own ignorance when confronted with it. Thus, he submitted himself to a teacher-student relationship with Gurdjieff.

The importance of the relationship between these two men cannot be stressed enough. Ouspensky was to Gurdjieff much like Plato was to Socrates: the former a razor sharp intellect and consummate communicator, the latter a man of exceptional _being_ whose mere force of presence was testament to a great deal of raw life experience, as well as the efforts he had made to transform himself.

Though Ouspensky has typically been regarded as Gurdjieff's 'chief disciple', this is mostly misleading. In fact, Ouspensky only studied deeply with his teacher for a few years (from 1915-18). From 1919-1924, he was vacillating, going back and forth and more than once breaking with Gurdjieff. By 1924, he was essentially complete with him (they met sporadically for a few more years until a final meeting in 1931 in Paris). The reasons for his break have never been clear, mostly because Ouspensky himself never fully explained it; however, it seems clear enough from the records that there was something in Gurdjieff's intensity that was ultimately too much for Ouspensky. He became convinced that Gurdjieff and the system (his body of ideas) must be clearly distinguished from each other. Gurdjieff's brash volatility, crude humor, and sudden changes in behavior doubtless alienated the intellectual and cultured Ouspensky who in the end believed it was risky to be associated with Gurdjieff. He actually went so far as to forbid his own students, in later years, from ever mentioning Gurdjieff by name. In light of his eventual break with him, Ouspensky's perception of his teacher was interesting. He once said,

> Mr. Gurdjieff is a very extraordinary man. His possibilities are much greater than those of people like ourselves. But he can also go in the wrong way…Most people have many 'I's. If these 'I's are at war with one another it does not produce great harm, because they are all weak. But with Mr. Gurdjieff there are only two 'I's, one very good and one very bad.[13]

As to the reasons behind this position, some senior students of the Gurdjieff Work have seen Ouspensky as being caught in an ego-trap from which he could not free himself. He was too attached to his own sense of 'right' and did not embrace the physical-emotional aspect of the Work. This created an imbalance in his development that made him unable to see his deeper character flaws, thus necessitating him to project these onto his teacher, whereupon Gurdjieff was perceived as a 'danger'.

A more prosaic psychological explanation is even more probable, being that Ouspensky, like Gurdjieff, was an autocrat and used to having the stage himself—and like so many males, came to feel competitive with his alpha-male teacher. He wanted to learn from Gurdjieff at the beginning and was convinced that Gurdjieff had something that he could learn about. And so, he repressed his more egocentric need for recognition long enough to gain the information from Gurdjieff that he wanted. Once he had this information, his 'inner leader' began to resurface, making it very difficult for him to remain in a subordinate position to another teacher, and a very autocratic one at that. The fact that Ouspensky went to England and set himself up as a teacher there (teaching Gurdjieff's material to boot) seems clear evidence that he was driven to teach more than anything. All that, combined with Gurdjieff's relentless pressing of Ouspensky's buttons, was more than enough to cause the full break.

In Moscow in 1912, Gurdjieff had begun to slowly form his first groups. Over the next four years, teaching mostly in St. Petersburg and Moscow, he drew to him some of his key students; in addition to Ouspensky, Dr. Stjoernval, Zaharoff, and Thomas and Olga de Hartmann. During this time Russia had become embroiled in the First World War; that, followed by the Russian Revolution of 1917 that brought down the Tsarist aristocracy and eventually led to the formation of the Soviet Union, made for a highly unstable atmosphere. From 1917 to 1919, Gurdjieff and his small band of followers were often in real danger and were constantly on the go, moving between Russia and the Caucasus region of Georgia and Armenia, staying variously at Tuapse and Sochi on the Black Sea coast, Essentuki in southern Russia, and finally at Tbilisi (then known as Tiflis) in central Georgia, midway between the Black and Caspian Seas. All the while during this time, Gurdjieff continued to teach and work with all of his students directly. It was the very antithesis of a staid monastic or ashram environment. This was live-fire work on self.

The Institute for the Harmonious Development of Man

It was in Tbilisi in Georgia in October of 1919 that Gurdjieff officially opened his Institute for the Harmonious Development of Man, with a nucleus of six students—Stjoernval, the de Hartmanns, Alexandre and Jeanne de Salzmann, and his wife Julia Ostrowska. (Ouspensky by that time already had his first break with Gurdjieff, and had returned to St. Petersburg—renamed Petrograd by then—although he would shortly rejoin his teacher, before breaking with him again not long after.) The political instability in Georgia by then was such that Gurdjieff had to leave within six months. At that time, his following had grown to about thirty disciples. In the spring of 1920, they went west to Istanbul, Turkey (then known as Constantinople).

There, in October of that year, Gurdjieff reopened his Institute.

During this time, Gurdjieff was beset with considerable personal loss—his father, along with one of his sisters and all her children, had been killed by Turks in 1918 and 1920 respectively. The hardships, both outer and inner, that he and his small group of dedicated students had to endure was extraordinary, and yet it also dovetailed with the very nature of Gurdjieff's system, which was to work directly with the harsh conditions of life, and to maintain presence of mind—clear attention—in the face of it all.

The Institute's duration in Istanbul was, as with its initial period in Tbilisi, around six months. By May of 1921, Gurdjieff had closed it owing to problems attracting students. At that point, Gurdjieff made the decision to relocate to Europe, and in August he arrived in Berlin, Germany. The next winter he visited London briefly, hoping to open his school in England, but plans for that fell through. However, in October of 1922, with the help of a wealthy English benefactress—Mary Lilian, the Lady Rothermere (wife of Lord Rothermere, the newspaper magnate)—he made a down payment on the Chateau de Pieure des Basses Loges, at Fontainbleau-Avon, forty miles southeast of Paris, France. At fifty years of age, Gurdjieff had finally found a long-term base for his teachings that would serve as his first true commune. After years of constant move, throughout Russia and Asia Minor, dodging revolutions and wars, he and his community of students at last were able to settle in surroundings that enabled them to deepen their practice of the Work. The Prieure was now the headquarters for his Institute (see Chapter 9 for a more in depth look at this commune).

The Work at the Prieure consisted of the essentials of Gurdjieff's System: hard physical labor accompanied by active meditations, chief of which were 'self-observation' and 'self-remembering'. Individual assignments were given to students fitting their unique requirements for growth. A special Study House was built for the practice and performance of the Sacred Dances and Movements, ancient rituals that Gurdjieff learnt during his years in Sufi monasteries.

It was not an easy place to be. This Work was unlike the sweet-coated dross and tepid sentimentality that passes for much new age or personal growth work nowadays. Gurdjieff was a fierce, unrelenting taskmaster, but capable of extraordinary compassion at unexpected moments. However, the basis of his system was effort and more effort. 'No growth is possible,' he would say, 'without conscious labour and voluntary suffering.' By this he meant that we cannot attain something without payment, or sacrifice—not in the sense of morbid self-punishment, but rather in the necessity of giving something up in order to make space for something new. What we 'give up' can be something intangible like low self-worth, or even laziness, or some other character defect like vanity or pride.

By 1923, Gurdjieff had drawn to him many of the seekers who would become major players in the unfolding drama of constant change that was his life, including J.G. Bennett and A.R. Orage, both of whom would prove to be instrumental in the further dissemination of Gurdjieff's System. Bennett in particular went on to become a teacher of significant standing, as well as a prolific author. Admired by many, he has also received his share of criticism for, as some saw it, mixing too many teachings together.

In 1924, Gurdjieff and thirty-five members of his community sailed to the U.S., where they staged demonstrations of the Sacred Dances in New York, Chicago, Boston, and Philadelphia. While there, he attracted several key people who would further his cause in America, such as Margaret Anderson, Jane Heap, Jean Toomer, and C.S. Nott. Later that same year, while back in France, Gurdjieff, a notoriously aggressive driver, had a serious auto crash, and was not expected to live. However, he recovered, no doubt aided by his powerfully crystallized will. Shortly after this, to the shock of everyone, he disbanded the community and Institute. This was revealed though in short time to be something of a ploy to rid himself of his less dedicated students, whom he no longer felt he had sufficient energy reserves to freely give them. He continued to work with a smaller nucleus that remained with him, students who were more supportive of him and less demanding of his energy. Gurdjieff's mother and wife passed away in 1925 and 1926 respectively. After this he began a phase of more introspective work, beginning his magnum opus, *Beelzebub's Tales to His Grandson*,[14] and working on numerous musical compositions with Tomas de Hartmann. This music was designed to evoke an opening of the 'higher emotional center' (see Chapter 5 for more on this) and when experienced in combination with the Sacred Dances, elicited an obvious sense of the transcendent and ineffable. The same was true of Gurdjieff's writings, though operating through the intellectual center. These were examples of what he called Objective Art, which had the capacity to catalyze the observer into an awakened state of consciousness. Such art was based on a form of higher mathematics that nowadays goes by the term 'sacred geometry.' Other examples of Objective Art are the Egyptian pyramids, Tibetan *tangka* paintings, the Taj Mahal, Stonehenge, etc. Gurdjieff distinguished these from subjective art, which includes almost all conventionally known forms of art.[15]

Gurdjieff's Work at the Prieure lasted for ten stormy years until its enforced closure in 1932. By that time he had effectively assigned many of his students to leave him, and even had to intentionally alienate some of them to do this. In this sense, Gurdjieff was authentic in that he understood the delicate task a true teacher has, i.e. having to know when it is right for a student to leave, in order to avoid the dangerous consequences of attachment and dependency. Such a leave-taking is rarely easy and often traumatic as the student has opened themselves completely to the teacher, much as a child to a parent and thus is highly susceptible to being hurt. Depending on the consciousness and compassion of the teacher, the separation can be engineered with grace, but that of course is not always the case. More than one teacher-student relationship has ended via a painful rupture of one sort or another.

It should also be noted that Gurdjieff appeared to engineer some of these separations as a means of keeping his own consciousness sharp, via conscious labor and voluntary suffering. To part from those he had great fondness for was his way of keeping himself from losing consciousness due to excessive ease and comfort.

Gurdjieff appeared uninterested in allowing himself to be deified, or his community to be turned into a cult. Personalities with cultic tendencies who gathered around him tended to find it difficult to stay long, if they did not cease their psychic dependency on him. (He even complained that while recuperating from his car crash in 1924 people would visit him who simply wanted to suck energy out of him—doubtless as much related to his commanding autocratic nature as to their dependency.) This periodic tendency to push students away, though sometimes causing pain for those attached to him, nevertheless marked him apart from the usual run of leaders in typical organizations, be they religious or secular, who are primarily interested in simply acquiring more and more subordinates. As 'the Oracle' said to Neo in one of the *Matrix* films, 'What do all men who have power want? *More power*.' That said, Gurdjieff was, without doubt, a master manipulator and so his true motive for pulling students toward him or pushing them away was not always clear. He did, unquestionably, have a 'planetary aim,' and was dedicated to that. That is, his life was not governed as the average person's life is governed, by personal aims. He had a powerful vision, and was entirely a Western bodhisattva—someone motivated by deep compassion for the human condition. As J.G. Bennett said, 'He was fundamentally good'. But he was also often ruthless. It is this quality, ruthlessness, that is so feared and yet respected by others. It makes for a sharply defined character, one who commands attention just by walking into a room.

In 1934, Gurdjieff met Frank Lloyd Wright, the famous architect, and the two connected very well, though it is doubtful that Wright became a student in any sense of that term, as is sometimes believed. Wright had married one of Gurdjieff's former students, Olgivanna Hinzenberg. Speaking of Gurdjieff, Wright, with an architect's eye for observation, once gave a fascinating account of the old Magus:

Gurdjieff, declaring all mankind idiots, divides them into three classes—those who take what they can get; those who get what they can take; those who get what they get...There is enormous ego in this man. Always deliberate in movement, not large although he seems so—with the skull bald and tall behind— forceful humorous luminous eyes. In him we see a massive sense of his own individual worth. A man able to reject most of the so-called culture of our period and set up more simple and organic standards of personal worth and courageously, if outrageously, live up to them. He affected us strangely as though some oriental Buddha had come alive in our midst...A kind, solid, fatherly man. All that went on about him seemed to impress him little and yet he would later give evidence that nothing escaped him, so highly are his powers of observation and concentration developed...perhaps the personality of Gurdjieff is somewhat similar to that of Gandhi only, of course, more robust, aggressive and venturesome in nature. Now a man of perhaps 85 looking 55, he has some 40,000 'followers'—he will not call them students or disciples—has 104 sons of his own and 27 daughters for all of whose education he has made provision and to which he has given his attention...His knowledge of human nature and all its foibles seems perfect, and he does not hesitate to use this knowledge for his own ends although with a conscience that sees to it that they get something worthwhile out of his meeting them. Not caring at all for America or Americans, he has come over here, as he frankly put it, 'to shear the sheep.' He will turn the wool into some kind of good work for humanity. His hypnotic powers have served him well in this connection, but he is more careful now in exercising them. American fruits and foods he finds unfit to eat—likes only our tomato juice and our dollars. But eats enormously just the same. The style of our money he approves. But the shearing I imagine is not so good. The wool is now so short. Notwithstanding a superabundance of personal idiosyncrasy, George Gurdjieff seems to have the stuff in him of which our genuine prophets have been made. And when prejudice against him has cleared away, his vision of truth will be recognized as fundamental to the man men need.[16]

The biblical numbers cited (doubtless sincerely) by Wright above — '40,000 followers, 104 sons and 27 daughters' — is a highly amusing example of Gurdjieff's bluster and willingness to pull anyone's leg, especially that of a famous man.

From his middle age and beyond, Gurdjieff, like Crowley, had recurrent financial problems and in his later years relied mostly on American disciples to fund his continued efforts to promote the Work. By 1938, Jeanne de Salzmann had emerged as Gurdjieff's chief deputy, running a successful group in Paris dedicated to the Work. She would eventually head up the international Gurdjieff Foundation and competently lead it for years after the master's death, outliving all the original students in the process until passing away in 1990 at the age of 101. It is an interesting fact that a number of Gurdjieff's prominent female students lived to advanced ages. Examples were Olga de Hartmann (94), Sophie Ouspensky (89), Olgivanna Lloyd Wright (86), Jane Heap (81), Annie Staveley (90), Solito Solano (87), Katherine Hulme (81), and Margaret Anderson (87).

Throughout World War Two, Gurdjieff resided in Paris, where he worked with a large group of French students. Now in old age, he remained mostly in his famous flat on Rue des Colonels Renard, entertaining students and seekers with his outrageous humor and lavishly prepared meals. During this time he developed the ritual Idiot Toasts, yet another of his methods designed to diminish self-importance. His writings were prepared for publication; these were, along with the years of their publication:

The Herald of Coming Good (1933) A slim volume later withdrawn from publication and repudiated by Gurdjieff.

Beelzebub's Tales to His Grandson (1950) Gurdjieff intended that this book be read first; its purpose being to break down the student's rigid and conditioned views of reality.

Meetings with Remarkable Men (1963) Later made into a film by Peter Brook in 1979. This book was to be read second, its purpose being to introduce to the student a new way of thinking and perceiving reality and the possibilities of being.

Views from the Real World (1973) A collection of talks given by Gurdjieff, mostly from the 1920s. It is not an official part of his canon, *All and Everything*.

Life is Real Only Then, When 'I Am' (1975) This was to be read third, its purpose being to teach the student how to interact with life and encounter reality.

Apart from *Herald*, Gurdjieff did not live to see the publication of any of these works, although he approved the final proofs of *Beelzebub* shortly before he died. Three of them—*Beelzebub*, *Meetings*, and *Life*—were termed collectively *All and Everything*, 1st, 2nd, and 3rd series. It is unclear what took these books so long to get published, although doubtless it reflects the difficulty the public had with understanding Gurdjieff's ideas, let alone having a means to recognize and appreciate who he was.

In 1947, Ouspensky died, according to some sources as a disillusioned drunkard, according to others as a genuine saint, but in reality probably a bit of both. He failed to reconcile with Gurdjieff, though he had been invited to Paris by the master shortly before his death. In 1948, Gurdjieff authorized Mme. Ouspensky, herself a respected teacher of the Work, to publish her husband's *Fragments of an Unknown Teaching* (later re-titled *In Search of the Miraculous*). Upon looking over the manuscript, Gurdjieff was impressed by Ouspensky's memory. He remarked 'For long time I hate this man. Now I love him'. This book was published in 1949. In October of 1949, in (probably) his late seventies, Gurdjieff's health failed and he died shortly after. His final instructions on his death bed were to Jeanne de Salzmann, who later that year organized the re-grouping of the scattered body of Gurdjieff students and communities under the collective banner of the Gurdjieff Foundation.

J.G. Bennett probably became the most influential and effective Gurdjieff exponent not affiliated with the Gurdjieff Foundation, opening his own school in England, which later spread to America. Bennett was a prolific author and became a guru in his own right, and he always acknowledged Gurdjieff as his main inspiration. Next to Ouspensky, he did the most to transmit his master's knowledge, despite receiving rough treatment from some, especially Ouspensky, who criticized Bennett heavily for teaching (in Ouspensky's opinion) before he was ready and without authorization. Bennett died in 1974.

During his life, Gurdjieff remained largely obscure and unknown, and when he was recognized, it was with more notoriety than anything else. Two of his students, Ouspensky and the literary figure A.R. Orage, were far more renowned. After Gurdjieff's death, however, his fame slowly spread. Like Crowley, he grew enormously in stature and recognition only several decades after his death. A large part of Gurdjieff's task was the transmitting of Eastern and Middle Eastern esoteric knowledge to the West, namely Europe and North America. In succeeding in this (though his success became clearly apparent only after his death), he was one of the chief forces contributing toward what became known as the human potential movement and related developments in transformational work of the late 20th century. Just a few examples, of great varying degree of quality: In addition to Ouspensky's body of work, that of J.G. Bennett and the Claymont Institute; Maurice Nicoll, Kenneth Walker, Rodney Collin; Maxwell Maltz's conception of 'psycho-cybernetics' based on the idea that our brain and nervous system are 'servo-mechanisms' that can be controlled by our consciousness—notice the link with Gurdjieff's idea that man is a 'machine'; Maltz's ideas were borrowed and developed by Werner Erhard via his est teachings; the entire Enneagram Personality System industry as developed by Ichazo and Naranjo; the Michael Teachings, a series of popular new age books alleging to represent a body of information 'channeled from fifth dimensional entities' but which is in fact heavily borrowing from Gurdjieff's ideas; common modern terms such as 'The Work,' 'Work on oneself,' and 'awakening,' now more or less household expressions amongst those involved in personal growth or transpersonal work, were all originally Gurdjieff expressions.

Ouspensky was an essential component of this accomplishment. More than any other, he brought Gurdjieff's ideas to large numbers of people in the West. In fact, his work, *In Search of the Miraculous*, the account of his years with Gurdjieff, has been far more widely read than any of Gurdjieff's own published writings. It is one of a small number of 20th century Western classics of spirituality, up there with Earnest Holmes' *The Science of Mind*, Maxwell Maltz's *Psycho-Cybernetics*, Crowley's *Magick: Book Four*, Helen Schucman's *A Course in Miracles*, and Alan Watts' *The Book*.

The jury remains out on Gurdjieff the man—he could be both kind and brutal, and above all, *intimidating*. As John Carswell put it, 'He had the power of controlled fury, which commands instant obedience.'[17] However, there is little doubt about the value and usefulness of the system he left behind, which is almost certainly all he would have cared about anyway. There is also little doubt about the influential impact he and his Work have had on so many tens of thousands throughout the world, the vast majority of whom never met him.

Gurdjieff, much like the protagonist of his magnum opus, *Beelzebub*, was a stranger in a strange land. He was exceptionally unique, a wizard from another world, but paradoxically he was also very human. Ultimately, however, like all true Magi, there was something unapproachable about him—or as his student Margaret Anderson put it, he was the 'unknowable Mr. Gurdjieff'. The essence of the man and his life was probably best summarized by this well known quote from his Russian disciple Rachmilievitch: 'God give you the strength and courage, Gurdjieff, to endure your lofty solitude'.

Chapter 3
Osho: The Most Dangerous Man
since Jesus Christ

I don't have any biography. And whatsoever is thought to be biography is utterly meaningless. On what date I was born, in what country I was born, does not matter. What matters is what I am now, right here.
Osho, *The Last Testament*

Everything that is valuable is esoteric.
Osho, *Beyond Psychology*

Esoteric means bullshit.
Osho, *From Bondage to Freedom*

The second and third quotes above vividly illustrate a quality of Osho's that anyone familiar with the rich tapestry of his life will attest to: the man was a walking, breathing contradiction. That his words frequently contradicted themselves was something he openly and cheerfully admitted many times—and seemed to revel in. If in that regard only, he was the quintessential rascal guru. He was also the archetypal spiritual rebel; indeed rebelliousness was the very heart of his teaching and his character. Even his book publishing house was named Rebel Publishing.

More pointedly, Osho's contradictoriness in his spoken words was itself *consistent* with his Zen master persona. In particular, it was impossible to set up any sort of Church around him, much less prepare any sort of holy book, simply because his words were so unpredictable. Doubtless that pleased him because more than any modern day guru he was vehemently anti-establishment and especially anti-organized religion.

He was a brilliant man, and probably one of the mostly intensely charismatic humans ever to walk the planet. He attracted tens of thousands of followers and admirers not just for the penetrating wisdom of his oratory, but for the impressive quality of his person. Like Gurdjieff he was not a large man, 5 ft. 6 at most, but he had an impressive, magisterial head with mesmerizing eyes and an extraordinary dulcet voice that, while changing over the years, always seemed to render everything around him in slow motion, almost as if he were speaking underwater. Power, self-assurance, and a kingly quality oozed out of him. Even his name, 'Rajneesh', which was originally a nickname given to him in his childhood but that stuck with him for most of his life, is based on the Sanskrit *raja*, meaning 'king'.

I had the opportunity in early 1986 to attend his nightly talks in Nepal, sitting not more than twenty-five feet away as he spoke every evening for several weeks straight. He had the ability to turn an entirely spontaneous talk in a hotel conference room in front of a hundred and fifty people into a deeply intimate affair, one where you felt like he was speaking personally to you as he discoursed about any and everything. I fully agree with Swami Paritosh, who, going by the pen-name 'Sam' in his book, *Life of Osho*, wrote:

'This gentle vegetarian' wrote the American novelist Tom Robbins. There, so far as I am concerned, speaks someone who never sat in front of Osho. Gentle vegetarian, my eye. He was scary, Osho; he was really scary…What was it he said? 'You open an abyss before them, and you tempt them to jump.' Well, that's what it felt like, just like that.[1]

My own experience with Osho was that he had the capacity to

operate as a very intense mirror; that is, if I sat in front of him in a negative state of mind, he could indeed seem 'scary.' If, however, I sat in front of him feeling relaxed within myself, he appeared tender and full of compassion. In keeping with the deepest truth of so-called 'guru-yoga', he was neither truly unkind nor wholly compassionate. Of course, he was capable of either of those manifestations of behavior, but more to the point, I was simply witnessing my own capacity for unkindness or compassion reflected back to me. He was, as the Zen expression has it, an 'empty mirror'. At least, that was his 'guru function', which he performed well enough. But what of Osho the man?

Childhood

Osho was born in the hamlet of Kuchwada, in Madyha Pradesh state in central India, on December 11, 1931.[2] He was given the name Chandra Mohan Jain. (The word *chandra* in Hindi means 'moon,' an interesting factoid as his controversial commune in Oregon, which existed from 1981 to 1985, called Rajneeshpuram, also went by the informal name of 'City of the Lord of the Full Moon'.) His parents were Digambar Jains of the Taranpanthi sect. The Jain religion is very old but is currently a minor faith in India. The origins of Jainism are unclear but it is known to have existed at least a few hundred years before the Buddha and over eight centuries before Christ.

The first nine years of Osho's life were lived in a very small village which did not have a school. He claimed to be 'uneducated' in any formal fashion for those first nine years, living only in an innocent, natural setting, and playing with abandon and great freedom. These were all hallmarks of the later man he would grow into—despite obtaining two university degrees, he remained deeply suspicious of conventional education and always vehemently opposed rote learning and educational dogma. His school year confrontations with his professors (both as a student and later as a professor himself) were legendary. In addition, he was always deeply concerned that people learn to be *natural* and uninhibited, doubtless a reflection of his own highly free formative years.

Osho was the firstborn of what was eventually to be a family of eleven children. At an early age, he was sent to live with his maternal grandparents who, in their last years, wanted to raise a child. He reports that his grandparents had some means, which kept them separate from the other very poor families in the village. Osho as a child was thus kept alone, not allowed to play with the other village children. He claimed that as a result of that he never had friends but he also claimed that he soon came to enjoy his aloneness greatly.

The English psychiatrist Anthony Storr, in his interesting but somewhat flawed study of gurus, titled *Feet of Clay*, made the observation that gurus almost never have friends, only followers:

> Many gurus appear to have been rather isolated as children, and to have remained so. They seldom have close friends. They are more interested in what goes on in their own minds than in personal relationships, perhaps because they do not believe that anyone else really cares for them. In other words, they tend to be introverted and narcissistic.[3]

Storr's observations are astute and probably accurate in many cases; however, they disallow for the possibility of a different sort of outcome to such an upbringing than the usual neurotic introversion and exaggerated sense of self-importance. This type of interpretation is mostly due to the psychiatrist's natural default tendency to pathologize suspect behavior, and to dismiss the possibility of true ego-transcendence. In the case of Osho, however, Storr's points about narcissism are pertinent, as Osho did appear to have an enormous sense of personal entitlement, along with his powerful charisma and intellectual acumen. (As an interesting aside, the obituary that appeared shortly after Anthony Storr's death in 2001 made note of the fact that for much of his childhood he was a lonely child who had no friends. One of his later books was titled *Solitude*. Given that, one may speculate as to how much of Storr's views about Osho's self-absorption arose out of his identification with him.)

In 1939, when Osho was not yet eight years old, his grandfather, whom he'd been very attached to, died. This death deeply affected him. In later years, when speaking of the event, he claimed to handle it in a very mature and wise fashion, even declaring it a transformation and an 'immense mutation', saying this is the natural by-product of losing someone you love deeply. He reported that his dying words to his father were:

> You have given me your love and you have given me your freedom. I think no child ever had such freedom as you gave to me. What more do I need? What more can you give? I am thankful. You can die peacefully.[4]

Those words, while profound and graceful, are certainly the words of an adult, not a seven year old boy. So while the passage sheds light on Osho's subsequent intense interest in death and in discovering a timeless realm beyond death, it also reveals one of his pronounced tendencies, that being to embellish, and almost always in such as way as to cast himself in a more impressive light.

He was in many respects, by his own admission, a difficult child and adolescent. His earliest biographer, Vasant Joshi, described him in his boyhood as 'egotistical, immodest, discourteous and even seditious'.[5] He was also very clever, creative, a natural leader, and possessed of enormous courage. His headstrong nature was probably molded in part by his grandparents who indulged him greatly for the first seven years of his life. He became used to having his own way. All this, combined with a zeal for reading and learning and his fearless independence, slowly honed him for a future life as a radical guru.

Years of Seeking

It's interesting to contrast the next phase of Osho's life with that of Gurdjieff's similar period. Both became exceptionally intense seekers of truth, wholly consumed with a burning passion to penetrate the mysteries of life. But while Gurdjieff's search (as he claimed) was very extroverted—forming a group called the Seekers of Truth and traveling far and wide through many dangerous lands—Osho's, more in keeping with the Oriental spirit, was much more internalized (although he did have many people in his life, including three important mentors—see Chapter 14 for more on that). He began experimenting with meditation in his early teens. In 1946, at just fourteen years of age, he experienced his first *satori* (sudden, though temporary, awakening).[6] In his late teens, around the year 1950, he began to pass through a type of nervous breakdown brought on by intense contemplation of the ultimate questions of life. In a sense, he had devised his own Zen *koans*[7] and was spending all of his time and mental energy in profound contemplation of them. This eventually brought him to a state of virtual intellectual exhaustion (he was also a heavy reader at that young age). He began to disconnect from the world around him, both interpersonally and physically. He claimed that at this time he took to running up to sixteen miles a day 'just to feel myself'.

There is often a fine line between authentic spiritual breakthrough and what is sometimes called depersonalization, or even outright mental illness. A good case in point is the story of Suzanne Segal, an American woman and spiritual seeker who one day while standing at a bus stop had a deep and direct experience of no-self, of the inherent emptiness of the separate personality. Whether because she lacked a supportive network or proper guide to confirm her realization, or because she simply wasn't ready, she did not respond to it well. The effects of this experience lingered for close to a decade as she grappled with the terrible fear provoked by her trying to hang on to the sense of individual self that had been shattered by her 'bus stop experience', as she called it. She eventually settled into the realization and moved beyond her fear, ending up writing a book about the ordeal and becoming a spiritual teacher.[8] Not long after, however, she was found to have a brain tumor and passed away in 1997.

Her case is interesting because it can be argued that Western culture, being more individualistic and egocentric, makes it difficult to relinquish ego in the classic mystic sense, and does not reinforce the Eastern realization that the personal self is essentially an illusion. There is certainly an Eastern cultural ego as well but as a whole the philosophical atmosphere, certainly in India, is more conducive to supporting a profound spiritual realization. Many wandering mystics, or *sadhus*, in India would probably end up committed to mental institutions in the West, as opposed to being sustained by daily alms. Some of them are probably pushing shopping carts around on city streets this moment.

As Osho neared the spiritual epiphany that would, as he understood it, become his enlightenment, he became more and more remote. His parents, concerned, took him around to mental health practitioners. One doctor, rather than pathologizing what was happening to him, apparently served to confirm Osho's spiritual state, remarking, with tears in his eyes,

> He is not ill. I have been searching for this state myself. He is fortunate. In this life I have missed this state. Don't take him to anybody. He is reaching home.[9]

Enlightenment

A climax in Osho's deep questioning was eventually reached, during which, as he claimed, his questions about the ultimate meaning of existence were not answered, but rather, the questions were destroyed by the fire of pure inquiry. He then entered a period of seven days where 'all hope disappeared'. This occurred in mid March of 1953 when he was twenty-one years old:

Seven days I lived in a very hopeless and helpless state, but at the same time something was arising. When I say hopeless I don't mean what you mean by the word hopeless. I simply mean there was no hope in me. Hope was absent. I am not saying that I was hopeless and sad. I was happy in fact, I was very tranquil, calm and collected and centered...[10]

This ended with a final day, on March 21, during which a deep deconstruction of his personal self seemed to occur:

I was becoming loose from my past, I was being uprooted from my history, I was losing my autobiography. I was becoming a non-being, what Buddha calls anatta. Boundaries were disappearing, distinctions were disappearing.

Late in the day, his process began to deepen and climax:

I used to go to sleep in those days near about twelve or one in the night, but that day it was impossible to remain awake. My eyes were closing, it was difficult to keep them open. Something was very imminent, something was going to happen. It was difficult to say what it was—maybe it is going to be my death—but there was no fear. I was ready for it...I went to sleep. It was a very strange sleep. The body was asleep, I was awake....near about twelve my eyes suddenly opened—I had not opened them. The sleep was broken by something else. I felt a great presence around me in the room. It was a very small room. I felt a throbbing life all around me, a great vibration—almost like a hurricane, a great storm of light, joy, ecstasy. I was drowning in it...a deep urge arose in me to rush out of the room, to go under the sky—it was suffocating me. It was too much! It will kill me! If I had remained a few moments more, it would have suffocated me—it looked like that...I reached to the garden where I used to go every day...

The experience culminated with an ecstatic confidence and sense of being totally finished as a separate entity:

> I looked around. One tree was tremendously luminous—the maulshree tree. It attracted me, it pulled me towards itself. I had not chosen it, god himself has chosen it. I went to the tree, I sat under the tree. As I sat there things started settling. The whole universe became a benediction.

What distinguished this experience from a more typical Zen *satori* ('sudden awakening') is that in Osho's case, he claimed the event resulted in a permanent shift in consciousness for him. He was literally reborn as a fully awake man, in whom the sense of personal identity and personal story had evaporated:

> And that day something happened that has continued—not as a continuity—but it has still continued as an undercurrent. Not as a permanency—each moment it has been happening again and again. It has been a miracle each moment.

Taking into account the whole process, beginning with the years of intense questioning and searching, Anthony Storr argued that Osho suffered what appeared to be a classic psychotic breakdown:

> ...this series of events sounds like a psychotic episode. It appears probable that Rajneesh suffered from a fairly severe depressive illness between the ages of nineteen and twenty-one which came to an end with a hypomanic state in the form of an ecstatic experience...there are strong hints that he suffered from further periods of depression after he became a guru...in March 1974, he withdrew from all activities and went into complete silence for the next few weeks. In 1981, he also went through a period of some months in which he failed to respond to those caring for him, and apparently did not even read...I think that it is

reasonable to conclude that, as in the case of many other leaders, his personality was both narcissistic and manic-depressive, manifesting itself in actual illness from time to time.[11]

I give space for Storr's views here because as an established Western psychiatrist who was not in any way connected to Osho or his movement he was a good example of how the Western psychoanalytic mindset would tend to interpret Osho's inner process, especially in light of the happenings in Oregon that became manifest some thirty years after this event. And in point of fact, Osho himself partly confirms Storr's views, describing the period leading up to his enlightenment as 'a time of nervous breakdown and breakthrough.'[12]

But Storr's view is limited because he does not really consider the break*through* part. The limitation of some of the conventional Western psychotherapeutic models is that they lack any comprehensive view of mystical states, although one psychiatrist who clearly did have a deep understanding of the matter, R.D. Laing, was acknowledged by Storr—and there have certainly been others, most notably William James back in the late 19th century, and of course, C.G. Jung. But much of the dim view Western psychoanalysis casts on the mystical experience has its roots in Freud himself, who dismissed most mystical experience as an 'oceanic' type of consciousness that is regressive and infantile, that is, based on old memories of 'oneness' with the mother.

The problem with Storr's diagnosis is that some elements of Osho's experience, as he described it, are consistent with a type of traditional mystical awakening, found in many different traditions, and in particular, the enlightenment experiences of the Zen tradition. Here are but two examples, taken from the classic text, *The Three Pillars of Zen*:

Am totally at peace at peace at peace. Feel numb throughout the body, yet hands and feet jumped for joy for almost half an hour. Am supremely free free free free free. Should I be so happy? There is no common person. The big clock chimes—not the clock but Mind chimes. The universe chimes itself. There is neither Mind nor universe. Dong, dong, dong! I've totally disappeared...oh, you are! You laughed, didn't you? This laughter is the sound of you plunging into the world. The substance of Mind—this is now luminously clear to me...I am at peace at peace at peace...I am grateful, so grateful.[13]

Or this:

I have it! I know! There is nothing, absolutely nothing! I am everything and everything is nothing!'...feel free as a fish swimming in an ocean of cool, clear water after being stuck in a tank of glue...and so grateful...but mostly, I am grateful for my human body, for the privilege as a human being to know this Joy, like no other.[14]

Lex Hixon, in his study of the enlightenment experience, *Coming Home: The Experience of Enlightenment in Sacred Traditions*, writes:

Enlightenment is the awakening to our primal harmony or, in another mystical language, to our rootedness in the Divine.[15]

The question then becomes, how does this 'awakening to primal harmony' manifest? What the world's wisdom traditions bear out is that while the underlying truths tend to be common, the manner of realization of these can vary greatly, depending on the disposition of the seeker. But to merely dismiss Osho's epiphany as a 'psychotic break' is to ignore the reality that it was not inconsistent with a genuine type of mystical experience—and not all of whom have such an experience are by default mentally ill people.

During his seeking years, Osho had attended Hitkarini College in Jabalpur, but was eventually expelled due to insubordination. He transferred to a different college, D.J. Jain, completing his under-graduate degree (in philosophy) in 1955 at the age of twenty-three. He then entered the University of Saugar where he earned a master's degree (again in philosophy) two years later. Of interest here is that he accomplished these academic feats *after* his claimed spiritual enlightenment in 1953. This is highly unusual. History bears out that most seekers who undergo a profound spiritual awakening generally retire from conventional life, and most commonly from academic pursuits (although in theory, the two need not be antithetical). A good case in point was Osho's contemporary, the American guru Adi Da Samraj (previously known as Franklin Jones, Da Free John, or a host of other appellations), who, like Osho, obtained a master's degree but who, unlike Osho, had not yet had his self-realization at that time. He then left academia to plunge into deep spiritual inquiry in India, culminating in his (as he claimed it) full awakening in California several years later.

The way Adi Da described it, it would have been almost incon-ceivable for him to return to academia after the event of his awakening. And that is much more the norm—accounts of radical spiritual realization typically occur *after* conventional academic education or outside of it altogether. There are more conventional exceptions to that tendency—as a case in point, the American psychotherapist and spiritual teacher Jack Kornfield ordained as a Buddhist monk in Burma as a young man, and after many years of meditation and deep insights he returned to America, married, and pursued a PhD in psychology. This approach is somewhat common in the case of seekers who do not claim a profound awakening or anything like full enlightenment—is it far less so in the case of seekers who have awakenings that they would describe as total or nearly total.

Osho was an interesting paradox in that regard, because despite his antinomian and highly body-centered philosophy, he was himself intensely cerebral. In general, he taught his disciples to 'live from the heart, not the head' and yet he himself had a massive private library of some 80,000 volumes and was a known speed-reader devouring up to ten or more books per day (see Appendix V for more on that).

The question as to why Osho pursued an academic training in philosophy when he was already supposedly completely enlightened has perhaps never been satisfactorily answered. The standard reply by followers who studied his life has been that he needed to be prepared for what awaited him in the future, that is, the many educated Westerners who would come to him. And it is true that the average level of education of his followers was relatively high (a majority were college educated). But this sort of explanation is too contrived. More conceivable is that Osho still identified with being an intellectual, and was not ready to abandon everything and go sit at the foot of a mountain, as the Advaitin sage Ramana Maharshi famously did, and as scores of other Himalayan 'cavemen' routinely still do.

The other possibility is that Osho was not yet convinced of the totality of his own enlightenment. This is suggested based on an incident that he reports happened during his university years. He used to attend a particular class wearing wooden sandals. His professor asked him why he was wearing these noisy shoes to class. He replied that he did so because the sound of the shoes helped to keep him awake—that is, he was using the shoes as a meditation device in order to keep his awareness present and sharp.[16] It follows that a fully enlightened being would not need to use techniques of this sort in order to be 'fully present.' Apparently, Osho was still working on himself, that is, he had not yet stabilized in the realized state. The point may seem trivial in light of the grand drama of his life but it bears significant implications, precisely because Osho's movement *initially* was, above all, a personality cult. That is, it depended crucially on his claimed spiritual state, much like how Christianity depends crucially on the belief in the resurrection.

Without the resurrection, Jesus is just another wise man, not one who has conquered death, and thus the essential Nicene creed—that Jesus *is* God—is gutted. Likewise, Buddhism is based on the assumed factuality of Gautama Buddha's full enlightenment. The doctrine of the Buddha means little if he himself did not fully realize what he preached. Similarly in Osho's case, his teaching was entirely based on taking his disciples from where *they* were, to where *he* was. As he said:

> I have to work on two levels: one is the level where you live, where you are, and one is the level where I am and where I want you to be.[17]

Whatever his actual inner state, after obtaining his MA, he applied for a teaching job at Raipur Sanskrit College, where in 1958, at the age of twenty-six, he was hired and then in short order asked to leave by college authorities who feared his radical teaching style and brash personality were alienating too many. In due course he transferred to the University of Jabalpur where in 1960 he became a full professor.

We can pause for a moment here to imagine the situation. Here is the 'Acharya Rajneesh' (as he was called then, *acharya* being the Hindi word for 'teacher'), a small yet vital and handsome young man in his late twenties with penetrating eyes, highly eloquent, brilliant and knowledgeable, a forceful, stubborn, and overbearing personality with strong anti-authoritarian tendencies, and (by his own understanding) spiritually self-realized to boot. It's easy to imagine that he must have been a holy terror and why he was kicked out of two colleges. But as usually happens, as many people who are intimidated and scared off by such a man, others are drawn to him. There are few things as powerful and magnetic in life as someone who challenges status quos and old conventions in a way that is both aggressive and eloquently well reasoned. (By all accounts, if the New Testament is to be believed, Jesus cut a very similar figure, although in his case he paid a heavier price than expulsion from colleges.)

Around this time, the young *acharya* also began doing a lecture circuit of his rather large country, an activity of his that continued for almost a decade up until the late 1960s. His talks were renowned for their fiery condemnation of various 'sacred cows' like celibacy, Mahatma Gandhi, and Hindu religious authorities. In large part no doubt due to his wide reading—Osho, at that point, had never traveled outside of India—he was strongly pro-Western in many ways, criticizing India for its technological and political backwardness.

Osho began formally teaching meditation via retreats or camps in the early 1960s and by 1966 he decided to devote himself full time to lecturing and leading these camps around the country, quitting his teaching post at the university. This marked the beginning of his complete entry into guru-hood. He had by that time already acquired an Indian following and was supported financially. In his talks, he began to aim his criticisms at more specific targets, particularly Hindu leaders, and his first major book, a collection of lectures called *From Sex to Superconsciousness*[18] published originally in 1968, served to cement his reputation as a deeply radical figure. India is a nation of strong sexual protocols and Osho's ideas about sex energy (doubtless influenced by Western figures like Wilhelm Reich whom he'd read) were highly inflammatory. Like Crowley, he began to acquire fame via notoriety as specifically connected to his views on sexuality. But unlike Crowley, Osho was forwarding such ideas during a time when much of the Western world was embracing a cultural revolution that included an attempt to become liberated from social and sexual inhibitions. The same year that saw Osho's book, *From Sex to Superconsciousness*, published also saw Aleister Crowley's name and legacy being gradually resurrected by The Beatles from their 1967 *Sergeant Pepper's* album. As one old tantric master was being brought back from the dead, another live one was launching his wild career.

Dynamic Meditation and the Mumbai (Bombay) Years

In 1970, at the age of thirty-eight, Osho introduced a meditation that proved to be one of his major trademarks over the years, a five step process lasting one hour called Dynamic Meditation. The term 'meditation' to describe this process represented a whole new understanding of what exactly meditation is or can be. It's difficult to appreciate just how innovative this technique was, and just how well Osho grasped the psychological needs of people at that time. The meditation itself (described in full in Part Four of this book) contains stages of deep breathing, cathartic release, jumping up and down while repeating a mantra, silence, and dance. It has been suggested by some that Osho crafted this process for Westerners, owing to their deep psychological repressions, but in point of fact when he devised this meditation almost all of his followers were Indians. So clearly he saw the problem of repression as something endemic to humanity, not just those of the Occident.

In September of 1970, he formally launched his spiritual movement, initiating followers into *sannyas*, which made them disciples in the classic spiritual sense of the word, that is, allegiant to one particular spiritual master. *Sannyas* is an ancient tradition in India—the Sanskrit word itself literally means to 'lay it all down', or as more conventionally understood, to 'renounce' the world in order to devote oneself entirely to spiritual discipline. Osho's concept was very different, however. Much in keeping with Gurdjieff's idea of the Fourth Way (way of the spiritual householder) Osho did not want his people to renounce the world, or desires (including sexual). He rather wanted them to renounce the ego/i.e., the tendency to be unconscious. He wanted his people to celebrate life, meditate, love, live joyously, and be connected to the world at the same time. Although this latter point was always problematic in light of the fact that the only way for a follower to be physically close to Osho was to live in either the ashram in Pune or the commune in Oregon, both of which were (and in the case of the Pune ashram, still is) largely self-contained environments more or less sealed off from the world around.

In keeping with his highly radical nature, Osho's version of *sannyas* was also unique in that not only were followers required to wear the classic orange robe of the wandering mendicant, they also adopted a new Sanskrit name and—in an innovation that skirted perilously close to personality-worship—wore around their neck a mala of 108 beads that contained a framed photo of Osho. Whatever his intentions, this device seems to have had the result of dividing up Osho's followers at the time between the casual onlookers and the serious seekers (and not to mention, the infatuated). The former left, the latter took the leap into full initiation.

It is interesting to pause here again and take a look at this 'device' (as Osho referred to it as). Osho had always been an admirer of Gurdjieff, but it is unlikely Gurdjieff would have approved of the use of the framed photo in the mala. One of Gurdjieff's definitions of black magic was the 'creating in people of infatuation'[19] and he was himself reputed to intentionally alienate people if he suspected they were becoming too attached to him. (This point has been disputed—that is, it's not clear to what extent Gurdjieff was 'intentionally alienating' others or to what extent they were simply being naturally alienated by his ego-manifestations.) The famous Advaitin sage Nisargadatta Maharaj—who was teaching out of a small room in Mumbai while Osho was beginning his work in that same city in the early 1970s—also was highly sensitized to the issue of attachment, and had a policy of allowing visitors to stay only for a week or so with him before they had to leave; and on occasion, he would throw people out (and some of those people were Osho disciples). Here again, the issue is clouded—Nisargadatta taught out of a small room that could only hold so many people, thus getting rid of people after eight days may have been purely logistical.

Osho, however, seemed to invite the opposite, that is, he actively sought to cultivate relationships with followers and directly encouraged the growth of his spiritual family. When people would leave him temporarily, as in traveling back to the West to resume work or other responsibilities, he would often say things like 'I will haunt you in your dreams'. These comments were generally made in a playful or affectionate tone but nevertheless they revealed something about his nature, that being that his way of working was very much based on the ideal of the spiritual community. He would say, repeatedly, that all that mattered was the disciple's connection with the master but, in fact, one of his aims was clearly to develop a powerful community or, as he would call it in later years, a 'buddhafield'.

Years later, in commenting on the issue Osho's close disciple, Juliet Forman wrote,

> Osho's whole message is that everyone is born with the same potential…at the most, Osho was our potential realized, a mirror for us…when we touched Osho's feet in those days in Pune, when we namasted him in greeting and he us, when we wore his photograph on lockets around our necks, we were paying respect to and reminding ourselves of what was possible within us.[20]

That is indeed the highest and best usage of such a device—what could be called the ideal expression of *bhakti* (devotional) yoga. The more difficult issue concerns to what degree it did in fact get used that way. Crowley was often accused of overestimating his students and his readers, writing in such a way that assumed their level of understanding to be higher than it was. Osho probably could be accused of something similar. While the locket device was a powerful learning vehicle and while Osho may have intended it precisely in the manner explained by Forman, the fact remains that people did become dependent to varying degrees, depending on their maturity, intelligence, underlying authority issues, and so on. (The locket became an issue when in late 1985 Osho invited disciples to drop it, which many did—only to be told by Osho that they had dropped it too quickly! Some began wearing it again, but not long after it was dropped entirely.)

In late 1970, Osho settled into the Woodlands Apartments in

Mumbai, which was to become home for the next three years. In 1971, he changed his name from Acharya Rajneesh to Bhagwan Shree Rajneesh ('Bhagwan' meaning 'the blessed one'—a title that was also used by the famous Advaita sage Ramana Maharshi, and so accordingly incited some controversy in India at the time). At this time his chronic health problems began to appear, asthma and diabetes being the most troublesome, as well as certain allergies. He became particularly sensitive to odors, something that in later years brought about the need for 'sniffers' at the gates before his lectures, disciples who would go to the trouble of closely smelling each person about to sit in his lectures. Anyone smelling of perfume or other strong scents was turned away at the gate.

Pune I, Rajneeshpuram, Pune II

Eventually, the climate in Mumbai was deemed unacceptable for Osho's health and chiefly as a result of that, in March of 1974, he and his followers moved to Koregaon Park, a well-to-do suburb of Pune, a mid-sized city about a hundred and fifty miles southeast of Mumbai. There, they purchased a group of buildings on a lush property and converted them into the Shree Rajneesh ashram. This was to become home for the next seven years for one of the largest and most radical personal growth experiments on the planet (a phase later to be known as 'Pune I'). During this time, Osho would initiate tens of thousands of people into *sannyas*. Several thousand of these disciples would be present in Pune at any given time; a few hundred resident in the ashram, many more staying in villas, hotels and simple huts nearby. The presence of the ashram proved a boon to the local economy, and despite some who objected to the content of Osho's teachings and the presence of so many 'hippie-like' Westerners, the community was by and large tolerated—until around 1980, when the inevitable problems began to arise as the number of disciples swelled.

During these years in Pune, Osho had a fixed daily routine that he would rarely vary from. Every morning he would lecture in the main hall for approximately ninety minutes. He would then return to his room and spend most of his day alternating between reading and napping. He read voraciously, up to ten or fifteen books a day. To read that many books in one day obviously requires speed reading, and doubtless skimming as well. This manner of reading seemed to be reflected in Osho's discourses, which while vast in scope and breadth of knowledge, were not particularly specialized. He delivered talks that were intended for wide audiences of intelligent spiritual seekers but not for esoteric specialists. However, his talks were generally recognized as brilliant. He had a particularly strong ability, in many ways similar to the mythologist Joseph Campbell, to weave many strands together, from religion, mysticism, philosophy, psychology, and science—and like Campbell he would do it all without notes and without pause in his delivery. He was a superb and mesmerizing orator.

In the evenings, he would then host *darshan,* a term that means 'vision of the divine' or 'to see the light of the master'. These meetings were small gatherings of a few dozen people in which Osho would talk to disciples one-on-one—greeting new arrivals, seeing people off as they were going back to the West, and bestowing initiations. He also would provide considerable guidance, often counseling everything from quarreling couples to confused seekers to those who were experiencing significant inner breakthroughs in their work on themselves. Many of these meetings were recorded and published as 'darshan diaries' which provided interesting glimpses into the intense dynamic between Osho and his *sannyasins*. Arguably these 'diaries' are amongst the most comprehensive and intimate portraits of a guru working with his disciples.

At this time, Osho was, in one sense, at the height of his powers. Ironically, one of most vivid descriptions of his intense charisma and personal impressiveness comes from his disaffected disciple Hugh Milne, who, in his otherwise generally critical book, *Bhagwan: The God that Failed*, wrote:

Many people have asked me how a sensible, independent person could be mesmerized by someone like Bhagwan [Osho]. The answer, as many sannyasis [disciples of Osho] would agree, is that once you had been affected by his energy and experienced the sensation of being touched by it, you knew that there was nothing like it, no bliss to compare with it. Once you had experienced it you had to go back for more, to try and regain that feeling of harmony and being at one with the universe...Bhagwan's touch could be just as addictive as the strongest drug.[21]

The main activities going on in the ashram were many types of meditation and alternative psychotherapies. The ashram was unique in this respect, as Osho was the first Eastern guru to fully embrace Western psychotherapy, both intellectually and experientially, in his work. The chief therapists at the ashram during the 70s, or 'group leaders' as they were generally called, acquired a fame and prestige within the community that at times would rival Osho's. Some of the more notable ones over that time were Michael Barnett (Swami Anand Somendra), Paul Lowe (Swami Ananda Teertha), Allen Lowen (Swami Anand Rajen) and Robert Birnbaum (Swami Prem Amitabh). By the early 1980s some of these therapists (such as Barnett and Lowe in particular) eventually left Osho, either believing themselves to be sufficiently awakened as to not need him anymore or simply feeling that their time with the master was complete. (Osho did, however, accuse some of them of competitiveness with him and an ego-based need to have their own exclusive followers. That noted, I personally cannot recall of a single case where Osho approved of anyone's leaving of him, unless it was clearly someone aberrant. In some twenty years of teaching, Osho never sanctioned anyone to leave him and go off and teach on their own as a 'master'.)

By the late 1970s, the rapid growth of the ashram, mostly due to Osho's rising popularity amongst Westerners, brought about the necessity of looking for a larger piece of ground on which to build a new commune. However, Osho was then (as always) highly controversial and was considered a problem by the Indian government and in particular by the prime minister at that time, Morarji Desai. The result was that several attempts to acquire land in remote parts of India were blocked. In addition, the tax exempt status of the Pune ashram was discontinued and back taxes were demanded. Then, in early 1980, a man claiming to be a Hindu fundamentalist stood up during one of Osho's lectures, accused Osho of insulting his religion, and threw a knife at him. The blade was apparently not well thrown and clattered harmlessly on Osho's podium, but it was considered an assassination attempt nonetheless. All these factors, plus a health issue with Osho's back—and the fact that Osho, reminiscent of Gurdjieff, was eyeing America as the next logical phase in the expansion of his work— prompted his followers to fly him to the United States in June of 1981, where he stayed for a few months at an Osho retreat center in New Jersey.

Shortly before traveling to America, Osho had entered into a period of silence that was to last until November of 1984. During this time he was mostly in seclusion, communicating only with a few disciples, such as his chief secretary at that time, Ma Anand Sheela, and his caretaker companion, Ma Yoga Vivek (Christine Woolf).

In June of 1981, Sheela purchased a 64,229 acre ranch in a desolate area in central Oregon, which became home to Osho's new commune. Hundreds of disciples toiled long hours for many months to gradually transform the place into a thriving town in the middle of nowhere. For the first three and a half years of the life of the commune Osho did not give lectures; videos of his discourses were played in the evenings instead. From the beginning, the commune was beset by numerous legal challenges and a hostile reception from surrounding political forces. Serious internal problems began to occur by 1984 and by September of 1985 the commune collapsed under the weight of several scandals, most of which appeared to center around criminal activities by Sheela and a number of her associates (brought on, at least in part, by intense local resistance from certain elements within the Oregon government to the presence of Osho and his people there). Osho was viewed by the majority of observers from the general public as the main source behind the criminal offenses, but in fact no real evidence was ever found to link him with Sheela's more serious crimes. (See Chapter 10 for a fuller discussion of the commune and Sheela.)

However, by then, Osho's reputation in the eyes of the mainstream media and general public had already been damaged by a number of factors, not the least of which was his collection of Rolls Royces (which at the end, numbered ninety-three). This comically large fleet of highly expensive cars was regarded as an elaborate joke by most of his followers, a parody of American consumerism, or simply the amoral, wildly irreverent act of a 'crazy-wisdom master'. Osho himself ultimately claimed they were a practical joke.[22] (The cars mostly sat there, unused—though he did usually take one of them for a daily drive to greet his disciples—and they were owned by the commune, not by Osho. After he left America the fleet was sold to a collector.) But despite that, many people came to associate him with these cars and many could not wrap their minds around the apparent incongruity of a 'spiritual master' with such a collection of decadence. As 'Sam', in *Life of Osho*, put it amusingly:

> Officially the Rolls Royces…were meant to be some kind of piss-take of capitalism—or, alternatively, they were meant to show that meditation was perfectly compatible with luxury. Either way they were not communicating any such thing. What they were communicating was…yuk! They were communicating taste-lessness.[23]

What I'd noticed over the years was that these cars tended to provoke people in ways that were always interesting to watch. All kind of moral righteousness would arise in those inclined to judge Osho as not aligning with the image of the humble saint, and their preconceived ideas of what religiousness and purity of character was. Others saw the humor in it all. Many of those who were on some sort of path of self-transformation but not aligned with Osho and his work were the harshest judges. And that more or less summed up my observation over the years: those not on some sort of 'inner work' path often ignored Osho or mildly judged him; those who were 'on the path' tended to be polarized into two camps, those supportive or those strongly against (with very few neutrals). Government and religious authorities may have opposed him but for different reasons: he was merely a threat to their power base in some way. It was amongst the so-called 'spiritual seekers' that he would find his most severe critics, because these were the ones who were potentially the most threatened by his radical approach that sought to overthrow centuries of mediocre spirituality. As to the matter of the Rolls Royces, some who criticized him were, needless to say, simply jealous of such material abundance. That said, Sam's view of the 'tastelessness' of the cars is not without merit, although rather than tasteless my own view is more that it was all simply *pointless*, that is, not very effectual as a teaching device—if indeed it ever was that.

During the fall of 1985, Osho was officially charged with breaking immigration laws and arranging sham marriages following a strange episode in which, after some of his disciples attempted to take him out of the country and he was arrested in North Carolina after his plane landed to refuel, he was subsequently moved through several jails over a period of twelve days. He was then deported from the United States in November of 1985 and returned to India. The next month, the Indian government decided to expel Osho's closest disciples, including his doctor, caretakers, and secretary, who were travelling with him (all of whom were non-Indians, which meant that the government only had to cancel their visas). Osho opted to leave so that these disciples could remain with him; he then went to Nepal where he stayed for just over a month (all this time continuing with his daily lectures). In early 1986, he went to Greece on the pretext of searching for a possible location for a new commune, but the Greek authorities threw him out after only a few weeks there. This was then followed by a bizarre period of travel in which he was kicked out of, or refused entry to, Switzerland, Sweden, England, Ireland, Canada, Holland, Italy, and Germany. Many of these expulsions were dramatic, with armed guards surrounding Osho's Lear jet as it came to a stop on the runway and manhandling the (for the most part) docile followers. In all of this, Osho's loyalty to his closest disciples was shown to be extraordinary, since at any time he could have simply gone back to India, where he could easily have found other disciples to take care of him. He was trying to find a different country so that this particular small group of followers could remain with him, owing to their visas having been cancelled by the Indian government.

In late March, one country in South America (Uruguay) finally invited him in, and there he went where he was able to stay for three months. During that time, he gave a number of lectures on more esoteric matters (such as *chakras*, dreams, altered states of consciousness, etc.), something he had not done for many years. But in July, the Uruguayan government had him expelled, following up on the same INTERPOL message that had been sent to all the other governments that had kicked him out, that specified Osho and his group being part of a ring of 'smuggling, drug dealing, and prostitution'. That, and the vengeful long arm of the Reagan Administration, was enough to keep them on the run during that period.

In July of 1986, after his expulsion from Uruguay, followed in short order by Jamaica and Portugal, Osho, doubtless wearying of finding a country that would accept both him and his followers, simply went back to India, staying at a friend's home in Mumbai for several months, thus returning to the city where he'd first launched his movement over fifteen years before. In late December of 1986, he then resettled in Pune, beginning a new phase of growth for the old ashram, usually dubbed 'Pune II'. He was to remain there for the final three years of his life. During that time he gave a series of lectures that were frequently interrupted by bouts of ill health. The cause of his sharp physical decline—he was only in his mid-fifties when his body began deteriorating—has been grounds for rampant speculation. He himself declared in late 1987 that his poor health was due to his having been poisoned by a faction within the U.S. government (the CIA). Osho's doctors suspected the poison used had been thallium, a highly toxic metal that is a known assassination tool of choice—sometimes called the 'poisoner's poison'. Other forms of radiation poisoning were also speculated on. However, over the years, this theory has been increasingly questioned and it is now suspected by many that Osho's own diabetic condition, combined with the extreme stress he'd been subjected to in the mid-1980s, along with possible nitrous oxide abuse, combined to wear him out (see Chapter 12 for a fuller discussion of this). On January 19, 1990 he passed away at the age of fifty-eight due to heart failure. His doctor had asked him to accept a pacemaker (which the doctor later stated would doubtless have prolonged his life) but Osho refused, one of his last statements being 'existence decides its own timing'.

About a year before his death, he had dropped his name Bhagwan Shree Rajneesh. After a brief, confusing period during which he went by various names and was even nameless at one point, he eventually accepted the name 'Osho', and since his passing the world has come to largely know him by this name, even though throughout the great majority of his teaching career he was known as Rajneesh.

Osho's community did not collapse with his death; on the contrary, it thrived, and despite the inevitable internal power issues, and the coming and going of many disciples, the overall movement continued to grow and the Pune ashram flourished, expanding and constructing a number of new buildings. As of this writing (twenty years after Osho's passing), it remains one of the largest and most successful personal growth centers on the planet. In addition, Osho's lectures have continued to be published; currently there are close to six-hundred and fifty titles bearing his name, translated into over fifty languages.

To briefly summarize Osho's life story is difficult, but what can be said without hesitation is that, as with Crowley and Gurdjieff, he was a force of nature and brought together, within himself, a remarkably vast spectrum of ideas and qualities. The views on him by the intelligentsia are wildly polarized, some referring to him as a genius and the greatest spiritual teacher of the twentieth century, and others as a mediocre thinker who was more flash than substance. But as with many impactful gurus, what they appear to create transcends their personal life and our interest in the events of their story. Osho was ultimately the source of a new psycho-spiritual philosophy, and a powerful network that connected hundreds of thousands of people. The last time I was at his ashram was in 1991, a year after his death, and I met many there at that time who had become involved in his work only after he was gone. At present time (2010), the general estimate is that the majority of seekers now present at his ashram (now called 'meditation resort') in India were not associated with him while he lived (or were even aware of him). The same is certainly true to a far greater degree in the cases of Crowley and Gurdjieff—neither had a significant following during their lives, but both became highly influential after their deaths.

That is all perhaps in keeping with the essence of what Osho claimed to stand for—the impersonal aspect of spiritual awakening, and how it does not depend on any one personality. At a talk in Mumbai in 1971, he was asked by a questioner, 'Excuse me for asking such personal questions, but who are you, and why have you come into the world?' to which he replied:

It makes no difference whether these questions are personal or not because to me the person does not exist. You cannot ask any personal questions because there is no one to be related to as a person. In fact, it is not presumptuous to ask personal questions, but to assume that a person is, is certainly presumptuous. The person is non-existent, a non-entity. In fact, there is no person…as far as I am concerned, I do not feel at all to be a person. The deeper one goes the lesser one is. And once someone reaches to the ultimate core of himself, there is no self at all.[24]

The irony, of course, is that Osho's followers rarely allowed him to be a nobody, but instead turned him into something else altogether—even to the point of capitalizing the 'H' in 'his' or 'he' when referring to him in print. He liked to say that his idea of the new person was a combination of Zorba the Greek and Gautam the Buddha—'Zorba the Buddha' he called it. But he himself was no Zorba the Buddha; more accurately, with his magisterial presence and extraordinary erudition, grace and sensitivity, he was a royal Buddha. And, it must be admitted, he made no real attempt to dissuade the type of devotion naturally paid to such a figure. I suspect that in the end, despite his earlier realization of the inherent emptiness of the self, elements of his ego-mind indeed survived the spiritual explosion he passed through at age twenty-one. It seems unlikely he was a fully realized being, but the point can be argued that almost no one ever has been. What is of central importance is the message, not the personality, because the message endures. And, as is clear for any who bother to study Osho's work and teachings, his message and legacy is a major key to unlocking the spiritual potential of humanity.

Part Two

The Teachings

Note to the reader: What follows in the next three chapters is, it goes without saying, one person's view. The teachings of these three men were vast and touched on so many disciplines and fields of life that they could not possibly be completely encapsulated in three essays. The next three chapters are an attempt to summarize some of their more important ideas.

Chapter 4
Crowley's Magick and Thelema

It is...of the very first importance to train the mind in every possible way, and to bind it to the Higher Principles by steady, by constant, by flaming Aspiration, fortified by the sternest discipline, and by continuously reformulated Oaths.[1]
Aleister Crowley

I am the flame that burns in every heart of man, and in the core of every star. I am Life, and the giver of Life, yet therefore is the knowledge of me the knowledge of death.
The Book of the Law (2:6)

Crowley had extensive spiritual influences and was extremely well read. Doubtless in part, because of that, his teaching represents more a progression from past traditions rather than a radically unique system seemingly appearing out of nowhere (as appears more the case with Gurdjieff's system, although in fact there is a historical basis to that as well). He called the method 'Magick' (adding the 'k' to distinguish it from stage magic and the endless trivializations of the word), and his system—which he recognized as a new religion— he named 'Thelema' (from the Greek word for 'will').

Crowley taught both mysticism (Yoga, mostly) and Magick, and although he highlighted their differences, he also saw them as ultimately pointing toward the same destiny. In *Magick: Book 4*, he wrote:

There is the general metaphysical antithesis that Magick is the Art of the Will-to-Live, Mysticism of the Will-to-Die; but—'Truth comes bubbling to my brim; Life and Death are one to Him!'

By 'Will to Die' he was referring to the death of the ego, via the traditional Eastern approach of subduing the ego (more the Hindu method), or seeing into its illusory nature (more the Buddhist approach) or relaxing, letting go, and accepting what is (the Taoist approach). By 'Will-to-Live' he was referring to the Thelemic approach of embracing the ego's energies and aligning them with one's true Will (a more Western approach tailored to a culture with its roots in Graeco-Roman individualism).

Magick

Crowley's definition of magick was the following:

Magick is the Science and Art of causing Change to occur in conformity with Will.[2]

He gave a practical illustration of this principle:

It is my Will to inform the World of certain facts within my knowledge. I therefore take 'magickal weapons', pen, ink, and paper; I write 'incantations'—these sentences—in the 'magickal language' i.e., that which is understood by the people I wish to instruct; I call forth 'spirits', such as printers, publishers, booksellers and so forth and constrain them to convey my message to those people. The composition and distribution of this book is thus an act of Magick by which I cause Changes to take place in conformity with my Will.[3]

Dion Fortune (1890-1946), a slightly younger contemporary of Crowley's and a former member of the Stella Matutina, one of the break-away groups from the original Hermetic Order of the Golden Dawn, took Crowley's definition and made an interesting modification to it. She called magick,

> The Science and Art of causing change to occur in consciousness in conformity with Will.

Fortune's is the more psychologized version, and it has been argued by some that hers is an improvement on Crowley's. But Crowley of all people was not remiss to the psychological basis of magick. He was exceptional for his time in terms of his grasp of the so-called principle of reflection—an idea found in many wisdom traditions— that says that what we encounter in life is (to varying degrees) a reflection of some aspect within us. It is in the nature of the ego to project, and to create the perception that all problems lie outside of us, having nothing to do with our own state of mind.

The core Hermetic principle in the famed Emerald Tablet is *as above, so below.* Those four simple words compress an enormously powerful and meaningful truth, that being that the entire universe is interconnected and interdependent. The idea is that reality is a hall of mirrors, ultimately reflecting back to us what the Zen tradition calls our 'original face,' the best and deepest truth of who we really are. However, this best truth cannot be properly seen until we first learn to recognize the less flattering reflections. Nietzsche once wrote, 'Be on your guard not to become the monster that you hunt,' but from another perspective, we *already are* the monster that we hunt. That is, we are not much different from the things in life we dislike the most. We can change our relationship with this 'monster'—with our undesirable life-circumstances, and undesirable inner traits—by making changes *within ourselves.* The keys of magick involve the art and science of making these changes within, in order to come into increasing alignment with our true, best self and its capacity for doing—as Crowley called it, our True Will.

Crowley comments further:

The most common cause of failure in life is ignorance of one's own True Will, or of the means to fulfill that Will. A man may fancy himself a painter, and waste his life trying to become one; or he may really be a painter, and yet fail to understand and to measure the difficulties peculiar to that career.[4]

With those few lines Crowley has nailed the chief cause behind suffering in life. It is, in a sense, the Western equivalent of Buddha's observation that the main cause of suffering is desire—that is, the desire to be something other than what we truly are, the constant attempt to escape our own intrinsic nature—both what we are, and what comes *naturally* to us. Crowley expands on this:

Every man and every woman has a course, depending partly on the self, and partly on the environment which is natural and necessary for each. Anyone who is forced from his own course, either through not understanding himself, or through external opposition, comes into conflict with the order of the Universe, and suffers accordingly. a man whose conscious will is at odds with his True Will is wasting his strength. He cannot hope to influence his environment efficiently. a man who is doing his True Will has the inertia of the Universe to assist him.[5]

With these ideas Crowley was anticipating much of the 'you create your own reality' teachings that were popularized in the 1980s New Age movement, ideas that found much of their source in Ernest Holmes' writings of the 1920s, and in earlier 'new thought' movements. As with all spiritual teachings, however, a type of fundamentalism inevitably appears. New Age fundamentalism took on the form of a clumsy, hardened view of this teaching that ends up encouraging those who seek to apply its principles to take a too facile view of things, and in particular, a too simplified view of cause and effect. The idea that thought creates reality holds true, but not all results that occur in our life are solely due to our particular, individual thoughts. For example, the fact that hundreds of thousands of people can perish at once in a natural disaster (say, an earthquake) does not mean that all these people were caught in the exact same frame of mind. It is a certainty that at least some of them were having happy and blissful thoughts just before the Earth swallowed them.

The idea that we only attain fulfillment in life by doing our True Will needs to be understood carefully, because the True Will, arising as it does from our true self, depends entirely on being *aware* of our true self. And this, it may be said, is where the *true work* begins. Without the introspective focus, the idea of True Will can easily be perverted. For example, Adolf Hitler once declared:

> The man who is born to be a dictator is not compelled. He wills it. He is not driven forward, but drives himself. There is nothing immodest about this. Is it immodest for a worker to drive himself toward heavy labor? Is it presumptuous of a man with the high forehead of a thinker to ponder through the nights till he gives the world an invention? The man who feels called upon to govern a people has no right to say, 'If you want me or summon me, I will cooperate.' No! It is his duty to step forward.[6]

There is an obvious similarity there between Hitler's words and some of the ideas of Nietzsche's Overman and Crowley's True Will. The crucial difference, especially with Crowley's idea, is that True Will cannot be manifested without strident efforts to break free of attachments. In Hitler's case there was an enormous attachment to power—and in particular, the desire for power over others. When great will is combined with great attachment, the result is great egocentric force, inevitably followed by suffering arising from tyranny—regardless of whether such tyranny is over others, or privately over oneself.

In order to become aware of our true self we need to cut through layers of conditioning—from society at large, from our family of origin, from our education, religious influences, even our spiritual ideas, and on and on. In doing so we gradually become aware of our degree of *falseness*, of just how far we have drifted off course from our true nature. To correct this, we need to do a tremendous amount of work on ourselves.

So we begin by self-discovery, and then we proceed into applying ourselves in the world. This latter is *accomplishing* our True Will. Neither task—finding ourselves, or applying ourselves—is even remotely easy, however, and this is borne out by the degree of suffering the human race has endured throughout history. Put simply, we suffer because we are not living our truth. Of course 'finding our truth' does not mean that all suffering magically ceases. On the contrary, there are levels of experience that might be said to correspond to initiations given by life. An initial ecstatic break-through in finding and exercising our True Will might be followed by a dry period or a period of what appears to be total collapse (Crowley's own life being a compelling example). At that point, we are being called to look deeper into the matter and reach for the next level of understanding and maturation.

One of Crowley's key sentences from *Magick in Theory and Practice* is:

Magick is merely to be and to do.[7]

This bears a striking resemblance to one of Gurdjieff's core principles, namely the inability of a person to *do* when he does not know how to *be*. As Gurdjieff said to Ouspensky: 'Our starting point is that man does not know himself, that he *is not*.'[8] Crowley's work, as with Gurdjieff's, was entirely about resolving this basic issue, although the two men used different angles of approach.

Crowley was unique in functioning as a kind of bridge between older and archaic systems of magic and a more scientifically oriented understanding of the matter. A term he had for his system was 'scientific illuminism'. He was trained in critical thought, was interested in and informed about science, and had a passion for rigorous comprehension of things. In a sense, he served to bring magic into the modern age, without abandoning the aesthetic value of its forms and ceremonies. In addition, his sympathy for and deep understanding of the Eastern paths (Raja Yoga and Taoism especially) made it possible for him to join these with the important elements of the Western esoteric tradition. Much as with Gurdjieff and Osho, he was a master synthesizer, an apostle of the universal school of perennial wisdom, but with a fiercely progressive edge.

Thelema

Crowley's work involved, as a main objective, the implementation of what he called the 'Law of Thelema.' *Thelema* is the Greek word for 'will'. It lies at the basis of Crowley's ideas. His famous maxims are:

Do what thou wilt shall be the whole of the Law

and

Love is the law, love under will.

The first expression is not actually original to Crowley. As he freely admitted, he borrowed it from Francois Rabelais, the 16th century French writer. Rabelais wrote a novel about an abbey in which the sole rule was *fais ce que tu voudras* or 'Do what thou wilt'.[9] Crowley developed the idea by, in a sense, linking it with the Taoist concept of selflessness, in effect taking Rabelais' idea to a much higher level. In one sense 'Do what thou wilt shall be the whole of the Law' can be reduced to 'do what comes naturally', or more specifically as 'follow your bliss', the famous expression of the mythologist Joseph Campbell. But this is not the lazy, drug-induced 'bliss' of the 1960s credo *do your own thing*. It rather refers to a profound commitment to both know and be aligned with one's deepest nature and highest calling in life. This is brought about by the following:

1. **Discover your True Will.** What actually is our True Will? It is the highest part of our nature, what awakens passion in us, and a sense of being aligned, on purpose, full of authentic enthusiasm for life. It is what makes us look forward to getting out of bed in the morning. It's what brings true fulfillment in life (regardless of the struggles that may accompany such fulfillment!).

Sadly, most people do not know, let alone are aligned with, their True Will. This is because the True Will cannot be recognized unless there is either natural psychological health, mostly due to having been raised with skill and love by psychologically healthy parents (rare in current times), or there has been considerable self examination—and that by nature is the hardest work of all. Most people are highly resistant to self-examination (or what Gurdjieff called self-observation). And as if that weren't enough, most people are already trapped by difficult circumstances or are living a life based on seeking approval from others (usually perceived authority figures, like family elders, employers, spouse, religious church, or other external factors, including 'God'). Ideally, to know our True Will—or, in the more Taoist sense, to 'do what comes naturally'— should be simple and straightforward; however, we have been conditioned in such a way as to be far removed from our natural self. And this is why we must work on ourselves, to literally become natural again. This is important because only a natural human being can correctly progress to loftier spiritual states.

The idea of 'do what you will' was co-opted by the 1960s counterculture movement as part of a general concern at that time with free will, but it actually means much more than that. The hippie expression was more about anti-authoritarianism, or what in psychology is called 'reaction-formation'. This is a stage a child or adolescent commonly goes through in which they will automatically do or say the opposite of what authority figures appear to do or say. *If you say left, I say right. If you say black, I say white. If you say no, I say yes.* And so on, all part of an attempt to differentiate from authorities, to establish one's personal identity.

Crowley's idea was much more sophisticated than simple anti-authoritarianism. He was, in a sense, taking some of Friedrich Nietzsche's ideas to the next level. Nietzsche believed that thousands of years of religious conditioning, particularly around the notion of *self-sacrifice*, had made humanity weak and susceptible to influence by controlling powers. But Nietzsche, although a brilliant thinker, lacked the circumstances to go beyond cognitive understanding and begin to deeply *live* his teachings. Crowley developed a system to help others embody in a *practical* way a spirituality that was not based on self-reduction, but one rather that employed a robust relationship with life—embraced sexuality, passion, self-esteem, empowerment, success, and so forth (all Nietzschean ideals). That Crowley himself did not always live these virtues is a given, but unquestionably he went further than many philosophers in meeting head-on the reality of his own ego structures.

Crowley's seed ideas were developed further in the 1960s human potential movement—and particularly in Osho's work—in which the notion that we could be self-loving, self-honoring *and* spiritual at the same time began to take hold. That is, that we need not hate ourselves, or psychologically crucify ourselves as 'sinners', or repress our primal energies, in order to move into alignment with our true nature.

2. Once in touch with your True Will—the path in life that makes your heart sing with passion and aliveness—then *follow it* with deep conviction. That's what he meant by the second part: 'shall be the whole of the Law'. That nothing, and no one, has the right to prevent you from following your True Will. (Decades later Wiccans added a few words to Crowley's maxim that softens it somewhat: *And ye harm none, do what ye will.* Or, 'as long as it doesn't harm anyone, do your True Will'. Arguably, this can be seen as a useful safety valve to guard against a self-absorbed militancy creeping in. As I suggest in Chapter 10, it was precisely the lack of this safety valve that was Ma Sheela's undoing and that contributed to bringing down Rajneeshpuram—a community that in other ways

was very much based on Thelemic precepts).

3. **Love is the law, love under will.** By this, Crowley was stating that love is the binding law of the universe, but not the typical love that most people experience (which is really more akin to attachment or sentimentality). His 'love under will' is love guided by the True Will—that is, love guided by awakened consciousness. That's a tall order, of course, because, as the Buddha pointed out twenty-five centuries before Crowley, it is personal attachment that blocks our spiritual awakening more than anything. So to be able to *truly love*—i.e., love minus manipulative attachments, or put another way, unconditional love that freely gives with no thought of reciprocity—is our highest potential. Christ is referring to this when he says 'love your enemies'. But in many ways loving an 'enemy' is easier than truly loving someone close to us, in such a way that is free of agenda. 'Love under will', or love guided by truth, may be said to be the highest test of wakefulness. This is a critical point because it may be safely said that no ideal more than 'love' has been abused throughout history—people have committed all sorts of atrocities in the name of the ideal of 'love', whether they be of the personal kind, or of the large scale sort. Another way of understanding this is that typical 'love' (as we normally think of it) has an opposite, that being fear or hate. True love—'love under will' or love guided by awakened consciousness—has no opposite, as it transcends duality and directly understands the interconnectedness of all. It is beyond ego and the very definition of Oneness.

Sex Magick-Tantra

All sexual yogas (whether the 'sex magick' of the Western esoteric tradition or the Tantra of the East) are based on the essential idea that through union comes knowledge, and that we all seek to be unified with our highest source. Most people, however, lack an operating conceptual model of higher possibilities and so tend to experience the natural longing for this 'union' either via the urge to form relationships (partners, marriage) or via the pull toward sex (the union with another body). The Bible itself uses the word 'know' as synonymous with the word 'sex'. To have sex with someone is, at least potentially, to know them by being intimate with them. Accordingly, the sexual function can be a key to profound realizations about the nature of self via relationship. Equally possibly (and far more commonly), it can be used by the ego to simply reinforce identification (I am nothing more than a body) and duality (the more I try to merge my body with yours, the more I see that we are in fact separate). As a result, the key lies in how sex is approached. Tantra involves attempts to work consciously with its powerful energies.

Crowley employed sexual energy and the sex act in his system in ways that have loosely come to be known as 'sex magick'. Though using different forms and methods, this can be understood as the Western equivalent of Eastern Tantra (there are many Tantras; we speak here of course of those that involve sexuality). Much of Crowley's work, especially as undertaken in his Abbey of Thelema in the early 1920s, involved intensive efforts with sex magick to free himself and his students of puritanical conditioning, self-loathing, and fear and disgust of the human body. His actual work with sex magick began when he engaged in homoerotic practices with his student Victor Neuberg during a period of time in North Africa when he was in his mid-thirties. He was at that time exploring, along with Neuberg, John Dee's 16th century system of Enochian (angel) magick when he experienced a psychic block in his ability to access subtle states of mind. He decided to break through this block by 'offering himself up' in a way that involved playing the passive role in homosexual acts with Neuberg. He claimed that this freed up his consciousness in such a way as to allow him to deepen the spiritual practices he was involved in at that time.

It would be easy to be cynical about such things especially given that Crowley was both bisexual and an admitted hedonist. But it was in matters such as these that Crowley was such a clear predecessor of the psycho-spiritual and tantric practices that began to proliferate in the West from the 1960s onward. One basic idea put forth in many related schools of thought (from humanistic psychology to tantra) is that our capacity for spiritual clarity—the experience of the subtler states of consciousness—is dependent on our level of psychological clarity. In other words, we cannot truly experience deep meditation, for instance, if we are held in the grip of strong psychological blocks. More specifically, if we are sexually repressed, it is unlikely that we can move deeply into authentic spiritual states like unconditional love, deep peace, or expanded wisdom. That would be something like living in a house with a wonderful upper floor, while the middle floors or the basement are full of junk, or in poor structural shape and about to collapse. Even if we could reach the upper floors, we would not be able to relax and would not wish to stay there long.

Sex magick, in common with Tantra and more recent experimental psychotherapies, works to break down barriers and free up blocks in the body-mind. That is one aspect. In addition, a key element of sex magick is connected to the orgasm, the peak of sexual excitation. Because sexual energy can be so powerful, it has the capacity to overpower the conscious mind and silence the internal dialogue (the typical idle chattering that our minds commonly produce). Mystics throughout history have recognized that a mind that is truly quiet (as opposed to merely suppressed)—a state Zen has termed 'no-mind'—is capable of profound realizations. There are a few different ways to reach that state of mental quietude, and sex is one of them. From that perspective, the main reason the orgasm is so intensely pleasurable is not merely because of biochemical processes, but also because when it occurs we experience a moment of total desirelessness. When truly free of desire—even if only for a few seconds—we experience a deep fulfillment, a blissful contentment. Certain drugs have the ability to bring this state of mind about, but the sex act accomplishes it organically. When the mind is quiet and open, much is possible, because the typical filters of the chattering conscious mind are not in the way, and are not distorting things, even if only for a few brief moments.

Owing to the times in which Crowley lived and taught, much of what he wrote about sex magick was in code, or via puns. This was necessary in order for him to avoid the chance of his books being banned, that being a real possibility in his time.

The Book of the Law

There can be no question that the strange little book received by Crowley in April of 1904 in Cairo, called *Liber AL vel Legis*—or as it is more commonly known as, *The Book of the Law*—came to be the cornerstone of his teaching. Although his *Magick: Book Four*, containing his key teachings on Mysticism, Yoga, and Magick, published some quarter of a century after *The Book of the Law* was written down, is generally accepted to be his magnum opus, it is still *Law* that is held to be his prime sacred work—even though, paradoxically, most Thelemites agree that Aleister Crowley was not the actual author of it.

It is perhaps ironic that the book generally accepted to represent the key piece of Crowley's work was claimed by him to not actually have been written by him, but rather dictated to him by a 'non-human' intelligence named Aiwass. (However, such a means of receiving a 'holy book' is not uncommon; most of the Old Testament was received in such a fashion, and Mohammed received the Koran from the angel Gabriel, so the legend says.) Further, the book was written down when Crowley was not yet twenty-nine years old. In virtually all cases, a man in his late twenties, no matter how bright and precocious, has not yet manifested his full wisdom, simply because he cannot have had sufficient life experience to mature his spirit. However, it is arguable that someone under thirty years old, or even under twenty, has the intelligence, sensitivity, and full capacity to *see* the truth, even if they have not had the time to fully experience it. In addition, a younger mind can—probably better than an older mind—function as a 'medium' for truth, or, Mozart-like, as a vehicle for that vast artistic impulse and capacity that we refer to, with great understatement, as 'talent'. It's common knowledge that

Einstein's revelatory realizations were accomplished in his mid-twenties, and that the greatest chess masters usually perform their highest feats during this young decade also. That brilliance is the province of the younger brain is usually not disputed.

However, brilliance is not wisdom. The latter is intelligence seasoned by experience, based in large part on the deepened capacity to recognize and avoid blind alleys, wrong turns, and matters pointless to spend energy on. Wisdom could be defined as the capacity to both understand truth, and to efficiently enable the ways in which it becomes practical and actualized (as opposed to idealistic and ineffectual)—or, to use Gurdjieffian terms, the ways in which *knowledge* and *being* become joined. All this may explain in part why Crowley did not initially recognize the value of *The Book of the Law*.

The story of how Crowley received the text of *The Book of the Law* is interesting and worth recounting. In 1904 he was in Cairo, Egypt, with his first wife Rose. They'd been there for about a month. After several months of magical inactivity, Crowley began practicing invocation again, in this case of certain Egyptian deities such as Thoth, Isis, and Osiris. One day while doing his invocations, Rose, seemingly inebriated or otherwise in an altered state of consciousness, began murmuring 'They are waiting for you'. The next day she was more specific: it was the god Horus who was waiting for Crowley. A few days later they went to the Boulak museum, where Rose—completely ignorant of Egyptology and knowing nothing about Horus—directed Crowley to a stele dedicated to the priest Ankh-f-n-Khonsu that depicted Horus in his form known as Ra-Hoor-Khuit. This impressed Crowley. In addition, the stele was numbered 666 in the museum catalogue (although Crowley says that at the time he 'dismissed it as an obvious coincidence').

Rose then told Crowley that the entity that was communicating through her was named Aiwass, an advanced disembodied adept who had been a minister of Hoor-paar-kraat (a manifestation of

Horus). She then directed Crowley to sit in his temple room in their apartment at noon on the 8th, 9th, and 10th of April, for exactly one hour each day, and write down what he heard. This Crowley dutifully did and for the next three days at exactly noon a voice—not quite booming but 'of deep timbre...perhaps a rich tenor or baritone'—was heard from over his left shoulder (according to his memoirs, he was alone in the room at that time, without Rose). He transcribed its words and, after the third day, he had *The Book of the Law*.

Crowley's role, as he saw it, amounted to introducing a new spiritual octave (to use a Gurdjieffian term) to humanity. As I suggest elsewhere in this book, this 'new dispensation' is not just the province of a few thousand Thelemites in the world—it rather represents something much bigger and, in fact, has already been picked up at least *in part*, via the work of the human potential movement and its offshoots, especially as it flowered in the 1960s. It is perfectly fitting that Crowley's image was resuscitated at that time by the Beatles, because, in fact, his very work and its underlying philosophy was (at least in part) getting life breathed into it, beginning in that decade by many who had scarcely heard of him and by more who were entirely unaware of what he actually said and taught. It goes without saying that *The Book of the Law* is not a purely 'humanist' work, owing to its occasional forays into the aggressively militant spirit and elitism, but the general overall tone of honoring the self and breaking free of allegiance to old paradigms is consistent with humanist psychology and its emphasis on self-actualization, self-direction, and freedom from moral constraint that suffocates a person's innate individuality.

The essence of the 'new dispensation' was seen by Crowley as humanity's entry into a new era, one he called the Aeon of Horus, or of the Crowned and Conquering Child. He believed that three essential ages defined the recent history of mankind: those being the Aeons of Isis, Osiris, and Horus. The first, Isis, is that of the Great Mother, and bears similarity with what J.G. Bennett called the 'Age

of the Great Mother Goddess,' and relates to the pre-Christian matriarchal societies that were strongly represented on Earth, especially
in the Near East, such as in ancient Sumeria and Babylon. The
second, the age of Osiris, or what Bennett called the age of the Solar
and Savior Gods, is about what Crowley called the Dying and
Reborn God, that is, male religious leaders and male deities who are
said to die and resurrect to become Lord of the other world (such as
in the myths of Osiris, Mithras, Dionysus, Quetzalcoatl, and Jesus).
This age is ruled by the spirit of sacrifice and of the denial of the
personal self. According to Crowley, it came to an end in the early
20th century to be superseded by the Aeon of Horus.[10]

That Crowley ultimately believed Aiwass to be a discrete,
discarnate entity—something other than a part of his own mind—is
clear. Over the years, he had variously seen Aiwass as his own
'Guardian Angel', as a god, 'praeterhuman intelligence', and even
Satan. The latter has caused confusion, with some dabblers
assuming that this implied that Crowley was indeed a Satanist. He
wasn't; he used the name 'Satan' as in the literal meaning of the
word in Hebrew—'adversary'—in this case, one who is *adverse* to the
old Aeon of Osiris, the Aeon of patriarchy and its glorification of
sacrifice. According to Crowley, Aiwass had come to herald the end
of the patriarchal Aeon (what astrology would generally call the
Piscean age), and as such would appear to be an adversary or enemy
to the status quo forces, particularly the Christian church.[11] Near the
end of his life, in referring to *The Book of the Law,* he wrote:

The author is quite certainly both more than human, and other
than human.[12]

This was consistent with his views later in life on the Holy Guardian
Angel. Like Gurdjieff and Bennett, Crowley believed in a hidden
'spiritual directorate' overseeing the affairs of humanity and
ultimately regarded Aiwass as an emissary of such a directorate. He
added:

The Book of the Law presumes the existence of a body of initiates pledged to watch over the welfare of mankind and to communicate its own wisdom little by little in the measure of man's capacity to receive it.[13]

And in referring to his role as the recipient of *The Book of the Law* he remarked:

Elsewhere I will explain why they picked out so woebegone a ragamuffin as myself to proclaim the Word of the Aeon, and do all the chores appurtenant to that particular Work.[14]

The Book of the Law is a slim volume, just three short chapters, written in what seems to be almost a poetic stream of consciousness, yet is, in fact, laced with profound insights and lyric beauty. Each chapter is concerned with one of the three Egyptian deities just mentioned. The first is Nuit (or Nut), the Egyptian sky goddess commonly seen on the ceilings of the royal tombs in the Valley of the Kings. She is equated to the age of Isis, to the innocence of Nature, and to the ideals of blissful tantric union and the womb of existence. The second is linked to Hadit or Horus, who represents the spark of individuality that arises in us from the infinite matrix of Nuit. And the third chapter is connected to two different emanations or expressions of Horus—the extroverted and martial Ra-Hoor-Khuit (who expresses some quite militant views in the Book), and the divine Child, Hoor-paar-kraat (the offspring of the union of Nuit and Hadit).

The Aeon of Horus is called that of the Crowned and Conquering Child because it represents the importance of the *individual* above all else—above nation, family, community, etc. The main idea is that as the power structures of the Osirian age gradually break down (the decline of royalty and colonialism being two notable ones, as well as, to a lesser degree, the secular power of religion—although in the case of the eradication of Tibetan Buddhism as a theocracy from

Tibet by the Communist Chinese, that one happened in a messy fashion), something potentially emerges from that, a type of humanism, but one that also embraces the profound paradoxes involved in the need to balance opposites.

Crowley, in a typically perverse fashion, characterized the new Aeon as being in part that of the 'master and the slave'.[15] He goes on to clarify, however, that by 'master' he means one who is adventurous and welcomes responsibility, and by 'slave' he means one who lives in fear, always controlled by the need for safety. Again, his emphasis is on individual empowerment and freedom brought about by living truthfully and courageously.

Crowley's whole effort was to join self-empowerment with the spiritual impulse (as opposed to the spiritual impulse being about self-sacrifice and denial of personal desire and joy). As the Book proclaims:

> Remember all ye that existence is pure joy; that all sorrows are but as shadows; they pass and are done; but there is that which remains. (2:9)

The Law of Thelema is about an attempt to introduce a robust element into spirituality, to make it fully embodied; thus, in effect, countering centuries of life-negative and body-negative religious conditioning. To that end, the concept of the Will becomes central. In addition to individuality and Will, another important idea put forth in the Book is that of intelligent integration of the best of all wisdom traditions—similar to what Huxley called the 'perennial wisdom'—while at the same time making it clear that we must let go of attachment to the past, including many of its symbols and doctrines (famously echoed in the line 'With my Hawk's head I peck at the eyes of Jesus as he hangs upon the cross'). Thus, the Book is of a deeply progressive spirit, seeking to move bravely into a new world in which such values as aliveness, joy, and individual freedom are sacred above all others.

There is a notorious 'Comment' appended at the end of *The Book of the Law*, where it says,

> The study of this Book is forbidden. It is wise to destroy this copy after the first reading. Whosoever disregards this does so at his own risk and peril. These are most dire. Those who discuss the contents of this Book are to be shunned by all, as centres of pestilence.

Insight into this seemingly strange comment can perhaps be gained from this line from *The Book of the Law* (II:19):

> Is a God to live in a dog? No!

That is a virtual paraphrase of a famous Zen Buddhist *koan*:

> Does a dog have Buddha-nature? No!

A *koan* is not something to be rationally comprehended; it is more a device to open the mind to a transcendent perspective. Much of *The Book of the Law* is clearly tailored to the same purpose. So 'study of the book is forbidden' can be understood as an invitation to open one's mind to its deeper meaning, much like a Zen *koan*, rather than trying to analyze it in a linear, simplistic fashion, passing it on as rigid dogma.

The Holy Guardian Angel

The idea of the Holy Guardian Angel (HGA)—a term apparently first used in the 15th (some argue 18th) century book, *The Sacred Magic of Abramelin the Mage*, has since the late 19th century at least been central to Western ceremonial magick, and particular Crowley's teachings. The HGA does not appear at all in *The Book of the Law*. Crowley's own views on it throughout his life do not seem to be entirely consistent. For instance, in his last book, *Magick Without*

Tears (written when he was in his late 60s), in speaking of the Holy Guardian Angel he wrote,

> He is something more than a man, possibly a being who has already passed through the stage of humanity, and his peculiarly intimate relationship with his client is that of friendship, of community, of brotherhood, or Fatherhood. He is not, let me say with emphasis, a mere abstraction from yourself; and that is why I have insisted rather heavily that the term 'Higher Self' implies 'a damnable heresy and a dangerous delusion.'[16]

Elaborating on this, he adds,

> Apart from any theoretical speculation, my Sammasiti and analytical work has never led to so much as a hint of the existence of the Guardian Angel. He is not to be found by any exploration of oneself.[17]

This is an interesting contrast to the Crowley of 1903 who wrote that 'the spirits of the Goetia are portions of the human brain'.[18] It is also apparent that in some of his earlier writings, the HGA was another term for the Augoeides, inner Genius, or silent, higher self. In a number of places in *The Vision and the Voice* (one of his earlier works), however, he seems to imply that he understands it to be a discrete entity. However it is understood, Crowley's emphasis in the latter part of his life on the objectivity of the HGA is interesting and, as with so much about him, is contrary; in this case, to more diluted spiritual teachings that tend to over-emphasize the point that everything is 'One' and/or a projection of the mind. More to the point, although the HGA may indeed be another term for the true Self, it will tend to be *experienced* as separate by most. A rough parallel here may be drawn with these two seemingly contradictory statements attributed to Jesus in John's Gospel:

I and the Father are one. (10:30)

You heard me say, 'I am going away and I am coming back to you.' If you loved me, you would be glad that I am going to the Father, for the Father is greater than I. (14:28)

It may be said that the 'Father' is both One with Jesus *and* separate from him— 'greater than I'— depending on perspective, much as how the HGA of a person is both One with him and distinct from him. This ties in with the idea of 'absolute' and 'relative' levels of reality (explored more in Chapter 8), that is, two essential levels of reality, the experience of which depends entirely on one's state of consciousness at the time.

Crowley taught a Qabalistic understanding of the HGA that is as follows and is very helpful for grasping the whole thing: in one view there are within us five essential domains of consciousness or being (this is a simplification), known by their Hebrew *sephira* names: Kether, Chokmah, Binah, Tiphareth, and Malkuth. They can be thought of as corresponding to the following archetypes:

Kether = Source (our true, ultimate nature)
Chokmah = King (the divine masculine in us)
Binah = Queen (the divine feminine in us)
Tiphareth = Prince (our higher self, or our holy guardian angel)
Malkuth = Princess (our physical, earthly incarnation—who we
    typically know ourselves to be when we say 'me')

According to the Qabalah, our true nature is Kether, or Oneness with all. We have fallen asleep, however, and come to believe (through the process of what Gurdjieff called identification) that we are all five levels of consciousness. Malkuth is our earthly, physical personality. Tiphareth represents our higher self. Binah and Chokmah represent our highest elements, the divine feminine and divine masculine, which together with Kether is essentially the 'holy trinity' found in different religions, what the Qabalah calls the 'supernal triad'.

The awakening process, the journey from Malkuth to Kether, reaches a critical stage when we 'attain the Knowledge and Conversation of the Holy Guardian Angel'—a stage that is often likened to a sacred marriage between the princess and the prince— between our earthly self and our higher self. The process is allegorized in different ways in many spiritual traditions, and in all cases it represents the very heart and soul of the journey of spiritual awakening—whether it be known as Christ-consciousness, the Buddha-mind, or the Oversoul. The bottom line is that through our sincerity of intention to awaken we achieve an inner 'alchemical union' with our highest part. Our being is touched and transformed (to vastly varying degrees, depending on many factors) by our direct experience of this higher part. Such a process can also be seen as simply 'awakening' to the already existing nature of this higher consciousness. This is union with the HGA and it, in turn, makes it possible for us to return fully to our native, divine condition (represented by the Queen, King, and Source).

Finally, it is instructive to note a parallel here with Gurdjieff's ideas of 'Objective Reason' and 'Objective Art'. By these terms he implied a level of understanding and expression that was of perfect clarity, completely free of subjective distortion or the delusions of the dreaming mind. Crowley's ultimate insistence on objectifying the HGA may be understood in a similar light, that is, as symbolic of something that is utterly free of subjective egocentric distortion.

The Three Schools of Magick

An important and interesting part of Crowley's teaching was his over-arching view of the history of spiritual traditions, something he defined in terms of three basic schools of Magick—what he called the White, Black, and Yellow schools. Along with the three schools he added his definition of what he called the 'Black Brother', a type of relatively advanced adept who fails to negotiate the ultimate stage of ego-dissolution (what he called 'crossing the Abyss') and turns back. This aborted development results in a person who ends up involved in misguiding human evolution. What follows is a capsule outline of Crowley's definitions of schools and the Black Brother:

White School: This is transformational work that views the universe as inherently real in an energetic sense, to be worked with and realized as an extension of one's self, much as with the Tantric schools of northern India that regard the universe as 'power' (*shakti*) rather than 'illusion' (*maya*). Put practically, this approach embraces life, as well as such ideals as robust joy, aliveness, the sexual current, and so forth. In *Magick Without Tears*, Crowley states that the Rosicrucians, such as they were, were the prime custodians in the West of this approach. Presumably, he's referring to ideas that took hold during the time that Francis Yates called the Rosicrucian Enlightenment of early 17th century Europe. Crowley himself claimed to be an emissary (or vehicle) of the White School. J.G. Bennett, in his voluminous writings, was referring to this school in his idea of the *Khwajagan*, or 'masters of wisdom', that he said occasionally injected specific energy and information into humanity from time to time when the need was there.[19] Bennett believed that Gurdjieff was an apostle of this school. Thus, according to Bennett, at least, Gurdjieff was the same as what Crowley claimed for himself, that is, a representative of the White School.

Crowley stated it like this:

We may define the doctrine of the White School in its purity in very simple terms. Existence is pure joy. Sorrow is caused by failure to perceive this fact; but this is not a misfortune. We have invented sorrow, which does not matter so much after all, in order to have the exuberant satisfaction of getting rid of it. Existence is thus a sacrament.[20]

Immediately following this, Crowley adds some telling remarks:

...Nietzsche expresses the philosophy of this School to that extent with considerable accuracy and vigour. The man who denounces life merely defines himself as the man who is unequal to it. The brave man rejoices in giving and taking hard knocks, and the brave man is joyous. The Scandinavian idea of Valhalla may be primitive, but it is manly. A heaven of popular concert, like the Christian; of unconscious repose, like the Buddhist; or even of sensual enjoyment, like the Moslem, excites his nausea and contempt. He understands that the only joy worth while is the joy of continual victory, and victory itself would become as tame as croquet if it were not spiced by equally continual defeat.[21]

Black School: According to Crowley, this tradition uses the approach *via negativa* in transformational work, that is, regards the universe as fundamentally an illusion to be transcended by way of 'shifting' from identification with form (matter, and in particular, the body) to that of the formless (pure, unobstructed consciousness). Buddhism and Gnosticism, according to Crowley, are of this school. Although it should be noted that Buddhism and Gnosticism are very different in how they see things, Gnosticism holding to the view that the 'true God' did not create this universe (that being the work of the Demiurge, or Ialdaboath as he is sometimes known—more or less identified with Jehovah of the Old Testament), and Buddhism of course denying the existence of anything like a 'true God', speaking only of the unknowable void. Both Buddhism and Gnosticism do, however, hold in common the view that supreme realization is both our birthright and our actual nature, a nature that we are merely asleep to at present.

Crowley did not have a high opinion of the Black School, viewing it as hopelessly negative. In his earlier years he spoke highly of Buddhism, but by his old age he had become sharply critical of it. He also ultimately assigned Christianity to the Black School as well owing to the essential defeatism he saw as implicit in the whole symbolism of the crucifixion as commonly understood. The fundamental message of his *The Book of the Law* is that existence is intrinsically *joyful*, not sorrowful (as in the Buddhist view) nor sinful (as in the Christian).

Here it should be noted that Crowley's grasp of Buddhism may not have been complete, mostly owing to the fact that the Tibetan teachings in particular did not become fully known and understood in the West until after his death. The first Tibetan master to deeply expound on the Vajrayana Buddhist teachings that are unique to Tibet, the controversial Chogyam Trungpa Rinpoche, did not begin teaching in the West until the late 1960s. He was soon followed by a number of Tibetan masters and the inevitable establishing of hundreds of centers for Tibetan Buddhism in the West. In current times, a well stocked metaphysical bookstore will usually have a large section of shelves groaning under the weight of volumes on Tibetan Buddhism, many of which explain in detail the rich and vast complexity of its teachings. But in Crowley's time only the essential doctrines of the Theravadin schools (native mostly to Southeast Asia) were understood. Even the Zen tradition, through the writings of D.T. Suzuki, was barely becoming known.

Crowley was an inveterate traveler but one (practically the only) place of importance he never got to was Tibet. This is significant because the Tibetan Vajrayana (Tantric) teachings are the most 'un-Buddhist' in appearance of all Buddhist teachings (doubtless because of the influence of the Bon shamanistic tradition of Tibet on them, and Indian Tantra), and they have the potential to upset Crowley's definition of the Black School. Tibetan Vajrayana is based on Mahayanist doctrine but also allows for the creation of the *mahasiddha* or crazy wisdom master, of whom Chogyam Trungpa was a good modern day example of (within the Tibetan tradition). This type of teacher is antinomian, largely flaunting tradition— Trungpa himself, while a revered Tibetan *tulku*, smoked, drank heavily, married an Englishwoman and slept (openly) with many of his students. Of course, such activities do not suddenly qualify him for some sort of special spiritual category—more than one guru has bedded his *bhakti* babes—but Vajrayana needs to be understood carefully.

The term Vajrayana derives from the Sanskrit *vajradhatu*, meaning 'indestructible realm'. It speaks to a reality that is both unbreakable (our true nature), and to a surrounding world that is vivid, alive, colorful, and infused with meaning. It is a worldview that is anything but Crowley's drab and negative definition of the Black School. It is in some respects closer in spirit to his depiction of the White School.

The fundamental point of the Vajrayana doctrine is escaping imagination and delusion and embracing reality. This was entirely in accordance with Gurdjieff's teaching (although his approach differed). Crowley's exhortation to embrace joy (in distinction to the 'life is sorrow' of Buddha's First Noble Truth) is not at all at odds with Vajrayana doctrine.

A good example is in the Vajrayana teaching of the *kleshas*. This is a term given to describe our 'defilements' or negative emotions (like anger, jealousy, pride, stupid stubbornness, etc.). In this approach the *kleshas* are not rejected or repressed but rather embraced as powerful energies that can aid in our awakening if properly engaged. The whole approach is essentially the psychological equivalent of a Western magician working with so-called lower class spirits. Thus, in the Vajrayana approach, existence is not seen as a 'curse' (anything but that) but rather as energy to be harnessed. However, the idea is that this 'energy' is best understood only when one has seen clearly into the nature of one's ego, grasping the idea that the ego is a conceptual construct only—thereby, in effect, realizing one's true nature as free of egocentric limitation. This idea is echoed in the Abramelin Working in different terms, a structured retreat in which the magician first purifies him or herself, attains direct insight in his true nature, and then—and *only* then—sets about taming, or harnessing, the lower energies (which can be understood as either 'demons,' or as the magician's own shadow side).

Yellow School: Crowley saw this as mostly represented by Taoism, in specific, its sourcebook the *Tao Te Ching*. The main feature of this school is its realization of the illusoriness of personal will. There is only the Will of the Whole (the Tao), so all awakening amounts to realizing the nature of the Tao and one's *a priori* non-separation from it. I believe that some schools of Advaita Vedanta would fall under this as well.

Black Brother: Crowley went to pains to clarify that this term has nothing to do with the Black school. He saw it as representing one who failed to properly traverse the abyss (the shadowy '11th *sephira*' of the Qabalah, usually referred to as *da'ath*). There is something of a parallel for this in Zen (and related traditions) in one who experiences *satori* (sudden illumination) but fails to integrate it, and then in effect becomes worse than useless in terms of how he can influence others. The logic there is that if one has not fully understood something, one can by definition only misrepresent it. The whole concept of the Black Brother is a problematic one, especially in Crowley's case, because an argument can be mounted that he himself fulfilled at least some of the criteria of such a person. He clearly was an advanced adept who certainly attempted to 'cross the abyss' of his ego and dissolve it in the fullness of enlightenment. But did he succeed? Those who superficially peruse his life tend automatically to assume that he did not. Those who are committed practitioners of his ideas and accept him as the self-proclaimed prophet of Thelema, tend to accept that he did.

A helpful key to all this lies in grasping the contrast between absolute and relative levels of reality. The absolute view concerns ultimate truth, the relative view concerns conventional truth. Absolute reality is 'All is One', and one who dedicates their life to realizing that inevitably encounters all the elements of their mind that resist 'dissolving into the absolute'. Relative reality is 'all is many,' and for one who lives entirely in this realm, life is essentially about contrast and differences—I love these differences, I hate those differences, I love you, but you I hate, and so on.

A competent mystic who practices sincerely will sooner or later have a taste of All is One, but it is entirely unlikely that he or she will be able to sustain such a state of being 24/7. To do so the best chance is to move to a Himalayan cave or somewhere else sufficiently remote, live and breathe the rarified atmosphere, and avoid humans as much as possible. Given enough time, a consistent felt-unity with one's interiority as well as with the surrounding environment may be sustained. But for one living in the human world—a marketplace mystic—the challenges connected to the issue of survival alone are sufficient to disturb one's consciousness on occasion, enough at least to cause ripples on the still lake of pure consciousness (or waves, for that matter). And when relationships are factored in, it becomes an almost impossible task to stay consistently 'awake'.

Crowley clearly tasted the Hindu *samadhi*, or what Zen calls One Mind, and he equally clearly was a zealous and committed practitioner of spiritual techniques. His intellectual grasp of esoteric principles was beyond reproach. But as a conventional personality he often stumbled badly, and many of his relationships with others ended up a train wreck. On this level, he was an ordinary human being. He was far from ordinary, however, in terms of the intensity of his spiritual search, and of the barriers he attempted to break through. And so, in the end, his very notion of a Black Brother may in part be a projection of elements of himself he judged and condemned. More to the point, however, we can use the idea of the Black Brother to examine the part of us that is not totally committed to our personal transformation. For all that may be said about the idea of a Black Brother, it is best understood as a failure of commitment, to not pursue things to the end. As the Tibetan master Chogyam Trungpa once said, 'Better not start on the spiritual path. But if you do, you had better finish'.

Crowley's definition of the White School was a novel and highly interesting attempt to define a new spirituality that he saw as badly needed in these times. Osho's philosophy and teaching, appearing some quarter of a century after Crowley's death, was a classic (by Crowley's terms) White School approach—disavowing the old life-negative ways, embracing a robust and embodied spirituality, fiercely alive and sensual, treating existence as a sacrament. Of this much at least, the old English magus would have approved.

Chapter 5
The Gurdjieff Work

If a man knows how to be mercilessly sincere with himself, then to the question 'What are you?' he will not expect a comforting reply.
G.I. Gurdjieff[1]

Gurdjieff's system at first glance seems to be presentable in a fairly defined fashion—after all, it *is* a system—but once its teachings are delved more deeply into, the multifaceted nature of both 'the Work' (the term generally given for Gurdjieff's system) and Gurdjieff the man becomes more clear. Gurdjieff, like many highly charismatic spiritual teachers, left no real successor behind (although he did appoint certain people to lead his work in various parts of the world, such as Jeanne de Salzmann and Lord John Pentland). As such, an element of his system inevitably died with him. A large part of the potency of any spiritual teaching lies in the quality of *being* of the one teaching it. It is this that largely distinguishes a living spiritual school from a stuffy institutionalized religion. And yet this same truth also carries a shadow issue, that being that we run the risk of glorifying charismatic teachers, or becoming too attached to them. It is this dynamic tension between the need for teachers who actually embody the teachings, and the need for seekers to uncover truths for themselves, independent of their teachers, that creates the minefield that the *real* spiritual path truly is.

When Gurdjieff passed away in Paris in 1949, his close student Jeanne de Salzmann remarked, 'When a teacher like Mr. Gurdjieff goes he cannot be replaced'.[2] And yet, while that was clearly true, it was also true that Gurdjieff's efforts had begun to bear fruit, demonstrated by the fact that while he was only marginally recognized in his lifetime—after all, he had to compete with such things as the two world wars, the Russian revolution, and the Great Depression—his fame gradually spread after his death. Today, sixty years after his passing, he is far more recognized than when he was alive. In no small part this is due to the publication of his major works—his magnum opus, *Beelzebub*, was published shortly after his death—but more so it is due to the work of his surviving students, many of whom wrote accounts of their years with him, and many of whom made real efforts to continue his work in organized form in various parts of the world.

The other thing that should be said about the Gurdjieff Work is that it is really a system of individual transmission, that is, each individual student in the Work gets guidance based on his character and needs. During my own time in the Work, the element that I experienced as most significant was the individual assignments that would be given out. These assignments were tailored to the individual and their growth requirements. This may be said to be the defining feature of an esoteric spiritual school, as opposed to a large scale organized religion where all members simply practice the same tenets and perform the same rites that everyone else is doing.

Man is a Sleeping Machine

If there is a concise statement that may be said to sum up the spirit and tone of Gurdjieff's teaching, it is that the average person is asleep. This is a powerful statement because typically we think of sleep and waking as two relatively distinct states of being. Most people sleep somewhere from six to eight hours per night. Over the course of a typical seventy-five to eighty year life that amounts to about twenty-five years spent in slumber and dreams. Clearly, while we spend a large amount of time in sleep, the majority of our life is spent awake. Or so we assume. Gurdjieff, however, signals an essential quality of his teaching right off the bat, and that is a type of uncompromising starkness. He bluntly asserts that most people are in fact asleep most of the time. What we think of as 'consciousness' is not true consciousness, but is rather a type of robot-like living in which we operate in an entirely mechanical way. Gurdjieff said:

> Man is a machine. All his deeds, actions, words, thoughts, feelings, convictions, and habits are the result of external influences. Out of himself a man cannot produce a single thought, a single action. Everything he says, does, thinks, feels—all this happens. Man is born, lives, dies, builds houses, writes books, not as he wants to, but as it happens. Everything happens. Man does not love, hate, desire—all this happens.[3]

There is a strongly Buddhist-like quality in those words, although approaching the matter from a different angle. What Gurdjieff's core principle holds in common with the Buddha's understanding is this: the universe runs on cause and effect—that is, everything that appears to exist does so only because of previous causes. The person that we seem to be right now—our body, our character, the current condition of our life—is all the result of an intricate chain of causes and effects stretching back in time. Looked at dispassionately, it soon becomes clear that if all things are produced by previous causes, then nothing can exist in any isolated, truly independent fashion. The inward correlate of that will be that there is no truly fixed, consistent self—much less any consistent will—existing inside of us. Our daily thoughts, feelings, moods, impressions, actions and so on, are produced by the sheer momentum of previous thoughts, feelings, moods, impressions and actions. A person is like a colony of worker bees with no Queen bee—no centralized controller or 'doer'.

And this is exactly what Gurdjieff asserts. Starting with the bold assumption that the average person in their current condition has no real free will, he adds the important explanation that the reason this is so is because we are inwardly fragmented. We do not have one 'I' but many—dozens, hundreds even. Each 'I' operates as an island unto itself, with its own agendas, and the lack of cooperation between them results in the average person accomplishing very little in their life. We are pushed around by various external and internal causes and forces, but the problem is that for the most part we fail to realize this. We think we are operating from some consistent inner command seat of awareness, that our ideas are truly *our* ideas, and that we have the ability to consciously intend and exercise will and choice. According to Gurdjieff, nothing could be further from the truth.

There is something very powerful about beginning from this understanding, because for one thing it puts everyone in the same boat. There is no wriggle room for the ego to assert that it is special. You begin only by seeing and understanding your own mechanical nature, and the universality of this condition. As Gurdjieff asserted, we are in a prison but we can only escape from it if in fact we realize we are imprisoned. To see this, to admit one's own extreme limitations, is potent because it disarms pretence, which in turn makes it possible for really significant inner work to begin. A rough analogy would be in a standard Alcoholics Anonymous meeting where a newcomer is invited to stand, say their name, and declare that they are an alcoholic. It's a crucial first step because it reverses denial and demonstrates the essential humility required in order to progress. Perhaps the single greatest barrier to inner growth is the belief that there is nothing truly wrong with us. As Gurdjieff said, a man is a machine who has the potential to become aware that he is a machine but this can only occur if he is first willing to see how mechanical he in fact is. According to Gurdjieff, the main cause of our mechanical nature and general unconsciousness is identification.

Identification

For the vast majority of people, who they *think* they are is not who (or what) they *really* are. The so-called 'I' of practically everyone is inconsistent (and largely illusory). Today 'I' like green, tomorrow it may be blue. Yesterday it was yellow. Saturday it may be purple. Now I like you, now I don't. Now I want to do this, now I don't. Today I want to be with you, yesterday I didn't, tomorrow maybe I will. Today I believe this, yesterday I believed that. Today I want to accomplish this, tomorrow it will be something different. And so on. Such simplified examples serve well enough illustrate the point but in many more subtle and sophisticated ways most people demonstrate the same lack of consistency. It all leads in the end to a maddening sense of ineffectiveness, of an aimless, meandering life lived for wrong reasons, just going along to get along—what Shakespeare referred to as 'a tale told by an idiot, full of sound and fury, signifying nothing'. What is the cause of this futility?

When we are in bed at night, asleep and dreaming, a fascinating thing happens. We actually forget that we are asleep and dreaming. We somehow think the dream is real. We don't know that we are dreaming. If the dream was pleasant, we might wake up disappointed that it was 'just a dream'. If the dream was unpleasant, or a nightmare, we wake up relieved that it was 'just a dream'. We don't know that we are dreaming because there is an absence of self-awareness. Only the external world—in the case of dreaming, the dream itself—is real. This basic absence of self awareness, to the point where only the external world has a sense of reality, is the essence of identification. An equivalent analogy: we are acting in a theatre play. When we forget that we are acting, and come to truly believe that we *are* the character that we are playing, we have become identified. Likewise, when we get caught up in thoughts and feelings and memories to the point that we think such thoughts, feelings, and memories solely define *who* we are, we are identified—and we will suffer accordingly.

The identification that occurs in our dreams at night is a good analogy for what tends to happen to us in our daily lives. By constantly identifying with things around us we eventually develop a convincing case that we are in fact one solid, separate entity, with a central, clearly defined personal self. For example, we may attempt to develop a certain career as young adult, acquire a circle of social contacts, project an image to the world in a certain way, etc. All of these eventually become points of reference to define who we appear to be, our basic sense of identity. If someone asks us, 'Who are you?' our natural way to answer would be to describe ourselves in terms of our cultivated identities: 'I'm a secretary, artist, carpenter; I'm a parent; I look like such and such; I have these personality qualities,' and so forth.

Even the more intangibles, like inner qualities, are somehow believed to represent some definable sense of who we actually are. There is a certain warm relief that usually accompanies the establishing of an identity for someone, especially if it is someone we do not know. 'Ah, that's who they are!' Once we can label someone in some way, identify them, there is a general sense of security connected to how we view that person.

But according to Gurdjieff, this need to identify others is deriving from a deep fear around identity in general—that is, the sense that we are a whole self, somehow in charge of ourselves, is a deep illusion, and at some level we suspect that, even if only vaguely. Due to constantly identifying we continually miss the reality that our sense of self is actually a mirage, sustained by memories, beliefs, opinions, negative emotions, and so forth. And because we are inwardly fragmented, we lack the ability to truly *do* anything. All our actions are mostly motivated by unconscious factors.

The Seven Centers

According to Gurdjieff, one of the root causes of our inner fragmentation lies in the malfunctioning of our 'centers'. He taught that we have seven basic centers, which are as follows:

Higher Intellectual Center: This can be thought of as the 'wisdom eye', the seat of what Gurdjieff called 'Objective Reason'—the ability to apprehend and understand Reality directly—to see the truth of things. Gurdjieff taught that in the average person this center is non-operative. It can only be properly known by one who has done a great deal of work on him or herself.

Higher Emotional Center: This center represents the higher aspect of the Heart, what might be called 'true love' and refined feelings of ecstasy, bliss, compassion, and so forth. Gurdjieff also asserted that this center, like the Higher Intellectual Center, is dormant in most people, which is why he said that almost no one is capable of true love.

Intellectual Center: This is the center of most people's typical cognitive processes—thoughts, memories, images, dreams, fantasies, and so forth. Some people are naturally inclined toward this center, a type Gurdjieff called 'man #3'.

Emotional Center: The emotional center is the typical feeling, emotional life of people—everything from the negative feelings to the so-called positive. Gurdjieff called a person primarily dominated by this center as 'man #2'.

Moving Center: The latter three centers (Moving, Instinctive, Sex) may be said to represent the foundation of our inner house. The moving center is self-descriptive, referring to the domain of body-movement, which will clearly be reflective of to what extent a person is aware of their body (or, as it is sometimes put, *in* their body). Gurdjieff referred to a person run mostly by the lower three centers as 'man #1'.

Instinctive Center: Refers to the realm of unconscious body functions.

Sex Center: Gurdjieff placed great importance on the sexual center, stating that when it does not function properly then it tends to negatively impact all other centers. For example, a person whose sex center is not working properly tends to be given to drama, vehemence, excessive imagination, and so forth.

Although there are indeed seven centers in the above scheme, in fact, only five of them operate in the average person (the two higher centers being essentially dormant). This whole model is of course abstract, an esoteric metaphor, representing the overall inner functioning of a person. It bears some similarities to the Eastern idea of *chakras*, which are traditionally described as seven centers of subtle energy that correspond to seven psycho-spiritual domains. But Gurdjieff's seven centers do not fit comfortably with the *chakra* system, and should be regarded as a distinct model. For one thing, the fifth from the bottom, the intellectual center, does not correspond very well to the fifth *chakra*, that being the throat center that is typically connected to communication. Intellect is more than just communication. The Instinctive and Sex centers do correspond to the first two *chakras* (survival and sex). But the third center, Moving, does not correspond to the third *chakra* (power). The fourth center, Emotional, is only a very partial fit with the fourth *chakra* (the heart). The sixth center, Higher Emotional, bears only a slight similarity to the sixth *chakra* (the 'third eye', usually equated with psychic and spiritual sensitivity). The seventh center, Higher Intellectual, or Objective Reason, is probably a close correspondence to the idea of the seventh *chakra* (connection with Spirit, or divine wisdom). So while there are some similarities between the two systems, there are more differences, and thus it cannot be said that Gurdjieff was really talking about the *chakras* in describing the seven centers.

In considering Gurdjieff's model of the seven centers it's important to bear in mind a key teaching of his in this regard, which is that the higher centers can only begin to function if the lower centers are first brought into balance. Psycho-spiritually, this makes perfect sense. A person cannot truly open up to their higher spiritual potential if they are not first a grounded, balanced, healthy individual. If they do try to bypass the lower centers they end up with an imaginary spirituality, based mostly on wrong ideas and delusion.

Concerning the sex center, Gurdjieff had some particular things to say. He taught that this center holds vast potential for creative and spiritual power but is rarely used that way. In fact, the energy of the sex center typically gets 'stolen' by the other centers, resulting in various disturbances generally related to an inability to handle its powerful energy. In this regard, Gurdjieff appears to be in accord with other teachings (such as those of Wilhelm Reich) concerning the idea that sex energy properly developed is an enormously powerful force on creative and spiritual planes—which makes perfect sense given that sex energy is the strongest of the biological forces.

There is a further organization in Gurdjieff's scheme, and that is that the first five centers are each themselves divided into three sub-centers—the moving, emotional, and intellectual parts. For example, we have the 'moving part of intellectual center', the 'emotional part of intellectual center', the 'intellectual part of intellectual center', and so on, resulting in no less than fifteen distinct sub-centers.

Of important note is what—in a stroke of Gurdjieffian practicality—is called the 'formatory apparatus' or center of 'formatory thinking'. This is thinking that is mechanical, repetitive, the type of thinking that is completely unoriginal—for example, in the (all too common) tendency to simply parrot something that we may have heard. 'This must be true because someone said it was true' (something that is all too common in personal growth or metaphysical circles). It is an example of the misuse of the intellectual center. In reality, most of the centers in the average person are not operating properly, are interfering with each other, competing with each other, and so forth—rather like a large dysfunctional family. One of the results of this is an inability to be truly *present* in whatever it is we are doing.

A typical Gurdjieff anecdote speaks to this: one day he was on a long drive with his student Maurice Nicoll when they stopped in the evening in order to eat. While having an impromptu picnic under the stars, Nicoll began to wax poetic about the night sky, in the typical way that people will often do. Gurdjieff, ever the teacher, rebuked him, telling him to drop his idle fantasizing and come back to the present moment and engage the activity they were actually involved with, which was eating a meal.[4] This is reminiscent of the classic Zen story of an advanced Zen student who comes down from the mountain and requests an interview with a Zen master. Before entering the Zen master's home he leaves his shoes and umbrella outside. When the student begins to ask his questions, the Zen master stops him and asks him on which side of his shoes did he leave his umbrella—the left or the right side? Unable to remember, the Zen master lectures the student on the importance of being truly aware moment by moment, which includes awareness of small things. As a result of this, the student spends another ten years studying under this master.

Further Barriers to Awakening

As mentioned above, according to Gurdjieff, the main thing that keeps us asleep is identification. There are two important elements to identification, those being what he called internal and external considering.

Internal Considering: This involves being overly sensitive to the ways in which we think others see us, judge us, or treat us—in one sense, the ways in which we allow others to get to us. It is an extremely important thing to see and understand. We can waste our whole lives being caught in the fear of being judged by others, and accordingly, living our lives based on a constant need for the approval of others. In this state we cannot remember ourselves—we cannot be present, awake.

External Considering: This is to put oneself in another's shoes and to understand things from their point of view. That might be called a right use of identification (empathy, tact, etc.). Gurdjieff stressed that this type of considering takes great strength and awareness and is truly only possible in a balanced person. In most cases there is a shadow side to so-called empathy, which is the potential to 'enable' others by identifying so much with their pain, suffering, etc., that one actually weakens them by not applying appropriate backbone when needed. Or, it is common to feel resentful that one's empathy or tact has not been reciprocated. When external considering slides into something negative it has in effect become internal considering again.

Buffers: This was Gurdjieff's term for what he called 'artificial appliances' that he said interfere with our best intentions to become more conscious. In this case, a 'buffer' is a psychological device that works much like a typical buffer between train cars, also called a 'shock absorber' in automobiles. When our car hits a pot-hole most of the impact is absorbed by the shock absorbers, preventing serious damage to the car or discomfort to its passengers. Buffers between train cars work in a similar way, absorbing the momentum of two train cars bumping together, preventing damage to the cars or injury to the people riding. In us a buffer works in a similar way, by cushioning the friction that occurs within us from two very different parts of ourselves. According to Gurdjieff, the average person houses within themselves many different and contradictory voices and if we were to see the real truth about just how fragmented and self-contradictory we are, we could very well go insane. We are prevented from doing so by the existence of the buffers, which in effect blind us to the reality of our own inner divisiveness. A close analogy would be an anesthetic given before an operation which functions to make us unaware of pain—a pain that otherwise would be there given the reality of the situation, and that in many cases would be unbearable.

Gurdjieff stressed that these buffers are created by us, although unconsciously, and they are built up slowly over time. As fortifications to defend against the painful truth—our own inner fragmentation—buffers effectively keep us from being conscious to any significant degree, or being truthful with ourselves. It follows that any person seeking to wake up is going to have to begin to see the nature of their buffers. This is not easy because the tendency is to become defensive, or to deny, when our buffers are pointed out, and for very good reason because it is through buffers that we have learned to survive and reach some level of comfort in our lives. Modern psychoanalysis refers to Gurdjieff's concept of buffers as 'defense mechanisms'. Some examples of these are lying, repression, projection, rationalization, sublimation, and so on. All of them are designed to protect us from facing the full reality of our inner conflictedness, and at the same time, they shield us from others in such a way that others cannot see too deeply into us.

Gurdjieff makes the point that buffers enable a person to 'always believe he is right' about any issue. This is an important point to see because it is the attachment to 'being right' about things that ultimately creates suffering and blocks any possibility for growth.

Lying: Gurdjieff paid special attention to the phenomenon of *lying*, something that he saw as far more pervasive and common in the average person than is typically believed to be so. One of the most difficult aspects of the awakening process is to begin to clearly see the nature and degree of our own untruthfulness, and yet it is absolutely essential otherwise we can never distinguish truth from falsehood. According to Gurdjieff, lying is created by our buffers, and yet it is also true that all buffers (defense mechanisms) are essentially forms of lying—that is, they prevent us from seeing the truth. In general, it can be said that most authentic schools of transformation help seekers begin to see the ways in which they are untruthful—an 'unmasking' process that can be both difficult and unpleasant—and that this level of work could be said to be what differentiates it from more tepid forms of 'feel-good' spiritual work.

Essence and Personality

Gurdjieff defined man as being comprised of essence and personality. According to him, essence is our truer self, what we born with, and what cannot be taken from us. In the average person, who does not make any effort to awaken in their lifetime, essence does not grow, remaining at an essentially infantile level. Personality, consistent with the meaning of the root of the word—*persona* (Greek for 'mask')—is the part of us that is false, not really ours, that has been grafted onto us by education, culture, and so forth. Because of identification, we come to believe that we are our personality but in fact this is a deception. An irony here is that in conventional thought to have 'a lot of personality' is considered a good thing, a sign of charisma, but according to Gurdjieff it simply means a person who has many layers of falsehood, someone who is very inauthentic.

Gurdjieff did not say, however, that the object of awakening is to destroy the personality. He rather said that in order to grow, essence needs to become active, and personality passive, but both of them need to work in balance. This may be thought of as a rough equivalent of the Buddhist concept of 'being in the world, but not of it'. That is, personality serves our basic functioning in the world, and our interrelating with those who are not on a path of transformation. Essence is the only part of us that can truly grow. It is the part of us that has the possibility of developing into our true individuality, or what might be called our potential higher destiny. But it is only a potential and has no hope of growing to its fruition if the personality continues running the show, which is the case in the average person.

This idea of essence, while similar in some respects to the idea of the 'soul' or 'higher self', is actually not the same because, according to Gurdjieff, the essence of most people is not developed; it is in fact primitive, immature, or as he put it with his characteristic superb bluntness, 'simply stupid'. The conventional religious view of the soul, or the typical New Age view of the higher self, is that it is naturally wise, evolved, and innately beautiful in everyone. Gurdjieff, ever the pragmatist, counters this with his austere view of the essence, saying that it can indeed become something wise, evolved, and beautiful but only in a person who makes sincere efforts to transform themselves. Otherwise it is largely base and primitive, merely a potential.

In fact, this view of Gurdjieff's dovetails well with the Tibetan Book of the Dead, which asserts that the 'after-life' experience of most people is a dreamlike journey through realms (called the 'bardo') created by confused thinking, with the end result being that we are simply drawn back into another womb, ready to begin the whole process of human life over again. There is no 'higher world' that we get a free pass to just because we are human. Whether or not such a view is ultimately accurate matters less than the essential point, which is that unless we use our life for waking up to our full potential as conscious beings, we have squandered it.

Self-Observation, Friction

The matter of *how* to awaken, to transform, according to Gurdjieff, is brought about entirely by the effort to observe oneself. Typically our attention flows exclusively outward to the object we are considering, be that a person, or a thing. Central to the idea of developing consciousness is to practice *divided attention*, which means to be simultaneously aware of both ourselves and what we are considering.

In addition, a key element needed in the awakening process is what Gurdjieff called 'friction', that being an energy that is generated by engaging the inner struggle between a 'yes' and a 'no'. Gurdjieff was a master at creating situations for his students in which they would have the opportunity to self-observe and generate friction that could be used for developing their consciousness. An example of this would be an interaction with another person in which our 'buttons are pushed' and we want to immediately react. To delay reaction intentionally, while consciously observing ourselves, generates friction—*energy*—that serves our awakening.

Gurdjieff also pointed out that a 'wrong' type of friction is possible, for example, in someone motivated by fanaticism or fear of authority, etc. He used the example of a brigand standing motionless with his rifle on the roadside for eight hours without moving, even though part of him is suffering greatly and would like to move. By his sheer willpower he develops a certain center of strength—a process Gurdjieff called 'crystallization'—but in this case, it is a wrong crystallization and can only be changed by a very painful process of inner deconstruction. Another analogy is that of a soldier who has been brainwashed for a wrong cause and needs to be de-conditioned. This soldier may have developed a very strong will but it is for a completely wrong purpose and it will effectively block further possibilities for growth. This is a crude example, but more common examples are happening all the time in people who fight for useless causes or pour tremendous effort into something that makes them a strong person for an entirely pointless reason.

'Right crystallization' begins to occur only when we make honest efforts to observe ourselves and struggle with our unconscious habits by not allowing ourselves to be controlled by them in an 'autopilot' fashion.

The Law of Three

It has been argued by some that Gurdjieff's more abstract philosophy—such as his 'Ray of Creation' and 'Laws of Three and Seven'—are less relevant than his more psychological insights and his practical methods. In particular the 'Law of Seven' (see below) has been criticized by some as incoherent. Nevertheless, these ideas form a central part of his doctrine and they need to be understood in order to grasp the deeper meaning of this work.

In Gurdjieff's *Beelzebub's Tales to His Grandson*, he devised specialized words (neologisms)—usually long and hard to pronounce—to represent many of his key ideas. He called his Law of Three the Law of *Triamazikamno*. This law is based on the idea that there is a natural interplay of three essential forces that bring anything into manifestation. Gurdjieff called these three forces those of affirming, denying, and reconciling—or, positive, negative, neutral. The basic idea is that positive things tend to be opposed, or balanced, by negative things. So we have hot and cold, up and down, positive and minus, love and hate, rich and poor, and so forth. Typically, we tend to leave it at that and see the universe as primarily based on this natural dualism. The Law of Three states that there are not two natural forces basic to the arising of anything, but in fact three—and that this third essential force often goes unnoticed.

The idea of a trinity shows up in religion (Christianity and Hinduism in particular). In a simplified manner we can see how it applies to the examples of dualism we just mentioned—hot, cold, mild; up, down, in the middle; positive, negative, zero; love, hate, indifference; rich, poor, middle class; and so on. In fact, wherever we look (if we look closely) we never truly see things coming in pairs, but in fact in a basic triangular structure. Even the way we enter into the world—father, mother, child—is based on this triangular model. And even in the case of two people together, there is still a third essential element present—that of the relationship itself. The relationship can be likened to the context. This can also be understood geometrically: two dots separated are connected by a line. The line is the third element. Or in the case of a sphere, there is the center point, the circumference, and the space in between that fills up the sphere.

In life this law typically takes the form of the following: an attempt to do something, say to start a business, is the positive, initiating force. This positive force is then sooner or later met by the negative force or what we generally call resistance. This resistance may take the form of financial roadblocks, health issues, laziness, and so forth. At that point a new and third force is needed to bring the project to fruition. This third force could take the form of anything—for example an investor who injects some necessary capital to make the business viable. According to the Law of Three, we always need this third force in order to bring anything to manifestation, and that in fact nothing happens without it. As Gurdjieff put it, 'The higher blends with the lower to actualize the middle'.

Another good way to understand this idea is via creation, destruction, and redemption. Seen in a natural setting this could be compared to a forest fire burning down a forest, resulting (eventually) in new growth. The lightning that struck the forest was the positive force, the ensuing fire that destroyed it was the negative, and the eventual re-growth is brought about by the force of reconciling. This third 'force' is essential for the re-emergence of the forest but would itself not be possible without the first two 'forces' (the lightening strike, and the fire). And so, in reality, all three forces of the Law of Three are interdependent and part of the timeless tapestry of cause and effect that runs the universe.

Another way of understanding this is in the way we see things unfolding in our lives. We have an idea (the positive force), begin to put it in motion, only to be met by unforeseen negative factors (resistance). Depending on how we deal with our resistance will determine to a large extent what kind of third (reconciling) result will unfold. If we handle the negative—our resistance or the resistance of others—poorly, then the third force will not have a chance to appear and do its job. And so the whole project is aborted. But if our approach to the negative is handled reasonably well (i.e. consciously/maturely) then we stand a much better chance of having the third force manifest in a way that will end in promising results.

The Law of Seven

The Law of Seven is a more complex idea and its applicability is less straightforward. According to Gurdjieff, this idea is based on the view that all events that are brought to completion have seven distinct and discrete phases to them that correspond loosely to the musical scale. Gurdjieff asserted that his law can only be understood by first postulating that the universe is comprised of vibrations (or forces) that interact with each other. He states that typically we assume that these vibrations proceed in a continuous manner, but that, in fact, they are discontinuous and do not develop uniformly, but rather with 'periodic accelerations and retardations'.[5]

Gurdjieff used the seven tone musical scale of octaves as a means by which to explain his idea (which is why his Law of Seven is also sometimes called the Law of Octaves). Using the standard do-re-mi-fa-sol-la-si-do musical model of notes, he explains that as the vibrations increase from the first 'do' to the last 'do' they do not do so uniformly, but rather arithmetically as follows:

do=1
re=9/8
mi=5/4
fa=4/3
sol=3/2
la=5/3
si=15/8
do=2

As is clear from those ratios, they are not consistent in their progression. At two intervals—between mi and fa, and between si and do—the rate of increase is actually retarded, that is, is less than at other intervals. When this process is applied graphically it yields something that begins as a straight line, and then at two intervals (mi-fa and si-do) veers off in a different direction, resulting overall in a crooked line.

Using this natural process as an extended metaphor, Gurdjieff proceeded to compare it to the sense of direction in general as it applies to average human life. He said that we tend to begin a project only to see it inevitably veer off in another direction. We can see this pattern readily enough throughout history. Religions begin with spark and hope, usually originating in a bright and charismatic leader who had genuine spiritual insights, and then over the centuries harden into intolerant dogma that in some cases become a polar opposite perversion of what they were originally intended to represent and accomplish. Or a business or organization begins with energy and enthusiasm and sooner or later deteriorates and collapses. The same applies to relationships in general, the body, and indeed all of life. A rough analogy for this idea is found in Buddhism where it is called the law of impermanence. Modern physics refers to it in its second law of thermodynamics, and in specific, the idea of entropy, which is based on the observation that energy tends to go from higher to lower states—for example, warm air in a house will rush out if the door is opened on a cold day, or a drop of bath oil will disperse if dropped into a bathtub. Put simply, things tend first to deviate, then to become disorganized and run down.

In Gurdjieff's scheme there is also the ascending octave (in addition to the descending octave), meaning that things can indeed 'get better' and appear to be going well for some time. But they cannot stay at the same level forever because (according to this law) everything sooner or later alters course. Great suffering occurs in human beings because of the strong tendency to be ignorant of this law and to expect things to remain the same forever. (The Buddha's 'Second Noble Truth', that suffering is caused by craving, refers to this because craving leads to attachment, and attachment resists the natural tendency of everything in life to sooner or later change course.)

It's at this point that Gurdjieff injects an interesting idea in his Law of Seven, something that puts the whole thing into a bigger context. He says that if 'shocks' are provided at the two intervals of retardation the whole octave can be given a 'right development'. In a descending octave, the greater shock needs to be given at the first interval, and in an ascending octave the greater shock is required at the second interval.

Translated into common terms, if your project, or relationship, is beginning to deviate, you need to stop the deviation relatively soon, near the beginning of the descending octave in order to ward off its collapse. Conversely, if something is going well (ascending octave) but is still beginning to get off course then a gradual adjustment (shock) is needed in the beginning and a stronger one later on (the second retarding interval).

Gurdjieff claimed that the Law of Seven lay behind the Biblical story of God's 'creation' of the universe in six days, resting on the seventh, although he said that it was an incomplete version of it. He also more significantly tied it directly to his blueprint for the universe, what he called the Ray of Creation.

The Ray of Creation

The designations in what Gurdjieff called the Ray of Creation line up like this, with the 'World numbers'—1,3, 6, etc.—referring to the number of laws governing each level:

1. World 1: The Absolute—do
2. World 3: All Worlds (The Universe)—si
3. World 6: All Suns (Galaxies)—la
4. World 12: The Sun—sol
5. World 24: All Planets (planetary)—fa
6. World 48: Earth (organic)—mi
7. World 96: Moon (inorganic)—re

Gurdjieff taught that the Ray of Creation could be thought of as both a descending octave and an ascending octave—that is, a process of involution (from the Absolute to the Moon) or evolution (from the Moon to the Absolute). He defined this 'Ray' as seven essential levels, each corresponding to a musical note and to a number, the meaning of which he claimed describes the 'number of laws' that are applicable within each of these domains. They can also be thought of as seven descending (or ascending) dimensions.

When seen as a descending octave, the two 'retarding intervals' are between the Absolute (do) and All Worlds (si), and between All

Planets (fa) and Earth (mi). Taking this as a guide, Gurdjieff then makes an interesting assertion: he claims the first retarding interval is the Absolute 'consciously manifesting a force' that leads to the creation of 'All Worlds', and that the second, the gap between All Planets and the Earth requires a very specific 'shock'. He claims that that shock is provided by organic life on Earth—that is, life as we know it somehow provides a key link in the cosmic chain that keeps us connected to the Absolute source of everything and to the cosmic forces that emanate from it.

In accordance with the diagram, Gurdjieff further claimed that human life on Earth is almost entirely influenced by 'planetary forces' (arising from 'All Planets', the level immediately prior to Earth). There is in this idea a concurrence with the basic hypothesis of astrology, that being that planetary configurations produce 'forces' or results on Earth—everything from global events, down to particular human traits and tendencies. This is, of course, not entirely without known scientific basis as gravity is known to be an 'invisible force' (or, in Einstein's terms, curvature in space-time) that bears effects—some obvious, as in tides caused by the Moon, others much less obvious as in slight perturbations in orbits caused by the effect of other bodies. On a human social level, we know this phenomenon also through mere slight changes in positioning. For example, you are sitting about ten feet away from your friend, talking to her. Then go and sit five feet away, then two feet away, then six inches away, and notice the changes (psychologically, biochemically, etc.) within both you and her. Or, go the other direction: fifteen feet, twenty, and so forth. The point is that changes in positioning in space produce an effect, according to the natural law of cause and effect, or in Gurdjieff's terms, interactive forces.

The idea behind the numbers that correspond to the different levels—beginning with 1 at the Absolute, down to 48 for Earth and 96 for the Moon—refers to increasing levels of density and lack of freedom. Seen from the diagram, Earth is at the second lowest level, that is, has the second highest number of laws by which it must abide. The higher we move up, the less laws, and thus the greater our freedom. This idea is paralleled in most esoteric teachings via the idea of the seven basic dimensions (physical, etheric, astral, mental, causal, spiritual, and absolute) or variations thereof, and of the seven 'bodies' that comprise each individual.[6]

Another thing that is apparent from this model is that we are not directly connected to the Absolute, and are not directly under its influence. Many levels or gaps lie between that ultimate level and our condition and these gaps are bridged by our efforts to work on ourselves. From this model also came Gurdjieff's infamous statement that we are nothing but 'food for the Moon'. His idea there is that higher levels on the Ray 'feed' lower levels by their mere presence, and that organic life on Earth is ultimately a type of food for the dimension 'below' us, that being represented by the Moon. Gurdjieff appeared to claim this literally, saying that the Moon was 'evolving' and that its destiny was one day to be alive like Earth. Some have struggled with this view of Gurdjieff's and more than one critic has parodied his 'food for the Moon' idea, but if nothing else it can be taken as a powerful metaphor that suggests that there is nothing innately special about life on Earth, and that ultimately we are just another part of the universal tapestry. Our anthropocentrism has always resisted this idea, much as how Copernicus and Kepler risked their lives by proposing that the Earth was not the stationary center of the universe. The seeming absurdity of us providing the Moon with 'food' aside, Gurdjieff's Ray of Creation makes us aware of any lingering anthropocentric tendencies that can get in the way of a deeper appreciation of the world around us, and of our essential role in the universe

The Enneagram

The enneagram (from the Greek *ennea*, meaning 'nine') is a circle divided into nine equal parts. This symbol appears to be unique to Gurdjieff's teaching and indeed there is no previous record of it being published anywhere prior to Ouspensky's *In Search of the*

Miraculous in 1949.[7] Gurdjieff first began talking about it around

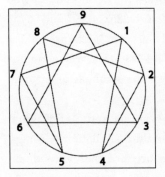

1915 in Russia to his early groups, which included Ouspensky.

He claimed that it was an unknown symbol to the world at large and that it had emerged from the body of work (the Fourth Way) that he claimed was ancient, self-supporting, and independent of other esoteric lines of work. From this it seems clear that Gurdjieff was claiming to transmit a teaching rather than to create one, although in other places he indicates more the latter. The best guess is that his teachings were an amalgam of original research and a transmission, or modification, of certain old and obscure traditions. This is reflected in the enneagram symbol itself because where exactly he got it from is unclear; some have suspected Sufi sources, others have claimed it has Eastern Orthodox roots, but no evidence has ever been confirmed for either, so Gurdjieff may have simply made it up.

Be that as it may, he utilized it as a map for specific esoteric teachings connected to the transformation of energies. He did not, however, use it as a map for personality types. The nine personality types commonly associated in modern times with the enneagram was actually the work of the Bolivian mystic Oscar Ichazo (developed further by the Chilean psychiatrist Claudio Naranjo) who in the late 1960s adapted Gurdjieff's symbol to a personality typology. By the late 1980s, the enneagram of personality types had become thoroughly popularized. Opinion is divided about whether this has been a good thing or not, with some seeing this as a debasement of Gurdjieff's original teachings and others as a natural evolution of them tailored to the needs of modern society.

According to Gurdjieff's original idea, the enneagram is basically a diagram that unifies the Laws of Three and Seven. The central triangle in the symbol represents the Law of Three and the six-pointed figure overlapping the triangle represents the Law of Seven. (That six points represents the Law of *Seven* may seem odd at first glance, but it is based on the idea that 1/7=0.142857142857 and so on, repeating in that sequence. The six points of the figure in the enneagram are connected as follows: 1-4-2-8-5-7-1, following the numeric pattern of the inverse of 7, hence the symbolic association with the Law of Seven.)

Gurdjieff connected the Law of Seven with the enneagram symbol itself via his teaching about the right assimilation of things. He taught that we have three primary sources of energy: food, air, and impressions, and that in the average person, of those three the only one we assimilate properly is food. In order to transform ourselves, to awaken from our depraved condition, we need to properly assimilate air—in other words we need to learn how to breathe consciously by combining self-remembering (mindfulness) with breathing. Doing so results in a 'shock' that prevents us from 'deviating' into less consciousness. That corresponds to the first shock for the first interval (between mi and fa). The second shock (between si and do) has to do with correctly assimilating impressions and this again requires more consciousness in order to bring about. He then proceeded to map this out on the enneagram symbol.

The enneagram is similar in some respects to the Qabalistic Tree of Life with its ten domains. Both are symbolic structures based on numbers and the interrelationship of these numbers. These symbols are basically contrivances, devices to make certain concepts more clear. They can be thought of as practical elaborations of the eternal law of cause and effect, showing how certain causes bring about certain effects and, most importantly, how greater consciousness can determine if this process of cause and effect will be helpful to us or not.

Conscious Labor and Voluntary Suffering

Gurdjieff's teaching is pre-eminently one of effort. He believed that the need for great effort to awaken from our condition is related to the origins of the human race. Because of the 'fall' of humanity, our fate is *work* and *suffering*—the former he related to the need to find food to eat, and the latter to the necessity to have children. Survival and procreation consume a huge amount of our time, energy, and concerns in life, and are also the source of our greatest hardships. Gurdjieff taught that by applying conscious labor and voluntary suffering we add consciousness to the natural work and suffering that is inherent in life and in so doing, we begin to evolve rather than stagnate.

The idea of conscious labor is clear enough. To work with mindfulness is to transform both the work we do, and more importantly, ourselves as we work. As an example, to dust one's coffee table with awareness—slowly, precisely, with excellence, while maintaining awareness of self—is to alter one's very relationship with one's immediate environment. We all know the feeling of satisfaction that comes from completing a task, especially if it is something we have been putting off. To do such a task while simultaneously observing oneself, or remembering oneself, enhances the experience because it brings us vividly into the present moment.

A bit more difficult to understand is the idea of voluntary suffering. This is related to the whole idea of sacrifice. According to Gurdjieff, the average person has no free will and no true being. They literally have nothing. But most people do not believe this. And so for those beginning to work on themselves they need to sacrifice several things, one of which is the idea that they have free will. This way they can be guided by another. In fact, what they are really doing is sacrificing their illusions of which there are many. And according to Gurdjieff, the ultimate illusion to sacrifice is suffering itself—or in more modern psychological terms what is called self-loathing.

We begin to sacrifice our illusions by voluntary suffering—that is, we see the main point, which is that we have no consistent center of being, and then we voluntarily relinquish our various illusions because we grasp that we truly have nothing to lose. This process of giving up our illusions is itself a type of suffering because many of these illusions we are very attached to. But because we are engaging the process willingly and consciously, it is called *voluntary* suffering.

Esoteric Christianity

The importance of Gurdjieff's ideas around sacrifice and voluntary suffering cannot be emphasized enough as they form an essential part of his teaching. In speaking about his own life, he referred many times to his various intentional sacrifices (which included consciously pushing away some of his closest students). The fact that he once called his system 'esoteric Christianity' is significant in this regard as the whole Christian doctrine is centrally based on the presumed sacrifice of Jesus Christ for the cause of humanity. By calling his teaching 'esoteric', Gurdjieff was implying that he understood the deeper teachings behind certain Christian principles and his ideas around suffering and sacrifice are related to that. It can be confidently said that an incorrect understanding of sacrifice has caused untold suffering, from gross to subtle levels, throughout history. Gurdjieff's idea that we must ultimately *sacrifice our suffering itself* hits on the root of the issue, which may be said to be collective self-rejection—the belief, deeply ingrained, that we deserve to suffer. And it is this belief that must be given up.

The image of Christ as suffering for humanity has often been interpreted as to suggest our inherent guilt (that Christ needed to singlehandedly transform), with a clear implication that we are intrinsically flawed and incapable of rectifying this situation on our own. Gurdjieff's teaching directly challenges this notion by asserting that not only can we change things, we can do so in such a way that frees us from suffering. And the key factor is consciousness. In this way, he was paralleling Crowley's idea of the new Aeon of Horus, the movement away from the old paradigm of the glorification of suffering and sacrifice—and relinquishing the idea that we are intrinsically flawed and guilty.

Gurdjieff's idea of esoteric Christianity is that it represented an ancient tradition rooted in ancient Egypt. However that may be, the crux of his Work was all about growing beyond our human limitations—in short, the importance of becoming truly *free*.

The traditional Eastern approach is all about seeing that the 'I' or 'self' that we think we are, is really non-existent, a great space of nothingness that we hang all sorts of things onto. A kind of mannequin that we dress up in all sorts of elaborate clothing, only to gradually realize that it's just a mannequin. Gurdjieff, however, although from Asia Minor was ultimately more a man of the West and not inclined to use such a model. He did say that the 'I' in everyone is fragmented, not whole, not even close, and thus, in a sense, nothing. But he also spoke about a 'real I', or a 'crystallized self' that could possibly arise in someone of great sincerity and who made great efforts—'super efforts' he sometimes called it. Gurdjieff also taught that this true self that arose via effort had the potential to be immortal, to literally survive physical death. Christians, of course, claim an over-arching dispensation has been in effect for the past two millennia, that being that we no longer need make effort to attain this immortality of consciousness. We need only attach ourselves, via devotional surrender, to Christ, who as supreme avatar of this age will then effectively piggyback us into this immortal condition of peace and fulfillment. In India, this process of surrendering to a spiritual master (whether they are in a body or not) is called *bhakti* yoga

Gurdjieff's version of 'esoteric Christianity' had within it a key component, that being an understanding around the process of *bhakti* yoga. He said that mere devotion or surrender was not enough, and that it was a serious error to assume so. His basic teaching was that there is no free pass to immortality and that merely declaring one's spiritual allegiance to a great master or deity (such as Jesus, Yahweh, or Allah) is insufficient. It *can* be helpful for inner purification, humbling the ego, and so on, but it is not enough, because it does not provide for the conditions to result in the essential qualities that yield overall maturity—the necessary ground for real transformation (as opposed to imagined transformation). Gurdjieff taught that we can't progress on this path if all parts of us are not going in the same direction. If one part meditates in the morning while another part of us is out committing arson late at night, then we are divided, fragmented, or what Gurdjieff called a 'lunatic'. This highlights the essential dilemma faced by all who aspire to an awakened life: can we be truly consistent? Without that consistency, Gurdjieff declared we will 'die a dog's death'.

Shakespeare's Prospero said it even better:

> Our revels now are ended. These our actors,
> As I foretold you, were all spirits, and
> Are melted into air, into thin air;
> And, like the baseless fabric of this vision,
> The cloud-capped towers, the gorgeous palaces,
> The solemn temples, the great globe itself,
> Yea, all which it inherit, shall dissolve,
> And, like this insubstantial pageant faded,
> Leave not a rack behind. We are such stuff
> As dreams are made on; and our little life
> Is rounded with a sleep.

Gurdjieff maintained that we just dry up and blow away, so to speak, when this whole show is over, like a sand sculpture that was impressive for a while, then gets reduced to an amorphous mass, and then finally nothing—*if* we don't see the whole picture and act on it. He maintained that only truth survives because only truth is real. Truth is best known by recognizing the falsehood in our lives and unmasking it, exposing it, simply seeing it for what it is—by seeing deeply into the mechanisms by which we fool ourselves, deceive ourselves, and lie to ourselves.

Sacred Dance, Movements and Sacred Music

Gurdjieff, at times, would identify himself solely as a 'teacher of dance', and in fact this was part of his repertoire, but he did not teach typical dance. He taught a complex series of dances and movements which are difficult to describe until they are seen but which could be loosely compared to the movements of Tai Chi, Qi Gong, or other Oriental martial art forms. Similar to Tai Chi, the Gurdjieff dances and movements are designed to harmonize mind and body. His body of dances is broad in spectrum ranging from six 'obligatory' exercises to women's and men's dances, to temple dances deriving from (or influenced by) Sufi and Tibetan sources, to a complex series of 'Movements' based on the enneagram symbol.[8]

Many who watch sacred dances (from whatever tradition) can sense a change in consciousness merely by observing the dancers. Gurdjieff was aware of this and doubtless it was a motivating factor in his decision to introduce his Work to the public at large via a series of performances of the dances and Movements, first at the Champs Elysees theatre in Paris in 1923, and then in America in 1924 in major cities like New York, Boston, Philadelphia, and Chicago. Hundreds came to see these performances and while not all were equally impressed, many were very impacted by what they witnessed and some decided on the basis of that to become involved in Gurdjieff's Work. Along with the sacred dances, Gurdjieff spent many years collaborating with his close student and accomplished pianist and composer, Thomas de Hartmann, on a series of haunting musical scores. This music would accompany the performances of his dancers. The combined effect of music and movement had the potential to elevate consciousness by helping the observer to remember that which in life is sacred, meaningful, and timeless.

Chapter 6
Osho's Teachings

I have been constantly inconsistent so that you will never be able to make a dogma out of me. You will simply go nuts if you try. I am leaving something really terrible for scholars; they will not be able to make any sense out of it.
Osho[1]

Of our three subjects in question, Osho undoubtedly had the most undefined 'system'. In fact—despite the profound scope of his thousands of hours of recorded lectures and the dozens of effective meditation techniques he devised—he can only marginally be said to have had any system at all. Looking back over the span of his life and teachings one is struck by how elusive it all was, especially if viewed from the perspective of historical analysis. Osho condemned, in no uncertain terms, any attempt to approach his work via systematic analysis. He was keenly aware that modern men and women, especially those from the West, are 'top-heavy', that is, over-identified with and over-valuing the mental plane. His whole effort was to push his disciples out of the comfort zone of their intellectu-alizations and into the bare immediacy of feeling, sensation, aliveness, and, in particular, the quality of meditative *being*. That did not, of course, imply that Osho thought that modern society was too 'intelligent'—in fact he regularly condemned modern man as 'stupid'. His point was, in complete agreement with Gurdjieff, that we have gotten dangerously out of balance. That in our overemphasis of intellect, our minds have, in fact, become duller, less capable of working efficiently. Moreover, because Osho was originally attracting to him a type of person—typically young, Western, educated, mentally oriented, anti-authoritarian—he worked with ideas and methods that fit best for these types of seekers. Put simply, he used what worked, helping his followers to remain alive, sharp and progressive, rather than becoming mere members of the 'dead traditions' (as he called them) that so many gurus and saints represent.

That Osho was a man of many faces is a given, but what makes it all the more difficult to get a hold of him is the fact that he spent so much of his time talking about the ideas of others. He was a consummate commentator, something of a literary Harold Bloom of the spiritual world. This commentary on others—whether they be Lao Tzu, the Buddha, Jesus, Morarji Desai, Mahatma Gandhi, Martin Luther, Freud, Marx, Gurdjieff, or Ronald Reagan—contributed to deflecting attention away from any possibility of systemizing his own teaching. Moreover, he was notorious for contradicting his own spoken words such that it is impossible to form any sort of 'inspired scripture' based on what he said. In one sense, it is somewhat pointless to assume that Osho was the leader of any sort of organized spirituality (which he continuously denied—despite the irony that a very large organization was indeed built around him and his work). In one sense, he was simply a very spontaneous, brilliant, charismatic, and eccentric Socratic intellectual/sage that many people happened to gather around. In that regard he was similar to some other rogue gurus, but he was unique in his inner balance of many outstanding qualities, the inevitable result of which was that Osho's destiny was to attract a very large crowd. But as he repeatedly emphasized he didn't want his teachings turned into doctrine, and would stop at nothing to prevent that.

That said, if one were forced to describe Osho's teaching with a two word definition it would probably be *radical acceptance*. Above all he stressed the need for a deep acceptance of what one becomes aware of within one's nature. He shunned all artifice and sought to establish a quality in his community of *totality of experience* on all human levels. His main argument was that the religions and priesthoods of history had conspired to make men and women unnatural and self-loathing. He sought to restore a balance of naturalness and self-acceptance, in which each person would be 'their own church' — very reminiscent of Crowley's 'Every man and every woman is a star'.

He did actually provide a list of 'commandments' — not once, but on two occasions, both times half in jest, but seriously enough for us to consider them. The first set of 'commandments' was written in a letter to one of his disciples early in his teaching career, in 1970 in Mumbai. He wrote:

You have asked for my Ten Commandments. It is a difficult matter, because I am against any kind of commandment. Yet, just for the fun of it, I write:

1. Never obey anyone's command unless it is coming from within you also.
2. There is no God other than life itself.
3. Truth is within you, do not search for it elsewhere.
4. Love is prayer.
5. To become a nothingness is the door to truth. Nothingness itself is the means, the goal and attainment.
6. Life is now and here.
7. Live wakefully.
8. Do not swim — float.
9. Die each moment so that you can be new each moment.
10. Do not search. That which is, is. Stop and see.

Several of them are standard Eastern spiritual precepts. It is known that in the letter Osho underlined four of them — numbers 3, 7, 9, and 10. But the three that stand out for me are the first three, because they are suggestive of that rebellious spirit that was such a hallmark of Osho's character and that stayed central to his philosophy over the remaining twenty years of his life.

In terms of this study, more to the point, they strongly resemble some of the precepts that Crowley transmitted in *The Book of the Law*. From that book, Chapter 3, line 60: *There is no law beyond Do what thou wilt*. Contrast that with Osho's commandment #1: *Never obey anyone's command unless it is coming from within you also*. Crowley is stressing that the supreme 'Law' is being aligned with our True Will—his term for the outer expression of our inner core of being—and that more to the point this is ultimately the *only* true law. Osho is also stressing the primacy of our inner truth, so much so that he exhorts us to not follow any external 'command'—in effect, *law*—unless it aligns with our inner truth. The wording is different from Crowley's but the general thrust is basically identical.

Also of note is #5: 'To become a nothingness is the door to truth'. This echoes an ancient theme in transformational work, that being that we must sooner or later cross a divide in which we are, effectively, stripped of everything—of all attachments and identifications. Crowley wrote extensively about this, calling it the 'abyss.'

Osho's ultimate vision was for his disciples to become the living embodiment of what he taught. In that regard I believe that his effort was, in effect, building on the earlier work of both Crowley and Gurdjieff. It can be said that Osho was the supreme syncretistic teacher. He used whatever worked, but he always resisted offering any clear cut formula. He was more interested in his people following a way of life based on such ideals as freedom, love, creativity, celebration, and meditation.

Back during the years of the Oregon commune in 1984, when Osho was still in his three and a half year period of silence, his secretary at the time (Ma Sheela) had attempted to create the beginnings of a definable religion. She called it 'Rajneeshism' and even created a small book—effectively, a holy writ—that was to represent the religion. (Around the same time, some within the community—

and this one was Osho's initiative—were bestowed with flamboyant sounding 'degrees' from the 'Rajneesh International Meditation University', or RIMU as it was abbreviated. Special spiritual titles, such as *arihanta*, *acharya*, and *siddha*, were given to the 'chosen few' as they were called.) A year later, in September of 1985 when Sheela and her small group of aids had been exposed for flagrant crimes and had fled the Oregon ranch and the commune was collapsing, Osho appeared and dramatically renounced Rajneeshism. In a strange reversal of the ancient theme of the priest burning the books of the mystic, this time the mystic denounced the 'priest' and all copies of the 'holy book' were gathered together and torched in a bonfire. At the same time Osho told his disciples that they need no longer wear shades of red or the mala containing the locket with his photo. (The next day many gleefully dropped the malas and red clothes. Osho then criticized them for the disrespectful and undignified speed with which they did this. The day after many put the malas and clothes on again. It was a strange and highly charged time where individual lessons were coming fast and furious—what Gurdjieff doubtless would have seen as a gold mine for self-observation possibilities.)

In retrospect, this whole affair was presumably excruciating for Osho as he had spoken out so vociferously and for so long against 'isms' of any sort. How and why he allowed Sheela to create this 'religion' is unclear. He claimed that it had been her idea but the fact remains that he must at some point have given it at least his tacit approval. (It has been theorized by some that he allowed the creation of this 'religionless religion' to satisfy the visa requirements of the U.S. Immigration department—as a 'religious teacher' he had a better chance of being permitted to stay in the country.) At any rate, the retraction of Rajneeshism by Osho himself has an irony to it but is also deeply interesting because it raises a natural question: what would Jesus (for example) have done if he had the opportunity to derail the religion created in his name before it caused serious damage? If we are to believe Osho he would have done exactly the same thing if he'd had the chance—and perhaps it would have been Paul, Matthew, Mark, Luke, and John fleeing to Europe as Sheela and her confederates did two millennia later (though without shekels or Swiss bank accounts).

Ultimately, Osho was only concerned with the awakening of the individual. He taught that masses do not awaken, only individuals do. But owing to his exceptional powers of oratory and personal charisma, he attracted a large and very devoted following and so inevitably his thoughts turned to the larger picture. In the 1970s, he usually lectured exclusively about enlightened mystics of the past and how their teachings were to be understood. By the 1980s, his lectures were growing more political and his political commentary was almost entirely limited to withering criticism of politicians and priests. Either way, his vision was clearly becoming more concerned with the bigger picture and the state of the masses.

His lampooning of organized religions increased in his later years—amongst other ribald remarks he once suggested that the Holy Ghost was probably God's genitals.[2] His manner of expression when speaking in such ways tended to accentuate the levity of it all as he had a deadpan delivery and a wide-eyed 'innocent' look. He was a master of dry humor, and probably no guru, let alone professional comedian, in history has made light of religions and religious leaders with as much gleeful irreverence as Osho did. However, all this did, naturally, attract a great deal of hostility toward him as well from established quarters of the powers that be, all the more so because Osho was not always joking. At other times his eyes would cloud over and with fierce intensity he would rip into the priesthoods in a way his followers saw as being like Jesus bringing a sword into a corrupt temple. A good example being when he denounced Pope John Paul II—whom he was fond of calling 'Pope the Polack'—as the antichrist himself:

Thousands of people have been killed by these people who represent 'the church'. And what peace have they brought to the world? You can see: the two world wars have been fought in the Christian section of the world; and the third world war will also be fought in the Christian section of the world. These people are representatives not of peace but of death. So I say categorically that the antichrist is already in the Vatican. He has started doing the worst that can be done to humanity. He is preaching to the whole world against birth control, against the pill, against abortion. That is enough, that will destroy this whole world through starvation, through poverty. Right now there are five billion people on the earth—and the earth is capable of supporting joyously not more than one billion people. One billion people can live on this earth in a dance, in ecstasy—but five billion people? And by the end of this century the population will be six billion. Out of sheer overpopulation—no nuclear weapons are needed—humanity can commit suicide. My answer is absolutely clear: Pope the Polack is the antichrist; all the popes have been—and not only in Christianity but in every religion.[3]

Nevertheless, in spite of all Osho's endless attempts to deflect attention, intentionally or not, from the possibility of clearly defining his teaching, a teacher's work is best known via his students—'by their fruits ye shall know them'—especially when those students have been sanctioned, as it were, by the teacher to represent him with their work. In Osho's ashram there were two main 'inner work' activities—those of group therapy, and meditation. Other 'situational work' was going on all the time as well—that is, specific work tasks during which one had the opportunity to 'work with awareness' and to notice how one's mind reacted to specific situations and conditions. Osho referred to his ashram as a 'buddhafield', an idea meant to indicate a concentration of energy brought about by the sustained effort of a group of committed truth-seekers. An environment like that, much as in any monastic setting with committed meditators, results in an ambience that is in constant vivid contrast to one's state of mind. In most places in life a typical state of consciousness will not be noticeable because it will not be noticeably different from most everyone else's—that is, everyone is equally sleepy. But to be sleepy amongst alert and mindful people soon throws one's sleepiness into high contrast, and makes it very uncomfortable to be in that state, something like an annoying alarm clock that won't stop until you wake up and get out of bed. That, at least, is the guiding idea behind situational work, and in Osho's ashram it was ongoing in every activity. (Life at Gurdjieff's Prieure was similarly set up, though on a much smaller scale, and with the master himself prowling the grounds.)

Psychotherapy in a Spiritual Context

Osho was unique in being the first Eastern guru to deeply embrace Western psychotherapy. In his ashram in the 1970s a number of 1960s-style group therapies were used, led by several experienced therapists. At that time the Pune ashram where Osho's experimental approach was unfolding rivaled the famous growth center in northern California known as Esalen.

The word 'therapy' derives from the Greek *therapeia*, meaning to 'heal' or 'cure' or 'treat'. The word 'psyche' derives from the Greek *psykhe*, a broad term that variously refers to 'mind', 'soul', 'spirit', or 'animating principle'. The term 'psychotherapy' thus refers generally to the healing of the mind or soul—the attempt to set right that which animates our consciousness.

Meditation in its various forms has been around for millennia. Western style psychotherapy is a relatively recent practice originating with Freud in the late 1800s but other forms of it were practiced in much earlier times, from the 'hypnotherapy' used by Franz Mesmer in the 1770s, to some of the efforts of the 16th century European alchemists, to the first insane asylums set up in Morocco and Baghdad in 8th century AD. Alan Watts, in his landmark book *Psychotherapy East and West*, argued that the Western parallel to the Eastern spiritual traditions is not Western religion, but rather Western psychotherapy. He wrote:

If we look deeply into such ways as Buddhism and Taoism, Vedanta and Yoga, we do not find either philosophy or religion as these are understood in the West. We find something more nearly resembling psychotherapy...the main resemblance between these Eastern ways of life and Western psychotherapy is in the concern of both to bring about changes in consciousness...[4]

Watts did allow, however, that there are also key differences between traditional Western psychotherapy and Eastern wisdom traditions and these have lay primarily in the definitions of 'mind', 'consciousness', 'psyche', and so on. He believed, however, that that gap was beginning to be closed as psychotherapy became less materially and empirically fixated—in effect, as it began to catch up to the wisdom of Eastern understanding of the mind. Watts wrote his book at the beginning of the 1960s decade which was to prove to be a key turning point in the history of psychotherapy.

The defining feature of traditional psychotherapy is the attempt to restore psychological health to the individual but this 'health' usually does not go further than the ideals of balance, adjustment, and 'getting along' in the world. Modern spiritually oriented psychology, which probably began with the efforts of the Swiss psychotherapist C.G. Jung, is the attempt to view the individual not as a subject of pathology but rather as a vast being waiting to be explored.

It can be safely said that most people undergoing psychotherapy are doing so primarily to develop their ability to function well in the world—to 'get along' with the elements of society, to learn to feel good about themselves and to 'fit in'. A small minority use psychotherapy in its more spiritual form which is to explore the nature of being, self, and individuality. Gurdjieff was one of the first to pioneer the expression 'work on oneself' and this 'work' has as its basis the view that we have an almost unlimited potential, a capacity to grow in consciousness such that may far transcend our ordinary day-to-day mindset.

What is the average day-to-day mindset of most people? Gurdjieff for one was not charitable in that regard, referring to humanity at large as essentially 'asleep'. Osho shared the view, frequently referring to the 'sheer stupidity' of human nature and to the fact that there have been literally thousands of wars over the past few thousand years. Crowley was equally trenchant in his criticisms— *The Book of the Law* makes ample references to the fallen state of the human condition. None of the global spiritual traditions would disagree with this viewpoint. All of them hold that there is something fundamentally 'off' in the average person—whether that be due to the effects of 'original sin' as conceived by conventional Christian doctrine or to the delusions of the conventional self as understood in both Hindu and Buddhist teachings—and that the only way to solve the problem is via sincere and sustained introspection. The downfall of humanity can be summarized as this: a failure to look in the mirror and truly examine who we are.

Psychotherapy is an attempt to do just that, but one of its defining features is that it is largely a shared practice; it is not generally undertaken in a solitary fashion. It is possible to self-analyze, and certainly possible to practice deep introspection on one's own, but in general such work is undertaken with a guide, mentor, or therapist of some sort. In this respect it is uniquely different from meditation which generally speaking is undertaken as a solitary practice (even if one is meditating in a room with many other meditators).

Osho instructed many of his Western disciples to undergo cathartic therapies such as encounter groups or Western type Tantra prior to attempting serious passive meditations like the Buddhist *vipassana* or Zen methods. His overriding concern was that Westerners would be prone to repressing their minds while meditating, rather than openly witnessing their thoughts. This is a crucial point to understand because it can be said that psychological and spiritual development proceed along parallel tracks. That is, it's possible to have genuine spiritual experiences and yet remain

somewhat stunted psychologically—that is, to have poor communication skills, self-esteem issues, dysfunctional relationships,
unhealed issues with one's parents, and so forth. As Israel Regardie
once put it, 'mystical experience is not curative of psychoneurosis'.
Equally so, it's possible to be reasonably grounded psychologically,
and yet to lack any sort of meaningful spiritual experience or
perspective.

It's fairly common, especially amongst spiritual seekers, to find
those who have used meditation or related practices to merely
distance themselves from their psychological pain, as opposed to
truly facing it and embracing it. In these instances meditation
becomes more a type of *medication* in which a person is capable of
'drugging' themselves via mastering what amounts to a more sophisticated type of repression. A mind with significant unhealed psychological issues which is given to repressing the pain associated with
these issues is not truly capable of deep meditation. And even if they
are, they are susceptible to disturbing psychological states that can
ensue when deep and sustained meditation begins to break down
the barrier between the conscious and subconscious minds.

A brief example here from my own journey can help illustrate this
point. Back in my early twenties I originally tackled certain elements
of the spiritual path with great gusto and intensity. On one occasion
I decided to undergo a self-imposed three week meditation retreat in
isolation. This took the form of basically locking myself into my
apartment and committing to many hours of daily meditation,
minimal food, and sexual abstinence. Naturally after a week or so,
this built up a tremendous amount of energy. One day about three
weeks into this experiment, I was sitting in meditation when
something seemed to 'snap' in my solar plexus region. I immediately
felt a strong foreboding that something powerful was about to
happen. I stood up and walked over to a mirror, deeply boring in as
I focused on the timeless *koan* 'Who am I?'

A great silence descended on me, a silence that was also full of
powerful energy. I recall the awe I felt as I looked at the reflection in

the mirror and realized deeply and tacitly that *no one* was looking back—I was rather faced with a great vastness, still, silent, and profoundly empty. In that instant I truly saw that personality is but a shadow, an elaborate pretence, and that fundamentally I did not truthfully *know* who I am—more accurately, I just *was*. I then walked down the hall and went into my kitchen. I sat down at the table and marveled at the vivid clarity of my surroundings—I recall in particular picking up a red dishcloth and sensing the immense aliveness of even this inanimate object. While enjoying the wildness of this awakening, I recall two things then happening: first, a sensation of a strong 'current' of energy moving up my spine. And second, a certain thought, that was something along the lines of 'I can't handle this'.

Right about at that moment the energy ascending my spine reached the general area of my heart and then seemed to stop, as if encountering some sort of block. Almost instantaneously I was plunged into a strange panic. My pulse rate shot up and a terrible fear engulfed me. I found myself partially reliving a terrible drug trip I had passed through as a young teenager about a decade before. To make a long story short, this panic attack gradually subsided but left me in a deeply disturbed state—dissociated and disconnected from my body, the world, everything. I felt as if reality was far away, at the end of a long tunnel. Even my arms seemed like long bones stretching out far from my body. Everything was grey and seemed to smell of death.

For three straight nights I could not sleep. Whenever I would close my eyes I would be greeted by a bright golden-yellowish light glowing inside my head. It was nightmarish. Years later, I happened to read about Gopi Krishna's epic horrors involving 'premature *kundalini* awakening' as described in his book *Kundalini: The Evolutionary Energy in Man*[5], but at the time I was less certain of what I was experiencing. I did, however, believe that it was essentially a 'spiritual emergency' (to use the term coined by Stanislav Grof)[6] rather than a psychotic break, and thus resisted conventional medical treatment. After a few days I went to the local Osho meditation centre (I was an initiated disciple of Osho at that time) and found one man who understood what had happened to me. He said that he himself had undergone something similar years before that had left him 'on fire for three years'. I could not have imagined surviving this for three years so I was not entirely convinced that my friend's 'on fire' and the horrid inner disturbance I went through were the same, but I deeply appreciated his empathy nonetheless. Within a couple of days the symptoms subsided and I felt myself again.

The bottom line is that what I experienced was a classic case of a psycho-spiritual disturbance brought about by a failure to do sufficient psychological healing of old wounds before engaging in intensive meditation practice. The intensity of my meditation efforts served as a type of 'cleaning chemical' that rather violently dredged up old psychic wounds and flung them without mercy upon my conscious ego. Overwhelmed by the force of it, I lapsed understandably into first panic, and then several days of feeling deeply dissociated from reality and my body.

That is a more dramatic example but the point stands that only a reasonably healthy and whole personality can embrace deep spiritual states. This is so because the psychic forces that can be unleashed by spiritual practice can be exceptionally intense, drawing as they do on the powerful energies held in the unconscious mind.

Osho was vividly aware of all this and because he was well-read in Western philosophy and psychology he understood the phenomenon of repression, but not only for that reason. He also recognized repression from his own Indian culture with the violent reaction many had to his teachings on the innocence of sexual energy. In this connection, it should be mentioned that Osho was well familiar with the work of Wilhelm Reich, the pioneer of 1960s bodywork methods whose radical teachings on 'orgone' energy and the importance of the sexual orgasm were highly controversial in his day. On more than one occasion Osho said that Reich could have been his disciple (and once even bestowed a posthumous initiation on him—reminiscent of Crowley's granting posthumous sainthood to certain figures). Reichian therapies were commonly used at Osho's ashrams for the purposes of releasing negative mental states that were believed to be locked into the body in the form of muscular 'armoring', the term Reich gave to 'knots' in the psyche that were originating in the repression of painful memories, and that manifested in the body.[7]

The whole issue of 'catharsis' (the direct purging of negative emotional states) remains controversial, with some claiming it is indispensible for necessary psychological healing and others claiming it basically useless and even potentially harmful. Osho supported its use, and his main meditation device—'Dynamic Meditation' (described in Chapter 17)—utilizes catharsis as an essential stage in the process. But most advanced teachers, including Osho, agree that catharsis in and of itself does not guarantee any permanent change or significant self-realization. This is because negative ego-based patterns will simply repeat unless there is proper cognitive understanding as to the root causes of the suffering, in addition to a necessary attitude of willingness to take responsibility for one's negative thoughts, feelings, and circumstances in life. Then and only then can meditation truly be effective.

Darshan and Transformational Group Therapy

Osho, for much of his teaching career, was not merely a guru or sage. He was also a psychotherapist, and perhaps nowhere was this more evident than in his *darshans*, private meetings that he used to hold in the evenings with small groups of disciples. The term *darshan* literally means 'to see' and in this context, to 'be in the light of the master'. During these meetings—which occurred from approximately 1974-1980—Osho would greet disciples arriving, see them off, and initiate new disciples. Invariably each one-on-one interview he would conduct with a disciple sitting at his feet would amount to a mini session in which Osho would offer advice, give assignments, and more mysteriously, do 'energy work' on the disciple (particularly from 1979 on, where the *darshans* focused more on energy transmission). This would consist of placing his fingers on certain parts of their body, most commonly the center of the forehead (or '3rd eye' in traditional yoga). Often these sessions would result in profound changes in consciousness for not just the one being treated but for others observing as well. How much of this was attributable to Osho's therapeutic skill or yogic *siddhis* (powers), or to the general suggestibility of an atmosphere of charismatic-type healing, is debatable. As with most things of this nature it was likely a combination of all of that.

The use of deep therapy—the 'groups'—was controversial in Osho's work, but it is without question one of the elements that put him on the cutting edge of transformational work. I myself participated in several of these groups in the 1980s and early 90s. I also had the fortune around that time to participate in transformational groups that were not part of the Osho organization and in the end I can conclude confidently that there was not much difference between them. The notable exception was that Osho's presence was always made apparent in the former, generally through large photos of him adorning the walls and, of course, in the ubiquitous lockets (complete with Osho's photo) worn by everyone, including the group facilitators (though this was discontinued around 1986). Glanced at by the average outsider it would all appear to be a form of cultic programming, but the outer trappings of, say, a traditional Eastern Orthodox or Japanese Zen monastery are not much different. Monks wear black robes that are all the same, chant the same words, follow strict regulations and protocols, and everywhere idols are seen, generally in the form of Christian or Buddhist saints.

Osho emphasized that there have always been two traditional methods of inner work: working alone, or working in a group. 'But,' he added, 'the West is totally group oriented.' The reason that group methods (such a group therapy) were needed for Westerners in general was, he argued, because Westerners have cultivated a stronger and more defined ego. The idea is that a strong ego suffers when alone but in a group setting it has a better chance of relaxing and dissolving (at least to some degree). A less defined ego can handle a solitary path—such as deep meditation, or a one-on-one relationship with a guru—with greater ease. The idea of 'group consciousness' helping to relax the ego can and has been grossly abused, of course, with fascist movements being a prime example. But used in an inner growth context the same effect can be made into a powerful aid for letting go of more harmful egocentric tendencies.[8]

Osho's therapy groups acquired, over the years, a significant reputation. Amongst his Western disciples it was practically considered a must to participate in at least some of these groups. For many, they became the primary means of social connection with other disciples. Most who passed through these groups gained an obvious benefit from them, emerging lighter, more relaxed and open, less neurotic, more engaged with life (although in many cases this would prove to be only a temporary opening as the old dysfunctional habits returned later). In the first phase of this work in Pune in the 1970s, the more dramatic groups, especially the Encounter group run by Paul Lowe (Ananda Teertha), became renowned for representing both the possibility of ego-shattering breakthroughs into higher states of consciousness, or, on occasion, bone-shattering exercises in experimental totality. It was not uncommon for bruises, black eyes, and occasionally a broken limb to occur. Significantly, Richard Price, one of the founders of Esalen, the famed growth center in Northern California, traveled to Pune in 1978 after taking initiation (officially becoming a disciple of Osho) by mail. Once there, he participated in some of the groups but after witnessing a group session where a woman broke her leg, followed by a discourse of Osho in which (as Price saw it) he appeared to shame the woman, he withdrew.[9] From the point of view of what Osho was trying to create in those days (and he was largely succeeding) the loss of Price, and potentially all of Esalen, was a setback. This was all the more so as many were coming to regard Pune as the 'Esalen of the East', one of the two pillars of truly cutting edge transformational work on the planet.

Osho was a sensualist, teaching that the body was to be respected and befriended and worked with consciously. His specialty since the late 1960s had always been active meditations that he had personally designed, such as his Dynamic Meditation and Kundalini Meditation, and several others. In the late 1980s he designed several new meditations, including the Mystic Rose (three weeks of three hours per day of, in the first week, laughing, in the second week crying, and in the third week silent witnessing), and various 'talking to the body' exercises. All this may seem ironic, giving the alarming decline in health of his own body in his fifties, but nevertheless his teaching can only be described as integral in that he sought to bring together all dimensions—the physical, therapeutic, meditative, and creative/artistic (he was a great aesthete, and his communes always reflected that, holding to a very high aesthetic standard).

Osho's Dynamic Meditation, designed to be a vigorous morning exercise, in many ways is an excellent metaphor for his entire teaching. The process is one hour long and takes place in five stages—ten minutes of deep, fast breathing, ten minutes of catharsis (emotional purging), ten minutes of jumping up and down shouting 'hoo!' followed by 'stop!' then fifteen minutes of motionless silence, and concluding with fifteen minutes of dance (See Chapter 17 for a more detailed explanation). The breathing represents yogic influences, the catharsis is the psychotherapeutic, the jumping up and down is the physical component, the 'stop!' is Gurdjieff's influence (it was one of Gurdjieff's actual techniques), the silent phase is classical meditation, and the final dance phase is an expression of Osho's emphasis on the body and celebration. Dynamic Meditation has always been front and central in his work, and has been held daily at 6am at his communes since the early 1970s.

Sex

The book that cemented Osho's reputation as the 'sex guru' was his landmark 1968 publication, *From Sex to Superconsciousness*.[10] Ironically, this book was only the first of over six hundred (to date) published under his name but it remains his most famous. It was radical at the time and caused an uproar in Indian society, a highly repressed culture at the best of times. Despite being first published over forty years ago, the book still sells, having been reprinted as recently as 2008 with a new subtitle: *A Book as Infamous as it is Famous*.

The main point behind Osho's teachings on sex was that, owing to the conditioning of religion and the effects of civilization in general, naturalness had been gradually lost, and with that, innocence as well. At one point in *From Sex to Superconsciousness* Osho made comments about nakedness, and how the fear of removing one's clothes was based on condemnation of the body. (Nudity was a practice occasionally used in Osho's later therapy groups at the Pune ashram, as an exercise in aiding people in moving beyond fear and inhibition. Crowley, for one, would have approved.)

The idea is simple: only a natural, innocent person can truly move into higher states of consciousness. By 'innocent' Osho did not mean ignorant, or inexperienced in life. He rather used that word (and it was a recurrent word in his teachings) to point toward a deep and natural acceptance of who one is, beginning with one's body.

The point is sound. As Gurdjieff taught, and as Crowley attempted to demonstrate, it is attachment and identification that lies behind practically all psychological suffering. The first and most basic thing the individual tends to identify with and become attached to (whether positively or negatively), is their own body. As one ages, a natural loss of identification with the body occurs. The body is much more real for a twenty-five year old than it is for a seventy-five year old, health conditions notwithstanding. But the idea of conscious work on self is that one need not wait for one's elder years to begin to enjoy the inner freedom of a deeper acceptance for, and thus less attachment to, one's body.

As Osho always emphasized, to be less attached to the body does not mean that one cares less for it, or that one enjoys it less. On the contrary, enjoyment deepens, as does the capacity for experiencing the sensory effects of the present moment with totality and intensity. Above all Osho's teaching stood for aliveness, because he was convinced that unless a person was actually in touch with their body, and with their sexual energy, their spirituality would be bogus.

Sex was a significant part of life as a disciple of Osho, although this was more so in the 1970s and early '80s. Toward the end of Osho's life in the late '80s, the emphasis of his teaching gradually shifted more toward meditation (and in particular, Zen). However, without question, the term 'sex guru' for Osho—though usually used pejoratively—was not without legitimacy, as his disciples were freely encouraged to explore their sexuality and sensuality as openly and as intensely as they wished. The irony with Osho was that he himself appeared anything but sexual; his image conforming more to the archetypal old wise man who is, as he more than once admitted, only 'hovering around the body'. Despite that, he claimed to have 'loved many women', although personally I had my doubts. For one, he spent so many years engaged in a massive reading venture (speed reading over ten books a day year in, year out, until the early '80s), not to mention being deeply engaged as a philosophy professor and later a guru greatly in demand, that it is unlikely he had much time to be a Lord Byron. Nevertheless, his understanding of sexual energy was profound and he was fearless in the face of withering Indian condemnation of his ideas. It is generally accepted that the assassination attempt on him in 1980 (where a local Indian tossed a knife at him as he lectured, only to miss) was connected to his criticisms of the sexually repressive elements in Indian religions.

Aloneness and Authenticity

Osho taught the value of many qualities of being, but two in particular stand out consistently in his teachings over the years: aloneness and authenticity. The first may seem very ironic, given that his community was often seen as a hotbed of relationships (and indeed it was, in many ways). And yet he continually returned to the theme of what it meant to be truly comfortable with oneself. More to the point, he taught that only one who is able to be comfortable alone can truly be with others. He once said,

If you can enjoy your aloneness, you can enjoy anything. And if you cannot enjoy your aloneness, you cannot enjoy anything. That is an absolutely fundamental principle.[11]

He also greatly valued authenticity, and frequently attacked the falseness of societal conventions. One of his prime arguments was that a person who lives authentically does not accumulate resentments and thus has very little (if any) need to forgive others later on. He saw all this as a function of one's ability to live truly alive, moment by moment.

Meditation: Inquiry and Witnessing

Perhaps no word more than 'meditation' underscores the limitations of the English language when it comes to its ability to describe subtle states of consciousness—one need only consult the Oxford dictionary to see this, it giving 'engage in contemplation' and 'plan mentally' under its entry for meditation. The word itself stems from the Latin term *meditari*, meaning to 'think over' or 'consider'. However, anyone who has practiced meditation or who understands something about subtle states of consciousness will attest to the fact that thinking or contemplation is only a preliminary aspect of one of the two main components of meditation, which is *inquiry*.

The other component is what the Zen Buddhist tradition has loosely referred to as 'no-mind': a state of relative mental quietude in which the mind relaxes its conceptual filters, thus allowing for a deeper attuning to the actuality of this moment. The essence of this second component is watchfulness or mindfulness, best known simply as *witnessing*.

Over the years of Osho's work, he frequently would create new methods, and as is well known about him he would often speak inconsistently about things. But he *did* consistently promote witnessing as the essential basis of meditation. At first glance it may seem that Osho did not talk about inquiry very much, at least in comparison to witnessing. But in point of fact, when we study the process as he described it that led to his own enlightenment, it is unquestionable that inquiry played a major role. He was given heavily to both doubt and questioning, and it was this doubt and questioning that led him to the place of deep witnessing that culminated in his major realization in 1953.

The renowned 18th century Japanese Zen master Hakuin Ekaku—who Osho more than once talked about—famously denounced Zen practitioners of his time for being 'lumps of coal in black robes', decrying the state of affairs in Zen practice then. Basically, what he was arguing was that meditation had deteriorated into a state of mere witnessing, minus the element of inquiry. The problem with witnessing without inquiry is that it runs the risk of resulting in a subtle state of deadness, a lack of sharpness, and an inability to penetrate past remaining ego barriers.

The great 20th century Advaitin sage, Ramana Maharshi, had his realization entirely via the force of inquiry. One day, at age sixteen, seized by a deep desire to know who he was, he lay down and simulated the experience of death. While imagining his body dying, he inquired deeply into his essential nature—'Who am I?' In a moment of powerful understanding, he saw directly that his essential nature was timeless, unrelated to the body, and had been there all the time, merely going unnoticed. He then left his home and settled at the foot of the holy Mt. Arunachala in southern India, where he remained for the rest of his life. His consciousness eventually stabilized completely in the realized state, but the whole process had been clearly initiated by inquiry.

The great contribution of the Zen tradition, especially after it was rejuvenated by Hakuin, is the understanding that an initial 'awakening' experience is usually not enough to result in our stabilization in that state. We must periodically practice inquiry as well as witnessing, in order to keep our intelligence sharp. There was perhaps no better living example of that idea than Osho, who while consistently emphasizing the importance of witnessing, was himself always inquiring into things, and encouraging his disciples to do the same.

A meditation practice that employs witnessing but lacks periods of inquiry tends to be incomplete, as mentioned. The reverse situation—excessive inquiry with a lack of witnessing—is something common to intellectually centered people and Osho regularly criticized this approach. He was one of few Eastern gurus to emphasize the difference between intellectuality and intelligence. The former was, for him, the province of the typical academic. Because he himself had spent many years in academia—being an undergraduate, then graduate student, and then professor until age thirty-four—when he criticized academic approaches, particular in the philosophical and religious fields, his words carried weight. His main point was that excessive intellectuality keeps us at arm's length from things, making it more difficult to experientially penetrate deeply into the essence of something. For example, when listening to music, we cannot experience it fully if constantly thinking about the notes, the scales, the lyrics, the instruments, the history of the particular piece of music, and so on. When looking at a sunrise, we cannot appreciate it as much if we are thinking about the thermonuclear processes powering the Sun and the chemical composition of the atmosphere. When having sex we cannot enjoy it as much if we are discussing the biology of sex with our partner. And so forth. For scientific observation of things 'arm's length' is beneficial and usually necessary, but for direct experience, for quality of *being*, it is a problem.

However, contrary to what some might suspect, Osho was not 'anti-intellectual', at least not in the true sense of that term. He did often disparage 'mere intellectualism', but he was deeply interested in intelligence and often used it as a metaphor for wisdom or spiritual clarity. Most of the enlightened sages of history that he regularly spoke of he also categorized as 'immensely intelligent'. For him, intelligence was more properly a sharp mind combined with a deep common sense. He used to mock the absent-minded professor type—Karl Marx being one he often poked fun at, for once famously forgetting his own name—and more than once indicated that such 'types' were as far from enlightenment as anyone else, if not farther. But, he asserted, when intellect is used in the service of inquiring into oneself, it becomes pure intelligence and a formidable ally on the journey to self-realization.

Osho saw simplicity as a virtue, as a natural by-product of an intelligence that sees to the heart of issues, and does not get caught up in wasteful thinking and common indulgences. The English word 'simple' is, paradoxically, a complex word with several possible ways of being used. Typically, it tends to be used in a pejorative fashion, such as calling someone 'simple-minded' or a 'simpleton'. Alternatively, it is also used to imply a certain clarity, as in 'simple, direct, to the point'. The key term there is 'direct'. Osho, brash and outspoken all his life, stood for *direct* communication in the realm of human relating. His disciples tended to follow this, most of them inclining toward direct, simplified communication whenever possible.

On the issue of communication in general, Osho exalted the quality of silence, which might seem ironic for someone as loquacious as he was. Long term meditators often notice that their minds tend to think more economically, that is, with less idle daydreaming or pointless internal dialogue. One of the basic ideas of the mystical path has always been that reality yields its 'secrets' more readily to a mind that is not cluttered with its own opinions of, and projections on, everything. The essential idea behind meditation is that consistent practice of it allows us to see things more and more clearly, as they actually are—both internally, and externally. Persisted with, we eventually reach a point where we begin to see through the mind's 'construction of duality', that is, the conditioned tendency to see everything as fragmented, disconnected, separate. We begin to see the interconnectedness of all things. Finally—and naturally not all make it to this point—we begin to see that nothing is truly separate, including our own consciousness. That wherever we look we see, as the Zen expression has it, our 'original face'.

Although Osho emphasized watchfulness as the heart of meditation, he did not support a passive withdrawal from life. He stressed that the natural development of meditation was to be able to remain meditative while engaged in the activities of life. He said:

> Meditation is not against action. It is not that you have to escape from life. It simply teaches you a new way of life: you become the center of the cyclone. Your life goes on...more intensely—with more joy, with more clarity, more vision, more creativity—yet you are aloof, just a watcher on the hills, simply seeing all that is happening around you.[12]

Enlightenment

A close reading of Osho's words on the matter of enlightenment show that he is in alignment with many of the classic realizers of the world's wisdom traditions. A litmus test often used for the understanding of someone in this area, are their views on *spiritual experiences*. Many who practice meditation or have had different kinds of altered states of consciousness become fascinated with spiritual experiences, and often, very attached to them as well. One area that most spiritual realizers agree on is that enlightenment is *not* an experience. It is, rather, the simple and direct recognition of our true self, the consciousness beyond all experience—what the American philosopher-sage Franklin Merrill-Wolf called 'consciousness without an object'. Osho concurred with this, saying:

> One of the most fundamental things to remember is that whatever you come across in your inner journey, you are not it.

You are the one who is witnessing it...even great travelers of the inner worlds have gotten stuck in beautiful experiences, and have become identified with those experiences, thinking, 'I have found myself'. They have stopped before reaching the final stage where all experiences disappear...enlightenment is not an experience.[13]

Going hand in hand with the idea that enlightenment is not an experience is the understanding that enlightenment is not a meditation or exercise either, and literally cannot be 'practiced'. Osho said,

You cannot practice your enlightenment...it simply is...it overflows you, it expresses in every gesture. It is all around you, but you don't have to practice it. It is your very nature. Do you practice anything that is your very nature?[14]

A problematic issue that was always connected to Osho was the question of why so few, if indeed any, of his disciples were ever recognized as enlightened by him while he was alive. A few that did leave him and later either declared themselves, or were acknowledged by others, as enlightened, were generally denounced by Osho. A good example was Michael Barnett, who went by the name Swami Anand Somendra when he was with Osho. He was one of the master's more prominent disciples and one of the chief therapists in the Pune ashram in the 1970s. In the early '80s, he left Osho, went to Europe, and set himself up as an independent teacher there. Barnett was a charismatic man and soon had his own commune and following. It was understood that he believed his time with Osho had naturally come to a completion, and that he was now enlightened himself. Osho, however, did not accept this and in a public talk dismissed Barnett as 'unhealed' and not ready to be a master. (As of 2010, two decades after Osho's death, Barnett still teaches in Europe.) Barnett is one example of several prominent Osho disciples (including Paul Lowe, known in his Osho days as

Swami Ananda Teertha) who left and were discredited by Osho. I personally do not recall one case of him ever sanctioning a disciple leaving and claiming themselves a teacher.

In 1984, during the Oregon commune years, a fascinating event occurred in which Osho one day summoned twenty-one of his closer disciples to his private residence. Once they were all gathered, he announced that they were to be divided into three groups. The first was now enlightened. The second would become enlightened sometime before Osho died. And the last would become enlightened after Osho died.

The way these twenty-one disciples reacted to this totally unexpected edict from the master was highly interesting. Some actually began to 'feel enlightened', something that demonstrated the power of thoughts to shape reality, and needless to say, the immense power of suggestion when it is tied to the words of someone one has invested a deep trust in. This 'enlightened feeling' had concrete effects: several began to feel deep peace, clarity, and profound acceptance of the here and now—all qualities traditionally associated with the idea of spiritual enlightenment. Yet others registered some skepticism. One allegedly offered to give his certificate of enlightenment to another 'unenlightened' disciple in exchange for the latter's Oldsmobile. Another who made the list of twenty-one awakened ones was discovered to have actually left the movement a short time before. Tracked down on a farm somewhere in England and duly informed of his enlightenment, he replied with a frown, 'Are you sure there hasn't been some sort of mistake?' Only one, a disciple named Maitreya, was said to have 'understood'. His only response upon hearing of his enlightenment—he was in the first group, declared enlightened now—was 'Osho is a rascal'.

After some six months, Osho gathered the group together again and told them that it had all been a big joke—or more accurately, an elaborate device. Told that they were not in fact enlightened, some laughed, but others mysteriously felt their 'enlightened state' suddenly dissipate. The entire experiment, regardless of Osho's underlying motives for initiating it, was an interesting glimpse into the relationship between authentic spiritual realization and blind trust in a guru. It was reminiscent, on a larger scale, of something Gurdjieff once did with a group of his students. As recounted by Fritz Peters, Gurdjieff once announced—coincidentally, also to twenty disciples—that now that the book he had been writing was finished, so, in a sense, was he, and that he was ready to announce a successor. He paused dramatically, looked piercingly around the room, and began to point his finger, slowly passing it over everyone—until he reached Fritz Peters, where he paused and pointed directly at him for several moments. Silently, Gurdjieff then dropped his arm and strode out of the room. Peters found himself in a type of trance state, trying to absorb what seemed to have just happened. He then got up to leave the room, but was immediately stopped by another student, who pointed out to him that Gurdjieff had not really appointed him his successor—he had only created a device for Peters to see his own ambitious ego. Peters later came to agree with that assessment.[15]

When I was attending Osho's talks in Nepal in early 1986, just before his infamous world tour, there was one disciple in the large group of Nepali followers who was alleged to be enlightened. His demeanor appeared consistently relaxed, centered, peaceful—a reasonable candidate for enlightenment. But the harder truth is that the lack of 'enlightened' disciples around Osho reflected real problems around the whole notion of enlightenment. My own sense was that there was always too much baggage connected to the idea. In a Gurdjieffian sense, the concept operated well enough as an 'aim', a light to orient one's life toward. But the problem with Osho was that his intense charisma, and the sheer adulation given to him, made him a remote figure on a mountaintop impossible to reach. As a result, the key thing that he was understood to embody, enlightenment itself, also became unreachable, if only in the minds of many of his followers.

This was, in a sense, confirmed when, not long after Osho's death in early 1990, a number of disciples drifted north from the Pune ashram, to Lucknow, and the company of the Advaita master Harilal Poonja. At that point, already eighty years old, Poonja had been a devotee of the famous south Indian sage Ramana Maharshi who had died in 1950. Operating through a low profile, Poonja taught a small circle of disciples (including Andrew Cohen, who later broke with him). After Osho's death, Poonja's community swelled by several hundred. Thrust into something of a limelight, Poonja was soon endorsing a number of disciples as enlightened and sanctioning them to conduct *satsang* meetings in the West. He was clearly impressed for the most part with the quality of seekers who came to him from Osho and saw himself as the guide who would usher many of them to the final step, that of actual self-realization. The time for therapy, manual work, and all sorts of different meditations was over. Now they had only to look deeply into Poonja's eyes, 'get it'—or as Poonja often put it, 'just keep quiet'—and that final step could happen.

The question of whether Poonja really represented a final step for many of Osho's disciples or whether he just had lower standards for recognizing enlightenment, is, of course, speculative. It would commonly be assumed by most who knew Osho that it is unlikely that he would have approved of or recognized Poonja, since he recognized so few and condemned so many. However, I do recall one talk in Nepal when Osho was asked what to do after he died. I still vividly remember his response. 'If, when I am gone, you find a master who is charismatic and awake, then go to him.' Despite the general sense that he was possessive of disciples, I think that underneath it all his interest in the liberation of his disciples was genuine.

Humor and Celebration

To a degree unusual for most Eastern gurus, Osho placed great emphasis on the need for dance, creativity, humor and celebration. Osho communal houses during the 1970s and 80s were renowned for their partying, but the reputation for sex and drugs at these parties was always exaggerated. The main thing going on during them was dance, and more dance. If there could be said to have been an activity that best represented Osho's disciples it would be dance — more so even than therapy or meditation. This was in keeping with Osho's emphasis on both the body and creativity. He repeatedly said that his vision for an enlightened society was one where its people could be free to dance in the streets, to be alive and vital, and he repeatedly spoke against the image of the long-faced, overly serious spiritual seeker. He admired sincerity, but was adamantly opposed to seriousness.

Jokes were a big part of Osho's lectures for many years, although more so as time went on. These were written by his disciples and then he would read them out at the end of his lectures. He usually delivered these jokes deadpan — in fact, despite his humor, he rarely laughed, generally inclining more toward an amused half-smile, clearly taking more delight in seeing his disciples laugh. As time went on, the jokes became increasingly ribald. They were in a sense a teaching device. He frequently told jokes with racist or sexist themes, the idea being to see that any sort of identification, be that with race, sex, creed, culture, body-type, social status, and so on, was bound to result in suffering sooner or later. The jokes were a means of laughing at oneself and thus an aid to become free of certain kinds of conditioning. For example, Osho often poked fun at Germans, Jews, Japanese, and the English, precisely because a large percentage of his disciples were German, Jewish, Japanese, or English. I have, over the course of several decades, sat in the presence of many gurus and teachers and I can say in all honesty that none had a better sense of humor than Osho. A few have come close; the Tibetan teacher Ponlop Rinpoche is very funny, as is the Canadian Theravadin Buddhist teacher Ajahn Sona, and Adi Da Samraj (who passed away in 2008) was a humorous man in his earlier years. But none could match Osho's combination of subtle wit and capacity for the rowdiest humor.

Part Three

Commentaries

Chapter 7
Kings of the Night

It is a lie, this folly against the self. Be strong, o man! lust, enjoy all things of sense and rapture:
fear not that any God shall deny thee for this.
The Book of the Law, II:22

In order to become an altruist, one must first become an out and out egoist.
G.I. Gurdjieff

I teach you to be selfish.
Osho

Let the Illusion of the World pass over thee, unheeded,
as thou goest from the Midnight to the Morning.
Aleister Crowley

Osho, Gurdjieff, and Crowley all had some interesting associations with the night—as well as with its old luminous nocturnal sentinel, the Moon. Crowley was dubbed 'the King of the Shadow Realm' (by his literary executor John Symonds). As Symonds remarked of Crowley, 'He lived through the night, not the day'.[1] To a large degree, this was literally true. Crowley, especially in his later years, was a nocturnal creature, sleeping during the day and writing by night. Gurdjieff seemed preoccupied with the glowing lord of the night sky and had some unique ideas about it, declaring that humanity was, by and large, 'food for the Moon'. He was often associated with the dark, called such things as a 'black panther' and the 'black devil of Ashkhabad'. Osho's commune in Oregon was nicknamed 'City of the Lord of the Full Moon'. His original Hindi name was Chandra Mohan Jain; *Chandra* means 'Moon'. His nickname in childhood that stuck with him for much of his life, Rajneesh, literally means 'king of the night' or simply, 'the Moon'.[2] Many times, Osho spoke of his deep fondness for the night and the Moon; his enlightenment at age twenty-one occurred in the middle of the night. Like Crowley, he too became largely nocturnal toward the end of his life, living in a room that was kept in deep darkness at all hours owing to his physical condition that made him overly sensitive to light.

In 1914, Crowley conceived the idea of inducing the birth of a higher dimensional entity in human form; this idea later took shape as a novel eventually published in 1929, titled *Moonchild*. An amusing anecdote relating to Crowley's interest in Moon symbolism was relayed by the journalist Tom Driberg in 1969 when, reminiscing about Crowley, he recounted the following:

> I first met Crowley when I was very young. He asked me to lunch in London. I was curious, but distinctly on my guard...The man I met was elderly, bald, stout, and dressed in good green Harris tweeds—not at all exotic, except that, as we sat down, he said 'Pardon me while I invoke the Moon.'[3]

In Crowley's Thelemic teachings, the night, or more specifically what he called the Night of Pan, holds great mystical significance, representing the dissolution of the ego on the way to self-realization. He symbolized this by the Latin term NOX ('night') and said it was the key to the current Aeon. The Moonchild of Crowley's novel was a great being from a higher world come to guide humanity (reminiscent of the 'Starchild' concept shown at the conclusion of the

1969 science-fiction film *2001: A Space Odyssey*). Two years after the publication of Crowley's *Moonchild*, Osho—named 'Moon'—was born.

Crowley's, Gurdjieff's, and Osho's connections with the Moon and the night go much further than commonalities of appearance and synchronicities, however. They relate primarily to two major areas: teachings that are pre-eminently concerned with the reconciliation of opposites, of the so-called light and dark realms of the psyche and in particular the long-disputed conflict between self and selflessness; and the living of a life that is a demonstration of that, in vivid, bold ways.

The latter of these, the personal journey, will be clear to anyone who studies the biographical data of the three men. Their lives were full and rich, packed with sheer experience and a fearless spirit that is reminiscent, more than anything, of Shiva the Destroyer from Hindu myth. Gurdjieff, in introducing his magnum opus, *Beelzebub's Tales to His Grandson*, expressed this well, declaring that the purpose of the book was,

> To destroy mercilessly, without any compromise whatsoever, in the mentations and feelings of the reader, the beliefs and views, by centuries rooted in him, about everything existing in the world.[4]

No more apt job-description for a Shiva-like figure could be formulated. There is no compromise, no asking for permission, no implicit 'respect of equals'; he simply brings his sword and hews away. Crowley and Osho were no less uncompromising and domineering. Both could and did wield a rough Zen sword on others, although with Crowley's sadomasochistic tendencies he just as often wielded the sword against himself. Osho probably holds some sort of record for insulting the most religious leaders and politicians ever. He would tacitly admit, near the end of his life, that his brazen approach hastened his death, believing that the American administration at the time (and the Vatican, according to other researchers), royally pissed off by his words and the criminal activities of a few of his disciples, decided to assassinate him via radiation poisoning (see Chapter 12)—but only after vindictively assuring that he would be barred from (or thrown out of) over twenty nations. Even if Osho was not assassinated, the fact is, he attracted an enormous amount of hostility. As the American author Tom Robbins once remarked,

> Osho is the most dangerous man since Jesus Christ. He's obviously a very effective man, otherwise he wouldn't be such a threat. He's saying the same things that nobody else has the courage to say. He scares the pants off the control freaks.[5]

The Kali Yuga

Hindu cosmology long ago put forth the idea that life on Earth as we know it progresses through a cyclical pattern of world ages. In this model, there are four such ages, each referred to as a *yuga*. The word is commonly understood to mean 'era' or 'age', but technically it is the same as the root of the word yoga, meaning 'yoke', and can be understood as a means of attaching sentient beings to the passage of time. The four ages are called *satya-yuga*, *treta-yuga*, *dvapara-yuga*, and *kali-yuga*. The first, *satya*, literally means 'truth', and this is a golden age in which truth dominates. It is the highest and purest of the four ages. During this time, wisdom, love, and goodness rule; the age is symbolized by the 'bull of dharma' standing whole, on all four legs. After the Satya Yuga a gradual decline begins, first with the Treta Yuga. At this point, the symbolic bull has lost a leg, and stands on three legs. This is then followed by the Dvapara Yuga and a further decline in virtue, where the bull has only two legs. The process ends with the Kali Yuga, in which all spiritual qualities— wisdom, understanding, love, virtue, truth, justice, peace, and so on—are at their lowest ebb. Darkness and vice predominate. The bull of dharma has only one leg left. It is barely standing.[6]

According to most interpretations of Hindu cosmology, we are currently in the early stages of the Kali Yuga.[7] The term *kali* in this case is not related to the Hindu goddess Kali, as is sometimes mistakenly assumed, but rather to a male demon that goes by the same name, who is regarded as a type of shadow expression of the god Vishnu. He is seen as a force of destruction and evil.

This is, of course, religious myth, but the literal meaning of 'myth' is 'story', and as we all know stories often reveal or reflect profound truths. The idea of a general decline or dark age can in part be related to the notion of the 'myth of progress'. This is the generalized idea (or belief) that humanity has been progressing, from primitive to advanced, in a linear, consistent fashion, and that, accordingly, a great and brilliant destiny awaits us in the future. Occasionally, people associate this idea with a simplified view of evolution, loosely understood as a natural process that leads from simple to complex, from dumb to smart, from unsuccessful to successful—in short, from less to more. The drastic recent rise in human population heightens the appearance of that.[8]

And yet, this idea is soon realized to be deeply flawed. For starters, it is acknowledged by most evolutionary scientists that the vast majority of species that have ever lived on Earth no longer exist. By some estimates, more than 99.9% of all species that ever appeared on this planet are extinct—despite the fact that millions still remain. Many were wiped out by natural disasters, most simply came to an evolutionary dead end, i.e. nothing evolved from them. In short, what that implies is that evolution is not purely and simply progress, it is more properly *change* (driven, as most biologists agree, by natural selection and genetic drift). In that sense, it is more akin to the Hindu idea of cyclical ages than it is to a simplistic notion of ladder-like progress.[9]

The idea that we live in any sort of Kali Yuga or 'dark age' may be laughed off by those dazzled by modern technology. Unquestionably, we live during a time when our medical, transportation, and communication technologies, in particular, are so far beyond what was known in only the recent past as to render that past very primitive in contrast. And yet a simple look at the amount of carnage and destruction that took place in the 20th century will quickly dissipate our enthusiasm. Approximately a hundred million people died in that century in warfare alone. Even as old afflictions have been eradicated (like smallpox) new ones appeared, such as AIDS, which as of 2010 has killed over twenty-five million people (with another thirty million infected). Overpopulation has become a critical problem. The jury is still out on the causes of global warming, but environmental pollution and wholesale destruction of entire ecosystems is a stark reality. A looming energy crisis brought on by the inevitable exhaustion of fossil fuel reserves, generally referred to as 'peak oil', is now universally accepted. The advent of the nuclear age brought with it the creation of new shadowy agencies (the CIA was created the same decade that the atomic bombs were dropped on Japan), and the greater need for overt and covert defensive forces in the world. Terrorist and counter-terrorist organizations are now legion, along with rogue nations with more weapons than food and the haunting specter of the suitcase nuke. Quite simply and indisputably, we live in a very dangerous time.

What the idea of the Kali Yuga refers to is a time of spiritual darkness—literally, the spiritual night. If, for a moment, we were to consider the idea that we live during such an age, what actually is meant by the idea of a 'spiritual night'? Clearly, examining the world as it is now, it is not that everything is without hope and that no light exists anywhere. On the contrary, there is far more awareness of higher values and of the importance of appreciating the various cultural contexts of these higher values than at any time in history, largely due to the advances in communication and transportation technology. The world is a much more accessible place than it was a century ago. Space and time have been collapsed to a large degree. On the social level, advances like Women's rights, the Civil Rights Movement, increased integration of races and cultures, Gay Rights, and so forth, all speak to a marked evolution of tolerance and compassion. However, the central point is that as much as positive factors have been enhanced so have negative factors. Put simply, as the light increases, so does the dark—as the Sun comes out from behind the clouds, so do shadows accordingly appear. Thus, the need to understand the contrasting nature of opposites becomes particularly critical.

In the Hindu myth, it is further taught that there is a specific form of spirituality that is best suited to such a time as the Kali Yuga, and that is Tantra. A key element of Tantra is that it does not deny the shadow elements of life but rather seeks to embrace them, in order to come to deep acceptance and understanding of the whole cosmic dance of duality—good and bad, light and dark, pure and impure, high and low, spirit and sex, male and female, rich and poor, formless and form, *numina* and phenomena.

As spiritual teachers, Crowley, Gurdjieff, and Osho, far more than most others of their kind exemplified the intention to embrace the polar opposites of life. As a young Golden Dawn initiate, Crowley set up his apartment in London with two main rooms, one a 'white' temple for white magic, the other a 'black' temple for black magic. In his *Liber Tzaddi* he referred to the adept whose body stretches from below hell to above heaven:

Many have arisen, being wise. They have said 'Seek out the glittering Image in the place ever golden, and unite yourselves with It.' Many have arisen, being foolish. They have said, 'Stoop down unto the darkly splendid world, and be wedded to that Blind Creature of the Slime.' I who am beyond Wisdom and Folly, arise and say unto you: achieve both weddings! Unite yourselves with both! Beware, beware, I say, lest ye seek after the one and lose the other! My adepts stand upright; their head above the heavens, their feet below the hells.

Echoing the timeless creed of alchemy and anticipating Jung, he said, 'The Great Work is the uniting of opposites'. Gurdjieff's pictorial image that represented his Institute depicted two celestial beings on either side, one an angel, the other a devil. Osho taught that the new man was to be 'Zorba the Buddha', the synthesis of the sensual and the transcendent, or the material and the spiritual. And yet as much as their teachings, it was who they were, and the way they lived, that was such an apt demonstration of this attempt to resolve opposites, and to live life in all its dimensions.

Since recorded history, humanity has struggled to resolve the inner conflict between the higher and lower nature—between the celestial and the animal, between the divine and the carnal, between self and selflessness. What modern Western psychology came to define as the 'ego', and what Eastern traditions have called the 'self', is rooted in the survival instinct. Human beings have been exceptionally successful at surviving a rugged past against great odds: harsh environmental conditions, predators, diseases. Until recently, the average person did not live much longer than the time needed to mate and create offspring to continue the species. Our entire history is dark with limitation and colored by the urge to survive at all costs. Beneath the thin veneer of a civilized mask, beneath all our cultural and scientific attainments, lurks a primal beast always semi-conscious of its mortality and the possibility of losing everything at any moment. We rail against an abyss of nothingness, pretending it does not exist, but always motivated by our deep fear of it—the fear of losing the things we are attached to, and of losing who we think we are—the fear of disappearing, of death.

The self, the ego—that centralized notion of identity that makes us claim things as 'mine'—is ancient, rooted in the impulse to protect, defend, control, conquer, kill. It is (necessary) selfishness incarnate. As human social structures became more organized over time, and as nations formed and grew, the need to control the primitive inner nature became more and more crucial. Impulse control became imperative. Moral codes were introduced—the various 'commandments'—and with these, the need for priesthoods to implement them and monitor their effectiveness. Long dead spiritual masters were gradually turned into mere icons of morality, figureheads representing a church and doctrine designed to control and govern the masses and preserve what learning there was.

The puritanical streak that runs through most organized religions has always been problematic, serving as it does to divide a person inwardly, to cause the person to turn against him or herself. This inner psychological struggle gets acted out within the literary canons of our world—Dante's *Divine Comedy*, Shakespeare's tragedies, Milton's *Paradise Lost*, Goethe's *Faust*. Religious myth is saturated with it: the struggle between Ahura Mazda and Ahriman, between Christ and Satan, between the Buddha and Mara. The 'dark' for most people is the forbidden fruit, the lure of sin, the attraction of the dangerous. It is compelling because it speaks to our alienation from this part of our nature. We strive to be good, virtuous, moral, faithful, upstanding, and so to gain approval in the eyes of others, all the while suppressing our 'unwholesome' nature, deadening it through dissociation, through endless distractions and indulgences, through fantasy and living vicariously. And when we act it out, we tend to do so secretively, furtively, always in fear of exposure or ridicule.

Amongst that small minority of humanity who have, throughout history, chosen to dedicate their lives to inner transformation, mystical wisdom, and philosophical and spiritual enlightenment, the struggle to come to terms with the self-centered side, the primal man or woman, the inner beast, has not gone away. In fact, this struggle intensifies, carrying with it the very real risk of deciding to shut the beast out altogether, only to have it erupt in consciousness later on, or to have it slowly erode one's spiritual practice—or even worse, to bestow a false spirituality, a bogus awakening based more on culti-vated behavior than profound realization—to become righteous and phony holy. Organized religion has been notorious for breeding hypocrisy, for encouraging a spurious spirituality ruled by moral dogma. This, in turn, has created pressurized people, inwardly controlled, easily set off by random external triggers.

The Left and Right Hand Paths

In order to truly understand what teachers like Crowley, Gurdjieff, and Osho were about, what they were doing, what their intentions were—and why things happened around them the way they did—it is necessary to have some grasp of the so-called Left Hand path, and its contrast with the Right Hand path, as they apply to the spiritual realm. This is, in part, because, whatever else may be said about them, Crowley, Gurdjieff, and Osho were teachers who were pre-eminently concerned with the creation of a whole man and woman—balanced, complete, and integrated—to a degree, and with a depth of insight, found in very few teachers.

The terms 'Left' and 'Right Hand path' are of course conventions, ultimately falling away as we penetrate deeper into the matter and begin to understand what it means to reconcile opposites. But in order to approach the whole issue, they can be helpful concepts, because they highlight an area that is notoriously difficult to see and understand—the issue of integrating the needs of the personal self with a spiritual life that by definition seeks to be transpersonal—'beyond' the self.

All three of these teachers of necessity had to address the so-called Left Hand approach in order to work with the insidious nature of repression brought on by centuries of religious, political, and social conditioning. Contrary to some misunderstood views of them, all three embraced *both* the Left Hand and Right Hand approaches. They unquestionably used basic Left Hand philosophical tenets to a marked degree. That in all three cases their work met with considerable resistance and opposition in the world is in large part attributable to these Left Hand views and methods.

The Right Hand path is understood by most people well enough—it is the conventional path of work on oneself, seeking transcendence of personal flaws and limitations and to purify oneself sufficiently in order to join with a higher principle. That 'higher' may be conceived of as a deity, the higher self, the Absolute, Nirvana, God, Christ, the Buddha-mind, the atman, and so on. In all cases, the personal self is subsumed by the transcendent. All major religions are (in theory) Right Hand paths, as are most conventional spiritual practices.

The Left Hand path differs from the Right principally by its conception of the personal self. It does not seek to overcome or dissolve the personal self but rather seeks to investigate it deeply and even to exalt it. It is, quite simply, 'self-centered', and for a very specific reason. Osho, in a talk, expressed the idea—in, it must be said, its *ideal* way—as follows:

> I teach selfishness. I want you to be, first, your own flowering. Yes, it will appear as selfishness; I have no objection to that appearance; it is okay with me. But is the rose selfish when it blossoms? Is the lotus selfish when it blossoms? Is the Sun selfish when it shines? Why should you be worried about selfishness? You are born—birth is only an opportunity, just a beginning, not an end. You have to flower. Your first and foremost responsibility is to blossom, to become fully conscious, aware, alert; and in that consciousness you will be able to see what you can share, how you can solve problems.[10]

In a poke at Buddhism that would have pleased Crowley, Osho also remarked, 'I don't teach the middle way, I teach the total way'. This is the key point—how to live a *full* life that is also awakened to our highest potential. The Left Hand, in this sense, can be thought of as representing the part of us that is typically fought against, denied, feared, and shunned—and, accordingly, it becomes the problem child within us, and at the same time, the key to our liberation. The Bible hints at this idea in its parable of The Prodigal Son. The return of a 'lost son' is cause for celebration, much as the proper re-integration of our denied and shunned personal energies results naturally in fulfillment and happiness.

Throughout history, in many cultures, the left has been associated with the troublesome, the radical, and the sinister. And the etymology backs this up: the Latin word *sinister* literally means 'from the left side'. In a broad range of cultures, from Chinese to Muslim to Hindu to the Judeo-Christian West, the left is associated with the unclean (Hindus and Muslims wash with their left hand after relieving themselves), the subversive, the clumsy, the improper, the untrustworthy, and so on. It even refers to being 'out of touch' as the expression, 'out in left-field' suggests. In many cultures, to shake someone's hand using the left hand is considered an insult. Further, statistics from a British study done in the 1970s showed a decline in percentage of lefthanders in older population groups, suggesting that lefthanders were compelled by various factors (including the practical matter of operating machinery) to switch to being right-handed.[11]

This extraordinary negativity connected to the left even extends to the spiritual path where the 'Left Hand Path' is often connected exclusively to anti-Christian values (such as Satanism) or to the ideas of mere selfishness and materialism. There is a great deal of confusion in this area, much of it being an echo of ancient ideas of dualism that have their roots in Zoroastrianism, as well as the 19th century European misunderstanding of Left Hand Tantric traditions from India. But in order to understand all this we need to look a bit deeper into the history of religious dualism—the split between the 'good' and the 'bad', between the so-called 'left' and the 'right'.

Dualism and the Conceptual Roots of 'Pure Good' vs. 'Pure Evil'

The notion of a singular and primary force that is wholly evil was birthed in Persia (modern day Iran) through what was known as the Zoroastrian Reformation, around 580 BC. At that time, Indian Hinduism had Shiva, Kali, Durga, etc., all fiery, destructive gods, but all equally ambiguous in nature, and certainly none opposed to the Will of the Absolute. Buddhism, which came a few decades later, had Mara, the 'prince of temptation', but his role was not much different from the Amerindian concept of the 'Trickster' as Raven or

Coyote, or the Celtic Grail myth archetype known as the Green Knight. The idea is that these are forces whose task it is to test humanity and without whom there would be no motivation for growth, but they are not identical with a wholly adversarial quantity like the Judeo-Christian Satan.

The ancient Sanskrit scriptures, known as the *Rig Veda*, finished (in its current form) perhaps by 1200 BC but very likely begun much earlier, was adapted by Zoroaster, who was born into the cultural descendent of the Vedic empire that stretched from India to North Africa and from the Black to the Caspian Seas. Persian Vedantism allowed for many different gods. The main ruling entities were Ahura Mazda and Mithra. At that time, there was no prime 'devil'.[12]

Mithra, a savior god whose birth took place in a sacred cave, was foretold by prophets, and was presided over by the appearance of a special star. At Zoroaster's birth in 628 BC, Persia had been recently unified, and was in need of a unifying religion. Bowing to political needs, Zoroaster included in his writings the presence of dual and opposing forces of Light and Dark: Ahura Mazda (good) and Ahriman (evil). The notion of such vivid dualism was politically useful, much in the same way 20th century state leaders frequently demonized their enemies (Iran vs. 'Great Satan', the USA; or Ronald Reagan vs. the Soviet Union's 'Evil Empire'; or George Bush Sr. vs. 'the next Hitler', Saddam Hussein). Zoroaster's Ahriman is the first identified character representing pure, unambiguous evil, in recorded history.

In Zoroaster's myth, one of Ahriman's servants was known as Azaziel, a demon of the wild who usually took the form of a goat. This is the oldest probable connection with medieval Europe's conventional association of the Judeo-Christian devil with a goat-like creature, especially through the imagery of Baphomet, the supposed ass-headed idol of the Knights Templar. Crowley himself paid homage to the image of Baphomet in his Gnostic Mass, believing it to be a symbol of unity. He also added,

> The Devil does not exist. It is a false name invented by the Black Brothers to imply a Unity in their ignorant muddle of dispersions. A devil who had unity would be a God.[13]

Astutely, Crowley pointed out that 'devils' tend to be the gods of older, vanquished civilizations—or as he put it, 'the god of any people one personally dislikes'.[14] This is, of course, all a variant of the idea that history is written by conquerors. The main idea to see here is that a split has been engineered in the collective mind of humanity, based on black and white morality and simplistic notions of good and evil. This split ripples down to many levels of culture, from a God or benevolent gods battling armies of darkness, to 'good' people vs. 'bad' people, to conscious vs. unconscious—and to the right hand vs. the left hand.

Crowley denied the existence of the Judeo-Christian-Islamic version of the Devil, but he did recognize the Devil as an archetype and had a Devil trump card in his own Tarot deck (the Thoth deck, designed by him and painted by Frieda Harris). In his commentaries on the Devil card, he had some penetrating insights:

> This card represents creative energy in its most material form...the formula of this card is the complete appreciation of all existing things. He rejoices in the rugged and the barren no less than in the smooth and fertile. All things equally exalt him. He represents the finding of ecstasy in every phenomena, however naturally repugnant; he transcends all limitations; he is Pan; he is All.[15]

Crowley subtitles his Devil card as The Lord of the Gates of Matter and The Child of the Forces of Time. Standard occult Devil symbolism (as in typical Tarot cards) equates the Devil to bondage and materialism—to such ideas as greed, control, tyranny, selfishness, and all the potential evil of matter brought about by our attachments to it. Crowley, however, perceives the issue from a different angle. He points toward an alternate approach to the usual attitude found in religion toward the body and material reality, commonly regarded as things to be shunned and renounced—seen as inherently sinful, or at best, mere illusion. He does not argue that attachment to matter and form leads to suffering, but reasons rather that the way to become truly free is not by denial and renunciation, but by robust joy and passionate involvement in life.

In the domain of psychology, C.G. Jung devoted much thought to this problem, referring to the 'Shadow', a symbol representing repressed instincts and impulses that is also the source of creative energy. On other occasions he referred to it as the 'whole unconscious'.[16] Basically, it is the part of us that we fail to acknowledge, that we are afraid to admit—our weaknesses, perversions, hang-ups, embarrassing fears, and so on. In many ways, it is the polar opposite of the surface personality, the face we present to the world. Jung wrote,

> What we call civilized consciousness has steadily separated itself from the basic instincts. But these instincts have not disappeared. They have merely lost their contact with our consciousness and are thus forced to assert themselves in an indirect fashion. This may be by means of physical symptoms in the case of a neurosis, or by means of incidents of various kinds, or by unaccountable moods, unexpected forgetfulness, or mistakes in speech... modern man protects himself against seeing his own split state by a system of compartments. Certain areas of outer life and of his own behavior are kept, as it were, in separate drawers and are never confronted with one another.[17]

These ideas are virtually indistinguishable from Gurdjieff's. What protects a person from 'seeing their own split state' are what Gurdjieff called 'buffers' (the modern term is 'defense mechanism'), and the idea of our inner 'compartments' never confronting one another was understood by Gurdjieff as our various inner 'centers' (intellectual, emotional, etc.) out of touch with each other. The whole point of his practical methods was to establish interconnectedness between these inner parts—to become whole.

Osho, Gurdjieff, and Crowley were all entirely occupied with healing the inner fragmentation of the person. To tackle this problem they, on occasion, moved deeply into exploring the Left Hand path and accordingly ended up using many approaches that addressed the repressed, shadow part of the mind. It is, however, important to understand that 'addressing the repressed part of the mind' has nothing to do with indulgence. The key lies in the angle of approach. Gurdjieff once said it simply and concisely:

Before you can help others, be of real use to others, you must know yourself and be able to help yourself. Now you are an egoist, your mind is always on yourself. You must learn how to be an egoist for a good aim, then you will be able to be a real altruist and help others.[18]

Gurdjieff taught *self*-remembering, not God-remembering. However, the key is not just being selfish—the key is how to be selfish *in the correct way*. The key ingredient, as always, is consciousness. Selfishness is problematic only if it is unconscious, knee-jerk, motivated by repressed hostility and resentment toward the world. *I did not get, so now I will not give.* This kind of self-absorption is arising out of an unconscious desire to punish others. It is also known as withholding, and leads inevitably to contraction, shrinking from life, playing small, diminishing self-esteem, and eventually collapsing inwardly in failure, despair, and depression (or, on occasion, exploding outwardly and destructively in rage).

The antidote to withholding is *extending*. But this extending, this reaching out to the universe, cannot be done properly without first learning how to be consciously self-absorbed—a state that is sometimes called 'selfing'. In order to do that it is helpful to let go of overly rigid attachments to morality, to being upstanding and 'nice' in such a way that renders us bloodless and one-dimensional.

Tantric Antinomianism and the Problem of Hypocrisy

The word 'antinomian' originates from the Greek word for 'lawlessness'. When applied to spirituality, it refers to a particular teaching that is not concerned with conventional ethics and is largely amoral (as opposed to moral or immoral). The spiritual antinomian approach embraces a wilder kind of spiritual awakening that is not founded on traditional codes of religious ethics and morality. Antinomianism is the opposite of what is called 'legalism', which in this context is the idea that spiritual awakening is impossible unless founded on a strict obedience to ethical codes. Tantric antinomianism in particular is at the other side of the spectrum from traditional Vedanta. In Vedantic philosophy, the world is understood to be *maya* ('illusion' or 'mere appearance'), but in Tantra the world is regarded as *Shakti* ('energy', or 'power') to be awakened to, with the ultimate goal being the union within us of power/energy (Shakti) with vast spacious stillness (Shiva).

As mentioned above, Shiva is the god par excellence who applies to Crowley, Gurdjieff, and Osho. (And not coincidentally, one of Crowley's many appellations for himself was 'Shivaji'). Shiva is unique in the world's pantheon of gods in that he is both an ascetic—the ultimate yogi, living naked in the wilds, absorbed in deep meditation—and a sensualist, a Dionysian, who with his Tantric partner, the goddess Parvati, is often aflame in sexual passion and blissful tantric union. Flaunting conventions, ignoring orthodox order, he is feared and loathed by established priesthoods. One of his manifestations was known as Rudra, meaning literally 'he who is feared'.

That Crowley, Gurdjieff, and Osho could arouse fear in others, with their 'take no prisoners' style of teaching, is a basic part of their legend—whether it was Gurdjieff telling the young and beautiful Jesse Dwight that if she took his key student A.R. Orage away from him he would make sure she 'burned in boiling oil'; or Osho calling Jesus a 'stupid young man', and declaring the twelve apostles to be all homosexuals;[19] or Crowley identifying with the Beast of

Revelation and signing his letters '666' — the chthonic, or *underworld* spirit, was always clear in all three. Crowley is often accused of being a Satanist and yet there is great irony in this because he rejected Christianity — as well as its simplistic antihero pantheon of Satan and his minions — wholesale. He enjoyed poking fun at the deep hypocrisy of religion conditioning, maintaining that in Christianity, as in all dualistic faiths, evil is merely the inversion of good. In that sense, the God of the priesthoods is the ultimate hypocrite, having created their Devil and yet shunning and condemning him. Societies in general follow suit, judging and fearing whatever is different, performing all sorts of atrocities in the name of attacking what it does not understand. C.G. Jung, in his book *Aion*, put it concisely:

...the dogmatic figure of Christ is so sublime and spotless that everything else turns dark beside it.[20]

The bloodless, plastic Jesus, the pure white robed man of Sunday School, is entirely a human invention, and his very existence automatically calls into being the devilish opposite — but this opposite is simply a projection of repressed darkness. It, in turn, demands a scapegoat, something to punish as a means of avoiding the reality of where this darkness is coming from in the first place — that is, from our own minds. (One of the most vivid examples of this need to scapegoat played itself out in the so-called 'Witch' trials of the Inquisitions — and yet it goes on daily still, via all sorts of travesties of justice involving discrimination, prejudice, religious extremism, and so on.) It was the conventional view of Satan that Crowley rejected, going to great pains to explain that the entire symbolism of the 'Beast' (especially in the Book of Revelation) is misunderstood, that it, in fact, was a foreshadowing of the end of an era — that of the Aeon of the 'dying God', that is the archetype of self-sacrifice and the glorification of suffering.[21]

Of the three, Crowley was most inclined to on occasion reveal his loathing of any weakness in himself. In a burst of darkly amusing antinomian frustration, he once declared,

> After five years of folly and weakness, miscalled politeness, tact, discretion, care for the feeling of others, I am weary of it. I say today: to hell with Christianity, Rationalism, Buddhism, all the lumber of the centuries. I bring you a positive and primeval fact, Magic by name; and with this I will build me a new Heaven and new Earth. I want none of your faint approval or faint dispraise; I want blasphemy, murder, rape, revolution, anything, bad or good, but strong.[22]

John Symonds, Crowley's literary executor, eventually took a dim view of his former teacher, believing that Crowley had 'fallen prey to unconscious forces'. He felt that the very same forces Crowley attempted to tackle head on—basically alone and isolated in Victorian repressiveness—eventually ended up swallowing him.

Looked at it on balance, I think the evidence argues against Crowley being consumed by the chthonic power of Shiva. He remained lucid to the end; arguably his best and most mature works, *The Book of Thoth* and *Magick Without Tears*, were written in his last decade. But it is probable that Symonds had a point in there somewhere and it was that any path that involves so-called Left Hand practices is high octane and fraught with risk. To face into the ego always invites the possibility that one will be frightened to death by what one sees. The demon Choronzon that Crowley encountered in the Algerian desert in 1909 was not unique to him; it is the darkest part of our own ego, the part of us that stubbornly refuses us entry into our highest potential and true spiritual birthright.

Most people live double lives. It is almost a given of human nature. The magical motto that the poet W.B. Yeats took, *Deus est demon inversus*—God and the devil are two sides of one coin—speaks to this. The whole culture of deceit has been getting unmasked increasingly in modern times. We hardly go a month without some scandal breaking involving some high profile figure who is found out to be just a regular human after all. These stories generally make good snicker-material but the real point is to be able to witness these things and at the same time have just one moment of suspending judgment. Because if we can't respect the sheer power and omnipresence of the shadow-side of human nature, then we run a real risk of condemning ourselves (when we're done condemning everyone else), and splitting ourselves into partitions.

The dictionary definition of hypocrite is: 'A person who pretends to have virtues, moral or religious beliefs, principles, etc. that he or she does not actually possess.' The word derives from the Greek *hypokrisis*, which means acting on a stage—playing a role that is not who one really is. The American sociologist Benjamin F. Martin put it this way:

> Hypocrisy is the art of affecting qualities for the purpose of pretending to an undeserved virtue. Because individuals and institutions and societies most often live down to the suspicions about them, hypocrisy and its accompanying equivocations underpin the conduct of life. Imagine how frightful truth unvarnished would be.[23]

Living the 'unvarnished truth' is indeed frightful and is a process that requires a deep degree of sincerity and commitment to undertake, if only because of St. Augustine's old lament, 'I can resist anything but temptation'. The trap within most Left Hand paths is to see a legitimate spiritual science as simply a glorified licence to indulge, an excuse to justify temptations. It can also easily drift into a kind of adolescent rebellion, and a search for special recognition from others.

However, the truth is that many of the humanistic and transpersonal forms of psychotherapy and inner work—everything from Primal Therapy to Reichian bodywork and Lowenesque bioenergetics to Red Tantra (as popularized by many Western seminar teachers who trained under Eastern adepts)—all embrace, to an extent, Left Hand philosophy. Not in the sense of glorifying the identification with the body, but simply in the sense of bringing consciousness into the gritty corners of human existence—in, as Jung put it, 'bringing light into the dark, not fleeing the dark'. In so doing, these approaches teach a deep acceptance of self, an approach diametrically opposed to the traditional spiritual methods of subduing, denying, or ascetically disciplining the self.

Crowley, for all his passionate defence of the teachings of his chief Holy Book (*The Book of the Law*), was far too sophisticated to fall into the trap of merely teaching an elaborate form of egoism. He wrote:

> It is better to conjure up the most obnoxious demons from the most noisome pit of Hell than to take one's own excitations for Divine benediction; if only because there was never a demon yet so atrocious as that same old Ego.[24]

In other words, the idea behind 'deeply accepting the self' is not to exalt the ego, or to believe for a moment that one's conventional personal self is a source of transcendent wisdom. It most certainly is not. But it is a source of immense mischief and suffering if it is merely denied, repressed, judged and condemned. Commenting on this line from *The Book of the Law* (II:22): 'It is a lie, this folly against the self. The exposure of innocence is a lie', Crowley remarked, 'The exposure of innocence is a lie'; for that means clearly enough Hypocrisy. So 'it is a lie, this folly against self' only means 'To hell with sentimental altruism, with false modesty, with all those most insidious fiends, the sense of guilt, of shame—in a word, the inferiority complex...'[25]

This was a major element of Osho's teaching as well. Arguably it reached a badly distorted expression in Ma Anand Sheela, his notorious secretary who played 'Judas' in the dramatic downfall of Osho's Oregon commune (see Chapter 10). But handled with some measure of skill and mindfulness, the result of letting go of false modesty and all related qualities that contribute toward hypocrisy, makes possible a deep healing of wounds founded on guilt, shame, and self-loathing.

My own experience within all of this has led me to believe that a gradual paradigm shift is occurring in which so-called Left Hand path and Right Hand path are beginning to overlap and join. The traditional Right Hand path is a straight arrow that aims right for spiritual source (however one conceives that to be) and seeks to dissolve the ego or personal self at its very root—whether that be devotionally, by surrendering to God or guru, or by meditation, by seeing into the illusion of the personal self. The pitfall of this approach has always been the problems of repression. Repression is by nature insidious and subtle, serpentine (perhaps an ironic term for a danger of the Right Hand path). It is repression that lies at the heart of the culture of deceit and pretence, and repression that leads to the inevitable explosions that sabotage years of spiritual work (the standard 'fall from grace'). And, if truth be told, the traditional Right Hand approach fails far more than it succeeds, if we measure such success by quality of being, let alone actual enlightenment.

The patron saint of the Left Hand path is Lucifer of the Old Testament, the quintessential archetype of both self and rebellion. Crowley, as is commonly known, identified with the biblical Beast of the Book of Revelation and utilized the averse pentagram in some of his rituals. The hero of Gurdjieff's magnum opus, *Beelzebub's Tales to His Grandson*, is of course Beelzebub—the name of which derives from the old Philistine Semitic god named Ba'al but which later came to be a name for Satan, consistent with the practice of newer cultures demonizing the gods of older ones. Gurdjieff once referred to himself—tongue at least partly in cheek—as the 'Ambassador from Hell'.[26] These are not knee-jerk anti-Christian sentiments. Gurdjieff was closely connected to the Russian Orthodox Church and an Orthodox priest presided over his funeral. He once called his own teaching 'esoteric Christianity'. His concern was with the truth, not mere rebellion against the status quo. And Crowley's identification with the Beast had nothing to do with mere reaction against 'good'. He was rather pointing toward a new era we are entering, one no longer dominated by the priesthood enforced ideals of plastic virtue, and one facing the truth of what thousands of years of inner divisiveness has resulted in.

However, truth very often hurts, and badly. The thick, dark, sleepy unconsciousness that has permeated humanity throughout history cannot be broken with only a soft touch. It needs a rough shaking from time to time. And that shaking often takes the form of a rebellion, a necessary phase in the process of integration, of the balancing of opposites. Osho said,

> Unless one is a born troublemaker one cannot become a buddha...I am Zorba the Buddha. I am a meeting of the East and the West. In fact, I do not divide East and West, higher and lower, man and woman, good and bad, God and the devil. No, a thousand times no—I don't divide. I join together all that has been divided up to now. That is my work.[27]

The Lucifer archetype is bold, self-affirming, authentically self-expressive. However, in Lucifer's very desire to legitimize his existence via rebellion, he separated himself from his source, God, which on the absolute level is the same thing as separating from his true self. In effect, he cut out a piece of his own heart. That's the shadow side of the Left Hand path—pride, which is the attachment to being special. So while the common difficulty with the Right Hand path is repression and denial of self, the shadow element of the Left Hand path is an inflated sense of self that goes beyond a healthy reversal of shame and self-loathing. It is the need to be special.

Uniqueness and specialness (in this context) are not the same thing. Each entity is unique, yet none are special. Gurdjieff once stated that the ego is essentially founded on vanity and pride. Vanity is fascination with oneself—self-absorption to the point of disconnectedness—and pride is the conviction in one's specialness.

A few years ago, I was running a workshop in Germany in which I set up a process whereby people in the room were to divide into two 'camps'—the angels, and the devils. They were then to attempt to sway those of the 'other side' to cross the floor and join the enemy. The process soon makes one aware of one's shadow elements, as well as one's capacity for puritanical moralism. In this particular case, the room divided up roughly equally, and after the usual boasting and haggling, several people switched sides. (Germans being generally self-controlled and somewhat inhibited, the devils were soon outnumbering the angels, as many of them secretly desired to be devils.) Then, at one point, an interesting thing happened. One woman in the group opted out of the process altogether and simply stood in a separate part of the room. Within several minutes, she had been joined by about one-third of the people. We then effectively had three groups. After, she admitted that the reason she formed her own group is that she had a strong resistance to being part of anything conventional. She had a deep need to be special, to stand out. In drawing one-third of the room into her improvised group, she unwittingly echoed the myth of Lucifer who drew one-third of the angels to him upon launching his rebellion.

The shadow side of the Left Hand approach may be the attachment to being special, but the intelligence of the Left Hand approach lies in its addressing the immediacy and power of the human condition in a physical body—self, will, emotions, sensuality, and sexuality in particular. In Left Hand Tantra, the body is worked with as a temple of the divine, and one's partner is to be regarded as no less than a direct expression of the divine. Sexual intercourse is not just some act of frantic compulsion or desperate gymnastics; it is a sacred act of conse-cration in which the outer union is understood to mirror the inner union of polarized energies resulting in a heightening of awareness of the sacred present moment.

The Right Hand path also aims directly for the sacred present moment, giving it different names, but the essential point to bear in mind is that consciousness itself is the alchemical force that transforms all limiting tendencies of mind into the gold of love-energy. Both Left and Right Hand paths seek this. The chief difference is that Left works from the sensory universe (via the body, and its immediate, localized sense of self) inward toward the numinous source. The Right seeks direct access to source.

Both approaches ultimately become complimentary in an integral approach, at which point the labels of 'Left' or 'Right' drop naturally, much as the distinction between self and not-self becomes less relevant. At this point, it is truly possible to live fully, present, alive to existence. As Gurdjieff said,

> When you do a thing, do it with the whole self. One thing at a time. Now I sit here and I eat. For me, nothing exists in the world except for this food, this table. I eat with the whole attention.[28]

Osho, Gurdjieff, and Crowley were pre-eminently concerned with the wholeness of a person, and all their teachings and work pointed toward that ideal. They were spiritual warriors, 'kings of the night,' superb at tackling the darker, grimier, and virtually invisible levels of the psyche, the nasty elements that stand in the way of such wholeness—both in themselves, and in others. That they stumbled at times—occasionally falling flat on their faces—is to be expected. The night is dark and sometimes you can't see everything.

Chapter 8
Self-Perfection and the Myth of the Infallible Guru

The Master is the Awakener. The Master awakens those who themselves wish to wake up. He rouses them from sleep, awakens them to Being, to Reality, to Life.

Henri Tracol (student of Gurdjieff)

Spiritual 'Rank': Self-Mastery, Enlightenment

Gurdjieff, Crowley, and Osho all had their particular form of spiritual 'rank'. For Gurdjieff, his main scheme classifying humans was as 'Man #1, 2, 3, 4, 5, 6, and 7'. Crowley, originally an initiate of the Golden Dawn which was itself founded by three Freemasons, an organization that is synonymous with graded levels, followed a path that was deeply intertwined with the notion of initiation and rank. He himself had been a Freemason. In the end he took to ranking himself, ultimately taking the title of 'Ipsissimus', a level beyond even that of the exalted Magus title. He saw himself as beyond the beyond—a kind of Western Taoist sage who has disappeared as a conventional personality and lives solely to implement his 'True Will'.

Osho's 'system of classification' was far simpler than Gurdjieff's and certainly Crowley's. In keeping with an essential Eastern approach, Osho basically categorized people into two levels—the unenlightened and the enlightened. He considered his own enlightenment to have taken place at age twenty-one as a culmination of many years (and, as he claimed, lifetimes) of deep and sustained inner work. He saw his own spiritual state as rarefied, and mostly exclusive. He dismissed most other contemporary gurus as not authentically enlightened (with the notable exception of J. Krishnamurti). Despite his criticisms of Krishnamurti's teaching style and methods, he saw him as enlightened, and in many ways seemed to grudgingly acknowledge him as his equal in realization. He did, however, strongly disparage Krishnamurti's attempts to awaken others, categorizing him as a failure in that regard. Osho called him 'a great mystic but a useless master'.

Problems inherent in classification schemes of spiritual 'status' are obvious, although it is also clear that such schemes can be helpful, providing a dangled carrot to reach for, a light at the end of the tunnel to dedicate one's efforts toward, what Gurdjieff called an 'aim'. In Osho's case, part of the problem lay in the very richness of his charisma. Because he was such a mesmerizing personality it was all too easy to assume that his spiritual state was equally impossible to equal. There was him up on the 'throne', the Awakened One, and there was everyone else. It is ironic to see that despite his consistent condemnation of organized religions, and in particular their deification of some anthropomorphic 'God', he himself largely assumed that role in the eyes of most of his followers. Intellectually, most grasped the idea that he was not separate from them, that he was some kind of 'nobody'—as he often stressed—but the fact remained that he was treated as if he were an ambassador from another planet, an untouchable paragon of enlightened perfection. He was made deeply special in the minds of his followers.

Gurdjieff did not work with the Eastern concept of enlightenment, although Osho retroactively categorized him as such, calling him a 'buddha'; the word means one who is awake. Gurdjieff's following was very small compared to Osho's—his fame did not really grow until after his death—but he was arguably Osho's equal in terms of how he was regarded with awe by his people. Despite being physically accessible—in particular in his last decade or so in Paris where he commonly had feasts on a nightly basis, during which his small apartment on Rue des Colonel Renard was regularly packed—he never ceased to hold great power over his immediate space and never appears to have abdicated the kingly role that came so naturally to him in the slightest. Like Osho, he was unshakeable in his position as representing a state of being to be aspired to, a distant mountain beckoning climbers to approach and try scale if they dare.

It is significant that, at the time of Osho's death in early 1990, very few (if any) of his disciples were acknowledged to be enlightened. Within a few years of his death, however, a number of followers drifted away from the Pune ashram, heading north to Lucknow, to sit in the satsangs of the Advaita master Harilal Poonja. Within a few years, a number of these erstwhile Osho disciples were being declared self-realized by Poonja. He subsequently authorized some of them to conduct *satsang* meetings in other countries on his behalf.

What had happened? Why were all these freshly realized people able to make the 'final leap' into the awakened state with Poonja (or indeed, did they?), but not with Osho? Why did not any of Gurdjieff's first generation students attain to the level their guide (they believed) was at? To attempt to answer these and related questions, we need to look at the whole notion of enlightenment itself. The very concept of self-transcendence itself needs to be examined.

Graduated vs. Sudden Awakening

The age-old dispute concerning the matter of spiritual awakening has been between the 'gradual' and 'sudden' schools of thought. The former argues that self-realization is always a gradual affair, a long drawn out process in which the ego is worn down, something like a rock reduced by water to a grain of sand, eventually disappearing altogether. The sudden view is that enlightenment by its very nature is a starkly black and white matter—as Osho more than once said, 'you are either enlightened or you are not'. In this model, realization is understood to occur in a flash of insight, in an immediate revolution of understanding. Especially in the 'sudden awakening' view, time is regarded as a construct of the conceptual mind and self-realization is understood to take place beyond the boundaries of conventional space-time. Zen refers to this as 'no-mind' but it can also be interpreted as 'no-time'. Because realization is understood to occur beyond time, it follows logically that (in this view) realization has nothing to do with the conventional flow of time. From this it is concluded that enlightenment cannot be a progressive affair.

If something occurs outside of time then it can be argued that this 'something' is not in some future but has *always been here*. We were simply unaware of it, owing to the distortions brought about by our conditioned mind. However one sees it, if spiritual awakening recognizes the ultimate illusory nature of time, then it follows that all awakening must be sudden, something like switching channels on a TV—or perhaps more aptly, pulling the plug on the TV altogether.

The gradual school will generally not quarrel with this reasoning nor dispute that many who come to self-realization do so in such a fashion, but still maintains that our awakening proceeds something like an elevating 'sine wave', in which the entire wave is itself ascending, as in the image on the right. The peaks of the sine wave can be said to represent actual peak experiences, 'small awakenings'. The valleys represent a period of integration, in which we learn how to apply the merits and wisdom of these peak experiences to our everyday life.

As can be seen, the peak of an early wave is, in fact, at a lower point than a valley in a later wave. This suggests that as spiritual maturation and wisdom deepens we come to understand that peak experiences are themselves a type of illusion, at least inasmuch as they are not an accurate gauge of our overall level of understanding. Even dark nights of the soul, which often follow profound spiritual awakenings, can be of equal or greater value than the peak experience itself. A later valley can be higher, i.e. more meaningful, than an earlier peak.

The gradual view is, of course, far more popular than the sudden view, if only because it seems much more practical and forgiving of our psychological weaknesses. Both Gurdjieff and Crowley promoted a gradual model, via their respective initiatory degrees and levels of attainment. Concerning Gurdjieff's 1 through 7 scale, Ouspensky, in *In Search of the Miraculous*, quotes Gurdjieff as follows:

Man number one, number two, and number three, these are people who constitute mechanical humanity on the same level on which they are born. Man number one means man in whom the center of gravity of his psychic life lies in the moving center. This is the man of the physical body...Man number two means man on the same level of development, but man in whom the center of gravity of his psychic life lies in the emotional center, that is, man with whom the emotional functions outweigh all others...Man number three means a man on the same level of development in whom the center of gravity of his psychic life lies in the intellectual center...Every man is born number one, two, or three...man number four is not ready made...he becomes four only as a result of efforts of a definite character. Man number four is always the product of [inner] school work....Man number five has already been crystallized...He has now one indivisible I and all his knowledge belongs to this I...the knowledge of man number six is the complete knowledge possible to man; but it can still be lost. The knowledge of man number seven is his own knowledge, which cannot be taken away from him; it is the objective and practical knowledge of All.[1]

There are some similarities between Gurdjieff's abstract scheme for ranking spiritual development, and the more structured grade system of the Golden Dawn and Crowley's Ordo Templi Orientis and A.·.A.·. The main difference is that Gurdjieff's scheme was strictly theoretical and, as far as I know, he did not talk of it very often, nor did he openly state his own level (and presumably no one ever bothered to ask). As to the authenticity of such levels, Gurdjieff was blunt. Asked once if he knew anyone who had reached the higher levels, he answered,

> It means nothing if I say yes or no. If I say yes, you cannot verify it and if I say no, you are none the wiser. You have no business to believe me. I ask you to believe nothing that you cannot verify for yourself.[2]

He allows for only four actual levels of attainment (stages 4 through 7), as the first three refer more properly to generalized personality types (the physical, emotional, and mental). It is easy to relate this to the standard Hermetic classification of the four elements:

Man number 1: Earth (the body)
Man number 2: Water (the emotional body)
Man number 3: Air (the mental body)
Man number 4: Fire (intuition; the initiation, awakening through the spiritual impulse)

And so on, with levels 5-7 representing deeper spiritual awakenings, ending with the seventh stage in which no possibility of 'losing' one's state is there anymore.

In Crowley's A.·.A.·. organization, the graded levels are similar to those of the Golden Dawn and older esoteric schools having roots in Freemasonry, with some differences:

Student

Probationer

Neophyte

Zelator

Practicus

Philosophus

Dominus Liminus

Adeptus (without)

Adeptus (within)

Adeptus (Major)

Adeptus (Exemptus)

Magister Templi (Master of the Temple)

Magus

Ipsissimus

Of the above, 'Student' and 'Dominus Liminus' are not actual numerically graded levels; they are preparatory and transitional levels, respectively. Each level has very specific requirements, such as a year long record kept of spiritual practices (Probationer), success in Yogic practices like *asana* and *pranayama* (Zelator), study of the Qabalah (Practicus), and so on. The higher levels represent extraordinary degrees of attainment, with the Adeptus Exemptus level representing a crucial juncture after which (according to Crowley) one either goes astray and ends up misrepresenting the teachings and misguiding others or becomes a 'Babe of the Abyss', one 'stripped of all attainments'. A Master of the Temple 'tends to his garden of disciples' and is a 'master of samadhi'; i.e., is what in the East would be conventionally recognized as 'enlightened'. A Magus is similar but has a very specific role to play, namely, 'declaring a Law' by bringing a great spiritual dispensation to humanity. This is in some ways similar to what the East calls a *mahavatar*, a great being who incarnates only rarely with a very intentional and specific spiritual task.

Crowley declared that prior to himself there had been seven men who had reached the classification of Magus, those being Thoth, Krishna, Gautama Buddha, Lao Tzu, Moses, the Resurrected One (who according to Crowley can be understood variously as either Osiris, Dionysus, Baldur, Adonis, Jesus—there having been a number of mystics who in legend died and were resurrected), Mohammad, and Perdurabo (Crowley). His main argument is that a Magus brings 'one Word' to humanity which overturns current dogma and initiates a new and needed spiritual current. As examples, he gave Krishna's *atman* (the true self); Buddha's *anatta* (no-self); the Resurrected One's 'IAO' (what Crowley recognized as the formula of the Dying/Resurrecting God that ended the older age of matriarchy); Mohammad's *Allah*, and Crowley's *Thelema* (True Will) which, as he saw it, represents the end the age of the patriarchy and of the Dying/Resurrected God.

It is of course natural to dismiss all this as a megalomaniacal flight of fancy on Crowley's part, but in his defense it should be noted that his attitude when writing about such things often appears self-critical rather than merely bloated. In his *Confessions* he describes a period of time (in New York City in 1915 at the age of thirty-nine), shortly before he claimed the grade of Magus, in which things failed abysmally for him, a period of isolation and darkness in which everything seemed to fall flat for him wherever he went. It could be argued that his own self-importance was being ground down by this, and that is in some respects how Crowley saw it. That did not, however, stop him from proceeding in 1924 to the final and supreme grade of Ipsissimus.

The controversial Western adept Adi Da Samraj (1939-2008)[3] developed a scheme that was similar to Gurdjieff's but somewhat more fleshed out. Echoing to a certain extent Gurdjieff's typology, Adi Da assigned the first three stages to the physical, emotional-sexual, and mental-will domains respectively—but unlike Gurdjieff, he was specifying a linear process that everyone normally passes through, taking approximately seven years for each stage. That is, by around age twenty-one a person should (under normal conditions) have completed these three foundational stages, resulting in a functional and healthy young adult.

As Adi Da wrote in his *The Seven Stages of Life*:

> Successful completion of these first three stages should include psychological individuation, full development of the will, and a strong moral character, oriented naturally toward the disposition of service. In short, to fully complete the first three stages of life is to be a true adult, an emotionally mature human being.

He then astutely observed:

> Regrettably, today very few adults have successfully handled the business of the first three stages of life. But maturity in the first three stages of life is only the foundation for true Spiritual practice.[4]

It is interesting at this point to pause and contrast Gurdjieff with Adi Da. The latter, born Franklin Jones in New York State in 1939, grew up in the radical and experimental 1960s decade and like many intense seekers of his time, eventually found his way to India and the guru-circuit, apprenticing himself to Baba Muktananda, one of the well known India gurus of the 1960s-70s. His spiritual realizations soon had him convinced that he'd surpassed his master—and indeed, most other masters—and he spent the next thirty-five years or so teaching and writing numerous books. He worked intensively with a relatively small number of followers (that perhaps numbered a few hundred), and passed away in 2008. Adi Da lived sixty-nine years, first as a young academic, then spiritual seeker, then guru. He lived most of his last twenty-five years on a remote Fijian island in the Pacific, cared for by devoted followers. Although a brilliant thinker of obvious profundity and a speaker and writer of great depth, his life was fundamentally soft. Gurdjieff, careening through two world wars and the Russian Revolution, was exposed to far harsher conditions and witnessed much more of humanity's heart of darkness. Accordingly, his blunt view of the common person, recorded by Ouspensky in *In Search of the Miraculous*, makes Adi Da's note above seem polite:

> A modern man lives in sleep, in sleep he is born and in sleep he dies.[5]

A bleak fundamental of Gurdjieff's teaching is that man is not born with a soul—and that without one, he will 'die like a dog'. (Gurdjieff's reference to 'dying like a dog' is interesting in that the dog is a symbol for death in many cultures—not least of which was in ancient Egypt, where Anubis, generally recognized as a canine-type god, is a chthonic deity of embalming and death). Consistent with some elements of ancient Egyptian mysticism, he believed that the soul could only be created by working on oneself—by becoming, at the least, a 'man number four'.

Adi Da characterized his fourth stage as the true beginning of the spiritual path, marked by a tendency to assume that the divine source is outside of us, and something that we begin to feel a yearning to serve in some way. His fifth stage is marked by a true psychic opening to higher energy states, and altered states of consciousness such as the 'spiritual ascent toward absorption in the divine light'. He views this stage in a light that reflects his yogic training. Gurdjieff's version refers more to the 'crystallization' of 'man number five' brought about by deep and sustained work on self, such that this level has achieved the first type of real inner unity—the beginning of a bona fide spiritual person, one truly no longer asleep.

Adi Da's sixth stage of life is, as he put it, 'marked by abiding in Transcendental Consciousness Itself', a stage in which one has truly gone beyond the illusion of the ego and the world. His seventh stage was a 'beyond the beyond' level, transcending 'all the conditional structures of human existence—gross, subtle, causal'. How he describes this seventh stage bears much in common with Crowley's definition of the Ipsissmus and with Gurdjieff's man #7.

Of interest here is that Adi Da claimed to be the only sage ever to attain to level 7 in his own scheme, a perhaps unfortunate declaration that caused many to not take him seriously. Crowley, always the mountain climber, also claimed to have reached the summit in his own scheme as well. Osho, although not having as structured a scheme as Crowley, Gurdjieff, or Adi Da, did claim full enlightenment. Only Gurdjieff steered clear of self-assessment as to his spiritual status, so if in this regard only he must be seen as the least self-aggrandized of the four. (Of course, there remains the possibility that he was, in fact, the only one of the four who was not fully self-realized, but we note, tongue-in-cheek, how unlikely this is especially given that Adi Da claimed sole status at the 'top', but which position he apparently shared with Crowley and Osho, even if he was unaware of it.)

But is there truly any value to such schemes of spiritual progression? Is transcendence of the self actually possible? Can a human being actually change themselves to any significant degree, let alone reach lofty heights of sustained self-realization?

I recall an amusing moment in a public talk by the American spiritual teacher Andrew Cohen that I attended years ago. It was the first time Andrew had been back to my city in about a decade. At one point during an exchange with the audience, a man stood and asked a question that seemed to irritate Andrew. He then peered at the man as if recognizing him, and asked, 'Didn't you ask that same question of me ten years ago?' The man shrugged and admitted that he probably had. 'Well then,' fired back Andrew in a somewhat resigned fashion, 'I guess *neither* of us has changed'.

The audience laughed but the point was well taken. Cohen himself once traveled extensively, interviewing a broad range of spiritual teachers, talking to their students, and so forth, and concluded that very few people ever truly change. That is, that 'spiritual growth' is on some fundamental level an illusion, and that 'work on oneself' doesn't really work for the majority of people.

Prior to understanding the idea of self-realization or enlightenment, it is important to look at the whole area of what motivates the desire for it in the first place. The important early 20th century German psychiatrist Karen Horney once wrote:

> No matter how frantically our Pygmalion tries to mold himself into a being of splendid dimensions, his drive is doomed to failure. He may at best be able to eliminate from awareness some disturbing discrepancies, but they continue to exist. The fact remains that he has to live with himself; whether he eats, sleeps, goes to the bathroom, whether he works or makes love, he is always there...even if he functions like a well-oiled machine, there are still limitations of time, of power, of endurance—the limitations of a human being. The best way to describe the situation is in terms of two people. There is the unique, ideal person; and there is the omnipresent stranger (the actual self), always interfering, disturbing, embarrassing...Moreover, even though he may discard factual disturbances as irrelevant or unrelated to himself, he can never escape so far from himself as to not register them.[6]

Horney questioned the entire process of what she called self-idealization, defining it ultimately as a form of 'neurotic pride.'
She added,

> Briefly, when an individual shifts his center of gravity to his idealized self, he not only exalts himself but also is bound to look at his actual self—all that he is at a given time, body, mind, healthy and neurotic—from a wrong perspective. The glorified self becomes not only a phantom to be pursued; it also becomes a measuring rod by which to measure his entire being. And this actual being is such an embarrassing sight when viewed from the perspective of a godlike perfection that he cannot but despise it.[7]

Her basic idea is that there is a correct and incorrect development, the former being healthy growth via nurturing our abilities and potentials, the latter being the 'neurotic process' in which we seek to relieve ourselves of conflict by various means—one of which is trying to escape ourselves via aspiring to some ideal self that we never honestly attain to.

It is a given that *aspiration* in and of itself cannot be seen as a fault, else how would anyone attain any level of accomplishment? But if the motivating factor is some desire to escape from ourselves prior to properly accepting what we are, then Horney is almost certainly correct and the result will be a forced or inauthentic development—a regular human wearing a spiritual frock. Doubtless, more than one guru has fallen prey to this, especially when they find themselves in a position in which they suddenly have more admirers or students or disciples than they realized, thus feeling compelled to live up to expectations.

However, it cannot be reasonably argued that all self-transcendence values are negated because of the difficulty of realizing them. It has always been a truth that valuable things are commonly difficult to come by. A great work of art, like Michelangelo's Sistine Chapel fresco, Leonardo's *Mona Lisa*, or of literature like Dostoyevsky's *Brothers Karamazov*, or of science like Newton's *Principia*, do not appear overnight, and they do not appear at all without tremendous effort and aspiration on the part of their architect. Spiritual or mystical aspiration is no different—for as many 'failures' in its domain, there are bound to be at least *some* realizers. In this realm more than any other, however, imperfections leap into appearance, because what is being aspired to is so enormous: nothing less than the transformation of one's entire being.

Einstein, Newton, Michelangelo, and their genius brethren, are rarely recorded to be superb exemplars of human character or disposition. Many such people were deficient in character in many ways, but this is usually considered irrelevant in light of what their accomplishments stand for. The spiritual realm is much more difficult to embrace because it is not based on things that we create or mere theories that we conceive; it is rather about the transformation of the person himself. As such, it is much more difficult to hide behind, or more to the point, cannot be hidden behind at all. Holding that in mind, it is essentially impossible to not have some measure of 'sympathy for the devil' when considering the plight of rogue gurus, but alas, it seems to be much more common to vilify such gurus for brazenly aspiring to lofty heights.

The inner conflict between the desire to attain to the true self and the daily realities of the conventional self can indeed be intense and no spiritual teachers were more aware of this than Crowley, Gurdjieff, and Osho. But in the final analysis, what was their spiritual attainment? And can this even be in any way properly evaluated?

Absolute Reality and Conventional Reality

First, it is helpful to have some conceptual framework on the nature of reality to work with. A concept found in several traditions, but probably most closely elaborated in Tibetan Buddhism, is the notion of absolute (or ultimate) reality vs. conventional (or relative) reality. The idea there is that there are two essential states of mind, one based on absolute truth, the other on relative truth. The latter is the world of appearances—bodies, trees, rocks, mountains, animals, stars, and so on—the entire universe of matter and energy and all that we perceive. The former, absolute truth, is the idea that nothing in and of itself has permanent existence, or is truly independent of anything else. An alternate, more Vedantic way of expressing that is that relative truth is the universe that we normally perceive, seemingly comprising separate objects in space and time, and absolute truth is the underlying reality that all is One, and that, in the final analysis, only this 'One' can be said to be truly real.

In the Buddhist tradition, the notion that all things arise from cause and effect, are always dependent on other things for their existence, and lack inherent, discrete existence, is called 'emptiness'. That this idea is easily misunderstood was once amusingly illustrated by the Tibetan teacher Ponlop Rinpoche, who once related that after giving a talk on emptiness a student asked him if the chair he was sitting on was also empty. 'Yes,' replied Rinpoche, to which the student retorted, 'then why if your chair is empty of existence does it support your body? Why do you not fall to the ground?' As Ponlop Rinpoche explained, the student was confusing absolute and relative levels of reality, adding 'He was trying to put my relative body in an absolute chair.'[8]

To see this idea from a more scientific viewpoint, we can say that the chair is indeed real—something we can see, touch, and sit on, and it does indeed support our body. But if we start to look more and more closely at the chair, what do we see? We see raw elements, like wood, and then eventually, the chemical composition of this wood. Sooner or later we get down to molecules and atoms. At the atomic level, we have subatomic particles and what appears to be a great deal of empty space. Looking beyond, we have quantum probabilities, and so forth. The more we break things down, the less we see anything solid or substantial.

Buddhism applies this idea not just to the universe of objects in space and time, but introspectively to the self as well. The more we look at ourselves, the less of a 'whole self' do we see. We see habits, tendencies, conditioned beliefs, memories, thoughts and feelings, and so on, all constellating around some presumed sense of 'I'. Eventually, we come to realize that the idea of any fixed, permanent self is an illusion created by identifying with our body, autobiographical memories, how others seem to view us, and so forth.

According to the Buddhist view, the real value in grasping the nature of absolute reality is that it can help us reduce the clinging to things (or to others) that inevitably gives rise to suffering. If we truly believe that we are a fixed, discrete, independent self, then it follows that we will believe this about others as well. Believing that we are here on our isolated island, and they are there on theirs, we automatically begin to believe that we need these others in order to maintain well-being, even to survive. We become dependent. We cling, and sooner or later, we suffer. The very belief in independent, discrete existence itself creates the belief in separation, and all the pain that that eventually entails.

Buddhism stresses that we are not involved in refuting the existence of the relative self—our bodies, our social life, our apparent identity in the world. All these things have their own conventional existence and need not be a problem. The problem comes from being ignorant of the deeper level of reality, because if we remain caught in believing that conventional reality is the *only* reality, suffering must sooner or later follow, generally in proportion to our attachments and our clinging. (It should be noted here that Crowley himself had serious problems with Buddhism, although he did at many times admire its logical cohesion. His disagreements with it came more to the fore as he accepted the teachings of *The Book of the Law*, which in places is opposed to Buddhist principles, especially the 'First Noble Truth' that 'life is sorrow'.)

Understanding the contrast between conventional or relative truths, and ultimate or absolute truths, is crucial if we are going to understand controversial spiritual figures like Osho, Gurdjieff, and Crowley (and many others). This is because in the case of teachers like them the contrast is particularly vivid. Crowley claimed being an 'Ipsissimus', an ultimate level of development, and yet ends up addicted to hard drugs and leads a life that in the domain of inter-personal relationships appears to be in large part a mess. Gurdjieff is regarded as a highly advanced master by many, and yet appears to others to be a volatile, hard drinking, chain smoking, Dr. Jekyll-Mr. Hyde type. Osho claims full enlightenment, yet dictates books while stoned on nitrous oxide, appears to be oblivious to his Oregon commune falling apart, and is given a fleet of ninety-three Rolls-Royces, which he accepts. The controversial Tibetan master Chogyam Trungpa is understood in his own tradition to be a *tulku*, a highly evolved being, and ends up dying at age forty-eight of liver damage brought on by years of hard drinking. (And there are endless other examples). How to account for all that?

More than one observer—many of whom were students at one point or another of any of these (or similar) crazy-wisdom type teachers—has gotten entangled in perceptions that focus exclusively on the conventional personalities of these teachers, thereby ending up invalidating all work done with them and by extension, all work done on themselves when with them (or their communities). This is clearly problematic. Further, many who are intrigued by the idea of walking a spiritual path find out about teachers like these and never bother stepping on the path in the first place, assuming that the whole thing is inherently corrupt because the gurus themselves are inherently corrupt. There is even something of a cottage industry that has sprung up around trashing spiritual teachers of any stripe. The Internet, that domain notorious for all kinds of people suddenly finding courage to express certain ideas, is rife with websites devoted to guru-bashing. (An amusing example of this is the site www.strippingthegurus.com, which is devoted to attacking a long list of well known spiritual teachers. Many of the points the author makes are valid, and some of his remarks are genuinely funny, but the whole thing suffers from the typical Achilles Heel of 'guru-critics' and that is the problem of context. Almost always such critiques are notoriously bereft of proper context.)

Many of the issues inherent in the problem of the 'Dr. Jekyll-Mr. Hyde' type guru are resolved when the contrast between absolute and conventional realities is clarified. Put simply, any guru, no matter how seemingly sublime, remains a human being, bound by the limitations and laws of nature that a human body-mind must conform to.

Most of the wisdom traditions recognize that there are different levels of illumination or enlightenment, beginning with enlightenment at the level of mind, and culminating in a supreme state of realization in which the entire body-mind is transfigured. What is also generally recognized is that, in the vast majority of cases, an enlightened teacher has only passed through the preliminary stages of awakening, at the level of the mind. Further, it is usually agreed on that such a level of realization does not completely transform the personality, and not necessarily even all neurotic tendencies. Georg Feuerstein, in his excellent work, *Holy Madness*, quotes the radical Indian guru U.G. Krishnamurti (not to be confused with J. Krishnamurti) as follows:

> The personality does not change when you come into this state [of enlightenment]. You are, after all, a computer machine that reacts as it has been programmed. It is in fact your present efforts to change yourself which are taking you away from yourself and are keeping you from functioning in a natural way. The personality will remain the same. Don't expect such a man to become free from anger or idiosyncrasies. Don't expect some kind of spiritual humility...it is for this reason that each person who comes into this state expresses it in a unique way, in terms which are relevant to this time.[9]

It can be safely surmised that neither Crowley or Gurdjieff or Osho were examples of complete enlightenment involving total transfiguration of the body-mind. All three, however, were almost certainly examples of awakened mystics at the level of the mind. In addition, all three had extremely dynamic personalities—powerful intellects, aggressive tendencies, autocratic, willful, arrogant, stubborn, energetic, and highly charismatic. It can also easily be noted that these personality qualities existed *prior* to their deeper awakenings, and without question continued to exist, in large part, *after* their awakenings.

This is an important point because there is an idea found in some spiritual philosophies that the personality is dissolved with enlightenment, or worse, there is the commonly found new age belief that the personality becomes 'nice'—unconditionally loving and graceful at all times—after a spiritual awakening. This view is clearly counter to all evidence. Occasionally, one finds a spiritual teacher who has a particularly smooth or easy-going nature, but almost always one finds out that this was their basic personality-type prior to their spiritual realizations as well.

Transference

A long standing problem in the area of relating to a spiritual teacher—and even more so, to controversial crazy-wisdom type teachers like Osho, Gurdjieff, and Crowley—has been the issue of what is known in psychology as 'transference'. The idea of transference in this context was first introduced by Freud, who noticed in his sessions of psychoanalysis with his patients that the manner by which he operated—listening impassively while encouraging the patient to open up and share their deepest thoughts and feelings—resulted in a dynamic between him and the patient in which the patient would eventually begin to project the image of someone from their past onto him. Most typically this would be a parent, or less occasionally, another important authority figure from their earlier years.

This phenomenon is actually quite common between any psychotherapist and their client, and equally so between any spiritual teacher and their student. It tends to be accentuated if the guru or therapist is remote in some way, or very charismatic. The disciple or client will often build a fantasy image of the mentor in their minds, in which they will (mostly unconsciously) use the mentor as a vehicle to re-experience old thoughts and feelings connected to childhood authority figures. Again, these authority figures are usually parental.

If the nature of transference is not eventually recognized, the danger lies in the possibility of not seeing the guru or mentor realistically, which can easily lead to resentment if one begins to imagine that one is being ignored, not being loved or appreciated enough, being disrespected, or what have you. Moreover, if the student or client has major unresolved issues from their earlier years, or had a parent who abused them or abandoned them or otherwise was very incompetent in their parental role, this increases the danger that they will, sooner or later, begin to see 'flaws' in their teacher or therapist and then seek to justify their perceptions by seeing only what they want to see. This is sometimes referred to as 'finding the thorn in the bush of a hundred roses'.

Crowley, Gurdjieff, and Osho all experienced a broad range of projections from others, and for a wide variety of reasons. Crowley, emerging as he did from Victorian England, was in particular subject to projections related to sex. When he was called the 'King of Depravity' or the 'Wickedest Man in the World' it was entirely related to sexuality. That he was openly bisexual, hedonistic, and highly exploratory, only served to paint a huge target on his back, making him fair game in the minds of many for all sorts of projected sexual deviancies. Had he lived a few hundred years before he would have been quickly burned at the stake, and doubtless tortured on the rack for good measure.

That Osho was massively projected on is obvious to any observer of his life, and the reasons for these projections are equally easy to see. Similar to Crowley, he made the re-visioning of sex and sexual energy a major part of his work, and he began this work in India, one of the most sexually repressed nations on Earth (partly a legacy of the 19th century British imperial rule in India). Everyone knows that in standard Hindi ('Bollywood') films, characters almost never openly kiss, let alone have sex scenes. And here comes Osho—back in the 1960s, at that—teaching that sex and sexual energy are valid means to reach the divine, and that in fact, cannot be avoided. Scandalous! He was vociferously condemned as a result.

In Gurdjieff's case, the types of probable transference he was subjected to tended to show up in some of his most important relationships, often with key male students, the two most well known examples being P.D. Ouspensky and A.R. Orage. Neither of these men were typical disciples. Both were formidable intellects and teachers in their own right. But both recognized in Gurdjieff some key qualities and knowledge that they knew they did not have, and that they wanted. And both broke with him at key times during Gurdjieff's attempt to disseminate his teachings. (Some believe that the loss of Ouspensky and Orage resulted in Gurdjieff's work being crucially diminished.)

Ouspensky's split with Gurdjieff has been well documented in William Patrick Patterson's *Struggle of the Magicians*, and further commented on at length in Gary Lachman's *In Search of P.D. Ouspensky*. These authors arrive at different conclusions. Patterson is of the view that Ouspensky's ego aborted his process with Gurdjieff, owing essentially to transference and projection, and Lachman suggests that Ouspensky from the start may have simply chosen a track that was not his optimum, i.e., he could just as well have opted to follow his own star from the beginning. Given Ouspensky's already established reputation as a brilliant esoteric thinker and published author prior to meeting Gurdjieff, this seems reasonable enough. But it too easily overlooks the point that Ouspensky was a sincere seeker and recognized all too well that his knowledge was mostly limited to ideas that he had not truly lived. In Gurdjieff he saw a man—rightly or wrongly—who represented *experiential knowledge*, and as an intellectual, it was this above all that he desired. He had been to the Orient, and like most 'spiritual tourists' what he found there were mostly dead monuments, or religious communities that required a complete renunciation of the world (as in monastic vows) in order to participate in their teachings. None of that was what he was looking for. It is to his credit that he honestly recognized this, and sought more, that is, real transformation, and a *living* tradition, and one in which he would not have to abandon his worldly life. For this he cannot be faulted, and accordingly he cannot be faulted for apprenticing himself to Gurdjieff.

I spent a number of years sitting with various gurus and studying under many teachers, and since the early 1990s have also run my own transformational groups during which time I have worked intensively with hundreds of people, so I have some degree of direct experience with the teacher-student dynamic. It is, needless to say, a particularly sensitive relationship, one in which the slightest shift in tone or mood can alter matters significantly. A particularly delicate matter that any teacher inevitably works with is the reality that many people secretly wish to uphold the idea of the infallible guru. Openly the idea is increasingly scorned as evidence seems to mount that the majority of gurus are 'bogus', or at the least, suffer from an overinflated self-importance. But what is meant by 'bogus'? Usually, it involves the complaint that the guru is somehow found out to be ordinary, having human desires and getting entangled in very human relationship scenarios. This becomes a big deal because there is the idea that stubbornly persists in many people that a guru or other spiritual figure should somehow be spotless, or at the least, beyond conventional human desires, like the Sunday School image of a blonde Jesus in white robes, God as a faultless old man surrounded by angels on the ceiling of the Sistine Chapel, or the Buddha as a placid and perfect statue.

Osho once remarked that of all the qualities he exalted, 'ordinariness' was the one he most cherished, and he urged his followers to embrace it above all else. I suspect that the reason he said this—and wearily, I think—is that he himself had grown tired of being seen by his disciples as anything but ordinary. He was tired of being seen as special (although he also tacitly encouraged it), and longed to bridge the gulf between 'awakened one' and 'everyone else'. It is a particularly large and lonely gulf, especially as it exists mostly in the mind of the one who is still stubbornly seeking an ultimate parental figure, the one (they think) they never had in the past.

It can reasonably be said that to see beyond the myth of the infallible guru is, in a sense, to truly mature as a spiritual being. Crowley and Gurdjieff in particular made this very attainable, because neither presented themselves as perfected beings (Crowley's 'Ipsissimus' proclamation notwithstanding). Quite simply, these were two complex, multidimensional men, the sheer contrast between their dark masculinity and their brilliant spiritual mentations being far more interesting than any notions of 'prophet' or 'solar god'. Osho, although presenting a more regal figure, nevertheless was full of humor and a deep warmth as any who truly knew him was fully aware of. Although his ideas were troublesome and dangerous to the status quo forces of politics and religion, he cannot be accused of abandoning his humanity solely in the name of animating an image of perfection. This latter took place mostly in the minds of his followers and the armchair critics.

That said, it is also arguable that Crowley, Gurdjieff, and Osho all enjoyed the 'divine play' between teacher and disciple, and much as they may have grumbled about it, it appears they also reveled in the dance. This is likely true with most crazy wisdom gurus. The stories of Gurdjieff (much like the autocratic Harilal Poonja) alternately growling at and being tender toward a student practically in the same breath, are legion. Crowley rarely passed up an opportunity to dramatize a relationship in some fashion; his process with his 'Scarlet Women' alone is worthy of a book length study. Osho did appear to grow tired of it all toward the end (and who can blame him?) and yet throughout most of his life he had an inexhaustible passion for his relationships with his disciples.

As always, we are left with the contrast between the light and the dark, between the reality that a guru is not perfect and the reality that we all like to pretend that maybe, just maybe, they are—or that more to the point, maybe, just maybe, enlightenment equals perfection. Alas, it does not, and things would be much less interesting if it did.

Chapter 9
The Spiritual Commune:
Paradiso and Inferno (Part One)

There is death for the dogs.
The Book of the Law (2:45)

He who does not make a soul, will perish like a dog.
G.I. Gurdjieff

The worse the conditions of life, the more productive the Work,
always provided you remember the Work.
Aphorism #3 at Gurdjieff's Prieure

Crowley, Gurdjieff, and Osho all designed and launched highly experimental intentional communities, each probably best described by the terms 'commune' and 'mystery school'. Crowley's was centered in a small house in Cefalu on the famous Italian island of Sicily. It lasted from 1920 to 1924 (although he had left by 1923). Gurdjieff began his Institute for the Harmonious Development of Man several times in different places during his travels through Eurasia, but established it most successfully at the Prieure, in Fontainebleau-Avon, which is about forty miles southeast of Paris, France. It was open from 1922 to 1932. Osho began two major centers for his work—his ashram in Pune (a hundred and fifty miles southeast of Mumbai), and the commune in the central Oregon wastelands, named Rajneeshpuram. Osho's Pune ashram has been a notable success, running from 1974 to 1981, and then again from 1987 to present times, where it remains open under its new designation as a meditation resort ('Club Meditation' as it sometimes jocularly referred to). It is, however, his American commune that lasted from 1981 to 1985—the same length of time, incidentally, as Crowley's Sicilian Abbey—which we will be considering in the entirety of the next chapter.

It is beyond the scope of this book to fully cover the intricacies of what went on in even one of these communes, let alone all three of them. So from the outset let it be clear that the following two chapters are not an attempt to approach the matter as a comprehensive recapitulation. Some essential facts will be outlined, but what will be looked at more will be the whole basis of the idea of intentional spiritual community—its value, its problems, its relationship to spiritual awakening, and ultimately, if it really works.

Communes themselves have been around for a long time. In 1970, shortly after the 'back to the land' heydays of the '60s, there were an estimated two thousand communes in the United States alone.[1] Few of these were intended to be mystery schools of inner transformation, however. The commune as mystery school has old roots, with the Essenes, the Jewish mystical group that flourished between the 2nd century BC and the 1st century AD, being possibly the first to experiment with such a way of living. Subsequent communes down through the centuries were often connected to apocalyptic ideas of the return of Christ, and many of these eventually evolved naturally into monasteries. By the turn of the first millennium in the West, some of the better known factions that lived communally were the Paulicians of Armenia, the Bogomils of Bulgaria, the Cathars of France, and the Anabaptists in several locations in Europe. Most of these, especially the more powerful ones, were problematic for the religious and secular authorities of the time, as they often resisted military service and the payment of taxes; in general, they were deeply anti-authoritarian and sought their own self-governance. Many ended up meeting a painful fate—being 'stabbed, crushed, and strangled' as Martin Luther, ironically himself a reformer—once demanded Church authorities do to them.[2] Not all communes, however, were stamped out by secular and religious authorities. There are examples of intentional communities living apart from society that thrived—the Oneida commune of New York State, a radical Christian sect which lasted for over thirty years in the late 19th century—being a good example. (Oddly, the Oneida commune met its demise via a tornado in 1878 and survives today as a silverware company.)

A Mystery School is not a Utopia

The first and most essential idea to grasp for anyone who seeks to understand the nature of a true school of inner transformation—what we can call in general a mystery school—is that it is *not* the same thing as a utopia. The failure to understand this basic point has been the cause of much confusion and disillusionment with spiritual schools—whether they be known as a monastery, ashram, commune, temple, order, fraternity, or what have you. Somehow, it is expected that such a community should be some type of consistent paradise if it is truly 'working'. Nothing could be further from the truth. The reason the vast majority of mystery schools are anything but utopian is that the whole purpose of their existence is to serve as a training ground in which to encounter one's ego, as well as an open screen on which the entire contents of the unconscious mind of the community gets projected. The result, predictably, is rarely heavenly. At its very best, it can be likened to a *tough* paradise, but just as often can be a tough and chaotic hell.

The idea of utopia exists partly as an outgrowth of religious fantasy. Historically, the term was first coined by the English lawyer, scholar, statesman, and advisor to King Henry VIII, Sir Thomas More (1478-1535), it being the name of a fictional novel he published in 1516. The irony is that the word, deriving from the Greek terms *ou* (not) and *topos* (place), literally means 'no place' or 'nowhere'. The

Greek word *eutopia*, however, means 'good place,' and so it is now accepted that More intended the word as a pun. Literally it referred to a place that was nowhere, i.e., did not exist, but was also meant to point to the ideal of a possible near-perfect world.

The Oxford dictionary defines utopia as an 'imagined perfect place'. The key word there is *imagined*. The idea that the original Greek root of the word means 'nowhere' is an irony that can never be lost on those who experienced Crowley's Abbey of Thelema, Gurdjieff's Prieure, Osho's Rajneeshpuram, or any other intentional community designed with a grand spiritual blueprint in mind. To be sure, many idealistic communities have survived for far longer than the above three examples, so the possibility of would-be Utopian worlds having a reasonable longevity is not at issue. What is interesting with the examples of the three subjects of our book is the nature of the *raison d'etre* of these communes and the means by which they came apart.

More's Utopia was situated on an island in the New World and described a society that was bound by a number of principles. Some indeed appear potentially utopian; others seem strange and are clearly an echo of More's early 16th century cultural milieu:

1. No private ownership. All goods are available from warehouses.
2. No permanent residency—homes rotated every decade.
3. No locks for doors.
4. Primary work is agriculture-related. Manual skills are emphasized.
5. People are not required to work more than six hours per day. Anything beyond that is optional.
6. Different types of Nature-based faiths predominate, all tolerant of each other. Only atheists are held in contempt.
7. Education is valued and encouraged. Scholars can attain positions of leadership.
8. Each household has two slaves, who are usually island criminals.

9. Priests can marry and divorce is legal.
10. Premarital sex is punished by permanent mandatory celibacy.

As we shall soon see, while several of the above points were indeed elements of the three communes we are about to look into, the overall notion of Utopianism bears scant resemblance to the chaos, drama, heartbreak, breakthrough, and breakdown that was to characterize so much of Crowley's, Gurdjieff's, and Osho's communes.

Crowley's Abbey of Thelema

The genesis of Crowley's magickal and tantric communal experiment, that ended up being his Abbey of Thelema in Sicily, was in 1920 in France in the small town of Fontainebleau, ironically enough. This was the same place that Gurdjieff was to settle in just two years later, opening his Institute for the Harmonious Development of Man at the old Chateau de Prieure in 1922. In February of 1920, Crowley, fresh from the World War One years that he'd spent in America, was living in Fontainebleau with his current mate Leah Hirsig, her two year old son from a previous marriage, and a second woman, Ninette Shumway (whom Hirsig had met on the boat coming over from America) as well as her three year old son. Add to that, Hirsig was pregnant and soon to give birth to Crowley's child. For health reasons Crowley sent her to London after the birth of their daughter (named 'Poupee'), and then made a decision to leave Fontainbleau. To help decide where to go, he did something he was to do many times in his life—he consulted his trusted oracle, the ancient Chinese divinatory system known as the *I Ching*.

According to Crowley, the oracle directed him to the small town of Cefalu, on the north coast of the Italian island of Sicily. He, Shumway, and the two little boys arrived there on March 31, 1920. Two days later he found and leased the villa that was to serve as the center for his new commune. It was a solid, five room house, with a central chamber that was to serve as the temple, connecting the rooms. About ten days later, Hirsig and their baby daughter arrived. He decided to call the house the *Collegium ad Spiritum Sanctum* (College of the Holy Spirit). His experiment had begun—himself, aged forty-four, Leah, thirty-seven, Ninette, twenty-five, two boys aged three and two, and a baby girl—in a house on the outskirts of a small Sicilian town. The philosophy and teachings of his commune were based on *The Book of the Law* that he'd mediumistically received back in 1904 in Cairo. The altar in the central chamber of the house featured a copy of the Book surrounded by his Golden Dawn-type magical implements.

They were soon joined by a student of Crowley's that he'd been in correspondence with for some time, the middle-aged actress Jane Wolfe. This excerpt from Crowley's *Confessions*, described with his patented rich verbosity, gives a revealing look at how he saw some of the work he was doing on Jane:

> During her first few weeks at the abbey, every day was one long battle. I hacked through her barbed wire of aggressive axioms. I forced her to confess the incongruity of her assertions. I drilled holes in her vanity and self-satisfaction. I dug her critical spirit out of its corner, and made her clean off the rust, sharpen the edge and the point, and polish the steel till it shone. When she saw it, she feared it all the more; but I forced her to grasp it and use it...she also found that the harder she struck at truth the stronger it stood. So in the end, she learnt the value of the critical spirit and made it one of her regular weapons.[3]

Crowley set up a strict training schedule for the women based on structured work in yoga, magick, and daily written journals that all were allowed to read. Needless to say, the relationships between them were complex and intense. Crowley had already been sexual with Shumway back in France, which according to him provoked intense jealousies in her toward Hirsig. But it was Hirsig who was his Scarlet Woman, his main tantric partner, and she was to play anything but a passive role. For a period of time, she acted out the dominant pole of a sadomasochistic process with Crowley that he claimed was undertaken intentionally and consciously by both of them.

Crowley invested considerable energy in redesigning the Abbey. One room in particular—which also happened to be the bedroom he shared with Hirsig—received his full attention, in the form of a vast mural Crowley painted on the walls that depicted, with Hieronymus Bosch-like intensity, a series of scenes designed to evoke the whole spectrum of feelings and responses related to repressed states of mind. In short, it was a kind of fantastic depiction of the collective unconscious of humanity—as much as that could be accomplished in one wall painting via Crowley's art work. He called it, fittingly, *Le Chambre des Cauchmars*—The Chamber of Nightmares. The idea was classic Left-Hand Tantra, that being to directly face one's deepest fears and walk through them with eyes open, that is, with awareness and presence and a fearless willingness to embrace all dimensions including that of the body and sexuality. The main idea was to be free of puritanical religious and social conditioning, thereby lightening and purifying the mind to make it more available for higher states of consciousness. This was, essentially, Osho's general method as well. Crowley's 'Chamber of Nightmares' was a primitive version of the therapy chambers at Osho's Pune and Oregon communes.

Drugs were liberally used at the Abbey as an aid in this process, the most common two being cocaine and heroin. Crowley himself was using these and other drugs on a regular basis at the Abbey. The usage of drugs like heroin might have seemed incredibly irresponsible of Crowley (and at least three people, including himself, became addicted to it while there) but in point of fact, at that time, he (and most other people) did not fully understand the addictive power of the drug. Heroin was first banned from manufacture and sales four years after Crowley opened his Abbey, in 1924 in the U.S. (Bayer at that time had an advertisement with Aspirin and Heroin side by side, the latter trumpeted as a 'sedative for coughs'—in what would prove to be a major embarrassment for Bayer).

Crowley also was not enacting the part of the remote guru—he was directly involved in the Tantric practices himself, in specific, with Leah Hirsig. As mentioned above, she at times took on a dominant role with him at his express wish. He wanted to encounter his deepest fears and weaknesses and thus went through an unusual process whereby he took an oath to be obedient to his Scarlet Woman (Hirsig). In so doing, he allowed her to perform various sadistic actions on him, including burning his flesh with cigarettes, and on one occasion forcing him to consume her feces. (It was this latter act, in part, that earned Crowley the British tabloid epithet of 'The King of Depravity'.)

To what degree these activities were attributable to simple sadomasochistic urges in Crowley (and Hirsig), and to what degree to genuine Tantric practice, cannot be easily judged with clarity. The intention was most likely as Crowley claimed, that is, a genuine attempt to overcome unconscious fears and puritanical conditioning via intentional role playing; however, the regular usage of drugs doubtless at times blurred the line between conscious work on self, and mere indulgence in repressed desires. The entire process was, however, dutifully recorded daily by both in their 'magical diaries', a fact that lends credence to the view that the whole enterprise was as Crowley claimed, a valid attempt at transformational work.

That dysfunctional affairs were afoot is a given. When Crowley's and Hirsig's baby daughter died in October of 1920 at seven months of age this was followed two weeks later by Hirsig's miscarriage. Both Crowley and Hirsig were devastated. Ninette Shumway, who had also gotten pregnant via Crowley, gave birth to a healthy boy, an occurrence that provoked painful jealousy in Hirsig. The latter became convinced that Shumway had worked some kind of current of black magic against her contributing to the death of her two children and asked Crowley to look at Shumway's diaries. To Crowley's shock, what he found seemed to confirm Hirsig's suspicions, and he had Shumway banned from the Abbey. However, this banishment lasted only three weeks and she was soon back along with their baby boy. Some kind of healing between all of them appeared to take place.

Other visitors appeared in due time, including the following who became students: Cecil Russell, followed by a couple, Cecil Maitland and Mary Butts, then Frank Bennett, and later Raoul Loveday and his wife Betty May. Of these, Bennett and Jane Wolfe appeared to gain the most out of the experience and both would remain loyal supporters of Crowley's work for the rest of their lives. Some, like Cecil Russell, who spent close to a year at the Abbey, would eventually pass harsh judgment on Crowley, particularly in relation to what he saw as a conflict in him between his intellectual and mystical sides. Russell saw Crowley as primarily an intellectual, unable to fully escape the linearity of his mind, concerned chiefly with his writing and publishing. He wrote,

> Ever hunting the happy phrase, modeling the merriest metaphor—even while fucking he was recording the Opus in his mind rather than endeavoring to establish *Ekagrata* [focused energy] to effect Samadhi![4]

Russell's criticism—although doubtless aided by the fact that Crowley, ever the rapacious bisexual, had desired yet failed to seduce him—is probably valid to a fair degree. There is a reason why very few self-realized mystics write autobiographies, much less massive ones like Crowley's *Confessions*. It is because there is often a corresponding loss of infatuation with the written (or even spoken) word in one who progresses far in meditation or related psycho-spiritual practices. While it is possible to retain a scholarly focus for one moving deeply into mystical practice, it is uncommon. Far more typical are to find scholars or intellectuals who write prolifically about metaphysical matters to be at best dabblers in actual spiritual practice (if practitioners at all), or to find serious meditators or committed spiritual practitioners (such as those who enter monkhood or other renunciate paths) to write only very occasionally, if at all.

There are exceptions to this of course and Crowley was one—a man who made extraordinary efforts at spiritual practice and who was also a powerful intellectual and prolific writer. The fact that Cecil Russell saw this dichotomy in Crowley likely implies that he had this going on within himself as well. As we will explore in the next chapter, the matter of Osho's Oregon commune, a teacher commonly draws to himself disciples who reflect many of his own characteristics regardless of their overall level of development—and regardless of the *teacher's* overall level of development.

At the Abbey, Crowley had elaborate names for some of his people—he called Leah Hirsig not just his Scarlet Woman but also the 'First Concubine of The Beast', and he referred to Ninette Shumway as the 'Second Concubine'. That these two women were in competition with each other goes without saying. Despite the stated magickal-conscious intentions of the whole setup at times it would all deteriorate into the standard dysfunctional family and in particular, the dysfunctional triangle. Some of the dramas were amusing, an example being an occasion when Crowley attempted to perform a sex magick operation with both Leah and Ninette. As the rite was being performed ceremonially, a row erupted between Leah and Ninette. The latter then fled into the woods in tears, Crowley in pursuit. When he finally retrieved her and brought her back, they both found Leah thoroughly drunk. When Ninette and Leah started fighting again, Crowley gave up, went into another room, and lost himself in opium.[5]

In retrospect, these 'smaller' details of Crowley's life tend to get overlooked, especially by those more interested in the sweeping abstractions of his Thelemic philosophy, but the difficulties of such 'left-hand' Tantric communal living can never be underestimated. I once had the occasion to question a spiritual teacher I knew who had shared a house with three other women, all of whom were his lovers. I asked him how he managed it. 'With great difficulty,' he allowed. There is a profound level of emotional tension and corresponding stress innate to such conditions. Whatever one may judge about Crowley's character for entering into these scenarios, it is a given that he must have possessed a marked capacity for enduring nervous tension, all the more so in this case as there were at least three small children present as well (none of whom were, far as is known, mistreated).

Crowley took an active interest in the two little boys, spending a fair amount of time with them, taking them for walks and on juvenile versions of rock-climbing. Part of his Thelemic creed was that children should be raised as naturally as possible, free of suffocating parental direction and excessive meddling and cloying and encouraged to discover their own true nature as opposed to being simply turned into clones of their parents or guardians. This turned out to be very much Gurdjieff's and Osho's approach to the matter as well. During the 1980s, I spent a couple of years living in Osho communal houses, one of which had no less than twelve children living in it. These youngsters were extraordinary in one main respect, that being the degree to which they were uninhibited, expressive—even if such expressiveness was on occasion of the unfriendly sort. Above all, they could never be assessed as being artificial or unnatural.

Seen from another angle, Crowley's Abbey of Thelema was not much more than a 1960s-style hippy commune time-warped back to the 1920s. Instead of sex, drugs, and rock n' roll, the primary activities in the house were sex, drugs, and ceremonial magick. But for one not attuned to the magical and mystical element, the whole thing would have appeared to be just a massive exercise in self-indulgence. And that is indeed how the general public as influenced by the British popular press largely came to see this venture of Crowley's.

The underlying point of the commune, consistent with left-hand Tantric work, was a deep and relentless exploration of the psyche, a type of wild applied psychotherapy, all anchored by the mystic's core belief that the essence of a human is both good, and intrinsically connected to a divine principle—the 'God within,' or what Crowley recognized as the 'Holy Guardian Angel'. Without this transcendent principle, the whole thing founders on the rocks of personal agenda, swallowed up by the need to control others and use their energy to bolster one's sense of self. Crowley, in utilizing drugs and a direct approach to the darker realms of the unconscious, was at all times dancing with the devil, skirting the razor's edge. In following such an approach, a strong faith in a divine principle of some sort is a prerequisite, needed as a foundation to hold the inner house together precisely because in any encounter with one's darker self the light can easily be blotted out altogether.

For Crowley, this faith went hand in hand with the power of the will, the need for discipline, and the determination to see something through to its finish. His views on this were aptly illustrated in his perception of his students Cecil Maitland and Victor Neuberg:

> The great value of such men as Maitland and Neuburg to me has been to strengthen my conviction that in the absence of will power, the most complete collection of virtues and talents is wholly worthless. Combine in one man the strength of Hercules, the beauty of Apollo, the grace of Antinos, the wisdom of Athena, the intelligence of Hermes, and every other gift of every other god, unless the anatomist is careful to supply a spine to support the structure, you will have a mollusc and not a man. You must have a fulcrum, not only to move the world, but to move a feather.[6]

Crowley was not there for the entire four year duration of the Abbey of Thelema (and not for the last year at all). He took several leaves of absence, usually to Paris for a few weeks here and there, but more often he would make weekend excursions to the nearby town of Palermo to frequent prostitutes, both male and female. Considering that at this time Crowley was already in his mid-forties, it gives a fair glimpse at how considerable his sexual appetite was. He was at all times straddling the fine line between high and low magic—the dance between mystical transmutation of the ego and the urge to be driven by lust.

It cannot be argued that events at Crowley's commune were free of baser forms of magic, or what is more conventionally called primitive shamanism or 'sorcery'. These were performed on occasion as well. An infamous example was a ceremony that combined both bestiality and blood sacrifice that Crowley devised when Cecil Maitland and Mary Butts had joined the commune. It called for the Beast's 'chief concubine', Leah Hirsig, to copulate with a goat. At the moment of the goat's ejaculation, Crowley was supposed to cut its throat, with the goat's blood to be used in the Cakes of Light (the Abbey's version of communion wafers). In the event, the goat developed cold feet and would not mount Leah, but Crowley killed it anyway. Leah, almost certainly high on heroin and sprayed by the goat's blood, asked what she should do. 'Take a bath' was Mary Butts' terse suggestion.[7]

It seems clear in the case of his students, Maitland and Butts, that Crowley 'lost hold of the bull', as the Zen expression has it. Maitland and Butts left the Abbey after lasting there for a few months, but they later claimed that despite some worthwhile meditative and introspective work there they'd also acquired drug addictions stemming from their time at Crowley's mystery school.

In February of 1922, Crowley temporarily left the Abbey, returning to Fontainebleau. (Gurdjieff was in England then giving talks; he was to arrive in Fontainebleau eight months later to open his Institute.) There, renting a room, Crowley systematically set about conquering his drug addictions using Magick and Yoga practice and keeping a detailed diary the whole time. The matter was worsened by his asthma attacks that flared up whenever he attempted to break the hold the drug had on him. He was caught in the throes of slavery to his physiology in what must have been a profound and abject lesson in humility. His success in this undertaking was sporadic; for the rest of his life he would struggle with heroin, alternating periods of being free of it, with long stretches of hopeless addiction. Not long after this, in June of 1922, Crowley dictated to Leah the novel *Diary of a Drug Fiend*, churning out 121,000 words in 27 days. The novel, about a young couple overcoming drug addiction and attaining to spiritual heights with the aid of a powerful magician named King Lamus (a character based on Crowley himself), was immediately published by Collins and went on to become a cult classic.

Without question, the darkest episode at the Abbey of Thelema and the one that led to the final ruination of Crowley's reputation with the general public, involved the young Raoul Loveday. Crowley had met him in London in the summer of 1922 when Loveday was but twenty-two years old. The young man had just married Betty May, a woman a few years older who had been twice previously married. Crowley was set to enter into yet another complex triangle, and as with Cecil Maitland and Mary Butts, he was again more interested in the man, seeing in Loveday great spiritual and occult potential, and in May, an annoying woman who was mostly in the way.[8]

Loveday decided to follow Crowley back to the Abbey in Cefalu much to Betty's protests, but she relented and accompanied him there. They arrived in the late autumn of 1922. Loveday plunged into Abbey life, a devoted and talented student of Crowley's Magick and Yoga, and progressed quickly enough. As an example of one of Crowley's methods, Raoul and Betty were assigned the exercise of not using the pronoun 'I' when speaking—and if they forgot and at any time blurted out 'I' they were to prick themselves with a razor blade. (Betty refused to do the exercise; Raoul, the obedient student, complied, and naturally ended up with many self-administered razor cuts). An irony here is that Crowley, a few years later, would suggest that some of Gurdjieff's methods involving punishment for lapses in awareness were 'morally valueless'. He'd either forgotten his own draconian punishments or had decided by then that such degree of harshness was ineffective.

At this point in the story it should be mentioned that by modern standards the Abbey was unhygienic—it lacked running water or toilets that flushed. Dogs and children wandered about, filth accumulated, and the diet of the commune members was not particularly good. It was a rough place, in such a way that the average modern denizen of Western society would have difficulty appreciating. In this environment it is not surprising that someone eventually fell seriously ill and that was young Raoul Loveday. He had been there not quite two months when he was sickened. A doctor from town was summoned and acute enteritis was diagnosed. His condition quickly deteriorated and a few days later he died. He was only twenty-three.

His young wife Betty was, naturally, distraught and blamed Crowley (who himself was devastated by Loveday's death). She returned immediately to London where she gave her story to the English press. She claimed that Raoul, while consuming large amounts of hashish, had been sickened by the effects of drinking cat's blood from a ritual sacrifice conducted by Crowley. The press embellished the story further, with the tabloid *Sunday Express* labeling Crowley 'one of the most sinister figures of modern times'.

As to what actually happened to result in Loveday's death, there appear to be different versions from Crowley's various biographers. Crowley's literary executor John Symonds, known to have developed a strong bias against Crowley, in his 1951 biography *The Great Beast* simply repeated Betty May's story that Loveday had indeed died from drinking the cat's blood. In his 1988 biography, *The Legacy of the Beast*, Gerald Suster wrote that Symonds' account was false and that 'the source of this scabrous fiction was a drunken Betty May who needed money from hack reporters in search of sensation'. He goes on to report that May's autobiography *Tiger Woman* confirms the 'sober truth' that Crowley had told Loveday and May to not drink the local water, that Loveday had ignored this when thirsty on a hot day, caught enteric fever, and died 'despite Crowley's care and nursing'.[9]

Richard Kaczynski concurs with Suster's view, reporting that Loveday died from drinking contaminated spring water and that Betty May fabricated the story of the cat-sacrifice in order to wreck vengeance on Crowley.[10] Lawrence Sutin reports that Betty May did indeed claim that Loveday died from the 'toxic effect of the consumption of cat's blood as part of a ritual sacrifice in which Loveday presided'. She described a lurid event that involved Loveday, under Crowley's direction, killing a cat and then drinking some of its blood that Crowley had accumulated in a small bowl. Sutin, however, goes on to affirm that Loveday was in fact sickened by drinking tainted mountain water.[11] Martin Booth describes the cat ritual in more detail but affirms that it did occur, that Loveday did drink some of its blood, and that, additionally, earlier that same day, he had indeed drank some contaminated spring water. He speculated that either the water or bacteria from the cat could have been the cause of the death.[12]

Crowley himself, in his *Confessions*, not surprisingly makes no mention of a cat sacrifice, only describing an illness that had been afflicting both he and Raoul, followed by Raoul's decline and subsequent death due to paralysis of the heart brought on by acute infectious enteritis. Crowley further claimed that Betty May had reached a peace with him at the end and did not leave on a bad note, but that once back in England, the yellow press, getting her drunk one evening, convinced her to sell a lurid story to their paper. There is justification for suspecting that this version of things has truth to it, because the *Sunday Express* was at that time teetering on the edge of bankruptcy and needed some good trash journalism to sell papers.[13]

Roger Hutchinson, in his generally unsympathetic *Aleister Crowley: The Beast Demystified*, reports that the *Sunday Express* stated that Loveday fell sick from eating 'black pudding made from goat's blood'. In a seemingly fair appraisal Hutchinson remarks,

Aleister Crowley was responsible for Loveday's death only insofar as he was responsible for running an unhygienic household, and for initially misdiagnosing the young man's complaint as a passing fever. The latter cannot be held too strongly against him: a qualified doctor was, after all, three times called up from Cefalu, and he failed to recognize the severity of Loveday's condition until it was too late.[14]

Ultimately Hutchinson is inaccurate, however, as Loveday's illness was not due to the hygiene of the house, but rather to the condition of the spring water in the surrounding countryside. Back in 1930, P.R. Stephenson, in *The Legend of Aleister Crowley*—the book that appears to be the main source for several of the biographers mentioned above—reported the contents of Betty May's autobiography as to this matter, where she admitted that Crowley had warned them not to drink the water, and that after a long walk on a hot day Raoul had ignored this warning, drank some spring water, and duly fell ill.[15]

The event of Loveday's death marked a turning point in Crowley's work at the Abbey. Shortly after, all residents left, except for the original triumvirate of Crowley, Hirsig, and Ninette Shumway. After the English press picked up on the story of Loveday and his wife, more stories spread to America and Europe, with various lurid headlines, and eventually it all came to the attention of Benito Mussolini, the newly installed dictator of Italy. He ordered Crowley's expulsion for reasons that remain a source of speculation. (Crowley himself blamed the influence of the Catholic clergy, although direct evidence for this is lacking.)

Crowley and Leah Hirsig departed for Tunis at the end of April, 1923. They had run the Abbey of Thelema for three years. A few of his students remained at the Abbey until late 1924, such as Shumway and Norman Mudd (who had arrived just when Crowley's expulsion notice did) but the mystery school element of the Abbey was effectively over after Crowley's and Hirsig's exit.

In light of some of the events, it may be difficult for all but the most committed Thelemite to understand how Crowley's work, especially at his commune in Cefalu, can be regarded as anything but self-indulgent egoism, let alone as 'spiritual'—his Latin name for the Abbey, 'College of the Holy Spirit,' notwithstanding. And yet, there was indeed a method behind the madness. Crowley was, from one perspective, a practitioner of Left Hand Tantra, or as it is known in India, *Vama Marga Tantra*. The whole essence of Tantra is affirming rather than negating, an approach Crowley developed into his own system and ultimately designated as the 'White School of magick', which involves utilizing Nature, as opposed to negating it and withdrawing from it (as in the classic way of the renunciate).

The main idea behind 'utilizing Nature' is to transform one's fears, to become free of attachments to form and flesh, so that one may authentically transcend the limitations of the physical universe. In the left-hand approach, this is accomplished by *facing into* one's ego, and experientially passing through the ordeals of desire and attachment directly, so as to avoid, at all costs, the consequences of denial, repression, spiritual artifice, and the like.

The more lurid aspects of so-called low magic, such as the drinking of blood, was certainly not a practice original to Crowley— left hand Tantra in northern India and other Himalayan regions have long had a particular practice that has involved a candidate or initiate drinking a substance that is a mixture of menstrual fluid and semen. Many of these rites (not just those of Indian Tantra) eventually evolved into ceremonies involving only symbolic representations of these substances—a good example from Christian ceremony being the drinking of wine that symbolizes Christ's blood, or the eating of wafers representing his flesh. Most do not stop to ponder where these rituals are originating from.

When Crowley emerged from his three year experiment at the Abbey of Thelema he was broke, addicted to heroin, and one of his prize students had recently died under his care. All that alone might have seemed cause to simply give up, but Crowley—in common with Gurdjieff and Osho, whose communes were also damaged by scandalous events—never allowed himself to be broken by adversarial factors. He soldiered on, staying with Leah for a while in North Africa, in the Mediterranean city of Tunis.

It is difficult to pass summary judgment on the Abbey of Thelema. Unquestionably valid esoteric work, of the controversial Left-Hand approach, took place there, although taken at face value, the commune was a failure. An eight month old girl died there (Crowley and Leah's daughter, Poupee), as well as a twenty-three year old man. At least one couple (Cecil Maitland and Mary Butts) claimed that their stay at the Abbey rendered them addicts. Another (Betty May) had had her life painfully altered, losing her husband (Raoul Loveday). Crowley himself became a heroin addict. On the other hand, others claimed to have benefited greatly from their time there, such as Frank Bennett and Jane Wolfe. Ninette Shumway seems not to have been negatively affected, at least, and the same can be said for Leah Hirsig. Bennett himself had attained the magickal title of major Adept as well at the ninth degree in Crowley's Ordo Templi Orientis school during his stay at the Abbey. These were not minor feats; Crowley had a very rigorous training curriculum that involved disciplined meditation, yoga, esoteric practices, and study.

Crowley himself claimed certain definite successes at the end of it all, in particular his view that those who completed their Magick-Yogic regiments there had vanquished all fears and inhibitions related to sexuality and the body, thus breaking the powerful conditioning of organized religion. This particular de-conditioning work was taken up in earnest forty years later by the human potential movement as led by such figures as Wilhelm Reich, Abraham Maslow, Carl Rogers, Arthur Janov, Fritz Perls, and the Esalen community in northern California. But it was in Osho's fledgling ashram in Pune, India, in the mid-1970s, where some of Crowley's core ideas reached their maximum development, where no effort was spared to help people be free of sexual repression and the deeply unconscious layers of shame programmed in by centuries of social, moral, and religious doctrine.

More to the point, the entire experiment of Crowley's Abbey of Thelema must be acknowledged for its sheer novelty. Although the Abbey would not have turned too many heads in the 1960s, four decades before that it was an extraordinarily radical venture, bringing to reality what Francois Rabelais could only dream up in his imagination four centuries earlier. If for no other reason than that, Crowley was the consummate trailblazer.

Gurdjieff's Institute for the Harmonious Development of Man

As one daring esoteric communal experiment was winding down in Cefalu in 1923, another was just getting into full swing in Fontainbleau-Avon—the Institute for the Harmonious Development of Man.

The Chateau de Pieure des Basses Loges, at Fontainbleau-Avon, forty miles southeast of Paris, France was originally built in 1310 as a hospital. In the 15th century it became a monk's priory and that remained its main function over the centuries—although at one point in the late 17th century it had served royalty, being a home of King Louis XIV's second wife, Francois d'Aubigne, the Marquise de Maintenon. It was a large estate, three stories high and capable of housing up to a hundred people, and it was set on forty-five acres of mostly uncleared pine forest—which accordingly led to the main press term at that time for Gurdjieff's movement, 'the forest philosophers'. Clifford Sharpe, the London journalist who coined the term, wrote in the *New Statesman* of March 3, 1923,

> The Gurdjieff Institute has been compared in the Press by Mr. T. P. O'Connor and others with various experimental 'colonies' which have been established in Europe or America during the past few decades. All such comparisons, however, are entirely mistaken, and would not be offered by anyone who had spent twenty-four hours at Fontainebleau, seeing all that there is to be

seen there. As far as the writer's knowledge goes, the only recorded institution with which Mr. Gurdjieff's school can at all plausibly be compared is the school which was established in southern Italy by Pythagoras about 550 BC.[16]

Sharpe's account was fair and informed; many such accounts were not, with Gurdjieff variously being referred to as the 'latest cult leader' or other pejoratives. An editorial from *The World Today*, of June 1924, summed up the common uninformed view of the matter:

Among the many bizarre cults to which disillusioned men and women have turned since the war for spiritual stimulation, none has obtained more disciples of note than the so-called 'Institute for the Harmonic [sic] Development of Man' at Fountainebleau.[17]

Meanwhile, Gurdjieff himself had written up a prospectus giving a theoretical overview of his intentions for the Institute:

The civilization of our time, with its unlimited means for extending its influence, has wrenched Man from the normal conditions in which he should be living. It is true that civilization has opened up for Man new paths in the domain of knowledge, science and economic life, and thereby enlarged his world perception. But, instead of raising him to a higher all-round level of development, civilization has developed only certain sides of his nature to the detriment of other faculties, some of which it has destroyed altogether. Modern man's world perception and his mode of living are not the conscious expression of his being taken as a complete whole. Quite the contrary, they are only the unconscious manifestation of one or another part of him.

From this point of view our psychic life, both as regards our world perception and our expression of it, fail to present a unique and indivisible whole, that is to say a whole acting both as common repository of all our perceptions and as the source of all our expressions.

On the contrary, it is divided into three separate entities, which have nothing to do with one another, but are distinct both as regards their functions and their constituent substances.

These three entirely separate sources of the intellectual, emotional or moving life of man, each taken in the sense of the whole set of functions proper to them, are called by the system under notice the thinking, the emotional and the moving centers.[18]

After moving into the Prieure, Gurdjieff immediately set his students the task of constructing on the site a large Study House, a separate building made in part from an old airplane hangar. This was to be the site of the performances of the Sacred Dances and Movements, a key component of Gurdjieff's system and the one that was by far the most impressive to visitors and journalists.

Barely over two weeks after Gurdjieff and his students took possession of the Prieure, they received one of their more famous guests, the New Zealand writer Kathleen Murry, who went by the pen name Katherine Mansfield. A prolific short story writer— usually recognized as one of the best of her era—she was only thirty-four when she came to Gurdjieff, partly in an effort to cure her pulmonary tuberculosis, and partly to satisfy a spiritual hunger. She was there for close to three months before dying in January of 1923 at the Prieure. Contrary to some rumors that 'the cult hastened her death'—or, as Wyndham Lewis described it, she was the 'famous writer in the grip of the Levantine psychic shark'—she in fact had exhausted all known medical treatments prior to coming to the Prieure, had been given only a few months to live by doctors in Paris, and was treated with civility and gentleness by Gurdjieff. Infamous for being a stern taskmaster with most of his students, with Mansfield his sole directive was for her to walk in the gardens, pick flowers, and rest.[19] Despite all that, the press inevitably attacked Gurdjieff as the 'man who killed Katherine Mansfield'. The rumor, with no basis in fact, dogged Gurdjieff and the Prieure for several years.

Needless to say, there was a great deal of work to be done at the Prieure—clearing forest, breaking stones, digging wells, cleaning the buildings, running the kitchen, and of course, constructing the huge Study House. Throughout it all, the main technique used by Gurdjieff's students was self-observation. The idea was to work very hard, to throw oneself with abandon into the physical effort, while at the same time directing awareness back to oneself—cultivating 'divided attention' as it was known. In short, this is to remain vividly aware of self (the subject) as one worked on whatever labor one outwardly focused on (the object), resulting in a heightened state of awareness in general.

Gurdjieff would prowl the grounds monitoring his student's progress with the physical tasks while at the same time noting their progress with the mental tasks. If he caught someone too deeply absorbed in their work to the point that they were becoming heavily identified with it he would call them out on that, and he would do so literally and emphatically, bellowing out 'Identification! Identification!' This was the key piece in Gurdjieff's whole teaching. His idea was that through identifying—literally forgetting who we are and believing that we have *become* the role we are playing—all of our suffering arises. An example would be working on a garden and realizing that something is not going well with the flowers we are tending to. If we are identifying strongly in that moment with being a 'gardener' then the chances are we will get upset over the flowers. We have become too deeply identified with being a gardener. As a result, we develop a corresponding attachment to seeing the flower bed work out perfectly. Identification leads to attachment, which in turn results in suffering when things do not conform to our expectations.

A flower bed is a simple example. A more difficult example lies in human relations. The more we identify with what it is that we do—'I am a policeman,' 'I am an artist,' 'I am a writer,' 'I am a privileged person,' etc.—then the greater the chance that we will be more easily upset when things related to our occupation, or how we see ourselves, do not turn out well. Looked at clearly, it can be seen that the cause of most severe acts in life that lead to suffering for oneself or for others are related to one's cultivated self-image being offended in some way—that we have not been seen, understood, appreciated, or recognized in some fashion.

'Who we really are' is, in this context, pure presence, or as Gurdjieff called it, *being*. He was of course adamant that one who is *not*—that is, one who lacks being—cannot truly *do* anything. Everything that they appear to do is, in fact, the result of mechanical cause and effect forces acting upon them. They are not much better than a robot. The Prieure, although appearing to an uninformed stranger as a peculiar cult-like environment centered around one eccentric man dominating several dozen others who all slaved to build and maintain a large retreat center, was in fact much more than that. It was a training ground for becoming free of identification and harmful attachments—in short, for waking up.

During the first two years of the Prieure, Gurdjieff was extraordinarily busy. Not only was he the spiritual guide at his commune as well as the administrative head, he was also occupied in running a number of businesses in Paris. Communication and transportation in those days was relatively primitive so this necessitated Gurdjieff regularly commuting the forty miles between Paris and Fontainebleau several times per week. On top of all that, he was forced to learn French from scratch.

When the Prieure opened in late 1922, Gurdjieff had already been a known teacher for a decade and accordingly, he had already acquired a loyal if relatively small, following—all told, around forty immediate disciples. A number of these were low profile Russians who had followed him to Europe (including several relatives). The more high profile ones, most of whom had been with him in the early years, were still with him and had moved into the Prieure—Dr. Stjoernval and his wife, Thomas and Olga de Hartmann, Alexandre and Jeanne de Salzmann, the former British Intelligence officer Major Frank Pinder, Olgivanna Hinzenberg (the future third wife of Frank Lloyd Wright), and Gurdjieff's own wife Julia Ostrowska. Ouspensky had gone to London where he had decided to set himself up as a teacher of Gurdjieff's system, although he was not mandated to do this and had been publically repudiated by Gurdjieff. Nevertheless, in a strange irony, it was through Ouspensky's efforts and teachings in London that Lady Rothermere had come to know of Gurdjieff, subsequently becoming his main financial benefactress.

Interestingly, Ouspensky's wife, Sophie, forced to choose between her husband and her master, chose the latter, and remained at the Prieure with Gurdjieff. She was in later years to progress into one of the stronger and more respected teachers of the Work, doubtless partly due to her courageous decision not to abandon her path with her teacher merely because her husband had decided that he'd had enough of that teacher. However, owing to Ouspensky's influence in England, a number of his own students eventually sought out the company of their 'spiritual grandfather' and made the journey across the channel to Fontainebleau-Avon. These included the well known English literary figure A.R. Orage, the psychiatrist Dr. Maurice Nicoll, as well as John G. Bennett, Dr. James Young, and Rowland Kenney.

Ouspensky himself had visited the Prieure in November of 1922 but he didn't last long, as he disliked certain elements of the atmosphere at the commune and later predicted that it would not last. What exactly these elements were has never been completely clear as Ouspensky was always circumspect in his criticisms, but some have suggested that in part it was related to the large group of Russians at the Prieure, many of whom appeared to not have the same level of commitment to the Work that the others had. More likely, however, Ouspensky's issues were related to his personal relationship with Gurdjieff. The latter had publically humbled Ouspensky at a talk in London about eight months before, declaring that Ouspensky was not authorized to teach, which wounded Ouspensky, coming as it did in front of his own students. The fact that he even went to the Prieure after that is noteworthy, but either way, he had reached his own personal wall with his teacher and was not ready or willing to go further. Additionally, life at the Pieure was very physical—hard labor during the day and practice of the Sacred Dances by night being a large part of commune life—and Ouspensky was not a physical man. He was above all a thinker and a visionary. If he had stayed at the Prieure he could have worked more on his connection to his body, but at that point he already had established himself successfully as both a teacher and an author, and so his motivation to face into his ego must have declined correspondingly.

Life at the Prieure was one big device, set up by Gurdjieff to provoke conditions that would enable students to see clearly their ego-defenses. Opportunities to experience 'loss of face' were constant, and whenever a person's ego would clearly show itself, Gurdjieff, like a ruthless hawk, would attack. It took a combination of willingness and awareness to understand that what was being attacked was one's vanity, one's pride, one's lazy mind—in short, one's ego—the very thing that was understood to be in the way of the higher development of the person.

It is critical to understand this point. Westerners in general are conditioned to be rebellious and mistrusting, individualistic and independent. The reality, of course, is anything but that—people in Western cultures are arguably as subservient or easily duped or dominated by herd mentality as they are in any other part of the world—but in general, appearances notwithstanding, the West is not guru-friendly, and the concept of 'spiritual surrender' is poorly understood, being generally confused with 'giving away one's power'. Because of all that, the work that went on at Gurdjieff's commune was all the more exceptional, and a testament to his charisma and personal impressiveness. He has been accused of being a master manipulator, and doubtless in some respects he was, but he also convinced a number of extremely intelligent and successful people to abandon themselves to his system, which points to the likelihood that his system was largely genuine and effective. More or less all of his close students would claim this, even into their old age, and that included people like Ouspensky who had gradually pulled out after only a few years of consistent time with his teacher.

In late October of 1922, A.R. Orage—who was to become one of Gurdjieff's key students—came to the Prieure having dropped his career in London as editor of the established literary magazine *The New Age*. Asked by his secretary what he was doing, he replied 'I am going to find God'. Orage had originally been Ouspensky's student but after attending one of Gurdjieff's lectures in London the year before, it was immediately clear to him that Gurdjieff was the more advanced teacher. And so, at forty-nine years of age, he crossed the channel and committed himself to the grueling task of waking up under the exacting eye of a stern taskmaster.

Once there, he was assigned minimalist quarters—a monk's cell, essentially—and given the task of digging seemingly senseless ditches. After completing his digging, he would be told to simply refill the ditch. Orage, an intelligent man, quickly caught on to what was going on and took the process in stride as a device, rather than allowing his ego to be offended by a teacher who at first glance was apparently manipulating and humiliating him. In other words, he successfully avoided identifying with being a ditch-digger. He kept some measure of 'space' between himself and what he was doing. (If he had over-identified with his task, he would accordingly have been offended by how he was being controlled and told that he was not doing it good enough.)

That is not to say that Orage did not suffer during this baptism by fire. Indeed he did, suffering physically (he had arrived overweight, out of shape, and soft from years of living the life of an inactive intellectual), and emotionally, often collapsing in despair and tears at the end of a grueling day. After a week or so, near the point of giving up, he decided to make one more effort—what Gurdjieff would classify as a 'super-effort'. In doing this, something in Orage shifted, and he began to feel a new surge of energy and to enjoy the menial work. That is, he connected with his body—he was, for the first time in years, truly *living* in his body.

Gurdjieff, ever the observant guide, noticed this and approached Orage telling him to stop his work and join him for coffee. Seeing Orage's potential, he had designs for him. Within a little more than a year, Orage would be Gurdjieff's main ambassador in America. Orage's English friends in the literary world had difficulty understanding what had happened to him—John Carswell remarked, 'The most notable English editor of his time had become a mysterious exile owing allegiance to an Armenian magus.' [20]

As it is with most schools of deep inner work, high drama was a regular occurrence at the Prieure. In the summer of 1923, Sophie Ouspensky cabled her husband in England and asked him to come to the Prieure, which he did, if reluctantly. Once there, he had a strained meeting with Gurdjieff in which the latter informed him that he was not satisfied with the progress of the Work, and in particular was having problems with the progress of a number of his students. Gurdjieff then called a general meeting in which he divided all of his students into seven groups. The upshot of this was that he asked everyone to leave except for four people—Orage, Pinder, Dr. Stjoernval, and Dr. Young. At the same time he told everyone that he was no longer working with Ouspensky, and that further, the reason he was asking certain people to leave was because their connection with Ouspensky was interfering with his work with them.

All this was part of the grand drama that Gurdjieff was to enact with Ouspensky over a number of years. The main issue was that Gurdjieff judged that Ouspensky was not ready to teach, and had not endorsed him to do so, and yet Ouspensky had gone off and done this anyway. The whole thing was very delicate because despite Gurdjieff's assessment of Ouspensky's level of development, the reality was that Ouspensky was useful to him in England. Many of Gurdjieff's key students, both at present and in the future, would come to him through Ouspensky—people such as Orage, Bennett, Maurice Nicoll, Kenneth Walker, and of course his main financial sponsor, Lady Rothermere. So Gurdjieff had to finesse the situation carefully, finding the balance between the teacher of spiritual principles and the pragmatist who needed students and capital to survive.

Gurdjieff was constantly creating situations that would enable Ouspensky to drop his willfulness, and undertake further and deeper work on himself with Gurdjieff as his guide. Perhaps predictably, all Gurdjieff's closest students agreed with his view of Ouspensky. Frank Pinder declared,

> All that Ouspensky had of value, he got from Gurdjieff, and that only with his mind...Ouspensky knew the theory, better than anyone, possibly—he had the knowledge, but he did not understand.[21]

The temptation to teach is an old and thematic issue amongst a teacher's disciples who have potential—either owing to the fact that they are already established in the world in some way prior to coming to their teacher, or because they simply have the intelligence and natural charisma to teach. The former was Ouspensky's category; the latter was the Englishman John G. Bennett's.

Bennett was an extraordinary young man when he met Ouspensky in Istanbul in 1920 when he was but twenty-three years old. At that time, he was already head of a section of British Intelligence in Turkey, and he was fluent in the Turkish language, something very helpful as Turkish was the *lingua franca* in those days of Eurasia. When Ouspensky moved to England and began teaching Gurdjieff's system there, Bennett was an enthusiastic attendee of his talks. Then in August of 1923, Bennett came to France to meet Gurdjieff at the Prieure. The magus immediately saw the young man's potential and expressed interest in grooming him for an important position in Gurdjieff's Institute. Bennett demurred, saying he lacked funds. Gurdjieff replied that he was not interested in Bennett's money, but in his work. He even offered to make Bennett his chief translator in America, and to support his living expenses. Despite all that, Bennett declined, saying he would go away and earn money on his own first. He did not return to Gurdjieff for twenty-five years, spending a few months with him near the end of Gurdjieff's life.

Over the years, Gurdjieff's three disciples with the most potential for helping him widely disseminate the teachings were Ouspensky, Orage, and Bennett, and yet all three struggled with their commitment to the Work. Ouspensky got caught up in teaching independently; Orage, after serving Gurdjieff faithfully for several years, eventually opted for a more conventional life with a young woman (Jesse Dwight); and Bennett had so many other things going on that he could not create the time needed to delve deeper into Gurdjieff's Work. Despite that, after Gurdjieff's death, Bennett would claim that Gurdjieff was always his main teacher and he would go on to teach his version of the master's system for many years after.

From January to June of 1924, Gurdjieff was away from the Institute, having taken about thirty-five of his students—especially those more gifted in his Sacred Dances—to America to promote his work in New York City, Boston, Philadelphia, and Chicago. It was in February of 1924, shortly after Gurdjieff had departed, that Crowley paid his first visit to the Prieure where he was given a tour of the grounds and had a private talk with Frank Pinder, whom Gurdjieff had appointed to run the Institute in his absence. Crowley was duly impressed.

Back in May of 1923, Gurdjieff had learned to drive an automobile, a development that was to have fateful consequences. From the beginning, he was a notoriously bad driver: very aggressive, frequently taking serious risks, such as reckless speeding, rarely respecting intersections, and shameless tailgating. Somewhat remarkably, he only had two accidents in his life but both were serious. The first of these accidents, in addition to nearly killing him, irrevocably changed both the nature of his work and the form of his community.

Shortly after returning from what had been a successful six months in America, on July 8, 1924, Gurdjieff was in Paris with Olga de Hartmann, who by then had taken on the role of his secretary. That day he did three things that were out of the ordinary. First, he had her find a mechanic to check his car, a Citroen. Then he signed over power of attorney to her should something happen to him. And finally and perhaps most oddly, he told her to take the train back to Fontainebleau, something he normally never did. It was a hot day and Olga was resentful about having to ride the train.[22]

In the drive back from Paris, Gurdjieff lost control of the car while trying to avoid another car at an intersection and collided with a large tree. His car was destroyed and he was found lying down on the ground (it is unknown if he crawled out or was thrown from the car). The injuries were bad, including a severe concussion. He was found by chance by a passing policeman on a bicycle and taken first to a hospital, then back to the Prieure, with a gloomy prognosis. Attending doctors were doubtful about his prospects for survival. He was in a coma for almost a week, after which he awoke, much to the relief of his disciples, and began a slow recovery over the next several months.

Several interesting things arose out of this accident. First, the inner Work at the Institute all but stopped during Gurdjieff's convalescence. More than anything, this revealed how crucial the system still depended on him, and how none of his students had yet approached a teaching level. In part, this was because Gurdjieff's autocratic character did not permit peers, and in part, because of the depth of understanding of the teachings he clearly had.

Secondly, when Gurdjieff had recovered sufficiently—almost two months after the crash—he gathered everyone together and told them he was closing the Institute. Gurdjieff had bluffed with this before but now it appeared he was serious. He told everyone that they could stay for two weeks and then must leave. He planned to sell the Prieure and then begin his Work elsewhere, with a small select group, whose names he would post shortly. He said that he felt 'empty' and was deciding from now on to live only for himself. This all did, in fact, turn out to be another sort of bluff—he did not close the Institute and some of his students did stay on (although a number did leave). But the nature of how he operated as a teacher from then on changed. He spent much less time working directly with people and much more time writing. He began, in December of that year, to work on his magnum opus, *Beelzebub's Tales to His Grandson*.

The third interesting development resulting from the car accident was the philosophical issue of why this mishap had occurred and what it might mean. Practically speaking, he crashed either because he drove poorly, or because of a mechanical defect in the car. Olga de Hartmann recorded that there had been a problem with the steering mechanism and that this likely caused the crash.[23] However, the greater issue at question was that Gurdjieff's system included a teaching about what he called the 'law of accident'. The general idea there is that the average person, asleep to their higher possibilities, is not much more than a machine governed by cause and effect forces, buffeted here and there by the winds of fate. This person—and for Gurdjieff, that meant essentially all of humanity— is subject to the law of accident, at mercy to the caprice of blind cause and effect. Gurdjieff further contended that the average person does not have the will to escape the law of accident, but he or she *does* have the capacity to obey another person—and from that, the possibility to gain sufficient consciousness and will such that escaping the mindless power of cause and effect, and seemingly 'unlucky' or 'unjust' occurrences, becomes possible. Of course, simply 'obeying' someone is not a guarantee of any liberation, and far more often is the cause of mischief and doom. But Gurdjieff was not talking about being blindly obedient to some secular cause—he was referring to the sacred, and in specific, to obedience to an awakened person—namely, himself.

Yet despite all that, Gurdjieff himself had gone and had an accident—and not just any accident, but a nearly disastrous one. As a result, some people connected to him became confused and alarmed, especially Ouspensky, who outright admitted that he was afraid. For how could a master, one supposedly awakened to a high level of consciousness and allegedly free from the arbitrary harshness of the law of accident, have such an accident himself? Ouspensky concluded reluctantly that it meant that something had gone astray within Gurdjieff's being and it was the same thing that he'd been sensing for some time and using as justification for breaking with his teacher. In short, he felt that Gurdjieff had not sufficiently purified or deconstructed his ego to the degree that he seemed to be claiming by setting himself up as a guru.

Gurdjieff, predictably, did not agree. His view was that the accident was caused by something he called *Tzvarnoharno*. This is a term that appeared initially in *The Herald of Coming Good*, a slim volume that was published in 1933. It was his first book, but he later withdrew it from publication, having decided that it was not properly understood. In the book he described *Tzvarnoharno* as a force that arose as a natural process amongst people that inevitably led to the destruction of any who tries to help humanity, and to all of their efforts. Put in more conventional psychological terms, he was describing the 'collective unconscious force' of common humanity that automatically opposes any counterforce that is attempting to wake people up. He remarked,

> ...I am now quite convinced—it was the last chord of the manifestation toward me of that 'something' usually accumulating in the common life of people, which...was first noticed by the Great, really Great king of Judea, Solomon, and was called Tzvarnoharno.'[24]

It is of course tempting to dismiss this interpretation of Gurdjieff's as

esoteric nonsense, a simple refusal on his part to accept any responsibility for what had happened (such as, for example, the reality that
he drove recklessly). But in fact his view is worth looking at. The
truth is, history is full of examples of the work of mystics or sages
being suddenly aborted or sabotaged. The more dramatic cases are
the crucifixion of Jesus, the poisoning of Socrates, or the execution of
the 9th century AD Sufi sage Al-Hillaj Mansoor. More commonly, the
impeding or sabotaging factors occur from within the community of
the mystic himself, and doubtless just as commonly, from within the
mystic's own psyche. But from whatever angle it is seen, it cannot be
argued that attempts at engineering deep transformative work, as in
the community of a spiritual guide of some quality, are not regularly
met with very strong resistance. That the new is generally resisted
by the established or the old, is obvious, and has been the prime
cause behind revolutions throughout history. The only thing that is
not obvious is the means by which such resistance manifests. The
fact that so much of cause and effect is blind, unconscious, by nature
makes it often impossible to isolate and identify the 'true cause'
behind things. This is all the more so in the spiritual or esoteric
realms.

Sages have always understood that as much as the average
seeker of enlightenment may claim that they are interested in truth,
and even go through the motions of devoting their life to such a
quest, there nevertheless remains a part of their mind that is actually
opposed to the whole process. From my own experience in this
field—three decades worth of it—I believe this applies to virtually
everyone. To wake up to one's true potential is to engage in a type of
warfare, one that may appear to be between oneself and the people
in one's life who have no interest in such matters—and who more
insidiously, may actively seek to interfere with them—but the
deeper reality is that the battlefield is enacted within one's own
mind. The denser egocentric tendencies do not wish to change in
any real way, and certainly do not want the freedom and responsibility that accompanies awakening to higher possibilities.

Whatever the cause behind Gurdjieff's accident, when he emerged fully once again after a long recovery, the direction of Work at the Prieure was forever changed. In one sense, although the Institute remained Gurdjieff's main base until 1932, it only functioned in high gear during its first eighteen months. From 1925 to 1932 Gurdjieff was heavily involved in writing—his Beelzebub not only ended up close to 350,000 words long (about four times the length of the average book), he also was forced to rewrite it several times owing to stylistic problems which, according to Orage, had initially rendered it unintelligible. Even when finished and published it remained an exceptionally difficult book, written in a purposefully dense and almost unreadable fashion, so as to compel the reader to make extra effort and maintain sharp focus and presence while reading. A later example of this type of writing is found in the 'inspired' text *A Course In Miracles*. Like Gurdjieff's system, it also purports to be a form of esoteric Christianity, i.e., what Jesus really taught, and although of an entirely different style, is equally dense and impossible to read quickly.

In addition to Gurdjieff's writing projects, he was also busy composing hundreds of musical scores with the pianist Thomas de Hartmann, and he was occupied with directing his work in America with A.R. Orage as his main coordinator there. Gurdjieff made a number of sailings between France and New York during the late 1920s. Orage, a brilliant and capable disciple, did an excellent job in America for several years but eventually his work with the old magus fell through due mainly to two matters: first, his tendency, as it was with Ouspensky, to over-intellectualize the work, and second, his relationship with Jessie Dwight (see Chapter 11). By 1930, many if not most of Gurdjieff's closest disciples had left him—some of their own accord, several (most notably the de Hartmanns) intentionally pushed away by their teacher.

To neatly encapsulate the meaning of a place like Gurdjieff's Institute for the Harmonious Development of Man in Fontainebleau is essentially impossible. This is because the work of any legitimate mystic is deeply personal, that is, wholly dependent on the inter-action between teacher and student—which needless to say includes both the mystic's skill level, and the student's willingness to actually do the work. In the larger sense, at the Pieure there was no 'community' and certainly no organization. When one reads the different accounts written by many of the men and women who were there and who worked on themselves directly under Gurdjieff's alternately baleful and compassionate gaze, one gets the overwhelming sense of just how out of control the whole thing was—not unlike Gurdjieff's motor car driving. This is the way it always is. A 'community' is but a concept, a label we attach to a collection of individuals, and in a mystery school with a teacher of Gurdjieff's character, the sense of illusoriness of 'community' is enhanced.

A further sense one gets from a number of the accounts is the relative innocence of people back in those times. Gurdjieff received his share of 'psychic attack' in his day but overall the sense is strong that he inspired deep trust in his students even if he was given to intimidating them regularly, or disturbing them with uneven behavior. Many of them were clearly in awe of him. He *was* the Prieure in the truest sense. The force of his presence was enormous, and if nothing else that presence allowed for the creation of condi-tions that heightened his student's capacity to know themselves. There is arguably no more worthy endeavor to engage in for one, who like Orage, had 'gone to find God'.

Equally arguably, however, is the notion that all such work fails in the end. Gurdjieff taught the path of effort and struggle, conscious labor and voluntary suffering, the need to earn a soul for oneself by blood, sweat, and tears. But did any of his disciples attain that peak he pointed to? It is questionable. It is in the nature of a dangerous magus to provoke, anger, and inspire many, but almost never do any come to share the top of the mountain with him. Such a teacher is a walking paradox: teaching about the possibility of reaching a sublime height, and yet at the same time seemingly making it impossible for this to happen. No man more than Gurdjieff exemplified that.

But let us ask one further question: is there in fact any 'peak' to be attained? In all likelihood there is not, at least as we typically conceive of that. There is simply the endless journey, beyond the distant goals that the ego loves to seize upon, and beyond the image of the teacher to contrast oneself with.

Chapter 10
The Spiritual Commune:
Paradiso and Inferno (Part Two)

History: an account mostly false, of events mostly unimportant,
which are brought about by rulers mostly knaves, and soldiers mostly
fools.
Ambrose Bierce, *The Devil's Dictionary*

The distinction between freedom and liberty is not accurately known;
naturalists have never been able to find a living specimen of either.
Ambrose Bierce, *The Devil's Dictionary*

The commune built by Osho's disciples in central Oregon in 1981
was arguably one of the most interesting and controversial intentional communities ever created. I was there at separate times in
1984 and 1985. I worked in landscaping and was a daily participant
in meditations and other activities. What I can attest to is the
extreme intensity of the place, a sort of undercurrent buzz beneath
the more outward show of meditative calmness or flamboyant
celebration. I can also assert the following: the place was a bona fide
mystery school, that is, an alchemical laboratory for working on
oneself, but in order for that to be clear you had to understand a few
things. First, you were entirely on your own. The commune was not
an especially social place, and not at all from the conventional point
of view. I remember more than once visiting the 'disco dance' area
and the usual thing to witness there was the vast majority of people

dancing on their own—in their 'own space' as the expression had it. And this was true of the place in general. If you went out for a walk in the small town (and it was indeed a town) you would mostly encounter people walking on their own, and most of these people were not inclined to be social—and certainly not in the usual artificial way. I emphasize these points to help dispel the myth that the Oregon commune was some sort of 'free love/sex cult', a slightly more Eastern version of a late 1960s hippie commune. Nothing could be further from the truth.

Whatever has been said about the place—and naturally, due to its spectacular collapse, most of that has been negative—it was still fundamentally a place based on the meditative spirit. It was not a 'feel-good' community (not by a long shot); it was mostly based on hard physical work, and the prevailing overall atmosphere was one of being pushed into self-observation. It was, if in that respect only, very Gurdjieffian but also very much like a more conventional Buddhist monastery, especially of the Zen type. I have spent time in both Gurdjieff communities and Buddhist monasteries and can attest to the similarities.

That said, there were elements to the Oregon commune that were radically different from anything found in the Gurdjieff Work or Buddhist communities. There was definitely a celebratory atmos-phere at times, and there was a strong Tantric component—not of the absolutely *vama marga* (left hand) type because the commune was strictly vegetarian—but this was not a community of celibates. Even with the beginning of the AIDS scare at that time and despite strict precautions taken by the commune to minimize the possibility of the transmission of disease, it was still a place that embraced sexual freedom. In addition, the whole commune existed in the shadow of a draconian leadership, the general strategy and tactics of which were not, it appears, fully known for some time by Osho himself.

I can also confirm that the commune was being illegally buzzed by American fighter jets that roared overhead unannounced and at incredibly low altitudes, practically damaging your ear drums in the process (according to several researchers these were from Whidbey Island Naval Base near Seattle; the purpose was to intimidate commune members and at the same time use commune buildings as targets for simulating bombing run trainings). On one such occasion I could easily make out the pilot inside as he flashed over my head. In addition, there were other, sinister developments arising from within the commune. I myself was something of a 'troublemaker' disciple and was in hot water more than once with the commune authorities. On one occasion, I was told to leave by one of the leadership 'lieutenants' prior to the sudden collapse of the commune in September 1985. I resisted and had an intense encounter with this person. On another occasion, I was followed by a commune helicopter for a lengthy stretch of empty road where I was the only person around; this came shortly after I'd been asked to leave (and had refused). There were other coercive tactics. I see these neutrally now, knowing that at the time the commune administration probably had their hands full what with the daily death threats against Osho from surrounding Oregonians. Difficult disciples from within their own ranks were doubtless cause for further unwanted tension. When the commune collapsed in a legal firestorm and internal corruption in the autumn of '85 it was tempting to feel righteous, but that too missed the point. It was, as many later correctly saw it, above all an opportunity for individual transformation. Despite all that happened there, it remains for me a memory of a fascinating mystery school. And it is to the story of this commune that we now turn.

Rajneeshpuram: City of the Lord of the Full Moon

Osho had quit his post as a university professor in 1966 to devote himself full time to spiritual teaching (made possible by the support of some followers). By 1970 he had settled in a large apartment in Mumbai but it wasn't until 1974 that he established his first commune, or ashram, as they are known in India. By the late 1970s as the world-wide number of his followers swelled into the tens of thousands, the need for more space became apparent. Emissaries were dispatched to various parts of India to find appropriate land for the 'new commune'. At that point, however, Osho was falling out of favor with the government of Morarji Desai due to various reasons, partly related to Osho's incisive criticisms of organized religions and politicians (and not to mention of Desai himself—he was fond of mocking Desai's Ayurvedic practice of 'drinking his own piss').

Throughout the 1970s, Osho's chief administrator had been Ma Yoga Laxmi, but by 1981 in what would prove to be a fateful change, she was displaced by Ma Sheela (Ma Anand Sheela). Sheela, a young woman of just over thirty years of age, had a fire and drive that Laxmi didn't, and Osho saw in her someone he judged to have the right characteristics to lead the administration of his organization through the next crucial phase of its growth.

Osho's many troublesome issues with his body began to plague him seriously in May of 1981 when at forty-nine years of age he was diagnosed with a chronic lower back ailment (a degenerative disc). He then made what would turn out to be a decision that would bear serious consequences—he decided to go into an extended silence, ceasing the daily lectures that he'd been giving for the past seven years. (There is an interesting parallel here with Gurdjieff's similar phase of prolonged withdrawal from his students following his serious car crash in 1924—a withdrawal that also proved to have a pivotal effect on the future of his work). Osho's silence would last for three and a half years.

That same month, a decision was made to fly him to the United States to treat his back condition—he was issued a medical visa based on the claim he was going there for medical help. He arrived in New York on June 1st 1981 and was ushered to one of his many worldwide centers, a building in Montclair, New Jersey that had been designed to resemble a medieval castle. He and his group of caretaker disciples stayed there for a few months. They first considered relocating to a piece of land one of the disciples had found in New Mexico, but Osho rejected that idea.[1] Shortly after that, Sheela found and purchased a large parcel of land in the central wastelands of Oregon. Called the 'Big Muddy Ranch' by locals and notorious for its poor quality of soil and sparse vegetation, the place was deemed attractive due to its remoteness, and to the possibilities it presented for building something from scratch that could conform to Osho's ultimate vision of a commune of awakened ones. It was very large, 64,229 acres, which is equivalent to a square of land approximately eleven miles long by eleven miles wide. As an analogy, a piece of land this size could fit seventy-five Central Parks and is half the size of all of San Francisco. The ranch was situated about eighteen miles southeast of Antelope, a tiny hamlet of around forty mostly retired folk.

This ranch was soon transformed and maintained by a small army of grunt disciples performing grueling labor, typically twelve hours per days, seven days per week, into a fully operational town—complete with hospital, post office, school, airport, and its own police force—that could sustain several thousand residents. During this time ('81-'84) Osho did not give lectures or meet with disciples. His sole means of contact with them was via the daily 'drive-by' in which disciples would line the side of the road as he cruised slowly by in one of his Rolls Royces, sharing a smiling communion with devotees excited to catch a glimpse of their master.

The commune was given the name 'Rajneeshpuram' and was legally incorporated as a city (although this was hotly disputed by certain government agencies—see below). First and foremost, however, the purpose of the commune was for it to function as a mystery school, a site for disciples of Osho to gather and work on themselves. In addition to all the trappings of a small town, two central features were Rajneesh Mandir and the 'Multiversity', which included the therapy chambers. The first was a very large outdoor auditorium that served as a meeting place in which to do group meditations, attend *satsangs* [2], watch videos of Osho's lectures, and after late 1984 when Osho broke his silence, to attend his live lectures. The Multiversity was arguably equally important. Not only was it extremely profitable, pulling in millions of dollars a year—money needed to finance the construction, maintenance, and expansion of the commune—it also played a key role in the social dynamics of the commune. The therapy groups were, in many ways, the most effective means of developing relationships within the commune. As mentioned, it was not a place just to 'connect' with people—it was a place for sincere seekers of truth and thus the emphasis was always on such qualities as authenticity, work on oneself, awareness of the moment, being 'in the body' (i.e., truly present), and so forth. For most disciples, the best place to develop these qualities was through a combination of experiencing the therapy groups, meditation, and hard work. And, of course, through the all important connection with the master, which was the main defining point that brought everyone together.

Rajneeshpuram survived for just over four years. During that time it accomplished many remarkable things—transforming dead land into successful and self-sustaining dairy and poultry farms, creating entire irrigation systems, power substations, transportation, and telecommunications systems being just some of them—to the point that it has been commonly recognized as one of the greatest modern examples of intentional community. Alas, it all collapsed rapidly in the autumn of 1985 in a flurry of criminal activities. In brief, the worst of it involved the following: Sheela and a close group of associates, convinced that a nefarious plan involving outside forces and/or Osho's closest disciples was afoot to assassinate the master himself, attempted to kill Osho's personal doctor (Devaraj), poisoned his caretaker (Vivek), conducted illegal wiretapping (much of the commune was bugged, including Osho's own bedroom), and poisoned a salad bar in a restaurant in the Oregon city of The Dalles, sickening over 700 people, in a misguided attempt to prevent voters from voting in a key state election.[3] (Despite all the poisonings, somewhat miraculously no one actually died in connection with these crimes, either in the commune, or outside of it.)

Those were only the most spectacular and flagrant transgressions. Endless 'lesser' abuses of power were ongoing. In the end, Osho claimed that he was unaware of Sheela's activities and when he found out he invited the FBI and other authorities into the commune to investigate. Shortly before this happened, Sheela and about ten others fled the commune in September of '85. Sheela went to Germany, but was later arrested and extradited to the United States, where she served just over two years of a twenty year sentence. Osho, after a strange sequence of events in which he suddenly left the commune, was arrested (along with a few disciples who were with him) in North Carolina, then transported slowly across the states back to Oregon, being forced to stay in a number of jails along the way. Once back in Oregon, on the advice of his lawyers, he pled guilty to the crimes of falsifying his visa documents and arranging sham marriages. He was fined $400,000 and deported. He returned to India with his inner circle of caretaker disciples. No evidence to link him with the more serious crimes was ever found.[4]

Three Poisons and a Wild Card

What went wrong? Despite the original lofty intention behind the commune—as a sacred meeting ground for Osho's disciples to practice and follow his teachings while being near their master at the same time—numerous troubles soon arose to interfere with that spiritual mandate. Three obvious and potent problems in particular began to develop, all of which combined to destroy the commune within those four years. These were, in short, political opposition from surrounding governmental forces, Sheela's own psychological state and her 'application' of Osho's teachings, and a deadly rift from within, between two key commune factions. There is a fourth, wild card issue, one that concerns Osho himself, and the degree of his responsibility; that will be discussed below. For now, let's take a closer look at the 'three poisons':

1. The presence of Osho's disciples in this conservative part of

America was never welcomed, doubtless aided by the fact that these were, by and large, intelligent, educated, attractive young adults, not drugged out hippies or adolescents with shaven heads chanting Hare Krishna. Further, a significant number of Osho's followers were affluent (though the majority were not), and most of these had willingly put their considerable material wealth at the disposal of Osho's work. Inflaming all this was that Osho was not a typical polite Eastern guru—especially during his lectures of the concluding Pune years of the late 1970s-early 80s he had been a fiery outspoken critic of politicians and organized religions in particular. To top it off, he would flaunt the wealth of his organization in part via his slowly growing collection of Rolls Royce cars (the ultimate symbol of decadence), and to really rub it in, his philosophy both allowed for and encouraged disciples to explore sex deeply and fully. He was seen as a hedonist who eloquently condemned Christianity and politicians. A more provocative man could scarcely be imagined.

But that was not all. A key element of Osho's movement was the requirement of all disciples to wear shades of red and a mala with a locket that contained a photo of Osho's face. The reddish clothing was not exceptional—committed members of religious groups (most notably monks and nuns) have worn only certain colors for centuries. Nor was the mala of one hundred and eight beads particularly noteworthy, that again being something traditional and common, specifically in the East. But a photograph of one's guru in a locket dangling from such a mala was not common—in fact, it was essentially unheard of, even in Asia, where behavior toward one's guru that seems subservient is relatively common.

Most of Western civilization—and we refer here to Western Europe and North America—has its roots in Roman and Greek history. A typical element of Greek conditioning in particular has been the idea of the rebel, the hero who battles gods, who defines himself or herself via conflict and contrast with others. It is the archetype of independence. In much of the world, the prime sense of responsibility is toward the family (India being a good example), or toward the nation (as in China), but in the West the prime responsibility—at least as the ideal to be aspired to—is toward the individual. America in particular represents the culmination of that ideal, having been birthed via a violent revolution that tore it away from its British roots. For Americans freedom is the chief ideal, and even if that ideal has been only marginally realized in reality—and probably not at all for the typical American—it remains omnipresent in the background, rendering suspicious anything that appears to be suggestive of loss of individuality. Needless to say, there is great hypocrisy within all this, especially amongst the staggering socioeconomic inequalities of a capitalist society, where a tiny minority of people own and control the majority of everything. But despite all that, the average small town American is conditioned to be deeply suspicious of anything remotely resembling a form of devotion that, a) appears to minimize the individual, and b) is obviously foreign.

The idea of 'minimizing the individual' was not actually what Osho taught—he taught, as he repeatedly pointed out, the minimization of the *ego* and the *promotion* of the individual—but his method in that was unabashedly Eastern and the reality is that for most Americans, including the media, this method was too foreign and threatening. The man in the locket must be a sinister manipulator with a gargantuan ego, the people wearing his locket must be brainwashed, case closed.

Owing to all that and more, Osho's movement was, as mentioned, never truly welcome in Oregon. From the beginning, officials at the highest level of Oregonian government were investigating ways to have the commune shut down. The attorney general of Oregon at the time, Dave Frohnmayer, was an immediate adversary and attempted to legally invalidate Rajneeshpuram's incorporation as a city by proving that it amounted to an unconstitutional merging of church and state. The Supreme Court eventually agreed with Frohnmayer, rendering the incorporation of the commune invalid, but their decision came in 1986 and was academic at that point, coming after internal events had already transpired to bring down the commune in '85.

In addition to Frohnmayer's efforts, the environmental group '1,000 Friends of Oregon' opposed the commune on the basis of its commercial activities on the land and sought also to invalidate its incorporation on that basis. Along with all this, there were regular threats of violence, and the Rajneesh Hotel in Portland was bombed in 1983 (although the bomber blundered, setting his device off prematurely and ended up maiming himself; no one else was injured).

Complicating all this was a series of events centered on the tiny village of Antelope, the closest community outside of the commune. Osho's disciples gradually took over this hamlet, by legal means that derived from some of them getting elected to the Antelope school board, and from some of them buying real estate. All this was seen as threatening by state-level officials (including Oregon's senators, who were now actively involved), and the effort to be rid of the commune was intensified. When the Antelope town council was taken over by Osho's disciples, and in a dubious decision the entire town renamed the 'City of Rajneesh', it all added to the inflammatory mix.

Max Brecher, in his exhaustively researched 1993 book, *A Passage to America*, concluded that there were high level conspiracies—all the way up to the Vatican—to shut down the Oregon commune from the beginning. Suspicions were rampant about the commune's seemingly inexhaustible supply of cash, suspected to be connected to illicit activities (drugs, etc.), although most of this money was coming from a number of highly successful European businesses (Osho restaurants and discos, mostly in Germany), and the Multiversity programs which were almost always booked up. Rumors of stockpiled weapons abounded, although in fact these 'stockpiles' were not found to be as significant as initially believed. (Here it can be mentioned that the Oregon commune had an officially sanctioned police force that had been trained by the Oregon State Police Academy.)

In addition, Brecher reported that he interviewed two mercenaries who claim they were offered a contract to assassinate Osho; one of the men claimed to have been employed as a hired hand by the CIA previously in covert ops in Central America. Both these men believed that the CIA was behind the assassination contracts. The men eventually bailed on the plan believing that it would have been certain suicide for them to attempt to kill Osho in a commune of thousands of zealous followers.[5]

Finally, several months after Rajneeshpuram had dissolved, the US Attorney for the district of Oregon at the time, Charles Turner, admitted that the government's principle aim was to destroy the commune from the beginning. He admitted this in answer to a question as to why Osho had not be charged with any serious crimes, also stating that there was no evidence to link Osho to any of the serious crimes.[6] (Turner himself was the object of an assassination plot by Sheela and several of her assistants; the last of these assistants was tried in court as recently as 2006.)[7]

All of these facts are important to bear in mind because anyone with a casual knowledge of Rajneeshpuram tends to believe that the commune self-destructed owing to internal, internecine corruption, and that was all there was to it. But in truth the commune was, from the beginning, besieged with legal challenges and a hostile reception from locals, media, and state officials. However, the response of the commune, as led at that point by Sheela, was fierce and combative. There was no 'Taoist approach' used, no yielding or practicing 'no-resistance'. The approach was entirely contentious, 'eye for an eye'. This approach was carried to ludicrous extremes, however.

2. The second major problem that faced the commune from the beginning had to do with Sheela's psychological state and her questionable grasp of her master's teachings. To what extent this all reflected on Osho is a separate issue, and is discussed below. But for now what can be safely said is that Sheela and her group of lieutenants—mostly all of whom were women—ran the commune with an iron fist, used their power in at times highly questionable ways, and showed little or no sign that they were involved in a personal spiritual practice (meditation, therapy groups, etc.).

Jill Franklin, who went by the name Satya Bharti when she was a close disciple of Osho and who had authored a couple of popular books on her master in the late 1970s, had this to say about the early days of the Oregon commune:

> Even in the ranch's first year there were more glimpses of ugliness than an intelligent person should have been willing to put up with.

That one sentence is really enough, but the rest of Franklin's paragraph is insightful and important:

> The handwriting was on the wall of every illegal building we erected and written into every letter of protest we sent off to local politicians accusing our adversaries of religious discrimination and bigotry. The us-and-them mentality that Sheela emphasized in mandatory general meetings and did her best to create by abrasive public behavior fostered an atmosphere where it was easy to suspend critical judgment. Whatever our Bhagwan [Osho]-appointed leaders did was necessary, imperative. The community was struggling for its right to exist. In a battle against opponents who wanted us out of the state, the country—who saw us as red devils, Christ killers, communists, and menaces to the 'American way of life,'—the community's frequent skirting of the law and its dictatorial internal policies seemed justified in many ways despite a queasy feeling of distaste that never left me.[8]

Her point is well stated. The 'feeling of distaste' speaks volumes and is testimony to the fact that Franklin never lost her sensitivity, was never completely taken over by Sheela's powerful personality and compelling agenda. The same cannot be said for many others. Sheela may not have won any popularity contests but her authority was so unquestioned by most that many in fact became very devoted to her. Not in the way they were devoted to Osho, but in the way a child can become attached to a parent who may not be all that likeable but who is, nonetheless, *present* in the child's life, and in Sheela's case, far more present than the other 'parent' who was spending all his time in silence in his room. Consistent with classic family dynamics, Sheela became the dominant parent primarily because she was forcefully *there*.

Connected to all this is a controversial topic, the issue of Osho's feminism. It is no secret that Osho had a highly developed feminine element in him—his appreciation of beauty in form, his masterful understanding of relationship, his body-centered spirituality, his elegant manner of expression, his trenchant condemnations of patriarchal power structures in politics and religion, and so on. As if to confirm all this he installed women into most of the administrative power posts in his communes. Sheela herself was famous for in turn assigning only women as her aids. The men around her, whether they were assistants or friends, were mostly gay men. There were no edgy Bodhidharma-types in her immediate realm, to put it mildly.

I was once listening to a talk given by an old Native Indian shaman named Sun Bear. In this talk he made the comment about how risky it can be to give exclusive power to women in a communal spiritual setting. He said that because of the centuries of oppression and marginalization of women, when they finally get power they cannot resist using it to its maximum and commonly abusing it as well. Sun Bear himself was a traditional patriarch, but in the case of Sheela and the Oregon commune there is a point in there that Osho essentially agreed with. He remarked in one of the press interviews shortly after Sheela left the Oregon commune in September, 1985:

Just one woman cannot destroy my respect for womanhood. I will go on giving chances again and again, for the simple reason:

for thousands of years women have not been given chance. So it is possible that when they get the chance—it is just like a hungry man who has been hungry for many days is bound to eat too much and is bound to become sick by eating. That's what happened to Sheela: she had never seen such big money, she had never seen so much power, in my name she had ten thousand people who could have died or done anything.

Sheela had no spiritual aspirations. Seeing that she has no potential, at least in this life...and this was my impression on the very first day she entered my room in 1970—that she was utterly materialistic, but very practical, very pragmatic, strong-willed, could be used in the beginning days of the commune...because the people who are spiritually-oriented are stargazers.[9]

Later, in a series of talks he gave in September of 1988 on Zen, he remarked,

The first commune was destroyed because of women's jealousies. They were fighting continuously. The second commune [the Oregon commune] was destroyed because of women's jealousies. And this is the third commune—and the last, because I am getting tired...Still, I am a stubborn person. After two communes, immense effort wasted, I have started a third commune, but I have not created any difference—women are still running it.[10]

The point here is obviously not to suggest that women cannot run organizations, but rather to highlight the area of the Oregon commune's relationship with the surrounding aggressive masculine energies embodied in the form of its many political enemies. If the commune was being run by someone psychologically unhealed with the masculine polarity (as Osho explicitly and implicitly suggested about Sheela) then that could potentially show up in the form of an unskilled approach that would backfire (which is what happened).

Given the facts, it can be reasonably concluded that Sheela did not demonstrate a balanced or valid expression of Osho's teachings and overall philosophy, because she lacked an introspective disposition—uninterested in meditation and having, quite literally, slept through her master's teachings. To top all that off she was too young, being thrust into a high-powered position during the relatively green time of her early thirties. She lacked the life experience and consciousness needed to deal with all the complex issues coming at her at once.

None of that is to imply that the Oregon commune would not have been destroyed had Sheela not been running it. It may have even if it had been run by a wise secretary who had been strong, non-defensive, and unthreatened by surrounding hostility. There is no way to know for sure. But it can be comfortably concluded that Sheela's disposition aided in and hastened the downfall of the commune.

3. The third major problem, in addition to the public and official perception of Osho and his disciples and Sheela's questionable level of development and understanding of Osho's vision, was ultimately the most serious. It was that a conflict was brewing from within the community itself between two key factions. The first of these was grouped around Sheela, a loyal band of about a dozen lieutenants (mostly women, dubbed the 'temple Moms'), all of whom had great power in the commune, in large part owing to Osho's self-imposed silence. During the time of his withdrawal, Sheela had assumed (in effect) dictatorial powers. Because Osho had emphasized the importance of 'surrender', the orders of Sheela and her assistants were rarely questioned and almost never rebelled against, because it was assumed that to rebel against Sheela was to rebel against Osho, which would defeat the whole purpose of being there in the first place. Osho had gone to pains to distinguish surrender from blind obedience—the idea was to surrender the controlling tendencies of one's ego, but not to blindly obey any so-called authority—however, this difference proved to be insufficiently grasped as events would show.

The second faction was that of the 'Lao Tzu residents', the group of caretaker disciples who lived closest to the master, in his residential complex called Lao Tzu House. These were basically his companion caretaker, Vivek, his doctor, Devaraj, his dentist, Devageet, his cook, Nirgun, his book editor, Maneesha, and one or two others. These disciples were not involved in the administrative running of the commune, so they lacked secular power in the organization, but they had tremendous status nonetheless simply by virtue of their proximity to Osho.

The entire experiment around Osho—especially from approximately 1970 in Mumbai up till the dissolution of the Oregon commune in 1985—was essentially a type of *bhakti* yoga, that is, a devotional path based on a deep personal connection with one guru, what Osho often referred to as a 'love affair with the master'. Although psychotherapy groups and meditation practice were essential elements within the organization, the whole thing was truly held together by each disciple's 'connection' to Osho. The idea behind this type of devotionalism is for it to become a means of deepening one's attunement with one's own higher nature, using the objectification of that higher nature—in the form of the divine, and in the case of a living guru, in the form of the guru himself—as a type of proxy link. However, inevitably in the course of such 'linking', the disciple develops very strong personal feelings for the guru, even at times forgetting that the whole thing is supposed to be a means by which to access a vaster and more profound level of impersonal love for all.

What appears to have happened in the case of Sheela and the Lao Tzu House residents was a fascinating drama that seemed straight out of William Golding's *Lord of the Flies*.[11] It became a textbook case of corrupted *bhakti* yoga, with Sheela developing powerful projections on her master and the 'family structure' around him. That is, she personalized the whole thing to such a degree that it became a dangerous situation precisely because of the power that had been invested in her. She began to resent those who were closest to Osho and in a spectacular example of amplified projection she began to perceive these people as actually dangerous to both Osho and to her own power base. She then followed this seeming logic like the relentless soldier that she was and accordingly plotted to have them eliminated. In her world it all seemed to make sense. And in a vivid demonstration of the problems inherent in dictatorship, those closest to her immediately bought into her perceptions, and as a result began to share the same or similar perceptions—the prime one being that Osho's closest caretakers were dangerous and had to be got rid of.

There has never been the slightest evidence that Osho's caretaker disciples were in any way a threat, either to him or to the secular regime of the commune as led by Sheela; however, it has been made clear that there was a significant psychological rift between the two factions. More than one source reported that Osho's doctor, Devaraj, the man who became the target of an actual assassination attempt, was 'not on speaking terms' with Sheela and her associates, and had not been for some time. Sheela was known to have 'hated' this faction since the days of the first India commune in Pune. However, what seems clear is that this animosity was motivated primarily by jealousy. 'Sam,' the pen name of the author of *Life of Osho*, argues that the contrary was also true, that is, that some or all of the Lao Tzu residents were also jealous of Sheela.

What was going on with Sheela? Why did she play the part she did in the disaster which followed? From the first the pressure on her must have been enormous. And the workload of running the Ranch was only the beginning of it—for Sheela had to moonlight as an ogress. In this strange scenario of Osho for and against his own religion Sheela was at the epicenter of all the contradictions. Sheela did it, they were all to say; Osho didn't know anything about it, it was all Sheela's fault. Making sense of her behavior is made even more difficult by the fact the main accounts of the Ranch were written by, or heavily influenced by, the accounts of the small group of sannyasins who lived in Osho's house—and there's a sense of jealousy of Sheela you can cut with a knife coming off all of them.[12]

It's interesting to contrast Sam's observations of Sheela with those of Rosemary Hamilton (Osho's cook), following a rainstorm and flood that caused damage during the early days of building the Oregon commune:

> One vivid picture of that flood stays with me. Sheela crossing the swollen river to keep her daily appointment with Bhagwan (Osho). Dark eyes blazing, long black hair streaming in the cold rain and wind, she forced a terrified, snorting black stallion through the yellow surging water—matching his brute power with her own, and winning. It was my first clear glimpse of why Sheela had been chosen to carve a city out of a wilderness.[13]

That Sheela was deeply attached to her master is not in question, and so the likelihood that she was not able to overcome her jealousy of those who were close to him is also a given. But the idea that others were jealous of Sheela probably has some truth to it as well. She was for several years the only one who had daily access to him, and who was his representative and spokesperson to the world. She was a chosen one, a golden girl, and such special status alone must have earned her at least envy in the eyes of many. Another passage from Rosemary Hamilton throws light on this, following her being appointed to the position of a cleaner in Osho's house:

> I watch my ego rise and preen itself as I come in through the gate as a cleaner: the rush of pride as the guard studied the list and nodded me through; the greater thrill when he no longer looked at the list; the envious stares of sannyasins who witnessed my easy coming and going through the sacred portal.[14]

It has long been a tradition in spiritual communities that serving one's teacher is a great honor, and in more devotionally oriented fellowships—which Osho's certainly was—to be near the guru is considered to be the highest blessing and one of the best possible opportunities to develop rapidly on a spiritual level. Accordingly, it is also a position prone to competition and jealousy.

Osho and Sheela: The Dangerous Magician and his Dangerous Daughter

A few key points stand out in any attempt to objectively analyze the matter of Rajneeshpuram and Sheela. First, Osho's self-imposed three and a half year silence was obviously pivotal, and while it cannot be said to have been *the* prime causal force—after all, Sheela may still have engineered all that happened even if Osho had been giving daily lectures—it was unquestionably a powerful contributing factor.

Secondly and more importantly, in assessing all this from the point of view of psychodynamics, we are inevitably faced with the need to address the issue of what, if any, level of accountability Osho had in Sheela's actions. There have been, naturally, widely diverging views on this. At one pole—represented by Osho-loyalists like Juliet Forman (aka Maneesha, Osho's chief chronicler) and George Meredith (aka Devaraj, aka Amrito, his doctor)—are those who see Sheela as a discrete entity who acted entirely on her own devices and whose criminal acts were in no way influenced by Osho's ideals or in any way a product of his vision or temperament. At the other pole are disgruntled ex-followers like High Milne or Christopher Calder, the latter of whom claims he was Osho's second Western disciple, and who goes so far as to describe the entire series of criminal events that befell the Oregon commune as having been fully orchestrated by Osho, implying that Sheela was nothing but a passive puppet manipulated by her guru's heavy hand.

An example of Calder's view is as follows:

In an attempt to subvert a local Wasco County election, Rajneesh [Osho] had his sannyasins bus in almost 2,000 homeless people from major American cities in an effort to unfairly rig the voting process in his favor. Some of the new voters were mentally ill and were given beer laced with drugs to keep them manageable. Credible allegations have been made that one or more of the imported street people died due to overdosing on the beer and drug mixture, their bodies buried in the desert. To my knowledge that charge has not been conclusively proven. Rajneesh's voting fraud scheme failed, and the derelicts and mental patients were returned to the streets after the election was over, used and then abandoned.[15]

That these homeless people were there and were fed and clothed (not to mention cigaretted) I can confirm, as I worked, ate, and smoked alongside some of them myself; however, it is regarded as common knowledge amongst most who have seriously studied the facts that this scheme was thought up and enacted by Sheela and her aids. Most agree that Osho green-lighted it, but it was a classic Sheela initiative.[16] Despite that nowhere in Calder's above paragraph (or in similar paragraphs in the article) does he even mention Sheela's name.

A bit more background information about Sheela is helpful at this point. She was born Ambalel Patel Sheela, in Baroda, India, in 1950. She became Osho's disciple in her early twenties. As is often noted, one who becomes a devoted follower at a very young age of an older, powerfully charismatic figure runs certain risks, because their ego-structure has not been firmed up yet by sufficient life experience. Being young they are more trusting and open, and lack comparative reference points. Accordingly, the guru can easily become the dominant center of their universe. I recall back in the early 1980s talking to a fellow disciple of Osho, a young woman of around twenty-five. In the course of chatting with her about discipleship I spontaneously blurted out, 'Well, you're not going to be with

Bhagwan (Osho) for your *whole* life.' She looked deeply indignant, as if I'd just gravely insulted her (which in a sense, I unwittingly had), but also looked at me with sympathy as if I was some kind of fool. She retorted, 'I am *going* to be with Bhagwan my whole life.' She said this with all the conviction of youth, as certain as the Sun rising tomorrow.

As a disciple, Sheela was noteworthy for a few things, one of which was an exceptionally strong personal energy, and the other was a strange habit of sleeping through her master's morning lectures. This latter fact is attested to in some surviving photos of the time: Osho lecturing on the podium, dressed in his simple white robe that in those days (the 1970s) he always wore, and before him, several hundred orange-robed disciples, all sitting, either listening attentively, or eyes closed in meditation. And there, amongst all of that, was an Indian woman in the front row lying on her side—snoozing.

Osho was known to have accepted Sheela's slumbering, even claiming on one occasion that while she slept he 'worked on her' (an expression he often used to indicate ways in which he would influence disciples on subtle levels—though he stopped using this expression toward the end of his life). But in hindsight, the strangeness of this habit of hers can be seen to be an interesting metaphor for her later fall from grace—the disciple who literally slept through her master's daily teachings on how to be awake. The irony is thick. And when seen in light of Sheela's remarkably flagrant violations of common sense and conventional laws during the fiasco of the Oregon commune collapse, the whole thing is all the more suspect.

By 'suspect' I don't imply anything conspiratorial, such as interpretations that Sheela was Osho's denied shadow element, the part of him that unconsciously wished to sabotage his own work, or related psychological sophistries. What seems clear rather is that Sheela was simply *much like* Osho in certain key ways—most noteworthy being her rebelliousness and need to cut a unique figure, to answer to nothing but her own highest call, and to steamroll anything that would get in the way of that.

It is useful to pause for a moment here and enter left stage Chogyam Trungpa, the brilliant and highly controversial Tibetan Buddhist master. In the late 1970s, Trungpa, breaking with tradition, had appointed a Westerner—his close student Thomas Rich—to be his 'Vajra Regent'. This was to be the man who would carry on with the vision of his teachings and community after he died. This of course is widely known to have ended in disaster. Not long after Trungpa passed away in 1987 due to liver damage incurred by alcoholism, Osel Tendzin (Rich's given Tibetan name) revealed that not only did he himself have AIDS, but that he'd slept with several of his students and knowingly infected at least one of them. The scandal rocked Trungpa's community and cost it a number of members, although it did survive (Tendzin himself succumbed to AIDS-related complications in 1990). But what is of interest here is to note the common patterns, much as how they transmit, from generation to generation, through a typical family. As Lawrence Sutin, in his excellent history of Buddhism *All Is Change*, observed:

> There is a discomfiting parallel between Tendzin's blatant denial as to sexual choices and the attitude of Trungpa toward his own constant drinking.[17]

Sutin's insight is glaringly obvious, and yet is the kind of observation that can be remarkably hard to make for those too close to such situations. Alcoholics are famous for their capacity to demonstrate denial, and those close to alcoholics (or other types of abusers/misusers) are equally famous for their capacity to enable, to develop thoroughly myopic vision in one eye. When all this is added into a spiritual mix, the result can be particularly strange, because for those deeply committed to spiritual teachings the need to believe that they (and what they are involved in) is truly special, beyond the pale, exempt from the laws of the universe, can be so pervasive that it overcomes common sense. Osel Tendzin himself admitted that the reason he went ahead and slept with the people he did, even knowing he had AIDS, was precisely the belief that he, and what he was involved in, was truly special:

I was fooling myself...thinking I had some extraordinary means of protection...[18]

And moreover, that it was his guru who had assured him that no wrong could come to him, as Stephen Butterfield recounts in his book *The Double Mirror*:

Tendzin had asked Trungpa what he should do if students wanted to have sex with him, and Trungpa's reply was that as long as he did his Vajrayana purification practices, it did not matter, because they would not get the disease.[19]

The main point here is not to highlight Osel Tendzin's or Chogyam Trungpa's character flaws, serious as they may have been, but rather to see that Tendzin was, in certain important ways, a reflection of his master. In the case of Osho and Sheela, the parallel is fairly straight-forward. There are too many traits in her that are easily recognized in Osho's well documented character (mostly documented by himself) not to see their similarities. During Osho's three-plus years of silence, Sheela was given enormous power and ran the Oregon commune essentially as a dictator. During that time she began to see herself as both a queen and a pope, and even dressed the part, decking herself out in red robes, and wearing her mala (the 108 beads with Osho's photo attached to a locket) with white pearls, wrapped around her head like some sort of garish Tantric miter—the pistol-packing pontiff herself.

The whole thing is absurd in retrospect, knowing now that she literally dozed through her master's teachings, never meditated, never underwent therapy, and never showed real interest in esoteric spiritual ideas. What, then, was she even doing there? Clearly she was infatuated with her guru, but equally clearly, she soon grew to become even more infatuated with her role. In the aftermath of the revelation of the criminal activities enacted by her and her confederates (attempted murder, an outrageous bio-terror attack, wiretapping, etc.), Osho's main argument was that he was not responsible for the actions of others. His funniest line was probably 'enlightenment means that I know myself—it does not mean that I know my bedroom is bugged'.

That may be so, and Osho's attempt to humanize enlightenment can only be appreciated, but the fact remains that he appointed a woman with the character traits that she had to an extraordinarily sensitive and important position in his organization. Why? The only reasonable answer is that he did so unintentionally, and unwittingly, precisely because Sheela was, at the deepest level, too close to him for him to see who she really was, and what she was really capable of. By 'close to him' is not meant a real intimacy, because she did not approach anything like a 'friend' to him (nor really did anyone else, for that matter). Rather she was, to a certain degree, a *reflection* of him in disposition. Despite the fact that she was nowhere near his intellectual equal, and had nothing like his spiritual zeal for transcendental consciousness—in short, comparatively speaking he was awake, she was not—she was nevertheless a close pattern-match with him on the level of certain character traits, perhaps most notably being a strong attachment to *being right* about things and a level of stubbornness connected to that, that goes far beyond being merely endearing.

In July of 1985, shortly before the commune fiasco erupted, Osho, while speaking about Sheela, was quoted in *The Sunday Oregonian* as saying,

Look at her. She is so beautiful. Do you think that anything more is needed? She can manage this whole commune. I have sharpened her like a sword. I have told her to go and cut off as many heads as she can.[20]

The last sentence in particular appears to confirm the view that Sheela was in many ways an echo of her master on the level of character. Osho without question 'cut off heads' in his many years of fiery discourse. Sheela was, in her way, trying to do the same—she was just infinitely clumsier.

Anyone who has ever listened to Osho talk about his past will, if they listen closely, free of sentimental attachment to his obvious grace, be struck by a few things. First and foremost is Osho's tendency to portray conflicts between himself and others in such a light that always, without fail, demonstrates Osho's righteousness. Time and again we hear stories of him encountering someone, 'calling them' on something, and they sooner or later admitting that Osho is right. He seems to have been the only man in history who never lost an argument, was never wrong, or was never put in his place by anyone. He always, without fail, is on the giving end of such encounters.

It's conceivable that that may have simply been the truth. Undeniably, he was a brilliant man, and equally undeniably, he was very contentious. In the area of spiritual one-upmanship he probably only had one modern-time equal, the cranky anti-guru guru U.G. Krishnamurti (not to be confused with his other, more famous rival, J. Krishnamurti), with whom Osho once engaged in an amusing war of words with U.G. calling Osho a 'pimp', and Osho returning the volley by declaring U.G. a 'phony guru'. Osho seemed always to have been at war with something or someone. He even famously exchanged hostile letters with Mother Theresa, calling her an 'idiot' and 'hypocrite' for—in his Nietzschean-like estimation— 'weakening' people by seducing them into the Church, and she returning the favor by insinuating that he was bound for hell and that accordingly, she would pray for him. To which he (justifiably, it must be said) responded, 'Who has given you permission to pray for me?'

I have personally been involved with several spiritual organizations and communities in addition to Osho's and I can confidently state that *sannyasins* (the name for Osho's disciples), while they could be amongst the most passionate, alive, intelligent, and affectionate— were often as well (particularly in the '80s) amongst the most abrasive and unfriendly. Osho valued authenticity very highly, and was contemptuous of 'English civility'—in a word, *niceness*— probably more than anything. Back in the heyday of the encounter-type groups of the 1960s-80s, the intention to 'become real,' coupled with the 'me'-emphasis of the Baby Boomer generation, gave rise to the prioritizing of authentic behavior. This could definitely yield a startling openness and aliveness but just as often could amount to simple unkindness in the name of 'being real'. It has been argued that Osho's community was not warmly welcomed by Oregonians in the early days (1981) of the commune, and while that is unques-tionably true, what is less commonly mentioned is that the general demeanor of Osho's disciples was often itself anything but warm and inviting. Some of that was an echo of Sheela's character and leadership style, but some of it was also the natural outgrowth of Osho's teachings on the importance of exalting the self above all else.

Osho was fighting his whole life—through his college years (which included expulsions), with professors, with religious leaders, even with other avant-garde gurus. That he handpicked Sheela, also a pit-bull, for such a pivotal position can hardly be surprising. And thus it stands to reason that he bears some degree of culpability in Sheela's criminal acts, even if only indirectly, and even if only psychologically. She was his devotee—in the language of psycho-logical alchemy, a Moon reflecting the light of her Sun. His decision to retreat into silence for over three years and allow a young woman in her early thirties to assume command over such a vast and sprawling fellowship with millions of dollars to play with, could only have occurred if he saw in her some quality that reminded him enough of something within himself—even if he was ultimately unaware of her more destructive potentials.

In September of 1985 shortly after Sheela and some of her lieutenants had fled the U.S., Osho appeared before the press in a series of somewhat strange interviews designed to flush everything out in the open. There, in a question about why he chose an intelligent but 'mean-spirited' woman to be his chief representative, he revealed his thoughts about Sheela, claiming that she had been a necessary evil:

> I could not put the commune in the hands of some innocent people—the politicians would have destroyed it...looking at the world, whatever happened, although it was not good, only bad people could have managed it. Good people could not.[21]

In a discourse a few days later, Osho claimed that he put Sheela in a position of power knowingly, declaring,

> I had chosen Sheela to be my secretary to give you a little taste of what fascism means. Now live my way. Be responsible, so that there is no need for anybody to dictate to you.[22]

In light of all that happened, this last comment of Osho's is dubious. If he knowingly chose Sheela to be in a position merely as some sort of elaborate device to give his disciples a lesson, then he did so knowing full well the potential dangers. That people were poisoned, and that some nearly died, underscores that point. It is rather more likely that Osho's remark was that element of his character structure (referred to before) surfacing—that being the need to reframe everything in such a way as to cast himself in the best possible light. 'Best possible light' in this sense refers to the crucial quality of *psychological knowingness*. As a master of wisdom, Osho must above all be seen to be wise, knowing. He can be seen to be innocent of more worldly matters but not of the deeper psychological issues. Without manifest wisdom in that area, his function as a fully enlightened master gets thrown too uncomfortably into question.

That Osho *had* tremendous wisdom and insight is obvious—and that he bore a critically important message and teaching for 20th century humanity is not in question. One has merely to read any one of his over six hundred books in print, or even to watch one of his many videos, to see that. Rather what is being highlighted here is his need to be seen as essentially infallible. The irony is that Osho regularly scorned the pretentious priesthoods and religious leaders of history for, in one form or another, presenting their infallibleness to a duped public. And yet he himself appeared to do the same. I am unaware of any public declaration by Osho that his appointing of Sheela as his *de facto* prime minister was simply a mistake on his part.

Finally, it should be noted that Sheela herself, after over twenty years of seclusion, surfaced in the public eye again. A series of videoed talks given by her were downloaded to YouTube in 2007. In these talks her manner of speaking is peculiar, with mannerisms oddly reminiscent of her master, as she presents her case and tries to promote her essential innocence. Judging by the viewer's comments attached to these videos, she has been unable to shake the general perception of the public that she and she alone, was responsible for the Rajneeshpuram Orwellian nightmare.

But the fact that she royally erred does not automatically exonerate Osho. She was not just his spiritual child, she was also his brainchild. He created the program, the vision, the view, the *raison d'etre* of his communes. It could not have been otherwise. Much as Judas must have been a close affiliate of Jesus, his betrayal, witting or unwitting, orchestrated or un-orchestrated, reflects at some level the rebelliousness of his master, even if that rebelliousness is of a far more immature quality.

The Jesus-Judas myth applies well enough to Osho-Sheela. In the end, Osho's essential argument that everyone is responsible for themselves is clearly true, but what is also true is that an initiative like Osho's *sannyas* has enormous impact and equally enormous consequences. Osho, though a man far ahead of his time, was still a man, and capable only of judgment that would reflect his understanding, his view, his characteristics. My main argument here is that his very nature and his very vision drew to him a certain type of seeker, one that inevitably would cause trouble.

The typical way of seeing such a thing is that Osho was not responsible for who Sheela was, but partly responsible for what she did. I see it differently. He was not responsible for her actions but he was, naturally, responsible for who *he* was, and thus, by extension, responsible for attracting to him a person *with Sheela's qualities*. And because of who she was, he gave her too much power, like a father giving the keys of his very fast and dangerous car to a favorite daughter who is not yet of driving age. And, to extend the metaphor—which also happens to be literal in this case—he did this because he himself also drove maniacally. That he did it with more skill than his 'daughter' is a secondary point.

Concluding Remarks

Gurdjieff, a master well acquainted with the traps of communal life based on higher ideals, once stated,

> It is no part of the master's role to take over the disciple's effort of understanding; the latter, and he alone, must make it for himself. The shocks, suggestions and situations calculated to provoke the disciple's awakening are there solely to prepare and train him to do without the master, to go forth under his own steam as soon as he shows himself capable of doing so.[23]

No better defense of Osho could be provided than Gurdjieff's words. But the problem with Rajneeshpuram was that Osho's prolonged withdrawal and Sheela's dominant reign began to confuse the issue as to who actually was the master. Osho may have been ultimately interested in the disciple's 'freedom,' but clearly Sheela was not. She was interested primarily in the survival of the commune at all costs and, needless to say, in the consolidation of her own power base. In that position, she did in effect attempt to 'take over the disciple's effort of understanding'. Once the basic principle stated in

Gurdjieff's quote is violated, a mystery school enters the grey area between spiritual training ground and cultic organization—or, in worst case scenario, a 'fascist concentration camp' as Osho himself put it.

One view of the matter has it that Osho himself was never truly happy in Oregon and that his withdrawal from public speaking, which had been his main and only substantial form of communication with his people for so many years, was actually a manifestation of a type of depression. But the very idea that he could be 'depressed' was absurd, sacrilegious to the many who followed him and believed wholesale in the idea that he was a fully realized being. But was he?

Back in the late 1980s, I read a book by the Canadian psychotherapist and one-time Osho disciple Robert Masters, titled *The Way of the Lover*. Masters had been present at the original Pune ashram in the '70s, and he had contrasted Osho's appearance in the '80s at Rajneeshpuram unfavorably with his bearing in the '70s. 'Bhagwan's face had lost its balance and luminosity, his eyes lost their timelessness and depth', he wrote, adding that Osho 'looked drugged, and appeared to be oblivious to it all'.[24]

At the time I had dismissed Master's remarks as those common of a disaffected disciple, especially one who had gone on to set himself up as a teacher and acquire his own following (as Masters had done in the '80s). Now, two decades later, I think he was correct, at least to some degree. There is no question that in many of the Rajneeshpuram videos Osho does not look like the blissful man he claimed to be. At times he looks tired, even uninspired, and—if I dare say—lonely. And how could he not be? This was a man with no peer, no real friends, no one with whom he could encounter his own self. Of course, in theory, full enlightenment eliminates the need for all that. After all, if you are one with everything, what need is there for a peer? Or for anyone at all? The question, then, hinges on the depth of Osho's self-realization. If it was not complete, then human needs remained, and if those needs were not met, then there would be unhappiness. The fact that Osho used nitrous oxide apparently for entertainment purposes (see Chapter 12) even if only occasionally, suggests that he was not completely content.

Content or not, one thing that is clear is that a fundamental idea was mistakenly applied at the commune. That idea was, essentially, Crowley's chief law of Thelema—'Do what thou wilt shall be the whole of the Law'. Many, if not most, of Osho's disciples had likely never heard of Crowley, but his teachings, as modified from Francois Rabelais's original ideas published in his *Gargantua and Pantagruel* in the 16th century, were highly evident in many of Osho's core ideas, and reached a distorted and incorrect expression in the very personality of Sheela herself.

Crowley's 'Do what thou wilt shall be the whole of the Law' follows no law but that of honoring the true self, aligning wholly and individually with one's highest truth, and not allowing anyone—or more to the point, one's own ego—to deprive oneself of that truth. This was essentially what Osho taught as well. However, it is an idea that is extraordinarily susceptible to being co-opted by the ego for its own agendas.

Sheela was a superb expression of antinomianism or 'spiritual lawlessness'—she was a true spiritual outlaw, and refused to allow anyone to 'mess' with her will. That part she got right. The only problem was she failed to find her *True* Will. She thus enacted a corrupted version of Crowley's Thelemic law, the ego's version of the True Will. This inevitably ends in disaster because it does not take into account karmic cause and effect. The True Will does not harm, but the same cannot be said for the ego's version, which simply tramples whatever is in the way. Sooner or later it meets something it cannot trample and is destroyed by the echo of its own reckless aggression.

Sheela made serious errors and committed serious crimes. Osho's error was in putting her in that position in the first place. But something in his nature allowed for all this to happen.

Finally, there is the 'bird's eye' view of things. As mentioned in the previous chapter, Gurdjieff proclaimed that his serious car accident in 1924 was not actually an example of what he called the Law of Accident, but rather was a manifestation of a type of negative force that opposes the arising of consciousness in the world—a force that he called *Tzvarnoharno*. One of Gurdjieff's basic ideas is that the universe works by a means of checks and balances, like an organic body, and has a self-regulated equilibrium. If anything disturbs that balance it is opposed, something like how bacteria or viruses in the body will be attacked by antibodies or white blood cells.

It is not hard to apply that idea to what happened at Rajneeshpuram and what happens in so many intentional communities guided by a strong principle of radical awakening. Almost all wisdom traditions agree that the ego (or self) is not a thing to be trifled with, that it is almost endlessly creative in its ways of surviving and corrupting any attempt to be free from its clutches. Above all, the ego is masterful at co-opting spiritual ideas and using them for its own agenda. In the case of Osho's Oregon commune and the regime of Sheela, this is clearly what happened. Individuals screwed up, and badly, but seen as an organic whole, Sheela (or whoever) was not the disease—it was, rather, *consciousness* that was the 'disease', and the threat. And this consciousness was duly set on by 'antibody' forces taking outer and inner forms—outwardly everything from Oregon's attorney general to the fears and prejudices of the average Oregonian or American watching on T.V., and inwardly everything from Sheela's crudely obvious ego and the sublimated ego of all sannyasins, to Osho's own characteristics.

In this bigger, absolute view, what brought down Rajneeshpuram in the end was not an *individual*, but rather a built-in universal factor, what the Gnostics (for one) personified as 'archons,' forces that impede any attempt to awaken. As Aleister Crowley's student Grady McMurtry once put it, 'Why does the gnosis always get busted? Every single time the energy is raised and large scale group illuminations are occurring, the local branch of the Inquisition kills it dead.

I think there's a war in heaven. The Higher Intelligences, whoever they are, aren't all playing on the same team'.[25] A closer to home version of this conflict is found within what most psycho-spiritual teachings call simply the 'ego', the element in the human psyche that is terrified of truth and freedom—and the enormous responsibility that both entail—and that will go out of its way to sabotage any legitimate attempt at movement in that direction.

Postscript: Shortly after this book was completed, on February 13th, 2010, a terrorist attack was made on a popular bakery across the street from the Osho Meditation Resort in Pune, India. At least fifteen people, some of whom were Osho disciples, were killed, and another fifty or so injured. The attack appears to have been the work of Muslim extremists, possibly the same group connected to the mass killings that were perpetrated in Mumbai in 2008 (where a hundred and sixty-six people lost their lives). The irony with the Pune bombing is that despite Osho's notoriety, the attack on the bakery associated with his ashram—twenty years after Osho's passing, and thirty years after a Hindu fanatic attempted to assassinate him—appears to be almost coincidental, its sole reason for its selection as a target being that it was highly popular with foreigners.

And yet despite such irony, there was something unsurprising about the attack. The Pune Osho resort, if nothing else, has been extraordinarily successful, a powerhouse commune and community that has drawn hundreds of thousands of seekers from around the world since its birth in 1974 (transforming Pune's economy in the process). As such, it, or nearby businesses such as the bakery attacked, inevitably became a tempting target for extremists bent on a vengeance arising from deeply egocentric agendas, precisely because of the success of Osho's community. The further and darker irony is that despite all the serious criminal scandals connected to the Oregon commune in the 1980s no lives were lost in any of the events that transpired. Now, a quarter of a century later, lives have been lost, if only due to a mindset that cares less about collateral damage—in the form of body parts—than its own agenda.

Chapter 11
Of Women and Sex

The best women have always been sexually free, like the best men; it is only necessary to remove the penalties for being found out.
Aleister Crowley

The sex center plays a very great part in our life. Seventy-five percent of our thoughts come from this center, and colour all the rest.
G.I. Gurdjieff

I have never been a celibate. If people believe so, that is their foolishness. I have always loved women—and perhaps more women than anybody else. You can see my beard: it has become grey so quickly because I have lived so intensely that I have compressed almost two hundred years into fifty.
Osho

Parts of this chapter may disturb some readers. Some viewpoints expressed here are, to say the least, politically incorrect by today's standards. But two of the subjects of this book (Crowley and Gurdjieff) were not products of today's standards; they were products late 19th and early 20th century patriarchy. Despite all their spiritual profundity, that has to be kept in mind. And even Osho, modern Tantric master that he was, said things at times that were intended to provoke if nothing else. While none of these men were exactly a Bluebeard or Henry VIII, if looked at from a certain angle some of the 'dark father' archetype can be seen in them, if only because of the extraordinary power they held over so many women. Crowley had a remarkable ability to cast spells (figuratively speaking) over women, seducing a long string of them throughout most of his adult life (as well as men, though less frequently). Gurdjieff was very much the same, although lack of a personal diary or memoir on his part makes more of his specific activities in this area harder to confirm. Osho interacted with and guided an extraordinary number of women, and although he was almost certainly less personally involved with them then our other two subjects were with their female followers, that really only refers to physical contact. Psychologically and energetically he was 'in the space' of far more women than Crowley or Gurdjieff likely ever even knew.

It is no exaggeration to say that Crowley, Gurdjieff, and Osho all had exceptionally intense and complicated relationships with women. One of the things that mark them apart from the more conventional guru is this very fact. (One is reminded of Tenzin Gyatso, the 14th Dalai Lama, who has lived a celibate life. Asked once in a public appearance a question about relationships, he answered 'perhaps you better ask someone else'.) In addition, all three were thoroughly red-blooded men who had no interest in denying themselves the pure sensual delights of physical interaction with women and the aesthetic appreciation of their beauty. Even Osho, who for many years projected the image of the archetypal remote wise man who seemed beyond the physical dimension altogether, regarded celibacy as an unnatural perversion, claimed to have 'loved many women,' and famously became known as the 'sex guru'. The label was not actually accurate—Osho was no Casanova, and there is no evidence he ever had anything like an ongoing primary relationship with one woman—but his teachings rightly or wrongly became associated with an extreme type of libertine spirituality. What Crowley (for one) could only envisage owing to the Victorian protocols and taboos of his time, many of Osho's followers, post-60s sexual revolution era, largely lived out in relative freedom.

Both Crowley and Gurdjieff fit the bill for what is usually (politely) termed the 'unrepentant patriarch', whereas Osho is generally known for a deeply progressive approach to the gender issue, and for making many efforts to empower women in his community (such as, for example, appointing them to most of the administrative power positions). However, in his case, my own sense is that the image of the 'feminized' Osho is misleading. It seems more likely that Osho's appointing of women to power positions was born out of a practical expediency rather than any lofty ideal to abolish patriarchal ways. His female disciples were particularly devoted to him and so were natural choices for important positions that required great commitment to his vision. And that is usually the case with most gurus. Osho's situation was no different in that regard. (Of course, that notion spectacularly backfired in the case of Sheela, as we saw in the preceding chapter— but she was an extreme anomaly in what otherwise was a large body of devoted and sane women.)

Crowley, the Great Whore of Babalon, and his Scarlet Women

If we are to begin looking at a man's connection with the feminine polarity by noting his relationship with his mother, then in Crowley's case the outlook at first glance is not promising. Speaking in the third person in his *Confessions*, Crowley wrote 'He always disliked and despised his mother. There was a physical repulsion, and an intellectual and social scorn. He treated her almost as a servant.'[1] She was a Christian fundamentalist and Crowley had concluded that religion had ruined her. By all accounts he resented the control she wielded over him as a boy, although he did rebel, and to such an extent that she called him the 'Beast,' after the Book of Revelation. Yet despite the negativity he shows toward her in his *Confessions*, at her death in 1914 he recorded in his diary that he'd dreamt of her passing just two nights before and had felt 'extreme distress'.[2]

However he may have regarded her, she unquestionably had strength and the imprint she left on him was probably more significant than he ever divulged. Much of Crowley's later work was concerned with the divine feminine—in the form of the deity Babalon—and much of his sex magick was largely similar to Eastern Tantric practices that exalt the Goddess. Despite some of the harsh things he on occasion had to say about women, they remained of paramount importance to him and were the central theme of his life, along with his magick and writing.

It is in the comparison between Crowley's ideas and the raw reality of his life—in particular, his relationships—that highlights more than anything the vivid contrast between absolute or abstract, and conventional or embodied, levels of reality. And it must be said here that regardless of how one judges Crowley's relationships, he was without question remarkably honest in revealing as much about them as he did via his writings. Gurdjieff was known to have had relations with many women but very little is known about them, or of the nature of his relations. In the case of Osho even less is known. Crowley's life, however, was largely an open book, and intentionally so on his part. It is rare in history that one finds the gritty details of intimate relationship told openly, especially by the guru himself. Far more common is for such information to only be known via second-hand sources.

In order to understand the basis of Crowley's complex personal relationships in the context of his 'Great Work' and the office of his 'Scarlet Women' as he called his Tantric partners, it is necessary to understand some elements of his Thelemic ideas as they relate to the Goddess archetype. In order to do so we first have to bear in mind that Crowley's Thelemic doctrine is based on the essential idea that (as of 1904) we are in a New Aeon, what he called that of Horus, or the 'Crowned and Conquering Child.' His view was that in the previous aeon (that of Osiris, or the Dying, Resurrecting God), the idea of the Virgin was central, relating as it does to a descent of Spirit into matter (the 'virgin birth'). In the present Aeon the deity known as Babalon, or the 'Great Whore', becomes central because she represents the opposite principle of the virgin—rather than the descent of spirit into matter, Babalon symbolizes the ascent (or re-absorption) of individual consciousness into the divine feminine. The 'whore' becomes an apt symbol because (spiritually, in this case) she welcomes all without reservation or discrimination. She invites and even longs for our return.[3]

It's important to understand what is meant by 'divine feminine' (as well as 'divine masculine'). This has nothing to do with conventional ideas of gender, or even goddesses and gods. It can more properly be understood in the context of the Hebrew Qabalastic Tree of Life, and in particular the *sephirot* (domains) known as *Chokmah* and *Binah*. (See Chapter 20 for more on Qabalah). The former means 'wisdom' and is associated with the divine masculine. The latter means 'understanding' and is connected to the divine feminine. Both can be thought of, in the context of an individual person, as elements of the Higher Self; that is, of the highest states of consciousness we are capable of experiencing.

Binah can be understood as the Mother of All, the archetypal womb that 'gives birth' to life.[4] As the first *sephira* immediately above the 'Abyss'—that null zone all seekers of truth must pass through in order to shed egocentric identity—*Binah* also represents the open space that we return to, the 'womb of the divine' that welcomes us home once we've abandoned the false conceptual constructs of the egocentric self. And so by connecting the goddess Babalon to the Qabalistic idea of *Binah*, Crowley is drawing attention to the idea that she is like a 'whore' who does not turn anyone away precisely because there is no 'separate' individual at this level. The illusion of separation and egocentric distinction is dissolved.

Binah can also be understood as a particular type of consciousness that is meditative, that is, is grounded in the here and now and is able to experience thoughts, feelings, sensations, and so forth, with no reference to a 'me' or 'I'. It is free of ego simply because at this level it is clear that ego does not actually exist. Rabbi David Cooper puts it like this:

> Ordinary mind-states have a wide range of emotions but usually a clear sense of personal involvement with the world...this sense of separation clouds our relationship with the world. In Binah consciousness on the other hand, we feel alert, mindful, bright, luminous, expansive, inclusive, soft, lucid. We integrate with everything that is happening around us, feeling connected, whole, relaxed.[5]

Crowley connected *Chokmah*, the divine masculine, with what he referred to by the Greek word *Therion*, or as he more commonly called it by its English equivalent, 'the Beast.' In the Qabalistic Tree of Life it is the highest domain of consciousness before the unknowable *Kether* (the Godhead). Chokmah is not a consciousness we can cultivate; it simply is there when we are ready (which is sometimes called 'grace'). In classic enlightenment traditions, it represents the final opening into non-dualistic awareness, but it cannot be controlled or forced—simply because at that level there is no individual ego to control or force things.

In Eastern Tantra, the ideas of the divine feminine *Binah* (Babalon) and the divine masculine *Chokmah* (Therion) have their approximate equivalents in *Shakti* and *Shiva*. *Shakti* is the dynamic, creative principle of existence—alive, moving, and the essence of form and appearance. *Shakti* shapes the universe much as how *Binah* gives form to the raw energy of *Chokmah*. She represents the beginning of duality, the distinction between 'I' and 'this'. *Shiva* is (in this context) the formless pure consciousness. He unites with *Shakti* to produce the experience of totality of understanding, or full enlightenment. By 'full enlightenment' is meant a state of complete understanding, freedom, and bliss that at the same time does not abandon the world of form (including, naturally, the body).

In Left Hand Tantra, or what is known in India as *vama-acara* or *vama-marga*, sacred intercourse with a consecrated woman is central to the practice.[6] In that regard, Crowley's magick with a Scarlet Woman consort was classic Left-Hand Tantra (by Hindu terminology). As Yoga scholar Georg Feuerstein vividly put it,

> If the Divine is everywhere, as the Tantric adepts affirm, it must also be present in and as the body...India's more ascetic traditions have typically looked upon the body as an inconvenience, even an obstacle, to the bliss of freedom. The body and bodily functions fill ascetics of whatever provenance with disgust and horror. The notion that the body is a bag of filth is as much at home with the ascetics of India as it is with the Gnostics of the Mediterranean.[7]

The Tantric approach is an attempt to embrace desire, and to enter into it with consciousness (as opposed to repressing it). It is an attempt to bring awareness into instinct, rather than fleeing in fear from instincts (of which the strongest force is the sexual). In so doing, Tantra aims to view material reality as an expression of the divine, rather than as a 'bag of filth'.

For Crowley, the goddess Babalon was essentially the same as the Egyptian goddess Nuit (or Nut). Years ago when I was in Egypt, I went into some of the tombs in the Valley of the Kings, across the Nile from Luxor. What was most surprising about these tombs was the ubiquitous presence of Nuit, who as a sky goddess is depicted in the form of a hugely elongated body arching across the ceiling in the tombs. All around her is the dark blue sky; she represents the womb of existence. Her name itself means 'night'. Standing in these tombs, the importance the Egyptians ascribed to the sky goddess is immediately apparent. Crowley interpreted Nuit/Babalon in a deeply mystical sense, as symbolic of the essential one-half of the cosmic principle that results in the appearance of any and everything. She is open space, the circle of infinite size. Her counterpart, recognized by Crowley as Hadit, is the point of manifestation that appears within Nuit's empty space. Working in tandem, Nuit and Hadit create the conditions for existence as we know it to arise.

To grasp this idea more clearly, imagine a blackboard that has nothing on it. Then place a black dot on it that is the same shade of black as the black background. Clearly, the dot will not appear. Symbolically it does not exist. But make the dot any other shade or color—say, for dramatic effect, pure white. The contrast between the white dot and the black background immediately causes the dot to leap into appearance. This is a crude example of how duality allows for consciousness to arise. We are conscious of things only via contrasting them to other things. Similarly with ourselves, we are conscious of our identity via contrasting ourselves to others.

As Crowley describes it, all of existence, which is nothing other than a play of consciousness, can *be* precisely because of this contrasting effect brought about by pure empty space (Nuit) and a 'point' in space (Hadit) that gives rise to *contrast*. (There is a state of consciousness that is beyond dualistic contrast altogether—Crowley wrote at length about this in his Yoga writings—known traditionally as *samadhi* in Hindu doctrine, or sometimes as 'consciousness without an object'. But in the case of *Nuit* and *Hadit*, we are dealing with the root principles of manifest existence as we typically know it.)

The symbolism is abstract and cosmic, but the implications—for modern women and men—are very specific and relate to the liberation of women and men in the truest sense. Not in the conventional sense—Crowley would not have endorsed any women's liberation that amounts only to aggressively competing with men, nor any men's movement that amounts only to men gathering to just bang drums and 'bond'—but rather to the idea of a woman truly realizing divine womanhood, and to a man truly realizing divine manhood, and to both moving beyond duality altogether. Gurdjieff and Osho, though employing different conceptual models, were working toward the same ideal. They were working toward the creation of women who are awake as well as truly feminine, men who are awake as well as truly masculine, and to the ultimate emancipation of both from the limitations of polarity-consciousness—'harmonious balance' as Gurdjieff referred to it, 'Zorba the Buddha' as Osho called it. But in all cases what is soon discovered is that transcendence of polarity—going beyond the man-woman dance—is not possible until this 'dance' is first embraced and deeply understood.

Put yet more simply, in order for a woman to become an enlightened woman she must first *be* a woman. In order for a man to become an enlightened man he must first *be* a man. By 'be a woman' or 'be a man' is not meant conforming to some generally approved stereotype—it refers rather to becoming truly comfortable in one's own skin, at home in one's gender, at peace with what we are in this world of form and appearance. Free of guilt and self-loathing it then becomes possible to see that contrast and duality need not breed suffering and contempt, but rather can be the source of all joy and creativity. That, at least, is one of the core messages of Crowley's *The Book of the Law*.

Looked at superficially, in terms of personal, biographical outline only, Crowley's life appeared to consist of a long hedonistic string of lovers (mostly women, but a few men as well) over an approximate forty year span from 1900 to around 1940. As mentioned, a number of these lovers he came to regard as his 'Scarlet Women'. That term has traditionally been associated with prostitution, but Crowley meant it as representative of the sacred role of Babalon, the 'divine whore' who symbolizes the open space of the primal source that leads us back to our true nature. That he chose such a provocative term was typical of his character, but there was also a specific design to it. Crowley sought whenever possible (sometimes consciously, sometimes not) to disturb people, to provoke their conditioning, and in particular, their moral conditioning. Once again, Osho was very similar to him in that regard (talking openly and frequently about sex, criticizing religious leaders, amassing an outrageous fleet of luxury cars, and so on). A basic idea there is that in order to move beyond conditioning we first have to see it—and that often involves an uncomfortable dislodging of such conditioning from the unconscious mind. Gurdjieff referred to the enduring of this phase as 'voluntary suffering.' In alchemy it is sometimes called the *nigredo* or 'blackening' phase, involving the facing into and breaking down of parts of our character that stand in the way of our development.

That said, to what degree Crowley's actions were done with conscious design and to what degree they were simply an unconscious catharsis in which he was still working out the kinks of his religiously oppressive and chaste Victorian upbringing, is not clear. Israel Regardie, in his *The Eye In the Triangle*, analyzed Crowley extensively and concluded that a number of traumatic events in his childhood—being repeatedly bullied at school, ill-treated by his uncle, losing his father at the tender age of 11, his animus with his mother, and so on—led to a strong sadomasochistic element in him that 'marred' many of his relationships with women.[8]

It is hard to disagree with Regardie when one actually examines Crowley's love life. But here again it must be noted how exceptional it is that his love life can be examined at all. Many gurus of the past had relationships that resembled train wrecks (even the Buddha abandoned his wife and infant child), or that involved a celibacy in which the guru's fantasy life, if there was one, was never revealed. With Crowley everything is wide open; he offers his life up as a demonstration of the inherent limitations of embodied life. That alone is of inestimable value, helping to break down puritanical ideas about spirituality that do nothing but reinforce guilt and fear. (And on that note, how many of us would willingly expose the details of our lifelong love life?)

The list below is of Crowley's main lovers, some of whom he considered to fill (if only for a short time) the office of Scarlet Woman. In several of these cases—notably Rose Kelly, Mary Desti, and Roddie Minor—they served as mediums or 'psychic aids' in helping Crowley access subtle levels of consciousness or 'praeter-human intelligences'. Others, like Leah Hirsig and Frieda Harris, were instrumental partners in the creation of a particular project (the

Abbey of Thelema in Hirsig's case, and the Thoth Tarot deck in Harris's case). Included are their years of birth and death (when known), as well as their initiate names and 'animal names' (in some cases) that Crowley, with humor and affection, gave to them. This list does not pretend to be comprehensive; Crowley is known to have had dozens of lovers beyond the ones mentioned here, and doubtless more children. Crowley's comments are in relation to Scarlet Women only; 'SW' indicates Scarlet Woman:

- Elaine Simpson. One of Crowley's first significant lovers, she was a fellow Golden Dawn initiate that he met in 1899. By 1900 they'd parted but he met up with her again briefly in 1906 in Shanghai, where they undertook some magickal work and a brief study of *The Book of the Law*.

- Rose Kelly, 'Ouarda' (1874-1932); Crowley's first wife. SW: 1903-09, aided in the receiving of *The Book of the Law* in Cairo in 1904. Crowley had two girls with her; one died before her second birthday. Crowley and Rose divorced in 1909. She was alcoholic and Crowley at one point had her committed to an alcoholic asylum. Crowley and Rose had a daughter, Lola Zaza (1906-1990), who as an adult disowned her father. An earlier daughter (Nuit, or Lilith—she had a string of exotic names), born in 1904, died of typhoid before her second birthday. Crowley's comment: 'My wife. Put me in touch with Aiwass; see Equinox 1, 7, 'The Temple of Solomon the King'. Failed as elsewhere is on record.'[9]

- Leila Waddell, 'Soror Agatha' (1880-1932); Crowley's lover from March 1910-October 1911. An important relationship for Crowley in that she appeared to have a measure of independence many of the others did not. She resisted Crowley's wishes for her to commit more deeply to magick. She was initiated into Crowley's A.·. A.·. but was never technically his

Scarlet Woman. Crowley was not monogamous with her. Of all his loves she seems to have been the one who fascinated him the most.

- Mary Desti, 'Soror Virakam' (1871-1931); SW: October 11, 1911-winter 1912; She replaced Leila, and was present with Crowley when they undertook the 'Abuldiz Working,' invoking a spirit guide by that name. Crowley: 'A doubtful case. Put me in touch with Abuldiz; hence helped with *Book 4*. Failed from personal jealousies.'

- Helen Hollis, 'the Snake' 1915. Not much is known about her. A brief lover.

- Jeanne Robert Foster, nee Oliver, 'Soror Hilarion' (1879-1970); 'the Cat' SW: 1915. Crowley: 'Failed from respectability.'

- Gerda Maria von Kothek, 'the Owl', 1916. Not much information is available on her.

- Alice Richardson, 'the Monkey', 1916. She was the English wife of the famed Indian art historian Ananda Coomaraswamy. As with all of his lovers, Crowley practiced sex magick with her. She became pregnant but miscarried while sailing back to Europe.

- Anna Miller, 'the Dog' 1917. A brief lover; through her he met Roddie Minor.

- Roddie Minor, 'Soror Ahitha', 'the Camel'; SW: October 1917-summer 1918. Crowley: 'Brought me in touch with Amalantrah. Failed from indifference to the Work.'

- Marie Rohling, nee Lavroff. Crowley: 'A Doubtful case. Helped to inspire Liber CXI. Failed from indecision.'

- Bertha Almira Prykryl, nee Bruce. Crowley: 'A Doubtful case. Delayed assumption of duties, hence made way for No. 7 (Leah Hirsig).'

- Leah Hirsig, Soror Alostrael (1883-1975), 'The Ape of Thoth'; SW January 1919-August 1924. She presided over Crowley's 'Ipsissimus' grade; was SW during the Abbey of Thelema years (1920-23). She bore Crowley a daughter named Poupee who lived only nine months.

- Ninette Shumway (1895-1989). She was Crowley's 'second concubine' (after Leah) at the Abbey of Thelema. She bore him a daughter, Astarte Lulu Panthea, born at the Abbey in 1920.

- Dorothy Olsen, Soror Astrid. (SW August 1924-October 12, 1926). She was Crowley's partner when he met Gurdjieff at the Prieure.

- Kasimira Bass, SW summer 1927-winter 1928. She was Crowley's partner when he first hired Israel Regardie as his secretary, described by Regardie in a memorable scene where Crowley and Bass fell to the ground and began having passionate sex right in front of the young and astonished Regardie.

- Maria Ferrari de Miramar (1894-circa 1955). Met Crowley in 1928; they married in 1929, separated in 1930, but never divorced.

- Bertha Busch, SW from September 30, 1931 to March '33. Crowley wrote about her: 'Best fuck within recorded memory of living man.'[10]

- Pearl Brooksmith, August 1933.

- Deirdre O'Doherty. She was much younger than Crowley. They were briefly lovers but did not live together. In 1937 she gave birth to his son, Randall Gair (given by Crowley the nickname Aleister Ataturk); he died as an adult in a car accident (date unknown).

- Frieda Lady Harris (1877-1962). She was the artist for Crowley's famous Thoth Tarot deck. She was not a lover and not a formal student of Crowley's, although he taught her a great deal nevertheless. She was first and foremost an artist. She merits mention here as a key relationship of his, even if nonsexual. Their friendship endured through the difficult five year process (1938-1943) of designing and painting the deck and at the end of Crowley's life, she was one of his few supporters.

Below follow some comments Crowley made about women in general. At first glance some of these views on women may appear to be consistent with prevailing Victorian attitudes of that time, or simply borderline misogynistic. But in point of fact what Crowley says is not much different from current prevailing views put forth by some popular writers of the 'men's movement', such as Robert Bly, Sam Keen, and David Deida.[11] As an example, I cite a series of extracts from Crowley's *Confessions* (written in the 1920s) and contrast them with some excerpts of Deida from his popular book *The Way of the Superior Man* (published in 1997). First, this from Deida, addressing men:

Your Purpose must come before your relationship...if a man

prioritizes his relationship over his highest purpose, he weakens himself, disservices the universe, and cheats his woman of an authentic man who can offer her full, undivided presence.[12]

Deida is basically saying that a man must have a primary passion for his life and above all for his work; and that a man who allows himself to be controlled by a woman (by prioritizing her) loses his masculine core, in effect becoming weak and unattractive to women anyway; Crowley said essentially the same thing seventy years before, although in a cruder way:

> I received my first lesson in what the religions of the world have discovered long since, that no man who allows a woman to take any place in his life is capable of doing good work. (Similarly, men may be as foolish over dogs as old maids over cats.) A man who is strong enough to use women as slaves and playthings is all right. Even so, there is always a danger, though it is difficult to avoid it. In fact, I don't think it should be avoided. I think a man should train himself to master what are commonly called vices, from maidens to morphia. It is undeniable that there are very few such men.[13]

The following comment by Crowley is strikingly reminiscent of Gurdjieff's three way power struggle between his prized student A. R. Orage, and Orage's young mate, Jesse Dwight:

> Again and again I have had the most promising pupils give up the great work of their lives for the sake of some wretched woman who could have been duplicated in a Ten Cent Store. It doesn't matter what the work is; if it is worth while doing, it demands one's whole attention, and a woman is only tolerable in one's life if she is trained to help the man in his work without the slightest reference to any other interests soever.[14]

Again, the wording is harsh. But compare the actual *content* of that paragraph (beyond the rough language) to David Deida's more appealing prose:

> She doesn't really want to be number one. A woman seems to want to be the most important thing in her man's life. However, if she is the most important thing, then she feels her man has made her the number one priority and is not fully dedicated or directed to divine growth and service...although she would never admit it, she wants to feel that her man would be willing to sacrifice their relationship for the sake of his highest purpose.[15]

Arguably Deida just has a more polished expression. But both men are ultimately saying the same thing: which is that men, in order to be men, need to put their work in life as #1, and their woman as #2. If they don't—if the put their woman as #1 and their work as #2— then eventually their spirit begins to wither and their women begin to lose their respect (not to mention their attraction) for them.

Crowley's added emphasis is on the capacity of a woman to help a man in his life's work, and this doubtless reflected his own struggles in that area with his various Scarlet Women. Here he continues with his points about the tendency of men to give their power away to women, the need for men to counter that with extreme focus on their work, and the innate, in Crowley's view, inability of women to work the way men can:

> The necessary self-abnegation and concentration on his part must be matched by similar qualities on hers. I say matched—I might say better, surpassed—for such devotion must be blind. A man can become his work, so that he satisfies himself by satisfying it; but a woman is fundamentally incapable of understanding the nature of work in itself. She must consent to co-operate with him in the dark. Her self-surrender is, therefore, really self-surrender, whereas with him it is rather self-realization.[16]

Deida (in effect) takes Crowley's words and gives them a facelift:

> Intimate relationship is never the priority in a masculine man's life and always the priority in a feminine woman's life. If a man has a masculine sexual essence, then his priority is his mission, his direction toward greater release, freedom, and consciousness. If a woman has a feminine sexual essence, then her priority is the flow of love in her life, including her relationship with a man whom she can totally trust, in body, emotion, mind, and spirit. Man and woman must support each other in their priorities if the relationship is going to serve them both.[17]

What Deida calls 'his mission' Crowley has called 'his work' and his 'self-realization'; what Deida calls 'the flow of love in her life' Crowley has called 'her self-surrender'. Surrender may seem a dubious word on Crowley's part, suggestive of some sort of submissiveness, but in fact the word 'surrender' is commonly used in many spiritual traditions when describing a deep, heart-centered devotion to something (as in *karma yoga* and *bhakti yoga*, for example).

I have provided this brief contrast between Crowley's and Deida's words in order to illustrate an important issue, which is the matter of post-modern spirituality and the question of whether it is truly more evolved or simply more attractively dressed up. Deida is a good representative of cutting edge understanding of relationship matters, but when you examine what he says and contrast it to early 20th century views of men like Crowley and Gurdjieff (see below), an argument can be made that it has all just been presented in a more passable fashion.

At any rate, there is the sense in Crowley's words that he is not just expressing very defined and, because of his rough language, politically incorrect views on women, he is also simultaneously revealing to us something of his struggle in this matter—that is, his deep fear of being engulfed by the feminine, and, almost certainly, his old lingering animus with his mother.

For many men, the Woman archetype represents a powerful, chaotic darkness, something that he fears can consume him and something that he must be on his guard to prevent being overwhelmed by—like a swimmer trying to stay above the surface of the water, always with an underlying fear of drowning. A man tends to identify with his rational, conscious mind, and often sees women (rightly or wrongly) as the power of the primordial, unconscious depths. The famous Swiss psychiatrist C.G. Jung once put it this way:

Woman is a very strong being, magical. That is why I am afraid of women.[18]

As the Sufi teacher Llewellyn Vaughn-Lee bluntly put it,

I had to encounter the dark, terrible power of the feminine of which most men are afraid.[19]

Despite his intellectual brilliance and profound spiritual insights, Crowley was clearly not a fully cooked egg in other ways. Nevertheless, his upside in his dealings with women was his untrammeled honesty. However arrogant he could get, he did not pretend to be otherwise, and his long, turbulent life with women was consistently conducted with an unflinching willingness to face whatever arose between he and them. In that regard he was ahead of his time, a predecessor of the post-1960s Tantric bohemian who seeks to move with totality into whatever presents itself. That he stumbled so often in this realm was to be expected, given his past and his disposition, but he cannot be accused of artifice or hypocrisy. His life is a fascinating study in the sheer contrast between a body of exalted and brilliant metaphysical ideas, and the stark reality of a life of painfully collapsed love affairs.

Finally, it must be noted that for every apparently harsh comment Crowley made about women, he made an equal number of supportive remarks that revealed his views as to what lay behind the oppression of women for centuries:

> Women under Christianity are kept virginal for the market as
> Strasbourg geese are nailed to boards till their livers putrefy. The
> nature of women has been corrupted, her hope of a soul
> thwarted, her proper pleasure balked, and her mind poisoned, to
> titillate the jaded palates of senile bankers and ambassadors.[20]

And here, in powerful and elegant prose, he affirms the ultimate
equality of men and women:

> We of Thelema say that 'Every man and every woman is a star.'
> We do not fool and flatter women, we do not despise and abuse
> them. To us, a woman is herself, absolute, original, independent,
> free, self-justified, exactly as a man is. We dare not thwart her
> going, Goddess she! We arrogate no right upon her will; we claim
> not to deflect her development, to dispose of her desires, or to
> determine her destiny. She is her own sole arbiter; we ask no
> more than to supply our strength to her, whose natural weakness
> else were prey to the world's pressure. Nay more, it were too
> zealous even to guard her in her going; for she were best by her
> own self-reliance to win her own way forth! We do not want her
> as a slave; we want her free and royal, whether her love fight
> death in our arms by night, or her loyalty ride by day beside us
> in the charge of the battle of life.[21]

Gurdjieff: the 'Man who killed Katherine Mansfield'

Gurdjieff was ruggedly masculine. Although very strong intellectually and emotionally, he did not have Crowley's literary and poetic
sensibility. He was, however, very manually oriented and skilled
and loved to tinker with things. As a young man in Ashkhabad he
set himself up as a universal handyman advertising his business as
'The Universal Traveling Workshop' and claimed to be able to repair
anything. He was also a master of elaborate dances. Like Crowley,

he had a powerful hold over women, who doubtless were captivated by the deep self-confidence he radiated, by the certainty and conviction with which he spoke. He had a strong understanding of the female mind. This was attested to if for no other reason than by the fact that many of his followers were exceptional, intelligent women. His male students were important and he did appear to lavish attention on at least three of them (Ouspensky, Orage, and Bennett) in the hopes of grooming them as successors, but in all cases these men did not achieve Gurdjieff's hopes. His women students, although generally of a lower profile than the men, were in large part more loyal. One of them, Olga de Hartmann, Gurdjieff once referred to as 'the first true friend of my inner life'. Another, Jeanne de Salzmann, emerged from a large group of followers as Gurdjieff's chief disciple at the end of his life, his 'Peter the rock'.

That said, Gurdjieff was, even more than Crowley, a patriarch. Although the principle point of his Work was to bring men and women into a state of inner balance, he nevertheless saw men and women as fundamentally different and made no bones about it. According to Fritz Peters, he once said the following (I've taken the liberty of converting Gurdjieff's broken English, dutifully recorded by Peters, into Standard English):

The nature of a woman is very different from that of a man. The woman is from the ground, and the only hope for her to arise to another stage of development—to go to heaven as you would say—is with a man. A woman already knows everything, but such knowledge is of no use to her, and in fact can almost be like a poison to her, unless she has a man with her. Men have one thing that does not exist in women, ever: what is called 'aspiration'. In life, a man uses this one thing—this aspiration— for many things, which are all wrong for his life, but he must nevertheless use it because he has such a need. Men—not women—climb mountains, go under oceans, fly in the air, because he must do such things. It is impossible for him not to do these things, he cannot resist this. Look at life around you: men write music, men paint pictures, write books, and such things. It's his way, he thinks, to find heaven for himself.

It is not necessary for a woman to do the work of a man in the world. If a woman can find a real man, then the woman becomes a real woman without the necessity of the inner work. But, like I tell you, the world is mixed up. Today in the world real men do not exist, so women try to become men, and to do men's work, which is wrong for her nature.[22]

Those remarks of Gurdjieff—spoken in the mid-1920s shortly after the voting privileges of women in most modern Western nations had first become a reality—would be denounced as sexist by many in current times, and indeed it is hard to defend Gurdjieff's remark that a woman 'must be with a man to go to heaven'. But teachers like Gurdjieff, Crowley and Osho were notorious for making statements that if taken out of context would seem to reflect badly on them. Fritz Peters, who provided the above quote, was reconstructing from memory words he heard Gurdjieff speak some forty years before he put them in his book. He was the same author, it should be mentioned, who provided the most outlandish version of the infamous Crowley-Gurdjieff encounter (covered in Chapter 13).

Even if we take the above quote at face value, the idea that a woman must be in relationship of one sort or another with a man in order to truly awaken to her divine essence is not unique to Gurdjieff. It is a variation of an old Gnostic theme, that being that the feminine spirit draws on something from the masculine spirit as part of its opening to higher truth. In the apocryphal Gnostic Gospel of Thomas, we read the following:

Simon Peter said to them, 'Mary should leave us, for females are not worthy of life.' Jesus said, 'See I am going to attract her to make her male so that she too might become a living spirit that resembles you males. For every female that makes itself male will enter the kingdom of heaven.[23]

Those words have long baffled, disturbed, and outraged many, and are probably no small reason why the entire Thomas Gospel has been considered non-canonical. Thomas' Gospel is also confusing to the New Agers because although it contains some decidedly Eastern-sounding wisdom (Jesus claiming to be one with the universe and so on) it ends with the seemingly sexist remark quoted above.

However, there is another perspective we can choose here. Instead of merely dismissing the quote as some sort of later editorial insertion by a patriarchal priesthood, we can understand it allegorically, as a psychological teaching about the relationship between the conscious and unconscious minds. Most world mythologies tend to equate masculine gods with the sky and symbols of ascending, and feminine gods with the earth and symbols of descending or grounding—'father sky, mother earth.' (As mentioned earlier in this chapter, there is a notable exception to that in the Egyptian sky goddess Nuit, but even there she symbolizes the womb of existence that is more akin to infinite space than to the sky 'above'.) In most mythic-spiritual traditions, the masculine symbolizes the abstract and the conscious, and the feminine the material and the unconscious. Even the words 'matter' and 'mother' have a common etymological root. From this perspective, the idea that a woman must 'become male' has nothing to do with gender; it is more a symbolic teaching about the unconscious becoming conscious. And that is unquestionably true. The unconscious in us must awaken and become conscious in order for us to evolve.

The mistake, however, is in judging the conscious as 'better' than the unconscious. Both have their critical function. 'Ascending' from matter to spirit is only one-half of the awakening process. Gurdjieff of all teachers was conscious of the need to bring consciousness 'down' into the body as well—or put another way, to understand that spirit and matter are ultimately not different. (See Katherine

Mansfield's remark below.)

Taken strictly as a reflection of his character, Gurdjieff's remarks on women above are interesting if for no other reason than that they reveal much about his nature. He possessed in great measure the masculine quality of 'courage under fire', that is, the willingness to speak his mind regardless of consequences or the judgments of others. The same was equally true of Crowley and Osho. That, paradoxically, often seems to be an attractive quality to women precisely because of the suggestion of strength it contains. In Gurdjieff's case in particular, he seems never to have allowed himself to be controlled by women in the slightest. Osho, by his own admission, was attempting something specific and radical (in terms of its novelty), that being to install women in most of the power positions in his organization. The complications that ensued from that decision were something he took in his stride and clearly saw as part of his life purpose. Crowley, likewise, held women as of paramount importance in the execution of his Great Work—after all, the Beast was not complete without his Babalon. (As an aside, many modern Western women today complain that there are few worthy 'Beasts' to be found.) Gurdjieff, however, was not concerned with exalting women, and perhaps for that reason he did not encounter exceptional difficulties with them beyond the normal matters (with the exception of Jesse Dwight; see below). He did, however, spend enormous energy in working with many of them, perhaps even more so in his old age.

Some glimpses of Gurdjieff's connection with the feminine polarity can be gleaned from his semi-autobiographical book *Meetings with Remarkable Men*. Of the Seekers of Truth that he joins forces with in the late 19th century, as described in the book, only one of them is a woman. As with Gurdjieff's wife she was Polish; her name was Vitvitskaia, and she was, by all accounts, a remarkable woman. William Patrick Patterson compared her to Mary Magdalene, the 'archetype of a feminine seeker'.[24]

Gurdjieff said he met her around 1890 when he was a very young man, barely twenty, at the beginning of his wandering years. She was described as 'beautiful and frivolous', and prone to depression. Her parents had died when she was young; she had later been defrauded and abandoned by some man, and ended up penniless and on the 'brink of moral ruin'.[25] The result was that she ended up 'poor' in all ways, but more along the lines of what Jesus referred to as 'blessed are the poor in spirit' — a type of emptiness that results from being freed of all encumbrances and tethers to one's past. In this state it is then possible to experience what Jesus further referred to when he said, 'Blessed are they which do hunger and thirst after right-eousness: for they shall be filled.' It means a great longing for truth can arise in one who has become 'poor', that is, *inwardly available* to the possibility of higher truths. Vitvitskaia later became an important member of the Seekers of Truth and became a trans-formed, awakened woman, specializing in an advanced under-standing of music and 'vibrations'. According to the story about her, as narrated in the book by Gurdjieff's 'essence-friend' Prince Lubovedsky, she died young of a sudden illness. The prince ends by declaring that of all the thousands of women he had known in fifty years of traveling the planet, she was the most unique.

Gurdjieff often said that his writings were to be understood on many levels, not just read as simple storyline. Historians of his life remain unclear whether Vitvitskaia (or Prince Lubovedsky for that matter) ever existed. But even as myth the story remains important because it is a rare example of a spiritual fable about a heroic journey from rags to spiritual richness in which the protagonist is a woman, not a man. There are far fewer female role models from history, actual or allegorical, centered on the spiritual life. Gurdjieff, for all his patriarchal bluster, was in many ways (along with Crowley) one of the first modern Western gurus to work in depth with women.

Like Crowley, Gurdjieff had a personality that tended to 'breed rumors'. Amongst those that periodically swirled around him there were the usual: that he was a Russian agent (the evidence is incon-clusive), a hypnotist (by his own account he was, although he claimed he renounced this skill in 1911); that he was Rasputin-like in his ability to seduce women (doubtful, although he did sleep with some of his female students); that he killed Katherine Mansfield (false); that he nearly raped a woman in the early years of the Prieure (unknown); that he flirted 'outrageously' with female students even as an old man in his last years (true—at least according to J.G. Bennett).

There is a highly amusing passage in Bennett's autobiography, *Witness: The Story of a Search*, in which he recounts the effect Gurdjieff had on some of Bennett's own English students. Bennett was a sincere seeker and (shortly before Gurdjieff's death at least) a devoted student of the master, but he was, by his own admission, a stiff Englishman. Doubtless, nothing he could have done would have prepared his English students for Gurdjieff's ribald nature. Bennett wrote,

[Some] were affronted by his behavior. They could not reconcile themselves to the drinking at his table and his obscene language. Several were terribly distressed by what they heard in Paris about his private life, and especially his relations with women. They took literally his boasting about his many sons and daughters and his irresistible appeal for women.[26]

On a darker note, the occult historian James Webb, in his scholarly and occasionally gossipy work *The Harmonious Circle* (1980), reports that one of the reasons Ouspensky may have broken with Gurdjieff was as follows:

Orage's explanation of the split is therefore of great interest. He always maintained that it was Gurdjieff's near-rape of Mrs. Y. in 1923-24 that finally decided Ouspensky. The date tallies, and the scandal was of such proportion that the explanation is very plausible. If Orage were right, this would explain Ouspensky's near obsession with Gurdjieff's integrity in his conversation with Mouravieff after Gurdjieff's [car] crash [in 1924]...[27]

As with Webb's account of Gurdjieff's encounter with Crowley in 1926 (see Chapter 13), he provides no source for the above, so nothing much can be concluded about it. I repeat it here only because Webb claimed to have spent nearly a decade traveling between Europe and North America interviewing people who had been involved in the Work, including some of Gurdjieff's direct students who were still alive in the 1970s when Webb was researching his book.

Regarding the noted New Zealand-born writer Katherine Mansfield, as mentioned elsewhere in this book, she came to Gurdjieff's Institute at the Prieure shortly after it opened in 1922, already with advanced tuberculosis. By all accounts, Gurdjieff treated her with kindness and only tried to make her comfortable; she died there a few months later. Because of her fame and youth (thirty-four years old) and because Gurdjieff was a new and unknown quantity in Europe at the time, it all made for a combination of factors that were ripe for the worst forms of gossip. Gurdjieff's name was whispered as the 'Oriental magician who had killed Katherine Mansfield'. It is interesting, however, to note that of all the women connected to both Crowley and Gurdjieff—and there were many—Katherine Mansfield was the only one of prominence who actually had some contact with both men. Her opinion of Crowley was not good—she referred to him as a 'pretentious and dirty person'.[28] Interestingly, when the Beast himself met Gurdjieff three years after Mansfield's death, the latter (according to Webb's account) also referred to Crowley as 'dirty'.

At any rate, there is no question that Mansfield trusted Gurdjieff, and although he was not able to affect any wonder cures on her she remained at his commune for the last months of her life and, according to what reports we have, she was content to be there. She went to him originally because she believed that 'he is the only man who understands that there is no division between body and spirit, who believes how they are related.'[29] Those are highly interesting remarks. Mansfield was a writer, and as such she was an intellectual first and foremost. Doubtless, she had a longing to be more connected to her body, to discover some semblance of spirituality in physical reality. That she recognized that element as present in Gurdjieff's teachings (which it was) and as being rare in metaphysical circles (which it also was) is a testament to her level of understanding.

She was eventually encouraged to attempt various tasks, like learning Russian, sewing and rug making—practical matters that she had not given attention to in her life. She remarked, 'All the things that I have avoided in my life seem to find me out here.'[30] That again is a pointed remark, underscoring a very common matter in a bona fide mystery school, which is that a student will invariably be guided to move into unknown territory. The idea there is that as creatures of habit we generally seek out the known and the comfortable, anything or anywhere where we know the ropes to some extent. In order to enter unknown territory we have to be more present, sharper, more alert, and this in turn creates in us (if we stay with the process) an expanded sense of being. This is, essentially, what Nietzsche was referring to when he said 'I give thanks for suffering!' To enter the unknown is often to suffer, but in so doing, to learn and to grow, which frequently ends in the quiet glow of accomplishment and joy.

There is, however, no evidence that Gurdjieff ever forced Mansfield to do anything, as her own copious diary notes attest to. He was always gentle with her, even as he would roar and bellow at healthier students. Mansfield's husband, Middleton Murry, was less convinced however. She had not been at the Prieure for a month before he began to suspect that she was being 'hypnotized'. This (in one form or another) is the fear of many men when their woman is in the company of a charismatic and powerful older man, but in Gurdjieff's case it was all enhanced because of the sheer mystery of his background.

She reported in one of her own accounts of being asked by

Gurdjieff to simply sit in a corner in the kitchen and observe things. The kitchen of any commune is invariably a lively place—much as it tends to be the center of energy in a typical house party—and doubtless Gurdjieff put her there to expose her to plenty of energy. While there she remarked on the liveliness of it all and had a special observation about Julia Ostrowska (Gurdjieff's young wife), saying she moved with the bearing of a queen.

Mansfield's last letter to her husband in England, shortly before she died of a sudden pulmonary hemorrhage, was poignant. She wrote,

> ...If I were allowed one single cry to God, that cry would be: I want to be real...but this place has taught me so far how unreal I am. It has taken from me one thing after another (the things never were mine) until at this present moment all I know really, really is that I am not annihilated and that I hope—more than hope—believe.[31]

Mansfield was buried in January of 1923 in the town cemetery in Avon near the Prieure. When Gurdjieff himself passed away nearly a quarter of a century later he was buried in a plot beside Mansfield's. After her death, her husband suspended judgment about Gurdjieff, but near the end of his own life he generously concluded: 'Katherine made of it an instrument for that process of self-annihilation which is necessary for the spiritual rebirth, whereby we enter the Kingdom of Love. I am certain that she achieved her purpose, and that the Institute lent itself to it.'[32]

Much more complicated than Gurdjieff's association with Katherine Mansfield was his connection with another strong willed young woman, the American Jesse Dwight. For some seven years he was to be locked into a difficult triangle with her and his close student A.R. Orage. It was not a 'love-triangle'—Gurdjieff and Dwight were not physically involved—but it was an interesting dynamic in which at times painful lessons unfolded for all three.

Gurdjieff and Orage were approximately the same age; Jesse was nearly thirty years younger. For much of the 1920s, Orage was Gurdjieff's point man in America, and as a brilliant intellectual and charming speaker who was deeply devoted to Gurdjieff, he was invaluable to the master. Jesse, however, was not a serious seeker and was more intent on starting a family with Orage and living a conventional life with him. Inevitably, Orage had to choose, and ultimately opted for his woman over his master.

It was while in New York in early 1924 that Orage, fifty at the time, met Jesse Dwight, an attractive and bright woman in her early twenties. Jesse became smitten with the handsome and articulate Orage while attending one of his lectures he was giving on Gurdjieff's system, and offered to organize talks for him at her bookshop, as well as to serve as his unofficial secretary at the same time. Their relationship began soon after and for the next seven years or so Gurdjieff battled with Jesse for the loyalty of Orage. At one point he famously said to her, 'If you take away my Super Idiot (one of his terms for Orage) you will burn in boiling oil!' On another occasion, when Gurdjieff insisted she sail to France and stay at the Prieure for a while, she shouted in his face, 'I hate you!'[33]

Orage, for his part, believed that he'd walked out on a previous marriage and was determined not to do so again. And so he was often torn between his love and devotion to his master, and his love and attraction for his beautiful young mate. By 1931 he'd chosen Jesse (who was his wife by then, and mother of two of his children). He did not live much longer, however, passing away suddenly in 1934 at the age of 61. When Gurdjieff was informed of his passing he is reported to have allowed a rare display of grief. 'This man,' he said, 'my brother.' For Gurdjieff, autocratic, patriarchal, unapproachable man that in many respects he was, this was a startling display of affection.

A number of remarkable women saw themselves as devoted students of Gurdjieff over the years—Julia Ostrowska (his wife), Olga de Hartmann, Sophie Ouspensky and Jeanne de Salzmann in particular. But of particular interest was the group of three women who began studying closely under Gurdjieff in 1935—Solito Solano, Kathryn Hulme, and Louise Davidson. This group came to be known as 'The Rope', and was later joined by Margaret Anderson, Jane Heap, Georgette Leblanc, Monique Serrure, Elizabeth Gordon, Dorothy Caruso, and Alice Rohrer. Most of the women were writers, intellectuals, and lesbians, and most were single. Many of them had daily contact with Gurdjieff until 1939 when the group came to an end.

Interestingly, Gurdjieff also assigned animal names to these women, much as Crowley had done with his 'Scarlet Women'. He called Solano 'the Canary'; Anderson was 'the Tibetan Yak'; Hulme was 'the Crocodile'; Rohrer was assigned two names, 'the Boa-constrictor' for her 'outer animal', and 'the Tapeworm' for her 'inner animal'; and Davidson was 'the Sardine'. Gordon was designated 'Mother Superior'. By all accounts, these women benefited from the fact that Gurdjieff, in his sixties at the time he was teaching them, had mellowed somewhat by then; Solano, in her diaries, reports that the tone of many of the meetings was lighthearted and humorous. Solano's story itself is particularly interesting; when she first met Gurdjieff in 1935 she was put off. She had been seated right beside him for an extended lunch with a group of people, and said he spent two hours muttering in bad English. She decided by the end of the lunch that she 'rather disliked him'. And yet, not long after, she was to become his secretary.

A number of the 'Rope' women later went on to write books about their years with Gurdjieff, and although it is clear that by this time he had mellowed, he was still frequently blunt and often crude. One of his favorite words was the French term *merde* (shit). Common expressions he would use were 'you are *merde* of *merde*', or 'your friend is *merde*; seeing his *merdeness* is good, as it helps you to see your own *merdeness*'. There is a strong sense that it was precisely this straightforward and earthy quality that drew so many women to him. He never pandered to sensibilities. He simply called it like he saw it. And because of his vast experience with human nature, what he 'saw' was more often than not spot on.

Regarding the function of sex in the context of a conscious life, Gurdjieff had some very pointed ideas. He taught that for the average (by Gurdjieff's terms, 'asleep') person, the main purpose of sex (outside of procreation) is as a medium to discharge negative energy. If sex energy is not released this way it becomes a toxic build-up. Accordingly, Gurdjieff warned against the dangers of confusing the sex function (in its typical use) with the idea of 'love'. It is more properly an act of necessary maintenance, something like changing the oil in a car from time to time. Most people who do not have a regular or semi-regular sex life tend to redirect their sex energy into fantasy, which is in the opposite direction of being awake. Gurdjieff referred to this wastage of energy as 'masturbation' and stated that there were, naturally, many kinds of masturbation, not all of them physical.

Gurdjieff's teachings here take on an interesting new light in this current era of Internet technology, in which graphic pornography of practically any kind can be found easily and for free by any person with access to a standard personal computer and Internet connection. Gurdjieff used the term 'involution' to describe a degrading of quality, and referred in particular to the involution of one's sex energy via excessive indulgence in fantasy. In that regard, modern access to pornography is something of a double-edged sword. The negative elements of it lie in the wastage of time involved in surfing porn sites; the dehumanization of women (and men, for that matter) by the tendency to see them merely as forms of flesh to be used and discarded; and the tendency to promote masturbation and thus contribute to wastage of sex energy in general. On the other hand, the fact that the pornography is graphically visual relieves the person watching it from the need for excessive inner imagination—there is little need to visually fantasize if one has only to access a porn site and can watch people 'in action'. In addition, there is the possibility that some can use pornography as a mean to release guilt by learning to embrace more fully one's shadow elements in the sexual domain. It is often said that one of the values of visual art or film is to help one get in touch with repressed thoughts and feelings. Similarly, porn can aid (at least in theory) in getting in touch with sexual guilt and related denied sexual thoughts and feelings—and learning to accept them. Transformation cannot occur prior to acceptance. We cannot transform anger, for example, without first acknowledging and accepting the reality that have anger within us.

Gurdjieff taught that sex, misused, is the main force behind 'slavery', that is the tendency to be controlled by our own unconsciousness. When improperly used its energy gets 'stolen' by other parts of us resulting in a person who is in the grip of an overactive mind—that is, who lives too much in idle thought and fantasy. He went so far as to claim that seventy-five percent of our thoughts originate from the 'sex center'.[34]

As for Gurdjieff the man, unquestionably he himself had a strong sexual energy. He is known to have alternated periods of sexual abstinence with periods of intense activity. By modern standards, Gurdjieff was no saint—in fact, he would have been pilloried in these times of extreme sensitivity to sexual protocols. He had sexual relations with a number of his female students as well as other chance encounters. According to Bennett, a number of his female students bore him children, and further, a number of them claimed that only those women who slept with him truly understood his work.[35] (That, however, is a claim that has been made by more than one follower of a celebrity.) Bennett further reported that Gurdjieff, despite his close involvement with many women and his many exceptional female students, always maintained that it was 'not the role of women to take responsibility and make decisions'.[36] If in this regard only, Osho would have disagreed. Or more accurately, Osho attempted to take Gurdjieff's work to another level. The jury is still out as to whether he succeeded or not.

Osho: the 'Sex Guru'

Few gurus of this or any time received as many snide comments about them as Osho did, as well as ludicrous titles geared toward mocking his modernized Tantric teachings. The 'Sex Guru' was the most common one, the 'Hugh Hefner of the spiritual world' being the funniest (and most absurd), all these stemming largely from his very first published book, *From Sex to Superconsciousness* (1968). This book was, like all of his books, a transcription of a live talk he gave — in this case, at a major convention of Hindu religious leaders. Osho had been invited to discourse on love. Predictably, and doubtless with relish, he spoke at length about how all so-called love, not to mention higher spiritual ecstatic states, were bogus if sexual energy was not first embraced and seen as completely innocent. An uproar resulted; Osho was summarily booted out of the conference.

Osho was surrounded by a great number of adoring female disciples and he would eventually utilize several of them as 'mediums' for his energy darshans. Much as Crowley used female students as mediums to contact (or help him contact) certain 'praeterhuman intelligences' and Gurdjieff used female students to aid him in the writing of his books, Osho used women as psychic and energetic conduits through which he could facilitate various extraordinary energy phenomena in the name of healing and energy transmissions.

To illustrate Osho's basic teaching on sex, he once related an old Buddhist fable of two celibate monks preparing to cross a river. Before they begin to wade across, an attractive young woman approaches them and asks one of them to carry her across as the river is somewhat deep. One of the monks agrees to do it. The other monk is aghast, as they both have taken vows to not only be celibate, but to never touch a woman either. And yet here is one of the monks agreeing to carry this young woman.

When they get to the other side of the river, the woman thanks the monk for carrying her and goes on her way. At that point, the monk who did not carry her turns on his companion, accusing him of breaking his vows. 'Why,' he demands, 'did you carry that woman?' To which the first monk responds, 'I let her go already. It seems that you are the one who is still carrying her.'

It's a clever parable and sums up well the whole relationship between attachment and repression of desire. That being that the more we repress ourselves, the more attached we become to the object of our hidden desires.

The problem has always been this: for one who seeks deep spiritual illumination, transcendence of duality, there is commonly a certain pull toward aloneness, the condition of the mystic who seeks ultimate reality. And this tendency has more often than not been manifest in many of the more prominent spiritual realizers of history. When Jesus is reported in John's gospel to have said 'I and my Father are one', he is not saying anything about a human mate. The Buddha famously became a deadbeat father, suddenly abandoning his wife and young child to go on a prolonged mystical retreat in the forest. Bodhidharma, the legendary father of Zen, is reputed to have become so fed up with human relations and human ignorance that he spent almost a decade facing a wall in meditation. And this pull toward aloneness is not an exclusively masculine trait—there are many accounts of female mystics retreating from relationship and even the world at large, in order to deepen their spiritual practice.

The pull toward aloneness was clearly there in Crowley despite his many romantic dalliances. Gurdjieff embodied the spirit of Percival of the Holy Grail myths in his early years of seeking and although he did eventually marry Julia Ostrowska, after her early death in 1926 he remained basically unattached for the last two decades of his life (though not celibate by any stretch). Osho, even more than Crowley or Gurdjieff in this regard, was a solitary figure. His immediate inner circle was usually a coterie of women and a couple of men (his doctor and dentist) but all were entirely his disciples. Unlike Crowley and Gurdjieff, he never married and seems to have never had anything like an ongoing love relationship with one woman. The woman who was closest to him, the Englishwoman Christine Woolf (Ma Yoga Vivek) was basically his caretaker and companion, and although she had sexual relations with him, it was nothing like the standard man-woman relationship—she was his disciple before anything.

Osho's relationship with Vivek was anything but typical, however. When he was sixteen years old, he had a girlfriend of sorts, named Sashi, who died in 1948. Years later he would claim that Vivek was the reincarnation of this girl. Vivek herself claimed to remember her past life as Sashi also. After two decades of serving Osho, Vivek suddenly died in December of 1989 at around forty years of age. The cause of her death is mysterious; she is believed to have overdosed on sleeping pills but whether it was accidental or suicide was never determined. Osho, ailing physically at the time and only a few weeks away from his own passing, had little to say about Vivek's death, except that she had long struggled with depression. Many commented on how little they knew her, and how she seemed a singular and somewhat isolated figure, of a strange quality of unknowable solitude that in some ways was a natural reflection of Osho.[37]

Osho on many occasions talked about his years of deep aloneness that preceded his awakening at age twenty-one, and he also intimated on more than once occasion in later years that he had always, essentially, been alone. He further claimed to enjoy it, connecting it to his first seven years when he was raised by his maternal grandparents in a very natural setting without other playmates.

Of course, the rumors would always be there. High Milne (at one point a guard of Osho's in Pune, later losing his prestigious position and subsequently renouncing his discipleship), claimed that Osho slept with a number of his earlier disciples, in events that were called 'special *darshans*'. He also stated that these women were once gathered together by Laxmi (Osho's secretary at the time) and told never to talk to others about it as it would cause too much jealousy and misunderstanding.[38] In his portentously titled book, *Bhagwan: The God that Failed*, Milne made further unflattering remarks about his former master:

> Though Bhagwan [Osho] placed so much emphasis on the physical side of sex, he was by all accounts hardly the world's greatest lover himself. Like so many who set himself up as sexologists, his own sex life left much to be desired. Many of the women who slept with Osho told me that far from practicing what he preached and making sex last for an hour or more, it was often all over in a couple of minutes...most of his sexual pleasure seemed to lie in foreplay and voyeurism rather than in active performance.[39]

In response to this, Juliet Forman, in a chapter of her book, *Bhagwan: The Buddha for the Future*, amusingly titled *The Guard That Failed*, wrote,

> ...that Milne, having found in Osho an excuse to live out his sex-obsessed nature, should then turn puritanical and comment on his own master's supposed sexual proclivities, is downright hilarious![40]

Her point is well taken, because the Achilles Heel in the master-disciple relationship is always (for the disciple) the tendency to project disowned elements of one's darker nature onto the master, as a convenient means to avoid assuming responsibility for one's own inner work. Crowley was a far bigger target than Osho for such projections, and indeed he received them wholesale. Gurdjieff was also heavily projected on at times. But Osho had something that neither Crowley nor Gurdjieff ever did: a very large following. As such he was a much more dangerous figure for those who see it as their 'duty' to safeguard morals and established values. When a Hindu fanatic stood up during one of Osho's lectures in Pune in 1980 and hurled his knife at him (missing), he was never charged by local authorities. The reason? Osho spoke freely and openly about sex. This made him a pariah to Hindu religious authorities.

India, despite the matriarchal presence in its pantheon of goddesses (Shakti, Radha, Kali, Parvati, Laxmi, etc.), is still one of the most patriarchal nations on Earth. There are Hindu scriptures that proclaim that a woman should worship her husband as God no matter what. Interestingly, one of the sects (the Digambaras) of the religion Osho was raised in (Jainism) maintain that a woman is incapable of enlightenment and must be born again as a man in order to achieve liberation (an echo of the Gospel of Thomas).[41]

India is of course not unique—for centuries women have been oppressed, on social and political levels. The so-called women's liberation, however, is mostly a Western phenomenon technically begun in France in the late 1700s, then gaining steam in the late 1800s in the United Kingdom and America in its so-called 'first wave'. This, in turn, led to what has been called 'women's suffrage', or the right of women to vote. The first country to allow women to vote was New Zealand, in the 1890s. It was not until around 1920 that many countries (including the U.K., U.S., Russia, Germany, and Canada) allowed full voting rights to women.

The oppression and marginalization of women has been a natural and expected result of these centuries of limitation, but a powerful side-effect since the early 20th century and in particular since the '2nd wave feminism' that developed in the 1970s has been rampant gender confusion amongst both males and females, especially in relation to common sexual and spousal relationships and the issue of 'roles'. By way of a psycho-spiritual therapeutic response, there seems to have developed two main approaches to dealing with the relationship turmoil and general dysfunction: the more Tantric approach (that Osho largely taught), and a more gender-separation approach favored by communities that specialize in 'men's groups' and 'women's groups'. The latter is more akin to traditional monastic settings where men and women are separated.

Gurdjieff used something of this approach at the Prieure, having his male and female students sit apart from each other at meals and being apart from each other when using the 'Turkish baths'.

'Men's groups' and 'women's groups' did eventually appear at Osho's Pune ashram by the late 1980s. Osho had said that both genders needed their own liberation, not just women. Commenting on Women's Liberation he said,

> Woman certainly needs a great liberation, but what is happening in the name of liberation is stupid. It is imitation, not liberation...real liberation will make the woman authentically a woman, not an imitation of man. Right now that's what is happening: women are trying to be just like men...this is not liberation, this is a far deeper slavery—far deeper because the first slavery was imposed by men. This second slavery is deeper because it is created by the women themselves.[42]

Osho's teaching always remained fundamentally Tantric, if only in the sense of embracing relationship rather than avoiding it. Some of the inner work that went on in this regard in the therapy groups was interesting. I recall one group I participated in many years ago in which all participants (about forty people) were asked to simply take their clothes off and stand facing each other in a long line (men on one side, women on the other). We were then invited to simply say or ask anything we wanted to say or ask about each other's body. Of course some had an easier time with this than others. But the end result was remarkable. Leaving the group, one was left with a clear sense of extraordinary inner lightness brought about by the simple act of revealing one's naked body to a group of (mostly) strangers. The mere act of confronting the primal identification with the body had the result of freeing up both energy and attention.

Most people carry a deep identification with their bodies to a degree not recognized. To be identified means (in this context) to believe that one is *nothing but* one's body, and more to the point that one's essential worth derives *only* from one's body. That of course is the fundamental delusion that all wisdom traditions have always attempted to address. The Gnostics went to a far extreme with their belief that the spark of spiritual truth in each person is literally trapped in matter, and thus, matter is inherently evil. The Christian concept of 'original sin' (that was formulated by St. Augustine) and the condemnation of Eve in the Book of Genesis have arguably contributed to centuries of sexual dysfunction, as people (especially women) come to associate the body with something 'bad'. The Serpent in Genesis was viewed by some Gnostic sects as the real teacher who had come to liberate humanity from ignorance. In many ways he can be seen simply as a symbol of sexual awakening. Osho, in his inimical style, made light of the peculiar myths of Genesis by once announcing to Oregonians during a press conference that 'if it wasn't for the Serpent you would all be still in Eden chewing grass.'

Most scandals surrounding 20th century gurus were related to sex and power. This was true in Crowley's and Gurdjieff's case, and the same can be said of Osho. While Osho was never accused of acts involving specific individuals, his entire movement was seen in a suspect light in large part because of the sheer embodied expressiveness of so many of its members. At this point it is helpful to review the Eastern idea of *chakras*. The word means 'wheel' in Sanskrit, and is generally taken to refer to seven (the most commonly used number) levels or realms of consciousness. They correspond roughly to:

1st *chakra*: Base instincts concerned with survival and immediate relationship to the physical environment.

2nd *chakra*: Sexuality, as well as basic feelings/emotions.

3rd *chakra*: Personal power.

4th *chakra*: Love and compassion.

5th *chakra*: Communication and truth.

6th *chakra*: Intelligence as well as psychic sensitivity.

7th *chakra*: Wisdom, connection with the soul or universal intelligence.

A common knock against the so-called New Age movement, especially as it developed in the 1970s-80s under the influence of a number of popularizations, has been that it encourages a leaning toward the higher centers (*chakras* 4 through 7), and an avoidance of the lower. Put in Jungian psychological terms, this involves a level of denial/repression of the more elemental energies of the lower *chakras* and of what he called the 'shadow'.

Part of what made Crowley and Gurdjieff stand out so much was their lower *chakra* 'activity'; that is, their forays into intensely 1st *chakra* physical adventures (mountain climbing and hunting in Crowley's case, world travel by both of them during a time when traveling conditions were still relatively primitive); their well known 2nd *chakra* exploits (intensely active sex lives, often with students); and their 3rd *chakra* activities (willingness to exercise personal power, including in some of its darker aspects, such as vengeance, brow-beating, manipulation, law suits, and so on). (The latter being more evident in Crowley's case.) Osho himself had also been intensely physical as a young man but in his case his attention became gradually diverted into the higher *chakra* activities of meditation and an enormous reading program.

Osho, Gurdjieff, and Crowley are, in a sense—at least in terms of how they lived their lives— representative of a progression from lower to higher *chakras*. Each taught a remarkably similar antinomian version of transformation, each embraced ideals of transcendent levels of reality, and yet each man required for his own path a different emphasis on personal experience. Crowley (despite his brilliant intellect, poetic sensibility, and mystical sensitivity) with his repressive Plymouth upbringing needed to explore the lower *chakras*; Gurdjieff, doubtless raised with more affection than Crowley, seemed to manifest more heart-centered traits (compassion, principally), although of course he could and did demonstrate severity and harshness fairly often. Osho, despite all his Tantric teachings and the sexual openness of his community, was himself centered very much in the subtle energies of the higher *chakras.* He used to say that he was only loosely tethered to his body and to this world, and for any who ever sat in person with him, his claim had the ring of truth. I can say with certainty that of all the teachers I personally experienced, he was the most extraordinarily non-physical. In his lectures his body would assume a position, generally one leg crossed over the other, and there would be no movement in the lower part of his body at all, often for up to two (or even three) hours. Only his hands and head would move, but only very slowly. He rarely blinked. All this can be seen in many videoed lectures of his freely available on the Internet. (The general cynic's response at this point is 'drugs!' but in Osho's case there is no evidence of drug usage to a degree that could explain such mannerisms).

To see the unusualness of this, one has only to sit in a standard public place and watch people. It is a sea of commotion, constant restless motion. Even libraries are anything but still. And casual observation of even most spiritual teachers giving talks will show a body that moves far more than it is still. In fact, I have only encountered one other teacher in many years of moving through various spiritual communities who demonstrated Osho's remarkably unforced stillness of body (that being the Canadian guru John de Ruiter).

Gurdjieff was described by some as 'cat-like' in movement—Olga de Hartmann said her first impression of him was of a 'black panther' coming into the room. The feline association is telling because felines above all have extraordinary body-sensitivity and economy of movement. (This latter phrase was exactly how Fritz Peters described Gurdjieff's wife, Julia Ostrowska.)

For Osho, the key lay in the second (sex) *chakra*, and on that point, Crowley and Gurdjieff were in absolute agreement. Gurdjieff used to say that the sex center in the average person tended to influence around 75% of their thinking. (He was not referring just to sexual fantasy but rather to the force and vehemence of sexual energy, which when frustrated, manifests in all sorts of problematic, neurotic ways.) Wilhelm Reich essentially said the same thing. Osho, in his trademark take no prisoners style, said 'I want to make it absolutely clear that people shying away from the truths of life are the enemies of humanity. Someone who says to you, 'Don't ever discuss sex' is humanity's enemy.'[43]

Crowley's position on sexual energy and its expression is summed up in these excerpts from the *Confessions*:

> The shocking evils which we all deplore are principally due to the perversion produced by suppressions. The feeling that it is shameful and the sense of sin cause concealment, which is ignoble, and internal conflict which creates distortion, neurosis, and ends in explosion...The sexual instinct thus freed from its bonds will no more be liable to assume monstrous shapes. Perversion will become as rare as the freaks in a dime museum.[44]

Osho's teaching, coming forty years after Crowley wrote those words, exactly parallels it in philosophy and spirit:

> Ninety-eight percent of Man's mental illness is because of suppression of sex. Ninety-nine percent of women's hysteria and related illnesses is because of sexual repression. If people are so restless, so agitated, so unhappy and suffering, it is because they have turned their backs on a powerful life-energy without trying to understand it.[45]

According to Osho, there is a key and historical link between sex and meditation, and it is this: Man's first experience of 'no-mind', that is, of a calm present awareness that is temporarily not conscious of time, was through the sexual orgasm. The intensity of orgasm is such that it has the power to overcome the thinking mind, resulting in a moment of pure desirelessness. This state is experienced as blissful. And so the natural tendency was for people to begin to look for other ways to recapture this state of blissful contentment. Osho asserts that from that intention, meditation was slowly developed—the attempt to recreate mental quietude that accompanies sexual orgasm without sexual activity itself.

Osho was, however, the consummate trickster teacher, demonstrated by the fact that he would invariably counteract something he'd said before with something different in the future. With regards to sex, after emphasizing its naturalness and importance, he later said it was nothing but 'stupid gymnastics'. What he meant, of course, is that sex that remains only sex is ultimately a kind of stagnation, a lack of growth. His main teaching was that sex was a doorway, not an end in itself. And this is why the label 'sex guru' for him was ultimately inaccurate.

Again, this was Crowley's position also. He maintained that the sole purpose of sex was to aid one to do one's True Will—what Osho had originally referred to as 'Superconsciousness' (although he would later drop that rather grandiose term, and speak more in terms of inner stillness and awareness). Crowley had reported that after the intense three year experiment at his Abbey, the participants naturally lost much of their interest in sex, simply because they had so totally indulged it in every possible way.

Osho emphasized that sex was the beginning, not the end. For him, meditation was the key, and in fact meditation is the only teaching that he never varied from his whole life. But like Crowley and Gurdjieff he was attempting to include all seven *chakras* (as it were) in his teaching and vision. For that to be, sex must be included and even emphasized, because of its power to disrupt and disturb.

The idea that Osho embraced all seven domains of human consciousness equally (that is, all possible human experience in a body) was an important point to understand about his teachings, because many were under the impression that his was the 'way of the heart' and that he exalted the heart above everything else. This was not actually the case. He clarified that point once as follows:

My way has been described as that of the heart, but it is not true.
The heart will give you all kinds of imaginings, hallucinations,
illusions, sweet dreams—but it cannot give you the truth. The
truth is behind both [head and heart]; it is your consciousness,
which is neither head nor heart. Just because the consciousness
can separate from both, it can use both in harmony.[46]

Echoing Gurdjieff's Law of Three, Osho added,

As your meditation becomes deeper, as your identification with
the head and the heart starts falling, you find yourself becoming
a triangle. And your reality is in the third force in you: the
consciousness. Consciousness can manage very easily, because
both the head and the heart belong to it.[47]

Chapter 12
Of Drugged Sages, Drunken Idiots, and Mysterious Deaths

I am the Snake that giveth Knowledge & Delight and bright glory, and stir the hearts of men with drunkenness. To worship me take wine and strange drugs whereof I will tell my prophet, & be drunk thereof!
The Book of the Law, II: 22

People wish to be settled; only as far as they are unsettled is there any hope for them.
Emerson

Of our three subjects Aleister Crowley would naturally be assumed to be the main star of this chapter. He practically wrote the book on combining a life of highly disciplined psycho-spiritual practice with a broad and deep range of drug exploration. Gurdjieff's drug of choice was primarily alcohol, something he used directly as a teaching aid, in his 'idiot toasts' and regular Dionysian feasts. Osho's role in this chapter is highly controversial and still unclear. His attitude toward drugs and alcohol was, as with everything else, beyond morality—his sole concern was with waking up. This Tantric acceptance inevitably resulted in considerable drug and alcohol exploration amongst many of his followers, although few used these substances to any significant degree. As an example, back in 1991 I used to conclude my day at Osho's ashram in Pune with a visit to the 'Osho Zen Bar'—the only alcohol-serving bar to be found in any ashram anywhere in India. (This bar no longer exists, having been closed down some time in the '90s.) It was nicknamed the Wunderbar, a plug at Osho's high percentage of German followers. Although outwardly appearing to be a typical Western style pub or bar, it in fact closed every evening at the tame hour of 10pm, to lyrics played on a loudspeaker of an Osho devotional song that went, *Home is where the heart is...*

Zen pubs aside, in Osho's case, a look into the matter of drugs is warranted in view of the manner of his surprising physical deterioration and death at the relatively young age of fifty-eight. He did, as is well known, accuse the Reagan Administration of orchestrating his death via slow-acting radiation poisoning, effectively re-enacting the drama of Socrates who was famously forced to drink hemlock as punishment for his rebelliousness and his 'corrupting the youth' of Athens. However, it also eventually came to be known that Osho used to undergo dental sessions during which, under the influence of nitrous oxide, he dictated at least three books. How he could dictate books while having his teeth worked on is unclear—or rather, what is reasonably clear is that some of these 'dental sessions' were not in fact that. The fact that he had many dozens of them would seem to emphasize that point. Accordingly, an argument has been mounted by some that he was in fact indulging in nitrous oxide usage to the point of addiction, and that this may have been a factor in his death. We will explore all this below.

Crowley, the 'High' Magician

Crowley's vast range of drug experimentation culminated with his addiction to heroin that he struggled with for the last quarter century of his life. Strictly speaking, however, Crowley's initial usage of drugs was as an entheogen; that is, employing a psychoactive agent for the purposes of psychological and spiritual (or shamanic, if you will) investigation. He argued in his 1908 essay, *The Psychology of Hashish*, that a classic problem confronted by meditators or practitioners of other forms of mysticism is something he termed as 'dryness' that 'hardens and sterilizes the soul'. He went on to suggest that occasional usage of drugs like hashish can aid in 'rolling away the stone' to get at deeper levels of the mind ordinarily not accessible to most meditators. He did, however, recommend that such drug exploration be temporary, and that meditative discipline be soon returned to.

Osho—who back when he was named Bhagwan Shree Rajneesh once famously replied to a question about his attitude toward drugs with, 'Are you kidding? My name is Bhagwan Shree Hashish'— mostly contended that the 'dryness' Crowley referred to is essentially repression, something endemic to modern Western man. He further argued that this repression could best be dislodged by deep psychotherapy that employs cathartic techniques (see Chapter 17). Given Crowley's Victorian upbringing, the 'dryness' he referred to may well have been the face of repression that he felt he could not fully break free from despite his courageous and outrageous character.

Be that as it may, Crowley's forays into the realm of mind altering substances began back when he was a young man living in London with his Golden Dawn mentor Allan Bennett. The year was 1899; Crowley was twenty-four, Bennett twenty-seven. Crowley, fresh from a large inheritance, was comfortable financially. Bennett, though Crowley's superior in esoteric knowledge and practical experience of it, was poor. The two struck up a close friendship and an arrangement—Bennett would abandon his hovel of a home that he was co-habiting with others and come live free of rent in Crowley's spacious flat in exchange for mentoring the younger man in the magical arts.

Bennett had asthma, which caused him great suffering (something Crowley described vividly in his *Confessions*) and he used drugs regularly to gain some measure of relief from it—opium, morphine, cocaine, and chloroform. This appears to be the origin of Crowley's lifelong usage of drugs. And so the irony: Crowley's first mentor in the occult arts—and Bennett was indeed a highly respected magician in London at that time—would also prove to be influential in launching Crowley's lifelong experiments and terrible struggles with narcotics. Bennett tutored Crowley in many of the fundamentals of ritual magic and occultism—invocation, evocation, divination, clairvoyance, study of the Qabalah, geomancy, skrying, tarot, and so forth. Along with all that, the two undertook certain experiments with drugs, particularly cocaine.

Back in 1899 most (by current definition) recreational drugs, such as hashish, opium, cocaine, and even heroin, were legal and easily accessible in pharmacies. The Dangerous Drug Act did not appear until 1920. It was in that year, coincidentally, that Crowley, at his Abbey of Thelema in Cefalu, composed a poem with the memorable lines,

Stab your demoniac smile to my brain
Soak me in cognac, cunt and cocaine
Heart of my heart, come out of the rain
Let's have another go of cocaine

Cocaine and heroin were Crowley's two main psychoactive aids, and to a lesser degree, opium and peyote. Cocaine, as is well known, has long been a drug of choice for those with money to burn, as well as for those in some tribal cultures. (Peruvian Indians have likened it to God himself.) The drug is renowned for producing a sense of effortless and fearless bliss. Negative states of mind (anxiety, despair, hopelessness, depression) are banished by the drug and all seems to be well in one's world. Of course, the 'fine print' dangers accompanying the benefits can be lethal. Overdosing on cocaine can destroy the heart, resulting in rapid death. And the blissful effects of it diminish over time if it is used chronically. Once habituated to, anxiety attacks, nervous tension, and even paranoia can easily result.

Heroin—a morphine derivative—was initially used mainly as a cure for morphine addiction. Ironically, the drug was originally promoted as lacking the addictive effects of morphine. This of course turned out to be spectacularly mistaken; heroin is the most addictive of the opiates. The word itself, oddly enough, is taken from the Greek *heros*, meaning 'hero', because of the euphoric, triumphant inner state it creates. Heroin derives from the opiate family, ultimately originating in the opium poppy, but cocaine derives from the South American coca plant and produces very different effects. Heroin loosely can be understood as a dissociative drug, resulting in a disconnection from pain and a general 'turning-off'. Cocaine is a stimulant, 'turning-on', livening and intensifying the vividness of the moment. Heroin aids in killing pain (although heroin addiction is one of the worst addictions possible, and creates a whole new kind of psychological pain that is much worse). Cocaine aids in feeling alive and rising above depressive, life-negative mental states, but easily creates dependency. Opium, the source drug for derivates like codeine, Demerol, morphine, heroin, etc., has been so popular throughout history that it even resulted in two large scale wars in the 19th century between Britain and China (the famed 'Opium Wars'). As a drug, it produces a smooth ecstasy that most people find seductively appealing, but the price is a rapid addiction to it that is hard to break.[1]

Crowley's peyote usage is another interesting example of how he was ahead of his time. He used to hold 'peyote parties' in both London and New York City on occasion, primarily for the purposes of mystical adventurism—in so doing, foreshadowing the popular interest in both mescaline (the psychoactive element in peyote) and more obscure drugs such as Ayahuasca, amongst Westerners in the latter half of the 20th century. Much of this had its origins in Carlos Castaneda's first two books published in the early 1970s, but Crowley was actively investigating such matters over a half-century before.

In 1917 during World War One, Crowley, forty-two years of age, was living in New York City with a lover, Anna Miller. Through Miller he met another woman, Roddie Minor, who became for a while his Scarlet Woman. At that time, Crowley practiced sex magick with both these women, as well as with Walter Grey, an African-American man. Anna eventually left and Crowley deepened his involvement with Roddie. She was a pharmacist by training and, in addition to being sexually and mystically adventurous, she was also open to recreational drug experimentation with Crowley, and this they did to a considerable degree. One day in early 1918, Roddie, after smoking opium, went into a trance state and started describing visions she was having. At first Crowley, writing at his desk, paid no notice to her—he had after all been trained in critical thought and was not gullible—but eventually Roddie murmured something that caught his attention. It was a reference to a mysterious 'egg under a palm tree' which just so happened to be an exact description of something Crowley and a previous partner, Mary Desti, had been instructed to find. This information came about while he and Desti had been in Zurich six years before performing a magical procedure he'd later call the Abuldiz Working. (The drug used on that occasion had been alcohol.)

Roddie then claimed that she was in contact with a 'discarnate entity' she called 'the Wizard', and she told Crowley that this entity wanted to communicate with him. (This was comparable to the events with Rose Kelly in Cairo fourteen years before when Rose told Crowley that the Egyptian god Horus wanted to communicate with him.) Crowley then 'tested' the entity with a cross examination ending with a technical question involving the spelling of one of his initiate names. The answers satisfied him. The entity then told him that its name was Amalantrah. Over the next six months or so, he and Roddie made frequent evocations of Amalantrah, generally via a combination of sex magick and drug sessions involving (mainly) opium and hashish.

In one such session, Crowley claimed that an entity made contact with him and manifested in his vision in a particular form. He made a drawing of it. Crowley had been an amateur artist (not one of his more commonly known attributes) of some talent. This drawing, which he displayed in New York City in 1919, has since gone on to some fame. In appearance it depicts a dwarfish figure, showing only the head and shoulders. The head is bulbous at the top, hugely out of proportion to the body (at least by human terms). The nostrils and mouth are very small, as are the eyes. The entity came to be known as 'Lam'.

The subsequent events stemming from Crowley and Minor's original Amalantrah Working are convoluted and if nothing else a powerful testament to the nature of cause and effect as it applies to the human creation of a mystical (and religious) tradition. In brief, the domino-like events—which require a temporary anthropological willingness to suspend judgment while following—transpired like this: it is believed by many modern occultists that Crowley and Minor opened a 'portal' of sorts, a type of shamanic bridge, between this world and a particular non-terrestrial dimension allowing for communication between that world and this one. This 'portal' was then believed to have been opened further by the efforts of Jack Parsons (rocket scientist and co-founder of the Jet Propulsion Laboratory) and L. Ron Hubbard (the later founder of Scientology) when in 1946 they undertook an operation called the 'Babalon Working'. This was a mystical procedure that has as its stated intent the effort to incarnate a 'goddess' on Earth, and thereby influence the course of civilization for the better. In effect, they were trying to enact what Crowley had described in his 1929 novel *Moonchild* (that being the term Crowley used for an incarnated superior being— essentially, a messiah). Parsons was young, enthusiastic, and a devoted student of Crowley's. His main reasoning behind the operation was that Crowley's New Aeon, that of Horus, needed a feminine counterpart—a higher dimensional goddess symbolized by the important Thelemic deity Babalon—to balance it.

Predictably, the 'Babalon Working' failed to produce an incarnated goddess. Crowley dismissed the whole enterprise as nonsense. In a letter to Karl Germer (who succeeded him as outer head of the Ordo Templi Orientis upon Crowley's death in 1947) he wrote, 'I get fairly frantic when I contemplate the idiocy of these louts'.[2] His perception on that matter may have been accurate. Hubbard and Parsons later had a falling out and in 1952 Parsons blew himself up in a lab experiment gone awry. Hubbard would later, after Crowley's death, refer to the Beast as 'my very good friend'—this despite the fact that they'd never met and Crowley had dismissed Hubbard as a con man after he'd bailed on a business arrangement with Parsons and run off with the latter's wife.[3]

At any rate, the fantastic tapestry does not end there: many occultists further believe that the actions of Hubbard and Parsons allowed for a 'widening' of the inter-dimensional breach, which in turn permitted deeper and more expanded contacts with extraterrestrial entities. Some groups, such as Kenneth Grant's Typhonian Order, dedicated themselves deeply to the study and exploration of this.[4] But in terms of interesting synchronicities, what bears mention is that the entity described by Crowley as 'Lam' and drawn by him bears considerable similarities to the visual form of a type of extraterrestrial known in the UFO communities as a 'Grey', or more elaborately, as a Zeta Reticuli (the name of an actual star believed by some to be their point of origin). Occultists are quick to note that Parsons' and Hubbard's failed Babalon Working took place in 1946; it was one year later that mass sightings of UFOs began.

This 'Grey' alien, complete with oversized bulbous head and huge insect-like eyes was famously depicted on the cover of Whitley Strieber's 1987 bestselling book *Communion* (subsequently made into a feature film in 1989 starring Christopher Walken). Although Strieber had been well known prior to *Communion* as a fiction author, he claimed his encounters with the Grey aliens—the 'visitors' he called them—were actual events. (Despite the seeming improbability of this claim, I have always thought that Strieber's experiences have the ring of truth and a legitimate shamanic feel to them, and I have no doubt that these were real encounters for him. His interpretation of what they mean is another matter, one the reader must make their own mind up about.) Strieber wrote several follow up books on the matter. Interestingly, he himself at one point had been involved with the Gurdjieff Foundation, attending group meetings between 1970 and 1983. He would later state that the visitors were 'true masters' and who offered themselves 'as guides' for him.[5]

An alien with a big head and a weak, small body would seem to be apt symbolism for the predominance of what Gurdjieff called the 'Intellectual Center' in modern man (since the advent of the 17th century Age of Reason, basically)—and in particular, the tendency to overemphasize this center in such a way that leads to over-identification with it. At any rate, it is significant to note that the now iconic image of bulbous-headed dwarfish aliens was originally precipitated by consciousness changes induced by drugs—most notably in this case, opium—from Crowley's and Minor's Amalantrah Operation in New York City in 1918. The issue of 'other-dimensional' contacts with spirit guides, alien beings, and the like, is of course highly problematic and not a matter that can be conclusively judged by intellectual analysis alone. Much as with all shamanic-type work, it is entirely experiential and is a specific domain of consciousness that needs to be properly entered in order to be understood, let alone legitimately judged. These experiences can no more be properly understood by detached intellectual observation than a foreign country can be truly known by studying travel books about it or by looking at maps of it. We need to actually go there to know it in any significant way.

The idea of communicating with inter-dimensional or extraterrestrial beings while in trance brought about in part by psychotropic agents (or, as in many cases like Strieber's, without such aids), is very old and is common in many tribal cultures. Mircea Eliade, in his landmark book, *Shamanism: Archaic Techniques of Ecstasy*, recounts many such examples, as does Graham Hancock in his more recent work, *Supernatural*. (In 1996, I was spending some time in the high desert of the American southwest and at one point made a stop in Sedona, an extraordinary town in northern Arizona that is populated partly by 19th century cowboys and partly by occult, spiritual, and New Age metaphysicians of all stripes. While there I wandered one day into a small shop that featured elaborately designed Hopi Indian *katchina* dolls. I was looking at a whole shelf-full of them and had decided to buy one when I remarked to the clerk that it was not easy to choose. She answered with all the wisdom of a kitchen-witch: 'You don't pick them, they pick *you*.' A moment later I 'chose' the Antelope Man doll. It was an exceptional work of art. But after examining it, it became clear how easily this thing could have been taken for some sort of extraterrestrial. The head was angular and looked something like a strange robot—and in fact, many amongst the Hopi regard them as inter-dimensional entities.)

Crowley left Roddie Minor in mid-1919, returning to Britain. Around that time his asthma, which he had developed several years after his mountain climbing expeditions (and which he believed were the cause of it, as well as his emphysema), began to worsen. An English doctor prescribed heroin as relief from the asthmatic spasms. This is where his heroin addiction began—in part due to the simple ignorance of medical authorities in those days. The following year, in 1920, he headed off to Sicily with his new partner, Leah Hirsig, to found their Abbey of Thelema. In the summer of 1922, Crowley went with Leah to London where he dictated to her the novel *Diary of a Drug Fiend* in a feverish twenty-seven days. The book immediately found a publisher and almost as immediately brought Crowley a fresh wave of infamy. At the time, he was still directing his Abbey in Sicily; he would not be expelled by Mussolini until the following year. He'd taken a break from the Abbey, traveling along with Leah to Paris and then to London.

Drug Fiend is over 120,000 words long; the reason Crowley could produce such a book in less than a month—a veritable Stephen King or Isaac Asimov rate of writing—was that the book was scarcely fiction, being more a thinly disguised recounting of Crowley's recent ventures with Leah at the Abbey. Basically, he was writing autobiography while dressing up the characters and storyline a bit. The fact that he could do such a thing is a testament as much as anything to the novelistic intensity and drama of his life.

Robert Anton Wilson referred to *Drug Fiend* as an 'epic of cocaine'. But the novel itself has a message that reaches far beyond drug usage, into the heart of Crowley's Thelemic teaching. The plot is simple enough: a young couple, Peter and Lou, having met at a night club while on cocaine, embark on an adventure of joint drug exploration (cocaine, and later heroin to calm their hyper-cocaine nerves). Soon they find themselves caught in the throes of addiction and descend into great suffering. The novel's section headings are borrowed from Dante's *Divine Comedy*; this part is predictably called *Inferno*.

They end up where most drug addicts end up, broke, and needing to do desperate things to survive (such as Lou turning to prostitution). They ultimately decide the whole thing is too painful and attempt, without success, to commit suicide. Sometime after this, they are led to a certain King Lamus, a magus who is based on Crowley himself. Peter and Lou enter Lamus' Abbey of Thelema (based of course on Crowley's actual Cefalu commune), where Lamus begins to teach and guide them. He allows them free drug usage while at the same time having them make daily journal entries of their experience. Along with this program of self-reflection, they are taught the basics of Thelema, in particular the idea of the True Will. One day Peter realizes that his True Will is to be an engineer. He had in fact been trained in this before but lost interest in it due to his having been spoilt by a large inheritance (since squandered). Lou also realizes her True Will which is to be a good and supportive wife to Peter. (Crowley remains ever the patriarch.) The drugs lose their power over them because they have both found and engaged their True Will. The idea—which is indeed sound—is that only the True Will, or the realizing of our highest passion, can overcome the self-defeating and self-sabotaging elements of the ego, in this case symbolized by the powerful dependencies created by narcotics.

This novel, released in a 1922 England that only just two years before had implemented the Dangerous Drug Act, caused a media uproar, and Crowley was duly castigated as someone attempting to corrupt English youth with foul ideas. The irony of course is that the primary message of the book is spiritual and healing, but the fact that the protagonists continued to use cocaine on occasion even after their awakening at the Abbey made it impossible to accept in the eyes of many.

Some comments should be made at this point about Crowley's asthma, which was a definite contributing factor behind his initial and ongoing drug usage. Israel Regardie, in his book, *The Eye in the Triangle*, argues that asthmatics are intrinsically fearful people, anxiety-ridden, and that asthma is in part symptomatic of this chronic repression of anxiety and fear. He believed that Crowley's own writings reveal that as a child he had been an 'insecure and frightened youngster'. He further claimed that Crowley, as well as his mentor Allan Bennett (also asthmatic), ultimately lacked the courage to properly recognize and embrace their fear and insecurities, instead covering it with bravado, adventurism, magical symbolism, and in Bennett's case, retreat into monkhood.[6]

There is *some* merit in Regardie's view. A Golden Dawn initiate and one-time secretary of Crowley's, Regardie was in later years influenced by the seminal Austrian psychotherapist Wilhelm Reich. One of Reich's basic ideas is that repressed emotional states leave behind a physical signature, resulting in muscular tension and subsequent 'character armoring' in the body. In effect, this is a type of psychological defense that enables one to not have to constantly feel their core-level fear—something like the psychological equivalent of a narcotic. Gurdjieff understood this concept also. His term for the inner mechanism by which we avoid facing our demons is 'buffers' which correspond essentially to the more modern psychological definition of 'defense-mechanisms'.

That Crowley had unresolved psychological issues—most notably his unhealed relationship with his mother, always a core-issue for both men and women—is clear enough. However, the problem with Regardie's view lays in the fact that Crowley, fear-ridden or not, did demonstrate remarkable courage at many points in his life. Climbing Himalayan mountains, hunting big game in southeast Asia, and summoning demons while alone in a dark, isolated country home in Scotland are not actions that are the province of cowards. Nor, it must be said, is plunging into relationship after relationship with complex, strong willed women. Regardie himself became asthmatic in 1932 and appears to have been far more monk-like than Crowley, being more like Bennett in that regard. And so, in Crowley's case, Regardie was likely projecting to some degree, that is, seeing a fear-ridden nature in Crowley that was as much, if not more, in himself.

Crowley emerged from his three year experiment at the Abbey of Thelema addicted to heroin and he struggled with this addiction for the remaining twenty-four years of his life. There were periods where he broke the addiction by dint of his powerful will and exceptional spiritual discipline, but these periods did not last. At his death at age seventy-two, he remained addicted. That he was still able to produce such a vast body of writings and maintained great clarity of thought until his last days is not surprising—more than one accomplished philosopher, scientist, writer, artist, musician, and even mystic has been heavily into drink or drugs of one sort or another. But Crowley was unusual in his tendency to go all out in whatever he did—which generally simply meant everything in excess. In the realm of drugs he was no different.

Gurdjieff, King of the Armagnac Idiots

Gurdjieff smoked like a chimney and at times drank like a fish. To that one might comment 'big deal', and indeed in Gurdjieff's time smoking was as commonplace as coffee drinking is now. An amusing story is recounted by Ouspensky when he describes an early visit to Gurdjieff in St. Petersburg around 1915. He describes a scene that 'astonished' him due to the fact that it consisted of a group of Gurdjieff's students sitting around in a room saying nothing. The silence impressed him, suggesting an almost monastic ambience created by the devoted truth-seekers. He then added that they did nothing but sit around smoking.[7] One can imagine this group of apostles huddled in a room absorbed in contemplation or self-observant silence, all in this great cloud of smoke, something like Zen Marlboro Men. In today's more Orwellian times, such a scene would doubtless result in someone calling the fire department, or the police for that matter.

On the issue of drugs, it's interesting to note that the very first topic that Ouspensky recalls discussing in his initial meeting with Gurdjieff in Moscow in 1915—at a 'small café in a noisy but not central street'—concerned narcotics. Ouspensky said to Gurdjieff,

> There are substances which yogis take to induce certain states. Might not these be, in certain cases, narcotics? I myself have carried out a number of experiments in this direction and everything I have read about magic proves to me quite clearly that all [spiritual] schools at all times and in all countries have made a very wide use of narcotics for the creation of those states which make 'magic' possible.[8]

Gurdjieff then responds at length, confirming that some spiritual schools indeed use narcotics, in particular hashish and opium. He further states that one of the main (and correct) purposes of using such drugs is to give a glimpse of what it is possible to attain by real work on oneself. The drugs are meant to open the mind up to higher possibilities; Gurdjieff admits that sometimes they are the easiest avenue for doing so.

That is, of course, exactly what the Peruvian-American writer Carlos Castaneda more or less claimed, in his best-selling (almost certainly fictional, though he claimed otherwise) books about his apprenticeship to the Yaqui Indian shaman don Juan Matus. Castaneda's first two books, *The Teachings of Don Juan* and *A Separate Reality*, were basically journals about his experiences taking peyote and related drugs under the guidance of an old and wise shaman. However, his third book (*Journey to Ixtlan*) changed course, as he was guided to undertake a number of psycho-spiritual exercises without any recourse to drugs. Don Juan explains that the drugs had been necessary to 'blast' Castaneda—an intellectual stuck in his head—and thereby open him up, but that ultimately they were to be discarded. One is reminded of Gurdjieff shouting at his student Rene Daumal 'Get out of your head Daumal! No more philosophy. Act, act, act!'[9]

The expression 'get out of your head' is often considered to be a fairly recent colloquialism stemming from the 1960s human potential movement, so it is interesting to see that Gurdjieff was already using it in the early 1940s. At any rate, the general view has long been that the most effective way to escape an over-active mind is either via something intensely physical—sex especially, but also labor or exercise—or by increased mindfulness of feelings and sensations. Or, via the time-honored lazy man's approach—drugs.

What does it mean to be 'stuck in one's head'? Contrary to some misinformed ideas, it has nothing to do with being 'intellectual'. It is entirely possible to be a balanced and harmonious individual and have a well developed intellectual component. Becoming enlightened does not mean that one no longer thinks or uses memory. What being 'in one's head' refers to, rather, is strong *identification* with thoughts, and a general neglect of feelings, sensations, and intuitions. This creates a 'top-heavy' person, one out of balance. To be strongly identified with thoughts means to get caught up in fantasy, idle and repetitive thought, rigid beliefs and perceptions, strong attachments to 'being right' about everything, and so on. Many neurotic states result from this, such as anxiety and all kinds of mental 'feedback loops' connected to obsessive states of mind. Depression is generally connected to over-identification with thoughts.

The capacity to get 'stuck in one's head' has very little relation to things like education level or intellectual development. A person with only marginal education, not given to intellectual study, can just as easily get 'caught up in their mind' as a PhD with a high IQ score. In other words, the issue is not the kind of mind we have, or its level of conventional training; the issue is our *relationship* with our mind. If we over-identify with thoughts we tend to lack perspective—in short, we lack consciousness in its greater sense. We get hung up on one tree and lose sight of the whole forest (not to mention where exactly we *are* in the forest).

Gurdjieff also told Ouspensky that drugs can, in addition to relaxing our attachment to our mind, be used to separate the personality from the essence (see Chapter 5 for more on personality vs. essence). He said that some drugs do so by effectively putting the personality to sleep. This can at times result in the person losing all of their ideals and beliefs, if those ideals and beliefs were nothing but cultural programming, that is, not truly their own thoughts and beliefs. Gurdjieff specified that the essence in everyone is different— in some it may be evolved, in some primitive and even 'stupid'— which would provide some sort of explanation as to why people respond differently when under the effects of powerful psychoactive drugs.

Ultimately, however, Gurdjieff's drug of choice was alcohol. J.G. Bennett reports that at the Prieure in 1923, 'Saturday was a feast day. Nearly every Saturday evening, there was a special meal with wines and spirits to drink.'[10] That is uncommon enough for a spiritual commune (if tame compared to Crowley's Abbey) but where Gurdjieff liberally used alcohol was in his famous Idiot Toast rituals. The general idea was that drink was a means to quickly bypass personality so that he could see deeper into his students. He said,

Alcohol opens, it shows many aspects of your interior; it is very important for knowing someone.[11]

Indeed alcohol—in specific, the psychoactive drug called ethanol, which is the type of alcohol found in booze—has long been the drug of choice the world over, utilized for any number of reasons. As with all drugs, its overriding purpose is to kill pain, whether psychological or physical. The Buddha's First Noble Truth is that life is sorrow, suffering, pain, and that this is a condition that none escape. Crowley himself ultimately disparaged Buddha's idea, proclaiming rather that life is inherent joy. Crowley's is certainly the more uplifting idea—and an awakened person does indeed perceive and express joy in being—but the Buddha, that supreme pragmatist, must be given his due. History bears out repeatedly the validity of his First Noble Truth. And most people unconsciously at least recognize this, otherwise mind-altering chemicals would never have been—and are arguably even more so today—so popular.

Not long after his car accident in 1924, Gurdjieff had begun his writing phase, tackling first his biggest project, *Beelzebub* (that ended up being over 1,000 pages long). While writing he would drink strong black coffee and his favorite alcoholic beverage, a type of French brandy known as Armagnac. (It is amusing to note that Gurdjieff wrote his magnum opus generally fuelled by alcohol or caffeine; Crowley dictated much of his massive *Confessions* while on cocaine or heroin; and even Osho dictated three books while influenced by nitrous oxide).

William James, in *The Varieties of Religious Experience* wrote,

The sway of alcohol over mankind is questionably due to its power to stimulate the mystical faculties of human nature, usually crushed to earth by the cold facts and dry criticisms of the sober hour. Sobriety diminishes, discriminates, and says no; drunkenness expands, unites, and says yes. It is in fact the great exciter of the Yes function in man. It brings its votary from the chill periphery of things to the radiant core. It makes him for the moment one with truth. Not through mere perversity do men run after it.[12]

James wrote that in 1902, a more innocent age to be sure, a time when heroin and cocaine could be gotten over the counter. Although his words are elegant and psychologically penetrating, he is writing from the mystical perspective, not with Alcoholics Anonymous (which did not exist then, having been founded in 1940) or abusive behavior and broken homes in mind. Alcohol has always been a potent drug but has become much more dangerous as technology has advanced. In James' time there were no drunk drivers, as there were no drivers (of cars, at any rate).

It has been sometimes said that nicotine suppresses anger, tetrahydrocannabinol (or THC, the active ingredient in marijuana and hashish) suppresses sadness, and alcohol suppresses fear. Anyone experientially familiar with those three substances can probably attest to that. The power of alcohol is, in a sense, much more basic than James' ideas of 'stimulating mystical faculties' and 'expanding'. His points are well taken but the probable reason alcohol appears to stimulate all that is simply because it blocks fear.

A fearless person is, naturally, capable of all sorts of things—taking all sorts of risks that can lead to advantageous results (many business ventures and relationships begin over drinks). But he is also incapable of sound judgment which is what makes him such a menace to himself and to others. Fear, though commonly disparaged as the worst manifestation of the ego's arsenal, has a key function when it comes to issues of survival and common sense. To fear the prospect of standing on a railway track in the face of an oncoming train is a good idea in general.

Although one or two people did emerge from their time with Crowley with a drug addiction of their own, I am unaware of any Gurdjieff student (during his life) who became alcoholic as a result of associating with him. Despite his drinking, there is no evidence that Gurdjieff was an alcoholic. He was, however, unique amongst prominent teachers in the West for utilizing alcohol as a teaching device. He first introduced his ritual called Toast of the Idiots in 1922 at the Prieure, but it was not until the 1940s at his apartment in Paris that he began hosting this ritual regularly. These ceremonial toasts would involve plenty of food as well as Armagnac and vodka. In referring to this Gurdjieff remarked,

> Alcohol was used by the ancient sages: not to get drunk, but to strengthen the power to wish.[13]

Gurdjieff was an old man then, in his 70s, but by all accounts his unpredictability and wild charisma were still largely in force. In the late 1940s in particular, after the war, his flat would be crowded on a nightly basis, people jammed in to an absurd degree, some literally standing on one leg due to lack of space. These evenings consisted of readings from Gurdjieff's manuscripts (*Beelzebub*, or *Meetings with Remarkable Men*, neither of which were yet published), as well as elaborate feasts that were usually prepared and cooked by Gurdjieff himself. He would also play music on his harmonium. Amongst all that were the ritual toasts of the Idiots.

By 'idiot' Gurdjieff did not mean the conventional fool. In additional to the usual definition, for him the word had a second, esoteric meaning. It was what he claimed sages of the past meant as 'to be oneself'. What is implied there is that a person who is getting free of the mass illusions of humanity is, in one sense, no longer playing by the conventional rules and so will look strange—mad even. (One is reminded of Dostoyevsky's novel, *The Idiot*, a term that referred to a character in the book that was in some ways based on Christ.)

Gurdjieff's scheme had a classification of twenty-one types of idiots, or twenty-one 'gradations of reason'. Idiot #1, the 'Ordinary Idiot', represents the most primitive or natural, and the eighteenth (not named by Gurdjieff) is the most advanced possible for a human being. Notably, this whole model is based on the same number of trump cards in the Tarot, if we subtract card #0, The Fool (who is, it could be said, the quintessential Idiot). The types were as follows:

1. Ordinary Idiot
2. Super Idiot
3. Arch Idiot
4. Hopeless Idiot
5. Compassionate Idiot
6. Squirming Idiot
7. Square Idiot
8. Round Idiot
9. Zigzag Idiot
10. Enlightened Idiot
11. Doubting Idiot
12. Swaggering Idiot
13. Born Idiot
14. Patented Idiot
15. Psychopathic Idiot
16. Polyhedral Idiot
17. No name, but is an 'advanced idiot'
18. No name, the highest possible for humans to reach.
19. A type of Idiot reserved for 'sons of God'. This includes Jesus Christ.
20. Also reserved for 'sons of God'.
21. Unique Idiot, which is God, or as Gurdjieff called him, 'Our Endlessness'.

At first glance this may all appear lighthearted but, in fact, it is a teaching of significant depth, tackling as it does some of the trickiest and most cunningly disguised aspects of the ego-mind. Interestingly, Gurdjieff used to say that type #18, the 'highest' possible for a human being, can only be attained after working backward from type #10—the Enlightened Idiot—down to #1, the Ordinary Idiot, so as to begin all over. This echoes to some extent Crowley's teachings on the Abyss, the initiation into the level of Magister Templi that he claimed to undergo in the Algerian desert with Victor Neuberg in 1909. It is an idea showing up in many different forms in various wisdom traditions: in order to go forward, to the highest levels of wisdom, we need to be essentially stripped of all our attachments, made naked before the divine—to go backward, in a sense. Bennett suggests that Jesus is referring to this when he specifies that we need to 'become as children again in order to enter into the kingdom'. We need to literally give it all up, in so doing demonstrating our deep love for, and absolute prioritization of, truth—and the corresponding willingness to realize it at all costs.

J.G. Bennett suggested Gurdjieff got the idea of the Idiot Toasts from a Sufi community, citing an ancient dervish tradition of ritual feasts; Gurdjieff's biographer James Moore casts doubt on this, owing to alcohol being forbidden in Islam. My own opinion is that Gurdjieff devised this particular version of a ritual feast himself. It bears all the marks of his character. His teaching, above all, was concerned with reducing ego in a direct, highly uncompromised way, and as an autocratic personality the approach of facilitating people into declaring their ego-idiocies in front of others would have fit naturally for him. Such work can be especially effective because it takes away any sort of egocentric specialness (it is very difficult to be special when you are an idiot just like everyone else), relieving the psyche of the strains of pretense, allowing one to be natural, human, humble, and open to the moment. It also allows for much humor. A certain myth that has persisted in some quarters about Gurdjieff was that his work lacked humor. In fact, this is untrue. There are many firsthand reports of much laughter during his nightly meetings in his crowded flat. Surviving audio tapes of some of these meetings confirm this. Gurdjieff can be heard talking, sounding much like a TIME magazine article that once described him as 'a remarkable blend of P.T. Barnum, Rasputin, Freud, Groucho Marx and everybody's grandfather'. Gales of laughter from the group around him can be heard as he regales them with stories.

Imagine the scene: dozens of people crowded into a small apartment, hard liquor being served, the air filled with smoke. Gurdjieff is holding court, dispensing Zen-like teachings moment by moment, utterly unpredictable as to what he might say or do at any moment. Various people are either toasting themselves or being designated by Gurdjieff as a particular Idiot. There is a Rabelaisian delight in all this, as well as the adventure of recognizing the truth of one's actual condition, i.e. that one is a nullity, something that is deeply refreshing once the power of pride has been overcome. That, at least, is the ideal it is based on.

There was a formal ceremonial setup for the Idiot Toasts. A 'director' for the ritual would sit on Gurdjieff's left (often his student, Bernard Lemaitre). He was responsible for coordinating things such as distribution of food, as well as being Gurdjieff's personal attendant. Left of the director sat the *Verseur*, the drink distributor, responsible for remembering who was drinking what and refilling when need be. To Gurdjieff's right sat *Monsieur Egout* (Mr. Sewer), who was often a visiting V.I.P., and who was given more food to eat than the others. On his right was *Monsieur Poubelle* (Mr. Garbage Can), who would receive any food that *M. Egout* could no longer eat. Right of *Poubelle* (and opposite Gurdjieff) was *Monsieur Bouche d'Egout* (Mr. Mouth of the Sewer). He would get occasional extra tidbits of food tossed at him by Gurdjieff. Next—sitting somewhere in the room but not at the table—was *Egout pour Sweet* (Sewer for Sweets). This was usually a young woman, and she replied 'present, Monsieur' when called on by Gurdjieff. She would then climb over the mass of bodies, reach Gurdjieff, where upon he would give her some candy.[14]

As Elizabeth Bennett put it,

> The exact repetition of the external framework left one free to attend to the shifting responsibilities of the inner world. Every moment in Gurdjieff's presence was a chance to learn, if one was sufficiently awake to take the chance.[15]

She captures well the spiritual function of ritual of any sort. Dabblers or dilettantes often complain when faced with discipline or structure in an inner work setting. A highly amusing example of this was shown in the 2002 German movie, *Enlightenment Guaranteed*, which involves a story of two brothers who flee their conventional lives in Germany for a Zen monastery in Japan. One of the brothers is a New Age-type guy — he meditates, and does Feng Shui for a living. The other is a conventional fellow, a husband, father and real estate agent. One day, the latter brother suddenly has his wife walk out on him, taking their four kids while she's at it. Devastated, he pleads with his New Age brother to take him with him when he goes on his planned trip to a Zen monastery near Tokyo. Reluctantly, the 'spiritual' brother agrees, and off they go. After several misadventures in Tokyo, they end up in the monastery, and it's the New Age brother who has the harder time with the monastic discipline. He soon finds out that his esoteric dabbling has, in a sense, made him even more ill-prepared for *real* spiritual structure than his so-called 'non-spiritual' brother.

In Gurdjieff's case, the augmentation of the Idiot Toasts ritual with hard liquor created a condition that forced the student to make a great effort to be consciously present. According to J.G. Bennett, these rituals did not involve more than '12 or 13 toasts' and he implied that no one was ever more than tipsy. This would likely be because the drinks came after the meals. Several toasts of Armagnac or vodka on an empty stomach would be enough to get many people more than tipsy.

Some of Gurdjieff's more high profile students were given the following Idiot designations: A.R. Orage: Idiot #2 (Super Idiot); J.G. Bennett: Idiot #8 (Round Idiot) and #11 (Doubting Idiot); Dr. Stjoernval: Idiot #3 (Arch Idiot); Jesse Dwight: Idiot #6 (Squirming Idiot), and so on. Apparently only one his close disciples, Jeanne de Salzmann, went beyond Idiocy of any sort.[16]

Jeanne de Salzmann announced after Gurdjieff's death that the Idiot Toasts would cease, as they relied too crucially on Gurdjieff's presence. There could perhaps be no greater testament to the sheer force of his character.

The Mystery of Osho's Death: Nitrous Oxide, CIA Assassination Plots, Black Magic

Osho's last few years alive in the late 1980s were quite bizarre. At various times, he changed his name, even going for a while with no name at all (giving fits to his publicity people); he also at one point declared, apparently entirely tongue-in-cheek, that the Buddha had entered his body, but that he ultimately had to kick him out because the Buddha couldn't adjust to more modern ways, such as Osho's Jacuzzi. Throughout late 1989, his health continued to deteriorate in a strange fashion. In mid-January of 1990, Osho claimed that CIA operatives, using black magic, were trying to kill him. A few days later, on January 19th, he died, of what was reported as heart failure. He was cremated almost immediately. The deathbeds of both Crowley and Gurdjieff had been mildly controversial, especially in Crowley's case, concerning what the last words of the magus were. (His funeral, in which his Hymn to Pan was read, caused an uproar, the rumor being—false, it should be noted—that it was a black mass). Otherwise, both Crowley and Gurdjieff passed with relative normalcy from this world, and both were in their 70s. Osho's death was far stranger, and is part of the lingering mystique of his relatively short life.

The story goes like this: in late October of 1985, just over a month after the sudden collapse of the Oregon commune and the exodus of secretary Ma Sheela and her confederates, the National Guard was getting into position to invade the commune. With that in mind, a small group of Osho's disciples decided to get him away from the commune as a preventative measure and to depressurize the situation (the biggest fear being that some disciples might come to harm if they tried to protect Osho from a sudden arrest and seizure by the FBI, which was already present in the commune at the time— Osho having invited them there to investigate the crimes that had happened). They flew him in a small jet across the country to Charlotte, North Carolina.

It's unclear exactly what Osho's people were thinking; owing to

Sheela's bio-terror attack on the salad bar in The Dalles, the whole Osho organization had been branded by the various government security agencies as a terrorist group. (This was regardless, of course, of the fact that Osho maintained that he had no knowledge of the crimes being committed—and indeed no evidence linking him to these crimes was ever found). And so, predictably, Osho and his few disciples were immediately arrested by a heavily armed unit at the Charlotte airport. They were carted off in shackles. The TV images of Osho walking shackled and flanked by armed agents looking furtively around were unforgettable.

The group spent three days in a holding cell in Charlotte. In the hearing that followed, the disciples—none of whom were identified as the particular disciples the authorities were actually looking for (presumably, those were Sheela and her lieutenants, who by that time were in Europe)—were released. Osho, however, was separated from his disciples and informed that he would be taken back to Oregon to undergo a new bail hearing.

It was at this point that things became a type of High Strangeness. A man can be transported from Charlotte to Oregon in no more than four or five hours. And yet the authorities opted to send Osho back by snail mail, so to speak—via a prison transport plane—in a journey that took ten days. During that time he was housed in six separate jails across the country. The public perception of all this became garishly distorted, a primetime 'true crime' tale of, as Swami Paritosh put it, 'the evil guru caught as he tried to flee'.[17] A live primetime interview from Charlotte of Osho with Ted Koppel on ABC news heightened the absurdity of the situation, with Koppel questioning Osho aggressively and with obvious (and predictable, under the circumstances) cynicism.

For a period during this obvious buying-for-time move by the authorities, Osho seemed to vanish. He could not be located for three days. Eventually the press found him in a jail in Oklahoma, of all places. It was in this jail where Osho claimed he was mistreated and fed something that he described as very suspicious—'two slices of bread with a strange tasteless sauce.' (Which sounded suspiciously like cafeteria quality French toast and industrial grade maple syrup—but assuming Osho knew what lousy maple syrup looks and tastes like, it would still suggest that his observation of its 'suspiciousness' was in hindsight otherwise he probably wouldn't have eaten it at the time.) He was made to sleep on a low quality mattress, which he and some of his doctors afterward came to suspect was hiding a radioactive source that would damage Osho's body in such a way as to leave no trace. He did, in the years that followed, experience great pain on the right side of his body in particular—the side he normally slept on, which would have been exposed to the mattress.

At the end of his brief stint in the mid-west jails, Osho was taken back to Oregon where in Portland he pleaded not guilty to all charges and then, on the advice of lawyers, entered an 'Alford Plea', a legal device that basically translates to 'I am not admitting guilt, but I agree that there is enough evidence against me to probably result in my conviction'. Osho was found guilty of making misleading statements on his immigration application and of arranging sham marriages (the latter arising from cases where non-American disciples would marry American disciples so that they could remain in the country). Osho was then fined $400,000 and deported. Within a short while his health began to deteriorate— slowly at first, more dramatically after a few years. The problem of what was causing his physical deterioration became a major mystery. The facts were that he had 'disappeared' for a few days while in prison custody and that he was regarded with deep suspicion by American authorities. So conceivably there was some incentive to eliminate him, and this is what the official position of the organization eventually became (as declared by Osho himself). But the other reality was that Osho had always had frail health and—in information that only became openly known in later years—he did make use of drugs (nitrous oxide, and possibly valium).

Osho had first appeared on the guru-circuit in the late 1960s, the time of Woodstock and the height of the recreational drug revolution. By 1974, when his work shifted into high gear with his moving from Mumbai to Pune and the launching of the Rajneesh ashram, many of the hippies, despite still looking entirely like hippies, had begun to gravitate from drug usage to meditation, Zen, yoga, and the esoteric. But drug usage itself—in specific, amongst Osho's disciples—did not entirely go away.

With Osho, far more than with Crowley or Gurdjieff (or even the alcoholic Tibetan *tulku*, Chogyam Trungpa), drug usage presents a difficult issue because, as has been touched on in other places in this book, his teaching depended vitally on who he was. The idea sometimes gets offered that what Osho did in his private life was no one's business but in the case of a self-declared Buddha as he was that idea seems absurd. Osho's whole teaching was based on the essential value of authenticity—in all domains of one's life. What exactly could he have to hide? He was supposed to be a man with no ego, no self, just a hollow bamboo. Obviously, he would have a private life in and of itself, but the idea that he would have secrets, something to be disguised or avoided or dodged, is not at all consistent with what he claimed to be.

Gurdjieff could be brazen and arrogant but stopped short of definitively pronouncing himself as special or great. He once even claimed that he was a small man compared to those who 'sent' him. Crowley, although capable of bombast with the best of them, was often disarmingly honest about his limitations. However, Osho carried himself with great dignity and elegance and consistently affirmed his own enlightenment. And so he set a high standard in terms of how he would be seen by others. Although he was anything but a moralist, and in fact regularly condemned the idea that morality was of any use without consciousness, he nevertheless was clear that his own enlightenment was brought about by the purest of intentions, free of any significant external causes, such as religious conditioning, spiritual puritanicalism, traditional meditation practices—or any sort of mind-altering chemicals. His path was to strip reality completely of its lies, revealing, only after great struggle, the pristine and naked truth of existence, and of his own being.

In September of 1985, three books by Osho appeared in print, and all three were reported by his dentist Devageet (in 2001) to have been dictated while Osho was under the effects of nitrous oxide. These books were *Glimpses of a Golden Childhood*, *Notes of a Madman*, and *Books I Have Loved*. Anyone reading these books, especially *Notes of a Madman*, will be struck by the different tone. I read this book when it first came out and even then, as a young and green disciple, it was immediately obvious to me that the book was different. Osho could never be accused of normative behavior but this book was peculiar, like some sort of extended session of free association.

Christopher Calder (who was an early disciple of Osho, though he left the community in 1975) claimed that Osho was a regular user of both valium and nitrous oxide. There are corroborating sources that confirm that view. Satya Bharti Franklin, in her *The Promise of Paradise*, reported a phone conversation with an early disciple of Osho's named Deeksha who also claimed that Osho had 'swallowed valium and Quaaludes by the handful'.[18] Hugh Milne claimed the same thing about Osho and valium. All three of these had, at one time, been close disciples of Osho.

An Oregon congressman at the time, Jim Weaver, visited the Oregon commune in 1986 and reported that, in addition to seeing the underground chambers and tunnels connected to Sheela's residence, he also found that Osho's bedroom featured nitrous oxide spigots by his bedside.[19]

In *Notes of a Madman*, Osho, high on nitrous oxide, said the following:

This is so beautiful. I feel so good. Actually, oxygen and nitrogen are basic elements of existence. They can be of much use, but for reasons the politicians have been against chemical of all kinds, against all drugs. The very word 'drug' has become dangerous. They are so against drugs because people can come to know themselves, and when people come to know themselves politicians lose their power over them, and they love their power. In the Vedas they call it soma, the essence, and since those ancient days until today, all those who know have recognized, either directly or indirectly, that chemicals can be of immense service to man. Man is chemistry, so is existence. All is chemistry. We cannot avoid its influence.[20]

Crowley would have approved. In *Magick Without Tears*, he wrote,

Again with drugs, it is the unknown which is the horrific factor. Most people get their information on the subject from the yellowest of yellow newspapers, magazines and novels...blank-eyed, they gasp when they learn that of all classes, the first place among 'drug addicts' is that of the doctor. But the crisis in which fear becomes phobia is the unreasoning aversion, the shuddering of panic, above all, the passionate refusal to learn anything about 'drugs,' to analyze the conditions, still less to face them; and the spasmodic invention of imaginary terrors, as if the real dangers were not enough to serve as a warning. Now why? Surely because in the sub-conscious lies an instinct that in these obscure medicines indeed lies the key of some forbidden sanctuary. There is a fascination as irrational and therefore as strong, as the fear.[21]

William James, writing back at the turn of the 20th century when Crowley was a young initiate in the Golden Dawn and Gurdjieff was wandering in Tibet, had this to say about nitrous oxide,

Nitrous oxide and ether, especially nitrous oxide, when sufficiently diluted with air, stimulate the mystical consciousness in an extraordinary degree. Depth beyond depth of truth seems revealed to the inhaler. This truth fades out, however, or escapes, at the moment of coming to; and if any words remain over in which it seemed to clothe itself, they prove to be the veriest nonsense. Nevertheless, the sense of profound meaning having been there persists; and I know more than one person who is persuaded that in the nitrous oxide trance we have a genuine metaphysical revelation.

Some years ago I myself made some observations on this aspect of nitrous oxide intoxication...one conclusion was forced upon my mind at that time...it is that our normal waking consciousness, rational consciousness as we call it, is but one special type of consciousness, whilst all about it, parted from it by the filmiest of screens, there lie potential forms of consciousness entirely different.[22]

Osho's death was not entirely sudden—his health had been declining since 1987 when an ear infection spread and caused him to become seriously ill, revealing that his immune system had deteriorated— but it still came as a surprise, and indeed a shock, to his many followers. When he passed away in his Pune ashram on January 19, 1990, he had only just turned fifty-eight the month before. He was not an old man, despite his long wispy white beard and archetypal wizardly grandfather appearance.

Osho's physical deterioration had worsened in early 1987 upon his return to Pune from Mumbai. His symptoms, as recorded by Juliet Forman, were noted as the following: hair loss, paralysis and spasms of the facial muscles, eye twitching, unsteady gait, pain in his extremities, muscular weakness, and depressed immune system. It was noted at that time that these symptoms seemed to come about after Osho's twelve days spent in the American penal system. By late 1989 he was in constant pain, especially around the area of his ears, mouth, neck, and shoulders.[23]

Shortly before Osho's death, he declared that he had been, in effect, slowly assassinated by the Reagan Administration. He said that doctors in England had determined that radiation poisoning, in particular thallium (a known assassination tool), had very possibly been used against him, although they could not absolutely confirm it. A dentist who looked at Osho's teeth deterioration concluded that deliberate radiation exposure was a strong possibility.

That there had been in fact 'high level interest'—at both White House and congressional level—in Osho was unquestionable. The crimes perpetrated by Sheela and others in Oregon came almost a decade before the Waco-Branch Davidian debacle, but only six years after the Jim Jones-Jonestown horror, and so the notion of the dangerously self-destructive cult was alive and well on the public radar. That, coupled with Osho's almost endless invective against politicians and organized religions—Christianity in particular— painted a large target on his back.

Nevertheless, it is far from clear that the U.S. government would have the necessary motivation to kill Osho, slowly or otherwise. Further complicating matters was the accusation, brought forth in some quarters, that it had been Sheela herself who had been poisoning Osho slowly by feeding thallium to a cow that was used for his milk.[24] (That angle would satisfy the 'butler principle', the idea that serious crimes are often committed by one very close to the victim). However, as information emerged over the years about Osho's nitrous oxide usage for 'dental sessions' that were far more numerous than the number of teeth in his head, research was invariably done comparing the symptoms of Osho's decline with both thallium exposure and nitrous oxide abuse.

What was found—and anyone can confirm this for themselves with a bit of research—was that Osho's symptoms more closely matched those of nitrous oxide abuse than they did of thallium poisoning. Just as one example, it is known that nitrous oxide usage can metabolically interfere with vitamin B12 stores in the body. Some symptoms of vitamin B12 deficiency are recognized as: twitching eyes, sleep disturbances, numbness and tingling in extremities, problems walking, referred to as 'ataxic gait' or more commonly as the 'drunken sailor gait', sharp pains in the hands and face, fatigue, clinical depression, etc.[25] Compare those to Juliet Forman's description of some of Osho's symptoms above. (A further theory was advanced by Christopher Calder that Osho's afflictions were all stemming from Chronic Fatigue Syndrome; admittedly, symptoms stemming from this disorder also appear to more accurately resemble Osho's symptoms than thallium poisoning. Additionally, the disorder was not clearly understood until recently; the medical term itself was only proposed in 1988.)

Thallium poisoning symptoms are associated with hair loss, pain, loss of reflexes, convulsions, numbness, muscle wasting, dementia, and psychosis. Heart rhythm disturbance can occur by three weeks after exposure.[26] While some of these symptoms were found in Osho's case, the problem is the time factor. He was allegedly exposed in October 1985, but did not die until over four years later, and did not really begin to fade until 1989.

Several other factors have been taken into account in this mix: Osho had been diabetic for many years, always had immune system problems (he was frail, asthmatic, and had several allergies), and, last but far from least, he had been subjected to enormous stresses during and after the Oregon debacle. He had been (at least in his subjective experience) betrayed by his 'prime minister' (Sheela), suffered the loss of an entire commune, and was rejected by at least twenty-one nations. All this was, to a large degree, taken for granted by both Osho's followers and by cynical observers. The former tended to believe that because Osho was 'enlightened' he would not be truly harmed by all these factors—he was, after all, 'beyond' the effects of psychological stresses resulting from a psyche still centralized by an ego, he of course being beyond ego. And the latter tended to dismiss the factor of stresses against him because they saw him as pampered and protected by his followers.

In reality, neither position was likely grounded in reality. Osho was certainly stressed by the process he'd been through from late 1985 until late 1986 when he finally settled back in Mumbai. This fact would not be mitigated by naive ideas about his assumed spiritual state or by cynical views of his assumed degree of protection.

So what killed Osho?

In a typical example of the 'unorthodox viewpoint' amongst Osho observers, Swami Parmartha, in his Web article *Osho in the Dental Chair*, remarks,

> I do not think the evidence that Osho received thallium is very convincing, the symptoms do not really match those Osho was experiencing. The 'official' line is, and he himself seemed to believe, that he had been poisoned by thallium. However Osho seemed really quite well between late 1985 and 1987, in Greece, and was in fairly good shape in the Himalayas, the world tour, and in Bombay too for almost two years. Any in-depth biographer has surely to note that Osho began complaining again of his symptoms in 1987, just when he would have been reunited with his dental chair.[27]

Those observations seem reasonable but they are not supported by the testimony of Juliet Foreman, one of Osho's closest disciples. In 1989 she wrote, describing the period from late '85 to early '86:

> After a few weeks in Kathmandu, Osho began to feel unwell. His stomach was upset. He was losing weight...Perhaps he was still suffering from the aftermath of the days in the American jails. Of course it didn't occur to any of us at this stage that something other than the general trauma of that experience could explain his ill-health; his painful back, his hair loss while in Kulu-Manali...On top of that he was having trouble sleeping and had a sense of weakness. He also began to suffer a spasm of the facial muscles, particularly around the eyes...Osho told Devaraj [his physician] that reading produced a sense of nausea and vertigo and of lights in front of his eyes.[28]

So it would appear that Osho was not 'really quite well' between late '85 and '87. I myself was present in Kathmandu for the entire month of February 1986, and I attended Osho's daily 'walk-by' that he did on the grounds of the Soaltee Oberoi Hotel, as well as his evening lectures in the main ballroom. He was at that point fifty-four years old; this was just three months after his incarceration in the American jails. Superficially at least, I'd have to agree with Parmartha: there was no obvious outward sign that he was unwell. I do not recall him missing any of the daily walks or lectures and in these lectures he seemed well enough. A friend of mine, a young Japanese disciple, stood up several times during the question-and-answer period that followed the nightly talks to ask Osho bold questions. In all cases, Osho's answers were responsive and sharp.

Of course that does not mean that Forman's observations are untrue. I have no doubt that she was reporting accurately what was going on with Osho's body, and I also have no doubt that the fact that Osho even did these evening lectures for his people—at a time when he could easily have just packed it in altogether—was testament to his courage and commitment. Nevertheless, he was not exactly bedridden. He was up and about and had all his wits, and for the casual observer he would have seemed fine. So whatever illnesses he had then would not have been enough to incapacitate him.

Nevertheless as Osho deteriorated, specialists were consulted; some concluded that rather than having been given thallium in his food, he may have been exposed to radiation via a mattress while in the Oklahoma prison cell in late 1985. Other researchers unearthed some suspicious facts, a noteworthy one being that the U.S. Marshall who signed Osho in at the prison was not a member of the prison staff and resigned his position and vanished the day after Osho was moved from the Oklahoma jail.

Worth mentioning here is the issue of *kundalini* energy, a phenomenon taken for granted in India, but not something scientifically recognized. Back in the early 1970s, Osho talked about the effects of *kundalini* on the body:

The moment the vital energy, the kundalini, begins to flow upward, sex energy follows. It begins to flow upward: the feet become cool and the head becomes warm. Biologically it is better for the feet to be warmer than the head, but spiritually it is healthier for the feet to be cooler because this is a sign that the energy is flowing upward. Many diseases may begin to occur once the energy begins to flow upward, because biologically you have disturbed the whole organism. Buddha died very ill, Mahavira died very ill, Raman Maharshi died with cancer, Ramkrishna died with cancer. And the reason is that the whole biological system is disturbed. Many other reasons are given, but they are nonsense.

Jainas have created many stories because they could not conceive that Mahavira could have been ill. For me, the contrary is the case: I cannot conceive how he could have been completely healthy. He couldn't be, because this was going to be his last birth, and the whole biological system had to break down. A system that had been continuous for millennia had to break down. He could not be healthy; in the end he had to be very ill. And he was! But it was very difficult for the followers to conceive that Mahavira was ill.[29]

And in a passage that would prove to be very ironic, Osho added:

There was only one explanation for illness in those days. If you were suffering from a particular disease, it meant your karmas, your past deeds, had been bad. If Mahavira was suffering from a disease, then it would have meant that he was still under his karmic influence. That could not be so, so an ingenious story was invented: that Goshalak, a competitor of Mahavira, was using evil forces against him. But this was not the case at all.[30]

These remarks of Osho were made in the early 1970s, almost two decades before his death. During those years much happened to him—he was subjected to all kinds of psychic and physical stresses. As his health declined, alarmingly in January of 1990, just a few days before he died, he claimed that he was being attacked by a type of mantra being used by one or more people sitting in the main hall where he sat with his disciples during the evening. In effect, he claimed that a kind of black magic—the same 'evil forces' used by Goshalak against Mahavira—was being used against him. He would ultimately declare that the CIA was behind it. His caretaker disciples did what they could to search for and find the perpetrators, standing and sitting in various strategic places during the evening meetings, to try and flush out the person or persons doing this. Predictably, no one was found, and Osho, seeing how the whole issue was upsetting his people, decided to suddenly drop the matter.[31]

The issue of so-called 'psychic attack' is usually brushed off, considered the domain of the credulous or of those unable to be accountable for their own nasty thoughts. And indeed most assumed cases of psychic attack are simply the repercussive effects of a person's own anger. However, if anyone doubts that thoughts can kill, they have only to stop and think about how all murders first begin with a thought. Inter-psychic forces are natural in more apparent ways: when someone close to us is angry with us a little bit of sensitivity can make that clear even if we are not in that person's immediate presence. We can know this simply because we have *conscience*. On that basis alone, we normally know when someone is angry with us, for the simple reason that more often than not *we* are angry with them. (For example, that Osho had harsh words for the Reagan Administration is amply documented.) That does not, of course, imply that every time we are angry with someone, they are angry with us, or vice versa. But consistent, prolonged negative emotional states tend to eventually find an external mirror to reflect to us what we are transmitting. We then perceive this as either attack from others or as 'self-attack' or internalized anger (which is likely one of the underlying causes of depression).

Osho was no fool. He knew that he'd deeply provoked many in

his life. Like Jesus and Socrates, he'd disturbed and angered people enough to pay a heavy price. The question comes down to how clear he was on deeper emotional levels—the realm of Gurdjieff's 'Emotional Center'. Followers of Osho have tended to assume that as an enlightened being he had no real issues in this area. But this is far from certain.

Osho himself, in a series of lectures given in the mid-1970s on the Tantric master Tilopa, had said some specific things about the power of thoughts and black magic:

> Somewhere the great physicist Eddington has said that the deeper science goes into matter, the more it becomes a realization that things are thoughts...if you go deeper into yourself, thoughts will look more and more like things. In fact, these are two aspects of the same phenomenon: a thing is a thought, a thought is a thing...you can kill a person through a thought just like you can throw a dagger. You can give your thought as a gift, or as an infection...that's why blessings can be useful, helpful. If you can be blessed by someone who has attained no-mind, the blessing is going to be true—because a man who never uses thought accumulates thought energy...if you attain to no-mind and your trend remains negative, you can become a dangerous force...black magic is nothing but when a man has accumulated thought energy without throwing out his negativity beforehand.[32]

At present, we are not in full understanding of psychic forces, whether natural or intentional, to pronounce certainty on the matter of 'psychic attack'. However, as one occultist once observed, only a tiny percentage of people have ever been subjected to an actual ritual curse, whereas one in every four persons experience some form of mental illness in their life. Psychological disturbance is enough to simulate the effects of an attack of sorcery.

If we put aside ritual curses or mental illness we are left with another possibility, something recognized via recent parapsychology experiments under scientifically controlled conditions, called DMILS (Direct Mental Interaction between Living Systems). In these experiments, a subject's electrodermal reactions are measured as they are 'subjected to' calming or arousing thoughts directed at them by another person in a different room. Careful controls are present, such as ensuring no contact, no way for covert communications, and so on. In repeated experiments of these kinds, a statistically significant result has been obtained appearing to demonstrate that we can indeed produce some sort of effect on another person via thought alone.[33]

The respected early 20th century occultist Dion Fortune, in her classic work *Psychic Self-Defense*, wrote:

> The commonest form of psychic attack is that which proceeds from the ignorant or malignant mind of our fellow human beings. We say ignorant as well as malignant, for all attacks are not deliberately motivated; the injury may be as accidental as that inflicted by a skidding car...the person from whom [the attack] emanates may not have originated it.[34]

Her point is well made, for indeed we are interconnected in ways that make it impossible to truly isolate anything. That the 'evil magicians' who were sending death-mantras at Osho were never found is apt symbolism; for even if they existed and had been found what would it actually have proved? That Osho provoked people to hostility? There was nothing new to be found there.

Osho died a few days after his claim that he was being attacked by black magic. It was a strangely macabre closing chapter for a man who throughout most of his life—and, according to his personal physician, during his actual moment of death—had been the embodiment of dignity. However, the issue of Osho's death will likely remain a mystery, a type of Zen koan like *why did Bodhidharma go to China?* His body was cremated within hours of his death; the evidence, if there was any, went up in smoke, and Osho, as he always maintained he would, dissolved into existence.

The story of his demise is ultimately secondary. A perhaps more useful approach to Osho's death is to examine our own preconceived notions, conditioning, belief systems, and expectations about perfection, spiritual authority, trust, surrender and rebelliousness, and all the matters related to his death. We do better to look deeper into the mirror, rather than attempt to validate our fears, suspicions, or attachments by seeking closure to a mystery that has no solution.

Chapter 13
Magical Warfare

I love the valiant; but it is not enough to wield a broadsword, one must also know against whom.

And often there is more valor when one refrains and passes by, in order to save oneself for the worthier enemy.

Nietzsche[1]

The Beast 666 meets the Ambassador from Hell
—or did he?

A relatively common fact of life is that renowned spiritual teachers only rarely meet each other, and even more rarely teach together. More commonly, their teachings do not harmonize, and on occasion they appear to not even like each other. This is all due to many factors, not least of which is that they are usually busy people. More subtly, there is often the case of the teacher's ego, or more specifically, what is known as the 'teacher-attachment' trait, the tendency for teachers to harden in their role as a teacher and minimize or ignore their own needs to socially and spiritually connect with peers. More insidiously, their followers or students often collude in various ways with the teacher-attachment tendency, projecting the image of the ideal parent onto the teacher and contributing toward the teacher's isolation. The followers, not wanting to share their 'ideal parent' with others, in effect prevent the teacher from active relationships with other teachers, much like clamoring children can absorb most of the time and energy of their parents.

Crowley, however, was not *always* so busy, and unlike Gurdjieff and certainly Osho, he was not hemmed in by his own disciples, doubtless in part because he didn't set himself up in anything remotely like a parental role (added to which, naturally, his abrasiveness was not precisely endearing). He is reported to have briefly met Gurdjieff in 1926 at the latter's Prieure in Fontainebleau. At the time, Crowley would have been fifty years old and Gurdjieff somewhere in his mid-fifties—both a couple of well-aged wine Magi at that point. Crowley had been fond of Fontainebleau, having been there many times, as early as 1911, a decade before Gurdjieff arrived. A number of pages in his *Confessions* mention his periodic visits to this town. Just prior to Gurdjieff's arrival and founding of his Institute in 1922, Crowley had leased a house in Fontainebleau in the winter of 1920. Shortly after this he left for Sicily where he was to found his Abbey of Thelema. By 1923, after the closure of the Abbey, he left Sicily for Tunisia, and by the following year was back in Europe.

Stanley Nott, a student of Gurdjieff who authored two worthy books on his master, met Crowley in the summer of 1926 in Paris, and went on to describe the meeting of the two Magi themselves:

One day in Paris I met an acquaintance from New York who spoke about the possibilities of publishing modern literature. As I showed some interest, he offered to introduce me to a friend of his who was thinking of going into publishing, and we arranged to meet the following day at the Select in Montparnasse. His friend arrived; it was Aleister Crowley. Drinks were ordered, for which of course I paid, and we began to talk. Crowley had magnetism, and the kind of charm which many charlatans have; he also had a dead weight that was somewhat impressive. His attitude was fatherly and benign, and a few years earlier I might have fallen for it. Now I saw and sensed that I could have nothing to do with him. He talked in general terms about publishing, and then drifted into his black-magic jargon.

'To make a success of anything,' he said, 'including publishing, you must have a certain combination. Here you have a Master, here a Bear, there the Dragon- a triangle which will bring results...' and so on and so on. When he fell silent I said, 'Yes, but one must have money. Am I right in supposing that you have the necessary capital?'. 'I?' he asked, 'No not a franc.' 'Neither have I.' I said.

Knowing that I was at the Prieure he asked me if I would get him an invitation there. But I did not wish to be responsible for introducing such a man. However, to my surprise, he appeared there a few days later and was given tea in the salon. The children were there, and he said to one of the boys something about his son who he was teaching to be a devil. Gurdjieff got up and spoke to the boy, who thereupon took no further notice of Crowley. There was some talk between Crowley and Gurdjieff, who kept a sharp watch on him all the time. I got the strong impression of two magicians, the white and the black- the one strong, powerful, full of light; the other also powerful but heavy, dull and ignorant. Though 'black' was too strong a word for Crowley; he never understood the meaning of real black magic, yet hundreds of people came under his 'spell'. He was clever. But as Gurdjieff says: 'He is stupid who is clever.'[2]

A few observations can be made of Nott's remarks. The time he met Crowley was not a high point in Crowley's trajectory—he was past his prime and struggling with drug addictions. In that sense, Nott's repulsion with Crowley's presence is not difficult to understand. Nott was a man who was working on himself and thus would have some degree of sensitivity. Crowley's life experience and intellectual depth would have been readily apparent (hence the 'magnetism' and 'impressive dead weight' presence) but his suspect health, financial weakness, and relative isolation at that time would have also been apparent on subtle levels.

The bit about Nott 'sensing' that he could have 'nothing to do with' Crowley is interesting because it suggests that Nott has achieved some sort of grounding within himself that would allow him to take such a position against an obviously charismatic and persuasive personality (something Nott himself admits about Crowley). It takes a certain trust in oneself to stand up to a strong personality. However, Nott's reasons for adopting this position seem vague, unreasoned, and probably based partly on Crowley's public reputation which was never particularly good.

And this is where Nott's relative clarity appears to end. He is quick to pass judgment on Crowley's lack of comprehension of 'black magic', yet offers no suggestion that he is truly familiar with Crowley's life work (in particular his writings). Perhaps even more telling, he seems to imply that Crowley actually was a black magician. Anyone truly acquainted with Crowley's life work knows this is nonsense. It is true that Crowley performed, on occasion, rites of ceremonial magic that involved the evocation of spirits from the 'Goetia' grimoires—some of what are conventionally known as 'demons' (though in reality they are simply the gods of older, vanquished civilizations)—and that on at least one occasion while in his early twenties he attempted to conjure some of these in some sort of misguided astral battle with his erstwhile mentor Samuel Mathers.[3] He also on another occasion claimed to be responsible for the sudden downfall of a publisher who had brought him grief. But in the epic sweep of Crowley's life, these small incidents have an almost comic interlude quality.

More to the point, Crowley himself had a very sophisticated grasp of different levels of magic and clearly understood that evocation magic like that involving the Goetic energies, or the Abramelin work, is at core a psychological process in which the magician encounters deep elements of his own unconscious mind—essentially a type of shamanic journeying (regardless of whether we see the 'spirits' involved as objectively real or not). Crowley also provided a very specific and uncompromising definition of black magic, a view consistent with the highest aspirations of the true mystic:

The Single Supreme Ritual is the attainment of the Knowledge and Conversation of the Holy Guardian Angel. It is the raising of the complete man in a vertical straight line. Any deviation from this line tends to become black magic. Any other operation is black magic.[4]

Interestingly, Crowley's view there is entirely aligned with Zen Buddhism, and its concept of *makyo*, a Japanese term that means 'the devil in phenomena'. It refers to the idea that a seeker of enlightenment sitting in deep meditation will commonly encounter visions from his unconscious, some of which may be quite convincing and spectacular. No matter what, however, he is counseled by the Zen master to ignore these visions — all of which are regarded as *makyo* — and persist only in the one-pointed witnessing of all that arises in his field of consciousness, without attaching himself to anything. The point being that *any* phenomena that arises in the mind as an image or symbol is a distraction from ultimate truth. What Crowley calls the Holy Guardian Angel is what, from one perspective at least (his later views of the HGA notwithstanding), Zen calls the Buddha-mind (the mind of ultimate truth). Nothing but that is a worthy goal for the true seeker. Crowley is in agreement with the Zen masters on that accord.

Gurdjieff himself did talk at least on one occasion about black magic in a rambling monologue quoted (or more accurately, reconstructed) by Ouspensky in *In Search of the Miraculous*. The gist of the talk is that Gurdjieff's view of black magic is that its prime quality is that it manipulates people into being dependent — what he called the 'producing in people of infatuation'. But that is of course a very broad definition and commonplace in occurrence. In the same talk, Gurdjieff stressed the mechanical nature of the average person and how they always *think* they are doing 'in the interests of good' as they understand it. As always for Gurdjieff, the issue of being awake vs. being asleep trumps morality and any significance of 'white' vs. 'black' magic.[5]

Given his teacher's views, it's not clear what special understanding of black magic Nott was referring to. At any rate, Nott's
observations are taken from his first book, *Teachings of Gurdjieff: A
Pupil's Journal*, which was published in 1961. Nott himself was born
in 1887, which would have made him probably in his late sixties
when he was putting this book together. Accordingly, one can
question the accuracy of the memory of his perceptions (even if
based on diary notes) drawing on events that occurred thirty years
before.

Nott followed up his account with an amusing anecdote apparently related by A. R. Orage, who was a close student of Gurdjieff's
and an established literary figure in England in the early 20th
century. The story took place at an earlier time:

> Orage said about this: "Alas, poor Crowley, I knew him well. We
> used to meet at the Society for Psychical Research when I was
> acting secretary. Once, when we were talking, he asked: 'By the
> way, what number are you?' Not knowing in the least what he
> meant, I said on the spur of the moment, 'Twelve.' 'Good God,
> are you really?' he replied, 'I'm only seven.'"[6]

It's a funny exchange, but little can be gleaned from it. Crowley may
have just as easily been playing with Orage, as the other way
around—or both men, equally renowned for their wit, may have
been pulling each other's leg at the same time. (Concerning
Crowley's reply to Orage, the esoteric significance of the number
seven is of course legendary; Blavatsky's Theosophy, which was the
dominant occult paradigm at the time that Crowley and Orage met
in the late 1890s commonly discussed the number seven in its
various doctrines, especially in relation to the seven subtle bodies of
Man.)

When initially researching this encounter of the Magi, I was
unclear as to when it took place, with some sources mentioning
1924, others 1926, but I soon realized that both dates were signif-

icant. This is because, although Crowley met Gurdjieff only once, he in fact visited Gurdjieff's school in Fontainebleau not once, but *twice*. One of Gurdjieff's chief biographers, James Moore, has this to say about Crowley's first visit, which took place in early 1924 when Gurdjieff was in America introducing his work in several major east coast cities:

> In Paris Major Pinder met Gurdjieff with news that was, none of it, particularly good. A gaggle of undesirable voyeurs had visited the Prieure, including D.H. Lawrence (who thought it a 'rotten, false, self-conscious place of people playing a sickly stunt'), and Aleister Crowley, the Beast 666 (who supposed Gurdjieff was a 'tip-top man...a very advanced adept').[7]

This is confirmed by Crowley's biographer Lawrence Sutin, who noted that Crowley visited the Prieure on February 10th, 1924, and was received by Gurdjieff's close student, Major Frank Pinder. Gurdjieff was in America from January to June of that year. Of his impressions of Gurdjieff and his work, Crowley had this to say in his diary, following his meeting with Pinder:

> Gurdjieff, their prophet, seems a tip-top man. Heard more sense and insight than I've done for years. Pinder dines at 7.30. Oracle for my visit was 'There are few men: there are enough'. Later, a really wonderful evening with Pinder. Gurdjieff clearly a very advanced adept. My chief quarrels are over sex (I doubt whether Pinder understands G's true position) and their punishments, e.g. depriving the offender of a meal or making him stand half an hour with his arms out. Childish and morally valueless.[8]

These remarks of Crowley are interesting (and also amusing in their own right). The fact that Crowley recognizes Gurdjieff's quality is significant, and is equally a testament to Major Pinder's ability to explain his teacher's work as it is to Crowley's broadmindedness.

The issue about sex is to be expected; Crowley's attitude toward sex was a foreshadowing of the approach adopted later by the counter-culture revolution of the 1960s, and more specifically, the psycho-spiritual atmosphere that later emerged from it, best represented by Osho's work. However, Gurdjieff approached the matter differently. His views were more classically Eastern, similar to Taoist or Yogic models where sex energy is regarded as a powerful force to be carefully regulated and conserved. Crowley's view was essentially psychological, concerned mostly with deep exploration and the avoidance of repression at all costs. This is a more 'left-hand Tantra' approach that is full of potential for both rapid growth, and rapid self-destruction, depending on how it is used. Crowley's judgment that some Gurdjieffian methods are 'childish and morally valueless' seems at first glance remarkably ironic—Crowley making pronouncements about morality? Crowley was also not averse to strict training methods, including harsh self-administered punishments for mental laziness, so his criticism here seems questionable.

As mentioned above, at the time of this meeting with Pinder, Crowley was already in his decline whereas Gurdjieff, despite being several years older, was near about at the peak of his powers. At the time of his early 1924 visit to Gurdjieff's center, Crowley was struggling with both heroin addiction and asthma attacks. (And, in fact, the most likely reason he went to the Prieure in the first place was because of Gurdjieff's reputation as a healer of drug addictions.) His finances were depleted and he had little support. Gurdjieff, however, was energized by a lively spiritual ashram that he was deeply engaged in running, had a supportive following, and had just set sail, along with thirty-five dedicated students, to America to give his first public demonstrations of his sacred dances in major urban centers like New York City, Boston, and Philadelphia (a series of events that proved to be quite successful).

But all this was soon to change. It was immediately after returning to France in the summer of 1924—and just a few months after Crowley's meeting with Pinder—that Gurdjieff had his famous car crash, in which he was seriously injured and very nearly died. (He was not an experienced driver having only learned to drive the year before.) He spent several weeks recuperating and when he emerged from his healing something in him had changed. He dismissed many of his students and began to focus more on his writing projects. It was exactly two years later, in the summer of 1926, when Crowley met with Stanley Nott (as recounted above) and made his second visit to the Prieure. His reasons for returning are unclear but it is significant that he returned at all. Clearly, there must have been something in Gurdjieff's school or teaching that interested him. Crowley had missed Gurdjieff during his 1924 visit, the latter being in America at the time, but in July of 1926, the two Magi met.

Of this second visit, in addition to Nott's account, there is this more dramatized version of the meeting, offered by esoteric historian James Webb, taken from his book, *The Harmonious Circle: The Lives and Work of G. I. Gurdjieff, P.D. Ouspensky, and Their Followers*:

Crowley arrived for a whole weekend and spent the time like any other visitor to the Prieure; being shown the grounds and the activities in progress, listening to Gurdjieff's music and his oracular conversation. Apart from some circumspection, Gurdjieff treated him like any other guest until the evening of his departure. After dinner on Sunday night, Gurdjieff led the way out of the dining room with Crowley, followed by the body of the pupils who had also been at the meal. Crowley made his way toward the door and turned to take his leave of Gurdjieff, who by this time was some way up the stairs to the second floor. 'Mister, you go?' Gurdjieff inquired. Crowley assented. 'You have been guest?'—a fact which the visitor could hardly deny. 'Now you go, you are no longer guest?' Crowley—no doubt wondering whether his host had lost his grip on reality and was wandering in a semantic wilderness – humored his mood by indicating that he was on his way back to Paris. But Gurdjieff, having made the point that he was not violating the canons of hospitality, changed on the instant into the embodiment of righteous anger. 'You filthy,' he stormed, 'you dirty inside! Never again you set foot in my house!' From his vantage point on the stairs, he worked himself into a rage which quite transfixed his watching pupils. Crowley was stigmatized as the sewer of creation was taken apart and trodden into the mire. Finally, he was banished in the style of East Lynne by a Gurdjieff in fine histrionic form. White faced and shaking, the Great Beast crept back to Paris with his tail between his legs.[9]

This account by Webb was published in 1980 and cites no sources. Stanley Nott, who unlike Webb was a direct student of Gurdjieff's and was present during Crowley's visit, makes no mention of such an outburst from Gurdjieff. Lawrence Sutin questions whether such an event took place:

> Webb portrays Gurdjieff's triumph—and Crowley's putative inner thoughts—with a heavy-handed novelistic touch. If this brutal banishment did occur, then it is remarkable that Crowley, who harbored animus toward so many rival teachers, never did so toward Gurdjieff.[10]

While it is clear from Nott's record that this meeting did in fact occur, as far as Webb's version goes, one would normally be inclined to agree with Sutin that it is unlikely that Crowley would make no mention of such rough treatment. (Although Crowley is silent on this matter, he did make disparaging remarks about Gurdjieff's famous pupil P.D. Ouspensky, calling him a 'verbose, ignorant quack' in *The Book of Thoth*). There is, however, the question of timing, as Crowley's published *Confessions* covers his life only up till 1924; the encounter with Gurdjieff took place in 1926. (Of course, Crowley kept diaries throughout his whole life, but in fact there are some known gaps in his diaries where he either stopped writing or what he wrote did not survive.) Additionally, Webb's account is difficult to dismiss entirely because it is in keeping with Gurdjieff's behavior and even his teaching methods. He was a volatile man in general. This account from J.G. Bennett describing the ordeal that Gurdjieff's nephew Valentin endured while assisting the old magus in 1935 in Paris, gives a vivid depiction:

> He also had to maintain his serenity in the face of Gurdjieff's violent onslaughts, which were frequent and terrifying. Those who witnessed Gurdjieff's rages can understand what it would mean to have been exposed week after week to them. His entire body would shake, his face would grow purple, and a stream of vituperation would pour out. It cannot be said that the anger was uncontrollable, for Gurdjieff could turn it off in a moment—but it was unquestionably real.[11]

Bennett goes on to add that he doubts that Gurdjieff's anger was always a 'teaching device' but that nevertheless, in the case of his nephew, it appeared to in fact strengthen him, if for no other reason, because of the consciousness he developed in enduring it. That, of course, will not work in all cases. The line between Nietzsche's 'what does not kill me makes me stronger' and simple damage wrought by trauma is a fine one.

At any rate, it should also be noted that between 1924 and 1926, Gurdjieff had gone through many taxing events—his car crash in the summer of 1924, followed by the death of his mother in the summer of 1925, and the difficult death of his young wife Julia Ostrowska in June of 1926 (he had tried hard to cure her of her cancer). In fact, Gurdjieff's wife passed away a mere couple of weeks before Crowley's second visit to the Prieure and meeting with Gurdjieff. That fact alone would provide a possible explanation for Gurdjieff's volatile behavior, if Webb's account is by chance accurate.

At the time of writing his book, Webb was dealing with an encounter that took place over fifty years before; one wonders who his source was. Of James Webb himself, a few interesting things can be noted: he was educated at the same place as Crowley (Trinity College of Cambridge), was only thirty-four years old when he published his *The Harmonious Circle*, and he committed suicide that same year (he had struggled with mental health issues). Webb was a brilliant young scholar who had written previous books on occultism, writings which included a discussion of the 'rejected knowledge' syndrome, the idea that knowledge spurned by the rise of science ends up being the focus of esoteric, literary, or artistic circles, functioning as a kind of tool for rebellion against the Establishment. He titled his first book *The Flight from Reason* (later reprinted as *The Occult Establishment*), in which he argued that much of the esoteric revival of the late 19th and early 20th century was based on a revolt against insignificance, a need to re-assert the primacy of Man that had been dealt a serious blow by the scientific method. Webb's largest work (*The Harmonious Circle*) was his last, in which he spent eight years researching and writing about Gurdjieff and the Work. He made many contacts in the worldwide Gurdjieff community and became deeply involved in the matter of his subject. That said, he remained fundamentally an outsider, an investigative journalist—not one who was actually doing the inner work.[12]

It is difficult to conclude much about his account of the meeting of the Magi. Because he did not mention his sources for it, and because his account differs so much from Nott's, the accuracy of his version must be considered suspect. However, Webb was unquestionably a sincere researcher. I suspect that he actually did hear a story with some basis in reality that had been passed down, but one that after fifty years had suffered the usual distortion. What he likely reported was that 'fish story'.

Unfortunately, Webb's version has been passed around apparently without much consideration by some. William Patrick Patterson, who has written several books on Gurdjieff's life, simply repeats verbatim the Webb version of the meeting of the Magi in his otherwise excellent video documentary *Gurdjieff's Legacy* (Arete

Communications, 2003), even referring to Crowley as 'the black magician' and suggesting that Crowley chose to visit the Prieure just a few weeks after Gurdjieff's wife's death as he 'may have sensed a psychological weakness' in Gurdjieff at that time (which is almost certainly untrue). Finally, an even more outlandish version (complete with the requisite distorted Crowley legend) of the famous meeting was recorded by Fritz Peters:

> Many years ago, Alistair [sic] Crowley, who had made a name for himself in England as a 'magician' and who boasted, among other things, of having suspended his pregnant wife by her thumbs in an effort to produce a monster-child, made an unsolicited visit to Gurdjieff at Fontainebleau. Crowley was apparently convinced that Gurdjieff was a 'black magician' and the ostensible purpose of his visit was to challenge Gurdjieff to some sort of duel in magic. The meeting turned out to be anti-climactical as Gurdjieff, although he would not deny his knowledge of certain powers that might be called 'magic' refused to demonstrate any of them. In his turn, Mr. Crowley also refused to 'reveal' any of his powers so, to the great disappointment of the onlookers, we did not witness any supernatural feats. Also, Mr. Crowley departed with the impression that Gurdjieff was either (a) a fake, or (b) an inferior black magician.[13]

Peters is primarily known for his book *Boyhood with Gurdjieff*, which describes five years he spent with Gurdjieff at the Prieure from 1924 to 1929. Peters was born in 1913, so these years encompassed his boyhood period of age eleven to sixteen. He published the above account in 1965 but he was only thirteen when Crowley met Gurdjieff. As a result, his view of the Crowley-Gurdjieff encounter is understandably childlike, doubtless distorted by banal gossip and probably the dim memory of an event that occurred forty years prior to his writing about it. For one thing the idea that Crowley, suffering from heroin addiction and broke at the time, would have sought out some sort of 'magic duel' is ludicrous. For another, the notion that Crowley thought Gurdjieff a 'charlatan' is completely refuted by Crowley's own words from his diary, referring to Gurdjieff as an 'advanced adept'.

And as a fitting anticlimax to these breathless depictions of the meeting of the Magi, we have the following description from Gerald Suster:

> It was Yorke who gave me an accurate account of the meeting between Crowley and another celebrated magus, G.I. Gurdjieff, for he was the only other person present. There are a number of false versions...according to Yorke, Crowley and Gurdjieff met in Paris for about half an hour and nothing much happened other than a display of mutual male respect: 'They sniffed around one another like dogs, y'know. Sniffed around one another like dogs,' Yorke chuckled.[14]

Gurus at War

The meeting of Crowley and Gurdjieff fascinates for many reasons that go far beyond the mundane nature of the alleged encounter and the various (often absurd) psychological projections of those describing it, not least of which is that it makes one consider the actual similarities of the two men. Both were noted for their appearance (shaven heads, during a time when shaven heads were not fashionable, and penetrating gaze); both had been world travelers and intense seekers; both had magnetic personalities and the ability to hold the attention of others; both were brilliant and capable of being conniving and manipulative with the best of them; and both ultimately formulated their own very unique system, based on not just the accumulated wisdom of the traditions they'd studied in, but also their own carefully thought out attempt to guide humanity to its next level of evolution. Both were concerned, fundamentally, with *planetary* aims, far beyond mere personal aims.

On a sheer human level, they even shared a common dark

chapter on their journey: they both briefly considered suicide during difficult phases of their middle-aged years: Crowley in 1923, shortly after the collapse of his Cefalu commune and his expulsion from Italy; and Gurdjieff in late 1927, upon suddenly realizing that the book he had been laboring on for three straight years (*Beelzebub*) was unreadable and needed a stylistic re-write.[15]

It is always interesting to note how often gurus steer clear of each other, like big alpha dogs marking out psychic territory. One would think that there would be plenty of common ground in which to establish a higher brotherhood of sorts—or at the very least, demonstrate active curiosity in each other's teachings. But in truth this rarely happens. Amongst the usual reasons offered— they have limited time, are meant to work only with specific conceptual models, practical methods, and particular souls, etc.—is also the more natural one, being that they themselves simply *do not want to.*

To their closest admirers, both Crowley and Gurdjieff were held to be nothing short of supernatural—Crowley the 'prophet' of a 'new Aeon' selected by advanced intelligences, the herald of a coming good; and Gurdjieff (who actually *wrote* a book called *The Herald of Coming Good*[16]) a 'planetary or solar god' (to use Orage's term) come to offer a crucial spiritual dispensation for humanity. What then prevents them— and other gurus—from being more outwardly connected to each other?

The issue has much to do with the dynamics of spiritual power. As an interesting case study, we can briefly consider here the saga of the Indian Advaita master Harilal Poonja—the elderly guru who received a number of Osho's disciples after Osho's death in 1990— and his one-time American student Andrew Cohen (who had never been an Osho disciple). Cohen, an American from New York, met Poonja in 1986 in Lucknow, India. At the time Cohen was around thirty years old, a former musician and a sincere spiritual seeker. As an adolescent he'd had a peak spiritual experience in which he'd tasted non-duality or the essential Oneness of life, in a manner that was potent enough to remain with him as a profound memory for many years, always to remind him of the possibilities inherent in human life. He pursued interests such as martial arts and music but remained fundamentally dissatisfied. While in India, he sought out and found Poonja who at the time was in his mid-seventies and although very respected as an awakened master by those who knew him, he was basically low profile and unheard of in the West. Cohen spent a short time with Poonja, a few weeks, and while with him underwent a powerful *satori* (the Zen term for 'sudden awakening') in which he clearly realized non-duality, most notably between Poonja and himself. This was underscored in his first book published not long after, titled *My Master is Myself*.[17]

That very description—*my master is myself*—lies at the heart of the ancient Eastern tradition of 'guru-yoga', something found in both Hindu and Tibetan Buddhist traditions. The essential idea behind it is to see that the spiritual teacher is, in principle, a reflection of the awakened self within the seeker. To regard one's teacher as the 'buddha-mind' as they put in some Buddhist traditions, is a generally trustworthy way to accelerate one's spiritual progress, because it gives a good opportunity to subdue the ego, which by nature does not trust in the higher values represented by the guru's teaching and seeks to maintain separation and ego-identity at all costs. (This was also the rationale behind Osho's 'device' of creating lockets for his disciples containing a photo of himself.)

Of course it is a given that such an approach carries a risk factor, because to regard one's teacher as a reflection of one's awakened self assumes that the teacher is a worthy representative of such. But a subtler point behind guru-yoga is that it has the power to override 'imperfections' in the guru. Put simply, it is possible to attain significant spiritual realization in the company of a flawed teacher. Likewise, it is also possible to experience considerable disillusionment and pain when associating with a teacher who turns out to have greater character flaws than one might have initially imagined.

Cohen eventually had a falling out with his master—largely over his perception that Poonja's behavior was seriously out of alignment with what he taught— documented in his somewhat harsh book *Autobiography of an Awakening*.[18] His decision to turn against his guru, and the subsequent backbiting that went on from both sides of the Poonja-Cohen camps, was reminiscent of a somewhat nastier version of Ouspensky's separation from Gurdjieff. In both cases, the student (Ouspensky and Cohen) decided that they'd seen and gathered enough subjective evidence that the teacher (Gurdjieff and Poonja) had serious character defects that compromised their work too much.

Poonja died in 1997 at the age of eighty-six; ironically, in the last decade of his life, he became very well known and attracted hundreds of devoted Western students, largely because of the publicity generated for him by Andrew Cohen. Many, if not most, of these students were former disciples of Osho who sought out a 'living master' after Osho's death in 1990. The jury remains out on the quality of character of both Poonja and Cohen, but anyone who studies their respective teachings will be struck by a simple fact: both were/are passionate teachers with skill, and both have inspired (and awakened, to some extent) many.

Cohen, as the younger of the two men, has met with criticism for what some perceive as a deeply disrespectful attitude toward an elderly teacher, but it can be argued that Cohen has more than compensated for that (if indeed such even needs compensation) by seeking out and engaging in a broad range of dialogue with many established spiritual teachers. For that alone he is to be commended, if only because of the rarity of it. As mentioned at the top of this chapter, spiritual teachers, especially well-established ones with a loyal following (regardless of the size of the following) very rarely spend any significant time with other teachers. Cohen has been a vivid exception to that trend. He has even taken it one step further by engaging in a series of dialogues and co-teaching seminars with the well-known American writer and theorist of consciousness studies, Ken Wilber.

Cohen's story, though mired in controversy and discord in his relationship with his root-teacher, is nevertheless a rarity in that he appears to be the first so-called 'enlightened' teacher in modern times to actively pursue dialogue with other teachers and even to co-teach with one of them. Psychological interpretations of this would be easy to come by, an obvious one being that Cohen may have been seeking to heal his relationship with the father-archetype (and thus vicariously with his now dead former guru), but nothing negates the fact that he has set an interesting and very unusual example.

A less involved and more amusing version of odd teacher-teacher dynamics can be found in the relationship between Osho and J. Krishnamurti. The latter was born in 1895, almost two generations before Osho, but during the 1960s and 70s they were probably the two most popular and notorious gurus in India. To use the term 'relationship' to describe their dynamic is being generous—the two never met in the flesh. But as extremely high profile gurus they were often exposed to each other's teachings or disciples, and frequently commented—often harshly—on each other. (These mutual insults reached something of a climax in the 1980s when Krishnamurti referred to Osho as a 'criminal'.)

In 2007, I was invited by the Theosophical Society in Toronto to give a talk and run a day-long workshop for about twenty-five of their local members. While there I had a chance to have a talk with a Mr. Pattal, the president at that time of the Toronto chapter, who hailed from India and who remembered the heady days of the late 1960s when Osho and Krishnamurti were the two main 'stars' of the guru-circuit in Bombay. He told me how seekers would gravitate from one to the other and of the subtle rivalries that would ensue. It has always been a long standing paradox that gurus who teach divine principles are themselves often seemingly light years apart, a fact that often confuses their followers and in worst case scenarios leads to the creation of rival religions that then usurp the original intention behind the creation of a spiritual community gathered around a teacher, wielding it instead as a weapon against the followers of the rival prophet. The Gurdjieff-Ouspensky split was a textbook example of that.

Krishnamurti's life spanned most of the 20th century and reads like the archetypal tale of a 'chosen one' who is fated from a young age to be an outsider. Groomed by the leaders of the Theosophical Society, that highly influential but uneven metaphysical organization founded in 1875 by Helena Blavatsky and Henry Steel Olcott, Krishnamurti was supposed to be an incarnation of a great world teacher, a type of Second Coming (sometimes compared to Maitreya, the 'next Buddha' of Buddhist canon). At the last moment Krishnamurti rebelled against this cosmic destiny, rejected the whole plan, and spent the next sixty-plus years wandering the world as a fiery and iconoclastic, profound teacher of spiritual awakening.

No doubt in part for his rebellious spirit, as well as the obvious quality of his understanding, Krishnamurti earned Osho's abiding interest and deep respect. When Krishnamurti died in 1985 at the age of 90, Osho remarked:

> He has died, and it seems the world goes on its way without even looking back for a single moment that the most intelligent man is no longer there. It will be difficult to find that sharpness and that intelligence again in centuries. But people are such sleep walkers, they have not taken much note. In newspapers, just in small corners where nobody reads, his death is declared. And it seems that a ninety-year-old man who has been continuously speaking for almost seventy years, moving around the world, trying to help people to get unconditioned, trying to help people to become free—nobody seems even to pay a tribute to the man who has worked the hardest in the whole of history for man's freedom, for man's dignity.

Those highly laudatory words were soon followed by less flattering observations from Osho:

Krishnamurti failed because he could not touch the human heart; he could only reach the human head. The heart needs some different approaches. This is where I have differed with him all my life: unless the human heart is reached, you can go on repeating parrot-like, beautiful words—they don't mean anything. Whatever Krishnamurti was saying is true, but he could not manage to relate it to your heart. In other words, what I am saying is that J. Krishnamurti was a great philosopher but he could not become a master. He could not help people, prepare people for a new life, a new orientation.[19]

These comments of Osho are problematic, given the benefit of hindsight. Osho may indeed be accurate in diagnosing Krishnamurti's weakness, but it's also apparent that the 'less heart-oriented' Krishnamurti did not leave behind a legacy of unsavory elements like the Oregon-Rajneeshpuram fiasco. The point that can be taken there is that 'ability to touch the human heart' can be a double-edged thing as is generally the case whenever passion is awakened. Krishnamurti was undeniably passionate but he did not have Osho's interest in cultivating close relationships with disciples, nor in setting up a large organization. So while Krishnamurti's approach remained much dryer and less involved interpersonally with followers, he also never had to deal with the immense disappointment that accompanies the destruction of a large commune and the dismantling of an entire vision.

The very paradox of the spiritual teacher is never better illustrated than in the interplay between Osho and Krishnamurti, both being seen as deeply enlightened by their followers (as well as by non-followers) and yet both having utterly different means by which to share their insights with humanity. Krishnamurti was dead-set against the type of guru-disciple relationship cultivated by Osho. He preached autonomy of spirit above all else, whereas Osho, particularly between the period of 1970-85, worked in a framework that was very much based on guru-yoga, where a deep level of trust and surrender is required by the disciple. After all, this was a man who not only gave personally crafted initiate names to each of his followers but also had them wear a locket around their necks containing a photo of himself. Seen by a disinterested outsider, such practices must have seemed deeply cultic, reinforcing dependency on the guru and little else. Experienced from the inside, however, the power of the process can never be underestimated. Guru-yoga is a potent and potentially deeply transformative practice because it allows for a vehicle in which certain elements of ego can be quickly vanquished, like fear, distrust, exaggerated independence, control tendencies—the list of undesirable traits that can be evaporated by an inwardly surrendered relationship with an authentic guru is almost endless.

However, all practitioners of faith-based traditions argue something similar. One need look no further than the tradition of the 'born-again' Christian. The point can be made that most faith-based paths differ from guru-yoga with a living master, being based on trust in a dead master, which is arguably much easier. Strong, *living* gurus are notoriously disruptive, and at best, not polite. To be near them is to be near a fire, and to be 'calcified' and 'dissolved' as the terms from alchemy have it—to be cooked in the heat and penetrating light of clear vision.

History is full of terrible examples of those who have 'surrendered' to a spiritual authority, only to turn out to be the latest example of intolerance and narrowness of understanding. Thus, guru-yoga and anything requiring the overriding of critical faculties by 'trust' and 'surrender' is intensely double-edged, because the point can be made that such a practice is really only intended for a mature seeker, one who can recognize clearly just what they are putting their trust in.

At any rate, the distance between Krishnamurti and Osho was great not just because of dissimilar character but because their very method and approach to the matter of awakening souls was almost diametrically opposed. And yet it can be easily argued that both shared a common level of understanding. The whole thing illustrates, once again, that enlightenment—the realization of truth—and the *teaching* of it, by whatever means, bear little relation. And this must be seen as one natural cause behind the typical disconnect between spiritual teachers.

Crowley and Gurdjieff may not have had much of a meeting back in 1926 in Fontainebleau, but the matter is likely academic. Even if their meeting had been more substantial, the odds that they would have agreed on much are very small. Even more likely is that the more they would have talked, the more they would have disagreed—not necessarily about core-level truths, but about the all-important matter of how to implement them, and above all, how to teach them.

Chapter 14
Transmission and Legacy

There are many magical teachers but in recorded history we have scarcely had a dozen Magi in the technical sense of the word. They may be recognized by the fact that their message may be formulated as a single word, which word must be such that it overturns all existing beliefs and codes.[1]
Aleister Crowley

Legacy: A gift from one who is legging it out of this vale of tears.
Ambrose Bierce, *The Devil's Dictionary*

I love Mankind. It's people that I can't stand.
Charlie Brown

Transmission: Of Three Wise Men and a Secret Message

There is one essential area in which Crowley and Gurdjieff at first glance appeared to differ substantially from Osho, and that concerns the subject of *transmission*. Although both Crowley and Gurdjieff made a number of unique contributions to transformational work, neither denied that they were representatives of something much greater than themselves. Crowley's prime mission as he saw it was to present an entirely new world view which had been transmitted to him—and through him—by Aiwass. That Crowley clearly saw Aiwass in an objective light has been established (see Chapter 4). He maintained that this entity was the voice behind *The Book of the Law* and Crowley identified himself as the herald of Aiwass. Beyond that, it is not always clear exactly how Crowley saw himself—at times he is awash in grandiosity, categorizing himself as a prophet in a select historical group (along with Thoth, Krishna, Buddha, Lao Tzu, Dionysius, Moses, and Mohammad), while at other times honestly confessing the sheer ordinary light he saw himself in:

> My simplicity is such that I often wonder if I am not half-witted…what courage I have comes partly from shame at being so sensitive and timid.[2]

Gurdjieff too saw himself as an emissary, saying, 'I am a small man compared to those who sent me'. His sources were famously vague and unconfirmed—Rafael Lafort's book, *Teachers of Gurdjieff*, in which the author (Idries Shah, using a pen-name) claimed to have visited and had conversations with Gurdjieff's original Sufi masters, has been quite thoroughly debunked and discredited.[3] John Bennett, who made a more comprehensive and sincere search in the Near East for Gurdjieff's teaching sources, had interesting but only indefinite results.[4] Nevertheless, the essential point here is that although Gurdjieff presented an original teaching, he did not claim to be acting alone. He openly stated more than once that he was the transmitter of an ancient knowledge. His job was merely to upgrade this knowledge, to make it useful for 20th century men and women.

Osho, at first glance, appeared to be acting entirely alone. Many times, he made the point of asserting that he'd never had a teacher—either in his life as Osho or in his 'previous lives'. This was part of the interesting paradox of the man: on the one hand brazenly declaring his unshakeable independence and yet on the other hand guiding others into becoming followers of himself. He used to claim, especially in his last years, that he was not a leader and that he had no followers—his disciples were just his friends—but this could be seen to be true only in the most abstract sense. His people were indeed his followers, for the most part being deeply devoted to him.

Many Osho disciples commonly had a collection of books that were all Osho's. One long time disciple once said to me, 'I feel no need to have any books that are not Osho's.' That may be 'friendship', but it is a highly exclusive type!

But is it really true that Osho had no teachers, or was not part of a tradition greater than him? More than once he stated that he was just 'part of existence' and in that sense he was indeed just another star in the firmament. As with Crowley's 'Every man and every woman is a star', he was an equal member of the family of existence. His independence, however fiery, however kingly, could not isolate him from the Totality. Moreover, in a collection of talks given in the early 1980s and compiled into a book titled *Glimpses of a Golden Childhood*, he did refer to teachers he had when he was young, beginning shortly after the death of his beloved grandfather. There were three main guides; all three were eccentric *sadhus*.[5] The first was named Magga Baba. ('Baba' in Hindi means 'father' or 'old man' but is a term often given to saints, gurus, and wandering holy men.) This *sadhu* apparently had taken some vow of silence because, according to Osho, he never spoke—except to Osho, and then only late at night. There is no evidence from Osho's words that Magga Baba ever said much; it was rather the quality of his *being* that rubbed off on Osho. He was a living demonstration of the idea that, as Gurdjieff said, a 'man of being' is greater than a 'man of knowledge'. As the American philosopher Emerson once famously wrote,

Who you are speaks so loudly I cannot hear what you say.

Osho's description of Magga Baba was curiously simplistic—the old man one day shows up in Osho's town, sits under a tree, and does basically nothing except on occasion to make gibberish sounds, apparently to scare away persistent curious bystanders. And yet why such a wandering old man should attract such attention—in a country where spiritual wanderers can be found practically on every street corner—is not made clear by Osho. The reader of his words is rather left to read between the lines, to see the point, which is that Osho is indicating that this man had extraordinary presence and quality of being. In addition, Osho makes it clear that Magga Baba could not be controlled in the slightest. Like a 20th century Diogenes, he does absolutely nothing that does not arise from the deepest core of his being. He is utterly true to himself. Osho said,

> Magga Baba had to be visited at least once each day. He was a kind of spiritual nourishment. He helped me tremendously although he never gave any directions except by his very being. Just by his very presence he triggered unknown forces in me.[6]

That is a classic description of spiritual transmission, the same process many disciples of Osho would assert was their own experience with the master.

After Magga Baba, the second wise man was Pagal Baba, an elderly wanderer Osho first met when he was twelve years old, and whom he immediately recognized as a 'saint', saying that 'His presence was luminous. You could recognize him among thousands.' (Osho usually used the term 'saint' in a mocking or derogatory fashion—claiming almost all so-called saints were not authentic—but in this case he clearly meant it as 'sage' or 'enlightened one'). They met while swimming together in a river. Pagal Baba functioned as a psychopomp for Osho, a guide to many realms both inner and outer. He took Osho to sacred sites such as the Himalayas, the Taj Mahal, the Ellora and Ajanta caves. He was also the man who encouraged him to obtain an academic master's degree. Perhaps more importantly, he introduced Osho to many creative people—'great artists and musicians' as Osho put it. These influences were all keys, the echo of which could be seen in much of Osho's vision as a philosopher and spiritual master. He embraced the grandeur of the Himalayas in his work in the form of values like silence and dignity; and he embraced the creative spirit utterly, being one of the very few gurus to emphasize art, music, and the creative impulse in his work with his disciples. In fact, Pagal Baba wanted Osho to become a musician, but Osho resisted, and eventually told the old mystic that music did not truly fulfill him, that it was a 'lower kind of meditation'. Pagal Baba agreed, but maintained that music was an effective bridge to deeper states of consciousness.

Osho's relationship with Pagal Baba had an interesting twist to it—Osho claimed that the reason that Pagal Baba was consistently kind toward him, in a way that Osho did not feel that he merited, was because Pagal Baba had attempted to murder Osho in a past life (by poisoning, although according to Osho the attempt failed). In this way, it was implied that Pagal Baba was seeking to balance his past deeds. But underneath this esoteric interpretation was perhaps a more revealing element that concerned the idea of transmission. Pagal Baba sought to pass something on to Osho and to be responsible for him in some way. As Pagal Baba grew old, Osho claimed that he saw some sort of shadow lurking in his 'aura' and although he was confident that it did not mean impending death, he felt he did know what it was. Pagal Baba confirmed Osho's perception and told him that the 'shadow' he saw was representative of the fact that Pagal Baba was waiting for a particular man to appear whom he could pass Osho on to—in effect, his next spiritual guide—but that this man had not yet shown up.

We in Western culture, with our heavy emphasis on intellectual training, information, and our diminished attention spans, may have difficulty in appreciating this kind of relating that is clearly directed by intuition. However, anyone who spends some time in India will become aware of certain things, one of which is that Indian men, in general, are much more intuitive than European or North American men. That 'intuition' itself is not always a reliable psychic function is a given, but it also makes possible all kinds of opportunities for growth because it has the potential of working through matters—and arriving at decisions—much more quickly than conventional rational thought.

Pagal Baba, in discussing with Osho this 'new guide' that he was awaiting to take over Osho's spiritual tutelage after his death, said an interesting thing:

You are very young and I would like someone like me just to be around you. In fact, this is an old convention, that if a child is ever going to become awakened, then at least three awakened people should recognize him at an early age.

Osho replied that he thought that was nonsense because, as he put it, 'nobody can prevent me from awakening'. The response is interesting, and vintage Osho: he frames it in antinomian terms. He cannot be controlled. Even in his youth he was showing signs of the spiritual 'outlaw' he was to grow into.

There was indeed a third Magi that showed up to guide Osho in his youth, and his name was Masta Baba. Unlike Magga Baba and Pagal Baba, he was a young man, in his mid thirties. His first meeting with Osho was unusual; Osho implies that Masta Baba immediately recognized Osho's caliber and acknowledged him with great formality of respect, repeatedly touching his feet. He then insisted that Osho call him 'Masto'—a term used by elders toward youth—and asked that he say it three times. Osho explained that 'in the East...unless you say a thing thrice it does not mean much.' Osho then added (showing, if nothing else, how Pagal Baba's ideas had influenced him):

...Unless three enlightened people recognize a child as a future buddha (awakened one), it is almost impossible for him to become one.

Osho goes on to mention that of all the remarkable men and women he met—and he claimed to have met many more than Gurdjieff did—these three were the most important, because they all recognized something in Osho, a potential greatness. He also remarks that his family was diametrically opposed to this kind of reinforcement, and that for them Osho was mostly a troublesome problem.

It is of course tempting, and not difficult, to apply a bit of psychoanalysis to that whole matter. The 'three wise men' apparently combined to reinforce Osho's deep sense of entitlement that had originally been nurtured by his grandparents who had indulged him in many ways for the first seven years of his life. He was treated like a prince, made to feel deeply special. The rest of his family—his father, mother, and many younger siblings—did not reinforce this, but rather opposed Osho's burgeoning self-importance. In so doing they applied the important counterforce—Gurdjieff's 'holy denying'—that allowed for a more balanced development of his character. If valid, that view is, of course, only concerning ego dynamics. There remains the whole higher aspect, the genuine love these men clearly had for the young Osho—who himself must have been greatly lovable—and the legitimate higher values they transmitted to him.

However the matter is seen, it is undeniable that Osho had mentors, wise men who took him under their wing and who appeared to both guide him and deeply respect his naturally rebellious nature. These wandering mystics were part of the great tradition of sages that is unified only by quality of being and depth of understanding. The only 'secret brotherhood' they are part of is the so-called 'invisible school'—masters of wisdom who roam freely, and mostly unknown, even to each other— throughout time.

Curiously, Gurdjieff also had three chief mentors as a young man—his father, Dean Borsch, and Father Evlissi (also known as Bogachevsky); as did Crowley—George Cecil Jones, Allan Bennett, and Samuel Liddell Mathers. In terms of the issue of transmission, at first glance, both Crowley and Gurdjieff represented a more defined lineage than did Osho. Crowley saw himself as the bringer of a new dawn, being a link in an ancient line descended back from—so he claimed—a minister of Hoor-paar-kraat (known by the Greeks as Harpocrates, the child version of the Egyptian falcon god Horus). To the Egyptians and Greeks he was the god of silence; to the Egyptians he was also connected to the rising Sun at dawn.

There are interesting connections in the symbolism of both silence and the rising Sun with Osho's work. Back in the early 1970s, when Osho had first created his trademark Dynamic Meditation technique, the forth and key stage in the method—where a voice booms 'Stop!' after which everyone is required to freeze in place and remain absolutely silent—was originally timed to correspond with the moment the morning sun first peaked over the horizon.[7] (The 'Stop!' method was of course borrowed from Gurdjieff). It was, in a sense, Osho's version of an Egyptian Sun adoration rite—and he hinted at his Egyptian connection in the presence of giant black pyramids he had built in the Pune ashram as his death approached. Crowley had a special term for those who had crossed the Abyss of ego-dissolution and emerged as awake to their divine condition he said they dwelled in the 'City of the Pyramids'. Osho's Pune center effectively became, shortly after his death, a city of pyramids, a fittingly poetic, if unwitting Thelemic, tribute to the master who (as his people believed) had returned to his divine source *prior* to death.

Crowley's prime document, *The Book of the Law*, is rooted in Egyptian mystical symbolism. There is a notable symbolic association here with Gurdjieff who sometime around 1890 famously found an obscure map belonging to an Armenian priest that featured a depiction of 'pre-sands Egypt'. William Patrick Patterson, in his video documentary, *Gurdjieff in Egypt: The Origin of Esoteric Knowledge*, argues that the reason Gurdjieff was 'seized with violent trembling' when he first saw the map is that it showed on it the Sphinx, which is generally accepted by most historians as having been constructed around 2,500 BC. If a map of 'pre-sands' Egypt showed the Sphinx then this implied that the Sphinx was much older than its conventionally accepted age, as that region of the Sahara has not known rainfall for at least seven thousand years— 'pre-sands' would then imply an Egypt of at least seven thousand years ago.[8] The argument continues that the Sphinx is thus likely a legacy of an antediluvian (pre-flood) society such as the legendary Atlantis first mentioned by Plato in his *Timaeus*.

The Egyptian Sphinx faces due East on the Giza plateau; the symbolism of the rising Sun was of immense importance to the ancient Egyptians, centering on the notion of rebirth (the Sun, personified as the god Ra, was thought to be reborn each morning, the Egyptians having no concept of a rotating Earth). The whole issue boils down to conquering death, and indeed that is what most Egyptian high magic was ultimately concerned with. The key point, however, is that these are not merely symbolic funerary matters or mythic mumbo-jumbo. Egyptian myth, which centrally involves the dead pharaoh being identified with Osiris, the resurrected Lord of the Underworld, can be more rightfully understood as symbolic of the initiatory process of the living—that is, how to attain one's immortality *prior to death*. In other words, how to become self-realized, enlightened.[9]

The point of course is not how old the Sphinx is or how far back into time spiritual transmissions extend. The point is realizing the bornless and the deathless—that within us that is beyond space and time. Gurdjieff taught about the need to 'create a soul' by working on oneself, so as to survive death. Crowley taught the goal of the Knowledge and Conversation of the Holy Guardian Angel, leading to the realization of our timeless, deathless Self. Osho taught enlightenment, the ecstatic merging with Existence. Each of these men was, in a sense, a manifestation of an archetypal wizard like Thoth or Hermes, the 'divine messenger of wisdom' who transmits the sacred teachings not of how to worship the divine, but rather of how to *know* the divine—so totally and intimately and directly that one becomes that. That is the 'Secret Message' of all bona fide adepts. To *become* that which we seek.

Symbolic connections with Thoth/Hermes/Mercury extend further: for ancient Hindus the planet Mercury (associated with Hermes) was named 'Budha' and understood to be symbolic of wisdom. Of special note is the Caduceus wand of Hermes, with its twin serpents signifying the resolution of opposites, the integration of spiritual with material, of 'psyche' with 'soma', of self and selflessness. As Rene Guenon pointed out, in some heraldic symbolism the serpent is replaced by the image of the flaming sword, what he calls 'a figure of wisdom and the power of the Word.' This 'Word' is what Crowley was pointing toward when he referred to the special dispensation brought by those occasional teachers who come to initiate an entirely new spiritual current—brought about in part by the sheer cumbersome weight and decadence of the old current. Inevitably, such teachers must face the tremendous weight of tradition, and the general overall resistance the human psyche has toward change of any significant sort. That is why, at least in part, their sword needs to be 'flaming'.[10]

Legacy: The Good, the Bad, and the Ugly

In the end, at the human level—consistent with all 'messengers of the divine'—the efforts of Crowley, Gurdjieff, and Osho did amount to failure to a fair extent. (It is almost axiomatic that a spiritual teacher's work becomes aborted, diminished, or destroyed outright by egocentric forces, whether from within or without.) Equally so, all three had successes. What follows is a very brief outline of some criticism and recognition of their respective accomplishments.

There is perhaps no assessment that is more representative of how Crowley is still regarded, even by the so-called spiritual cognoscenti, than a passage found in Andrew Rawlinson's massive six-hundred page text on 20th century Western gurus, *The Book of Enlightened Masters*. The part in question appears in Rawlinson's entry on Crowley's mentor and friend Allan Bennett:

> ...everything suggests that [Bennett] straightforwardly abandoned esotericism and became a Buddhist. But it is certainly true that magic and Buddhism could be seen at that time as aspects of the same truth in a way that they cannot now. So it is

hardly surprising that when Bennett went to Ceylon in 1898, he should hand over his esoteric manuscripts to a fellow magician. It is perhaps slightly more surprising that his trusted confidant should have been Aleister Crowley. In fact, Bennett, who was a little older than Crowley, was actually Crowley's teacher in the magical arts. Of course, everything that Crowley says has to be taken with a shovelful of salt.[11]

Despite this dig at Crowley, Rawlinson then goes on for several hundred words to rely substantially on Crowley for his entry on Bennett, quoting extensively from Crowley's *Confessions*. Perhaps even more oddly in the entire (otherwise excellent) book, with its hundreds of entries on Western spiritual teachers—a number of whom are relatively obscure or of questionable quality—there is no entry for Crowley. This is all the more ironic owing to the subtitle of the book (*Western* Teachers in *Eastern* Traditions), given Crowley's travels and studies in the Orient and his excellent writings on Eastern pathways.

One of my intentions in writing this book was to aid in restoring Crowley's reputation to a more rightful standing. He is, in my opinion, probably the single most unfairly maligned mystic and teacher of recent times; perhaps a modern day equivalent of Apollonius of Tyana or Simon Magus. Even most of the modern spiritual teachers, writers, or other 'authorities', whether they are academically or practically oriented, will not touch Crowley with a ten foot wand. Many are remarkably ignorant of what he actually wrote and taught. In general, he is either maligned or given a dubiously researched evaluation. More commonly, he is passed over in silence.

As an amusing example of this, John Hogue—considered one of the preeminent scholars of the life and work of the famous 16th century French seer Nostradamus—once went to the trouble of compiling a chart comprised of a dozen prominent 20th century gurus who seemed to have attributes forecast by Nostradamus centuries before. The chart lists eight essential traits Hogue claims that Nostradamus specified as being key to the 'founding of the coming spiritual revolution'.[12] These traits were the following:

Clues: Visionaries:	East	Hermes	Outlawed	Red	Mars	Moon	Travels	Bird
Osho	*	*	*	*	*	*	*	*
Gurdjieff	*	*	*		*		*	
Maharishi		*	*	*	*			*
Rev. Moon	*		*	*		*	*	
Adi Da			*	*	*	*		*
Krishnamurti		*	*			*		*
Prabhupada		*	*	*				*
Abdu'l-baha		*	*	*				*
Yogananda		*			*			*
Meher Baba		*						*
Sai Baba	*			*				
Hubbard			*			*		

As we can see, in the Messiah Olympics Osho scored eight points, with Gurdjieff and others in hot pursuit with five. Meher Baba, Sai Baba, and L. Ron Hubbard bring up the rear. (For any wondering, Hogue is not a disciple of Osho. Although, unsurprisingly, this chart was reprinted in the Introduction to Juliet Forman's *Bhagwan: The Buddha for the Future* in an article written by Osho's doctor and close disciple George Meredith.) Hogue's means of classification may at first sight seem obscure, but he has his method to the apparent madness. For example, 'East' does not mean merely 'from the East'—it means, according to Hogue's interpretations of Nostradamus' quatrains (four-line prophecies), 'a man from the East who finds his teachings welcomed in the West'.[13]

What is interesting is that of Nostradamus' eight criteria, Crowley easily fits the bill for seven of them, only 'missing' that he was not 'from the East'. And yet in many ways he was: he made extended journeys and stays in the Orient, was the first Western magus to integrate Eastern Yoga into the Work, and he headed up an organization called The Order of the Oriental Templars. As for the rest: Crowley's association with Hermes requires no comment; he was far more than 'outlawed' in the way most of the other gurus were, he was *vilified* (only Osho was treated worse); 'Red', 'Mars', and 'Bird' are all symbols running rampant throughout his key works. (Just to note but one: his prime holy book, *The Book of the Law*, is usually printed with a flame or wine red cover, and is a doctrine that centers on the Egyptian falcon god Horus who is decidedly martial in places of the text.) 'Moon' is found (amongst other places) in his important novel *Moonchild*; and 'Travels' needs no comment, Crowley being one of the greatest pre-jet era globetrotters ever.

I cite Hogue's survey not because I think it is of any profound significance (it is entertaining nonsense) but because it typifies Crowley's remarkable ability to fly under the radar of modern writers and scholars of the spiritual and esoteric. He was a kind of European equivalent of the American mystic Richard Rose, who was once described as 'the greatest man never known'. Crowley, of course, *was* known, but like Rose his wisdom is generally not.

That said, Crowley's failures are very human and apparent. His remarks about his various 'Scarlet Women' generally end with the comment 'failed', and although it is the women he is giving failing grades to, this would obviously include him. His epic struggles with his drug addictions throughout the last third of his life bears ample testimony to the limitations within himself he was dealing with. More than one biographer, observer, or student of Crowley's life has remarked on his difficulties relating to people. Lon Milo DuQuette put it very simply: 'He was not good with people and often alienated those who loved him dearest.'[14] That is undoubtedly true. However, it goes without saying that that assessment applies to much of the human race. The part of the mind that contributes toward relationship sabotage and breakdown is the part that tends to become activated in the presence of those who know us best.

Crowley's tumultuous relationships were simply an overt and dramatic expression of the human condition (consistent with his intention to make much of his life an open book). As the American Zen master, Charlotte Joko Beck, once remarked,

Relationships don't work. There never was a relationship that worked.[15]

Zen master Beck was no nun; she was in her late fifties when she made those remarks, had raised three children, and been married for many years. She was referring rather to the context of egocentric relating, which is always based on the agenda to make others help us feel good about ourselves (which, alas, is the foundation of most conventional relationship). In typical dysfunctional relating we do this because we are too concerned about what others think of us (what Gurdjieff called 'inner considering'), and because deep down we do not have a high opinion of ourselves. The sole purpose of relationship is as a learning ground, a means by which to develop our capacity and skill to relate to the universe that surrounds us. But the ego-mind seeks to manipulate others into doing that work for us—'just love me and everything will be fine.' However, if we don't believe we are healed and whole on the inside, no amount of 'love' coming from the other will make that the case, and sooner or later we will hate the other for reminding us of our inner dysfunction. That is basically the standard recipe for most relationship issues.

From this follows the natural question: was Crowley, as a man who had experienced profound spiritual depths, as an 'Ipsissimus' and self-declared (or gods-declared, as it were) prophet of the new religion of Thelema, supposed to be beyond such things? Clearly not. Prophets who are also flawed human beings abound throughout history. A better question might be what exactly is a prophet? The word derives from the Greek *prophetes*, meaning an interpreter or spokesman for the gods. A prophet is a 'divine' messenger. Of course one person's divine is another person's diabolic, so the task for a prophet who wishes to be useful is to cut through lifeless doctrine and bring to life the timeless message of spiritual revelation and inner awakening.

Crowley was a walking testament to the very image of the unrecognized genius known only for his silly press reputation. It is easy to dismiss the tabloid hysteria. The key issue, however, lies in Crowley's own inner attainments. In 1909, in the Algerian desert with Victor Neuberg, he claimed, in a crucial juncture of his life, to 'cross the Abyss' and become a 'Magister Templi'.

The whole issue of the 'Abyss' warrants close examination. Crowley used the term to describe that vastness that any aspiring truth-seeker must inevitably face and pass through—a vastness that represents the ultimate emptiness of the ego, and the need to transcend its appearance. The problem is that by 1906 Crowley had taken to self-initiation. Much as with Gurdjieff's journeys with the 'Seekers of Truth' we have only his word to go on the matter. In most esoteric traditions, realizations are confirmed by someone else so as to guard against the particular delusion known as grandeur (or in more traditional terms, pride). Gurdjieff claimed that he had such confirmations, but in the end his claims were similar to Crowley's in that they amount to a proclamation. How are these proclamations to be trusted as truth? There is no way to know for sure. A young woman once sat in front of the Advaita master Harilal Poonja and boldly asked him, 'How do I know that you are enlightened?' He replied, 'As you are now, you cannot know. First become enlightened, then such questions will not matter.'

It is the perfect response, and the only worthwhile one because all spiritual awakenings are ultimately a type of self-initiation. For while we may not be able to confirm in any way Crowley's claim to have passed through the Abyss, it is nevertheless undeniable that he provided a beacon, a powerful light that pointed toward something shrouded in darkness. As J. Daniel Gunther clarified in his *Initiation in the Aeon of the Child*, Crowley was no Messiah; he was rather a Scribe who pointed toward something very great.[16] Much as

Gurdjieff did with his coarse language, smoking, drinking, and womanizing, and Osho with his fleet of luxury cars and trenchant indictments of politicians and religious leaders, Crowley deflected people with his seemingly vulgar tendencies and abrasive personality. But, in a sense, it was natural that he was this way because he was teaching about the resolution of opposites—literally, the way to go beyond good and evil, beyond the dance of moral polarizing that has for too long been the bane of humanity. He could do this precisely because he was such a conflict of light and dark himself. His prime value is as a messenger, a pointer, and in that regard he is no different from all gurus and teachers.

Crowley never underwent in-depth psychology aided by a skilled facilitator. He had much internal 'clearing' to do around his mother whose control over him as a child he resented. He lost his father at the tender time of pre-pubescence. He was bullied in school. He appeared to have a near compulsive need to be desired and approved of by women. And he did not show evidence of having much compassion, except very sporadically at best. In short, he was undeniably egocentric. The essential difference between him and many other gurus, teachers, and prophets is that he made no real effort to cover this up, to be deceptive about his human foibles.[17]

The standard psychological critique of Crowley is that his biggest single failure was inadequately embodying in his own life the lofty values that he so brilliantly taught and wrote about. The critique continues that even though he had penetrated to levels of mind and Being that few reach, it was in the simple, profane details of his life that he came up short—and that because of this he was ultimately no more than an intellectual—not a bona fide mystic or transformed man.

However, this assessment falls short because it assumes that we can see the entire big picture of what destiny awaits a given person as they commit themselves to the inner work of transformation—and in particular, to one who assumes a guru role and offers a teaching of substance. Some die young and painfully (Jesus). Others live into old age with large and devoted followings (Buddha). Yet others begin as black magicians, undergo enormous purifying suffering, and end their days in a remote cave (Milarepa). Still others found numerous meditation centers, help hundreds of people, and yet die of liver damage brought on by years of heavy drinking (Chogyam Trungpa). The Sufi idea of *malamat,* of the 'way of blame', bears mention here, it being a manner of being adopted by a mystic that ensures that others will be offended or alienated by the mystic's behavior. This can serve several purposes, one of which is helping to prevent excessive dependency in followers, by making a master—via his bizarre behavior—basically impossible to mimic and thus throwing the disciple back upon himself. According to Sufi teachings, this is also a means God has of assuring that his closest devotees, his chosen 'sons and daughters' (gurus and prophets) who do his work in the world, do not become mired in pride and self-importance. And so in theory the closer one gets to truth, the more one attracts blame from the world so that all vestiges of pride are ground down, making more space for the divine in one's heart. In other words, *malamat* is not just for the disciples, it is also for the master.

Crowley, Gurdjieff, and Osho all bore evidence of this way and its intentionality at least at times in their lives. But the main point here is to remember that one man's feast is another man's famine; appearances deceive, the most apparently virtuous all too often turn out to be otherwise, and many of the 'scoundrels' and 'failures' conceal the purest gold.

On a more esoteric level, the occultist S. Jason Black criticized Crowley for declaring that the Goetic spirits (entities conjured in Goetic ceremonial magick) are in fact just 'portions of the human brain'. Black comments that 'This single remark has misled thousands of sincere seekers, and created an excuse for even more thousands of dilettantes. Never in his life did Crowley have a real familiarity with psychology...'[18] While the latter remark, about

Crowley's grasp of modern psychology, is probably mostly correct, Black neglects to add that Crowley's psychologizing of the Goetic magick likely saved just as many thousands from getting too caught up in mental projections or falling prey to mental illness outright. Black's point is that esoteric work since the early 20th century is too often influenced by psychology, the idea that it's 'all just in your head'. And it is true that the inner can be emphasized to the point of getting out of balance, just as with one fixated on externals and ignoring their own mind. But if the point is ultimately to see beyond duality, to rise to egoless consciousness, then it is essential that we see the interdependence of mind and external reality. Back at the turn of the 20th century, psychology was in its infancy and in matters of spiritualism (such as through séances, and so on) prevailing views put heavy emphasis on external spiritual manifestations. By emphasizing the role of the brain and subjective consciousness in such matters, Crowley was bringing some needed balance to the matter.

Crowley's legacy survives principally in his prolific writings, and in the two occult organizations that bear his imprint—the Argenteum Astrum (or the A.˙. A.˙. as it is typically represented) and the Ordo Templi Orientis (or O.T.O. as it is more commonly referred to). The former was founded by Crowley and George Cecil Jones in 1907; it is a 'secret' group insofar as members do not know of each other, with but one exception: their immediate superior, a mentor who is at least one initiatory grade higher than themselves. At a certain point, if successful in the inner work, a member can take on a student themselves. This group is much more rigorous in testing inner work discipline and success in that than the O.T.O. The idea of avoiding contact between members outside of one's teacher (or one's student) has the benefit of circumventing most potential problems arising from the messy politics of relationship that have plagued so many mystery schools and spiritual communities. The downfall is the absence of appropriate social reinforcement that is the strong suit of community.

The O.T.O. is believed to have been founded around 1895 by the Austrian chemist and Freemason Karl Kellner (1851-1905) and the German Theodore Reuss (1855-1923) in either Austria or Germany. Clear records do not appear until 1904 (coincidentally the same year Crowley received *The Book of the Law*). At Kellner's death in 1905, he was succeeded by Reuss as head of the O.T.O. Kellner himself is considered the 'spiritual father' of the organization. It is a public organization with historical connections to Freemasonry, although since 1918 it has had no formal relationship with Freemasonry. As with the Golden Dawn, the O.T.O. is structured on initiatory degrees, as well as dramatic rituals including its central rite, the Gnostic Mass, a sort of Thelemic parallel of the Roman Catholic mass written by Crowley in 1913 while traveling in Russia. The O.T.O. to this day, numbers its memberships in the low thousands (of whom about 1,200 are in the U.S., as of 2008). A far larger number of people, however, have read Crowley (no doubt many of those surreptitiously) and that number is likely slowly increasing.

While Crowley's surviving literary legacy is entirely legitimate, of high quality, and powerful, his reputation has been only slightly rehabilitated since his 'rebirth' into public consciousness in the late 1960s via the Beatles. Despite a number of fair and excellent works on his life and teachings that have appeared since the turn of the 21st century in particular, he remains not very well known to the public at large outside of Britain, and if recognized, is still regarded with suspicion and generally misunderstood. Outwardly the *Sunday Express* and *John Bull* tabloid headlines of the 1920s, along with his expulsion from Italy in 1923 and from France in 1929, severely damaged his image. The only significant biography on him that was available during the 1950s and 60s was John Symonds' *The Great Beast*, and although an important work, was largely negative and served mostly to reinforce a negative public perception of him. Inwardly, Crowley brought much of this on himself for his own reasons. Nevertheless, it is a high probability that with the passage of time his eccentricities of character will slowly fade into the background as his lofty ideas come to the foreground, and their merit increasingly, and deservedly, recognized.

Gurdjieff famously abandoned his primary work in the mid-1920s following his near-fatal car accident, and decided to switch to writing, recording his teachings for posterity—partly in 'scrambled' form—in his books. His work, although influential to some, never really took off in a major way. Gurdjieff was one of the most profound and seminal spiritual figures ever and yet he remains relatively unknown in the mainstream. When I give talks in various cities around the world I often ask the question, 'Who here has heard of Gurdjieff?' and very commonly not a single hand will go up in a group of thirty or forty people. When I Google the three subjects of this book (as of late 2009), I get returns as follows:

Osho: 2,960,000
Crowley: 764,000
Gurdjieff: 737,000

And that, as far as I've noticed, about accurately reflects the public's awareness of these men. Gurdjieff, though controversial, was not as sensational as either Osho or Crowley. He is, in some ways however, the most personally appealing of our three Magi. He was intensely human, even amongst his profound search for truth. This combination of his basic humanity—his love of his parents, of animals, his supporting many of his followers who had no money, even his filling his apartment in France with bad art just to support local starving artists—all spoke to a fundamental warmth. That he could be domineering and brutally rough with his most serious students—and that he had more than a touch of a Machiavellian opportunist in him—rounded him out as human in every way. That he combined it all with such a fierce search for esoteric wisdom under conditions of utmost political and geographic hardship, and that he finally succeeded in establishing a ray of light in the murkiness of Europe in the insane first half of the 20th century, is testament to his quality.

Gurdjieff's legacy has been complicated by the number of groups that arose as spinoffs from his original core group. This process had, of course, begun long before he'd died, when Ouspensky first separated himself and began his own independent line in England in 1921. Later examples of this included the non denominational church called the 'Fellowship of Friends', founded in 1970 by Robert Burton, a community that was originally based on Gurdjieffian-Ouspenskian teachings (although more recently has come to embrace a number of other traditions). Burton himself had had limited time in the Work, and according to Patterson (1998) his only mentor had himself never been instructed by an authentic Fourth Way teacher.

In this, there is a somewhat amusing connection between Burton's school and Crowley's original training ground (The Hermetic Order of the Golden Dawn). During the 1970s, when the phenomenon of the marketing of spiritual teachings was getting into gear (mostly via the remarkable savvy of Werner Erhard), members of Burton's school violated a basic tenet of Gurdjieff's Work—that being never to solicit the teachings—and began to promote their school by inserting impressively designed bookmarks, complete with their school's contact information, into all books they could find on Gurdjieff's Work in bookstores and libraries. As a result of this, several thousand people contacted them via the bookmarks and the Fellowship of Friends expanded remarkably.[19] Back in the 1980s, the major esoteric bookstore of my city was plagued by a recurring problem, which was that endless bookmarks were being inserted into all books dealing with the Western esoteric tradition (several large bookcases worth of). The identity of the organization on the bookmarks? It was a local chapter of the Golden Dawn. Apparently, they had picked up the bookmark marketing technique from Burton's 'Gurdjieff' school. (It should be stressed that since the 1980s there have been several different organizations calling themselves 'The Golden Dawn' or slight modifications of that name.)

The idea of marketing savvy in pushing spiritual teachings may seem nothing more than a reflection of materialistic, superficial, and intensely competitive times, but in fact it all has roots far before Werner Erhard and related acolytes. Gurdjieff himself was one of the first to charge money for spiritual teachings, and quite often, significant amounts. This was, however, balanced by the fact that he more than often let many receive his teachings for nothing; on occasion, he even subsidized students, and what money he made went to travel expenses, the upkeep of his massive Prieure, and/or the support of extended family members. His basic premise was that, for the average person, unless they pay for something they tend not to value it. And there is unquestionably great truth to this. Gurdjieff, however, was more than just a spiritual master; he was also a businessman, and this combination made him both a trailblazer and precedent-setter in a highly double-edged fashion. Many of his businesses were entirely apart from his transformational teachings and he can be said to have juggled these roles mostly with skill. The same cannot be said for many who followed in his footsteps. The Achilles Heel of integrating business with the Inner Work is that the Work more often than not gets diluted by the need to make it marketable. The temptation to manipulate for gain creeps in too easily when money is involved, which is one of the reasons monastic vows in most traditions involve a pledge of poverty, along with the understanding that peddling the teachings is a grave sin.

But what Gurdjieff, as much as any modern master understood, is that we are living in a new era. Old paradigms have fallen like Berlin Walls. What Crowley elaborately heralded as the new Aeon of Horus, of the Crowned and Conquering Child, many others have promoted in different terms and described with different cultural filters. All agree, however, that something major is afoot. Since the world wars of the 20th century, we have been in a quantum shift of some sort with unprecedented spikes in population and technology. Gurdjieff's main legacy may be said to be his strident effort to address the sheer power of this shift by moving transformational teachings from the monasteries and mountaintops to the urban realm—to the 'real world'. There was an edge of urgency in his vision—as he said, 'Unless the wisdom of the East joins with the energy of the West, the world will destroy itself.'

Gurdjieff's chief failure lay in his relationships with his three key male students—Ouspensky, Orage, and Bennett—the ones he hoped would be able to transmit and continue his work, like three loyal sons. None were able to, at least not as Gurdjieff wanted. In two of these cases, the problems (if we can call them that) can be attributed to competitiveness. Both Ouspensky and Bennett clearly wanted to be independent teachers, not apostles or lieutenants. Orage was more surrendered to his master but fell out with him over the issue of control, mainly. Gurdjieff was an autocrat, a domineering force, and by all appearances he could only be handled by others in periodic doses. The intensity of his presence ultimately alienated others—when he wasn't busy intentionally alienating them himself (which unquestionably he did at times, especially with Olga de Hartmann and Fritz Peters). However, I don't think it is an accident that his work was ultimately continued after his death under the leadership of a female disciple. There is a competitive element in the male psyche that ultimately makes it harder for them to share power, let alone function as devotee. Osho suffered similar problems with his key male disciples (like Michael Barnett and Paul Lowe). Crowley also fell out with numerous key allies, most of whom were men.

I'm reminded of the scene in Martin Scorsese's 1988 film *The Last Temptation of Christ* (based on Nikos Kazantzakis's controversial novel) where, in a dream sequence, Jesus meets a preaching Paul and complains to him that he is misrepresenting his teachings. Paul answers by thanking Jesus for telling him that, because he realizes that he prefers the dead Jesus to this live one, precisely because the dead Jesus is easier to represent and adapt to his own views and versions of the teachings. That arguably sums up Bennett's work to at least some extent. If Jeanne de Salzmann was Gurdjieff's Peter, Bennett was his Paul, the man who launched a teaching and philosophy that drew heavily from Gurdjieff but that ultimately moved off on a different trajectory.

In the final analysis, this cannot effectively be judged as good or bad, however, because transformational teachings by their very nature depend largely on who is transmitting them. Although the idea is appealing, a teaching cannot truly be completely separated from the one who is teaching it. And so, as much as the Christs and Gurdjieffs of the world will always appear, so will the Pauls and Bennetts. Likewise will the different branches, denominations, and sects. The real problem only arises when teachings become political—concerned with numbers, influence, and secular power. Bennett, for all that may be said about him, was no politician. He was almost as pure a seeker of truth as Gurdjieff. The same can be said for Ouspensky and Orage. And thus the argument that Gurdjieff's 'three wayward sons' resulted in some sort of 'deflecting of the octave' and a corruption of his legacy, does not hold, anymore than the argument that one branch of Tibetan Buddhism is inferior to another.

When Gurdjieff's chief disciple, Jeanne de Salzmann, passed away in 1990 at the ripe age of a hundred and one, most of his well known original disciples were gone. The International Association of Gurdjieff Foundations, the main organizational arm representing his work, has four chief branches, those being the Gurdjieff Foundation (New York), the Gurdjieff Society (London), the Institute Gurdjieff (Paris), and the Fundacion Gurdjieff (Caracas). In the early 1990s it was estimated that there were 'between five and ten thousand' directly involved with the Work as connected to these centers and smaller satellite centers.[20] By 2010 almost all first generation Gurdjieff pupils are gone. And thus with the unfolding 21st century his Work enters an interesting phase, one which over the next few generations will determine whether it drifts into a more formalized quasi-religion, maintains its esoteric quality and power, or fades away altogether.

In the end, Osho's teaching was based crucially on the quality of who he was (even if who he was, was ultimately but a meteoric appearance, albeit a dazzling one). Osho taught about enlightenment and he himself claimed to be enlightened. While he did not regularly go around trumpeting this fact, he never denied it either—with the exception of one infamous dental chair session when, under the influence of nitrous oxide, he implied that his 'enlightenment' was not fully realized. That particular session was actually published in the small book titled *Notes of a Madman* (reminiscent of Dostoyevsky's famous *Notes from the Underground*); in it Osho said:

Wipe that tear from my eye, I have to pretend to be enlightened, and enlightened people are not supposed to cry.[21]

A subsequent edition of this book appeared in which those words were altered. Ma Sheela was reputed to on occasion edit out select parts of Osho's words, both on audio and video. To what degree she did this is unknown but generally speaking it is accepted that her alterations were minimal, if and when they occurred. However, even if Osho said during one impaired dental chair session that he was not in fact fully enlightened, the issue is still secondary in light of what he consistently claimed about himself and what he claimed to represent—the ancient tradition of the enlightened sage. That was the only 'tradition' he ever claimed membership in and so it can be safely said that he himself—certainly in the eyes of his followers— was the living testament of what he taught. The story of his deep struggle culminating in his luminous awakening at age twenty-one is part of the standard legend for all disciples of Osho's. Without that enlightenment, the entire basis of his teaching is thrown into question.

Osho's singular great achievement is arguably in his meditation methods that he left behind. His most well known one, that most distinctively bears his mark, Dynamic Meditation (see Chapter 17) is a compact, high octane metaphor for his greatest accomplishment— the joining of East and West, the amalgamation of meditation and therapy.

Without question, Osho was more impactful in a broader and more practical way than either Crowley or Gurdjieff. But in the end he left open many unresolved matters and the impact of his teaching on global consciousness—while of a much longer reach than either Crowley's or Gurdjieff's—has still been, it must be admitted, minimal. This is to be expected: the domain of inner transformation has long been the province of the individual, not the masses. (In and of itself, 'minimal impact' means little; the work of Jesus had little impact for many decades after his death, being kept alive only by small and scattered Jesus-communities, many of which had differing views of their master's teachings.) And yet it would be dishonest to pretend that Crowley, Gurdjieff, or Osho were not interested in humanity at large. They were twilight bodhisattvas, Magi of a dark time in search of a means to provide a key to emancipate the human race. Their vision was large and ultimately, despite their apparent bombastic and autocratic ways, utterly impersonal.

All these men had periods where they appeared ridiculous, and yet as the occult historian James Webb aptly put it, 'all of us are looking ridiculous at practically every moment'. There is something intrinsically absurd about the human condition. Nature in itself—inorganic matter and organic life—moves along as it does, flawless even in its intense imperfections. But we humans, being self-conscious, have the capacity to enter into an exquisitely wise perspective—or much more commonly, into a perpetually awkward and absurd misstep, like a terrible dancer on a floor with Nijinskys.

That Osho was a force of nature is undeniable, and that he was brilliant, equally so. Inevitably however, his stature was at times overblown. A good example was a strange legend that began circulating in the 1970s that Osho had been recognized by the 16th Karmapa of Tibet, Rangjung Rigpe Dorje (1924-1981). A disciple of Osho's, Swami Govind Siddharth, claimed to have had a private audience with the Karmapa (who is head of the Karma Kargyu sect and roughly second in overall stature to the Dalai Lama in Tibetan spiritual hierarchy).[22] According to Swami Siddharth, the Karmapa had recognized Osho from his photo in Siddharth's locket as being the 'greatest incarnation in India since the Buddha and a living Buddha', adding that 'Osho speaks for the Akashic records also, the records of events and words recorded on the astral planes.'[23]

It sounds dubious—Tibetan Buddhism does not recognize terminology like 'astral plane' or 'akashic records'—these are Theosophical and Hindu terms. A close disciple of the 16th Karmapa, Lama Ole Nydahl, commented on Swami Siddharth's claim:

> Disciples of Bhagwan Shree Rajneesh [Osho]…had just published a book with a few humble claims that were new to us: that Karmapa had pronounced him the greatest Bodhisattva of all time, the man to bring Buddhist Tantra to the West. Karmapa, who did not even know him, was as diplomatic as possible, but the guru's disciples were not very pleased with his reply. Once again I could only shake my head at the enormous naiveté of people in spiritual matters. It is shocking how readily they give up both discrimination and common sense.[24]

Osho's failures were interesting. Probably one of his more outlandish proclamations concerned the appearance of AIDS. In 1983 he prophesied with specificity an AIDS holocaust, with 'two-thirds' of humanity being wiped out by the disease by the year 2000. In doing so he drew from Nostradamus' quatrains that predicted a 'nameless disease' spread via 'milk and blood' (the word 'milk' being a code word used by 16th century folk medicine practitioners for semen).[25] Other Nostradamus words were cited as prophetic material to support the idea that Osho's disciples were special and would survive the coming catastrophes.[26] I remember speaking then with a senior disciple of Osho who had once been his press secretary back in the early days of Pune. In 1983 he told me that an 'underground city' was being built in Oregon beneath the commune, and that we were going to retreat there for 'six years' during an upcoming war.

(It seems that an 'underground city' was indeed being built though it never got past the initial stage of serving as Sheela's weapons cache bunker.)

The scholar's term for prophecy gone wrong is 'prophetic disconfirmation', and it is often cited as being a key to the demise of many organized religions and cultic groups. Crowley's Thelemic teachings put forth the view that the Book of Revelation in the Bible is an example, in effect, of a prophetic disconfirmation, because it has been interpreted incorrectly. Crowley, with his heavy Christian conditioning, developed a vision of the future that was in part based on re-interpreting Biblical scripture. Accordingly, he saw the lurid visions of Revelation as pointing toward a new and brilliant Aeon that two millennia ago could only be seen through eyes of fear—and thus was, to the ancients, terrifying.

Oriental religions, and particularly the Jain and Hindu traditions that Osho grew up in, are not apocalyptic by nature, being based more on the notion of cyclical time. Things go around and come around only to begin again. The conception of time in Western religions is linear, not cyclical, generally pointing toward an apocalypse, a culmination that involves wholesale change, usually catastrophic. Be that as it may, a self-realized teacher does not by nature give himself over to prophecy, being more concerned with the actuality of life and the immediate spiritual needs of his followers. This was another example of how Osho could surprise; the fact that he made the AIDS prophecy shortly toward the end of his three and a half year self-imposed silence would suggest to the average thinking observer that he had lost some clarity. That is arguably true (and is, in fact, what J. Krishnamurti claimed about Osho at that time). But it is equally so that it was yet another example of his sheer unpredictability, his Trickster nature, and the impossibility of ever getting a clear fix on who he was. Of course, more than one *confidence* trickster has employed the same inconsistency of behavior, and this is where Osho's manner would tend to so thoroughly confuse (in particular) the spiritual dilettantes and dabblers. It was impossible to appreciate Osho at a casual glance; one would invariably be alienated by something.

A guru who is teaching about healing, mindfulness, enlightenment, and celebration, and who suddenly starts making apocalyptic predictions, might seem out of sorts, but in fact mystics throughout history have been known to on occasion make predictions or prophecies. Many of these prophecies were probably later editorial insertions, words put into the mouth of the teacher (such as Buddha's alleged proclamations about Maitreya Buddha). But the deeper symbolic point behind such predictions is that it highlights the fact that spiritual awakening is by nature both adventurous and dangerous, because it is working against the grain of something. That 'something' is the enormous resistance of what can be loosely called the status quo. Most predictions involve the need to meet in the future some difficult challenge. And as history has repeatedly borne out, profound mystics, and their community of followers, have traditionally met strong resistance from endless outer circumstances. (Resistance from inner circumstances—individual ego strategies and relationship dysfunction within the community—are of course a given.) The AIDS catastrophe Osho predicted may not have panned out the way he saw it but it can be argued that while he may have got the details wrong, he got the idea of an imminent threat right—only it was his own work that would soon be harshly attacked, with the crash of the Oregon commune coming just a few years after his AIDS prediction and his own death not long after that.

Spiritual teachers have traditionally been opposed in proportion to how dangerous they appear to be to the status quo. The Latin term *status quo* means 'the state in which'—the existing state of affairs. We become attached to matters as they are because we fear change. We fear change because it is, at the deepest level, the sole consistent fact about all phenomena. All is change. Nothing is fixed, consistent. Copernican and Keplerian science began to reveal this clearly in the 16th and 17th centuries as it became known that Earth is part of a moving clockwork of cosmic bodies (as opposed to stationary points of light in the sky). Darwinian evolution drove the point home—species evolve, arise, and fall away, their only constancy being perpetual change (even if, in some cases, such change is immeasurably slow).

The fact that things arise and fall away is one impediment on the path of inner transformation because it makes people very controlling, seeking to hold to whatever they have in quiet (or loud) desperation, in order to not face the dirty underlying truth, which is that none of this is going to last. As we cling to what we have, turning a blind eye to the abyss that is under our nose and guarding fiercely against the fear of abandonment, we naturally resist higher truth with its sharp, uncompromising light. Worse than resist it, we are threatened by it, and actively seek to destroy it.

The seminal 20th century psychotherapist, Wilhelm Reich, taught that humanity has long been caught in the grips of what he called the 'Emotional Plague'. It was his term for what afflicts the average person who has been repeatedly stymied and suppressed, who is incapable of being a *natural* person as a result. Such a person tends to feel very threatened when a truly natural person comes along. Above all, Osho taught the idea of the Natural Man, one unhindered and unburdened by the weight of dead traditions and artificial morality. Accordingly, his teaching was deeply threatening to established spiritual doctrine.

Amongst truth-seekers or the so-called religious, it was rare to find any, while Osho lived, who were neutral toward him. It was from this group that he would find his most loyal supporters, naturally, but also his greatest detractors. The rest of the world was largely indifferent. In early 1986, shortly after Osho had been refused entry to West Germany, he declared,

> You should be happy and rejoice the day I cannot find any place to stay anywhere in the world...I may be the first man in the whole of history who is being persecuted around the world...It means I have threatened all the powers of the world—religious,

political, social. A single man, single-handedly, has been able to prove the impotency and poverty of all great powers, great theologians, great organized religions. What more reward can I receive?[27]

Legitimate insight or insufferable grandiosity? Probably both, and that is par for the course. 'Larger than life' means larger in all ways — in light, wisdom, grandness, and ego. Asked once if he had an ego, Osho replied, 'Of course, and my ego is big — it is exactly the size of the whole universe.' Osho was not a representative of the humble saint's rotary club — egoless or not. He was born a lion and died a lion, complete with a lion's sense of humor.

The problem of the politics of succession has not spared his surviving movement. There was no individual successor (there rarely is for larger-than-life gurus) but he did appoint a body of twenty-one close disciples — called the 'inner circle' — to carry on his work, mostly in an administrative context. The number he chose is of interest if only in passing: he claimed his enlightenment occurred at age twenty-one, and in 1984 he declared twenty-one of his disciples to be enlightened (although later revoking the claim and declaring it had all been an elaborate joke/device). The number is also the product of Gurdjieff's key Laws of 3 and 7. But whatever his reasons for choosing the number twenty-one (and doubtless he would have claimed it unimportant), the original group itself did not remain intact for very long. By 1994, four of them amicably departed (and were replaced), and by the late 1990s an effort was initiated to begin de-emphasizing the personality cult element. The Pune commune was no longer referred to as an ashram but rather as a meditation resort, and was greatly expanded in size and complexity. Osho's name was removed from certain features (like the meditations) and many of his photos taken down. This was seen as part of Osho's own stated vision to never have his movement fossilize into a religion paying homage to the outer form of a dead master. Some from within the inner circle resisted this and left, setting up Osho centers mostly in India and Nepal that retained a greater degree of sentimental homage to the master. However, the Pune resort has been (and remains as of 2010) a marked success, the true Esalen of the East, attracting many seekers now who have only a passing or marginal awareness of Osho the man.

Be that as it may, Osho's legacy is notable and undeniable, mostly for his revolutionary efforts to bridge Eastern and Western transformational technology but more principally for his accent on honoring the self and the ending the 'enslaved' condition of the average person. What Crowley and Gurdjieff were pointing toward—a new spirituality that is self-inclusive, that steers away from puritanical models and personal debasement, that is individually empowering as well as enlightening in the true sense of the word—Osho carried effectively to greater numbers of people. I personally know of literally hundreds of people whose lives were powerfully and positively impacted by Osho's work. Also, it should be mentioned that a large number of teachers, facilitators, and writers in the field of human transformation in the late 20th and early 21st centuries were in fact initiated disciples of Osho, although many no longer openly acknowledge this for various reasons.[28]

Chapter 15
Return of the Magi:
Of Rogues, Prophets and Prophecy

It is a mistake to look too far ahead. Only one link in the chain of destiny can be handled at a time.
Winston Churchill

Saint: *A dead sinner revised and edited.*
Ambrose Bierce, The Devil's Dictionary

Rogue Mystics

The English word 'rogue' has several meanings—dishonest, scoundrel, tramp; a wild, fierce and unpredictable animal (as in a rogue elephant); disobedient, a renegade, uncontrollable. In the case of our three Magi, 'uncontrollable' would be a most fitting assessment of them as rogue mystics. Be that as it may, the key issue that has consistently plagued the image of such teachers has been in the area of the usage of power. When a seeker accepts a teacher (and vice versa), a relationship ensues between them that is not balanced. That is of course the case with many (if not most) relationships in life, but in the case of spiritual teachers the power imbalance can be enormous because the teacher's image contains an element of what Joseph Campbell called the 'supernatural aid'—that is, the teacher's presumed link to a higher realm of understanding that is beyond the grasp of the seeker. Accordingly, it indeed seems (to the seeker) that the only way is to trust the teacher if one wants access to these 'higher realms'.

The Italian Renaissance philosopher, Nicollo de Machiavelli (1469-1527), is renowned mostly for his infamous book, *The Prince*, published posthumously in 1532. Scholars are unanimous that Machiavelli has been largely misrepresented on the basis of certain ideas expressed in that book, but nevertheless the term 'Machiavellian' has entered standard lexicon and in the language of modern psychology in particular. It refers to the use of cunning and duplicity in order to get what one wants. It is a particularly skilled type of manipulation, the essence of which is 'never tell anyone the truth of why you did something unless it is *useful* to do so'.

The Machiavellian impulse is usually considered the province of cunning politicians, chameleon-types who simply adapt to what is needed and tell others what they want to hear in order to buy their allegiance and support, or of tyrants who maintain their power on the basis of Machiavelli's insight that it is better for a leader to be feared than loved. But in reality, every powerful spiritual teacher or influential mystic has a touch of Machiavellian nature in him. The only difference is (ideally) that such capacity to manipulate is done with a loftier intention in mind. The teacher can (in theory) hold this loftier intention in mind because he has the growth and devel-opment of his student as his aim, as well as a planetary aim (the awakening of the human race). Of course there is great room for error here because the moment a personal agenda slips in is the moment that the behavior becomes manipulative in a way that compromises the purity of the 'teaching device'.

That Osho, Gurdjieff, and Crowley all employed manipulation tactics is undeniable and all equally admitted openly doing so on many occasions. Does this make them 'bad'?

The unconventional view on the matter is this: In some respects, the issue transcends morality because something much bigger is at stake. As John Selden once quipped, 'The world cannot be governed without juggling.' (The image of the juggler is apt: in the old Tarot decks this was one of the names for the Magician card, an archetype that is part trickster, part sage.) To enter into a dark realm and work with the denizens there you have to know something of their ways. People who are sleeping deeply do not generally respond to a light touch. They usually require stronger approaches to be roused. Their dream must be entered and the laws of their dream-world learnt and used. That this requires a particular skill—akin to that of a juggler—goes without saying. It has been said before, 'the greater the teacher, the more difficult the students he or she will attract'. And this makes perfect sense. A master of the more difficult faces of the ego must know the ego from the inside out. To break others out of prison, he must know something of prisons himself.

The conventional view is this: Gurus who use power in ways that are at times openly manipulative and result in chaos amongst their followers are deceptive and dangerous individuals who have simply duped everyone. As Napoleon once remarked, 'One must change one's tactics every ten years if one wishes to maintain one's superiority.' Underneath the rogue guru's charismatic wisdom is merely the base instinct of wishing to maintain his position and the craft and cunning to do so. All his apparent changes and selective use of particular teachings at particular times are nothing more than Napoleon's creed dressed up in a transcendent package.

The problem, however, with the 'conventional' view is that it denies people the right to grow through their experience. By simply condemning rogue mystics and gurus, we remove all accountability from their followers and reduce them to powerless and pathetic victims. Over the years, I've been repeatedly surprised at the hostility people have for unconventional teachers like Osho, Gurdjieff, Crowley, Trungpa, Adi Da Samraj, Andrew Cohen, and their like; the same kind that is reserved for criminals and tyrants of the worst order. It's as if the very attempt to operate unconventionally in the spiritual realm is some sort of obscene violation of all codes of decency. My own suspicion about this attitude of righteous condemnation is that it is related to the persistent power of religious conditioning, and in particular, the puritanical and simplistic ideas of what it means to be 'spiritual'. I've known a remarkable amount of people who while outwardly professing freedom from religious programming or even 'intellectually liberated' atheism, inwardly appear to have all the vehemence and inflexibility they perceive in the very same 'religious nuts' and 'cult leaders' they condemn.

Be that as it may, it cannot be denied that our three dangerous Magi left as much trashed debris in their wake as they did flowers of wisdom and growth. That this would be so is inevitable given the times during which they taught. Our best approach if we choose to learn from them is to simply be accountable for our own inner growth while enjoying their fearless cutting edge wisdom.

Of Outsiders and Djartklom

I have, throughout parts of this book, highlighted some of the parallels between Osho and Crowley (a summary of these connections can be found in Appendix I). I have felt this important because, in one sense, what Crowley conceived of Osho sought to actualize with wildly varying results. (I speak here not just of the Cefalu-Oregon experiments, but of an overall approach to living.) Crowley's conception of the True Will builds, to a degree, on the existentialism of Kierkegaard and Nietzsche, at least *some* elements of which saw fruition in the 'third force' psychology (beyond Freudianism and Behaviorism) developed in the 1950s and 60s by Maslow, Rogers, and others—the idea of the true realization of human potential and *self*-actualization rather than the self-sacrifice that has been such an intrinsic part of the depraved and enslaved history of humanity. This was naturally followed by the development of transpersonal ideas in a therapeutic context, all of which Osho attempted to integrate with the Eastern wisdom traditions, principally of Tantra, Advaita, and Taoism.

Crowley and Osho independently located and shaped some of the very finest ideas and keys of transformational work and attempted to render them intelligible for the world in a way that conforms to the needs of the present time. (Crowley's and Osho's ideas embodied more than just the main principles of humanist psychology, of course, but the underlying thrust of their work has been paralleled by leading edge ideas in modern psycho-spiritual teachings.) It must, however, be noted that all inner growth paradigms have their warts and blemishes; the human potential movement has not been spared that. Its shadow side is basically narcissism, concern with self-actualization to the point of self-absorption, and preoccupation with feelings at the expense of action—arguably a degree of neurotic feminization that has been a natural counter force to centuries of heavily neurotic (not to mention abusive) masculine spirituality. Gurdjieff, for one, did not endorse a feminized spirituality doubtless because of our three Magi he was the least feminine. (Crowley certainly had strong masculine qualities, but his endless dramas with women and bisexual exploration reflected in part his strongly developed feminine side and his urge to come to terms with it.) Osho, again similar to Crowley, had highly developed masculine and feminine qualities; his decision to empower women had fateful consequences as he himself repeatedly pointed out.

All that aside, there is to be noted a fundamental link between Osho and Gurdjieff, a realm that they share, that Crowley stands apart from. Put simply, Osho and Gurdjieff were gurus, masters (character tendencies notwithstanding). Crowley, however, sits uncomfortably in such a designation. He is more properly a rogue prophet, mystic, and scholar. As an actual *facilitator* of people's growth, as a 'guru', he appears to have been mostly ineffectual, and indeed there is little sign that he was ever interested in such a role to begin with. I do, however, see him as one of the Magi of humanity because of the overwhelming power of his commitment to both walking the inner journey, and to explaining this journey to humanity with skill, unprecedented depth, and relevancy for current times.

In Colin Wilson's seminal 1956 work, *The Outsider*, he talked about a thematic character in world literature who reflects the essence of the seeker of truth. Wilson's Outsider has, for the most part however, not located what he is somewhat blindly looking for. He or she never quite fits in, is deeply curious about himself and why he is here, and attempts to resolve the deepest questions of life with very little support or reinforcement from a mostly cold surrounding world. The Outsider has within him the seeds of potential, the necessary sensitivity to recognize what Gurdjieff called 'the terror of the situation,' and, in varying degrees, the courage to do something about it—to break free of societal conventions and set out on the great journey in search of the Grail of wisdom. The Outsider is the man or woman beginning to wake up from an ancient slumber.

Magi like Crowley, Gurdjieff and Osho were all initially Outsiders who had already found the Grail—or at least, one version of it. To what degree they drank of its elixir and successfully absorbed it is moot and cannot be fully known. But they definitely had it in their hands. That each journeyed long and hard for their prize is beyond question. That each met with fierce resistance on their journey is undeniable. All change tends to be resisted, and the greater and more potential the change, the fiercer the resistance from the world at large. The crucifixion of Jesus, historical veracity aside, can be taken as representative of the collective ego's drive to destroy whatever seeks to flood it with light and to flush it from darkness. All truly radical and great thinkers and teachers have almost universally been prosecuted and punished by the world, generally to the degree that their message rouses others from sleep.

Crowley was brutally attacked by the media and intelligentsia of his day because at the bottom of it all he was challenging—with a headlong rush—the entrenched Judeo-Christian doctrine. All scandals associated with him that the press would triumphantly bandy about were connected to a few basic themes: sex, self-aggrandizement, and occult practice. The first is deeply threatening to the puritanical conditioning found so commonly in the West, especially the northern European cultures that would form the foundation of

North American society. The second violates the self-sacrifice and glorification of suffering that is such a psychological pillar of Western religion. And the third activates the terrifying archetypal image of the overpowering and condemning Jehovah of the Old Testament, who is cursing women, preaching the killing of witches and magicians, and sending Floods to control humanity.

Osho and Gurdjieff each faced this resistance as well to the point of being in large part destroyed by it. Osho may not have been literally assassinated by CIA slow acting radiation or mind control operatives but without question he deeply offended the status quo, which vengefully went after him. Gurdjieff's despair around being able to properly transmit his profound teachings climaxed in 1935 when the American senator, Bronson Cutting, who was seriously considering funding the re-opening of his bankrupt Institute, died in a plane crash days before meeting Gurdjieff. After a long series of frustrations, he was so upset by this that he disappeared without trace for several months.

In *Beelzebub's Tales to his Grandson,* Gurdjieff wrote about something he called *Djartklom.* It was a complex idea that touched on many things, but it is chiefly about the capacity to awaken, and what is needed to bring that about in an Outsider, in a seeker. Gurdjieff mentioned that there were two ways—either by the sheer force of the teacher, or more naturally from within the seeker himself.

The parallel between Osho and Gurdjieff is that both passed through this phase, that is, from being a powerhouse guru who could transmit energy directly to their disciples and facilitate their awakening, to one who moved beyond this and settled more into the role of beckoning the disciple to walk on their own toward the light. This shift occurred in Osho more or less between the end of the first Pune phase (1981) and the end of the Oregon experiment (1985). And that is why I think the Oregon commune represented his own personal 'final initiation', something that took him to a higher level where he ceased hoisting his disciples on his own energy, to one where he instructed them to truly walk on their own. The same happened for Gurdjieff when he crashed his car in 1924 in France. After that, he gradually shifted primarily to writing and guiding only those students who seemed truly ready to commit to the path. Prior to that, he was a sheer energy source who created 'artificial *djartklom*' in his students on the basis of his own magnetism and power. It is true, according to many reports, that he was still blasting people with the sheer intensity of his presence even in his old age in his Paris apartment, but he lived more for himself after the peak years of the Prieure in the early 1920s had passed.

Beyond Prophecy

Gurdjieff's student, John G. Bennett, though well known in Gurdjieff circles, was largely unheralded in his time and even now, over thirty-five years after his passing, is mostly unrecognized. This is something of a shame because he was an effective teacher and a prolific author of excellent and substantial works. At the end of his life (in 1974), he was working on a book that summarized his life work. It was called *The Masters of Wisdom* and was published posthumously by his wife in 1977. The day that Bennett died he had just decided to begin the final chapter. His wife reports that, although Bennett wrote enough notes on the chapter for them to later put in into publishable form, he never did complete it. He had written an entire book on the history of the Masters of Wisdom but died before he could comment on their influence on humanity in present times. Elizabeth Bennett wrote: 'What he intended to say about the present day Masters of Wisdom never materialized.'[1] It was a strange twist of irony—Bennett, one of the greatest esoteric historians ever, died before he could make his final pronouncements on the true efficacy of the secret global fellowship that (he maintained) has been our guiding hand for time immemorial.

This idea has been explored before of course (most famously by Blavatsky) and particularly after the publication of Bennett's book. Many of the attempts at exploring the idea of 'hidden masters' have been clumsy, some downright embarrassing. A few have had some interesting things to say. But the vast majority have focused only on outer matters—control, politics, conspiracy, a liberal dose of dubious science to boot, and more than one blaming it all on aliens. Most such writing inclines entirely toward speculation. Some speculation in these matters is inevitable but by and large it misses the point. As Gurdjieff pointed out repeatedly when speaking of the body of his writings, the point of his books is for them to function as tools for greater self-understanding, not to indulge in the storyline.

I first read *The Masters of Wisdom* in the early 1980s. At the time, I was captivated by the romantic ideal behind the premise of Bennett's book which is that there is a 'hidden directorate' (as he called it), an unseen fellowship of advanced beings—who he called the *psychotelios*—who have been guiding humanity for many thousands of years since before the beginning of recorded history. In 1985, I followed up this interest by setting out myself on a long journey to seek masters of wisdom. At one point I ended up in Kashmir, in northwest India, and paid a visit to the town of Srinagar. I went there in part to investigate the legend of the Tomb of Roza Bal. One of the legends connected to this tomb is that it was the burial ground of Jesus. This particular legend is Muslim; the Koran explicitly states that Jesus was not crucified, that someone was crucified in his place and that he himself survived and lived to an old age. The Kashmiri legend holds that he traveled across Persia and Afghanistan, eventually settling in Kashmir where he fathered a family and lived into old age. Predictably (and reasonably) this has all been ridiculed by many Western scholars as provincial Muslim propaganda, but the legend was intriguing enough for me at the time to check it out.

I recall sitting in the Roza Bal tomb in meditation on a dark, cold, rainy day in December in which I was the sole visitor there. The sounds of barking dogs and street merchants faded as I settled deeper into the inner silence. Then at a certain point a question arose in me. *Why are you here?* A sound question in which can be seen the plainest common sense; or which can be taken as a Zen *koan*. Either way an answer—via my own intuition informing me—came just as readily:

I am not here. Stop seeking me. Wherever you look, you will not find me.

It was the very antithesis of the famous expression of Christ in the Gnostic Gospel of Thomas:

I am the light that is over all things. I am all: from me all came forth, and to me all attained. Split a piece of wood; I am there. Lift up the stone, and you will find me there. (Thomas, 77)

As it happened, the answer I received apparently did not entirely satisfy me: about a decade later I found myself wandering through Jerusalem, while on my way to Egypt. There at the Church of the Holy Sepulcher, site of the original hill of Golgotha where Jesus was allegedly crucified, I repeated the process I'd been through in Kashmir years before. The same answer arose, but with a bit more clarity this time:

I am not here. Stop seeking me. Be still and know that I am.

The wise men of Matthew's Gospel, although never actually numbered, have traditionally been regarded as three. The title of this book, *The Three Dangerous Magi*, may seem to naturally suggest the idea of prophecy, if only because the 'three' Biblical Magi were indeed connected in purpose to a fourth and (in Christendom at least) supremely important entity, the Christ child. If teachers like Crowley, Gurdjieff and Osho were (even if unknowingly) part of a sequence of modern Magi—of Bennett's *psychotelios* or hidden directorate—were they pointing toward a final Master of Wisdom, someone in whom all wisdom traditions of recorded history are brought to a culmination and completion?

They weren't—at least not as we would conventionally understand it. *The Book of the Law* makes reference to one who 'cometh after' the Beast (Crowley) and 'who shall discover the Key of it all'.

Some Thelemites have regarded this as an explicit indicator of a post-Crowley messiah of sorts (initially thought by Crowley himself to be his brilliant student Charles Stansfeld Jones, though he later repudiated that idea) whom some followers of Osho would argue has already come and gone. But that line is easily countered by another in *The Book of the Law* that proclaims:

Expect him not from the East, nor from the West; for from no expected house cometh that child. Aum! All words are sacred and all prophets true... (1:56)

Prophets and prophecies have abounded throughout history. In the West, the year 1000 AD brought with it much turmoil and fear as would-be prophets of the time brought their messages of apocalyptic doom. This was repeated at various junctures throughout the next millennia. More recently, there was the 'harmonic convergence' of 1987 popularized by Jose Arguelles and then the inevitable shrill warnings leading up to 2000 (including the infamous 'Y2K' non-event). The latest in this line is the 2012 phenomenon, allegedly connected to Mayan prophecies about 'end times' (but which was almost certainly more a case of the Mayans running out of calendar space).

The common psychological feature in most such prophetic movements is of course fear and in particular the fear of change. C.G. Jung pointed out long ago that it was likely no accident that UFO sightings suddenly began happening in various parts of the world during the late 1940s shortly after the Second World War and in particular the unleashing of atomic weaponry (the American bombings of Hiroshima and Nagasaki in 1945). Jung was on record, especially in his later years, as stating that he regarded UFOs as probably real phenomena, but he also saw them as projected mandalic symbols of psychic healing and wholeness. The underlying point is that during times of great stress we humans seek outlets and can literally call forth into our reality all sorts of 'signs' and 'portents' that are designed to relieve us of our stress and general anxiety. That does not mean that these signs cannot have actual objective existence. Sometimes they do, but the essential issue here is that our consciousness is not separate from the world around us and the objects we perceive arising within it. Understanding this is the golden key, the secret at the heart of all occult, mystical, and spiritual doctrine. The failure to understand it leads to dysfunction on all levels, including a hysterical attitude toward prophecy and the failure to understand the 'signs'. It's possible of course to see signs in anything, and prophecy more than anything has been susceptible to this tendency of the human mind to project meaning where none lies except in the fantasies generated by the restless mind seeking to escape reality in its present-time condition.

Biblical legend has it that the Magi of the East followed a rather peculiar star that pointed toward the Christ child in the manger as the fulfillment of prophecy, and as the consecration of the divine in the body of Earth. Crowley, Gurdjieff, and Osho, and all other legitimate modern Magi, came to point to a new dispensation, toward the 'inner Child' of truth and wakefulness. They were ambassadors of a dawning knowledge, a new understanding, a new view—and most crucially, how to *implement* that view. This understanding, this view, holds that the divine does not lie in the remote sky, or in mother earth, or in some church, mosque, temple, synagogue, monastery, or in any human messiah. It lies *within* as our own basic nature, to be revealed, made, realized—the wording may differ, but the message is the same. The 'manger' is our body; the 'Messiah to come' is our own true Self, our own True Will, our own true Being. As Osho said, 'The way is in,' and as Crowley wrote in *Liber Tzaddi*:

In either awaits you a Companion; and that Companion is Yourself.

Ye can have no other Companion.

Of course, masters of past times also taught that truth is within—whether that be Jesus saying 'The kingdom of heaven is within', or the Buddha teaching a method that leads to the realization of one's innate buddha-mind. What is changing now, however, is the angle of approach. The days of emphasizing sacrifice or worldly renunciation are over. The sovereign truth of one's inner nature is to be realized via disciplined practice but without mortifying ourselves or turning our back on the universe at large; on the contrary, to live authentically, self-respectfully and consciously, is to be profoundly in relationship with all things.

In the end, when we study the person and life of a profound and difficult sage, what are we left over with? Can we truly *know* them?

Margaret Anderson, one of a circle of literate women who gathered around Gurdjieff in his later years, wrote a small book about her time with him and titled it *The Unknowable Gurdjieff*. Prior to publishing, she sent the manuscript to John Bennett and he had some pointed remarks. He wrote to her:

> ...the only specific criticism that I would make of your book is that you do not sufficiently convey the 'unknowableness' of Gurdjieff...[he] was and has remained unknowable, so that each person who meets him could discover little more than a reflection of himself.[2]

My own journey 'in search of wise men' in the Orient had culminated in Nepal in February of 1986 when, shortly after visiting the shrine of the legendary sage Shivapuri Baba, I found myself sitting in front of Osho every night for a month straight as he gave spontaneous talks at the Soaltee Oberoi Hotel in Kathmandu for about a hundred and fifty, mostly Nepali, disciples. What became quickly apparent over the course of the month was that there was, in the ultimate sense, no Osho. There was of course the man, complete with his somewhat amorphous personal identity, displaying his usual remarkable grace, charisma and eloquence. He did seem to be a bit tired at times (and evidently was not too well then, that being only a few months after his ordeal in the grubby American jailhouses). But the sense of a defined entity, consistent and predictable, sitting there in his chair, was clearly an illusion. The sense of a *presence* was marked, and vast. Something *was* very much there, to a degree and with a depth and quality that I had not experienced before (and I had met, even by then, many remarkable men and women). This was by all definitions an *uber*-remarkable being.

But what was really going on in his presence, in his discourses? It was not about the dissemination of information. Much of what he was saying was interesting; occasionally the words would sound a bit absurd. I remember in particular one remark he made about how planet Earth was the only planet in the universe with life. An American couple was seated behind me, newcomers to Osho. The man whispered to the woman, 'This is off the wall!' I don't recall seeing them after that lecture. Who knows, maybe Osho was right, and there is no life elsewhere in the universe (which, after all, we don't yet know for sure). But what was so surprising about his remark was how it seemed like something a religious fundamentalist might say. And that was exactly in keeping with his nature. He was masterful at keeping everyone off balance, preventing them from forming a hardened view of who he was—like Gurdjieff, he was deeply unknowable. As much as he could make on the face of it, such a seemingly silly remark that only Earth has life in the universe, he could and did follow that up with statements about how the reality of evolution negates the possibility of the Judeo-Christian God existing. He could go from one extreme statement to another in such a fashion that you could never truly know him through his words. Those who held him accountable to a standard of perfection would often become confused.

He once told the story of J. Krishnamurti sampling some ties in a clothing store, throwing them this way and that, unable to make up his mind about which tie he wanted. A woman, a student of Krishnamurti, happened to see him doing this and immediately decided that he could not possibly be enlightened. Osho ridiculed the woman as an example of the absurd standards we set in our minds for spiritual figures, most of which is a vestige of puritanical conditioning. In effect, we have made the strange correlation between spiritual realization and a sterile idea of perfection that rejects human qualities—a plastic Jesus, a stone supermarket Buddha.

John Bennett stressed an important point about the Magi in *The Masters of Wisdom*, and it was this: they are 'neither human nor divine...neither perfect, nor infallible' but have 'vision and powers' that 'far transcend even the wisest of mankind'.[3] Around such teachers, most of the world has gathered into one of two polarized camps: the cynical skeptics and the indiscriminate followers. The former certainly far outnumber the latter particularly in current times. There is of course some good in this. The capacity to make correct judgments is essential to the healthy development of the individual. Far too many disasters have resulted simply from blind trust or devotion. But the inability to see the essential message of valid teachers of wisdom as anything but malign, deceptive, or of ulterior motive has prevented many from being aroused from sleep, from recognizing the 'terror of the situation.' Cynicism has killed as many spirits as blind trust.

If Bennett had a weakness it was a tendency to incline toward a certain idealism that had the ultimate result of him being very hard on himself. He was a study in English perfectionism—and in that sense a good example of the typical sincere spiritual seeker who struggles with their own humanity. We can probably take his comment on 'vision and powers' with a grain of salt. I doubt that highly advanced or self-realized beings have 'powers' as we would *typically* understand that. They are more akin to a vast spaciousness through which things simply happen—and some of those 'things' can indeed be extraordinary.

I'm reminded of the stories that some people reported in connection with the famous 16th Karmapa of Tibet, Rangjung Rigpe Dorje (1924-81). All sorts of miraculous events were commonly reported to occur in his presence, including a medically documented case of his body—particularly the area around his heart—remaining 'impossibly' warm for several days after his death in a Chicago hospital.[4] But was he truly 'doing' any of this? There is a level of development in which it is indeed possible to obtain certain powers, the effect of what Gurdjieff called concentrated *hanbledzoin* (psychic force). Yogic tradition refers to this as gaining facility with the *ajna chakra*, or 'third eye'. Buddhism refers to it as a potential trap (owing to the inevitable attachment to such powers) with the result of becoming what is termed a 'jealous god'. Gurdjieff himself stated that he intentionally renounced his powers around 1911, in order to purify himself at deeper levels. Crowley clearly talked at length about this in his discussions of the Black Brother and the failure to properly 'cross the abyss'. One who attains to the levels defined by the Tree of Life as *Binah, Chokmah,* and *Kether* is no longer under the spell of *maya*, or dualistic delusion, and perforce understands that free will (in the conventional, egocentric sense) is entirely illusion. One who attempts to reach these highest levels yet fails to relinquish the grip of ego and its various and sundry approaches to 'doing', falls back and becomes a Black Brother, or what Gurdjieff called a Hasnumuss.

But this is all a metaphor, in one important sense, for what we are doing with our own mind. To flirt with spiritual principles, with transformational methods, and to only become half-baked by them—or worse, to use them against others or to reinforce our own ego—is in a sense to become a jealous god or a Black Brother ourselves. This is far more common than most might suppose. The so-called spiritual path is littered with the astral corpses of awakened wannabes. And I've seen far more than one person using spiritual principles to browbeat another or merely to dismiss the sad unwashed and unawakened masses. The ego is masterful at co-opting anything, and above all it seeks to co-opt spiritual principles and use them to its own benefit. A prime way of doing this is via what the Tibetan master Chogyam Trungpa called 'spiritual materialism', essentially a type of narcissism in which we use our knowledge of spiritual principles to both disconnect from and feel superior to others.

Bennett's point, however, was sound: even the most advanced

Magi are not perfect. That is shocking to the moral sensibilities of the average person. The idea of a 'perfect master' is a legacy of religious indoctrination, puritanical ideology that is necessary to control masses by keeping them forever feeling inferior—'I am unworthy of liberation and freedom'—and thus easier to control. Those who think little of themselves are easier to manage for powers that be compared to those who have authentic self-respect. The very image of a perfect saint demands its opposite, the perpetually stained and flawed seeker who never arrives at the Grail. Until the image of this flawless saint, this plastic Jesus, is relinquished, we will forever project impossibly high standards onto spiritual teachers, while at the same time keeping ourselves stuck in a perpetual immaturity in relation to this sterile image of perfection.

One day while attending Osho's talks in Nepal I was wandering the markets of Kathmandu when I stopped at a bazaar where I saw a table with a pile of photos on it. There on top of one of the piles was a small Polaroid snapshot of Osho; directly in the background of the photo peering over his white hat was a familiar face: it was me. It seems that someone took a photo of him just as he was walking by where I stood in the line of his daily 'walk-by' on the grounds of the hotel. The effect was one of me standing directly in his 'aura' if you will. I had the picture blown up when I came back to Canada. It's an odd photo, and one that I ultimately came to regard as something of a pictorial Zen *koan*: Where does the master end and the disciple begin? What is the nature of identity? Who are you, who am I?

One day in late February '86, Osho left Nepal for Greece. He went only with a small group of caretakers. He was not to be followed there. The next day I went for a walk in Durbar Square in the heart of Kathmandu. It was the one and only time I neglected to put my wallet and passport in my travel belt, leaving them lazily in my open jacket pockets. At one point while sauntering through the Square I was jostled lightly. The place was crowded so I hardly took notice. A short while later I realized I had been relieved of my wallet and passport. A hassle subsequently ensued as I had to convince the border authorities that I had not sold my passport on the black market. I was eventually let go and I went to the Canadian embassy in New Delhi for an emergency passport.

The symbolism was not lost on me. I had 'lost my identity' on the last day of my month-long *darshan* with the master. Gurdjieff had many passports, all with a different date of birth. In the end no one really knew who he was. Osho was a different face for everyone who knew him. Crowley was a study in conflicted, mostly shadowy, reputation, but his death summed up his life: he was alone, and ultimately, unknown.

We are all unknown and unknowable, our personalities and the endless dramas of our life being but shimmering images on the surface of an inner ocean seen from afar. The closer we get to the images the more they break up, and as we come fully upon them there is nothing there. Just a vast ocean, an abyss, a pure absence. And in that absence, an unspeakable immensity.

To come close to our own image, to see into the abyss, to gaze upon what Zen calls our original face, is a metaphor for living life with conscious intensity, with totality. Osho, Gurdjieff, and Crowley, whatever might be said about them, all did this and with gusto. They were revolutionary as spiritual teachers by virtue of this alone—in effect, teaching by demonstration that the more we live our lives with consciousness, totality, and intensity, then the more we glimpse the vastness of our true nature, and the less we are defined by the smallness of our personal agendas. In resolving and balancing opposites—the light and the dark of our own nature—in embracing the fullness of life and our very selves, in being both lofty and grounded at the same time, we bring together East and West within us, wisdom and energy, vastness and fullness. We become a child of a new Aeon, a harmonious human being, a Zorba the Buddha. We are a star in the inner sky, and we are at home. In their own reckless and inimitable style the three dangerous Magi all pointed toward that inner star.

Part Four:

The Inner Work

Chapter 16
The Importance of Practice

In order to be free from the laws of space and time, you yourself must change. This change depends on you, and it will not come about through study. You can know everything and yet remain where you are. It is like a man who knows all about money and the laws of banking, but has no money of his own in the bank. What does all his knowledge do for him?[1]
Gurdjieff

A man is a god in ruins.
Emerson

Summing Up: The Inner Work of the Magi

Thus far, this book has focused to some degree on the life stories of the personalities we knew as Osho, George Gurdjieff, and Aleister Crowley. I deemed it necessary to explore the narrative of these stories to a certain extent to provide the human counterweight, if we may call it that, to balance the theoretical basis of their ideas and teachings. This is important I think insofar as it helps as a reminder of the essential truth that we too are limited personalities and must bring to bear upon the raw material of our personality the full measure of our sincerity to awaken. We all have a story, a script that we live out in the drama of our life, and while we are all called to something greater, our life story bears the signature of our soul's struggle to self-realize.

As we recall from Gurdjieff's Law of Three, an event requires three elements to bring it into being: an active (or affirming) force, a passive (or denying) force, and a reconciling force which is the result of the first two interacting. The Law of Three can in one respect be applied in the following way to the process of inner awakening:

1. The theoretical basis of the teachings and ideas. (Affirming).
2. The personality and its story. (Denying).
3. The practical application of the teachings—the Great Work. (Reconciling).

The 'practical application' of the teachings, or what we call here for simplicity sake 'the Work', is a result (in this example) of two previous factors, those being the *teacher* and the *teaching*. These three elements can also be understood in terms of:

1. Creative: The Ideas of the Teaching
2. Destructive: The Personality of the Teacher
3. Redemptive: The Practical Inner Work

It might seem odd, at first glance, that the teacher should be designated the 'denying' or 'destructive' position, but this does not require a great deal of thought to see how it fits. The teacher by virtue of being a human being has limitations, no matter how advanced they may be. Inevitably, they cannot *perfectly* exercise the theory of their own teachings. But the 'interaction' of who they are with the theory of their teachings results naturally in the practical methods that they develop and offer. These methods then become the fruits that they make available to others.

Gurdjieff also defined the three forces as:

1. I can.
2. I am.
3. I wish.

This in turn can easily be applied to our own process. 'I can' corresponds to the ideas of the teachings we study. 'I am' corresponds to our personality. And 'I wish' designates the practical Work; that is, actually putting into action a wish by making effort.

A common objection often raised at this point, from many who are involved in some Eastern schools of thought such as Advaita or Taoism, is that we need not make effort to awaken, because there is no real separate self to attain to anything and therefore no one and nothing to truly 'work on'. Additionally, since there is no separate self there cannot be any such thing as free will; and so again, inner Work is pointless.

This, however, is the view from the absolute level of reality. It ignores the conventional or relative level. More to the point, it neglects the fact that the inner Work is ultimately an inherently joyful process, even if at times daunting, frightening, disturbing, and deeply frustrating. Above all, engaging the inner Work safeguards against the possibility of becoming inauthentic, phony holy, or a mere spiritual moralist. At the very worst, it simply shows us the deep futility of struggling against who and what we already are. Whether that process is understood as 'efforting' to enlightenment, or 'dropping effort' to realize that we are already enlightened, makes no difference. All that can be said for sure, however, is that no one ever arrived at a realized state without *doing* something beforehand. The idea that I 'need do nothing' (as the phrase from *A Course In Miracles* has it) may be ultimately true but rare is the person who can fully penetrate this most profound of all Zen *koans* and live it out in the gritty details of their life. And even if one can, it must first be initiated by a burning desire for truth, such as that which seized Ramana Maharshi when he was a young man. That deep desire is rare, but practical application of the Work can strengthen the flame that burns in our heart.

Crowley, Gurdjieff, and Osho can also be seen in the light of a three-fold scheme, summarized very generally as follows:

1. Crowley: Know thyself
2. Gurdjieff: You do not know yourself.
3. Osho: You *are* what you have been seeking, but you must first become unburdened before you can understand this.

The heart of Crowley's work can be summarized as *know thyself*. Everything he attempted can be reduced to a rugged and fearless effort to explore the depths of his own ego, his own conditioning, and to embrace beyond that the egoless consciousness he called by names such as the Holy Guardian Angel or the Augoeides or the Atman. As his student, Gerald Yorke, once put it, 'Crowley did not enjoy his vices! He explored them to overcome them.' That he offended so many was inevitable, given the era he lived in—an uptight time of severe behavioral protocols. Even his grander cosmic proclamations, most notably the advent of the Aeon of Horus, can be understood simply as a clarion call for people to shake off the shackles of the miserable past—the self-loathing legacy of Judeo-Christian programming—and learn to actually delight in and enjoy the wonders of existence. It was a clarion call entirely echoed by Osho, who, due to his nature and the time he lived in, was able to take the message to a higher and more influential level (even if his ride was decidedly rough along the way).

The heart of Gurdjieff's work can be summarized as *you do not know yourself*. He provides the perfect counterpoint to Crowley's essential message. While Crowley teaches the way to uncover the true self and its True Will, Gurdjieff shows us the stark reality of why we—in our current condition—have no true self or True Will to begin with. And so while one seems to contradict the other, in fact they complement each other perfectly when their core ideas are clearly understood.

The heart of Osho's work can be summarized as *you are what you have been seeking, but you must first become unburdened before you can begin to understand this*. In order to walk this path, face into your ego honestly, release its pent up tension, anxiety, and negative emotion.

Then be a silent witness. Settle into your natural self. And, finally, celebrate the energy awakened by this via creativity, conscious sensuality, laughter, enjoyment of all that life offers—live *totally*.

Osho's ultimate message is Tantric (live totally with awareness) and Zen (be still and see the truth), but he takes these teachings to a more comprehensive level by integrating them with modern psychotherapy. The modern Western man or woman is too neurotic, too burdened by the legacy of dysfunctional family lineages (exacerbated by the sheer trauma of the vast bloodshed of the 20th century) to be able to simply realize that they are intrinsically whole and complete, or 'already enlightened'. As Dennis Waite points out in *Back to the Truth*, his comprehensive book on Advaita Vedanta, there is a 'neo-Advaita' of recent times that focuses entirely on the 'need do nothing' angle. This approach is highly problematic because it easily invites denial, repression, and an attendant shallow depth of realization.[2]

Osho's effectiveness lay in his breadth of spirit that embraced cutting edge wisdom, in particular, the psychotherapies of the human potential movement—Reichian bodywork, breathwork, active meditations, group therapy of many varieties, and so on. (This was what Israel Regardie was getting at when he emphasized that any student of the Western esoteric tradition serious about the inner Work should first undergo psychotherapy of some sort.) The point that remains to be clarified is that we are not referring to more conventional Freudian psychoanalysis, which is based on the essential aim of normalizing a person assumed to be merely neurotic or otherwise dysfunctional. The human potential movement, which blossomed in the 1960s, is founded on the idea that human beings are vast realms of untapped potential—not merely faulty devices needing to be repaired so that they can function in the world. The essential element is a shift in attitude, a movement away from the idea of intrinsic flaw—along with its brethren of sin, sacrifice, and necessary suffering—toward one of exploration, investigation, self-discovery, and realization of potential. (Which is, essentially, in accordance with Thelemic ideals.)

The format of Part One of this book followed a progression from Crowley to Gurdjieff to Osho, reflecting the historical progression of the Great Work of transformation. Needless to say, I am not implying that Crowley's work is less effective than Gurdjieff's, or that Gurdjieff's is less effective than Osho's. I believe that a person could attain their full inner potential by following any one of the three approaches. However, not all individuals access their full potential by remaining with only one given path, and this is increasingly true in current times. Part of that is due to the information explosion that has happened with the rise of the Internet, but part of it is also due to the complicated time in history we inhabit, with its huge population spike, one that demands a comprehensive approach to inner work. The needs of current time seekers are complex and wide-ranging. (No one understood this more than Osho, which is why he referred to his mystery school as a 'multiversity'.)

The format of Part Four of this book—The Practical Work—is reversed, beginning with Osho's work, followed by Gurdjieff, and then Crowley's. This again is done with considered intention. Crowley's work belongs more to the classical realm of Yoga and High Magick, and although potent, is difficult for many seekers to embrace in current times owing to a number of factors, not the least of which are psychological repression, relationship dysfunction, and the general diminished capacity for attention. Crowley was a specialist, an intellectually advanced magus who can only be appreciated by those who desire to penetrate deeply into the mysteries. But such a one must be ready, unburdened, inwardly light and healthy on foundational levels.

Osho was not a specialist. Although brilliant and a master of syncretism, he did not quite have Crowley's comprehensive knowledge of particular esoteric pathways. Osho's specialty was in guiding modern men and women from where they are, to deeper within themselves, with the key piece to that being *where they are*.

Crowley was not so good in this area. His major Achilles Heel, as frequently cited by students of his life, was his seeming inability to realize that most were nowhere near his level of comprehension. (However, I'm not entirely convinced that he could not realize this. I suspect more that he was simply not drawn there.) If Osho is a massive tree under which many can take refuge, Crowley is a rare and exotic gemstone that can only be recognized by few.

Gurdjieff straddled between both. He had some of Osho's grandness of spirit, the effort to reach out to the world (via his sacred dances, music, writings, etc.). Yet, try as he might, he too was ultimately more of a specialist magus like Crowley. He was, however, more adapted to modernity than Crowley (despite the latter's emphasis on the new Aeon). Gurdjieff emphasized methods of inner work that were largely free of complex esoteric language or ritual. The heart of his work is self-observation, in itself the key to the awakening process. However, he died before the human potential movement arose. Despite his brilliance and sheer originality, he lacked Osho's grasp of modern psychology, not being exposed to the extraordinary blossoming of wisdom that occurred in the 1960s.

Taken as a sum, the body of work of these three teachers is powerful and more or less all-encompassing, leaving no stone unturned on the journey Home.

Those who seek should not stop seeking until they find. When they find, they will be disturbed. When they are disturbed, they will marvel, and will reign over all. And after they have reigned they will rest.
Gospel of Thomas (2:1, 2)

Chapter 17
Osho's Practical Work

It has been argued that Osho's core teaching can never be effectively summarized. It is true that for many years his work relied principally on his presence. His dying words—'I leave you my dream'—left it reasonably clear what this dream was—microcosmically, the flourishing of his Pune ashram, and macrocosmically, an awakened humanity blossoming into its full potential. But for the individual disciple who sought to chart out their own progression, the 'dream' was perhaps less clear, as Osho's general parting advice—'the way is in'—is anything but precise. He openly stated more than once that he purposefully intended there to be no 'system' or 'doctrine' left behind that could be said to represent him, although it was never clear to me whether that was deriving from his character-driven need to be rebellious or from a genuine antinomianism that naturally resisted any conversion of his work to doctrine and dogma. The reason why this is problematic is that while organized religions have been undeniably toxic is so many ways, surviving doctrines of inner work can indeed be helpful—a reasonable example being Tibetan Buddhism, which has thrived for over a millennia by transmitting very structured oral and written guidance.

At any rate, Osho did leave behind a considerable body of work, both theoretical and practical. This work consists of four pillars:

1. His recorded spoken and written words.
2. His practical techniques; namely, the meditations.
3. His therapists (group leaders, meditation instructors, etc.).
4. His central ashram in Pune, now officially referred to as a meditation resort, guided administratively by twenty-one disciples originally hand-picked by Osho in 1989 (although over two decades later the makeup of this group has changed).

The third—the therapists—are trained psychotherapists, counselors, or other specialists (all with varying degrees of skill and experience) who since the early 1970s have run the workshops at the ashram in Pune, or in other parts of the world, in Osho's name. (Most of the original therapists have since left). They are, in a sense, a type of subculture within the greater Osho community—after 1988, Osho even assigned them a special clothing (black robes with white sashes) in contrast to everyone else's maroon robes. This did raise some questions about whether or not the therapists had in fact unwittingly assumed the role of the 'priesthood' that Osho so often disparaged. Given Osho's regular condemnation of hierarchies within religious communities, it might have seemed odd that he would promote a different appearance for his therapists. But in fact it is not hard to see the effectiveness of the device. Some of Osho's therapy groups could be quite large, up to fifty participants or more, and in such a setting, where things can get chaotic, it helps to be able to quickly identify the group leader. But more to the point, the different appearance helps to establish a setting where the seeker is able, to some extent, to let go of control issues, accept the fact that they are there to work on themselves, and let the therapists do the facilitating. (For example, leaderless therapy groups are known to be mostly ineffectual, resulting in clashing egos and little else.) It contributes toward useful boundaries, something like a chain of command that supports maximum effectiveness in the position one is in. Additionally, the therapist's 'uniform' can help at times to provoke authority issues a bit more clearly into consciousness so they can be seen and addressed.

That said, Osho did take a certain shine to the color black near the end of his life—in addition to creating the black robes for the therapists, he also decreed that certain new buildings to be constructed in the ashram in the early 1990s were to be pyramidal in shape, and black on the outside. These were still being built when I was last there in 1991, but since their completion shortly after, they are impressive structures. The entire Pune ashram is extremely impressive and still thriving two decades after Osho's passing.

Catharsis

Aleister Crowley, who along with being an adept in Magick was also an adept in Yoga, once famously summed up the practice of Yoga as: 'Sit still, stop thinking, shut up, get out.' The Advaitin master, Harilal Poonja, reduced that even further to 'be quiet'. Few would argue that these men correctly summarized the essence of mysticism. Osho, however, argued that most modern men and women are literally incapable of sitting still, stopping thinking, or shutting up, which is why they cannot 'get out'. They lack the cohesion of will, and are too full of tension, anxieties, and neuroses of all kinds to properly engage classical mystical training.

Osho was the quintessential modern master. His enormous breadth of reading kept him fully up to date with cutting edge psychology. He was the equivalent of a top notch doctor who actually bothers to read the latest journals submitted by his peers (even if he is critical of most of what he reads). As a result of his learning, a major idea that Osho embraced was the psychological concept of catharsis. The word originates from the Greek terms *kathairein*, meaning 'to purge', and *katharos*, meaning 'pure'. (Medically, it is associated with 'purging the bowels'). To 'cathart' psychotherapeutically is to mentally and emotionally purge in order to become pure—a 'purity' that has nothing to do with morality, but rather is more akin to the action of a cleaning agent.

The idea of catharsis is, naturally, connected to the idea of repression. Reich, Lowen, Rogers, Janov, Perls, and many of the 1950-60s human potential psychotherapists came to the view that modern men and women are very repressed and that such repression interferes with (or blocks altogether) any sort of movement toward higher consciousness or (what Kurt Goldstein and Abraham Maslow called) self-actualization. The idea behind cathartic therapies, as well as some of Osho's active meditations, is to create the inner space necessary in order to properly move into meditation. The idea behind all this is simple and straightforward (even if the realization of it is anything but):

1. We live in a time of unprecedented technical sophistication and almost equally unprecedented psychological and spiritual dysfunction and damage. Computer, television, smart phone, and related communication technologies have severely compromised the capacity of many people to focus attention on anything. (And in particular on each other—modern social networking sites allow for more connections with others but in general greatly diminish the quality of connections.) Attention-deficit disorders are rampant, brought on in part due to the almost absurd glut of information and entertainment possibilities. Technology brings extraordinary advantages but at an exceptional cost. The cost is the erosion of the capacity for attention. This manifests in all sorts of ways:

A. Relationship breakdown: needless to say, we cannot actually 'be' with someone if we are not actually 'present' with them.

B. Performance issues: we cannot work if we cannot focus. (Most success in life is related to capacity to focus.)

C. Depression: the constant shifting of attention to adapt to rapid changes in our perceptual field leads naturally to repressing parts of our nature as we seek to constantly adapt to the latest changes. We literally do not have enough time to truly feel and sense what is happening for us internally, and so the only alternative is repression. (Think of a typical early 21st century Hollywood action movie—no scene lasts longer than a few seconds, before it is on to the next scene, and usually the camera is intentionally shaking instead of being held steady, rapidly zooming in and out. This is all done to try and capture attention in a way that makes it easier and easier for those watching to make no effort. In effect, these kinds of films are damaging people's capacity to actually *develop* attention, something like how junk food is easy to eat but damages the body.) Repression ultimately contributes significantly toward depression, because the constant with-hold of thoughts, feelings, and energy consumes energy itself. The subsequent energy depletion leads to an overall numbness and disconnectedness.

2. We have extraordinary natural spiritual capacity that lies dormant.

3. We can begin to experience this natural capacity by calming and clarifying our minds, physically relaxing, and developing the ability to direct our attention inwardly. (By 'calming' and 'relaxing' is not meant a dull, sleepy indifference, but something more akin to an alert ease. Think of a cat reposing restfully, with its eyes open, alertly watching what goes on around it.)

4. We cannot even begin to relax and be present—let alone realize our true nature and full spiritual potential—if we are too repressed, too inwardly contracted (like a fist), too full of anxiety, tension, and the memories (conscious or not) of past hurts, pains, and traumas. We cannot be truly present because our attention is trapped in these memories, fears, anxieties, and so on. There is barely enough attention left over to actually be *here*. So-called 'attention-deficit' disorders have become more common (or more recognized, take your pick) in current times, yet attention-deficit is, in one sense, the basic condition of humanity. When Gurdjieff said that 'man is asleep' he was referring to this.

Repression itself arises due to many factors but essentially it originates from a decision, made at certain key points in time, to hold ourselves back. The natural movement of life is to extend, to expand, to move outward in some fashion, even if slowly (much how life evolves, and the universe is ever expanding). Many years spent continually holding oneself back, closing inwardly, results in developing the habit of holding oneself back in general—playing small, sacrificing unnecessarily, selling out, and so on.

To re-emphasize the needs of the self is central to the theory of the human potential movement and while demonstrably helpful it has not come without its own shadow element. Some of the problems associated with this have been the risk of increased self-absorption, over exaggerating the value of feelings (at the expense of decisive action), and using one's 'inner process' as a justification for not getting on with life, and in particular, not taking responsibility for basic issues. That said, the benefits have almost certainly outweighed any liabilities with countless seekers being helped to unburden themselves of patterns of tension and anxiety-ridden self-loathing. This is something I have seen time and again with my own eyes. Therapies originating from the human potential movement of the 1960s are potent and work, if they are applied with sincerity. At present, nearly a half-century later, such therapies are still regarded as 'alternative'. However, what exactly they are alternative from has never been clear, since 'mainstream' psychotherapy is something of a misnomer, there being, arguably, as many different approaches in psychotherapy as there are therapists.

What follows below are a few of Osho's key meditations. In all cases he was the creator of them.[1]

Dynamic Meditation: This is Osho's most recognized technique. I practiced it extensively in the 1980s (and still on occasion). It is extremely effective, especially if done regularly for a few weeks. It is, however, a 'working' meditation, requiring significant effort and endurance. More than one person has struggled with it, failed to stick with it, or been intimidated by it at first sight owing to its vigorous nature. The term 'dynamic' to describe it is an apt fit. The meditation was devised by Osho around 1970, a time when the majority of Osho's disciples were Indians. Over the next few years the meditation underwent some adjustments, doubtless influenced by the influx of Westerners who came to Osho in the early 70s.[2]

Dynamic Meditation is a one-hour process best accompanied by the CD that has been created to guide people through it. (This CD, along with a few other Osho meditations, is widely available and can often be found in a well stocked personal growth bookstore.) It was designed to be an early morning meditation and seems to work best at that time, preferably on an empty stomach. The eyes are kept closed for the whole meditation, except for the fifth and final stage (the dancing) where they can be opened or kept closed as one prefers. Also, it is ideal to be able to do this meditation with others, and in a space where you can be as loud as you want. If this isn't possible the whole meditation can be done silently, with body movement and internalized voicing of the mantra 'hoo!' (see stage four). The meditation can also be done alone, although it does require some discipline to make sure you don't cut corners and not properly complete the stages. Blow your nose well before beginning to make sure your breathing passages are relatively clear.

Dynamic Meditation is done in five stages. The first three are ten minutes each. They are:

1. Deep, fast breathing, done in a standing position, eyes closed, ten minutes. It is okay to move the body a bit while breathing, such as some slight arm and knee flexing, but hold your feet firmly in place, and do not move from where you stand. The rapid and full breathing charges the body with energy, while at the same time slowing down the conscious mind considerably. This is because the sheer amount of attention required focusing on the breathing leaves less attention over for rambling thoughts. However, the mind is not entirely 'slowed down'—in fact, the unconscious part of the mind can become more active, as blocked feelings, thoughts, and so on, can surface as the rapid breathing activates energy. The effect is similar to the 'fire breath' of *kundalini* yoga, except that here the breathing is preparing you for the direct 'release' work of the next stage.

2. Catharsis. The energy built up by ten minutes of rapid full

breathing is allowed to express naturally via catharting—this can take the form of yelling, crying, laughing, or spontaneous physical movements. Pillow pounding is also good. The only way to 'go wrong' with this stage is to stand there frozen, doing nothing. If that seems to be happening, simply make some sort of noise. This stage is all about expression. Of course, be careful not to hurt yourself or anyone else, or to break anything around you. It is especially important to keep the eyes shut during the catharsis stage.

(A comment should be made here about the value of catharsis. Although without question helpful, catharsis in and of itself does not aid in significant transformation unless the deeper patterns underneath are brought into consciousness and worked with. This is important to bear in mind. Cathartic therapy is helpful for most people, but should never be thought of as some kind of magic pill. It is merely a cleaning agent. If we continue to ignore our inner patterns, the 'dirt' will simply accumulate again.)

3. Jumping up and down, hands held straight up in the air, loudly shouting 'hoo!' as you do. Imagine this noise coming from your belly, as you jump up and down. If you cannot make noise, simply say 'hoo' as you jump, or 'shout' it mentally. If you have physical problems that prevent you from jumping (especially back issues) or you are not in reasonably good cardiovascular shape, then rhythmically flex your knees so your torso moves up and down, feet never leaving the ground, keeping your hands raised as best you can. Ten minutes, eyes closed. This stage is the most difficult, but if done with totality can free up extraordinary energy and vitality.

4. At the end of the third stage a voice booms 'Stop!' (If you don't have the CD, use an alarm clock.) The idea is to freeze in position immediately. Let your arms come down slowly and naturally. Simply remain standing in silence for fifteen minutes. If you feel nauseous or weak, it is okay to sit down, but do so very slowly and mindfully, especially if in a group, so as not to disturb others. Just be a silent witness to whatever is going on inside of you. Try not to move your body. If you must adjust yourself or scratch, do so slowly with

awareness.

5. The last stage is a fifteen minute dance, eyes open or closed, as you wish. If you do not have the CD, use music that is lively and rhythmic, or dance to the silence. The idea of this stage is to celebrate and enjoy the energies that were awakened in the first three stages and the inner peace and silence that has been touched in the fourth stage.

Dynamic Meditation in particular is effective if done regularly. I've known people who have done it for a year straight or more, never missing a day, and some have claimed it to be more effective than years of psychotherapy. I first began doing it in January of 1983 at an Osho center in Canada, at 7am in a fairly large room with a couple of dozen people. Within a few weeks I felt an extraordinary sense of inner cleansing, inner peace, overall lightening of mood and greater clarity of thought. In 1984 at the Oregon commune, I used to participate in early morning Dynamic Meditation in the Rajneesh Mandir building with up to a thousand people at a time. The experience was unforgettable. I remember likening it to the power of a 747 jet, in which the combined group energy would literally push things through (and out) of your psyche with what seemed like minimal effort. The unburdening, purifying effect made it much easier to work productively or to meditate more profoundly.

Gibberish: This meditation is simple. It is thirty minutes long. The first fifteen minutes are spent sitting, eyes closed, making gibberish sounds—babbling, talking in a made-up language, in general letting out nonsensical sounds. The idea is direct catharsis of internal dialogue. Just babble like an idiot—but with intensity and awareness—nonstop for fifteen minutes. Then, for the last fifteen minutes, you lie on the ground, feeling yourself connect to the Earth with each exhale. This is a grounding technique, always helpful after catharsis.

Kundalini: Despite the name of this meditation, it is not connected to anything from more traditional Kundalini Yoga, where specific breathing exercises are usually employed. Osho's version is more physically oriented and active. It is in four stages, and as with Dynamic Meditation, is best done with the accompanying CD (although this one can more easily be done without it).

1. Standing in place, begin shaking the body, and do so for fifteen minutes nonstop. This shaking should be easy and relaxed. An effective way to do it is to imagine that you have no head (something like Douglas Harding's 'headless way') which can aid in relaxing the neck muscles and feeling more present on a sensory level with the body. As with all Osho active meditations, totality and intensity are key. The idea is to shake the body in such a way that your awareness seems to dissolve into the shaking—there is only the shaking, nothing else. In other words, you are not forcing or even truly 'doing' the shaking, it is rather happening naturally through you. However, if nothing is happening and you are just standing there like a five thousand year old Egyptian statue then push the shaking a bit; give it a kick-start. Eyes can be open or closed, although I have found it more effective to keep the eyes closed.

2. After fifteen minutes, begin dancing (if you do not have the CD, use some rhythmic or tribal-type dance music that features drumming). Allow your body to lead the dance; that is, try not to interfere with your conscious ideas of how you should dance. As with the shaking, dance totally, such that the 'dancer' seems to disappear and only the dance remains.

A comment here: over the years, I've noted that the main stumbling block to this meditation seems to be a failure to dance with totality. Many people—men in particular—tend to dance in such a way that it appears as if they are calculating their budget, thinking about tomorrow's activities, or remembering their last sexual encounter, while they dance, and it is a poor dance indeed: the body bobbing slightly up and down, arms and shoulders rigid, and so on. The best way to counter this is to really shake with totality in the first stage, and try to lose some control and rigidity in the second, dance stage.

3. The third stage is also fifteen minutes, in which you simply sit down and bear witness to whatever is happening in the body and mind. The music that accompanies this stage on the CD was performed in the early 1970s by Georg Deuter and features a somewhat abrasive and primitive sounding synthesizer that is almost reminiscent of recordings of Gurdjieff's accordion playing in 1940s France. However, I have found Deuter's strange music quite effective for centering inside.

4. The fourth and final stage, also fifteen minutes, is simple: just lie down on your back, relax, and remain aware. Many people fall asleep during this stage, especially in the ashram where this meditation is usually done at the end of a very full day. Falling asleep is okay but to really make use of the process, try to retain consciousness even as your body relaxes and moves toward sleep.

Nadabrahma: This meditation is also one hour long. There is a CD that goes with it as well, but of all of Osho's CD-accompanied meditations, this one can most easily be done without the CD.

1. For thirty minutes, sit with eyes closed and simply hum. The humming should be loud enough that you can hear yourself (which might sound obvious, but if you do this with a group of people, it's surprising how loud the group humming can be). I have found that the louder you hum, the better, although not to the point where you are forcing it.

Many of the esoteric traditions boiled down the essence of reality to two elements: light and sound. Light is equated to consciousness and the masculine, and sound is equated to energy and the feminine. The humming is all about sound and energy. Done with calm vigour for thirty minutes, you begin to feel a natural vibration, a pulse, an energy-presence. The idea is to lose yourself in the humming. Imagining yourself to be a hollow bamboo can be helpful.

2. The second stage features two sub-stages of seven and a half

minutes each. In the first, for seven and a half minutes, very slowly move your outstretched hands, palms up, tracing two circles, side by side. The hands are parallel to the ground. The circle begins at your navel with the hands together then your hands separate and form the two circles mirroring each other. For the last seven and a half minutes, reverse direction, palms down and parallel to the ground, tracing two mirroring circles. Again, move very slowly, almost as if you are barely moving at all.

3. Complete the meditation by sitting quietly for fifteen minutes.

Zazen: Of course, Osho did not create meditations like Zazen or vipassana, but they were and are used in his ashram. His prime recommendation was for a seeker to do therapy, or his active meditations (above) before attempting the classical passive meditations like Zazen or vipassana.

In a sense, Zazen is the simplest technique of all, and in some ways, the most challenging. In essence, it involves just sitting and being witness to whatever is happening or arising in this moment. In the Soto sect of Zen Buddhism they call this *shikan-taza*, a Japanese term that means 'nothing but precisely sitting'. It speaks to the ultimate aim of transformational work, which is to recognize one's inherent wholeness. The meditation can be done sitting with eyes open or closed, and it can also be done while driving, standing in line, or doing anything that requires nothing more than 'auto-pilot' responses from you. However, in the beginning you will find it easiest to attempt this in a sitting posture with the eyes closed. Let the back be straight, but not rigid. Relax the breathing, let the belly be soft. Hands can rest comfortably in your lap, left hand on top of right. If you prefer eyes open, lower your gaze downward at about a forty-five degree angle, and keep your gaze soft. Let go, and be relaxed and yet alert, sharply watchful, and calmly observant.

Remember that the point of Zazen or other passive meditations involving witnessing is not to get anywhere. The practice is never goal-oriented, it is process-oriented. The moment you start thinking about attaining something with the meditation, the ego-mind has crept back in. Just note these thoughts, and return again to the bare witnessing.

It should be noted here that contrary to many teachings and books, 'witnessing' is not the deepest stage of meditation. What we normally think of as the 'observer' is, in fact, simply the ego watching itself. To attain to a state of pure witnessing shows definite progress, but as long as we still locate ourselves as the witness—'I am watching *this*'—then there is still duality and thus, still delusion. When witnessing is persisted with it leads to something vaster and more profound than mere observation. Raja Yoga calls this *Samadhi*; others have called it 'consciousness-without-an-object.' It is a state of pure awareness in which all apparent separation is directly seen and understood to be an illusion generated by confused and deluded thinking. This can be understood as 'Oneness' rather than consciousness, because it is not conscious *of* anything—it is simply pure Being, pure consciousness-without-an-object itself.

However, in the beginning, we simply stay with witnessing, and practice. Osho called meditation neither an art nor a science, but rather a 'knack'. The knack of witnessing with minimal interference from idle thought takes some practice, but does come with time. Eventually, as our practice deepens, we catch glimpses of pure awareness that is beyond duality. These glimpses are what the Zen tradition has referred to as *satori*. As practice is persisted with, realization deepens and stabilizes. Comparatively few make it this far.

Chapter 18
Practical Exercises from Gurdjieff's Work

Remember yourself always and everywhere.
G.I. Gurdjieff

The heart of Gurdjieff's practical teaching can basically be reduced to three essential points:

1. We are asleep.

2. We are asleep because we are inwardly divided. This shows up via the basic inconsistencies in our life. We are not a whole person. We are, effectively, a 'crowd' of people, each with its own agenda. Monday, I like green; Tuesday, it is purple; Wednesday, I sign the check; Thursday, I want a refund; Friday, I 'love' someone; Saturday, I 'hate' them; Sunday, I begin a project; by Monday, I have abandoned it. We are not capable of *truly* doing anything in our life because we have no presence, no inner integrity of being. We are not whole. Everything we think we 'do' is merely the result of past causes. We function on auto-pilot, and multiple auto-pilots at that.

3. We do not see our inner divisiveness because, essentially, we've become skilled at lying to ourselves. We do this because we have 'buffers'. These buffers are like shock-absorbers, and they basically protect us from seeing the 'terror of the situation'. The terror of the situation is, put simply, that we humans live in a kind of madhouse, and that we all are, to varying degrees, crazy. If we saw this clearly and suddenly, it would overwhelm us. So we have developed many

strategies for blinding ourselves, preventing us from seeing the reality of the situation. These strategies, the 'buffers', are what psychology refers to as 'defense mechanisms'—such as repression, projection, identification, and so on.

Self Observation

Gurdjieff's foundational technique is self-observation. The key to self-observation is being disinterested. The word 'disinterested' is often confused with the term 'uninterested'. The latter is exactly what it implies—no interest in something, indifferent toward it. 'Disinterested' can also mean that but more often it refers to a type of objective detachment—what is sometimes called being 'unbiased by personal interest', something like how a referee will (ideally) officiate a sports match. The referee is not uninterested in the game—on the contrary, he is intensely interested in it. He just has no attachment to its outcome. He is able to witness it with the calm objectivity of a good scientist.

When engaging in self-observation, our goal is to learn to observe ourselves in such a fashion. Gurdjieff employed, at times, a decidedly more dramatic metaphor: he would recommend to his students that they observe themselves 'as if God is observing you'. Our attention is generally heightened when we know others are observing us also. Imagining God or a hypothetical ultimate Overseer as watching us lends a vivid effect and heightened intensity to our attempts to observe ourselves.

Self-Remembering

Self-remembering lies at the heart of most forms of inner Work on self. It has gone by various names over the centuries within the various spiritual traditions, but it always boils down to the art of maintaining an elevated state of awareness throughout our daily life activities.

The foundation of self-remembering is *divided attention*. The idea is simple: imagine an arrow pointed away from you, at a target. That is typically how our attention functions—it 'flows' from us, toward the object we are observing. While observing this object we are normally only marginally aware of ourselves (the subject). If the object we are observing is particularly absorbing, we can lose almost all sense of ourselves while in the act of observing. It's almost as if we are not there. This is normally how attention works. In order to self-remember, you must 'divide' your attention. This can be imagined as the arrow of attention having two points to it, one on both ends. As the arrow points toward what you are observing (say, a tree), the other end of it is pointing back toward yourself. At first, this may seem a bit forced and difficult, but with practice it gradually becomes more natural.

The world we live in is highly distracting (and never more so than in today's high tech world). As a result, our attention is getting continually 'trapped' in external events. Attention can be thought of as a commodity that can be used, apportioned, exhausted, and so forth. When attention is consumed in one place, it is not available elsewhere, and we then experience that as unconsciousness (but only after the fact!). However, the interesting thing about attention is that it can be developed and enhanced, to the point where it seems as if we have 'more' attention, and indeed we do.

Self-remembering via the practice of divided attention generates energy from within. Often it will seem as if the practice is consuming energy, much as we may feel tired after a meditation session. But these are short-term effects. The long term effects of self-observation, as they are with traditional sitting meditation, are increased vitality, presence, clarity, the proper functioning of boundaries, enhanced capacity for attention, and better overall psychological health. (This is, of course, a simplification. All inner development goes in cycles, with highs and lows).

It should be understood that with all meditation methods, including self-remembering, we are not trying to force the mind to be still. Forcing leads nowhere, except to just repression of thoughts and feelings. Self-remembering is not about repression. It is rather an act that allows us to be more involved in our life in a real fashion—as Gurdjieff once famously described it, 'everything more vivid'—while at the same time being able to see things more clearly and truthfully as well.

In the beginning, practice self-remembering whenever you remember to do it. If you forget do not berate yourself, because the moment that you realize that you forgot is, in fact, the moment that you are self-remembering! Simply note that you forgot and then proceed to self-remember for as long as you can. You can practice while driving, eating, going to the washroom, walking, etc. In the beginning, it's good to try this method when not engaged in anything complicated or serious, but over time you can do it in increasingly complex situations. It will never undermine your safety; on the contrary, to self-observe or self-remember makes you more present, more alert, and more responsive. It is the polar opposite of 'zoning out'.

Exercise #1: Divided attention. Throughout the course of your day, practice directing the arrow of attention both ways, outward and inward. At first, do this with simple circumstances, such as sitting in a coffee shop: be aware of both the coffee you drink and you as drinker. Be aware of the people in the shop, and you as observer. You can also try this when talking with someone. In the beginning it is difficult and you will forget yourself quickly and many times. That is normal.

Exercise #2: The Red Light meditation. Whenever driving, when stopped for a red light, remember to take note of yourself—objectively, as if you were observing a stranger. Be mindful of your body, your breathing, your feelings, your thoughts. See all these without judgment. (Note: when observing feelings, this does not mean to cease to feel. Allow the feeling to be there, while observing yourself in it at the same time). If you do not have a car, you can use another routine activity as an anchor for your attention, such as washing your hands. Whenever washing your hands, simply remember, '*I* am washing.'

Exercise #3: 'Many 'I's'. Begin to notice your inner inconsistencies. Notice how you are not truly 'one consistent self.' Again, try to see all this without judgment. If you find judgments arising, simply observe them as well. (The Eastern traditions, particular the Buddhist schools, teach that there is no real 'I' inside at all, and this is another valid way of approaching the matter. However, whether we see our inner nature as 'many selves' or 'no self at all' is arguably a theoretical issue only. What matters is the directing of attention inwardly. Put simply, we do the work first, and worry about philosophy later.)

Exercise #4: Inner considering. This was Gurdjieff's term to describe our tendency to give too much weight to what others think of us. It is one of the greatest impediments to awakening. When caught in inner considering, we cannot self-observe or remember ourselves. For this exercise, simply begin to notice how you 'give power' to others by being overly concerned with what they think about you. At first, with this exercise as well as Exercise #3, you will only be able to see your inconsistencies and ways of 'inner considering' in terms of how you've already been up to this point—in other words, through hindsight. In time, you will be able to catch these patterns as they arise in the moment. With persistence, you'll be able to change a habitual ego-pattern as it is happening. This is the beginning of the development of real will, the ability to truly 'do'.

Exercise #5: Changing things. Consciously change things in your life. My original teacher in the Work once gave me an assignment to put my watch on the other wrist for a week. It seemed trivial at the time, but such exercises quickly reveal how mechanical our behavior can be. Very simple alterations of mundane routines help to break up unconsciousness. In part, we fall asleep in life because all the reference points around us become so familiar. This is why, for most people, the older they get the faster time goes, and why childhood seemed to drag on forever. It is because when we are young the reference points around as are mostly unfamiliar, new, and our attention gets trapped in them. The effect is of time 'slowing down'. When older, we've 'seen it all before' and so our attention is less focused. Accordingly, less of us is actually present. It's like drifting off to sleep in an afternoon nap and waking an hour later when we thought we were asleep for only a few minutes.

'Changing things' is of course the heart of the Work, because it leads to the capacity to truly be able to *do*. It begins like this: notice a negative behavioral pattern you have, say of being overly critical of your partner. Try to catch yourself in the act. (It will not be easy at first because of the inner 'buffers' that function as blinds.) With repeated practice of self-observation and divided attention, you will one day truly see yourself in the act of criticizing. That is the beginning of the awakening of *conscience*—the ability to truly recognize when we are acting out of negative ego-factors. With continued practice (according to Gurdjieff), you begin to develop a finer quality of energy within you that enables the alchemical work to transform negative patterns into something more rarefied— consciousness itself.

However, in order for this process to work, we must develop the willingness to suffer consciously, because when we seek to criticize our partner and bite our tongue as it were, we are going to suffer accordingly. This is what Gurdjieff referred to as 'voluntary suffering'. All therapeutic process work and meditation is ultimately based on the same thing—being purified inwardly as we consciously resist our old unconscious patterns and gradually break free from their grip.

Exercise #6: Lucid Observation. This is my own term for a technique found in many wisdom traditions. It is the practice of remembering, at any given moment during the course of the day, that 'I am dreaming'. At night when we have a dream where we become vividly aware (within the dream) that we are in fact dreaming, we are having what is known as a 'lucid dream'.[1] One of the methods used to stimulate lucid dreams at night is to practice, periodically throughout the day, holding the thought 'I am dreaming right now'. The exercise is not, by a long shot, idle fantasy; many spiritual and philosophical traditions assert that all of life is a type of dream anyway. Regardless of our views on the objective nature of reality, the fact is that we can heighten our awareness of the present moment simply by telling ourselves that we are in the midst of a dream. (This does not, of course, mean that we subsequently *act* as if we are dreaming!) The type of awareness we have in a lucid dream is a close parallel to the quality of our awareness when we are truly observing ourselves in waking life—both are characterized by a sense of vivid presence, of truly being here.

Exercise #7: Self-Remembering. Attempt to remember yourself as the one who is having this thought, or the one who is having this feeling, body sensation, etc.—that is, hold the sense of 'I am' whenever possible throughout your daily activities. This does not mean that you can't engage in regular activities or thinking that requires your full attention. It simply means that you remember the sense of 'I am' when having such thoughts, feelings, and so on. In the beginning, self-remembering can seem like a tedious mental exercise, in that you have to make a mental effort to remember, 'I am'. But over time, this 'I am-ness' becomes less and less a thought and more an overall sense, and one that becomes easier to remember. Persist with it and you will see the benefits.

Buffers, Defense Mechanisms

All of our inner fragmentation and the inconsistency it manifests contributes toward keeping us in a kind of trance-state; effectively, in a kind of waking sleep. Society at large generally contributes toward this trance-state by discouraging any sort of self-observation. When we self-observe, by remembering ourselves throughout the day in so-called ordinary situations (self-remembering), we begin to gain energy, vitality, and clarity. In the beginning, however, we must first overcome the 'shock' of beginning to see our own unconsciousness, our own fragmentation.

To see our inner contradictions is humbling and can even be disturbing. If we saw them all at once we might even go mad. So we have a natural defense in this regard, what Gurdjieff called our 'buffers.' A buffer is a psychological shock-absorber that allows us to shift from one sub-personality to another, without too much of a shock. Buffers are known in psychology as 'defense-mechanisms'. There are, needless to say, many. What follows are just a few.

1. Lying: This is much more frequent than is commonly assumed. Most people lie several times throughout the course of a typical day, and often without being conscious of it. In this regard, lying is more than just distortions of the truth, or 'white lies', but refers to any kind of misrepresentation of truth. For example, saying 'A' when we really mean 'B,' or not saying anything at all—'forget about it'. In a sense, all defense mechanisms are forms of lying. In general, we lie in order to protect ourselves, but the deepest sort of lying is used in protecting ourselves from seeing fully our inner disconnect. Consensus levels of lying can become very destructive, as for example when an entire society has been programmed to believe a certain way that is not in accordance with reality—what has sometimes been called 'mass psychosis'.

2. The Innocent Mask: This is a type of denial or avoidance of facing oneself. 'The world is a mess and I have nothing to do with it.' It is a resistance to growing up, but more insidiously, it keeps us from properly recognizing our more unsavory traits and capacities.

3. The Angry Victim: This characterizes our habitual, knee-jerk tendencies to blame others or the world for our difficulties. Victim-consciousness is a powerful buffer that blocks us from seeing clearly just how we are contributing to our own suffering. (This should not be confused with 'victim-bashing'. Recognizing the Angry Victim is simply acknowledging our resistance to taking responsibility.) The hallmark of the Angry Victim is righteousness. *I am right that I have nothing do to with my troubles.* My own experience is that this is one of the fiercest of the ego's buffers. People will commonly choose death over the willingness to be wrong about something. In fact, most religiously motivated wars are ultimately based on this.

4. Suppression: The deliberate effort to control a desire that we think is unacceptable. For example, you want to help someone, but fear that others will judge you or attack you if you do. So you suppress your desire to help them. Or, you are attracted to someone, but fear the consequences of your attraction, so you suppress the feeling. The suppression may be so effective that you switch from your sub-personality 'A' that is attracted to that person, to sub-personality 'B' that isn't. This then translates into 'I am no longer attracted to you'. In effect, we are protecting ourselves from directly experiencing the sheer confusion of our ambivalence.

5. Reaction Formation: This is a technical psychological term that is useful to understand. It is a defense mechanism for denying a feeling that is unacceptable. It occurs in order to help us not remember or relive an old painful memory. For example, we may have been ridiculed long ago for holding a certain belief—say, in God. Later in life, we become militantly atheist, and violently denounce any talk about God. Whenever we experience a strong knee-jerk reaction toward something, reaction formation is often the cause, and we in fact have feelings that are completely opposite of our strongly held convictions. Another example would be to hate the opposite sex and scorn them at any chance, when deep down we badly wanted the love of our opposite sex parent, and deep down we still want the love and approval of the opposite sex. Reaction formation is common with adolescents, who will use it to attempt to differentiate from their parents. 'If you say white, I'll say black.' Adolescents will often assume the opposite point of view merely to assert that they are different from the other person. But many adults still do this because they never properly differentiated from one or both parents.

6. Repression: This is the totally unconscious splitting off of parts of the mind, so as not to feel pain or other difficult feelings connected to the memories of what is being repressed. Mass society (including religion) in general serves to encourage repression in people, and especially repression of their vitality (including their sexuality). When an element of a person is repressed they generally are out of touch with it. Oftentimes, self-observation and/or meditation is not sufficient to dislodge or reveal deeply repressed material. Sometimes this can be done only via deep therapy (individual or group work) in which we can begin to see our blind spots.

7. Attack: This is a particular nasty buffer that only seems to appear in a minority of people (which is doubtless fortunate). It takes the form of a certain vicious destructiveness that no longer cares about the consequences of its actions. In effect, it is a fire-breathing dragon that is a very strong buffer engaged in protecting something very vulnerable. This buffer seems to be present in some individuals who have passed through certain traumas or types of abuse. It protects the person from seeing and feeling the totality of their wounds. (In its more extreme forms it is one of the root factors of psychopathic tendencies, alongside genetic predisposition.)

Exercise #8: Spend a week noticing, as best you can, one of these buffers at work in you. Just observe them at work as free from judgment as you can be, like a biologist observing wildlife in the field. Keep a journal and note down your observations.

Resistance

In my own work with self-observation methods both with myself and others, I have repeatedly witnessed the extraordinary power of resistance to keep us from doing these exercises. Resistance as a general topic in transformational work is of crucial importance. It can be understood in light of Gurdjieff's Law of Three scheme as the negative or 'denying' force that arises in us in opposition to a positive intention.

I have noticed over the years that there are different levels of resistance—often in the form of a 'first wave' and 'second wave'. First wave resistance is the typical opposition we experience inside of ourselves to any sort of effort to be more aware and alert. Many people abandon self-observation work when they meet their first level resistance. Some forms this resistance can take are:

1. Failure to prioritize ('I have more important things to do.') These generally take the form of practical matters to attend to throughout the course of one's typical day. Although we understand the point that it is entirely possible to self-observe while doing practical matters—and that, in fact, this is the best time to practice— we still somehow convince ourselves that the self-observation will be interference or a nuisance. So we either consciously dismiss the practice, or unconsciously dismiss it (what we call 'forgetting').

2. General resistance to change. People in general do not want to change. Of all the so-called chief features of the ego, stubbornness tends to be the most common, and stubbornness is at root the fear of change. The source of this resistance lies in our early years in life where we were repeatedly controlled by others or by external circumstances. As a result, we tend to associate any sort of change as being controlled by someone or something. We may think we want to change, but deeper down we prefer to be 'left alone' to do our own thing. (The problem, of course, is that we do not really know what this 'thing' is, even though we like to think that we do.)

3. Wrong motivation for doing the Work. This one is particularly difficult to detect at first, and usually takes some time for us to

become aware of. In a nutshell it is this: we get involved in transformational work for reasons other than the clear desire to know ourselves. Examples are: doing it because our partner is doing it. Or doing it because we seek to recreate our family dynamics within the community of the teacher or guide we are working with, and give our past a 'happy ending'. More specifically, we may project parental quality onto our teacher or guide, and seek their approval by doing the Work 'properly'. (Of course, if we choose to work alone, we do not face those potential problems, but we face the equally problematic issue of blind spots, that is, failure to see our ego-dynamics the way others can. This is particularly important when it comes to the deeper ego defenses, as these are often clearly visible to others and yet virtually invisible to ourselves.)

4. Fear of doing the Work. There is one particular fear that is especially insidious. This fear, in my experience, is the most potent of all and sabotages more efforts at becoming more conscious than any other. It is the fear of being wrong. By 'being wrong' I am not referring to the simple wrongness of believing that 2+2=5 (putting aside, for a moment, any esoteric philosophical objections to that). I am referring to the 'wrongness' needed to discover our greater potential, our True Will. This wrongness is needed because we tend to have an attachment to being right. If deep within we do not believe that we can be awake, free, happy, wise, and so forth, than we have an attachment to believing that we cannot be any of these things. In effect, we want to 'be right' about that. The awakening process requires us to be willing to be wrong at core levels about who we think we are. In short, our entire self-image gets overhauled, and eventually, erased altogether as we become less identified with personality.

'Second-level' resistance can be even more difficult to work with. This is the resistance that arises only after we have pursued the practices for some time, and successfully overcome many of the early forms of resistance. In some traditions, second-level resistance is called the 'dark night of the soul'. It refers to a period of our work on self where things seem to run dry and flat. The Work has lost its novelty and much of its shine. Our ego has returned via the back door and co-opted the methods we are using. It does this by convincing us that we now know the ropes, understand this stuff, have seen how it works, and so on. We manage the near-miraculous feat of becoming bored with our inner process.

Often times, the solution to breaking out of second level resistance is to assume greater responsibility in our life in some fashion. On occasion, this takes the form of becoming trained to guide others. All of us are teachers, even if few of us are destined to teach transformational principles in a formal way. However, over the years I've encountered many who have been perpetual students or followers for their whole adult lives and have often been in fear of developing their own capacity to help others in some way. For many, developing leadership, facilitating, helping or healing skills of some sort is a key to overcoming second level resistance. Alternatively, instead of these kinds of skills what may be called for is increased self-expression— tackling a creative project, such as via art, music, writing, building, and so on—in order to break through the ego's core programming that informs us that our contribution to the evolution of the human race is unimportant or worthless.

Chapter 19
Practical Exercises from Crowley's Work

I'm sick of you always teaching, teaching, teaching, as though you were
God Almighty and I some poor, bloody shit in the street.
The Earl of Tankerville (Crowley's student)

The Magical Diary

Crowley was a very meticulous man when it came to the practice of
self-observation. His nine hundred and fifty page autobiography is
in large part a chronicle of his life-long struggles to know himself.
Cambridge educated and yet governed internally by a strong
mystical impulse, he brought together reason and spirit—the 'aim of
religion and the method of science' as he called it—in one of the
most comprehensive ways ever accomplished by an initiate of the
mysteries.

One of the elements of Crowley's work that is most effective to
employ was his practice of keeping a diary or journal, a regular
account of progress with one's spiritual practice. This is a surprisingly potent tool to use, but one that tends to get neglected by
students of transformational work. It works for a variety of reasons,
including the following:

1. Commitment. The greatest single barrier in engaging the Work
is lack of resolve. As we begin to look at ourselves we inevitably
come to the disturbing realization that we are not whole beings—we
are fragmented, inwardly divided, and accordingly, unable to truly
accomplish much. Because of this, spiritual and esoteric fellowships

down through the centuries have devised ways to 'lock in' the seeker or candidate; to hold their feet to the fire in the face of the squirming the ego tends to do once encountered with the prospect of looking at itself. There are various ways to hold oneself in place, to demonstrate and deepen commitment with the Work. One of the best of these is keeping a regular diary or journal dedicated solely to one's inner practice.

2. Learning. This one may sound obvious but it is of crucial importance. Along with weak resolve, another major detriment to the awakening process is failure to retain key lessons. When our memory is not working to support our growing, we end up reinventing the wheel too many times. Reincarnation is, in one sense, a grand metaphor for this process of forgetting key lessons and simply repeating them again in the future with no idea that we have already been over this ground. Keeping a journal enhances learning for natural reasons, foremost of which is that the mere writing down of an idea tends to clarify and strengthen it in the mind. Additionally, there is the opportunity to revisit previous journal entries to take note of progress, repetition, or stagnancy. Observation of progress gives rise to appreciation; observation of repetition or stagnancy allows for the possibility of changing these patterns. Ignorance thrives in the dark. Writing about things keeps the light on.

3. Creativity. Some may think of themselves as more creative or less creative than others, but in reality all human beings are endowed with the capacity for creative thought. The mere act of recording impressions, experiences, and observations of one's inner practice generates the possibility that original, creative ways of expressing the timeless truths of the path of transformation will arise.

4. Introspection. We live during an age when extroversion is encouraged, and although many cultures reinforce a more intro-verted disposition, much of human society is based on dealing with externals—material possessions, personal relationships, one's own

body, and so forth. The entire universe around us tends by nature (via our senses) to pull us outward, away from ourselves, into the 'other', into 'things'. Journaling is effectively a meditation, one that helps us keep paying attention to our mind and its manifestations. It keeps the light trained within.

Yoga

Crowley's universal spirit showed in his sincere attempt to integrate Eastern disciplines—in specific, Raja Yoga—with the Work of the Western esoteric tradition (namely, Theurgy, or High Magick). He saw clearly that the East was more advanced in certain realms of the inner disciplines; in particular, the practice of focusing the mind for the purpose of moving beyond ordinary consciousness. His first mentor in Western esoterica, Allan Bennett, had himself gone to the East and immersed himself in Yoga and Buddhism, something that would have lent powerful legitimacy to Eastern practices for the young Crowley.

Human experience can basically be designated as of three essential domains: the unconscious, the conscious, and the so-called superconscious (admittedly not a great term, but 'trans-conscious' or 'beyond the ego' are probably even clumsier. English is not a spiritually technical language, to put it mildly). The lower realm (the unconscious) and the higher realm (superconscious) have something in common, and that is that in neither does the 'I' exist. Egocentric consciousness belongs only to the middle level, the level we humans typically abide in. (Some animals appear to exist here as well to at least some degree, namely those with self-reflective awareness—i.e., they can recognize themselves in a mirror—such as apes, dolphins, and elephants.) Of course, in this ego level there is a vast gradient; one person may be only marginally conscious, little better than sleep-walking, while another may have reached a considerable level of awareness while still retaining a clear sense of a separate self. The point of Yoga, however, is to train the mind in such a way as to allow us to move in a safe and gradual way into the higher egoless realms of wakefulness—to know our true inner potential.

Crowley first seriously practiced Yoga shortly after his training in the Golden Dawn while staying in Burma with Bennett in 1901. It was in this year that he claimed to experience *dhyana*, a term that translates as 'meditation' (and from which the word 'Zen' derives), but, in fact, it refers to a specific (and advanced) stage in concentrative practice. In his magnum opus, *Magick: Book 4*, Crowley would be the first to combine classical Eastern Yoga and ceremonial Magick into a coherent system.

The Yoga Crowley learned and later taught is generally known as Raja ('royal') Yoga, or as 'Ashtanga' ('eight-limbed') Yoga. 'Royal' Yoga does not mean it was a yoga created only for princes and princesses. It refers rather to the idea that the 'mind is king' and must be trained to tame the body and 'rule' as an enlightened inner sovereign over the realm of one's being. As with Buddha's Noble Eightfold Path, Ashtanga Yoga provides eight essential steps to achieving *moksha* (liberation or enlightenment).

Most treatments of Ashtanga Yoga begin with the moral guidelines of Yama and Niyama (Cf., for example, Swami Vivekanada's classic text *Raja Yoga*, transcribed from his public lectures given in the 1890s, where Chapter One, 'The First Steps', begins with a discussion of Yama). Crowley, however, relegates Yama and Niyama to third and fourth place respectively in the order he discusses the eight principles in *Magick: Book 4*. He begins instead with discussions of Asana and Pranayama. Amusingly, Crowley remarks that many of the moral virtues of Yama and Niyama are 'those of a slave, invented by his master to keep in order.' [1] However, in this regard, Crowley is on the mark, pointing out that the real purpose of the moral guidelines is to calm the mind to allow for actual inner exploration (an agitated mind cannot meditate effectively). In other words, Crowley is stating that morality must follow consciousness, not the other way around, if we are to actually make some real inner progress and avoid mere puritanical pretentiousness. (This was yet another viewpoint of his that Osho was to strongly echo many years later when he condemned the piety of Indian religious authorities while guiding his disciples into developing an alert consciousness that was as free as possible of moralizing.)

1. **Asana**: Fittingly, this word in Sanskrit simply means 'sitting down'. It refers to the importance of governing the body by practicing a specific posture and holding it until a certain 'mastery of squirming' is achieved. As Osho once put it, 'above all, don't wobble.' *Asana* refers to the body, but the practice is also a metaphor—and an actual method—for disciplining the mind. Owing to the mind-body connection, as the body becomes still the mind tends to follow suit (provided one is not dealing with significant repression; see Chapter 17 for more on that).

There are a number of *asanas*; Crowley suggested four specific ones. These are known as The God (sitting in chair, back straight, knees together, eyes closed); The Dragon (kneeling, rump on heels, toes back, head and back straight, hands on thighs); The Ibis (a more difficult one: standing on the right leg, holding the left ankle with the right hand, forefinger of left hand on lips); and The Thunderbolt (sitting, left heel against anus, right foot on its toes, heel in front of the groin, arms over knees, head and back straight).

Anyone who has ever seriously tried these knows how much effort it can take to make any progress. (I remember once participating in a morning meditation at a Rinzai Zen Buddhist center. After only half an hour one of my legs fell asleep as I sat more or less motionless in the semi-lotus posture. When the teacher rang his bell to indicate everyone to stand and perform the walking meditation, I stood and almost fell down, discovering firsthand the perils of trying to walk on a sleeping leg.) Crowley advised that 'success' in any of these postures had been obtained only when one can sit motionless for one hour. He cited the vivid image of placing a saucer upon the head filled with water. The whole hour must be endured without spilling a drop. According to tradition, great self-mastery can be attained via *asana* methods alone (although Gurdjieff, for one, famously disputed this, believing that mastery of *asana* only develops one of the five basic centers—the 'moving center'. Raja Yoga agrees, regarding *asana* as only a preliminary stage).

2. Pranayama: Most spiritual traditions recognize a type of universal energy that to this day remains essentially undetected by empirical means. In Hindu traditions, this energy generally goes by the term *prana*. The word has several meanings in Sanskrit but is most commonly associated with breath, spirit, or 'spirit-energy', in that way being a close parallel to the Latin term *spiritus*, the Chinese *chi*, the Polynesian *manna*, the Theosophical 'astral light', and so on. Despite the close connection of *prana* to the breath and various breathing practices, *pranayama* is much more than that. As Swami Vivekananda points out, 'breath has very little to do with it. *Pranayama* means the control of *prana*'.[2] What actually is *prana*? According to Hindu doctrine, all of existence is comprised of two essential elements, those being *akasha* and *prana*. The former is responsible for creating all known forms—everything from atoms to galaxies, being the subtle energy that is their essence (while at the same time being extremely difficult to detect by physical senses). The animating principle or manifesting power that shapes *akasha* is *prana*. These two have a rough parallel in the Qabalah in the form of *Chokmah* and *Binah*. The former is the essential factor behind all manifest existence—the spark of creation arising from the Godhead—and the latter gives coherence to it.

In *Book 4*, Crowley actually spends most of his time in his chapter on *pranayama* talking about mantra yoga, recommending the usage of a mantra—a short expression of sacred words repeated over and over—as a reliable means to govern the mind and bring control to the breathing. He gives a few examples, such as the famous Tibetan Buddhist *Aum mani padme hum*, and the Advaitic *Aum Tat Sat Aum*. Crowley comments, 'You have not begun to master a mantra until it continues unbroken through sleep,' adding, 'this is much easier than it sounds.'[3] In *Liber E*, he also provides a basic procedure for regulating the breath: assuming one of the *asana* postures given above, practice breathing as follows: the thumb of your right hand closes the right nostril while you slowly exhale out the left nostril to the count of 20 seconds. Then inhale through the left nostril to the count of 10. Switch, closing your left nostril with your left thumb. Exhale through the right nostril to the count of 20 then inhale through that nostril to the count of 10. Then switch back to the other nostril, and so on. Do this for one hour. He recommends increasing the counts (30 and 15, rather than 20 and 10) as you become comfortable with the practice.

3. Yama: Crowley translated this word as 'control'. Although, according to yoga scholar Georg Feuerstein, it means a specific kind of control, namely, 'restraint'.[4] It is generally the first 'limb' of the eightfold work. It is the general moral framework upon which the spiritual life is based. The main idea (which Crowley always stressed) is that an agitated mind cannot discipline itself meditatively. A moral life tends to satisfy the conscience, which in turn helps to calm the mind.

In classical yogic doctrine, there are five *yamas*: *ahimsa* (do not harm); *satya* (be truthful); *asteya* (do not steal); *brahmacarya* (either celibacy or right sexual conduct); and *aparigraha* (do not overindulge in material possessions—live simply, with no more than necessary). In *Book 4*, Crowley predictably skewers many of the ideas connected to *yama*. He translated the first one, *ahimsa*, as 'non-killing'. With vintage Crowley puckishness, he proclaims:

...this constant worry, this fear of killing anything by mischance is, on the whole, worse than a hand to hand conflict with a grizzly bear. If the barking of a dog disturbs your meditation, it is simplest to shoot the dog, and think no more about it.[5]

Both Dennis Waite and Feuerstein, however, state that a more accurate translation of *ahimsa* is 'not injuring' or 'not harming'.[6] As Feuerstein points out, there is an interesting problem that arises in the Hindu holy text known as the *Bhagavad-Gita*, where the Lord Krishna exhorts his disciple Arjuna to participate in a great war and not worry about killing others. That would certainly seem to constitute 'harming', which is why Feuerstein mentions that many Hindu scholars accordingly choose to see the *Gita* as an allegory. (It was Krishna's war-like attitude that led Osho to once famously declare that 'If I was Arjuna, I would have slapped Krishna in the face'.)

It should be noted that Crowley made his above outlandish statement about dogs to illustrate the absurdity of moral injunctions taken too literally; a good example, and one he cites, being the Jain preoccupation with the accidental killing of insects. Some Jains actually walk around wearing a mask to guard against this. Osho, born a Jain, also denounced the exaggeration of *yama*.

4. Niyama: This word also means 'restraint'. Crowley more or less passes over it in silence in *Book 4*. Technically, the term constitutes five essential practices: *shauca* (purity); *samtosha* (contentment); *tapas* (asceticism); *svadhyaya* (study); and *ishvara-pranidhana* (devotion to God). All have the ultimate purpose of calming the mind to prepare it for deeper meditation.

Crowley recommends that the student follow his own moral codes, based on what will least excite his mind. Emphasizing the problems of moral relativity he writes, 'The cleanliness that will assist the surgeon in his work would prevent the engineer from doing his at all.'[7]

5. Pratyahara: This is the first consciousness-proper level; the four previous levels dealt with the body, breathing, or behavior. The word translates as 'withdrawal', or as Swami Vivekananda called it, 'gathering inwards'. This refers in particular to the relationship between our physical senses and the objects we perceive through them. To 'withdraw' here means to disconnect consciousness from sense perception. This is accomplished via a simple witnessing meditation: just observe the movement of thought in the mind, with no attempt to control it. Over time—perhaps considerable time—the mind will eventually calm down, and when it becomes truly silent for consistent periods of time, *pratyahara* has been accomplished.

Some schools of Tibetan Buddhism call this type of meditation *shamatha*, and provide some helpful guidance to sustaining it: 1. Do not prolong the previous thought. 2. Do not beckon the future thoughts. 3. Rest nakedly in the nature of fresh awareness of the present moment.[8]

In *Book 4*, Crowley provides an interesting chart depicting graphically the gradual control of the mind, until it reaches 'absolute control'. The issue of control has always been problematic in the context of some Eastern teachings, however, as the natural question to follow is 'who is doing the controlling?' However, the problem is resolved when we bear in mind that the word 'control' is a term of convenience. The issue of a 'controller' is, in fact, not relevant to the main objective, which is slowing down the thought processes to the point where we stop identifying with things, whether external objects, or internal thoughts. In so doing, we begin for the first time to truly be 'at rest'.

6. Dharana: The word means 'concentration'. It is, in some respects, the opposite of *pratyahara*, which is essentially choiceless awareness. With *dharana* we are attempting to put our full attention on one particular object—for example, visualizing a blue triangle, and trying to mentally sustain the image. Crowley warns of the terrible struggles that await the practitioner at this stage, as the object that he attempts to hold in his mind does not remain static and proves almost impossible to sustain, something like a bad TV reception that seemingly can't be fixed. He points out that the will power developed in *asana* (see above) will be one's only saving grace here.

He recommends practicing at first with a notebook and watch, and for no more than ten minutes in the beginning.

Although Crowley mentioned this stage in the context of eight-limbed Raja Yoga, it is the Tibetans, once again, who have almost certainly taken the practice of visualization to its most comprehensive level. There are extraordinarily advanced visualization practices in some branches of Tibetan Buddhism, some of which involve a solitary meditator attempting to hold in his mind an image of something to such an extent and duration that the image eventually 'comes alive' for him and even manifests in physical reality. Practices like this may seem to flirt perilously close to psychosis, but *dharana*, as Crowley intends it, is really only a stepping stone to the real goal, which is the transcendence of duality altogether.

7. Dhyana: As mentioned, this word translates in English as 'meditation.' Hindu doctrine is explicit that true meditation is the highest attainment of the seeker, greater than intellectual skill. It remains only to understand what this meditation is.

Swami Vivekananda, echoing Patanjali, refers to *dhyana* as the stage that allows for an 'unbroken flow of knowledge' about the object one is concentrated on. In describing this stage in *Book 4*, Crowley brings to bear all his Cambridge critical faculties as he decries the silly excesses of religious pundits who relate this stage to all sorts of glorious nonsense and fantastic powers (essentially the Eastern equivalent of Jesus walking on water, etc.). And unquestionably he is correct. We in the West are well acquainted with religious fundamentalism as it shows up in the big three Western monotheistic faiths (Judaism, Christianity, Islam), and of the problems therein. We are less acquainted with Eastern fundamentalism, but it is certainly alive and well on a doctrinal level. A classic example of this Yogic fundamentalism is the notion that spiritual awakening is 24/7 bliss, or that miraculous powers always accompany spiritual awakening.

The main point that Crowley stresses about *dhyana* in the context of Raja Yoga is that it represents a stage of meditation practice characterized by a sudden bridging of the gap between subject (meditator) and object (what the meditator was focusing on in the previous stage). He rightly describes this stage as 'catastrophic' for the ego, also using the word 'annihilation' to explain what happens here to normal egocentric consciousness. Crowley gushes on at length about the experience, although in his case it is certain that the egolessness he tasted was a temporary state, and nowhere does he deny that either. This is an important point because another common misconception many have about the more advanced spiritual stages is that they are permanent and irreversible. Time and again gurus and saints have demonstrated, if not by their words then by their actions and lives, that this is clearly not so.

Feuerstein (1990) points out that the personality is completely restructured by repeated practice of this stage, but that ultimately meditation practice must be dropped as well. This would be necessary if there remains identification with being a 'meditator' or 'spiritual person'.

8. Samadhi: This word translates roughly as 'acquiring truth', or in more spiritual language, as 'Oneness with God'. It is basically the intensification and stabilization of *dhyana*, involving the full realization that the ego or separate self does not ultimately exist, and that separation of any sort is a misperception brought about by confused and deluded thought. Classic yogic doctrine calls it the union of the *jiva* (psyche) with the *atman* (true Self). Crowley wrote that most of what is written about *samadhi* is rubbish, and even accuses the great Patanjali of 'raving' over it.[9] He prefers the simple description given by Yajna Yalka, calling it 'the taking away of everything that hides the lordship of the soul'. It goes without saying that this level of realization is only the domain of the most sincere and persistent seekers of truth.

After all his consideration of Yoga and his own practices in it, the thought may occur to some that it is strange that Crowley follows it up with the work and teachings of the Western esoteric tradition, hopping from Yoga to Magick as if flying to London after suddenly finishing with Paris. One may wonder, what is the point? If one's ego has already been transcended by yogic practice, would it not be completely redundant to undertake yet another Great Work of transformational of an entirely different discipline?

This is actually where Crowley's strength begins to show, where his higher calling really shines through. Like Gurdjieff and Osho, he was involved not only with the Great Work of transformation, but also with the very modern Great Work of bridging East and West. He had to go to the East but he could not stay there as his work and teachings belonged in the West. And of all the Western concepts he best understood, it was the topic of the Will that he specialized in. He went to pains to differentiate Mysticism from Magick, the distinction between East and West. As Osho was a man of the East, and Gurdjieff a man of the Central (Asia Minor), Crowley was a man of the West (Europe and North America).

High Magick and the Nature of Ritual

Crowley was originally trained in the Hermetic Order of the Golden Dawn, an esoteric fellowship that flourished in England in the late 19th century. There was a great deal of theory taught in this school (alchemy, Qabalah, tarot, geomancy, and so on). It self-destructed in the early 20th century due mainly to the collapse of a number of relationships owing largely to shoddy communication—although it later reconstituted and exists today in several different branches of varying legitimacy. Despite the heavy emphasis on theory, the Order did teach some practical work, mostly via its rituals. These are complex exercises that combine a number of factors within them (movement, toning, mantra, visualization, breath, etc.).

Ritual walks hand in hand with human nature and has been part of most cultural institutions throughout history. Much of drama, for example, has its basis in ritual, going back to ancient times when a tribal shaman might wear the trappings of a particular animal and perform a dance that would attempt to express his deep connection with the spirit of the animal he was hunting, or learning about. The mystery schools of ancient Egypt and Greece regularly conducted specific rituals for the purposes of causing desired changes both inwardly within the self, and outwardly in the world. All spiritual schools, Western or Eastern, utilize ritual to one degree or another, whether it be the *mudras* of Tibetan Buddhism, the yogas of Hinduism, the dances of Sufism, the movements of the Gurdjieff Work, the ritual forms of Kung Fu and Tai Chi, the rituals in Christian mysticism, the Catholic mass, and so on.

The theurgical purpose of ritual—the basis of so-called high magic—is to elevate our consciousness to its highest peak, so that it can join with our greater self and ultimately with the divine (or disappear into it, effectively). The usage of the combination of fixed movements, specific intonations of sounds, and other 'props' such as material tools, incense, candles, etc., is all designed to *focus* the mind on this lofty goal. A particular contrast we can make here is the *koan* of Zen Buddhism. A *koan* is a particular question or problem that has no real rational solution (such as 'who are you?' or 'what is another person?'). The Zen practitioner is instructed to focus with all their mental strength on these seemingly absurd questions and think of nothing else. Done effectively, this eventually leads to a deep break-through when the rational part of the mind 'gives up' as it were, and the consciousness shifts to a higher level in which a sense of profound unity with all things is experienced (called *satori*—a Japanese word referring to 'sudden illumination').

Ritual magic works in a similar way; the focus and absorption in the ritual can result in an altered state of consciousness; however, the deeper point is not so much to become altered in consciousness, but rather to relax and quiet the parts of the mind that are typically on autopilot most of the time—babbling away and so blocking our natural ability to experience the inherent profundity of each moment. The calm, still mind is the portal to wisdom. (Calm and still does not, of course, mean diminished capacity to think; it rather means that we are able to think more efficiently and clearly when we need to, but also able to be truly quiet inwardly). In addition, regular practice of any legitimate esoteric ritual leads to a change in one's overall mental state, as one becomes naturally oriented toward deeper and loftier values.

The effectiveness of legitimate spiritual ritual comes from three main factors: First, *totality of expression*. The more intensely involved one is with the ritual, the more effective it will be. Second, a *clear and powerful enunciation* of the sacred words that are used. The spoken word demonstrates our presence and sincerity of intent. (Which does not necessarily mean loud; intensity of presence is more the key). And third, *repetition*. The more we do a specific ritual, the more we feel the positive effects. The same is true with all contemplative practices.

The basis of so-called natural or practical magic, sometimes called 'thaumaturgy'—or, as it is known by the more popular modern expression, 'the art of manifestation'—is to bring about desired changes in one's life via creating an inner demonstration of those changes first within oneself. (The recent mega-popular book *The Secret* is entirely about this). This is the basis of 'sympathetic' magic, wherein the practitioner brings about a change in internal patterning by first imitating what it is he or she seeks. Put simply, we must become that which we desire. If we want more love in our life, we must become more loving. If we want more patience, we must become more patient. If we want more abundance, we must become more abundant inwardly first—that is, demonstrate abundance in thought and action. Put in esoteric language, we first change our state of mind, or what is sometimes called our 'energy' or our 'vibration', and then our immediate world around us tends to reflect this change, at least to some degree.[10] This idea can be summed up as: *resources follow commitment, not the other way around*. Jesus referred to this when he said 'seek first the kingdom of God'. The committed practice of any ritual that employs sacred mythic structures—such as names of the divine and geometric symbols representing the idea of higher realities—aides in the transformation of one's state of mind.

The Lesser Banishing Ritual of the Pentagram (LBRP)

The Lesser Banishing Ritual of the Pentagram (LBRP) is one of the foundational practices of the Western esoteric tradition—roughly the Western equivalent of a combination of *asana*, *pranayama*, and *mantra* yoga, though more complex. It is a compact, particularly 'high octane' example of a ritual exercise because of the numerous elements in combines in one package. The ritual has unclear origins, although it appears to have been devised in the late 1880s within the Hermetic Order of the Golden Dawn, possibly by Crowley's initial mentor, Samuel Liddell Mathers. Crowley learned and practiced this ritual during his time in the Golden Dawn, and later used it as a base to create his Star Ruby ritual, which he believed represented an upgrade of the LBRP. The LBRP, as with many exercises from the Western esoteric tradition, is essentially a form of applied Judeo-Christian and Qabalistic mysticism with Pythagorean elements (although it is not recognized within traditional Jewish Kabbalism). Space prohibits a full analysis of the elements of this ritual; what follows below is only a description of the elements of it. A number of works can be found explaining the ritual in depth, a good one being Israel Regardie's *The Middle Pillar: The Balance between Mind and Magic* (edited by Chic Cicero and Sandra Tabatha Cicero, Llewellyn Publications, 2000).

A Word on Banishing

The idea of 'banishing'—a common element found in Western esoteric ceremonial work—may seem suspect in the eyes of practitioners of modern spiritual pathways, many of which make common usage of ideas from humanist psychotherapy or fluffier new age teachings in which the general approach is to embrace openly rather than reject—that is, accept rather than banish. But, in fact, a version of 'banishing' is alive and well in modern psychology, and it is known as 'boundaries'. To have healthy boundaries is an essential element of healthy relating. Boundaries themselves are ultimately a function of mindfulness, of being present. When we are alert, mindful of our body, grounded in the here-now—actually *present*—then our boundaries tend to operate in a healthy, self-respecting, natural manner. We do not let people trample on us, but neither do we unnecessarily trample on them or push them away. However, we cannot always rely on our ability (or even effort) to be consciously present. Sometimes we have to learn to simply say 'no', and quickly. That is true with our inner tendencies as much as it is with outer difficulties. To 'embrace' one's laziness may be appropriate at times but, more often than not, will simply result in more laziness. Sometimes we need to proactively discipline ourselves, and to simply say 'no' to negative patterns.

A banishing ritual accomplishes many things, but a key—especially in the case of the LBRP—is that it calms and clarifies the mind by banishing negative internal chatter. This is something similar to firmly and compassionately controlling your unruly child, or calming down your barking watchdog. The purifying and calming effect on the mind then has a natural outer reflection. The world tends to treat us the way we treat ourselves. (This is true in most general cases—I am not referring to extreme examples such as times of war, natural disasters, or serious accidents and illnesses, which are governed by more macro-level laws of cause and effect.) If our mind is relaxed and free of negative self-talk or idle chatter, it is common to find that our outer life proceeds with greater harmony as well. Most spiritual austerities or yogic *sadhanas* have this effect; the LBRP is merely one way, though I have found it to be a particularly effective tool owing to the number of potent elements it contains. The whole ritual employs Hebrew terms from the Qabalistic Tree of Life (see Chapter 20). The ritual begins and ends with a shorter ritual, called the Qabalistic Cross.

The Qabalistic Cross

The exercise called The Qabalistic Cross is a short sequence that draws upon the shape of the cross, visualization of white light, and four Hebrew words. (Hebrew is used because the Qabalah is the basis of Jewish mysticism. Apart from that, the LBRP does not address Jewish theology. Some have also advanced the view that as Sanskrit is the chief sacred language of the East, so is Hebrew the chief sacred language of the West. That is somewhat arbitrary, but there is no questioning the antiquity of Hebrew in a purely historical sense. Do not worry too much about correct pronunciation of the words, as many Hebrew speakers do not themselves agree on the 'right' pronunciation.) The ritual is performed as follows:

1. Stand facing the east. Visualize yourself about twelve feet tall. Imagine a ball of white light above your head. Lifting your right hand, imagine bringing the light down to the center of your forehead. Intone the sound 'Ah-tah'. (All sounds should be made strongly, unless you are in a situation where you must be quiet. In that case, enunciate the words clearly and with intensity.) *Atah* is the Hebrew term for 'you are' (or 'thou art').

2. Bring the white light down by bringing your right hand down from the center of the forehead, to your groin area. Imagine the white light shooting through your legs, into the Earth, grounding you. Intone the sound 'Mal-koot'. (Alternatively, in this second stage you can touch the heart area, while sounding 'Mal-koot', instead of the groin area—this creates a subtly different quality of energy. You can experiment with both and use the version that feels best for you). The Hebrew word *Malkuth* is the name for the tenth and last *sephira* in the Qabalistic Tree of Life. The word means 'The Kingdom'. 3. Bring your right hand up to your right shoulder, imagining the white light being drawn up there. Intone the sound 'V'Geb-oo-rah'. *Geburah* is the name of the 5th *sephira* in the Tree of Life. It means 'The Power'.

4. Transfer your right hand to your left shoulder, imagining the white light being drawn over as you do. Intone the sound 'V'Ged-

oo-lah'. This word means 'The Glory'. It corresponds to the 4th *sephira* in the Tree of Life, which is called *Chesed*.

5. Bring hands folded in prayer position, or clasped, on your upper chest. Intone, 'Le-oh-lahm, Amen'. *Le Olahm, Amen* is generally translated as 'forever, unto the ages, Amen'.

At the end of the Qabalistic Cross ritual, you should see yourself standing in the center of a bright white cross. Rest there for a minute or so. A good sign that you have done this ritual, or any ritual, well, is that your mind will be fairly quiet. You may also feel a sense of expansiveness, or power, or general sense of well-being.

(Note: Crowley amended the Qabalistic Cross ritual at the second stage to add one step—a movement from the forehead to the heart center accompanied by sounding the name of his Holy Guardian Angel, 'Aiwass'. This is then followed by bringing the light down to the lower groin area. This amendment has proven a controversial issue amongst practitioners of Golden Dawn and Thelemic-type high magick. Some use the Aiwass invocation, many do not).

The LBRP

Having done the Qabalistic Cross exercise, you now proceed with the Lesser Banishing Ritual of the Pentagram.

1. Facing east, take two steps forward, in a clockwise semicircle (as if you were stepping around an altar, which you can use if you have one). When there, trace a large 5-point star (pentagram) in front of you. Begin with the lower left; go to the top, back down to the lower right, up to upper left, across to upper right, down to lower left. In standard Western theurgy, this direction is the 'banishing Earth' direction.

2. Then, with your left foot, take one six-inch step forward, and thrust into the center of the pentagram with your hands in the 'enterer' position, in front of you like a diver, head lowered. When you finish your thrust, intone 'YUD-HEH-VAV-HEH'. (All these words are Hebrew terms for the Divine. Say the words clearly and

with intensity of presence.) Then step back with your left foot and bring your left finger up to your lips, a gesture called the 'sign of silence'.

3. Then move clockwise, to the south, and repeat the above, except this time the name to intone is 'Adonai'.

4. Face the west, repeat the above, intoning 'Eh-Heh-Yeh'.

5. Face the north, repeat the above, intoning 'Ag-lah'.

6. Face the east again. Spread arms out. Visualize four twelve-foot tall archangels surrounding you. Say boldly, 'Before me, Raphael.' Draw the sound out on the name of the archangel, so it is, 'before me, Raaaaa-phaelllll.' See Raphael in violet and yellow, holding a caduceus wand. Then repeat, 'Behind me, Gabriel.' ('Gah-breee-ellll'). See Gabriel in blue and orange, holding a chalice or grail. 'On my right hand, Michael' (pronounced 'Mee-chai-el'). See Michael in red and green, holding a sword. 'On my left hand, Auriel ('Oh-ree-elll'). See Auriel in browns and golds and greens, holding a pentacle (circular object with a 6-pointed star in it). Then say, 'About me flame the pentagrams and in the column shines the six-rayed star.'

7. Step backwards, clockwise semi-circle, ending up back where you started, still facing east, standing once again behind your altar. End the ritual by repeating the Qabalistic Cross.

Crowley made no bones about how he saw Magick in relation to Yoga. Although the felt both complemented each other very well, he ultimately preferred Magick and saw it as more comprehensive. The main reason being that he understood Magick as principally about extension to the world, whereas Yoga he saw as a natural intro-version. In that sense, he regarded Magick as ultimately more appropriate for the Western mind, doubtless owing to our cultural roots in Greek individualism and the Western emphasis on extro-version and self-expression. In a sense, Crowley was providing a useful caution (and a foreshadowing) about the tendency to make everything uniform, to blandly mix and assume that all pathways in fact say the same thing—a tendency that became pronounced in the movement toward syncretism in late 20th century trends of new age thought.

What can be said is this: at ultimate levels, all bona fide transformational pathways must, in fact, lead to the same place. However, this cannot be authentically realized until one has persevered with a particular tradition beyond one's general levels of resistance. A dabbler is one who perpetually starts but never finishes, and accordingly cannot say that they made the journey. Only one who has completed their chosen road to Rome can truly evaluate its overall significance, let alone compare it to a different path and see the commonalities.

Moreover, there is an undeniable need to come to terms with our incarnation. Thich Nhat Hanh, the well known Vietnamese Zen monk and social activist, after many years of teaching, concluded that people did best by embracing the roots of the tradition they were born and raised in. I've encountered countless Westerners over the years who have embraced Eastern pathways like Yoga or Buddhism, and yet know next to nothing about Jewish, Christian, or Islamic mysticism (principally, Qabalah, Gnosticism, Sufism), the Hermetic and Neoplatonic traditions, or Gurdjieff's Work. The reason for the attraction to Eastern esoteric systems is not hard to see; Western organized religion is a failure in many regards, in ways too extensive to go into here. When one seeks to flee from something, one often moves as far away as possible from it—the other side of the world is good enough. That and the fact that many Eastern traditions are, in fact, superbly honed systems for individual awakening does not hurt. And yet returning home, a sincere seeker will equally often find hidden gems that were for so long right under their nose.

Part Five

Historical Influences

Chapter 20
Historical Influences on Crowley's Magick and Thelema

Any proper consideration of the background of Crowley's core ideas begins with a look at what exactly 'magic' (to use the traditional spelling in this historical consideration) is. It is safe to say that this topic is one of the most poorly understood by the general public, and this misunderstanding has only been amplified in recent decades by the proliferation of fictional literature that purports to deal with the matter of magic (such as Tolkien's *Lord of the Rings*, Lucas's *Star Wars*, or Rowling's *Harry Potter*), when, in fact, such fantasy is as far removed from the deeper meaning of 'real magic' as most tabloid reporting is from actual events. To get a hold on magic in its proper esoteric context, it's necessary to take a look at its historical roots. This is of course a vast subject; space permits here only a brief overview of the matter.

A Brief History of Magic

Throughout history, magic has always had two main dimensions—what are sometimes loosely called 'high magic' and 'low' or 'elemental magic'. The latter has been known variously as *thaumaturgy* (Greek for 'make miracles') on occasion as 'sorcery', or by the more modern term 'the art of manifestation'. This is the version of 'magic' that is mostly commonly thought of by the general public when hearing the word (aside from the typical sleight-of-hand 'stage magic'). This type of magic is basically about producing effects externally; that is, it is mostly a type of manipulation or control utilizing specific 'keys' to attempt to bring about a desired external result. In its more primitive form, it has been called 'sympathetic' or 'imitative' magic, which is based on the idea that by mimicking something, or by producing a likeness of something, we can in turn affect that thing by doing something to its likeness (as in the burning of an effigy, for example).

Prior to the scientific revolution, magic—or *shamanism* as it can also be rightly called in its more basic form—was practiced for thousands of years, possibly as far back as 14,000 years ago when the Paleolithic carvings in the cave of *Les Trois Freres* in southwest France were first done. In this cave, one of the images depicts what appears to be a man dressed up as an animal performing some sort of ritual dance (with the image fittingly known as '*Le Sorciere*'). The earliest known civilizations, those of ancient Sumeria, Egypt, China, etc., all show clear evidence of the existence, and esteemed status of, magicians and their art.

Much of magic has always been based on the idea of *correspondence*, and in particular the hidden or unseen connections between things. (The word 'occult' derives from the Latin word *occulere*, meaning to 'conceal'). In this connection it is very useful to understand an issue of logic that has been a problematic part of the history of magic for millennia, and that is what has come to be known as 'magical thinking'. Magical thinking is based on the *post-hoc* fallacy. This is a confusing of causal linkages of events—in this case, the observation that event 'A' comes before event 'B,' therefore event A *must be* the cause of event B.

The following sheds some light on the potential dangers of this kind of thinking. I have an out of print copy of Rossell Robbins's 1959 *Encyclopaedia of Witchcraft and Demonology*. The book is remarkable in that it was compiled by an educated and rational man who comes down hard on organized religion for perpetuating the witch burning craze that resulted in tens of thousands of unnecessary deaths between approximately 1450 and 1750 (mostly in

Germany and France). It's gruesome reading overall, but instructive in illustrating the potential horrors that can derive from the *post-hoc* fallacy. To give but one of many examples itemized in this book, the author reports the following on just page 4 (and the book is almost six-hundred pages long):

> A woman in Scotland is burned as a witch for stroking a cat at an open window at the same time the householder finds his brew of beer turning sour.[1]

And the book is full of examples like that. It was common for someone to make a casual observation of supposedly linked events (in the case above, the beer turning sour just as this woman happened to stroke her cat) and immediately assuming something sinister and *linked* by the events. That becomes the basis of all super-stition—most of which is harmless (such as the routines of many professional athletes, like hockey players growing beards during their playoff runs)—but some of which occasionally deteriorates into the worst human folly and depravity. Most unjust persecutions and many wars were motivated by magical thinking.

Beyond the issue of a confused understanding of cause and effect, however, lies the deeper meaning of magic and that has been to understand the *true* correspondence, or right relationship, between things. This intention to reveal demonstrable truth gradually evolved into the scientific method, perhaps nowhere better illus-trated than in the outgrowth of modern astronomy out of ancient astrology, or of modern chemistry from ancient alchemy. The esoteric teachings have always maintained, however, that many of these true interrelationships are not immediately apparent to the physical senses, and thus remain mysterious, concealed, or 'occult'. The famed science-fiction author Arthur C. Clarke once wrote that 'any sufficiently advanced science is indistinguishable from magic'. This is an important truth because, by appearance, much of modern technology is a form of 'low magic'—that is, it is capable of producing extraordinary external affects in such a way that most who use it have no understanding of how or why it works.

Back in the 1920s when Gurdjieff was laboring away on his massive *Beelzebub's Tales to His Grandson*, his favorite office for writing was a certain café in Paris. There, armed with pencils and cheap notebooks, as well as his black coffee and on occasion a shot of Armagnac, he would scribble away, sometimes for hours on end. Today, over eighty years later, I also frequently write in cafes. But I do not work with lead and paper. I write this down on my sleek laptop aided by my Blackberry and memory stick. To Gurdjieff, magus of the early 20th century, these tools would have appeared to be sheer sorcery, and doubtless he would have been fascinated by them (much as he was with the automobiles of that time).

The relationship between magic and science is an important one to understand because, during the key transition period of 16th-17th century Europe, these two domains largely overlapped. Isaac Newton, generally considered to be one of the greatest, if not *the* greatest scientist ever, was also a deeply committed student of alchemy, long held as one of the cornerstones of magic and the esoteric path in general. In fact, he is known to have spent more time absorbed in his studies of alchemy and the occult than he did on physics and mathematics. John Dee, respected mathematician, cartographer, and court advisor to Elizabeth I, considered by many to be *the* scholar of 16th century England, was also a known astrologer, ceremonial magician, and conjurer.

Alongside low magic has always existed a more subtle form of magic, what is generally known as 'high magic' or, on occasion, by the Greek term *theurgy*. This type of magic is far more unpopular (and even generally unknown), requiring as it does deep commitment and honest self-examination. It is a path of working on oneself, of awakening one's divine potential. *Theurgy* literally means 'divine-working'. It refers to the practice of inner transformation brought about by attempting to align with higher elements of the psyche (sometimes personified as gods or deities or other spirit beings). It was this type of magic that ultimately interested Crowley, as it does all who enter into the Western esoteric tradition with a view to discovering the deepest mystical truths.

Although a knowledgeable student of the world's wisdom traditions, Crowley, as with all late 19th and 20th century esoteric practitioners, was influenced by several key sources of inner work. The main one was what might be called the tradition of the Renaissance magus. There were four main influences behind the Renaissance magus, and these were Neoplatonism, Gnosticism, Hermeticism, and the Qabalah.

Neoplatonism and Plotinus

'Neoplatonism' is a modern term applied retroactively to a philosophical and mystical movement that began around the 3rd century AD primarily with the work of Plotinus (205-270 AD), who was attempting to develop and refine the original ideas of Plato (428-348 BC). A few hundred years after Plato's passing, his teachings had faded somewhat from public consciousness and the Neoplatonists began a revival of his work with enough significant changes to merit the *neo* ('new') addition to their self-description as Platonists. In addition, the Neoplatonists were also largely mystics, in the sense that they were concerned with their own personal transformation and *experiential knowledge* of the divine, over and above their intellectual investigation of ultimate matters. This concern with direct experience in contrast to book learning was strongly evident in Crowley's approach.

Plotinus spent his early adult years studying philosophy in Alexandria, Egypt, and also spent two years in India, but lived most of his later life in Rome, where he established himself as a teacher. Plotinus was an ascetic by nature and considered material reality, and in particular the body, as essentially a negative element, something to be transcended. His cosmology consisted of a Triad of higher principles that he called 'the One', the divine Mind, and the world Soul.[2]

The One is indivisible, unknowable, and perfect; it bears resemblance to the non-dual ultimate reality of the Eastern Advaita Vedanta, perhaps owing to the time Plotinus spent in India. His version of the One elevated the divine to a level of reality that was effectively beyond anything knowable, such as thought, being, or even non-being. The One cannot be categorized in any fashion as it is prior to all things, and thus prior to all conceptual designations. This again is consistent with the ultimate reality of Advaita, which is described as *prior* to consciousness or being. Plotinus even denies that the One possesses self-awareness as we normally understand that to be. The closest we can come to identifying the One in material reality is to associate it with such qualities as wisdom, truth, beauty, goodness, and pure potentiality.

Although he had serious disagreements with the Gnostics, Plotinus shared with them the view that the One (ultimate source) could not possibly be a *consciously intending* Creator God, thus dissociating it from the material universe. This is also similar in some respects to the Buddhist idea of the Void, the perfect emptiness that is beyond being and non-being and that is the ultimate reality. Perhaps paradoxically, Plotinus declared that the One, though beyond all conceptualization, is still the source of everything, including the universe. But the One does not create consciously and intentionally the way the Judeo-Christian God is traditionally understood to do. It is rather a natural, spontaneous emanation of itself that results in the One causing the universe to be. In other words, the universe as we know it is simply the inevitable and entirely natural end result of the existence of the One. The Neoplatonists saw this as a more streamlined and elegant metaphysical explanation for the cause of the universe, rather than the awkward Judeo-Christian idea of *ex nihilo* ('something from nothing'), the attempted explanation for how God as 'first cause' willfully created the world.

Next down from the One is what Plotinus called the divine Mind. This Mind is the all-that-is, the supreme level of Being, and is the effective Creator God of existence. The divine Mind is followed by the world Soul, which itself has a higher and lower element. The higher part of the world Soul is transcendent, beyond matter, and the lower part imminent, what we commonly know as Nature. Thus, the lower part of the Soul in Man is his natural self, and the task of this lower nature is to join with the higher, transcendent part of the Soul. This united Soul is then to be reunited with the divine Mind, which is its source.

So Plotinus saw existence organized hierarchically as follows:

1) The One (unknowable, non-dual reality, or 'great void')
2) The Divine Mind
3) The Higher World Soul
4) The Lower World Soul (Nature)

This can be seen to be essentially a refinement and development of Plato's original scheme. The major refinement lies in Plotinus' conception of the One, which is more fully realized than Plato's term for this (what he called the 'Form of the Good'). Plotinus' One is much closer to the sophisticated view of ultimate reality in Indian Vedanta.

Plotinus believed that in rare cases the Soul may reunite with the divine Mind, and pass even further into unity with the One. According to his student, Porphyry, Plotinus himself experienced this 'union with the One', a spiritual process called *henosis* by the Neoplatonists, several times in his life. Plotinus's *henosis* corresponds closely to the Zen Buddhist term *satori* ('sudden illumination'), which refers to a momentary awakening that does not necessarily vanquish the ego (let alone deeper character defects), but that is an important experience in one's overall spiritual maturation nonetheless, giving as it does a glimpse of ultimate reality.

Another noteworthy element of Plotinus' teachings was the idea that happiness is not dependent on material conditions and thus is an inner quality that can be attained by all, regardless of their status in society, precisely because happiness is attainable *only* in consciousness. This all went hand in hand with Plotinus' basic idea that matter itself (and the body) is deeply problematic, needing to be escaped via detachment from the world and deep immersion in and identification with the higher levels of the Soul. As we will see, this was a point of departure for Crowley, who sought to embrace the physical dimension in his spiritual paradigm.

Gnosticism

The word 'Gnostic' derives from the Greek word *gnosis*, meaning 'knowledge', but in particular, spiritual knowledge attained via direct insight. The Gnostic tradition arose roughly around the time of Christ as a parallel and different view of the meaning of Christ, as contrasted to the way Christianity (the Church) slowly developed in the first three centuries AD. There are many forms of Gnosticism but most hold in common a few essential views. One of these is that the true God did *not* directly create the world, that it was created by a powerful, though imperfect, lesser god (sometimes named the demiurge, or Ialdobaoth) with a specific agenda, which has resulted in an imperfect universe (the Gnostics argue that the true God, being perfect, is not capable of creating imperfection). Some schools of Gnosticism view the figure of Jesus Christ as the embodiment of the supreme and true God; others believe that Christ, while the Redeemer of the world, is only half of the divine principle, with the other half being Sophia, the wisdom aspect of the divine.

Many Gnostic traditions reject the Yahweh of the Old Testament and claim that the role of the Serpent in Genesis has been misunderstood—that the Serpent was actually a liberator, not a usurper. And yet, Gnosticism still largely recognizes Christ as cosmic Redeemer, the one who provides the bridge 'out' of this flawed universe of separation and fragmentation. Gnosticism teaches that 'Christ' is actually found within all sentient beings, being but a designation for the ultimate divine spark within that only waits to be revealed or discovered. This journey of rediscovery is enacted within each individual who seeks *gnosis*. The awakening individual is, in effect, acting out on a micro level the evolution of the universe at large, the Gnostic schools thus according great significance to each individual's self-realization.

A crucial difference from traditional Christianity is in that Gnosticism negates the physical resurrection, and eliminates the special status of the historical Jesus of Judea, by presenting Christ or Christ-Sophia as the universal spark of divinity that is accessible to all via *gnosis*, the mystical awakening brought about by full inner spiritual transformation.[3] This inner transformation eliminates the need for any church or priesthood. One can see why Gnosticism became a heresy and was mostly obliterated by the 4th century AD, around the time the Gnostic Gospels cache of Nag Hammadi (in northern Egypt) was buried. This cache of texts was discovered in 1945, near the end of Crowley's life, but the elements of Gnosticism as an esoteric form of Christianity were known and understood in the late 19th century. The influence of the tradition bears its mark in the name of Crowley's famous mass, called the Gnostic Mass, and to the ecclesiastic section of Crowley's Ordo Templi Orientis, called Ecclesia Gnostica Catholica. (Given Crowley's own harsh criticisms of Christianity, and his formative background with Plymouth Brethren family, his affinity for Gnosticism is easily understandable.)

The key Gnostic point recognizes Christ as the representation of our internal divine spark. This by extension recognizes the historical Jesus as a 'Christed One', but it also recognizes every other human as a potentially Christed One. That idea lies at the highest ideal— even if not always aspired to—of the Renaissance magus and of all esoteric practitioners, who seek to achieve union with the divine. Meaning anyone can awaken to their divinity by specific psycho-spiritual practices and by their own sincerity of intention. 'Divine intermediaries' like churches, popes, and priests, are not needed. Of course, other Christian sects down through the centuries have occasionally argued what appears to be something similar in certain respects—for example, Martin Luther's view that 'all baptized

Christians are a holy priesthood', which was part of the basis for the 16th century Protestant Reformation—so there are some common points between the Western esoteric tradition, as rooted in Neoplatonism and Gnosticism, and some Christian denominations. The prime difference lies in the fact that in general the esoteric traditions assert that each individual has the capacity to join with ultimate divinity, to become 'one' with it, whereas Christian doctrine holds the one supreme God (and his manifestation as Trinity) as forever superior and distinct.

Hermeticism

The term 'Hermeticism' or 'Hermetic' derives from the name Hermes Trismegistus ('Hermes Thrice-Blessed'), the quintessential archetypal magus. This name is, in turn, deriving from the Greek god Hermes but has come to also be associated with the older Egyptian deity known as Thoth, the god of wisdom, writing, magic, etc. What is meant here by 'Hermetic' is the entire field of spiritual metaphysics and ritual practices (including *theurgy*, or high magic) that was a central part of many of the mystery schools of old, most of which traced their roots back to ancient Greece and Egypt. These mystery schools can be thought of as very old precedents of the mystery schools that arose to prominence in the late 19th century, such as the Rosicrucian Society of England, the Esoteric Section of the Theosophical Society, the Golden Dawn, and the Ordo Templi Orientis. Needless to say, these all represented the tradition that was a prime influence on Crowley. The Egyptian roots of Hermeticism are important to notice in this regard. Crowley was not an Egyptologist but his connection with this ancient culture was clear in terms of where he received his *Book of the Law* (Cairo), and his usage of the 'stele of revealing' (a funerary artifact of 8th century BC Egyptian priest Ankh-af-na-khonsu) in the creation of his religion of Thelema.

Hermeticism arose out of the meeting of the two great Western cultures of antiquity, Egypt and Greece, mostly following the conquests of Alexander the Great in the early 300s BC. The rational philosophy of the Greeks, led by Socrates and Plato, met the esoteric spirituality of the Egyptian priesthoods, and the resulting cross cultural mix was a body of spiritual teachings and practices that eventually came to be loosely known as Hermeticism. The basic ideas of Hermeticism are consistent with all legitimate spiritual paths, being a disciplined attempt to escape from the prison of the human condition, and awaken to (or *re*-awaken to) our innate connection with the divine.

In older times, individual spiritual teachers or authors were rarely remembered or credited with anything, and thus most early Hermetic teachings and writings are attributed to the mythical Hermes Trismegistus. Few early Hermetic texts survive, possibly owing in part to the torching of the famous Alexandrian library, but one that did survive was the *Corpus Hermeticum*. This was a group of fifteen books written in the second or third centuries AD, likely in Egypt. One of these books, called the *Tabula Smaragdina*, or *The Emerald Tablet of Hermes*, has been translated many times and has long been considered one of the cornerstones of Hermetic philosophy. The following passages are a common translation of some lines from *The Emerald Tablet*:

1) This is true and remote from all cover of falsehood:
2) Whatever is below is similar to that which is above. As above, so below. Through this the marvels of the work of one thing are procured and perfected.
3) Also, as all things are made from One, by the consideration of One, so all things were made from this One, by conjunction.
4) The father of it is the sun, the mother the moon.
5) The wind bore it in the womb. Its nurse is the earth, the mother of all perfection.
6) Its power is perfected.
7) If it is turned into earth, separate the earth from the fire, the subtle and thin from the crude and coarse, prudently, with

modesty and wisdom.

8) This ascends from the earth into the sky and again descends from the sky to the earth, and receives the power and efficacy of things above and of things below.

9) By this means you will acquire the glory of the whole world, and so you will drive away all shadows and blindness.

10) For this by its fortitude snatches the palm from all other fortitude and power. For it is able to penetrate and subdue everything subtle and everything crude and hard.

11) By this means the world was founded

12) And hence the marvelous conjunctions of it and admirable effects, since this is the way by which these marvels may be brought about.

13) And because of this they have called me Hermes Trismegistus since I have the three parts of the wisdom and Philosophy of the whole universe.

14) My speech is finished which I have spoken concerning the solar work.[4]

The Rosicrucian mystical tradition, arising in 15th-16th century Europe, and later to become a strong influence on both Freemasonry and the Golden Dawn, was itself influenced by the Hermetic ideas. The ancient Egyptians were known to place heavy emphasis on ritual as well as the exalting of certain powerful archetypal deities, some of whom were linked with the stars in the sky. From this derived the famous Hermetic maxim, *As above, so below*. What this refers to is the essential Oneness of all things and in particular how the higher realms are mirrors for the microcosm of the human being—or, how matter and energy is, in their ultimate essence, a mirror of consciousness, linked to it by a complex but largely hidden network of correspondences.

A key basis of the ritual of ceremonial magic has been the invocation of the 'gods' and 'goddesses' which are understood as archetypal energies that have a corresponding significance within both humanity, and the individual. By invoking a particular deity, using ritual, intention, emotion, and visualization, the qualities of the deity are 'absorbed' or, perhaps more accurately, activated, within the practitioner. Such an activation then presents the possibility of experiencing everything from a healing, to total identification and merging with the quality of the deity—which is ultimately understood to be an aspect of the practitioner's own spiritual essence.

Certain forms of these practices exist also in schools of Vajrayana (Tantric) Tibetan Buddhism, and have even shown up in a very simplified form in some modern metaphysical teachings that have taught the practice of creative visualization—a practice designed to generate internal energies that (in theory) will result in manifesting outwardly and attracting to oneself one's desires.

The whole area of invoking gods and goddesses is ultimately seen to be an inner phenomenon, meaning that the external form or existence of such deities is eventually recognized to be of lesser significance in light of the primary purpose of the invocation, which is to awaken the higher qualities within. However, it is not difficult to see here how the original science of invocation became externalized into a ritual that did not require the wholehearted passionate commitment of the seeker. This, in essence, becomes the outward form of most religions.

In other words, what this suggests is that the inner practices of the invocation and activation of awakened qualities (personified as the 'gods/goddesses') has degenerated many times into empty rituals that were performed by people who no longer understood all the purposes behind them. At that point, the externalized archetypes become the gods or even the 'God' who must be obeyed and feared. It was only in the underground mystical schools of these traditional religions where the original inner art of invocation was preserved, which involved a deep and profound participation on the part of the seeker, resulting in mystical awareness and spiritual awakenings.

The Qabalah and the Tree of Life

The fourth—and arguably the strongest—major influence on Renaissance magic was Jewish mysticism, which is essentially the study of the Qabalah. The word *Qabalah* means 'to receive', which is suggestive of the legend that the original Hebrew mystics received this knowledge long ago from angelic sources. There are, in truth, three main versions of the Qabalah—a traditional, or dogmatic Qabalah, which is based on the original Hebrew source books; a mystical Qabalah that has been used heavily by practitioners of the Western esoteric paths, and a so-called unwritten Qabalah, which involves an inner, mystical journey into the heart of its symbolism.[5] Crowley was heavily involved with the latter two versions.

The entire Western esoteric tradition has three prime sources: the Egyptian, Greek, and Jewish mysteries. Of those three, the Qabalah is, in the view of many, the most essential, as it provides the most comprehensive road map to the spiritual realms—mostly via an elaborate map known as the Tree of Life. The mystical interpretation of the Tree of Life adapts well to other esoteric systems such as astrology, tarot, alchemy, and the notion of mystery school initiations that represent levels of understanding.

The Qabalah even interfaces with modern psychoanalysis. One particularly interesting study was first published by David Bakan in 1958, titled *Sigmund Freud and the Jewish Mystical Tradition*, in which the author argues persuasively that the entire technique of interpretive psychoanalysis as begun by Freud had its origins in Qabalistic forms of interpretation.[6]

Jewish mysticism and the Qabalah are based largely on the *Zohar*. The *Zohar* is the name for a series of books that are a mystical interpretation of the Torah (the five books of Moses that are the heart of the Old Testament, i.e., Genesis, Exodus, Leviticus, Numbers, and Deuteronomy). In the conventional religious view, the Torah forms the basis of understanding Man's relationship with God. The *Zohar* is similar to the Gnostic element in Christianity in that it seeks to understand the more mystical aspects of its faith. That is, it is primarily concerned with the *esoteric,* and how the relationship between Man and God can best be used for the individual's spiritual transformation and ultimate union with the divine.

The origins of the history of Jewish mystical thought are unclear but it is known that the *Zohar* first appeared in an organized form in Europe in the 13th century AD, roughly around the same time that the French poets, Christian de Troyes and Robert de Boron, were writing the Grail myths (esoteric interpretations of Christianity). Jewish mystics of the 13th century had hit upon a profound concept, that of the 'Void' or formless reality that is beyond creation. In this view, God is beyond both matter and spirit and manifests in two essential ways: one, as the infinite, unknowable Source, and two, as the Creator of the universe.

The formless, unknowable Source—the Void—is called *Ain*, meaning 'no-thing'. Technically, there is nothing that can be properly said by way of defining *Ain*, because in our current condition we lack the capacity to know it directly. It cannot be grasped by thought, only pointed at. This is strongly paralleled by the notion of the Tao in Taoism, and the famous lines of the *Tao Te Ching*:

> The Tao that can be told, is not the eternal Tao.
> The name that can be named is not the eternal Name.[7]

The second aspect of God, the interactive force that generates the universe, is known via its 'emanations', resulting from an original spark from *Ain*. These take the form of four basic levels of reality, referred to as the World of Emanations, World of Creation, World of Formation, and World of Actions. The first (Emanations) is the domain of the Infinite Light of Creation (*Ain Soph Aur*); the second (Creation), is the domain of the formless agents of the Infinite, such as archangels; the third (Formation) is all the non-physical dimensions of form (subtle planes); and the fourth (Actions) is the physical domain. The physical universe was created by a dimmer version of the brilliant light of the Infinite. As a result, the physical universe is essentially a darker 'copy' of the higher realms.

Although it is not clear to what extent Jewish mystical thought may have been influenced by Plotinus or Plato, what is clear is that the idea of Plotinus' 'The One', the Jewish *Ain*, and the Buddhist notion of *Dharmakaya*, the formless Void from which all things originate and return to, are all strikingly similar, differing only in ideas about how this ultimate Reality can be understood or related to.

A slightly more comprehensive version of the Tree of Life explains the map in terms of six levels: Yechida, Chiah, Neshamah, Ruach, Nephesh, and Guph. The first three (Yechida, Chiah, Neshamah) represent elements of the Higher Self and the universal life force; the next, Ruach, represents the ego-personality, with its five elements of reason, will, desire, memory, and imagination; the next, Nephesh, represents the so-called animal-soul, or instinctive, energetic aspect; and the last, Guph, is the physical realm, including the material body. The idea is to have these different aspects of the person communicate with each other, so that the entirety of the person is known—a type of integral self-knowledge that includes the whole picture. The problem, however, is that for the average person what dominates their life is the Ruach, or ego-personality— the conventional sense of 'I'. The Eastern spiritual approach is to subdue this 'I' so that our true self emerges gradually into awareness. The Western esoteric approach is a bit different (although the end point of the journey is the same, as it must always be). In this approach, the Ruach is not seen as an obstacle to vanquish, but rather something to be consciously connected to the other domains—the Higher Self, the animal self and material world. This approach was a strong influence on Crowley's teachings.

Finally, there is the most commonly recognized form of the Tree of Life, consisting of the ten *sephirot* (domains of consciousness and reality) plus one 'shadow-*sephira*':

1. Kether: The Crown (the root and source of consciousness and life; the Godhead).
2. Chokmah: Wisdom (primal masculine manifestation, pure energy).
3. Binah: Understanding (primal feminine manifestation, that which creates non-material forms).
X. Daath: Knowledge (the 'shadowy eleventh sephira', not recognized as a true *sephira*; symbolic of the Abyss passed through by all who aspire to transcend the ego).
4. Chesed: Mercy (creation of material forms).
5. Geburah: Strength (the principle of the necessary limitation and destruction of forms. Chesed generates forms; Geburah gives cohesion to these by shaping them, discarding what does not work, etc.).
6. Tiphareth: Beauty or Harmony (represents the 'higher self' of a person, the doorway to the higher realms of consciousness).
7. Netzach: Victory (the domain of instincts, emotions, desires).
8. Hod: Glory (reason, communication).
9. Yesod: Foundation (the images and constructs of the material world, the essence of matter, sometimes related to the 'etheric plane' in esoteric thought).
10. Malkuth: Kingdom (the physical universe).

Crowley was a great scholar of the Qabalah and utilized it heavily in his work and writings. His book *777 and Other Qabalistic Writings of Aleister Crowley,* written at a relatively young age, is a collection of essays on the Hermetic Qabalah and considered to be one of the most comprehensive works ever written on the matter. As with all his works, it is not a primer for beginners.

Ceremonial Magic

One of the main esoteric practices that influenced Crowley, and that he himself was to become a master of, was ceremonial magic. Magic is, in many ways, a solitary practice; a rite performed on one's own is typically called a *ritual*. When done in group form it is usually referred to as a *ceremony*. Drama, in its original form, has always been connected to the mystery schools, especially those of ancient Greece and Egypt. When a drama is enacted, whether in ancient Greek tragedies or in modern stage productions (not to mention on the Hollywood or Bollywood silver screen), changes in consciousness can potentially occur in those observing. The English word 'ceremony' derives from Latin *caerimonia*, meaning 'awe, reverent rite'. This is connected to the idea of what Gurdjieff referred to as 'Objective Art'—his term for the power inherent in certain forms of high art to evoke a heightening of consciousness in those witnessing it. It was one of the main purposes behind the staging of his sacred dances (the 'Movements') that he had his students perform during live productions in places as well known as Carnegie Hall in New York City. The modern psychotherapeutic version of this is called 'psychodrama', which involves participants role-playing specific characters with the express purpose of 'getting in touch with' the qualities embodied in that character. This can be very useful if, for example, one is repressing certain traits, thereby suffering the effects that come with that type of repression. The psychodrama can, in theory, help free up the energy that can be locked up in such repressions.

The traditional Renaissance magus would use a few different approaches to personal development, some of which were:

1. Meditation, prayer, and ritual
2. Invocation (the assumption of god-forms)
3. Evocation

It's the third one, evocation, that has had the most dubious reputation in the minds of the average person, who has tended to associate it with the stereotypical wizard in a circle conjuring evil spirits to do his bidding. This stereotype has been in part promoted by the arts; Christopher Marlowe's 16th century play *The Tragical*

History of Dr. Faustus, about an unwitting scholar who sells his soul to a devil in exchange for temporary powers (later re-imagined by Goethe in his famous play *Faust*), became so iconic as to practically become part of collective consciousness, even entering the English language as the word 'Faustian', a term given to someone who sells out his conscience for immediate practical gain.

It's in this 'Faustian' sense that Crowley (and others like him) have been most typically judged and found wanting by a societal consciousness that is heavily conditioned by standard Christian values. But anyone who seeks to understand the Western esoteric tradition has to come to terms with the practice of evocation, and what it is actually about. Not to mention, if the Bible is to be believed, Christ appears to have been a master-magician— converting substances (water into wine), performing exorcisms, evoking spirits (Lazarus), and transcending death itself (his resurrection). These of course are argued by Christian theologians to have been *divine* miracles brought about by Christ's divine condition, but outwardly—in appearance at least—they seem to be the same as miraculous feats claimed by other wonder-workers, including those of the literary Faustian kind.

The idea of the 'grimoire' (deriving from the old French term for 'grammar') as a handbook of secret codes and symbols designed to evoke spirits (usually angels or demons) and have them do the magician's bidding, is basic to the tradition of the Renaissance magus. The fundamental idea of the grimoire is rooted in Jewish mysticism and in specific Qabalistic magic, being based on the idea of the spiritual power of the spoken word. In the very first book of the Old Testament, *Genesis*, we read:

In the beginning God created the heaven and the earth. And the earth was without form, and void; and darkness was upon the face of the deep. And the Spirit of God moved upon the face of the waters.

And God said, Let there be light: and there was light.

Of note is that God did not just *think* 'let there be light', nor did he silently and impulsively will it into being—the doctrine is that he also *spoke* the words. He immediately follows this up by *saying* 'Let there be a firmament in the midst of the waters.' 'Let the waters under the heavens be gathered together into one place.' 'Let the earth bring forth grass,' and so forth. Clearly, this is a God of verbal power. Even the New Testament echoes this idea, with the first words of John's gospel being:

> In the beginning was the Word, and the Word was with God, and the Word was God.

The idea of the power of words to command results and bring about specific changes is universal, and is very common in Hindu thought in particular, especially in the various *mantras* employed in certain kinds of yoga, 'sacred words' that when chanted are believed to bring about specific and desirable changes in consciousness.

Of the magical grimoires most associated with the Renaissance magus, most famous are the texts known as the *Greater* and the *Lesser Keys of Solomon the King*, as well as *The Sacred Magic of Abramelin the Mage*.[8]

The *Solomon* grimoires, although attributed to the legendary Jewish king and magus who is recorded to have lived and reigned a thousand years before Christ (although historical evidence for him is scant), were certainly not written by him. The legend of Solomon as a powerful magician is recounted in the collection of ancient Persian, Indian, and Arabic tales known as *The Thousand and One Nights* (or sometimes as *Arabian Nights*), which features a tale where Solomon, unhappy with a particular 'genie', has it locked into a brass bottle and tossed into the sea. The bottle is sealed with 'Solomon's seal', making it impossible for the genie to escape.

The term 'genie' derives from the Latin word *genius*, originally referring to a type of spirit-guide or guardian angel assigned to each person at birth to guide and watch over them, though in the broader sense a 'genie' (or *jinn*, to use the Arabic term) could be of benevolent or malevolent nature. According to legend, Solomon was rewarded for a demonstration of humility and given vast powers, including a magic ring that contained the Seal of Solomon that gave him control over demons. This notion lay at the roots of the grimoires written in the 14th-15th centuries, known as *The Key of Solomon* and the *Lesser Key of Solomon*, or the *Goetia* as it is more commonly called. The books deal with the preparation for, and summoning of, various orders of spirits. The classic so-called Solomonic method of ritual magic involved the usage of the magic circle, fortified by holy names (mostly Hebrew), sacred symbols (including the pentagram and hexagram, or Star of David), and the 'triangle of art', in which spirits are evoked into.

The other grimoire of note, *The Sacred Magic of Abramelin the Mage*, was published by Crowley's Golden Dawn superior, Samuel Mathers, in the late 19th century. The original document has been around reputedly since the 15th century in one form or another (although more recent scholarship suggests it may be a more recent work from the 17th century). It's a manual describing in detail a course of practice for a six month retreat in isolation in which the magician seeks to attain two main things: the invocation of the Holy Guardian Angel (HGA)—which in one sense can be thought of as the higher self, or the rarefied aspect of one's being (although, as Crowley stressed, the HGA is typically experienced as a separate entity at first)—and the summoning and commanding of various orders of spirits (including angels and demons). The book specifies that the invocation of the HGA must occur first, and then and only then, to be followed by the summoning of the spirits. The idea there is that we can only properly manage these spirits *after* we've linked up with our deepest core-truth (the HGA).

Psychologically, the entire matter of ceremonial magic can be seen as a kind of shamanic journeying or investigative psychotherapy. The summoning of the spirits can be understood as the bringing forth of hidden aspects of ourselves, our more unsavory elements (laziness, anger, jealousy, vengefulness, etc.) and then disciplining these aspects firmly, much as one would with a watch dog that is behaving unruly.

In the right understanding of *high* magic, ceremonial magic is ultimately not about manipulating reality and achieving profane desires, Faustian stereotypes notwithstanding. It is much more an ancient system of psychology in which the magician seeks to confront and understand his or her own mind and soul. It is the practice of personal transformation. As with most spiritual traditions, a more mundane version of it exists, this being concerned with the manipulation of external events ('low magic'). This type of magic need not necessitate moral compromise—manifesting useful change in one's life is done naturally by any confident individual anyway—but the deeper esoteric work of the magus was always about personal awakening and union with the higher self, or Plotinus's 'journey back to the One'.

Crowley understood all this, and was psychologically sophisticated enough to label the 'evil spirits' of the magical grimoires as 'portions of the human brain' (a view that has proved to be controversial amongst modern occultists). He himself attempted the six-month Abramelin Operation at his famous Boleskine house on the shores of the Scottish Loch Ness. He failed to complete the six months, however, as Samuel Mathers called him to London on some urgent business. Generally speaking, it's not considered good practice to suddenly break a committed spiritual retreat, and some think that Crowley's subsequent problems stemmed from this (not just because he had unwittingly released 'evil spirits' as some naively assume). However, it should be noted that the mere act of shutting himself away for six months in a lonely country house during a dark Scottish winter in order to delve into his psyche via deep meditation and the ritual conjuration of spirits is noteworthy enough. How many have the courage to do something like that? In fact, the Abramelin Operation is notable for how very few would-be magicians have actually attempted it, let alone completed it. (Israel

Regardie once remarked that Crowley was the only person he'd ever known who had.) Crowley claimed that he completed the process a few years later while walking across China, visualizing the operation in his mind. His experience as a skilled chess player, a game that requires strong visualization capacity, doubtless aided him in this way.

In addition to the esoteric traditions just outlined, Renaissance high magic was shaped by several key figures, all of whom were Crowley's influential forbearers. A capsule outline of a few of them follows:

Marcilio Ficino (1433-1499). Ficino was an important early humanist philosopher and scholar of the Italian Renaissance, as well as a magus, Neoplatonist, and astrologer. He headed an informal version of Plato's Academy in Florentine, a gathering of intelligentsia that proved to be very influential. Ficino made translations of such key sources as Plato, Plotinus, and the *Corpus Hermeticum*, and attempted to integrate Platonic ideas with Christian doctrine. Like many of his time, Ficino was accused of heresy and had to answer to the Pope, but in his case an adequate defense saved him from conviction. Ficino's translation of key Hermetic texts was one of the main causes of the resurgence of Hermetic high magic during the Renaissance. Most of the magical revival of the Renaissance and modern (19th century and on) era can, in a sense, be traced back to the key efforts of Ficino. He was one of the very first to aspire to integrate all world wisdom traditions and to recognize the primordial source from which all religions derive. A Vatican librarian, Agostino Steuco, first coined the term 'perennial philosophy' in 1540 in an attempt to describe Ficino's work.[9] The term 'perennial philosophy' was further popularized by Aldous Huxley in the 20th century and has now come to be recognized as the standard expression to define a universal wisdom tradition.

Johannes Trithemius (1462-1516). A German monk, scholar, and magus, Trithemius was a complex character whose combined paths as Christian monk and later abbot, along with cryptographer and occultist, was a fitting reflection of his times, when many disciplines of learning overlapped each other. Trithemius spent most of his adult life as a Benedictine monk and abbot of a monastery in Germany. He wrote numerous works, most notably books on steganography (secret communication) and cryptography, as well as spiritually oriented works on angel magic (which appear to have been a type of precursor to the later work of John Dee and Edward Kelley). Some of his works, originally thought to have been magical grimoires involving means for invoking spirits, were later discovered to be simple cryptograms and ciphers, using occult language as a cover. Some historians have argued that Trithemius may have been the source behind the powerfully influential *Three Books of Occult Philosophy* (see entry on Agrippa, below).

Giovanni Pico della Mirandola (1463-1494). Italian magus and philosopher, notable for his precociousness (he lived only thirty-one years). A student of Ficino, Pico's great contribution to the Western esoteric tradition was being the first to deeply integrate Qabalah into the Renaissance high magic revival. At twenty-three years old, he wrote his famous '900 theses', a sort of manifesto of religious mysticism synthesizing Christian doctrine with Hermetic and Qabalistic magic, and offered to defend it against all comers. This manifesto landed him in hot water with the religious authorities of his time who denounced parts of it as heretical, and he had to flee Italy for a while as a result.

Henry Cornelius Agrippa (1486-1535) was an important German scholar, magus, and alchemist who is usually credited with writing the key *Three Books of Occult Philosophy* (published in 1531), a massive encyclopedia of Renaissance high magic, and a work that influenced many subsequent practitioners of Western esoterica, in particular the founders of the Golden Dawn. Most modern practitioners of the Western esoteric tradition have been influenced by the Golden Dawn, and since Agrippa is considered by many scholars to be *the* main influence behind the Golden Dawn, it therefore follows that Agrippa has had a profound effect on modern Western esoteric study and practice.

John Dee (1528-1609) was one of the key figures of Renaissance high magic. Dee was the proverbial Renaissance man himself, being a scholar of many different disciplines, including mathematics, navigation, and the entire occult field. At one time in the late 16th century, he had one of the largest libraries in Europe (around 4,000 volumes, an exceptional number in those times). He also had something of a special relationship with Queen Elizabeth I, being her private counselor and court astrologer.

Although Dee was a great intellectual and a sincere seeker of truth, he apparently did not see himself as psychically sensitive, and thus he sought out the help of certain self-professed clairvoyants to aid him in a subject that became of pressing interest to him in his later years, that being the means by which to receive inspired teachings—in particular, from what he understood to be angels. In this matter, he attracted to him Edward Kelley, a complex character (once convicted of forgery) who appeared to possess remarkable psychic abilities, including the sensitivity needed for mediumship. Spirit-mediumship—or 'channeling' as it has come to be popularly known since around the 1960s—is not a recent phenomenon, despite the publicity it has received since the 'new age revolution' of the 1980s. Officially sanctioned mediums, sometimes called state Oracles, have existed since ancient times, being found in Tibet, where the state Oracle on occasion provided guidance even for the Dalai Lama, and further back in time in Greece, with the Delphi Oracle. Large sections of the Bible are also clearly mediumistically inspired, an obvious example being John of Patmos' controversial Book of Revelation.

Dee and Kelley worked in close collaboration for a number of years using a complex set of magical paraphernalia including a 'shew-stone' (crystal ball) for skrying purposes. 'Skrying' is that term commonly associated with perceiving things in the proverbial crystal ball. (The modern term for this is 'remote viewing'. Another form of the 'crystal ball' is the 'dark mirror', glass painted flat black, which serves as a good visual device in which to perceive elements of the 'astral dimension' or unconscious mind, depending on how one chooses to see that.) With Kelley allegedly receiving the information via this method and Dee working to make sense of it, the two of them proceeded to build an entire sophisticated language and system of symbolic keys that has come to be known as Enochian magic (or Angel magic). This system remained largely unknown until some three hundred years after Dee's death when it was revived and modified by the Golden Dawn in the late 19th century. The system of Enochian magic remains controversial (mostly concerning the quality of energy it brings forth, which is disputed), but what most who practice Golden Dawn-type work agree on is that the Enochian system is complex, potent, and requires years of study and practice to understand and appreciate. Crowley made a deep study of this work and Enochian magic was one of the systems he used.[10] Like Dee and Kelley, he also employed what was effectively a type of mediumship (or 'channeling') in receiving the key, *The Book of the Law*, in Cairo in 1904.

Giordano Bruno (1548-1600). Italian philosopher, magus, and proto-scientist burned at the stake in 1600. One of the noted issues backed by Bruno was the Copernican heliocentric view (that the Sun is the center of the solar system, not the Earth) as first put forth by Copernicus in 1543. It is interesting to note the charges brought against Bruno in the trial that led to his execution, some of which were: holding views about the Holy Trinity and Virgin Mary that contradicted established Church doctrine; supporting the idea of reincarnation; a belief in the idea of many worlds beyond our solar system; and of course, the heliocentric view. Essentially for these views, most of which he refused to recant, he was convicted as a heretic—which gives a good idea of the spiritual vise grip the Church held on society in those days, obvious given the sheer commonality of Bruno's 'heretical ideas' in current times.[11]

Emmanuel Swedenborg (1688-1772), was a Swedish mystic and scientist who was one of the first to intellectually convey profound experiences of altered states of consciousness, what in current times would be considered shamanic journeying or trance channeling. He claimed to visit entire other dimensions in his inner traveling, and wrote in detail about the afterlife realms. He was a student of dreams and employed breathing methods and meditation techniques. Some of his psychic feats (that included 'remote viewing') were confirmed by others and difficult to explain away. He was the author of a number of major works, including his twelve volume *Celestial Secrets*. In some ways he can be considered a patron saint of the better elements of the so-called New Age movement that flourished in the late 20th century, despite living two centuries before, during a time that did not encourage such visionary exploration.

Count of St. Germain (1710-1784). St. Germain is a strange figure in history, mercurial and largely legendary. His inclusion here (as with Cagliostro, below) is warranted more on the basis of myth than anything else, for St. Germain is the archetypal wizard, reputed to have been the reincarnation of any number of grand historical figures. He has been claimed by several 20th century occult fraternities as a patron saint, and he is often 'channeled' by new age mediums seeking to bring forth wisdom from the 'secret brotherhoods' that allegedly watch over humanity.

Count Alessandro di Cagliostro (1743-1795), was an assumed name for the Italian explorer Guiseppe Balsamo. He claimed to have studied in many sacred schools of transformation while on his travels through Europe and the Middle East; reminiscent of Gurdjieff, there was nothing to corroborate these claims. Throughout his adventurous life, he seems to have been a mix of confidence trickster and genuine occultist, although to call him a 'magus' might be too generous. Much as with St. Germain, his legacy seems to amount to mostly Merlinesque myth and legend.

Eliphas Levi (1810-1875). Born Alphonse Louis Constant (later changing his name), Levi was a key figure in the 19th century esoteric revival and in some ways is the father of modern magic. His works *Transcendental Magic* and *The History of Magic*, though considered flawed by later scholars, were nevertheless highly influential and important treatises that brought together most of the major teachings of the Western esoteric tradition into a coherent whole. His work and ideas had a major influence on the founders of the Golden Dawn. He was the first to integrate the Tarot, Qabalah, and ritual work in a way that is still practiced today by the majority of Western mages.

All of the above personalities are important parts of Crowley's esoteric heritage, so much so that he even claimed that three of them—Dee's skryer Edward Kelley, Count Cagliostro, and Eliphas Levi—were previous incarnations of him. In a sense, however, they were all his 'previous incarnations'—archetypal figures who saw their twentieth century echo in the complex magus from England.

Yoga

Crowley was a world traveler from an early age and like many committed seekers he eventually made his way to the Orient. He had a good reason to visit Sri Lanka (then called Ceylon) in particular, as his old friend, former Golden Dawn brother and first mentor in magic, Allan Bennett, had moved there in 1900. In 1901, Crowley visited Bennett and both of them studied Yoga under Shri Parananda (with Bennett later that year ordaining as a Buddhist monk and taking the name Ananda Metteyya). This period of time left a lasting impression on Crowley and he was to incorporate elements of Raja Yoga into his future system of inner work. His later publication *Eight Lectures on Yoga* (1939) has been considered by many one of the better early works on Yoga by a Westerner.

In the final analysis, Crowley was a Western magus not an Oriental mystic and he made this clear despite his deep affinity with Eastern wisdom. Nevertheless, elements of the classical yogic path to enlightenment are directly embedded in his model of graded initiations as a candidate advances from neophyte to magus. Part One of *Book 4* (Crowley's magnum opus) is called *Mysticism*, and elaborately subtitled *Meditation: The Way of Attainment of Genius or*

Godhead considered as a development of the Human Brain. This section of
the book begins with an introductory essay on the various attempts
by the world religions to address the suffering inherent in the human
condition, leading into a consideration of how to end this suffering
by achieving the goal of mysticism, that being the realization of non-
duality. This is what he refers to in the classical yogic terms of
'joining subject (self) with object (universe)'—i.e., how to become
'one with all'. The essay is followed by what is essentially a technical
primer on Raja Yoga, and the various stages of spiritual development.

Buddhism

Here in the early part of the 21st century, Buddhism is relatively well
established in the West with many hundreds of Buddhist centers and
monasteries representing all main Buddhist traditions—Tibetan, Zen,
Theravadin, etc.—found throughout Europe and the Americas. But
back in Crowley's earlier years, when Allan Bennett was first teaching
him the elements of ceremonial magic at the end of the 19th century,
this was certainly not the case. Buddhism at that time was a foreign
tradition not well understood. Tibetan Buddhism in particular was
practically unheard of and Tibet itself mostly unknown. *The Tibetan
Book of the Dead* was not published in English until 1927. Zen
Buddhism was largely unknown until the efforts of the Japanese
scholar D. T. Suzuki, who published a number of works on Zen in
English in the 1920s-30s. Theravadin Buddhism, traditionally
regarded as the oldest branch, originating in India with Gautama
Buddha circa 500 BC and spreading through Southeast Asia, was
known somewhat earlier in the West, and it was this tradition that
Bennett ordained in, in Burma in 1902. (According to the Buddhist
scholar, Stephen Batchelor, Bennett was the second Englishman ever
to ordain as a Buddhist monk, following Gordon Douglas who took
the vows in Thailand a few years before Bennett.)[12]

Crowley himself, though originally in accord with Buddhist
principles, later rejected the religion as he began to develop his

system of Thelema. This appears to have been brought about through the revelation of his key text, *The Book of the Law*, that he 'received' in 1904. Initially, he struggled with the matter. In the *Confessions*, he wrote:

> The fact of the matter was that I resented *The Book of the Law* with my whole soul. For one thing, it knocked my Buddhism completely on the head. 'Remember all ye that existence is pure joy; that all the sorrows are but as shadows; they pass & are done; but there is that which remains.'[13]

Over time this position solidified for him. Near the end of his life he wrote: ·

> When the Buddha was making experiments and recording the results, he was on safe ground: when he started to theorize, committing (incidentally) innumerable logical crimes in the process, he is no better a guesser than the Arahat next door, or for the matter of that, the Arahat's Lady Char.[14]

Yet despite Crowley's dismissal of elements of Buddhism, his own foundational text, *Book 4*, begins with the following:

> Existence, as we know it, is full of sorrow. To mention only one minor point: every man is a condemned criminal, only he does not know the date of his execution. This is unpleasant for every man. Consequently every man does everything possible to postpone the date, and would sacrifice anything that he has if he could reverse the sentence.[15]

He goes on to qualify this statement, by saying that:

Practically all religions and all philosophies have started thus crudely, by promising their adherents some such reward as immortality.[16]

And yet he does not really deny the reality of this idea either. The Buddha's 'First Noble Truth' is: Life is *dukkha* (suffering). That is, the very nature of the human condition is rooted in hardship, struggle, sorrow, and suffering. According to the Buddha, this is above all because we are ignorant of our true nature and assume ourselves to be something that we are not—namely, an unchanging, permanent self. This fixed self then has the tendency to become attached to things and to suffer accordingly—which is why one of the virtues of Buddhist philosophy is traditionally regarded as non-attachment. Crowley's life tended to demonstrate this as his character was inclined to resist prolonged intimate attachments. All his numerous entanglements and sexual relationships with others notwithstanding, he was in many respects a 20th century European parallel of the ancient wandering Oriental mystic (and he even called himself the 'Wanderer of the Waste'). Whether this arose from an inability to establish and maintain relationships, or from a natural—and wise—inclination to resist entrapment, is debatable, though probably there is truth in both.

At any rate, Crowley's relationship with Buddhism appears somewhat conflicted. On the one hand, he ultimately dismissed what he perceived of as its 'joyless' approach; on the other hand, elements of Buddha's Noble Truths—not to mention the Buddhist ideal of detached and disciplined examination of the mind—are found throughout his life and writings. In *Book 4*, in discussing the founders of the world religions, he wrote:

The only one who explains his system thoroughly is Buddha, and Buddha is the only one that is not dogmatic. We may also suppose that the others thought it inadvisable to explain too clearly to their followers; St. Paul evidently took this line. Our best document will therefore be the system of Buddha; but it is so complex that no immediate summary will serve; and in the case of the others, if we have not the accounts of the Masters, we have those of their immediate followers.[17]

Ultimately, the main reason Crowley rejected Buddhism was because of what he perceived as the *via negativa* of its doctrine; this was significant because his Thelemic teaching embraced the idea of a robust joy as opposed to a more contemplative asceticism. He also perceived a nihilistic element in Buddhism that he disliked. However, as discussed in Chapter 4, it's possible that his grasp of Buddhism was not complete, owing to the fact that many important Buddhist developments over the centuries, especially in the Mahayanist and Vajrayana schools as manifested in Tibetan and Zen Buddhism, were not generally well known or clearly understood in the early parts of the 20th century.

Taoism

Crowley is known to have had a deep respect for the *Tao Te Ching*, the sourcebook of Taoism, generally accepted to have been written by a Chinese sage who may have lived anywhere from the 6th to the 3rd centuries BC, traditionally known as Lao Tzu (which simply means 'old master', adding to the enigma of the author's identity). In Part One of *Book 4*, Crowley wrote in a footnote:

> We have the documents of Hinduism, and of two Chinese systems. But Hinduism has no single founder. Lao Tzu is one of our best examples of a man who went away and had a mysterious experience; perhaps the best of all examples, as his system is the best of all systems.[18]

Coincidentally, Osho also, on more than one occasion, cited Lao Tzu as the wisest of all sages. He thought so highly of him that he named his living quarters at his ashram in Pune 'Lao Tzu House'. He said:

You can forget Mahavirs, Buddhas, Krishnas—Lao Tzu alone is enough. He is the master key.[19]

Crowley, in *Magick Without Tears*—written near the end of his life and considered by many to contain some of his wiser thoughts—wrote, in referring to the *Tao Te Ching*:

It is impossible to find any religion which adequately represents the thought of this masterpiece.[20]

From 1905 to 1906, he had walked across parts of China during which time he claimed to have connected deeply with the spiritual essence of the *Tao Te Ching*. He believed that the core of his teaching, *Do what thou wilt shall be the whole of the Law*, was mirrored perfectly in the *Tao Te Ching*. He wrote:

...the supreme classic of this subject is the Tao Te Ching...the Book of the Law states the doctrine of Tao very succinctly: 'Thou hast no right but to do thy will. Do that and no other shall say nay. For pure will, unassuaged of purpose, delivered from the lust of result, is every way perfect.' (AL, I: 42-44). 'Thus also the Sage, seeking not any goal, attaineth all things; he does not interfere in the affairs of his body, and so that body acteth without friction. It is because he meddleth not with his personal aims that these come to pass with simplicity.' (Tao Te Ching, VII:2)[21]

Crowley was also an enthusiastic student and practitioner of the *I Ching*, the ancient Chinese divinatory system. He frequently mentions his various consultations of it throughout his writings.

Chapter 21
Historical Influences on
The Gurdjieff Work

Perhaps I stole it.
Gurdjieff[1]

While we are on uncertain ground in trying to understand what individuals or possible 'secret brotherhoods' influenced Gurdjieff, we are on more solid footing in considering the particular *known* wisdom traditions that impacted him. His past, prior to the year 1912 or thereabouts, is unsubstantiated, but the nature of his teaching system, although unique in formulation, bears influences that are reasonably clear. Ouspensky in *In Search of the Miraculous* reports that Gurdjieff told him he'd visited, amongst other places, Egypt, Tibetan monasteries, Sufi schools in Persia, Bokhara, eastern Turkestan, dervishes of various orders, the Chitral (a valley in present-day Pakistan), and Mt. Athos, a sacred mountain in northern Greece that is the site of some twenty Eastern Orthodox monasteries.[2]

The Greek Influence and Pythagoras
Gurdjieff's paternal heritage was Greek and his father, being a bardic poet—someone who knows by heart hundreds of poems, songs, and instructional tales—was a strong influence on his son. That, combined with the deep influence early Greek philosophy had upon the later Western esoteric tradition, merits looking briefly at

some of the early Greek ideas, particularly the figure of Pythagoras and the famous allegory known as Plato's Cave.

Greek tradition taught about three essential forms of knowledge, those being:

1) *Pathesis:* Knowledge by way of feeling.
2) *Mathesis*: Knowledge by way of intellectual understanding.
3) *Gnosis*: Knowledge by way of deep experiential realization.

One type of *gnosis* would be the combining of full *mathesis* (clear thought and focused attention) and deep *pathesis* (embodied feeling; that is, mindfulness of feeling and sensation). That, at least, was Gurdjieff's approach. Many of the classical Greek philosophers were concerned primarily with rational understanding but the later Neoplatonists, like Plotinus, Porphyry, and Iamblichus, appeared to have more of an emphasis on personal *gnosis*. The mystery schools with their rites of initiation (such as those of Eleusis and Orpheus, etc.) could be said to have been more concerned with *pathesis*, and the development of what Gurdjieff would later call the 'higher emotional body'. In India, this path has been represented in part by *bhakti* yoga or the devotional relationship with the divine. These schools doubtless had their versions of *mathesis* and *gnosis* as well; however, many of the mystery schools that developed and arose following the conquests of Alexander the Great (up to 323 BC) did so as a kind of rebellion against the dryer rationalism of classic Greek philosophy. Some of these mystery religions were much older, also.

Pythagoras (570-495 BC), often acknowledged as the grandfather of Western philosophy, was also the archetypal seeker of wisdom and in many respects Gurdjieff's life is a kind of echo of him. Pythagoras was reputed to have widely traveled, having been initiated by many teachers and schools of wisdom, and eventually founded his own mystery school in Italy. In addition, Pythagoras appeared to have a strong balance between a mystical and rational nature, developing a type of number-mysticism founded on his idea that 'all things are numbers' from which the basic elements of geometry and the mathematics of music began to develop. Gurdjieff's usage of the musical scale, Ray of Creation, and Laws of Three and Seven are also founded on number-mysticism, of which Pythagoras is commonly regarded as the father of. (However, owing to his antiquity and the fact that none of his original writings survived, the historical records defining Pythagoras' life are scant. But the ideas are there, and would have been accessible to Gurdjieff via different means.) Of note also was Gurdjieff's idea of 'Objective Art', art based on harmonious proportions, also an idea found in Pythagoreanism. The mathematics of octaves, based on proportional fractions, is also attributed to Pythagoras as is the idea of the 'music of the spheres' stemming from the idea that planets move on the basis of specific geometries and numbers, which in turn correspond to musical notes and thus to a type of cosmic symphony.

Pythagoras' life virtually amounts to myth, almost a type of Greek Merlin—although not quite. He did exist, but little else can be said for certain about him; even the vaunted Pythagorean Theorem is debated by scholars as to who actually devised it. In this regard, Pythagoras is an apt symbol for the nebulous 'Masters of Wisdom' J.G. Bennett spent so much time seeking. The very facelessness of these distant masters reminds us not to get hung up on the personality but to look beyond to the ideas themselves.

Socrates and Plato

In a sense, much of the Western esoteric tradition finds its philosophical basis in the ideas of Socrates (470-399 BC) and Plato (428-348 BC). The early 20th century English philosopher-mathematician, Alfred North Whitehead, once famously wrote 'The safest general characterization of the European philosophical tradition is that it consists of a series of footnotes to Plato.' Plato was a student of Socrates, although historians are unclear how much of his thought derived from his teacher, and how much was his own. For example, many of Plato's key ideas are explained in his book, *The Republic*[3], and yet in this book all these ideas are narrated by the character Socrates. For sake of brevity we are going to refer to these as 'Plato's ideas' but all that matters of course are the ideas themselves, most of which form much of the foundation of Western metaphysical and esoteric philosophies.

A key element of Plato's thought that influenced the world view of the Western esoteric tradition was the idea of what he called 'Forms'. In the sense that he meant it, a Form is the deeper essence of all objects and qualities in the universe. It is the invisible template, the original perfect prototype upon which the material expression is modeled, as it were. According to Plato, behind (or before) the shape of the material human body is its invisible Form. Likewise for a tree, or a rock, or a planet, or an inner quality like peace or goodness; these all exist first as intangible Forms.

Plato argued that the existence of Forms was the only way to explain certain abstract mental phenomena that have no known correlates in the physical world. For example, we are unaware of anywhere in nature where a perfect circle or a perfectly straight line can be found. And yet, mysteriously, we are able to conceive of them. Further, much of human civilization has utilized such geometry. The world we construct, everything from buildings to tables to books and printed words, are laid out in geometric precision in a tidy order that is not found in the natural world.

The Western esoteric idea around the various planes and higher dimensions of existence was likely influenced by the notion of Forms, especially in the teachings of the 'mental plane' or what is sometimes called the 'fifth dimension', an order of reality marked by higher mental abstractions and archetypes that are universal and not subject to time and space. Plato also taught that the Forms are not subject to time and space. In part, he defined wisdom as the ability to naturally grasp the existence of the Forms, thus suggesting that our minds are directly linked to the deeper spiritual reality that lies behind the material world. In that sense too, he foreshadowed the Western esoteric teachings, especially the Hermetic maxim 'as above, so below'—the higher order of Forms is simply a mirror for the lower world of material expression.

Plato's own student, Aristotle, objected to the idea of the Forms, pointing out that simply because we can conceive of an abstract prototype of an object does not mean that that abstract prototype (the Form) must in fact exist. As the grandfather of Western science, Aristotle's simple objection to Plato's notion of Forms sums up well the longstanding division between metaphysics and practical science. But in reality, the issue of whether or not Forms truly exist is academic. From the point of view of inner work on oneself, all that matters is our ability to understand the relationship between our mind and reality as it applies to the domain of our own experience.

Plato also taught that the soul is immortal and pre-exists our body which is why, according to him, the process of learning is more akin to a process of *remembering*. The reason why we can conceive of perfect geometric forms or abstract qualities like greenness or wetness is that we were born with the ideas of the Forms representing these things already in place. As we mature, we re-awaken our knowledge of these Forms. This whole notion of 'recollecting' our true nature was utilized much later in certain spiritual traditions, like Sufism, with its God-remembering meditations, and in the Gurdjieff Work with its self-remembering method for raising consciousness.

One of the key well-known and important metaphors described by Plato was his 'allegory of the cave'. In this fable, a group of prisoners live in a cave that is closed off from the world. They sit facing a wall. Behind them is a big fire and between the fire and the people a series of objects are placed by puppeteers. These objects cast a shadow on the wall of the cave that the people are looking at. All they can see are the shadows. As a result, they conclude that the shadows are the actual thing.

According to Plato, a person who begins waking up to reality becomes aware that the shadows appearing on the wall are, in fact, caused by the combination of the light from the fire and the objects between the fire and the people. The firelight is simply casting shadows of the objects onto the wall. Thus, the awakening person becomes directly aware of the *cause* of things (the firelight and the objects), as opposed to only witnessing *effects* (the shadows).

But Plato takes the analogy deeper. In the story, one of the prisoners is taken outside of the cave where he becomes aware of the existence of the Sun as the source of all light. Plato symbolizes the Sun as the Form of Goodness, the archetype of divine light. The man who has left the cave also now sees that the objects in the cave were merely copies of deeper realities, living forms that exist outside the cave, such as a living dog, whereas in the cave there had been only a facsimile of a dog. The objects in the cave owe their existence to the real things outside of the cave upon which they are based. And the fire in the cave owes its existence to the Sun, much like all that we perceive in reality owes its existence to the Form or archetype of Goodness and Light.

The final piece to Plato's allegory is that the person who escapes from the cave and into the light of reality has a moral obligation to return to the cave and attempt to help others escape. He may, in fact, be ignored, or worse, killed by the cave dwellers who will likely feel threatened by his 'crazy' ideas of a greater reality outside of the cave, but it remains his duty to try to reach them anyway. This ideal is mirrored in Mahayana Buddhism in the notion of the Bodhisattva, the self-realized person who delays his own final liberation in order to assist others in waking up. There is also a parallel in Gurdjieff's analogy, comparing sleeping humanity to life in a prison and of the necessity for one desiring to get out of the prison to find someone else who has already escaped, or at least knows the way out.

Plato's cave allegory foreshadowed the early 20th century ideas in Freudian psychoanalysis concerning projection, the psychological tendency to see things in our outer world that are, in fact, arising from our own minds. Plato described the source of all appearances as the 'Form of the Good' and implied that it is outside of us, but the view can just as easily be taken that this resides deep in our own soul as the undiscovered part of our nature. Ignorance of this undis-covered part of us causes us to misunderstand reality, much as psychological projection causes us to misperceive things and imagine things to be 'out there' that are, in fact, no more substantial than shadows.

Of great importance in grasping Plato's word view is in under-standing what he called the 'divided line'. This is basically the blueprint of all later esoteric ideas around the structure of the universe according to a ladder of planes or dimensions. In Plato's scheme, a line is divided into two main sections, the 'Intelligible' and the 'Visible'. There are four smaller subsections: 'ideas' and 'images' within the Intelligible, and 'things' and 'images' within the Visible.

Plato envisaged a cosmic structure where the *ideas* of the Intelligible realm are a higher order than the *images* of the Intelligible. The Intelligible realm is the realm of the invisible, of that which lies 'behind' the physical universe. Similarly, the *things* of the Visible realm are a higher order of reality than the *images* of the Visible. The lengths of the smaller four subsections on the line are not all equal. The smaller length of the Intelligible ideas represents the greater degree of clarity and truthfulness of its domain. The largest length, that of the Visible images, represents the greatest degree of illusion.

In the theory of the Western esoteric tradition, reality is often divided into five planes (sometimes with a greater number of sub-planes). These five planes are commonly known as the physical, etheric, astral, mental, and spiritual. They roughly correspond to Plato's scheme as follows:

Spiritual = Form of the Good (which lies just beyond the Intelligible ideas)
Mental = Intelligible ideas
Astral = Intelligible images
Etheric = Visible things
Physical = Visible images

According to Plato, if we rely solely on our perception of Visible images, we are essentially in the realm of mere opinion. If, however, we look deeper into things, we can go beyond opinion into direct knowledge—much like the man in the cave who discovered that the shadows on the wall were, in fact, the mere reflections of tangible, 'more real' objects that were behind him.

Plato does not stop there, however, but pushes deeper. He proposes that the Intelligible images are, in fact, the *real forms* of Visible things—i.e., that the invisible Form is *more real* than its visible manifestation, just as the living things that the man discovered outside of the cave are more real than the statues in the cave that were modeled on them. Further, the Intelligible images themselves are deriving from a yet higher order of reality, that being the Intelligible ideas. These latter are themselves arising from the ultimate source, the Form of the Good.

And now comes Plato's key point: our knowledge of the highest levels—the Form of the Good (God) and the Intelligible ideas—is *a priori* knowledge; that is, it is *independent of experience*, or our physical senses. It is our birthright, and something that is recoverable via self-knowledge and pure reason and insight. Such a view lies at the very basis of the esoteric traditions, being that we hold within us the key to a profound understanding of reality and that our very makeup as human beings endows us with the faculties to rise to the highest levels of the sublime and the good. Plato wrote in *The Republic*:

> When the soul is firmly fixed on the domain where truth and reality shine resplendent it apprehends and knows them and appears to possess reason, but when it inclines to that region which is mingled with darkness, the world of becoming and passing away, it opines only and its edge is blunted, and it shifts its opinions hither and thither, and again seems as if it lacked reason.[4]

Over the centuries, Plato's core ideas came in for plenty of criticism, especially his ideas of the Forms, being based as it appears to be on something imaginary. Gurdjieff, while stridently opposed to the imaginary in general, nevertheless spoke about 'higher bodies' (such as the higher mental body and higher emotional body) which, although not directly observable, are understood to represent a higher level of truth, Man's greater potential. In that, we see a clear echo of Plato's root idea that there are levels of truth beyond our day to day experience of things that can only be reached by 'breaking out' of our more mundane consciousness. In addition, Gurdjieff spoke often of the need to wake up, comparing it to getting out of a prison. Plato's cave dwellers represent essentially the same thing, caught in a prison of their own making and unaware that they are *in* a prison. Gurdjieff said:

> You do not realize your own situation. You are in prison. All you can wish for, if you are a sensible man, is to escape. But how to escape?...one man can do nothing...no one can escape from prison without the help of those who have escaped before.[5]

That notion is a close echo of Plato's idea that the cave-dweller only gets out with the help of someone who has already gotten out of the cave.

Eastern Orthodox Christianity

Gurdjieff claimed on more than one occasion that his Work was essentially the secret and true Christian teachings. In response to a question put to him once about the relation of his work to Christianity he said,

> I do not know what you know about Christianity. It would be necessary to talk a great deal and to talk for a long time in order to make clear what you understand by this term. But for the benefit of those who know already, I will say that, if you like, this

is esoteric Christianity. We will talk in due course about the meaning of these words.[6]

The mere fact that Gurdjieff refers to his system in that way suggests that he never entirely separated from his Christian roots, even though he went to great lengths to make it clear that his version of 'Christianity' had little in common with the religion as it is practiced in the world today. In regard to that, he once said that 'the Christian form of worship' was inherited from ancient Egypt, long before the early Pharaonic period known as the Old Kingdom (beginning around 3,500 BC). To that he added,

It will seem strange to many people when I say that this prehistoric Egypt was Christian many thousands of years before the birth of Christ, that is to say, that its religion was composed of the same principles and ideas that constitute true Christianity.[7]

With Gurdjieff, it was often unclear if he was, essentially, making things up. Ouspensky himself, even as he dutifully reports Gurdjieff's claims, admits his own doubts, observing that Gurdjieff never divulged details about the mystery schools he'd claimed to have studied in and at times seemed to contradict himself when referring to them. Nevertheless, Ouspensky does not overlook the obvious, which is that Gurdjieff *was* in possession of considerable knowledge and practical techniques for transformation of the individual. In the spirit of all sincere seekers, this latter is what primarily interested Ouspensky.

Gurdjieff was born in northwest Armenia and grew up in northeast Turkey. These areas are not far apart and are located in the Caucasus region, the name given for the area of land that lies between the Caspian and Black Seas. This area is interesting in that it straddles so many varied cultures, being a crossroads for Europe, the Middle East, and Asia. The immediate countries of the region are Armenia, Georgia, Turkey, Azerbaijan, southern Russia, and Iran (known as Persia in Gurdjieff's time). The two dominant religious lines there in recent history have been Eastern Orthodox Christianity and Sunni Islam. Gurdjieff was born to Eastern Orthodox parents and was initially tutored by Father Dean Borsch, a local priest of the Orthodox faith. And so, despite the uncertainty about Gurdjieff's early years, one thing that is indisputable is that it was the Orthodox Church that was his first spiritual influence.

It's interesting here to stop a moment and contrast Gurdjieff to Crowley, who was also born and raised as a Christian. In Crowley's case, largely due to his animus toward his mother, he came to resent the tradition (Plymouth Brethren) that she so fanatically espoused and, Nietzschean-like, harshly rejected the main faith of his culture. Gurdjieff, however, in all likelihood because he seems to have had a close relationship with both of his parents and with Father Borsch, came to retain elements of the Christian teaching in his Work—by claiming that he taught the 'true' Christianity—even as he rejected the current state of it.

The Eastern Orthodox Church was formed in 1054 AD when it broke with the Roman Catholic Church in a process that was known as the 'Great Schism' which involved a split between the powers in Rome and those in Constantinople (present-day Istanbul). In current times, the Eastern Orthodox Church claims about twenty percent of all Christians. Most of Russia and the Eastern European nations are heavily Eastern Orthodox. Theologically, the Eastern Church is similar to the Western Roman Church in many respects, such as honoring the same seven sacraments (Baptism, Confirmation, Eucharist, Penance, Anointing of the Sick, Holy Orders, and Matrimony) but it is different in some important aspects, first of which is that it has no pope. Thus, final authority in decisions lie not in one person but in councils of bishops wherein the 'guidance of the Holy Spirit' is believed to operate as clearly as Roman Catholics believe it does through the Pope. In general, power is less centralized in the Eastern Church, where the view that the Holy Spirit works through all Christians is believed more strongly. This is demonstrated by the fact that laymen of Eastern congregations elect their clergy as opposed to the Roman Church where these are appointed. In addition, Eastern Orthodox priests may marry.

Of the three main lines of Christianity (Eastern, Roman, Protestant), the Eastern Orthodox probably has the most mystical tendencies, claiming as it does the heritage of the Desert Fathers and other solitary seekers of illumination. I have been to St. Catherine's monastery in the Sinai region of Egypt, which is run by a handful of Eastern (Greek) Orthodox monks, and can attest to the extraordinary remoteness of the place and the purity of the desert air, so tailored for mystical introversion. The Eastern Church more readily supports the idea of asceticism, based on the Biblical injunction from Mark 10:21 to 'take up the cross and follow me'. The St. Catherine's monastery, in addition to its austere isolation, also claims to be one of the two oldest Christian monasteries on the planet.

In considering the mystical side of Eastern Orthodoxy—the side of the faith that would ultimately have most interested Gurdjieff— what is of particular interest here is the *Philokalia*, a group of writings put together by Eastern Orthodox mystics between approximately the 4th and 15th centuries AD. These writings are intended as spiritual guidance for monks following the contemplative path. Before looking at some of the aphorisms of these writings, it is useful to bear in mind that Gurdjieff's system was not about mystical intro-version or asceticism—it was, centrally, about waking up within the midst of the typical conditions of life—the life of the householder. Nevertheless, he did employ techniques that were not dissimilar from those used by contemplatives.

The following ten *Philokalia* aphorisms—termed the 'Spiritual Directions of Ephrem the Syrian'—at first glance appear to be standard ascetic moral training for a would-be contemplative and a number of them (especially the first one!) may not seem to have much echo in Gurdjieff's teaching. But looked at more closely, we begin to see clear parallels:

1. Monk, neither desire meat, nor drink wine, lest your mind coarsen...Be not addictive to meat and wine-drinking, lest you make your mind incapable of receiving spiritual gifts.

2. God created man free, therefore for man are praise and punishment. Let spiritual seekers receive praise and laurels, and the negligent and criminals—punishment and pain.

3. The wandering eye causes much suffering to the one who follows it. Keep your eyes from wandering lest you find no straight way to chastity.

4. Wisely avoid adverse meetings to keep yourself in goodness.

5. If you want to conquer lust for wealth, love selflessness and sparing way of life.

6. If you want to conquer anger, develop meekness and generosity.

7. If you want to conquer lasting grief, mourn nothing transient; and if someone reviles at you, dishonors or irritates you, do not grieve, but, on contrary, be glad!

8. Grieve only if you have committed a sin, but even in this case do not grieve too much, otherwise you may become desperate.

9. If you want to conquer conceit, do not desire praise, laurels, nice garments, respect, favor, but like to be blamed and slandered by people, and reproach yourself as the most sinful among sinners.

10. If you want to conquer pride, do not say that your deed was done by your hands and might; say that with God's help and guidance it was done, not by my power and efforts.[8]

The general overall tone of the instructions is that of urging disciplined self-perfecting which is of course a hallmark of Gurdjieff's teaching. In particular, we are drawn to point #7 wherein the monk is exhorted to appreciate those who, in the modern vernacular, 'push his buttons'. This is a classic Gurdjieffian approach and, in fact, is found more or less in the fifth of Gurdjieff's famous list of thirty-eight aphorisms he had posted at the *Prieure*:

> Remember you come here having already understood the necessity of struggling with yourself—only with yourself. Therefore thank everyone who gives you the opportunity.[9]

Points 5, 6, 8, 9 and 10 are all seen in Gurdjieff's work in terms of making specific efforts to not be controlled by impulsive reactions. This is a path of applying willpower toward spiritual purification. The only significant difference found in Gurdjieff's approach is the Fourth Way idea of applying these teachings in conventional everyday life rather than in the monastery. Part of the inner asceticism of the *Philokalia* teachings involves a daily remembrance of the reality of death. This too is echoed in Gurdjieff's aphorism #33:

> One of the best means for arousing the wish to work on yourself is to realize that you may die at any moment.[10]

In addition, the ongoing remembrance of God is stressed—something found in Gurdjieff's teaching as 'self-remembering' which, while different in terminology, leads to the same experiential state of mind, that being inner silence and a sense of becoming vividly attuned to the present moment. This is connected to what the *Philokalia* refers to as 'watchfulness', clarity of awareness that arises as a result of the perpetual effort to remember the highest truth.

Another essential area in which Gurdjieff's teaching may be said to resemble Eastern Orthodox Church doctrines is on the issue of the nature of the soul. In Eastern Orthodoxy, more so than in Roman Catholicism or Protestantism, the emphasis is on the Resurrection—the need to die and rise again with Christ as symbolized by the Easter celebration. The 'resurrection body' is not something we are granted by birthright; we have to in effect earn it. Gurdjieff argued a similar thing in regards to the soul. He maintained that the average person had no soul but had the possibility of creating one via inner work.

The whole notion of 'creating a soul', seemingly unique to Gurdjieff, is, in fact, very similar to the idea of attaining a resurrection body via proper faith, contemplation, and action. And the further connection with ancient Egypt—specified by Gurdjieff as being the 'true source' of esoteric Christianity—is not difficult to see either, as Egyptian belief also revolved around the importance of attaining to salvation in the Other World via the vehicle of the *Akh*, which was the name given to the higher self that resulted from the *ba* (soul) and *ka* (life-force), uniting in the spirit-world after the death of the body. It was viewed by the Egyptians as immortal but was something that was *attained*, not simply given.[11]

A key concept to understand in Eastern Orthodox doctrine is that of *theosis*, a Greek word that means to 'make divine'. It lies at the very heart of the mystical objective, which is to attain to a deep intimacy with God or even, as is also sometimes put, to become 'one with God'. In Eastern Orthodoxy, there are generally held to be three stages to this process, those being *katharsis* (purification), *theoria* (illumination), and *theosis* (divinization).

Katharsis, or necessary purification, was referred to by Gurdjieff as 'conscious labor and voluntary suffering'. *Theoria* in Greek means 'contemplation' but in specific the ability to view something in a dispassionate manner—that is, to be a witness, which leads to correct seeing or illumination. Gurdjieff's self-observation was entirely about this. How to observe ourselves—and in particular our mechanical reactions—without getting caught up in the drama of things.

Lastly, it should be noted that when Gurdjieff died in France in 1949 his funeral service took place in an Eastern (Russian) Orthodox Church. As J.G. Bennett noted,

It is probable that Gurdjieff retained his contact with the Greek and Russian Orthodox tradition throughout the whole of his life, and certainly when I saw him at the end of his life, the sense that he was a member of the Russian Orthodox Church was quite strong with us.[12]

Sufism

The esoteric current of Islam, commonly known as Sufism, had a strong influence on Gurdjieff. He claimed that throughout his wandering years (from approximately 1887 to 1910) he met many great Sufi masters, usually known as Dervishes. This is almost certainly true as Gurdjieff spoke Turkish, which at that time was the *lingua franca* of Central Asia, and Sufism was the dominant esoteric tradition throughout that region.

In the centuries before the term 'Sufi' became known in the West, the two ways of most commonly describing the figure of this kind of mystic were via the Arabic word *fakir* and the Turkish word *dervish*. Interestingly, both terms mean 'beggar' or 'poor man'. The Hindu equivalent of this is the *sadhu*, the wandering mendicant who has abandoned all possessions. In all cases, this is a person who in theory has renounced the world in order to dedicate himself wholly to the pursuit of realizing God. The word 'Sufi' is believed by some to derive from the Arabic term *suf*, meaning 'wool,' and is generally thought to refer to the simple garment worn by a homeless mystic.

There are many different orders within Sufism. In terms of orthodoxy, these range from those that are little more than side-branches of traditional Islam, to those that verge on the heretical or are even regarded as being outside of Islam altogether. Consistent with most esoteric schools from any tradition—such as Christian Gnostics or Jewish Kabbalists—the goal of Sufism is the deep transformation of the individual, and the awakening to God-consciousness. To be 'conscious of God' is to be directly aware of one's limitless and eternal nature along with the wisdom, peace and compassion that arises from that state.

Despite the fact that individual Sufis often do belong to a particular order or Sufi community, the power of the tradition lies in the reality (such as it is) of the individual's spiritual awakening. The essence of all esoteric traditions has always been the transformation of the individual. As such, any significant transmission of knowledge that Gurdjieff received always came from the personal connections that he was able to cultivate with individuals. More than anything, the essence of the esoteric path—and Sufism in particular—is that it is possible to attain to intimacy with the divine here and now, not just in the afterlife. A traditional believer in 'the Book' (Jew, Christian, Muslim) has faith that, via devotion to their tradition alone, paradise will be reached after the death of the mortal body. The committed Kabbalist, Gnostic, or Sufi (in theory) seeks to realize this exalted state *while alive*. This general sentiment is strongly reflected in Gurdjieff's teaching.

Sufis generally believe that their tradition derives straight from the prophet Muhammad (570-632 AD) and that it was the intended line of spiritual transmission for those who had the capacity to attain to deep inner illumination and oneness with God. Muhammad was a warrior but he was also a mystic, and the Koran has a number of verses that describe his various mystical revelations. A typical passage in that regard is *Sura 53:6-18*:

The Lord of Strength; so he attained completion,
And he is in the highest part of the horizon.
Then he drew near, then he bowed
So he was the measure of two bows or closer still.
And He revealed to His servant what He revealed.
The heart was not untrue in (making him see) what he saw.
What! do you then dispute with him as to what he saw?
And certainly he saw him in another descent,
At the farthest lote-tree;
Near which is the garden, the place to be resorted to.
When that which covers covered the lote-tree;
The eye did not turn aside, nor did it exceed the limit.
Certainly he saw of the greatest signs of his Lord.

Four main Sufi orders still thrive in current times. These are the Naqshbandi, the Qauddiri, the Cheshtiya, and the Mujaddiyya. Smaller orders also exist, such as the Mevlevi, Halveti, and the

Mawlawis, also known as the 'whirling dervishes'. The Naqshbandi Order was founded in Bokhara, an ancient city that is located in present-day Uzbekistan. Gurdjieff claimed to have spent time there somewhere around 1900. The area is just north of Afghanistan and about half-way between his home region of the Caucasus and Tibet where he also claimed to have traveled to, so this claim is consistent.

Looking into some of the teachings of the Naqshbandi Sufis, we find some interesting and clear parallels with Gurdjieff's system. First amongst these worth mentioning is the idea of the 'spiritual householder'. Naqshbandi Sufis do not withdraw from the world but rather aspire to achieve a right balance between inner and outer lives. This, of course, was the heart of Gurdjieff's 'Fourth Way', the path of the householder who avoids monastic seclusion and seeks to transform within the very gritty intensity of ordinary life. The Naqshbandi also have a basic list of Eleven Principles. Depending on the source, these principles are sometimes translated differently but basically they amount to this:

1. Conscious Breathing: Just what it implies, awareness joined with breathing. This is very similar to the well-known Buddhist method of *vipassana*, except that in this case the mindful breathing is combined with God-remembrance.
2. Watching Your Step: This one is sometimes interpreted literally, that is, to always look at one's feet when walking, as a demonstration of both humility and single-minded focus. At other times it is interpreted metaphorically, as clarity of intention and focus on one's highest goals in life without stumbling over basic responsibilities that need to be handled.
3. Travelling Home: This again has a practical and symbolic meaning—the first being the willingness to go where you must in order to find appropriate spiritual guidance, and the second being the traveling of the inner journey home to God.
4. Solitude in Company: This is the Sufi version of the Buddhist 'way of the lotus,' that is, how to be *in* the world, but not *of* the

world. That is, it is the practice of staying calm and centered, with the aid of God-remembrance, when in the midst of the noisy marketplace of life, but at the same time, not avoiding life either.

5. Remembering: This is the heart of the idea of *Zikr* (sometimes spelt *Dhikr*) which is a mind training based on the remembrance of the Higher, be that via sacred names, or remembrance of truth. The goal is to dwell in constant remembrance of the supreme reality of God.

6. Restraint: Cultivating patience and self-discipline. .

7. Watchfulness: Cultivating alertness. Sometimes called Soul meditation; focusing on God's presence, while remaining mindful of idle thoughts that may intrude in the meditation.

8. Recollection: Remembering what is good from the past, and staying mindful of one's body.

9. Time-awareness: Noting how one's day was spent, how one is using one's time. To be accountable for this and to not waste time.

10. Awareness of Numbers: Refers to the importance of maintaining discipline in meditation by counting the number of meditations one is doing, such as keeping track of the number of repetitions of sacred names, etc.

11. Heart-Awareness: Exactly as it sounds, to hold consciousness in the heart as one remembers God.[13]

Most of the above exercises are found in the Gurdjieff Work with the main exception being that Gurdjieff replaced God-remembering with self-remembering, in effect adding a more Western-oriented psychological element to the purely spiritual practice of the Naqshbandi. Most notable from the eleven-point list is the heavy emphasis on discipline and watchfulness, something that was always a trademark of Gurdjieff's approach.

Tibetan Buddhism

Gurdjieff claimed to have visited Tibet around the year 1900. He indicated that he spent a couple of years there learning some of the language and absorbing some of the teachings of Tibetan Buddhism or 'Lamaism', as it was referred to at that time in the West. (He also claimed to have taken a wife there and fathered two children.) At that time, few if any Westerners had penetrated into Tibet. For several hundred years, the odd Christian monk or traveler might make it across the mountains into Tibet, but by and large it was a land and culture very poorly understood outside of Tibet in Gurdjieff's time.

Geographically, Tibet is referred to as the 'roof of the world' and with good reason. Most of the country is plateau resting at an average of fifteen thousand feet, tilted toward the east where it is drained by five major rivers. It is ringed by several huge mountain ranges. The world's highest, the Himalayan, is on the south; to the west lies the Karakorum peaks, and beyond them Ladakh and Kashmir. The Kunlun and Altyn ranges rear to the north, impeding the way to the central Asian deserts and further, Mongolia. To the east lies an inhospitable vastness of desert plateau and brackish lakes. Tibet is vast and windswept and, although in the southeast valleys there are some trees and vegetation, most of the country is arid and harsh—cold, dry, barren—but of an austere beauty with majestic mountains, deep blue sky, vivid moonlight, and turquoise lakes, all suggesting the power of both the *silent* and the *energetic*.

Over the centuries, rumors of the great spiritual powers of some Tibetan mystics began to filter into the West, and by Gurdjieff's time, although the land and its spiritual tradition was still not well understood, it *was* recognized that some mysterious Tibetans had attained to certain extraordinary abilities and wisdom. Gurdjieff, already a seasoned traveler by 1900 but still only around thirty years old, could not resist the lure of Tibet, and off he went.

The Tibetan culture is typically associated with something ancient and mysterious but its recorded history only reaches back to around the 7th century AD, the period that marked the origins of the Tibetan written language. Though it is believed that Buddhism was known in Tibet as early as the 5th century AD, it did not make significant inroads until the time of Tibet's second great 'Dharma king' Trisong Detsun (circa 790-858 AD). The famed Silk Road, which passed through Bokhara (home of the Naqshbandi Sufis), along with other pan-Asian trade routes that connected China with the Middle East and Europe, have existed since pre-Roman times but they always skirted the Tibetan plateau, winding around it north of the Kunlun mountain range. Such natural isolation resulted, for a long time, in a Tibetan culture of fierce, proud people, given easily to warring aggression and with xenophobic tendencies.

Prior to the entry of Buddhist teachings from India, the main religious tradition of Tibet was shamanism, going by the name of *Bon*. Buddhism and the *Bon* tradition initially co-existed uneasily; however, after a period of conflict, they not only accepted each other but in many ways combined teachings. This is why Tibetan Buddhism is quite different from Theravadin (or Zen) Buddhism as it contains more than a strain of shamanism. One of the unique elements within Tibetan Buddhism is its Vajrayana, or Tantric, schools. These include teachings that are considered to be very powerful, potentially offering a rapid path to awakening, though paradoxically stressing that there is no actual 'short-cut'. The radical Tibetan master, Chogyam Trungpa (1940-1987), was the first to systematically introduce these teachings to the West in the late 1970s.

There are a number of lineages within Tibetan Buddhism but the four main ones are (in order of age) the Nyingma, Sakya, Kargyu, and Gelugpa. The first three are sometimes designated 'Red Hat' schools and the latter, the Gelugpa, a 'Yellow Hat' school. Each of the four traditions has its senior *lamas* (masters). The most famous of these, the Dalai Lama, represents most Tibetans in secular matters; (and since the 1959 Chinese annexation of Tibet, via the official 'government-in-exile' located in Dharamsala, northern India.)

Although he is of the Gelugpa tradition, he is not the actual spiritual head of that lineage (that being the office of the Ganden Tripa, as of 2010 held by Khensur Lungri Namgyal).

As mentioned earlier, an interesting connection that has been suggested by some researchers between Gurdjieff's travels and Tibetan Buddhism lies in the name of the secret mystery school that Gurdjieff claimed to have been initiated in—the Sarmoung Monastery. Gurdjieff's biographer, James Moore, deduced that this monastery, if it really existed, was likely somewhere no further than five hundred miles east or south of Bokhara in the proximity of Western Tibet (just north of Afghanistan).[14] In Eastern Tibet lies a complex of approximately nine monasteries, called Surmang. The similarity of this name with the one of Gurdjieff's account (as first pointed out by William Patrick Patterson) is of interest mainly because of the time Gurdjieff claimed he'd spent in Tibet, although it should be said if the two places are the same then Gurdjieff was not telling the whole truth as the Tibetan Surmang complex is not within a 'twelve day (blindfolded) horseback journey' from Bokhara, the time he said it took for him to get there.

At any rate, attempts have been made to correlate some of the teachings within Tibetan Buddhism with Gurdjieff's system, although these parallels appear to be a bit more contrived than the similarities between Gurdjieff's teachings and Naqshbandi Sufism and the Eastern Orthodox Church. Nevertheless, they are worth mentioning. Some of them are:

1. Both Buddhism and Gurdjieff's Work stress the importance of a critical mind and the need to verify one's own experience—to not accept something just because it is said to be true but to find out for oneself. The Buddha is recorded as having stressed this point in the *Vimansaka Sutra*:

Do not accept anything on mere hearsay. Do not accept anything by mere tradition. Do not accept anything on account of rumors. Do not accept anything just because it accords with your scriptures. Do not accept anything by mere supposition. Do not accept anything by mere inference. Do not accept anything by merely considering the appearances. Do not accept anything merely because it agrees with your preconceived notions. Do not accept anything merely because it seems acceptable. Do not accept anything that the ascetic is respected by you.[15]

Aphorism #27 at Gurdjieff's *Prieure* expressed the same viewpoint compressed into a few words:

If you have not by nature a critical mind your staying here is useless.[16]

2. The emphasis on mindfulness. Both self-observation and self-remembering, core techniques in Gurdjieff's system, are forms of mindfulness, which in general can be said to be *the* central method in all Buddhist traditions.

3. The usage of dance. This connection is specific to a possible link with Gurdjieff's work and the Tibetan tradition. Dance as a means of cultural and spiritual expression is found only in the Tibetan forms of Buddhism (doubtless stemming from the Tibetan *Bon* shamanistic legacy). If Gurdjieff, in fact, went to Tibet and if he was granted permission to stay in a monastery, he may have gained access to witnessing some of these sacred dances. From what I've been able to see there is little resemblance between Gurdjieff 'movements' and Tibetan dances, but the main point here is that Gurdjieff included the body in creative expression in his spiritual practices, as do the Tibetans.

4. The reality of impermanence. Gurdjieff's aphorism #33 was:

One of the best means for arousing the wish to work on yourself is to realize that you may die at any moment. But first you must learn how to keep this in mind.[17]

Awareness of death, the impermanence of life, and the need to utilize these to strengthen commitment for one's spiritual practice is an integral part of Tibetan Buddhist teachings. There is even an exercise in Tibetan Vajrayana practice where a monk retreats to a graveyard—in Tibet these were called sky burials, where the corpse is left in the open to be picked apart by animals (usually vultures)—in order to sit with and contemplate upon the bones and thereby deepen his grasp of the impermanence of all things.

5. An interesting link between Gurdjieff's teaching and Tibetan Buddhism is found in the idea of the Tibetan *tulku*, or reincarnating *lama*. According to Tibetan Buddhism, when the average person dies they are largely propelled by the force of karma—which in this case can be understood as 'habit'—through the *bardo* (after death realms) and into their next incarnation. The whole process is essentially involuntary. However, they believe that a *tulku* has the ability to consciously navigate their way in the *bardo* and thus choose their next birth. What is noteworthy here is Gurdjieff's teaching that the average person has no real say in their destiny, they are merely blown around by the winds of cause and effect—what he called 'mechanicality.' However, he maintained that someone who reached a certain stage of development was capable of actually exercising will in the higher sense of that word (very similar to Crowley's idea of the True Will). While Tibetan Buddhism denies the existence of the soul as a discrete thing, it does agree with Gurdjieff that conscious development carried to sufficient degree allows for some measure of freedom particularly from the mechanical laws of cause and effect believed to operate in the afterlife.

Finally and somewhat contrarily, concerning suspected links between Gurdjieff's Work and Tibetan Buddhism, there is an amusing anecdote on this matter related by William Patrick Patterson in his book, *Eating the 'I'*. At the time, Patterson was a student of Lord John Pentland, the man Gurdjieff had appointed to lead his work in America, but he had also connected with Chogyam Trungpa Rinpoche, who as a young man had just began his teaching career in America (this was in the early 1970s). During an interview with him, Patterson asked the famous *lama* what he thought of the practice of self-remembering. Trungpa shrugged off the question, appearing uninterested. Patterson persisted at which point Trungpa admitted that he 'didn't give a damn about it'. Asked why, he said that the method only 'makes jealous gods'. This is, of course, a reference to a class of beings designated in Buddhism as being powerful but fundamentally deluded.[18] The anecdote is an interesting example of the contrast between Eastern and Western approaches to awakening; the former being based on submission of the ego, and the latter being more concerned with 'aligning' the ego with the higher self. Accordingly, it would be expected that an Easterner would take a dim view of many Western approaches regarding them as dangerously prone to self-aggrandizement—or to becoming a 'jealous god'.

Gnosticism

Gnosticism is discussed more in the chapter on Crowley's historical influences, but it can be safely said here that the Gnostic tradition had a strong influence on Gurdjieff's teachings. Many Gnostic schools have generally identified themselves as 'esoteric Christianity' and this of course was one of Gurdjieff's names for his system. It should also be noted that there is evidence for the existence of some Gnostic traditions prior to the Christian era—the most likely original source being ancient Egypt. And this is also consistent with Gurdjieff's claims, as he once hinted, that his system originated in ancient Egypt.[19] While it is unlikely that he had clear proof about this and that he even may have been completely bluffing, he may have been largely correct anyway owing to the probable link between some of the occult teachings of ancient Egypt and elements of Gnosticism as they existed shortly before (and during) the time of Christ.

Gurdjieff taught that humans are not born with souls, but rather must develop one through strong efforts at working on themselves.

Those who fail to do this simply become 'food for the Moon' at death. Although he seemed to mean this literally, some have interpreted this idea of his to indicate that the Moon represented a lower dimension and that at death the energy of the average person is simply dispersed to that realm. Taken in that symbolic fashion, the idea is really not much different from the simple reality that at death the body gradually decays and its elements are reabsorbed by the Earth. The idea of 'food for the Moon' may seem very strange but the idea that there is a subtle, as yet scientifically undetected, 'lower dimension' that absorbs energy from dead organisms is not such a leap. However, the important point here is that Gurdjieff added the key idea that a person who develops a soul can escape this fate and rise to a higher reality at death. This is very similar to the Gnostic idea of the three categories of humans: pneumatics, psychics, and hylics (also called somatics). In this Gnostic view the hylics—which constitute the majority of humans—are 'matter-bound', fixated on matter and wholly uninterested in the realm of spirit, and cannot hope to achieve liberation at death. Only pneumatics and psychics have this possibility. So what Gurdjieff's idea has in common with the Gnostic view is that only a small minority of humans have hope for survival beyond death. This is also echoed in the words of Christ, 'He who has ears to hear, let him hear!' (Mark 4:9).

Theosophy and Blavatsky

The Theosophical Society was founded in 1888 by the famous 19th century Russian writer and mystic, Helena Petrovna Blavatsky, along with the American lawyer, Henry Steel Olcott. The primary charter for the organization was to provide the intellectual basis for the esoteric unity of all world faiths—the underlying shared truths under all the outer doctrinal differences. Blavatsky attempted to do this (with mixed results) via her two massive volumes *Isis Unveiled* (1877) and *The Secret Doctrine* (1888). The Society ultimately flourished, despite the usual controversies, and exists to this day with branches in dozens of countries. During the late 19th century, it was one of the prime forces in the esoteric domain.

The most likely area in which Gurdjieff may have been influenced by Blavatsky was in the idea of the 'hidden masters'. Blavatsky famously claimed to receive much of her spiritual inspiration and guidance from the 'mahatmas' which she maintained were invisible spiritual masters. This idea was echoed also in the Hermetic Order of the Golden Dawn which spoke of 'Secret Chiefs' who guided the Order from invisible realms. Gurdjieff too based some of his claimed sources on remote masters—those of the Sarmoung Brotherhood somewhere in or near Afghanistan—who, owing to their never having been traced, were effectively unseen as well.

Also, there is the matter of the usage of the number 7 in esoteric teachings. For Gurdjieff, this number clearly had importance as seen in his Law of Seven (Octaves) and in his Ray of Creation, which features seven essential realms. Although the number 7 features widely in many worldwide wisdom traditions, Blavatsky did make serious use of it as well, primarily in her model of the human being, which she saw as being comprised of seven essential 'bodies' or domains of being. These were the *atman* (Self), *buddhi* (higher intellect), *manas* (mind), *kama* (desire), *linga sharina* (etheric double), *prana* (life force), and physical body. These were of course taken directly from Hindu yogic doctrine but it must be borne in mind that, during her time (late 19th century), Hindu doctrine was not well known, and so she played a key role in disseminating this information to the Western public at large. Gurdjieff, as a serious seeker living in major Russian cities during the early 20th century, would certainly have been exposed to these ideas; it is reasonable to assume that they served as a partial template for his own models of the seven levels of a man, Law of Seven, and Ray of Creation.

Because Theosophy was both new and flourishing during Gurdjieff's formative years, it has been assumed by some that it must have had a strong influence on his ideas. While it is unquestionably true that Theosophy heavily influenced many occult and esoteric communities and writings of that era and that it was present in Moscow and St. Petersburg when Gurdjieff was first there around 1910, there is not much evidence to substantiate a truly significant link between Theosophy and Gurdjieff's work, especially in the practical domain. Theosophy, despite all its esotericism, remained primarily an intellectual venture. Gurdjieff's work is above all transformative, that is, concerned with *direct experience*. In that sense, it has far more in common with some of the practical Sufi or Buddhist approaches outlined above. Gurdjieff did employ some intellectual maps (such as his Ray of Creation and enneagram) but these have always been seen as secondary to the highly experiential nature of his practical exercises. In short, Gurdjieff's work places a much greater demand on a seeker than does Theosophy.

Chapter 22
Historical Influences on Osho's Teaching

To cover the influences behind Osho is not as easy because his range was vast, even vaster than Crowley's, which is saying a great deal. Of the three he is, as a teacher, the most difficult to pin down. Nevertheless, several traditions can be identified as having been a pivotal influence on Osho's general overall teaching and those are Zen Buddhism, Taoism, Tantra, Gurdjieff's practical ideas (not his cosmology), Western humanist and transpersonal psychotherapy (especially Wilhelm Reich), and Western philosophy, in particular, the figures of Nietzsche and Socrates—the latter two to a degree probably not generally recognized.

Friedrich Nietzsche

In looking at Osho's life it should never be lost sight of that he was, as much as anything else, a student of the perennial philosophy, including the Western intellectual tradition. Add to that he had been an academic—if a restless one—for fourteen years, from his entry into college in 1952 until he quit his teaching post in 1966. During those years and for many years after, he read voraciously. He was unquestionably one of the most well read, if not *the* most well read, spiritual guru ever (even Crowley, a highly literate man himself, falls short of Osho in this regard). He was no homeless, grubby wandering *sadhu*. Despite his frequently hostile attitude toward conventional academics, he was himself a refined intellectual. That he also happened to be a radically awakened adept did not detract from this. His massive library, which ended up totaling an estimated 80,000 volumes (see Appendix V), was with him to the end of his days.

In the early 1980s, Osho dictated a book that he called *Books I Have Loved*.[1] It was exactly that, a list of 167 books that were his favorites, including commentary on all of them. Of that entire list—which includes some of the most notable classics of Western and Eastern literature—the very first book he mentioned was Friedrich Nietzsche's *Thus Spake Zarathustra*. He said:

> Even if Nietzsche had not written anything else but *Thus Spake Zarathustra* he would have served humanity immensely, profoundly... *Thus Spake Zarathustra* is going to be the bible of the future...it will be the first on my list.[2]

Given that Osho was an Indian and that he was steeped in Oriental philosophy, this crowning of a controversial 19th century German philosopher's famous work on his list of favorite reads is significant. As to the man himself, Osho had a mixed judgment: he believed that Nietzsche was a towering genius but that he lacked proper spiritual guidance, and that this was the prime reason for his eventual mental disintegration. He said that Nietzsche had the intelligence necessary for a potential Buddha. Anyone familiar with the deep suffering in Nietzsche's life could find sympathy for Osho's idea. Nietzsche is the archetypal isolated thinker, with few social contacts, fewer peers, poor, unhealthy, deeply lonely, generally engrossed in his thinking and writing, suffering a psychotic break in his mid-forties and dying at fifty-five—before ever truly being recognized.

It is a natural thing for genius to go unrecognized while it lives. Far more brilliant thinkers have achieved worthy recognition and appreciation after death than while they lived. Crowley and Gurdjieff were themselves vivid examples of this in the esoteric realm. In the case of Nietzsche, acclaim for his work was tainted for many years by some unfortunate associations with Nazism, although in actuality it is believed by most historians that Hitler himself was not truly familiar with Nietzsche's ideas and probably had not studied him in any serious way. Others in the Nazi hierarchy had, however, and some did their best to appropriate a few of his ideas and try to apply them to a fascist ideology.

The concept that has been the hottest philosophical potato within Nietzsche's rich spectrum of ideas was his notion of the *Ubermensch*, a term that has been translated in various awkward ways. The German term *mensch* is not gender specific, so the most common translation of the word—'Overman'—is not entirely precise. A more problematic translation has been 'superman', suggesting, as it does, elitism and dominance. It doesn't take too much imagination to see how these terms could be co-opted by one seeking to justify abusive agendas, such as the right of one people to dominate another.[3]

However, Nietzsche's idea, as expressed in *Zarathustra*, aims much higher—not toward simple elitist dominance, but toward a purity of understanding and a radical awakening of spirit. Essentially, the Overman is his version of the enlightened man. He says that this man will be to the average man as the average man is to an ape. The black and white severity of this contrast is reminiscent also of Gurdjieff, and his view of the sleeping man in contrast to the waking man. Osho, however, was arguably even more uncompromising, insisting on a level of enlightenment that resulted in a person who was utterly distinct from the 'unenlightened'—that is, the common man.

Nietzsche's idea of the Overman is one who *overcomes* his mere humanity, rising above the mediocre masses. This was always a favorite theme of Osho's, stressed by him in so many ways. Like Nietzsche, he was a trenchant critic of mediocrity (as was Crowley). And like Nietzsche, he was a vocal proponent of the idea of a 'God-free' universe, claiming openly many times that he did not *believe* that God did not exist, but rather, that he *knew* that God did not exist. It is true that in his earlier teaching years he did make reference to 'God', but generally used the term as a symbol for ultimate reality. By the 1980s, he became more vocally anti-religious and began to regularly denounce the term 'God' altogether and in particular the Christian God. His views in that regard were largely aligned with Nietzsche's sharp criticisms of Christianity.

The idea of a Godless universe was, of course, echoed in one of the most famous of Nietzschean declarations, vocalized in *Zarathustra* as 'God is dead'. His idea was that the Overman was of the Earth, putting him in opposition to the Christian idea of other-worldliness. Nietzsche was emphatic in stressing the importance of living for today, and for where we are—not for tomorrow, and not for some abstract heaven. In this light, Nietzsche connects the Overman to the idea of an *embodied* spirituality—that is, a way of life in opposition to the notion of world-denying asceticism. Here again we see a clear influence on both Osho and Crowley. Osho's entire teaching was based essentially on the importance of a truly embodied consciousness. He was often contemptuous of ascetics and those who retreat from the world to monasteries and caves, frequently branding them as cowards who were motivated more by fear of the human condition—and in particular of human inter-action—than they were by desire for enlightenment.

Nietzsche's Overman is motivated by a love of life, and of this Earth. His view in this matter was stridently anti-Platonic, that is, he wholly rejected Plato's scheme of higher worlds lurking invisibly beyond this world. In that sense, Nietzsche was contrary to a great deal of the Western esoteric doctrine, which has much of its basis in Plato. He was adamantly opposed to blind faith, insisting on the need for individuals to apply personal will to break through their limitations and to find their emancipation through their very own selfhood.

Though brilliant, Nietzsche was also a product of his times, a condition that not even the most radical intelligence can fully escape. The 19th century saw the birth of scientific materialism—sometimes called scientism, an appropriate term as it is suggestive of a new kind of faith—and while Nietzsche was no scientist, he did give voice to the long-standing urge to break entirely with the credulous blind faith of our Medieval heritage that had left such a long standing imprint. He was pre-eminently concerned with freedom, an understandable fact given the virtual slavery humans have lived in for most of recorded history—slavery to others, slavery to material reality, slavery to the harshness of life.

Ultimately, however, Nietzsche hit a ceiling from which he could do no better than move horizontally. In 'killing' God, in negating the notion of religious faith, he also abandoned the idea of transcendence beyond the self. And it is here where genuine mystics like Crowley, Gurdjieff, and Osho part company with him. Ideally, the development of a human is in three general stages: pre-ego, ego, and trans-ego. The first stage, that of pre-ego, is the child, what Crowley likened to the Aeon of Isis. It is our instinctive self, linked to Nature and blindly trusting in gods or a God above us to rule with justice about all things, dispensing punishments and rewards accordingly. The second stage, that of the ego, can be likened to adolescence and young adulthood (Crowley's macro-parallel was the Aeon of Osiris, of the Dying and Resurrecting God). It is the phase of the individual. Rightly established, it results in a person who is imbued with correct self-esteem, that is, a self-image that is free of self-loathing, self-rejection, and the need to repress one's true voice. A correctly developed ego is a powerful individual, one capable of living cooperatively with others, without relinquishing his or her own highest potentials in life. As Nietzsche accurately diagnosed, this stage had developed incorrectly throughout history in part because of the iron fist inside the velvet glove of organized religion. The result has been mostly the opposite of the qualities mentioned above: poor self-image, self-esteem issues, repression, and a general faulty ego-structure.

However, even in the case of a correctly developed ego, it still needs to be further refined, opening to a greater sense of that which is truly *beyond* ego (trans-ego), thus seeing deeply into the interconnectedness of all things. The danger inherent in not embracing this third stage—which may be likened to that of the (ideal) mature adult—is that there is the risk of ego development becoming overcharged, resulting in an individual who commands power over others in such a way that no longer allows for their correct development. The Fascist modification of Nietzsche's Overman ideal would be an example of this on a socio-political level. Buddhist tradition hints at this in what it calls 'jealous gods'. Gurdjieff called it 'wrong crystallization'. Crowley referred in part to this in his ideas of the 'Black Brother', an individual who attains marked development and accompanying powers but who balks at taking the next level, that of transcendence of ego, thus aborting and distorting his development and making himself a potential menace to others.

Osho believed that Nietzsche's eventual insanity was ultimately connected to his insular state, his deep isolation, a view that can be seen to suggest that Nietzsche came to directly face the dry austerity of the Overman who lacks faith—not the immature faith of a child or adolescent, but the mature faith of a true adult who simply recognizes that he is not truly alone (even if he cannot see beyond himself). Although Osho had a broader scope of understanding than Nietzsche because he embraced the transcendent as well as the empowered individual, it is arguable that, in the end, Osho himself directly encountered the limitations of the Overman, witnessing the dissolution of his work in Oregon, and then the dissolution of his body toward the end of his life while he lashed out at powers that be (the American government).

Despite Nietzsche's limitations, he was a singlehanded force of nature when it came to the establishment of a new type of worldview that was part and parcel of the terrible struggle of humanity to free itself of thousands of years of endless forms of slavery. Nietzsche was a herald of a new view of freedom. His influence on so many key thinkers of the 20th century, including Osho, was vast, even if this influence was itself a flawed work in progress, fraught with as many dangers as blessings.

Socrates

Over the years, Osho frequently mentioned his admiration for Socrates. He tended to cite him as one of the rare examples of a man so dangerous that he was, essentially, killed for his wisdom. (According to the records, Socrates was executed in 399 BC at the age of seventy for 'refusing to recognize the gods recognized by the state, and for corrupting the youth' with his teachings.)[4] Osho often mentioned Socrates in the same breath as Jesus, and he was one of the very few sages that he never criticized.

Socrates is a distant and shadowy figure, almost as difficult to define as Lao Tzu, the mysterious founder of Taoism. He was born around 469 BC in Athens. Different historical accounts of what he taught and especially of the type of man he was do not always align with each other, but there are enough common points of agreement that allow us to get a sense of what this seminal figure in Western philosophy stood for. As recorded in Plato's *Apology*, Socrates during his trial (that resulted in his being condemned to death) proclaimed:

> For I spend all my time going about trying to persuade you, young and old, to make your first and chief concern not to care for your persons or your property more than for the perfection of your souls.[5]

That level of commitment is typically common to radical sages, those who insist on the 'all or nothing' approach. If there was one quality that could be said to have captured Osho's essence it would be that of *totality*. Whatever he did, he went all out at and in choosing the spiritual path at an early age, he dove with total abandonment into that. Socrates' statement to put the 'perfection of the soul' above all else is the universal call of the bona fide mystic and Osho regarded it as his call too. While Osho was not an anti-materialist, he did stress the need of a true initiate on the spiritual path to abandon anything in the way of their inner development.

The essential idea is that wisdom must be uncompromisingly prior-
itized if it has any hope of arising within one's self.

Socrates resisted the idea that he was anyone's master, saying:

> If any man says that he ever learned or heard anything privately
> from me, which all the others did not, be assured that he is lying.[6]

Those words are interesting to contrast with these remarks of Osho's:

> Because people love me, they have called me a 'master of
> masters'...as far as I am concerned, I simply think of myself as just
> an ordinary human being who was stubborn enough to remain
> independent, resisted all conditioning, never belonged to any
> religion, never belonged to any political party, never belonged to
> any organization, never belonged to any nation, to any race.[7]

Socrates was renowned for dialectics (especially in its simple form of
questioning and answering), and in particular, something called
'Socratic method'. This is basically a type of cross-examining, via
constant questioning, of anyone who holds a strong belief about
something, so that they can deepen their understanding of the issue
they hold beliefs about—or until they are shown the inevitable
contradictions held in their views.

Like Socrates, Osho was a highly skilled debater and a merciless
questioner of anything smelling of dogma or righteousness. Back in
his college days, he won awards for official debate contests, but the
same ability to charm people with relentless probing of traditional
values and beliefs also won him enemies and got him twice expelled
from college.

Socrates has also been associated with what might be called the
idea of 'divine ignorance', or the 'wisdom of not-knowing'. He is
reputed to have been self-effacing to a degree that was not mere
humility, but rather reflected a profound insight about the true
nature of *knowing* itself, famously declaring,

The more I know, the less I know.

This stems from an incident where the Greek Oracle of Delphi proclaimed Socrates the wisest man in Athens. Socrates objected to this, believing that he had no real wisdom at all. To prove his point he then set about questioning several so-called wise people in Athens, to find out if they indeed knew more than he. What he found in each case, however, was that the people he was questioning actually believed that they were wise when he could see that they were not. In the end, Socrates concluded that the Delphi Oracle had been right all along, and that, in fact, he was the wisest person in Athens—but only for the reason that he alone realized that he was not truly wise at all. That is, he had the wisdom of recognizing his own ignorance.

The ignorance Socrates refers to is not the simple ignorance of being ill-educated but rather the profounder ignorance born out of the realization that conventional knowledge cannot truly penetrate to the heart of matters. For example, we can ask ourselves the simple question 'what is the color green?' Even with modern knowledge of wavelengths and reflected light and so on, we are still left with the realization that all of our knowledge amounts to conceptual designations. They do not explain the thing in itself, for the simple reason that conventional thinking separates us from what it is observing. This basic separation allows us to make detailed observations about the *appearance* of the thing, but not to truly know it as a *direct experience*.

The wisdom of 'not-knowing' is a theme commonly echoed in the Zen tradition in particular, and it was an idea that Osho consistently turned to. He was a vocal critic of pretentiousness in all its guises, and perhaps never more so than in the realm of *spiritual* pretentiousness. A major aspect of his work lay in pointing out the limitations of detached intellectual observation and the presumptuousness of the theological and religious 'authorities' who proclaimed to know higher truth, God's plan, and so on.

Socrates' manner of death is well known; having being condemned to death in a dubious trial, he drank a poison and slowly died. There is arguably some parallel for this in Osho's life, if only in a mythic sense. In 1987, Osho went public with his belief that he had been (literally) poisoned by the American government when he was briefly incarcerated in an Oklahoma jail in late 1985. Subsequent views on the matter have cast serious doubt on this but the fact remains that, like Socrates, Osho was a deeply defiant man, rebellious, brilliant, and highly critical of established authorities. Like Socrates, he was dangerous in that he also 'corrupted youth,' even if such 'corruption' was nothing more than trying to pull intelligent minds away from mediocrity.

Gurdjieff

Osho was a great admirer of Gurdjieff. His sole criticism related mainly to his observation that students of the Gurdjieff Work had acquired a disposition that was too serious. The ideal of laughter was always important to Osho and his vision, and he saw this element as lacking in Gurdjieff's Work. (In point of fact, Gurdjieff did have a good sense of humor, but it is true that much of his Work was conducted with a gravity and seriousness and that he was indeed a sharp critic of what he considered to be the negative manifestations of conventional humor.)

Gurdjieff's 'stop' exercise, a practice that involved a sudden cessation of all activity often in the midst of something very engaged, like dancing, in order to clearly observe oneself, was used by Osho in his key technique, Dynamic Meditation. But where Gurdjieff's ideals were probably most employed was during the first couple of years of the Oregon commune when only determined back-breaking labor succeeded in transforming a desert wasteland into a thriving town. Gurdjieff drove many of his students very hard in the early years of his Fontainebleau commune all the while teaching them a type of conscious labor that made hard physical work a direct meditation. This is not an idea original to Gurdjieff—

many monastics of different traditions combine their meditation or contemplation with hard physical work. But Gurdjieff had a unique approach in which he integrated self-remembering and self-observation with physical toil. Osho (or more accurately, Sheela) adopted something very similar in the early days of the Oregon ranch, even going so far as to replace the word 'work' with 'worship'. You did not get up at 6am to work at landscaping or washing dishes, you rather got up at 6am to *worship* at landscaping or washing dishes. The idea is that what was being 'worshipped' was the vision, the ultimate purpose of the commune, as the vehicle for the *sangha*, the spiritual fellowship. The commune (ideally) functioned as an oasis for thousands of seekers of truth around the world and thus was worthy of worship as a type of *karma* yoga.

That was the idea at any rate. While it cannot be said to be a completely accurate rendition of Gurdjieff's ideas around labor and toil, the spirit was similar, and almost certainly partly inspired by Gurdjieff's vision. Hugh Milne, an early disciple of Osho, claimed that 'Gurdjieff was the main role model for Osho who, needless to say, had read all of Gurdjieff's works...in particular Osho liked the way Gurdjieff rebelled against authority and kept testing the strength of his disciple's faith.'[17]

Although it is true that Osho frequently mentioned Gurdjieff in his discourses, in many ways their teachings were not aligned and almost certainly Gurdjieff would not have approved of some of Osho's work, most particularly the cultivation of disciples (giving names, a clothing color scheme, and especially, the mala with the locket of Osho's photo). Gurdjieff resisted anyone getting too attached to him, and although he did try to keep some people near him that he eventually lost to others (such as the young J.G. Bennett and later, A.R. Orage), the evidence is that he did not want followers. Osho, however, seemed to encourage this (despite in his last years claiming that he was not a master but only a friend).

In addition, Osho differed from Gurdjieff in the area of what may be called 'soul-psychology'. Gurdjieff emphasized that a human

being is not born with a soul but rather must 'grow' one by cultivating their consciousness. Osho, however, in keeping more with
traditional Vedic teachings, taught that our true nature is already the
case and that we just have to become aware of it by developing our
capacity for meditativeness—that, in effect, we do have a soul, but
are simply out of touch with it. It may be argued that these two
different approaches to the matter of 'soul' or 'true being' are
ultimately a matter of technique—that is, each approach will have an
effect on the seeker that may motivate them in different ways. Both
Gurdjieff and Osho were masters of 'situational growth', that is,
creating conditions for their followers to encounter themselves. This,
in the end, was more important to them than mere theory. That said,
the main element of Gurdjieff's Work most found in Osho's approach
was the emphasis on what we can call 'mindfulness in the marketplace'—awareness in everyday life. This was Osho's primary
teaching, the one approach he never really wavered from his whole
life.

Wilhelm Reich

Reich (1897-1957), the radical Austrian psychotherapist, was a very
strong influence on Osho's work to a degree not recognized by most.
Osho once posthumously and informally bestowed *sannyas* (initiation) on him (reminiscent of Crowley's declaring certain historical
figures as 'saints' of his Gnostic church). Osho left behind no church
(unless we can speak of a meditation resort as a new kind of church)
but if he did, Wilhelm Reich would have been one of its chief saints.

Reich was originally a student of Freud but moved off in a
different direction, beyond Freud's exclusive concern with neurotic
symptoms, toward the development of a theory that embraced the
entire character of a person—what Reich came to call character
structure or 'body armoring'. His main idea was that a sexually
dysfunctional and inhibited person tends to develop muscular
'blocks' and tensions that effectively shut them down, make them
less alive, and more prone to negative mental states accordingly. He

believed that the sexual orgasm—and in specific what he called 'orgastic potency'—was the key to mental health, seeing it as an 'emotional energy regulator'. Orgastic potency was his term for orgasmic health, the ability to properly release sufficient energy during orgasm. He argued that when such energy is not properly released, it backs up in the body and manifests as chronic muscular tension, anxiety, and in more severe cases, strong negative emotions like hate and sadistic tendencies. He believed that this tendency manifested at macro levels also as fascism and other forms of cruelty, tyranny, and oppression.

Reich's work was revolutionary and contributed to a host of derivative alternative therapies that flowered mostly in the 1960s, in particular Alexander Lowen's Bioenergetics (and related bodywork methods), Leonard Orr's Rebirthing, and Arthur Janov's Primal Therapy. All of these therapies and related methods were used at Osho's Pune ashram (as well as the Oregon commune) and are still in use at the Pune resort as of 2010. In some ways, Osho's entire body of practical work was a cross of Buddha and Reich— meditation and transformational, experiential therapy. Osho always had a keen (and sympathetic) eye for rebel geniuses who ended up being unjustly persecuted; Reich's sad death in an American prison in 1957, after his teachings had been censored and his books burned by the Administration of that time, was something Osho had particular empathy for, stating that Reich was 'too intelligent and therefore too dangerous for the mediocre masses'.

Alan Watts

The English philosopher, mystic, and intellectual Alan Watts (1915-1973) bears mention here, he being one of the very first thinkers to attempt to bring Western psychotherapy and Eastern disciplines, particularly Tantra, together in a theoretical framework. Osho may have been the first Eastern guru to seriously utilize Western psychotherapy (especially in group format) in his ashrams, but Watts was writing about the synthesis of therapy and meditation, of

Eastern and Western transformational pathways, as early as 1961, via his key work *Psychotherapy East and West*. Osho read a number of Watts' books, and was especially impressed by three: *The Way of Zen* (1957), *This Is It* (1960), and *The Book: On the Taboo Against Knowing Who You Are* (1966). The last in particular Osho favoured; all three were included on his list of 167 favourite books. Significantly, he ended his series of lectures on his favourite books by dedicating them to Alan Watts.

Tantra

Osho spoke a great deal about Tantra, especially earlier in his career in the late 1960s and 70s (but less so in the 80s). The version of Tantra he taught was more aligned with the northern Indian schools and less so with the Tibetan Vajrayana traditions. At times, he referred to it as the 'royal path', contrasting it with Yoga which he viewed as a 'warrior's' path. Osho, although a combative personality for much of his life, was at heart more of a king and a magician than a warrior and so his considering Tantra to be a superior teaching to Yoga was understandable in that regard. Osho was no yogi. His was the spirit of a spiritual hedonist and many of his followers adopted a hedonistic lifestyle. The term 'Tantra' became synonymous for many in the West with a lifestyle of casual sensual indulgence with consciousness—or at least, that was the idea. How many successfully added the 'consciousness' part is moot.

'Tantra' is one of those words that most people on some sort of personal growth journey have at least heard of but usually know little about. The word is often loosely associated with sexuality and certain mystical states of consciousness. The truth, as always, is far more involved and vast, and at the same time remarkably ordinary and down to earth.[8]

The word *tantra* derives from the Sanskrit language and translates as 'weave', as in a continuous thread or tapestry. This is significant inasmuch as the essence of the Tantric vision involves an embracing and accepting of all the energies in the universe, much like a thread that weaves its way through the entire cosmos ultimately making contact with everything, rejecting nothing on its journey. Historically, the roots of Tantra were birthed in north India around 500 AD in the Hindu religion. About a hundred years after that, the Buddhist version appeared, though the facts are not clear and some suspect that Buddhist Tantra originates with Gautama Buddha himself around 550 BC. Despite its mysterious origins, it is generally accepted that Tantra, as a unique form of spirituality, was established by the 6th century AD throughout the area that was the cradle of the Indo-Aryan civilization.

Esoteric Hinduism, which is essentially most forms of Yoga, was influenced by Tantra, as were the cults of Vishnu and Shiva (two-thirds of the Hindu Trinity). In Buddhism, it resulted in an entire new school of lineage, generally referred to as the 'Vajrayana' (Way of the Diamond Thunderbolt). This teaching was taken by the Indian master Padmasambhava, north over the Himalayas into Tibet during the 8th or 9th century AD, where, after an initial struggle with the entrenched shamanistic tradition known as Bon, it took hold and established itself. It is in Tibet, it is generally accepted, that the Tantric path became most highly evolved, and it was only after the 1959 Chinese invasion that these teachings were dispersed to the West, following the destruction of thousands of Tibetan monasteries by the Red Army, and the subsequent exodus of many advanced Tibetan teachers (*lamas*) of Tantric Buddhism.

Traditional Indian Tantra has usually been associated with worship of the divine feminine, in particular the goddess Shakti. The general idea that marks Tantra apart from other Hindu teachings (such as Vedanta) is that the universe is regarded as a play of energy (*shakti*) to be harnessed and utilized to both manifest things and attain to self-realization, rather than merely illusion (*maya*) to be overcome. In that sense, Tantra is approximately the Oriental equivalent of the Western esoteric path of high magic (*theurgy*). There are also 'lower' Tantras just as they are forms of low magic, or sorcery, mostly concerned with manifesting selfish desires and controlling others.

That Indian Tantra is rooted in a deification of the divine feminine is significant in looking at its influence on Osho's teachings because he had a great and abiding interest in the feminine. He severely condemned the dominance of patriarchal power structures throughout history and was a champion for the empowerment of women. Osho often defined Tantra as follows:

Yoga is suppression with awareness; Tantra is indulgence with awareness.[9]

For that idea he was criticized by the Yoga scholar Georg Feuerstein who called it 'a glaring oversimplification.'[10] (Here he was probably correctly identifying Osho's main intellectual weakness, the tendency to teach with a broad canvas and on occasions to blandly oversimplify). Feuerstein did acknowledge, however, that Osho warned his followers not to use Tantra as mere license to indulge but rather as a path to transform oneself. He concluded, however, that few of his disciples actually heard or understood this message.

On that score, Feuerstein was probably correct as well. There is a hidden 'dark side' to Tantric teachings if practiced in a fashion that lacks structured guidance, and it is the same dark side that is latent in the Western esoteric tradition, that being the potential for lazy indulgence, ego inflation and self-aggrandizement. The line between this and genuine transformation can be unclear at times. That said, every spiritual tradition has its shadow elements and it would not be accurate to entirely blame a misapplication of Tantric antinomian ideals for the shortcomings in Osho's community that contributed to the collapse of his Oregon commune, although there is likely some connection there.

Taoism

Taoism has its roots in the legendary teacher Lao Tzu who is thought to have lived in China anywhere between 600 and 300 BC. The name is an honorific that simply means 'old master' adding to the general enigma about the man. Some scholars even suspect that Lao Tzu may represent a composite of different characters. As is mentioned in the chapter on Crowley's historical influences, Osho shared an equal veneration for this ancient Chinese tradition. He went so far as to identify himself completely with Lao Tzu in such a way that led some to believe that he was claiming Lao Tzu as a 'previous incarnation' of him. More likely, however, is that he was simply expressing his deep affinity for the principles of the *Tao Te Ching* as taught by the figure of Lao Tzu.

In some ways, Lao Tzu's ideal of the awakened man as expressed in the *Tao Te Ching* can be seen as the next stage of development of Nietzsche's Overman. The key point, however, is that this sage-like stage cannot be properly reached unless one's ego-development has proceeded correctly. Osho identified deeply with Lao Tzu, doubtless in part, because of Lao Tzu's very enigmatic nature—he is as much a non-entity as a real person, a mysterious presence who offers refined wisdom of the highest order. Osho spoke often of his 'disappearance' with his radical awakening at age twenty-one and no figure in the history of the wisdom traditions embodies the idea of 'absent presence' better than that of Lao Tzu. Even the Buddha himself does not match that, having, as he did, something of a defined personal history and life story.

Lao Tzu's teaching is all about self-transcendence, of understanding and realizing the natural state of non-separation with the totality of life itself. This is non-duality in its purest sense where nothing but the totality, the Tao, truly exists. Connected to this is the important idea of *wu-wei*. The Chinese term *wu* means 'without' and *wei* translates as 'effort'. The idea of *effortless action* is central to Taoism and was a key element of Osho's philosophy. Chapter 2 of the *Tao Te Ching* expresses the idea as follows:

Therefore the Master
acts without doing anything
and teaches without saying anything.[11]

To 'act without doing anything' and to 'teach without saying anything' does not mean that one literally does nothing, or that one is always silent. It rather means that one is free of ego-conflict, ambivalence, and the tendency to be unnatural or disconnected from the immediacy of this moment. Gurdjieff refers to this as the state of harmony between the various inner centers (moving, sexual, instinctive, emotional, and mental). Crowley speaks of this when he talks about doing one's True Will. The main idea is that spiritual awakening is the most natural of all conditions but only seems unnatural or unattainable owing to our generally deluded state. *We are the ones in the way of our emancipation, nothing else.*

Zen Buddhism

The Zen tradition proved, in the end, to be of central importance in Osho's teaching. For the last year or so of his life, he chose to lecture only on the topic of Zen, devoting daily talks to practically every known Zen master from the Japanese and Chinese traditions. A significant number of his disciples were Japanese and many, doubtless, appreciated the attention he lavished on the Japanese Zen tradition in particular during these lectures.

The word *Zen* is a Japanese transliteration of the Chinese word *cha'an*. The Chinese word is, in turn, deriving from the Sanskrit word *dhyana* which translates loosely into English as 'meditation'. As Zen is of the Buddhist tradition and as the Buddha lived and taught in northern India, Zen itself has its roots in India. It did not reach its full development until centuries after the Buddha, in China in particular by around the 6th century AD, then shortly after in Korea and finally in Japan by around 1200 AD. It is the Japanese version of Zen that eventually became most well known in the West mostly due to the efforts of D.T. Suzuki, the Japanese scholar and meditation master who wrote numerous scholarly books on Zen Buddhism that were translated into English and other languages in the early to mid-1900s.

Legend has it that the Zen tradition began with an event in the

Buddha's life when he was giving one of his many sermons. On this occasion, the Buddha did not speak but instead merely held out a flower in his hand. For some time no one said anything, uncertain what the Buddha was doing. At one point, someone in the gathering laughed and the Buddha summoned him forward. This person was Mahakasyapa and he became recognized by posterity as the 'first Zen master', the one to receive, from the Buddha, the 'first Zen transmission'.

The moral of the story is simple and is the heart of Zen: spiritual truth ultimately lays not in intellectual apprehension, but rather in a moment of deep and radical insight—what the Japanese Zen tradition calls *kensho*, or *satori*, both words that refer to a sudden and profound illumination or awakening. Zen tradition refers to this type of understanding by saying that it does not 'rest on words or letters' but is rather a 'special transmission outside of the scriptures'. The idea is that this chain of transmission was passed down from the Buddha's original encounter with Mahakasyapa to the present day, although there is no real historical evidence to back this up. Nevertheless, the story of the Buddha's 'flower sermon' that allegedly began the Zen transmission is valid as myth, and accurately conveys the essence of Zen.

The Zen tradition proper is considered to have begun with the semi-mythical Indian monk, Bodhidharma, who made a lengthy journey to China around 520 AD. While there, he is reputed to have had a strange encounter with an emperor in which he appeared to insult the emperor (although according to the legend he was, in fact, giving him a high teaching which the emperor failed to understand). This resulted in him being banished, after which he wandered about settling near the site of the renowned Shaolin monastery (estimated to have been founded around 480 AD and made famous by the early 1970s TV series *Kung Fu*). Once there, he proceeded to live as a recluse for many years, absorbed in deep meditation.

The first clearly documented Zen lineage begins with Huineng (638-713 AD) and the famous story (some say fable) of his radical awakening as a young man. After this awakening, Huineng sought out further guidance and was accordingly directed to a particular monastery. Once there, he was assigned the task of husking rice for many months. At a certain point, the master of the monastery, feeling his years left on Earth to be growing short, decided to appoint a successor. To facilitate this, he staged a competition of sorts in which he asked his monks to submit a poem that articulated their level of understanding. Only one poem was submitted and that by his head monk, Shenxui. The lines he offered were these:

The body is the tree of salvation,
The mind is a clear mirror.
Incessantly wipe and polish it;
Let no dust fall on it.

The master of the monastery was not displeased with this offering, but nor was he satisfied, realizing that his head monk, while having a reasonably competent understanding, lacked a profound insight and had not penetrated to a deep enough understanding. Soon after, however, Huineng found out about the head's monk's offering. He was illiterate and so had someone translate it for him. Immediately, he saw that it could be improved upon and he countered it with the following:

Salvation is nothing like a tree,
Nor a clear mirror;
Essentially, not a 'thing' exists;
What is there, then, for the dust to fall on?[12]

When the master of the monastery read this, he realized that Huineng had a superior understanding to his head monk even though he was illiterate, not yet a monk, and had been doing nothing but husking rice since he'd been at the monastery. And yet the master appointed him his successor, confirming his realization. The story is classic Zen as it so vividly demonstrates the essence of the key

Buddhist teaching called the Heart Sutra and its famous line:

Emptiness is form, and form is emptiness.

This expression may be said to lie at the heart of Zen. In order to understand it we need first to understand the Buddhist idea of *shunyata*, which is loosely translated as 'emptiness'. This emptiness is *not* the Western philosophical idea of nihilism. Technically, nihilism refers to a 'nothingness' in which the universe is intrinsically meaningless and purposeless and all values are contrived. The Buddhist idea of emptiness, though understood in slightly different ways by different Buddhist denominations, basically refers to the idea that everything in reality is but an *appearance*, lacking intrinsic existence.

One way of grasping this idea is by the following: consider what we call the human body. What exactly is it? Looked at closely, what we call the 'body' is simply a conceptual label given to a collection of body-parts—head, arms, hands, legs, feet, organs, and so forth. But what, then, are these body-parts? Let us take the hand. What is it? Looking closely again, we see that the term 'hand' is merely a conceptual label given for a collection of parts—fingers, skin, bones, nails, etc. And what, then, is a finger? It is a collection of smaller parts.

And so on. This process can be followed endlessly, always ending up with something more and more primary, until we begin to understand that *everything* we recognize in the universe is, in fact, a conceptual designation, an idea, and thus, ultimately a mere appearance. There are truly no 'things in themselves', anymore than there is a body with no body-parts. Wherever we look we see only the externalization of our *ideas*, all the way down to subatomic particles and empty space.

So if nothing exists inherently and independently in so-called objective reality, beyond it being an externalized concept, then what about if we look within? What then? Clearly (as Gurdjieff taught) our 'I' is not consistent as it can be related to many things—moods, feelings, memories, values, thoughts, and so on. What we call 'I' is a composite of many different mental states. And because it would be crazy to refer to one state as 'me'—I am anger, I am fear, I am this memory (but not that one), etc.—then the same thing can be concluded, that being that this 'I' has no real inherent existence as something specifically and separately definable. 'I' is not a discrete thing isolated from everything else.

So what's left over? In some schools of Buddhism they call it 'luminous emptiness', a kind of continuous whole in which there is no real division between mind and universe. That can be called *absolute* reality. Then there are *conventional* realities to be recognized, such as the reality of 'I feel hungry' or 'I am tired' or in our conventional relationships with each other and so forth. In the investigation of absolute reality, conventional reality is not ignored or denied.

So does this ultimately mean that we don't really exist? No. You exist. I exist, but only as *inter*dependent, transitioning, relative realities. You, or I, do not exist in any inherently real, independently isolated, fashion. The belief that the self is disconnected from the reality it finds itself in, isolated and separate from everything else, is the illusion. The teaching on emptiness reveals that fundamental illusion.

Zen makes profound use of the idea of emptiness in its overriding concern with the need to realize the nature of absolute reality. It is, above all, a practical path that is concerned with direct experience. The Zen parable of the fingers pointing toward the Moon illustrates this idea, with the fingers representing words, teachings, doctrines, methods, and the Moon symbolizing enlightenment. We are not to become attached to the fingers—to the teachings—but rather are to direct all our effort and aspiration toward (metaphorically) the Moon, the direct realization of our true nature, or what the Zen tradition has sometimes called our 'original face'.

Osho's love of Zen is understandable. His personal history and especially his awakening process in his early twenties as he described it is very Zen-like in its approach—full of one-pointed focus on finding the truth no matter what, and a radical transcendence of conventional thinking. In the last year of his life, he turned exclusively to Zen in part as an expression of his fatigue with interpersonal conflict and drama (not surprising, given the intense drama played out in the collapse of the Oregon commune). During this last year, he ceased answering questions from his disciples on matters of relationships or other issues related to their 'personal story'. In Zen, he saw the purest reflection of impersonal truth that embraced a higher level of heart—what he called the wisdom of 'silence'. He said:

> All religions except Zen are dead...I call Zen the only living religion because it is not a religion, but a religiousness...it does not discriminate between the mundane and the sacred. For Zen, all that is, is sacred.[13]

Crazy Wisdom

When all is said and done, the tradition that most closely fits Osho—to the extent that *any* tradition can fit him—is probably that of the 'crazy wisdom master', albeit a very particular version of one. For all his talk about Zen throughout the last period of his life, Osho was no traditional Zen master and arguably not a very good example of even a non-traditional one. He was rather in a strange category all by himself, a fact that aligns him closely with the wild and unpredictable *mahasiddhas* of ancient days.

The term *mahasiddha* means 'great adept' and traditionally has been used to refer to a group of eighty-four famous Buddhist mystics of the Himalayan regions reputed to have lived during the early centuries of the transmission of Buddhism from India to Tibet (roughly from the period 800 to 1100 AD). Two outstanding features of these mystics were their unpredictable behavior and the fact that they tended to defy categorization, transcending religious traditions of any sort. They were pure embodiments of antinomianism or 'spiritual lawlessness'. They could not be pinned down and defined (except as one almost impossible to define—itself a definition admittedly, but about as loose as one can get).

Osho was renowned for contradicting himself, a remarkable fact given his quality of intellect and vast scope of erudition. But he had an extraordinary ability to convince you that what he was saying *this* time was the truth. Many effective charlatans and confidence tricksters have the same ability, granted, but in Osho's case, he usually gave the impression that his current words were a natural evolution from anything he'd said previously on the matter, and that, in fact, he was changing his tune because now the people around him were ready to hear a more uncompromising version of the truth. Nowhere is this clearer than in his comments on such revered figures as Jesus and Krishna. He began in the 1970s praising Jesus as a great master, and by the mid-80s was criticizing and lampooning him more and more. In the 1970s he described Krishna as a fully enlightened one and by the 80s was saying that if he'd had the chance thousands of years ago when Krishna lived he would have 'slapped him in the face'. Anyone close enough to Osho soon realized that it was pointless to try to make any sort of doctrine out of his words and this is a classic manifestation of crazy-wisdom style. Even to try to classify Osho as a modern day example of 'crazy wisdom' is itself dubious, but it does, nevertheless, help to shed light on the fact that Osho, although utterly unique, was not an isolated figure, that he did have brothers and sisters in spirit.

Another 20th century crazy wisdom-type guru—the controversial Tibetan Buddhist master Chogyam Trungpa—once said:

Who thought of the idea of enlightenment, actually? Who dreamt up God? Who proclaimed himself as god over the earth? It seems that the whole thing is full of shit, actually, if I may use such language.[14]

In the crazy wisdom approach nothing is taboo, everything is fair game for questioning—or for using as a teaching. The term 'crazy wisdom' is a rough translation of the Tibetan *yeshe cholwa*, meaning 'wisdom gone wild.' It suggests a complete transcendence of reference points and the quality of reflecting truth indiscriminately, much as a mirror reflects an object that is put in front of it, regardless of what that object might be.

The issue of 'crazy wisdom' is easily misconstrued. Trungpa himself, in giving a lecture on it, once prefaced his remarks with the following:

> The subject that we are going to deal with is an extraordinarily difficult one. It is possible that some people might get extraordinarily confused.[15]

The reason the idea of crazy wisdom is so easily misunderstood is that it is, admittedly, very susceptible to wrong representation, not to mention abuse of its ideas. The difference between crazy wisdom and mere *craziness* is entirely the level of consciousness and overall maturity involved. The ancient *mahasiddhas* of the Himalayas were renowned for their ability to turn a seeming crisis into a vehicle for liberation, or a teaching. They also had a marked ability to express sublime truths via paradox or seemingly absurd behavior. The crazy wisdom teachings of northern India and Tibet are rooted in Tantra which, as discussed in Chapter 7, proclaims itself an appropriate teaching for 'darker' times, of which, according to Vedic doctrine, this time is one (usually referred to as the *Kali Yuga*). According to tradition, the crazy wisdom master is the type of teacher who is necessary for *crazy* times. (Of course it is arguable that the entire history of human civilization has been essentially insane, but there is no question that the 20th century, despite all the scientific and social advances, was also the darkest hour in history, if only in terms of sheer bloodshed and global conflict.)

The essence of Tantra, as well as its more extreme expression in crazy wisdom, is an embracing of both the light and dark polarities of life. Everything is ripe ground for spiritual growth, including materialism and sexual energy. Osho, with his infamous cynical appellations of 'Rolls Royce guru' and 'sex guru', clearly fit this notion—at least in appearance. Beyond appearances though—however distracting his may have been—lay the more interesting nature of his teaching approach, which was a consistent attempt to work skillfully with what was presented to him by life. How well he truly handled what came at him is another matter. For now it suffices to say that 'crazy wisdom' clearly had its mark in Osho, if only in the sheer wildness of his intelligence and the frequently bizarre circumstances around him he had to deal with.

Advaita Vedanta

Osho, born into a Jain family, was a child of India and in the final analysis his teachings on meditation were basically aligned with the essential principles of India's great Vedantic traditions. Regarding meditation he taught:

> Meditation is nothing but a device to make you aware of your real self—which is not created by you, which need not be created by you, which you already are. You are born with it! You are it. It needs to be discovered.[16]

That, of course, is the essential idea behind the great Hindu and Jain doctrines. In specific, the ideas of Advaita, a sub-school of Vedanta, were echoed in Osho's core spiritual values. One of the great exemplars of the Advaita Vedanta tradition, the south Indian sage Ramana Maharshi, was admired by Osho and was one of the few major mystics who escaped his criticism.

The Sanskrit word *advaita* literally means 'not two', referring to the idea that Reality is One, indivisible, and that all experience of duality—of apparent separation—is created by the mind's faulty understanding. According to Advaita, part of the awakening process involves the growing ability to discriminate between the eternal, or absolute reality (the true self), and transitory, relative reality. There could be no better summary of Osho's philosophy. He was pre-eminently concerned with distinguishing the real and valuable from the false and unimportant, all the way from the domain of social values, up to the highest spiritual truths that Advaita is concerned with. While he was no world-denying ascetic—after all, he promoted the ideal of Zorba the Buddha, or the enlightened sensualist—he did stress the need to dedicate one's life to the realization of the infinite and the timeless. He was a vocal critic of the folly of wasting one's life in trivialities or concern with conventional pursuits—with that which falls away. In that regard, at heart, he was an Indian mystic, a spokesman for one of the oldest schools of philosophy on the planet and one of the most uncompromising— even if he moved in the form of a wild and modern sage decked out in impressive robes and enjoying expensive cars.

Vedantic teachings derive from the Upanishads, the ancient Hindu source texts. The key historical figure behind Advaita Vedanta was the 9th century AD Indian philosopher-mystic Adi Shankara. From Shankara came the famous three lines that are often seen to represent the heart and soul of Advaita:

The World is not real
Only God is real
God and the individual's soul are not separate

This means that as a seeker of truth goes deeper and deeper into their consciousness they eventually come to the realization that all appearance of separation is illusion. There simply *is* no separate self at all, and nor has there ever been. This is equivalent to the realization that the true nature of consciousness is oneness with the All, with the totality of existence—that is, nothing is truly separate. Ramana Maharshi expressed this essentially as:

The World is not real
Only God is real
God is the World[17]

Those lines appear, at first glance, to be self-contradictory, a strange logic that seems to be implying that A is not C; B is C; therefore B is A. This, of course, seems to be absurd. But the seeming paradox found within the words is resolved by understanding that they denote different levels of consciousness. 'The world is not real' refers to an initial breakthrough in understanding in which we begin to see that everything in reality is mere appearance, constantly shifting in form, impermanent, dependent on previous causes to bring it to appearance, and that 'things in themselves' lack inherent, discrete existence. Looking deeper, we eventually realize that 'only God is real,' which means only the totality exists, the entirety of existence. Finally, we come to realize that this totality is not separate from its parts, and that, truly, everything is a valid expression of the totality, of the All. Buddhism has its own version of this idea in its expression 'Nirvana is Samsara'. That is, the absolute is ultimately understood to be not separate from the relative. William Blake gave poetic expression to this idea when he wrote:

To see the world in a grain of sand,
And heaven in a wild flower,
Hold infinity in the palm of your hand,
And eternity in an hour.

Osho's work was the very definition of cutting edge—he was less a 'rich man's guru' than he was simply a guru of modernity—and he sought always to integrate transformational work with the gritty realities of life. He himself was no worldly person—more than once he mentioned how he never handled money, or much else, for that matter. As a young man, his sole material passion was his massive collection of books. But his philosophic concern was with living consciously in the world and directly facing the challenges of life. He always sought to promote the view that ultimate reality was not some dissociated mystical state, but was to be found in this very world—in the stars, the trees, the moon, the river, the body, and in the very simple things of life. He taught to realize the eternal within the ordinary.

Appendix I
The Osho-Crowley Parallels

There is an interesting fact that I initially suspected, but that became clearer to me as I was researching this book. Stated simply, it is this: it is well known that Osho frequently talked about Gurdjieff and that elements of Gurdjieff's Work can be found in Osho's teachings and methods. However, to my knowledge, Osho was basically unaware of Crowley or at the least, never talked about him. The interesting irony there is that in several important respects Osho actually had much more in common with Crowley than he did with Gurdjieff. Some common points between the two:

1. Joining East and West. Both men (as well as Gurdjieff) were exceptional in that regard. Crowley was the first, to my knowledge, to make a serious attempt to bring together Eastern Yoga (Raja Yoga in specific) with Western Hermetic and Qabalistic ceremonial Magick. Osho was the first, again to my knowledge, to comprehensively combine Eastern meditation and the general Eastern approach toward enlightenment with Western psychotherapy in an ashram setting. (Both Crowley and Osho kept these East-West practices relatively distinct even while using them together. Gurdjieff differed here by blending Eastern and Western practices into a specific methodology that was original at least in some ways.)

2. Attitude toward sex and the self. Both Crowley and Osho were antinomian—that is, operated entirely outside of spiritual and religious conventions—to a high degree. Both were highly charismatic men who clearly had a strong effect on the opposite sex. Both espoused a general philosophy of sexual exploration, and both were

strongly opposed to celibacy, sexual repression, and religious attitudes toward sex and the body. Sexual exploration in the Osho community was natural, expected, and widespread. While orgies in the various Osho communal houses were not exactly daily occurrences, there were very few monogamous couples and even fewer celibates. Both Osho and Crowley embraced the concepts of joy, celebration, laughter (although Crowley's often difficult circumstances made it hard for him to actually live out some of his ideals) and the exalting of the individual, and both had a Dionysian nature and pro-Nietzschean outlook. Their shared admiration for the latter was clear; Crowley declared Nietzsche one of the prophets of his religion and Osho chose Nietzsche's *Thus Spake Zarathustra* as his #1 book from his list of 167 favorite books. Crowley's Thelemic creeds of *Do what thou wilt shall be the whole of the Law* and *Love is the law, love under will* are absolutely central to Osho's teaching, although expressed in different wording. (A natural rejoinder here would be that Crowley's two maxims could be considered general enough so as to apply to the teachings of many philosophers and gurus, but that does not hold up well when the teachings of many philosophers and gurus—and most importantly, how they lived their lives—are closely examined. Space prohibits a detailed analysis, but suffice to say I am familiar with the teachings of many Eastern gurus and none come close to not just Osho's naturally 'Thelemic' teachings, but the way in which he lived his life as well.) One small example was Crowley's ideas around laughter. In *Little Essays Toward Truth*, he wrote,

The common defect of all mystical systems previous to that of the Aeon whose Law is Thelema is that there has been no place for Laughter. But the sadness of the mournful Mother and the melancholy of the dying Man are swept into the limbo of the past by the confident smile of the immortal Child.

He was referring to his ideas about the previous Aeons of matriarchy (Isis, the 'mournful Mother') and patriarchy (Osiris, the 'dying Man') and to the present Aeon of Horus (the 'immortal Child'). For any who knew Osho, the billing 'the confident smile of the immortal Child' fit him as well as anything. He was a classic embodiment of the *Puer Aeternus* archetype, an ageless Child and a Pan and trickster (amongst many other things) *par excellence*. But beyond the tempting nonsense of indulging in prophecy, more to the point is the content of the teaching. Osho was entirely pro-laughter; he undoubtedly told more jokes than any mystic in history. His YouTube video (that has been up since 2007) featuring a talk he gives on the various meanings of the English word 'fuck' is delivered with deadpan effectiveness and is (for most people) extremely funny. It is a master performance and one that would be virtually inconceivable to imagine being given by any other Eastern guru.

Osho, though highly critical of most philosophers, mystics, and gurus, was almost unanimously supportive of Gurdjieff and clearly had a great personal affection for him. He did have one main criticism of him and it was that his system was a bit too serious, lacking in humor. However, that view may be an example of the difficulties in understanding a teaching that was not fully captured by the modern wonders of technology. (There is an actual tape recording in 1948 of a student of Gurdjieff's explaining to him what the new-fangled tape recorder is and how he can actually hear his voice recorded and played back to him. Gurdjieff listens for a moment and then tells him to 'shut it off.'.) In fact, Gurdjieff did have an excellent (and equally ribald) sense of humor. One of the few tape recordings of him that survives has him regaling a group of students with an old tale about a bottle of scotch while the people in the room periodically roar with laughter.

3. Attitude toward drugs. Osho began teaching near the latter days of the hippie era and so was naturally exposed to many Westerners who had had ample exploration with drugs. Osho was known to have used nitrous oxide on a number of occasions, osten-

sibly connected to dental work, but he also dictated three books under the influence of this drug. I lived in several Osho communal houses in the 1980s and most house parties had the usual contingent of pot smokers out on the back porch. Recreational drug use among Osho disciples was not rampant but it was fairly common. At least some of Osho's disciples, especially in the 1970s in India, supported themselves through the drug trade.[3] Crowley's explorations with drugs are, of course, legendary, finding their natural continuation in people like Timothy Leary, Ram Dass, Robert Anton Wilson, and Terrence McKenna. Osho did not appear to use drugs significantly (beyond nitrous oxide and possibly valium); however, the sheer openness of his teachings (essentially, 'embrace rather than avoid') made it natural for many of his followers to use recreational drugs.

4. Bombast and braggadocio. Both Crowley and Osho were frequently given to sweeping condemnations of large institutions, like religions and governments, as well as individuals, in particular other spiritual teachers. Osho in particular was a trenchant critic (calling Swami Muktananda a pervert, U.G. Krishnamurti a phony, Mother Theresa a hypocrite, Nisargadatta a dirty old man, saying Krishna deserved to be slapped in the face, etc.). And both had no qualms about referring to themselves in highly special terms. Crowley's grandiosity showed in more esoteric ways; he did considerable research into his past lives via what he called the 'magical memory' (a type of yogic mind training), and in addition to a number of common incarnations, many of which he reported were generally negative in tone and accomplishment, he also believed himself the reincarnation of a number of important personages. Amongst these were Eliphas Levi, Count Cagliostro, Edward Kelly, Pope Alexander VI, and—interestingly enough—a sixth century BC Chinese disciple of Lao Tzu, named Ko Hsuan. Of interest with this latter personage, is that a school for children in England that for many years has been part of the global Osho community is named the Ko Hsuan School. (Whether this is the same historical figure referred to by Crowley is unclear—although both claimed them to

be ancient Chinese sages—but an interesting coincidence, never-theless, owing to the relative obscurity of this sage.)

Osho spoke of one past life in particular, that being his last one before his current. In very few of his public talks did he speak much about esoteric matters but in a series of lectures given early in his teaching career (late 1960s-early 1970s) collected together as the book, *Dimensions Beyond the Known* (1975), he did so. In these talks, he claimed to have had a life in Tibet at some time in the 1200s AD. In that life, he said that he was nearly enlightened and was ending his life with a fast that would lead to 'full knowledge' but that his effort was aborted when he was murdered. (Satya Bharti, one of Osho's early disciples from the 1970s and author of *The Promise of Paradise*, claimed to be the reincarnation of the young boy who had killed him back around the year 1270 AD in Tibet—she also indicated that Osho more or less confirmed this.)[4]

5. Medical condition. Both Crowley and Osho were chronic asthma sufferers.

6. Early life losses: as small children, both had a younger sister who died (Crowley when he was four, Osho at five), and both described a similar reaction to this death.

7. Both evolved personalities in youth that showed pronounced features of remoteness, rebelliousness and arrogance. Throughout their lives neither had anything resembling a monogamous long term relationship with one woman. Crowley was technically married to Rose Kelly (his first Tantric partner) for six years but was not monogamous and was often apart from her. His relationship with Leah Hirsig may have been his deepest but in his five years with her he was not monogamous either. Osho doubtless had sex with a number of women but does not appear to have ever had a sustained primary partner.

8. Short lived communes. Both created particular Tantric communes (Crowley's Abbey at Cefalu and Osho's huge Oregon experiment) that, in both cases, lasted approximately four years before scandals and political forces destroyed them. Crowley's

Abbey was comparatively tiny, with perhaps at most a couple of dozen people involved. However, what he called his 'chamber of nightmares' room in his Abbey was designed for psychotherapeutic catharsis and was thus a primitive precursor of Osho's sophisticated therapy chambers run by qualified psychotherapists, but the purpose was exactly the same, to free the mind of burdensome conditioning so that the candidate could more easily enter the subtle, meditative states of consciousness.

9. Both had razor sharp intellects and both were scholars of the perennial wisdom traditions. Both were as deeply educated about world religions and transformational methods as probably anyone has been with the possible exception of some specialized scholars like Frithjof Schuon, Mircea Eliade, Rene Guenon, or Joseph Campbell. Unlike academic scholars, however, Crowley and Osho were in the tradition of the 'crazy wisdom' masters who are more concerned with plunging headlong into a direct confrontation with the full energies of their egos and deeper being. What makes them unusual is that they were also scholars of their own tradition.

10. Esoteric connections. In Crowley's Thelemic teachings, a seeker on the journey back to their Divine Source symbolically passes through a zone of darkness (called the Abyss) where they are completely purged of ego. There, they confront the demon Choronzon, who is a sort of ultimate tester. Emerging on the other side, the seeker awakens fully to their divine state and comes to dwell in 'the City of the Pyramids'. The last year of Osho's life can be imagined to have paralleled that symbolic sequence: the year was spent almost entirely in an 'abyss,' (his room, darkened to pitch black and cooled to ease his physical pain), confronting a 'demon' (the agonizingly painful breakdown of his body). As his death approached, giant black pyramids were erected in his ashram. About a year after his death, the ashram became, effectively, a 'city of pyramids'. Additionally, there is a strange line of prophecy from Crowley's *The Book of the Law*, written in 1904, that in this connection is too tempting to pass up: 'I am the warrior Lord of the Forties: the

Eighties cower before me and are abased.' Osho was not the only mystic to undergo dramatic events in the 1980s, but he was one of the few—arguably, the only one—who sought to introduce radical change in the world via a revolutionary spiritual template that was exercised with considerable aggression; that is, with the same warrior-like attitude that some sections of Crowley's key book are imbued with.

11. Political awareness. Both men denounced the politically oriented mind and both were clearly mystics first and foremost, and yet both also retained a sharp interest in, and critically observant eye of, global political machinations. In particular, both promoted a planetary awareness that eschews patriotism. Osho on endless occasions remarked on the absurdity of patriotism and of the existence of nations in general. Crowley once wrote, 'All advanced thinkers, all men who realize the divine plan, desire and intend the solidarity of humanity; and the patriot in the narrow and infuriated sense of that word is a traitor to the true interests of man.'[5]

12. This last I offer mostly in jest, because it is a coincidence, but amusing all the same. All serious students of Crowley's ideas recognize the significance of the number 93 in his teaching, and many Thelemites commonly greet each other with '93'. (This is because in the Greek Qabalah where letters are assigned a numeric value, the word *Thelema* sums to 93; additionally, the name of Crowley's Holy Guardian Angel, Aiwass, in Hebrew sums also to 93). Osho's disciples gathered for whatever reasons a large collection of Rolls Royces for him that in the end was considered to be one of the most extravagant fleets of cars ever put together by anyone, let alone by an Eastern guru. The exact number of Rolls Royces accumulated for him before his fleet was sold off? 93.[6]

Appendix II
Crowley and Chess: The Royal Game and the Inner Work

Gurdjieff used an interesting term to refer to an esoteric teaching that is passed down through the centuries in a sort of encrypted form—he called it a 'legominism'. According to Gurdjieff, a legominism is a means of transmitting esoteric knowledge that is, on the surface, disguised by some sort of intentional mistake—or what he called a 'lawful inexactitude'. He considered his magnum opus, *Beelzebub's Tales to His Grandson*, to be a legominism. William Patrick Patterson, in his three-part video documentary on Gurdjieff's life and work, refers to three particular legominisms in addition to Gurdjieff's *Beelzebub*: the Great Pyramid-Sphinx complex, the Tarot, and the 'royal game'—chess.

Patterson mentioned elsewhere that it was his teacher, Lord John Pentland, who had told him that chess was a legominism, although where Lord Pentland was getting this from is unclear. That the Giza pyramid complex, Tarot, and chess are all fascinating objects of study that are full of symbolism is clear but how exactly their symbolism is to be understood has always been much less obvious. The challenge with symbols is that they are once removed from whatever it is that they are pointing at. As in the classic Zen parable of the fingers pointing toward the moon, it becomes problematic when we fixate on the fingers—just as getting attached to symbols and forgetting what they are pointing toward leads to confusion and ultimately delusion. Many established religions suffer from this problem, the tendency to glorify the symbol and overlook the truth that it is intended to represent.

I have meditated inside of the King's Chamber of the Great Pyramid and since the mid-1970s have been both a student of the Tarot as well as a chess player, so naturally Patterson's remarks interested me. The iconic power and deep mystery of the pyramids and Sphinx are commonly recognized and the Tarot—which has grown tremendously in popularity since the mid-19th century—is a basic element of the Western esoteric tradition, long appreciated as a rich source of psychological and spiritual symbolism. And it is interesting to note that both the Tarot cards and the modern form of chess are believed by historians to have first appeared at roughly the same time—during the 15th century—and at roughly the same place—in southern Europe, Italy and Spain in particular. (Chess is believed to originate from an older game from India or possibly China, but at that remoter time it had essential rule differences that, in effect, made it a different game.)

However, the strong parallels between Tarot and chess end with their time and place of origin. This is because chess, though utilizing archetypal symbols of royalty (kings and queens), clergy (bishops), military (knights and castles) and the common man (pawns), has largely resisted esoteric interpretation. That is in all probability because the game is so uncompromisingly competitive—in symbolic terms it is a fight to the death. The very term 'checkmate' is most commonly believed to derive from the Persian words *shah* (king) and *mat* (stymied, ambushed, defeated)—literally (in the context of chess) 'the king is defeated'. To checkmate your opponent is to disable the king in his realm, to control, subdue, and overcome the master of the house—at which point the game is over. This is accomplished by clear logical and spatial reasoning capacity and by no other way. There is no 'chance' element in the game of chess, only inasmuch as holding out for the 'chance' that your opponent plays a weak move. But even if he does, he has still done so willfully and is thus the architect of his resulting weakened position.

Because of the intensely intellectual component to the military strategy of the game, the clear rich symbolism of the pieces themselves has been largely ignored and is usually not a serious consideration for the average chess player. Put simply, chess and metaphysics have traditionally been like oil and water, a very unnatural mix. The Tarot cards are commonly accepted to be an esoteric system used for psychic divination or the investigation of psychological and spiritual symbols, but historically there is no clear evidence that they were used for anything other than casual gaming purposes until the mid-18th century. That is no longer the case, with the standard poker deck assuming the role of gaming while the Tarot has entered into the domain of metaphysics, even being joined by some esoteric practitioners with the Qabalah. .

That said, there is no clear evidence that any students of metaphysics or the occult sciences have seriously attempted to make of chess an esoteric system. The Hermetic Order of the Golden Dawn did devise a modified form of chess called 'Enochian chess' but according to some former Golden Dawn members and esoteric authorities (such as Israel Regardie) not much came of this game and very few, if any, Golden Dawn members actually played it.

Crowley and Chess

In most short biographical descriptions of Crowley we find, along with usual 'occultist', 'mountain climber' and 'big-game hunter', the title 'chess master'. He mentions in a few places in the *Confessions* his involvement in the game and how he eventually had a sudden and complete realization of how he was not fated for any sort of career as a tournament chess player. The following is from the period of his life when he was a student at Cambridge in his early twenties:

> My one serious worldly ambition had been to become the champion of the world at chess... I had frequently beaten Bird at Simpson's and when I got to Cambridge I made a savagely

intense study of the game. In my second year I was president of the university and had beaten such first-rate amateurs as Gunston and Coles. Outside the master class, Atkins was my only acknowledged superior. I made mincemeat of the man who was champion of Scotland a few years later, even after I had given up the game. I spent over two hours a day in study and more than that in practice. I was assured on all hands that another year would see me a master myself.

I had been to St. Petersburg to learn Russian for the Diplomatic Service in the long vacation of 1897, and on my way back broke the journey in Berlin to attend the Chess Congress. But I had hardly entered the room where the masters were playing when I was seized with what may justly be described as a mystical experience. I seemed to be looking on at the tournament from outside myself. I saw the masters—one, shabby, snuffy and blear-eyed; another, in badly fitting would-be respectable shoddy; a third, a mere parody of humanity, and so on for the rest. These were the people to whose ranks I was seeking admission. 'There, but for the grace of God, goes Aleister Crowley,' I exclaimed to myself with disgust, and there and then I registered a vow never to play another serious game of chess. I perceived with praeternatural lucidity that I had not alighted on this planet with the object of playing chess.[1]

And yet he never dropped the game entirely. Israel Regardie, in *The Eye in the Triangle*, mentions how he used to play chess almost nightly with Crowley when serving as his secretary in the late 1920s:

During the period that I stayed with him and served as his secretary, there was a nightly session after dinner—almost a routine or ritual—of chess-playing. After a while I came to loathe the game. It took me many years before I was able to return to it again for pleasure. Crowley not only enjoyed the game, he was a competent player. It addition, it was one of his contentions, which at that time was quite unintelligible to me, that by playing chess with someone, he was able to obtain a fairly clear picture of how he operated psychologically. Some people play a cautious game, others are more reckless in their expenditures of pieces. Some start out with a flair, and wind up after a dozen moves not knowing what they want to do or where they want to go or how to do it. Still others reach their best performance only toward the end of the game, after they are through probing their opponent's defenses and aggressive tactics. These attitudes are basic to the individual's general functioning, and operate in most areas of his life.[2]

Crowley's life-long passion for the royal game has long been of interest to me. About the same time I discovered Crowley (mid-1970s), I also discovered the En Passant Chess Café in Montreal, thus beginning my own life-long affair with (and at times addiction to) this most fathomlessly complicated of all games. Chess, on the face of it, is not a human activity typically associated with the path of the mystic. Chess players tend to be intellectuals more than anything and *competitive* intellectuals at that. The spiritual path has always tended to neutralize much of the competitive edge and for perfectly valid reasons—arriving at a glimpse of the Unity of All does not mesh with pouring concentrated mental focus into the effort to checkmate your opponent's king. The goal of the mystic has always been to abolish (or transmute or transcend) the ego, but competitive chess is far from an egoless game.

In *The Eye in the Triangle*, Regardie writes how the feat that impressed him the most was Crowley's blindfold chess. He then goes on to describe a typical evening with Crowley where he would play both Regardie and Gerald Yorke at the same time—blindfolded—and invariably win both games (all the while drinking brandy and smoking cigars). The feat sounds very impressive and indeed it does require a definite level of ability with the game. But what Regardie does not mention is that any chess player beyond a certain level of strength is capable of blindfold play. I remember my astonishment when as a young lad I walked into the Café En Passant one day and witnessed Leo Williams, a local Montreal master, playing no less than *twenty* players blindfold at the same time. I still vividly recall Williams sitting in an adjoining room about twenty feet away from the players, with a black blindfold on. He was hunched over, his back to the players. The intense concentration on his face was obvious. He gave these 'blindfold simuls' from time to time and invariably won a majority of the games. But even Williams was not the top player in the city. There were several local masters who were rated higher than him in standard one-on-one play.

'Blindfold' chess is chess where a player (usually of expert strength or higher) will take on another player without sight of the board. That is, he will have to carry in his imagination a picture of the board and remember how the position of the pieces is changing with each move. 'Simuls' are events where a chess player (again, of at least expert strength or higher) will play a number of players simultaneously. The simul world record changes frequently, usually being surpassed every few years; the current record for this is 360 boards at once, set in early 2009 by the Bulgarian grandmaster Kirli Georgiev (he won 284, lost 6, and had 70 draws).

A 'blindfold simul' is where an accomplished player will play, while blindfolded, more than one player at the same time. Thus, technically, Crowley's games against Yorke and Regardie were blindfold simuls. The confirmed record for such play is 34 boards at once, by the late Belgian-American grandmaster George Koltanowski in 1937 (the Polish grandmaster Miguel Naijdorf played against 45 boards blindfolded in 1947, but his play conditions were not as strict as Koltanowski's and his result is not considered official). So, as we can see, while Crowley's feat against Regardie and Yorke is impressive, it is nowhere near the level of skill exercised by more advanced masters of the game.

To describe Crowley as a 'chess master' is probably not techni-cally accurate, at least by current definitions. The standard rating system in place in international chess circles, devised by the Hungarian-American physicist and chess master Arpad Elo and implemented by the International Chess Federation (FIDE) in 1970, is generally recognized as follows:

1200-1400:	Class D (beginner)
1400-1600:	Class C
1600-1800:	Class B
1800-2000:	Class A
2000-2200:	Expert, or Candidate Master
2200-2400:	Master
2400-2500:	International Master
2500-2700:	Grandmaster
Over 2700:	Super Grandmaster (of which they are currently around thirty in the world).

The world champion (as of this writing in late 2009, the Indian grandmaster Viswanathan Anand) is usually around 2800. The rankings (master, grandmaster, etc.) beyond 2400 (the approximate beginning of international master strength) are not fixed; that is, they are dependent on specific tournament results rather than precise rating number.

Chess is an extraordinarily hard game to play well, let alone to master. Since the late 1990s, computers have officially overtaken humans and now the strongest chess programs can consistently defeat the best humans. This is an exceptional accomplishment and a testament to the brute calculating power of computers, the best of which will compute millions of possible moves per second thus overcoming a grandmaster's combination of reasoning and intuition.

No one is able to play chess well automatically, anymore than one can play a violin automatically. Even the most naturally gifted spend years at hard work studying and practicing the game. The average good club player will generally reach a rating strength of between 1500 and 1800. Anything over 2000 requires serious effort, and in particular, serious study. To progress beyond 2200 (the approximate beginning of master strength) is only possible for one who commits significant time to the game.

As Crowley admitted, he did in fact commit significant time to chess, making, as he described it, 'a savage study of the game'. As best as I've been able to glean (I am a class 'A' level player myself) in particular from looking at some of Crowley's published games is that he achieved a playing strength of somewhere between 1900 and 2100 (between class 'A' and expert, or candidate master, level). That in itself is no small achievement and only possible for one who has devoted many hundreds of hours to play and study.

The following are two games Crowley played in 1894; the first, where Crowley was one of several opponents playing the well known English master Joseph Blackburne in a 'simul,' shows some of his comments:

Blackburne, J – Crowley, A
Blackburne simul Eastbourne, 1894
1.e4 c5 2.Nf3 Nc6 3.d4 cxd4 4.Nxd4 e6 5.Nc3 Bb4?
Crowley: 'Unwise.'
6.Nxc6 bxc6 7.Qd4 Bxc3+ 8.bxc3 Nf6 9.Ba3 Qa5!
Crowley: 'A strong counterattack.'
10.Bb4 + = c5? 11.Bxc5 Nxe4 12.Bb4 Qd5
Crowley: 'Better than Qf5 because of g3.'
13.Qxd5 exd5 14.Rd1 Bb7 += 15.Be2?! a5 16.Ba3 Nxc3 17.Rd3
     Nxe2!
Crowley: 'Perhaps better than taking the second pawn. The two
     bishops are always dangerous and the pawn might have been
     regained with the better game.'
18.Re3+ Kd8 19.Kxe2! d4
Crowley: 'Temporary insanity.'
20.Re7 Re8 21.Rxe8+ Kxe8 22.Kd3 f6 23.Kxd4 Kf7 24.c3 Re8 25.Rb1
     Bc6 26.c4 Re2!

Crowley: 'This forces the exchange of rooks, and consequently the draw. Bishops of opposite colors and pawns even can result in nothing else.'

27.Rb2 Rxb2 28.Bxb2

Crowley: 'Mr. Blackburne proposed a draw which was accepted.'

28...Ke6= ½-½ (draw).

Crowley–Shoosmith, 1894

1.e4 e5 2.f4 exf4 3.Nf3 g5 4.Bc4 C37 KGA: King's knight's gambit 4...d6 5.0-0 h6 6.d4 Ne7 7.Nc3 Bg7 8.e5 OOB 8...d5 9.Bb3 c6 10.Ne2 Ng6 11.g3 g4 12.Nxf4 Nxf4 13.Bxf4 gxf3 14.Qxf3 Be6 15.c3 Nd7 16.Bc2 Nf8 17.Qh5 Qd7 18.Bd2 Bg4 19.Qh4 Ng6 20.Bxg6 fxg6 21.e6 Bxe6 22.Rae1 g5? 23.Qg4 0-0-0 24.Rxe6 h5 25.Qe2 h4 26.Bxg5 Rdg8?? 27.Re7 Qh3 28.g4 Bxd4+ 29.cxd4 Rxg5 30.Re8+ Rxe8 31.Qxe8+ Kc7 32.Qe7+ 1-0 (white wins).

The fact that Crowley played chess and played it well is another part of the enigma of the man. I know of very few serious spiritual seekers, mystics, or philosophers, let alone advanced esoteric adepts, who were also competent chess players. The two realms are just not very compatible. But Crowley was obviously no ordinary sort. And although his chess playing is usually mentioned only as a curiosity, I think it reveals an element of his character that merits looking further at.

There have been a number of attempts at probing into the psychology of chess. I recall reading Alexander Cockburn's *Idle Passion: Chess and the Dance of Death* back in the late 1970s. The author applied a somewhat grim and very Freudian interpretation to the basic elements of the game. However, I thought the book had some excellent insights and suspected this even more so when, in later years, I heard of the hostile reaction some chess players had to the book. Exaggerated defensive reactions are often suggestive of something to be defended and thus equally suggestive of underlying matters that have not been addressed.

Attempts have been made to interpret chess symbolism as relating primarily to the struggle to overcome the father (the king). It is known that the rules of the game changed in the 15th century when the queen was first given the vast powers she has since enjoyed as the strongest piece on the board (which was the birth of modern chess as we know it). Cockburn cites Kenneth Colby's idea that 'the innovator [of the queen's new powers] was probably a weakling who identified with the weak King and desired to create a strong woman who could contend against the world for him.' Such psychoanalytic theorizing may seem contrived, but as with all psychological theories all that really matters is its applicability.

In this case, can we see within Crowley a need to join with the feminine in an effort to 'contend' with the world? Without question, he did attempt this to some degree with his various primary women lovers, a number whom (in his mind, at least) held the office of what he called the 'Scarlet Woman'. (As explained elsewhere in this book, Crowley did not equate the Scarlet Woman with a 'prostitute', but rather with Babalon, a term that he saw representative of the Great Mother archetype and ultimately with the manifest universe itself.)

Alexander Cockburn theorized that many serious male chess players have a strongly latent homosexual impulse, but I would suggest a modification of that. It is more likely that many serious chess players (male or female) have a strong psychological association with the feminine principle and are seeking to come to terms with it—by trying to master a game that features, as its most powerful piece, the queen—and thereby to exercise this power within themselves. Crowley, for all his negative views of women and his clear resistance to relationship commitment, was certainly never free of them. In fact, women were deeply important to him. He appears to have exemplified the love-hate dance that typifies many men who have multiple lovers and relationships over the course of their lives.

In chess, the queen may be the most powerful piece but she is not the most important. The game entirely revolves around the king and cannot exist without him. The moment he is 'ambushed' and immobilized the game is immediately over. Moreover, the queen, despite her powers, is on occasion sacrificed in order to win the game. That is, she is a means to an end. She can 'die' (be captured), 'reincarnate' (when a pawn reaches the eighth rank and promotes to a queen), and 'kill' (checkmate) the enemy king, but the universe of the chessboard does not revolve around her. It centers on the king.

How does such symbolism relate to the Great Work of transformation that Crowley (for one) dedicated his life to? When young Aleister walked out of the Berlin Chess Congress tournament in 1897 resolving never to play tournament chess again, so repulsed was he by the various present chess personalities, he was making a leap—undergoing an initiation of sorts—from mere chess player to one ready to work with the living, breathing chessboard of the esoteric 'Great Work'. And this is a chessboard best symbolized by the ancient art of alchemy.

Chess as Alchemy

The Great Work, as Crowley himself was to state, lies in the 'uniting of opposites'. Chess, if nothing else, is a vivid representation of that idea fleshed out in stark form—opposing armies marching against each other across a battlefield mapped out in black and white squares. The checkered floor often depicted in Masonic images reflects this essential mystery and it also lies at the heart of alchemy, part of which is a process called the *mysterium coniunctionis*—the 'mysterious conjunction'.

Alchemy is an ancient art that, in many ways, lies at the foundation of the process of inner transformation. As an inner science, it is common in many forms of transformational work including those of modern times, being recognizable in disciplines as varied as Gurdjieff's system to Jungian psychoanalysis. The word 'alchemy' has uncertain origins, but is sometimes thought to stem from the Arabic *al-khimia*, possibly deriving from the Coptic word *khem* which means 'black land', another name for Egypt. Thus, 'alchemy' may simply mean 'of Egypt'. The black land refers to the soil around the Nile valley, which was rich with nutrients when the waters of the Nile would recede after the annual flooding. Another view holds that the ancient Chinese were the first to practice the art, and the Chinese word *kim*—which refers to the production of gold—migrated to the Middle East where it became the word *kem*, and later, *al-khimia*.[3]

The Arabic term *al-khimia* also means 'the art of transformation' and this applies to both physical levels (thus being the basis of the later science of chemistry) in which the alchemist of old was interested in transforming base materials, like lead, into more exalted materials like gold, as well as to the inner practice of alchemy which involves the transformation of the individual from unconscious 'raw material' to the 'finer material' of self-realization and divine illumination (enlightenment). It is to this latter science of alchemy, the inner art of transformation, that we are concerned with here.

The prized goal of alchemy, in the more traditional sense, was the substance known as gold. Gold has some interesting chemical properties—it is the most ductile of all metals, meaning, it can be reshaped into endless forms without fracturing. It is also largely immune to most corrosive agents of air or water and resistant to corruption by fire (which is why it was always valued in making jewelry). Thus, its great strength and brilliant color make it a powerful symbol for that which is both radiant and indestructible within us, i.e., our highest nature and true inner self.

Alchemy posits that all things in the universe originate with the *prima materia* (First Matter). Things only appear to be different because they contain different combinations of material, but when these combinations are stripped away, what is revealed is the First Matter. This 'First Matter', taken as a spiritual symbol, bears close resemblance to Plotinus' 'The One' (building on Plato's 'The Good,' or ultimate Source behind all things). All this points to the de-conditioning process that lies at the heart of most paths of spiritual transformation—that is, the deconstructing of that which is false, or untrue about us, to reveal that which is true and real, i.e., our actual, divine self.

This process of deconstruction can also be seen as a *constructive* process, and in some Hermetic schools of alchemy that is how they saw it—the physical body, being associated with Saturn (or lead) being transmuted into the 'solar body', or gold. Christian mysticism refers to this as the resurrection body, a body of light that is immortal and that we attain only through deep and profound practice.

Ultimately, whether we choose to see the process of transformation as deconstructive (dissolving the ego impurities) or constructive (transforming and thus heightening our 'vibration' so that we attain a more rarefied consciousness) is more a matter of perspective and less important than actually engaging the work. But in point of fact, the process of alchemy actually involves both of these actions through what is referred to as *solve et coagula*—the dissolution and coagulation—the deconstruction and re-construction of our inner being. Or put more simply, to separate and recombine. There is a clear and interesting symbolic parallel here in the Egyptian myth of Osiris who is killed by his brother Set, has his body dismembered, and then is reconstructed by the gods Isis and Thoth as part of his resurrection in the *duat* (Otherworld)—a symbolism that is pure alchemical *solve et coagula*. It defines the heart of the spiritual process of 'breaking down' and being 'reborn'. The Great Work of alchemy is ultimately to realize the fundamental interrelationship between mind and matter, between self and world, between heaven and earth, finally ending in the non-dual realization (All is One) that lies at the heart of all spiritual paths.

If Lord Pentland was, by chance, correct and chess is indeed a legominism—that is, a type of spiritual teaching preserved in code— then it's reasonable to speculate that the very dualism of the game, based on the black and white forces playing on sixty-four black and white squares, represents this timeless struggle to balance 'opposing' forces within the personality. When we play a game of chess we are gradually stripped away of our pieces—whether but a few as in a fast game where one side is quickly defeated—or in a drawn out struggle terminating in an end game with a bare skeleton of an army remaining. Warfare of any sort is not just destructive but is also a *deconstructive* process, much as the Great Work of transformation is—a peeling away of elements of the personality, a reduction of manpower, to arrive at some sort of graduation to another level. This 'other level' may be represented superficially by winning or losing, each with its natural lessons contained therein. The loser is humbled, the winner is made proud. In terms of the teachings of spiritual alchemy, it is the loser who is gaining the steeper lessons because the winner's pride will eventually be destroyed by something.

In alchemy, the prime symbols of royalty, the king and queen, carry rich meaning. The king is typically connected to the solar principle, the Sun that lies at the center of all. Much as in chess, in our solar system the Sun is the center of all and is irreplaceable. The queen is commonly connected to the lunar principle, the body that reflects the light of the Sun. Crowley chose the number '666' as representative of him in part because it is, in some esoteric systems, symbolic of the Sun or the masculine principle. But he also identified with it as it represented, in his interpretation, a key to moving out of the old Aeon of patriarchy and into a new Aeon of an enlightened consciousness that is based on the resolution of opposing forces— much as in the resolution of opposing forces on a chessboard.

Chess is a mathematical, geometric expression of the art of relationship. It is entirely about the dance of relating between the opposing forces of alchemy, the primal poles of duality—white and black, male and female, active and passive, creative and destructive—in contrast and struggle. As with all things, it has a positive and negative face. The positive face of chess has to do with mastery of opposites and contrast by learning how not to identify with the game—put simply, not being attached to outcome. We suffer in life because we over-identify with the role we play and then become attached to how things 'should' end—be that a chess game, or a love relationship, or a business venture, or a creative project. The picture we form in our mind never quite matches the way things turn out. And so we either let go and allow things to be or we resist, tighten inwardly, struggle and suffer, wanting things to be other than how they are.

Chess, replete with archetypal symbolism, is the most fiercely competitive of all games. On the intellectual battlefield it is ego-incarnate. And, as such, it is a powerful alchemical key for mastering competition—how to lose with grace, and how to win with wisdom. Losing prepares us for wisdom, just as all 'losses' in life do. Winning cultivates the ground for grace, just as all 'triumphs' in life do. In so doing, the sacred 'inner marriage' is fulfilled and we emerge—one day—both graceful and wise.

Appendix III
Gurdjieff, Beelzebub,
and Zecharia Sitchin

I bury the bone so deep that the dogs have to scratch for it.
G.I. Gurdjieff

Gurdjieff's magnum opus, *Beelzebub's Tales to His Grandson: An Objectively Impartial Criticism of the Life of Man,*[1] is volume one of his *All and Everything* trilogy. The book is an extremely difficult read; long, convoluted and full of strange neologisms (devised words) penned by Gurdjieff. He wrote and re-wrote it many times over a period of approximately a decade from 1924-34. It was not published until 1950 but for many years readings used to be done from the manuscript to Gurdjieff's students at various meetings, often in his apartment in Paris after the Institute at Fontainebleau closed in 1932.

The book is an allegory about an angel named Beelzebub who, in his youth, revolted against apparent injustices in the design and ordering of the universe. He tried to right the problems himself which resulted in terrible damage everywhere, and for his punishment he is exiled to the solar system 'Ors' (our system) where he lives on Mars and is given the means for interplanetary travel. Others exiled with him were sent to live on Earth. Some of these angels demoted to Earth (reminiscent of the *Nefilim*, the 'giants' or 'cast down' angels, of the Old Testament) caused problems by interfering with human civilizations. These Earth-bound angels eventually summoned Beelzebub from Mars to help, where he begins his trenchant observations of humanity.

The following is a brief overview of some of the main ideas and neologisms taught and created by Gurdjieff in *Beelzebub*:

Evolution and Involution: A key to grasping Gurdjieff's ideas is in understanding the relationship between evolution and involution. The simplest way to view this is in relation to Gurdjieff's idea of the Ray of Creation (see Chapter 5). Evolution is the process that proceeds from the lowest level (represented by the Moon) to the highest (the Absolute). It moves from unconsciousness and semi-consciousness to full consciousness, and has to make efforts to overcome the mechanical nature of unconscious forces while doing so. This represents the standard journey of awakening as described in most wisdom traditions. Involution describes the reverse process, the movement from the Absolute to the seventh and lowest dimension symbolized (in Gurdjieff's system) by the Moon. This is moving from full consciousness to increasing levels of mechanicality and unconsciousness.

Gurdjieff stresses that humanity is not separate from the organic processes of Nature and thus humanity is not meant, in the collective sense, to spiritually evolve, for if it were to do so the equilibrium of the greater planetary world of which it is a part of would be disturbed. This is why the realm of spiritual awakening has always belonged to individuals only—the odd person here and there who strives to awaken—and why there has always been and continues to be, even in this scientifically and socially 'more advanced' time, tremendous resistance to the awakening process. Gurdjieff claimed that there are actual planetary forces that inhibit attempts to become more conscious, an idea paralleled in some Gnostic teachings where these forces are termed 'archons'. The science-fiction film *The Matrix* was based on this idea, where the inhibiting forces were personified as the 'Agents'.

Concerning the Moon, Gurdjieff's idea that humanity is 'food for the Moon' has been frequently lampooned. (One respected psychiatrist studying Gurdjieff's theory remarked, reasonably it must be said, 'how can anyone subscribe to such nonsense?'). At first glance, the theory does seem absurd, and it should be pointed out that Gurdjieff basically stopped teaching it several years before he opened the Institute in Fontainebleau in 1922. His idea was that the Moon is 'evolving' and gets its energy from the Sun and Earth and that the Moon 'controls' all negative events on Earth. It can probably best be understood as a symbol for the lowest dimension. In that way, it would correspond to more mythic and psychological interpretations of lunar symbolism, which usually regard the Moon as being representative of the unconscious mind and its primitive and chaotic impulses (a meaning commonly found in the Tarot, for example).

Kundabuffer: This was Gurdjieff's term for a special organ that, according to his protagonist, Beelzebub, was once placed in human beings at the base of their spine. It had the effect of keeping humans spiritually and psychologically closed, inwardly contracted, mechanical, unconscious, and practically blind—in essence, enslaved. The organ was introduced in humans by a 'higher power' with a specific intention, which was to keep us from seeing our actual condition, that being merely 'food for the Moon'. It was thought that if humans saw their actual condition it would be too much for them and so the organ Kundabuffer was introduced to prevent us from seeing the cold reality of the situation. It can be, in that sense, regarded as a buffer against seeing deeper truths. A close analogy for this can be seen in *The Matrix* films where humans are attached to pods, fed, and implanted with computer programs that enable them to live in a fantasy world—never realizing their true condition, which is simply to serve as a power source (a 'human battery') for the machines that control the world.

Gurdjieff said that the 'organ Kundabuffer' was, in fact, removed from humans a long time ago but that the effects continue to linger, preventing humanity from waking up. Another way of understanding this is by the way the ego-mind keeps us asleep via its extraordinary ability to remain distracted by the trivial and mundane and to derive apparent satisfaction from this. There is a teaching in Buddhism to the effect that 'only one who has truly suffered has the motivation to awaken'. If, however, we fail to see our suffering we have no motivation. Kundabuffer is an apt symbol for that element of the ego that blocks us from seeing the 'terror of the situation'—our *true* and *actual* suffering that is inherent in our condition. In effect, it dupes and numbs us into accepting the mundane, mediocre, and worthless, and more, into believing we are unworthy of seeing beyond this.

There is something of a relation between Gurdjieff's idea of Kundabuffer and the Hindu idea of *kundalini*. The latter is regarded in most Hindu yogic schools as a subtle energy or force that resides 'coiled up' at the base of the spine. This force can be awakened by yogic and meditation exercises so we are told, resulting in a speed-up of our overall spiritual evolution. Gurdjieff, however, took a dim view of *kundalini* saying that it was merely the force of imagination—the strange ability we humans have to 'dream that we are awake'. My own understanding of what he is saying there is that awakening is not about cultivating altered states of consciousness. These are side-tracks or what the Zen tradition calls *makyo*—impressive phenomena that naturally arise in meditation practice but which are to be discarded. During Gurdjieff's time, occultism, spiritualism (mediumship), and what today is known as parapsychology were all increasingly in vogue, something like an earlier version of the 1980s New Age decade. Accordingly, he sought to downplay the notion of altered states of consciousness and rightfully saw it as a major distraction from deeper states of awakening.

Hasnumuss: A Hasnumuss was Gurdjieff's term for a person who is innately destructive, or as he described it, lacks 'Objective-Conscience'. A Hasnumuss is similar in some ways to what Crowley called a 'Black Brother'. They are driven by the compulsion to destroy others and derive satisfaction from leading others astray.

Hanbledzoin: The 'blood' of the Kesdjan (astral) body. It is vital energy, animal magnetism, and may be understood as a natural force that emanates from a healthy, balanced, powerful individual. Gurdjieff claimed to have this force in abundance; he also claimed that certain powers arise naturally from this force such as the ability to hypnotize (or capture the attention of others) as well as read the minds of others. He further said that he consciously renounced these powers in 1911 in order to develop other aspects of his being. A rough analogy would be a wealthy person giving away their wealth in order to experience the lessons that come with hardship.

Heropass: This was Gurdjieff's term for 'time'. According to Bennett, it is a compound of the Greek terms *hero* ('holy one') and *pass* (the masculine form of 'All'), thus meaning 'The Holy One who is All'. Gurdjieff would refer to it as the 'merciless Heropass', a reference to the flow of time and the inevitable running down of all things (similar to the Buddha's teachings on impermanence). Gurdjieff taught that by working on oneself it is possible to 'overcome the merciless Heropass'—that is, overcome the limitations of time.

Kesdjan: Gurdjieff's term for the 'astral' body or subtle energy body. Most esoteric traditions recognize this as a body comprised of a type of energy that is at present beyond the capacity of our sciences to detect.

Trogoautoegocrat: This term is used by Beelzebub to describe the 'Law of Reciprocal Maintenance'. The basic idea behind it is that 'being' and 'time' are, in their natural state, mutually destructive. Modern physics makes reference to this in its idea of entropy, which has to do with the idea that things energetically run down given enough time (from hot to cold, from organized to disorganized, and so on). This whole process is counteracted by the universe 'eating itself' so to speak. Substances and energies are exchanged throughout the cosmos—organisms survive by eating other organisms thereby holding off the naturally decaying effects of time. Put simply, the universe is an affair of mutuality, giving and receiving. To engage this process is to gain energy, to avoid it is to lose energy.

Triamazikamno: The Law of Three. See Chapter 5.

Heptaparaparshinokh: The Law of Seven. See Chapter 5.

Djartklom: A complex term that implies a few things: it is a force that divides Okidanokh (see below) into three essential parts— affirming, denying, reconciling—giving us the opportunity to 're-blend' these three within us and in so doing, achieve a higher state of consciousness. Such awakenings can occur spontaneously— walking in nature for example, and suddenly feeling alive and vividly present—but usually we then shift to mere enjoyment instead of using it as an opportunity to form the wish that we do not want to return to being asleep again. This is connected to the idea of 'remorse of conscience', a type of inner anguish brought about by an intense realization of how asleep we have been.

Etherokrilno: This is the formless basis of all material in the universe. A rough equivalent in Hindu terminology would be *akasha*.

Okidanokh: The cause behind all phenomena, the active element. A Hindu parallel would be *prana*.

Common Father Endlessness: The Source of All.

For a couple of years, between 1999 and 2001, I was part of a private and informal online group of researchers from around the world engaged in study of the so-called 'secret history' of the human race.

This involved looking into ancient scriptures and texts from Sanskrit, Sumerian, and Hebrew sources amongst other things. In the course of this research, we inevitably looked at some of the more speculative and radical ideas such as those of Zecharia Sitchin, Immanual Velikovsky, William Bramley and others. Sitchin and Velikovsky in particular have had dubious reputations with academic historians and scientists and indeed, much of their linguistic, historical, and astronomical speculations do not hold up well to scientific rigor.

Nevertheless, while examining some of Sitchin's interpretations of the ancient Sumerian records, I was struck by some similarities I found between them and Gurdjieff's cosmological ideas as presented in *Beelzebub*. As to whose is the older writing there can be no question. Sitchin was not born until 1922; his first book, the highly successful *The 12ᵗʰ Planet*, was originally published in 1976. Since then he has written a series of works outlining his theories.[2] There is no evidence that Sitchin was ever aware of Gurdjieff. The correlations are striking and interesting to note in part because Gurdjieff claimed that the Sarmoung Brotherhood (the legendary esoteric society that allegedly trained him) originated in Babylon circa 2500 BC. Sitchin claimed that his sources were the Sumerian records dating from roughly the same time.

Cosmology in *Beelzebub's Tales to His Grandson*

In the distant past, when the solar system is young, a civilization exists on Mars. At that time, a large comet-like body named Kondoor of a 'vast orbit' enters the solar system for the first time. Owing to errors in calculations by 'Sacred Individuals' (advanced intelligences) who deal in matters of 'world creation and maintenance', Kondoor intersects Earth's orbit too closely and a collision ensues. The result of the violent encounter is that two fragments of Earth break off.

As a result of the disaster, a commission of highly advanced beings headed by an archangel named Sakaki are dispatched to the solar system. A complex series of events follows involving sacred substances and special commissions by the overseeing protectors of Earth. The larger of the two fragments broken off from Earth, named Loonderperzo, later becomes our present day Moon. The second much smaller fragment currently goes undetected though it was known by the civilization that existed on Atlantis, and went by the name Kimespai, meaning 'never allowing one to sleep in peace' (perhaps an obscure reference to the potential lethal power of a colliding asteroid or comet).

Beelzebub reports that this occurred in extremely ancient times and that, prior to the collision, Earth could easily be seen from Mars (i.e. was closer). Beelzebub continues by explaining that the Earth and the Moon's, now unstable orbits, could only be stabilized if they were supplied with the sacred substance 'Askokin'. In order to produce this substance, Earth requires the existence of certain intelligent beings (humans) who are duly created by the Archangel Sakaki. At this point in Gurdjieff's narrative, Beelzebub learns that the High Commission decides that if the created humans were ever to discover the humble purpose of their existence they may destroy themselves en masse. In order to guard against this possibility, an Archangel implants the organ *Kundabuffer* into all humans at the base of the spine. This organ serves to keep humans basically limited in consciousness so they can never know their origins and the truth that the substance they produced was more important than they were.

There is then a twist of irony in Gurdjieff's tale. At a certain point, the substance no longer needs to be produced and the organ *Kundabuffer* is removed from all humans. However, because humanity has been plagued for so long by the effects of this organ, a memory imprint has crystallized, and the negative effects continue.

Sitchin's Thesis

During the Solar System's 'youth' (aged between five hundred million to one billion years old) an intruder planet appears (named

Nibiru by the Sumerians and Marduk by the Babylonians). Nibiru enters the solar system in a retrograde orbit. Its first close encounter is with Neptune where Sitchin speculates that a 'bulge' in Nibiru was torn away to become Neptune's moon Triton. The next encounter is with Uranus where the result is the formation of Uranus's four major moons and that planet's unusual orbital tilt. Passing within the orbits of Saturn and Jupiter, Nibiru's orbital path is permanently altered. In its interaction with the Saturnian system, a moon of Saturn is dislodged and after making a convoluted journey, ends up in the outer reaches of the solar system to become the planet Pluto.

Nibiru continued inward from Jupiter toward the planet the Sumerians named Tiamat. According to Sitchin, the Sumerian records maintain that, at the time of the original arrival of Nibiru, Tiamat was a young, unstable system complete with numerous moons, the largest of which was named Kingu. As Nibiru, along with its seven moons, approached the Tiamat system, a massive collision ensued. One of the Nibiruan moons smashed into Tiamat. In the encounter, all of Tiamat's small moons (except its larger moon Kingu) were redirected into new orbits becoming comets with elliptic, retrograde orbits. Kingu remains in orbit about the severely damaged Tiamat.

Nibiru continued around the Sun but was now trapped into a solar orbit. On a return orbit, Tiamat is hit again by another Nibiruan moon and broken in two. One half becomes Earth, orbited by Kingu, our present day Moon. The other half of Tiamat is crushed into numerous small pieces to become the 'hammered bracelet' or asteroid belt. On its way out the solar system, Nibiru has final encounters with Uranus, Neptune, and Pluto that result in alterations in their makeup and orbits. The Nibiruan orbital interval is 3,600 years.

Comparison #1:

Gurdjieff: Long ago Kondoor, a large body of a vast orbit, intrudes into the youthful solar system

Sitchin: Long ago Nibiru, a large body of a vast orbit, intrudes into the youthful solar system.

G: Kondoor collides with Earth.

S: The Nibiruan moons collide with Tiamat (Earth in the past).

G: When Kondoor strikes Earth one major and one smaller chunk is broken off.

S: Earth is battered twice and the second time is broken in two.

G: Earth-Moon system is created as a direct result of the Kondoor interaction.

S: Earth-Moon system (half of Tiamat and Kingu) is created as a direct result of the Nibiruan interaction.

Comparison #2

Gurdjieff: An original catastrophe (from interaction between Kondoor and Earth) results in a situation where a special substance (askokin) is extracted from Earth for the purposes of stabilization (between Earth and its Moon with greater cosmic ramifications).

Sitchin: An original catastrophe (from an interaction between Nibiru and its moons and Tiamat/Kingu) results in a situation where a special substance (gold) is extracted from Earth for the purposes of stabilizing the situation on Nibiru.

G: The human race is created and allowed to evolve strictly for the purposes of generating this special crucial substance (askokin).

S: The human race is created strictly for the purposes of generating and expediting the creation of this special crucial substance (gold).

G: The human race is purely functionary, a 'cosmic cogwheel' that was not created for any portentous, divine cause.

S: The human race is purely functionary, a drone race originally designed to operate to serve a much greater cause (the Anunnaki or Nephilim, the Biblical 'fallen angels').

G: Certain of the Overseers (High Commission and one

Archangel) deem humanity unqualified and incapable of understanding their ultimate purpose for existing on Earth. Things are concealed, with far reaching consequences.

S: It is implicit that certain of the Overseers (Anunnaki) deem humanity as subservient and unqualified to understand its true origins and not deemed worthy of true freedom. Things are concealed, with far reaching consequences.

There are some differences (Sitchin connects our moon to Kingu, former satellite of Tiamat), but the collision, change in orbit, and downsizing of Earth, are in both his and Gurdjieff's accounts. Also, the mysterious second fragment blown off from Earth, referred to by Beelzebub as 'Anulious' is similar to Sitchin's 'Hammered Bracelet' asteroid belt.

The ultimate message of Gurdjieff's writing was wholly concerned with the end of enslavement and his entire life work was based on devising inner psycho-spiritual methods to overcome the effects of this 'enslavement'. Sitchin was not concerned with such matters. Though the details of their cosmologies are different, the similarity of the themes between the Gurdjieffian and Sitchinesque models of the history of the solar system makes one wonder about a common mythic-archetypal origin.

Sitchin's work has been heavily discredited by scientists and many of his ideas are believed to be irreconcilable with the known laws of physics (though he himself often denies this). Gurdjieff's work is accepted to be pure fiction, a spiritual allegory. When we discard the astrophysical elements of their respective models, we're left with the main common denominator that humanity is the pawn of an older race. That is an ancient theme echoed in many world mythologies, one that can be seen as a powerful metaphor for Gurdjieff's central idea that in our present state we are incapable of *doing* because we are incapable of *being*. That is, we have no real free will, and are thus in effect controlled by forces around us. World myths tend to personify these forces as gods or aliens, but whether these gods or aliens exist is secondary to the main issue of our own unconsciousness and inner enslavement.

Appendix IV
Osho, John Dee, and the Greatest Library in the World

Osho was, without question, the most literate Eastern guru in memory—and possibly the most well read mystic ever. From his teenage years, he began collecting books and by the time he was twenty years old he was already very well read. Throughout his college years, both as an undergraduate and later as a philosophy professor, his collection continued to grow. Near the end of his life in the late 1980s, it was estimated to be around 100,000 volumes. Osho himself mentioned the figure of 150,000. The Danish professor Pierre Evald, who is also a disciple of Osho's, did a study of Osho's library and estimated the actual number to be closer to 80,000.[1] He reports that about 70,000 of these have been read, signed and dated by Osho. The remaining 10,000 have been gathered since 1987 at which point Osho was no longer reading (he said in an interview in 1985 that he'd basically stopped reading in 1981).

For a private library, the figure of 80,000 is extraordinarily large (and indeed, Evald suggested that it may be the largest private collection in the world). As a point of comparison, an entire main library in a mid-sized city might hold around a million books, barely ten times more than Osho's collection.[2] The most important library of the ancient world, in Alexandria in northern Egypt, is estimated to have had a collection of several hundred thousand scrolls. However, an entire piece of writing—what we would now call a 'book'—could take several scrolls to contain and so the actual number of 'books' in the Alexandria library would have been smaller, perhaps around 100,000, similar to the size of Osho's library. The Alexandrian library was famously destroyed in a series of calamities, most notably in what are suspected to have been burnings instigated by Julius Caesar (accidentally), a fourth century Christian bishop (intentionally) and a seventh century Muslim Caliph (intentionally).

In England in the late 16th century, during the time of Queen Elizabeth I and Shakespeare, the largest library in the country (and possibly all of Europe) belonged to the queen's court astrologer, advisor, and magus, John Dee. He had around 4,000 volumes.[3] Much of this collection was eventually destroyed by a mob, convinced that Dee was a conjurer of spirits. He was, amongst other things, but what today would be regarded as 'channeling' unfortunately was, in those days, highly suspect and possible grounds for being burnt at the stake. Dee survived, but alas, many of his books didn't.

To give some idea of the impressiveness of Dee's collection, the main library at Cambridge University in the late 16th century only had about 450 books in all.[4] In fact, Dee's library was the true academic center of England at his time and was known to have received visits from a number of notable people, including the queen herself. As for content, his collection reflected the fact that he was a Renaissance magus: he had works on science (he was one of the leading mathematicians, cartographers, and navigators of his time), as well as the complete works of the major Greek philosophers, the Neoplatonists, poetry, theology, alchemy, magic, and so on.

Osho may not have been a conjurer of spirits (at least in the classic sense) and nor was India's head of state sufficiently open to use him as an advisor,[5] but one thing he did have in common with Dee was that he was a man with a universal outlook and (especially in his younger years) an interest in reading anything of quality he could get his hands on.

Osho said that for much of his life he read twelve hours per day, sometimes eighteen hours.[6] This again is reminiscent of Dee who famously recorded that he allowed himself only four hours sleep a night, two hours for eating and other essentials, and eighteen hours a day for study. Assuming that Pierre Evald's estimate is accurate and that Osho had read about 70,000 volumes of his collection; and assuming that Osho was reading consistently from around ages fifteen to fifty (that is, around 1946 to 1981 when he gave up reading) then that would suggest that in roughly 35 years he read about 2,000 books per year—or, around six books per day. And when it's considered that he did not actually retain a copy in his collection of every book he read—Evald reports that there are libraries in northern India that still have Osho's name on them as the only person who ever borrowed the book—then we can safely assume that the number he read is even higher. Osho was a known speed reader and it was reported by those close to him, who used to supply him with books, that he was devouring between ten and fifteen per day. So the above figures would indeed seem to be legitimate.

Any way it is looked at, Osho's accomplishment in this realm is extraordinary. Evald—in his critically researched and balanced study—simply calls him 'the greatest bookman of India and the most voracious reader worldwide in the 20th century.' He further claims that Osho actually read between 150,000 and 200,000 books in his lifetime. That indeed translates as his followers claimed to between twelve and fifteen books a day over thirty-five years. Even if we use a 'low' figure of ten books per day, this works out to about a book per hour of available reading time. The average book is about 60,000-80,000 words long. This means Osho's speed reading amounted to at least 1,000 words per minute. The average reader can comprehend and retain about 150-300 words per minute; high achievers can approach 600 words per minute. Speed readers, however, are capable of spectacular rates: the current record holder is a man named Howard Berg who can read (if you can believe it) 25,000 words per minute.[7] He has been repeatedly tested on this and demonstrated his ability to actually recall in detail what he reads. That rate is sufficient to read the Bible in half an hour and Leo

Tolstoy's *War and Peace* in just over 20 minutes.

Sam, in *Life Of Osho*, reports that in the mid-1970s Osho was a 'recluse'. He ominously notes, 'After the morning lecture he went back into his house...and stayed alone in his room. No one knew what he did there.'[8] Perhaps the mystery is hereby solved. However, the most remarkable paradox about Osho has always been the substance of his teachings: emphasizing Being, heart, mindfulness, the body—but never the intellect. And yet there he was, with one of the most extraordinary intellects of any mystic ever—and a bibliophile to top it off.

Shortly before Osho died, he gave specific instructions for his library: no more than three books to be lent out at any given time. It appears as if he left his body with at least one remaining worldly attachment.

Appendix V
Resources

Osho

There is a tremendous amount of material published crediting Osho as author—approximately six-hundred and fifty titles as of 2010. They are transcriptions of thousands of lectures he gave daily from 1968-1981 and from 1985 to 1989. Because they are transcriptions, they generally have a conversational tone to them and tend to make for easy reading. Highly recommended is *Autobiography of a Spiritually Incorrect Mystic* (St. Martin's Griffin, 2000), a compilation of talks where Osho delves into his life story and work. In addition to his books, Osho is a popular presence on Internet video sharing sites such as YouTube where a number of his lectures (both in English and Hindi) as well as some media interviews from 1985 can be viewed. Watching the videos is valuable. Osho was very personally impressive in a way that cannot be fully captured via his books, audio CDs, or photos. There are several quality websites dedicated to his work:

www.osho.com (the website of the Osho Resort in Pune, formerly Osho's main ashram)
www.sannyas.net
www.oshoworld.com
www.sannyasnews.com
www.oshoviha.org
www.rebelliousspirit.com

Gurdjieff

Gurdjieff's writings comprise the following:

The Herald of Coming Good (This book was written in 1932, after Gurdjieff had completed his main three works, and first published in 1933. He later repudiated it).

Beelzebub's Tales to His Grandson

Meetings with Remarkable Men

Life is Real, Only Then, When I Am

Views from the Real World: Early Talks of G.I. Gurdjieff (A compilation of talks)

Approved by Gurdjieff: *In Search of the Miraculous* by P.D. Ouspensky

The 'Gurdjieff International Review' is an excellent website full of useful information connected to Gurdjieff, his work, and a number of his students:

www.gurdjieff.org

This page in particular lists the contact URLs for all Gurdjieff Foundation websites:

http://www.gurdjieff.org/foundation.htm

Crowley

Crowley was a prolific author. Below are listed some of his more well known works:

The Collected Works of Aleister Crowley. Crowley's early prose and poetry.

Liber AL vel Legis: The Book of the Law. His key text, received by him in 1904 in Cairo with the aid of his wife at the time, Rose Kelly. The text can also be found included within other books, most notably the more recent editions of *Magick* (see below), as well as the excellent *Portable Darkness: An Aleister Crowley Reader* (edited with commentary by Scott Michaelson)

The Law is for All

The Vision and the Voice

Magick: Liber ABA: Book 4, Parts I-IV (includes Magick in Theory and

Practice)
The Confessions of Aleister Crowley
Eight Lectures on Yoga
The Diary of a Drug Fiend
Moonchild
The Book of Lies
The Holy Books of Thelema
777 and Other Qabalistic Writings
Magick Without Tears
The Book of Thoth

The website for the Ordo Templi Orientis is
www.oto.org
To contact the A.˙.A.˙.
Chancellor
BM ANKH
London WC1N 3XX ENGLAND
Other sites of interest:
http://lib.oto-usa.org (site for many of Crowley's texts in online
format)

Appendix VI
Biographical Accounts

The amount of material published on these three men and aspects of their work is vast; although curiously, beyond the year 2000, there has not been much put out on them. Most of the works below were published in the last quarter of the 20th century. What follows is nothing like a precise list, merely one writer's subjective appraisal of some of the best works on these men and their ideas.

Crowley:

Everyone who knows something of Crowley knows that many harsh things have been written about him, but that trend has been gradually turning around, beginning with Regardie's efforts, and increasing with several objective studies that came out around the turn of the 21st century. The trend will probably continue in that direction as more people look to his ideas than to the endless interpretations of his behavior.

The Confessions of Aleister Crowley, by Aleister Crowley, edited by John Symonds and Kenneth Grant. (Originally published in 1929 by Mandrake Press; more recently in 1989 by Penguin Arkana as a 950 page trade paperback.) The detailed autobiography (or 'autohagiography' as Crowley called it) of a deeply controversial magus and philosopher. The book only covers the first forty-eight years or so of

Crowley's life, up till the end of the Abbey of Thelema, but it may be safely said that the majority of his most interesting experiences and significant work took place during these years. Not only did Crowley live a fascinating life, cramming into it adventures that most men would require at least two or three lives to experience, he is also an excellent writer, making this a thoroughly enjoyable read. The only drawback is the length, but it is the kind of narrative that can be picked up at any point as Crowley frequently goes into lengthy digressions. This is an invaluable document, the rare case of a genuine and controversial mystic telling his own story in detail. It ranks up there with St. Augustine's *Confessions*, Jean-Jacques Rousseau's *Confessions*, and Adi Da Samraj's *The Knee of Listening*.

The Legend of Aleister Crowley, by Israel Regardie and P.R. Stephenson (first published in 1930 by Mandrake, most recent printing in 1990 by New Falcon). To my knowledge, this was the first of the many Crowley 'biographies'; although to be more precise it is really a collection of many press reviews written about Crowley in the early part of the 20th century, along with commentaries and rebuttals by Stephenson and Regardie. Most of the press reviews back then were of course critical of the Beast, and some were written in such a way that it is hard to keep a straight face reading them. Stephenson (he wrote most of the book) is to be commended, however, for recognizing Crowley's genius and for having the courage to respond to his many lazy critics. Regardie's Introduction to the book, written in 1969, is full of his usual forthright manner and opinionated vehemence that always makes him great fun to read.

The Great Beast: The Life and Magick of Aleister Crowley, by John Symonds (originally published in 1951, just a few months after the repeal in the U.K. of the Witchcraft Act). Colin Wilson referred to this book as an 'appalling classic'. Symonds met Crowley late in his life and was appointed his literary executor by the old magus. He came largely to reject both Crowley the man and his doctrine of Thelema.

Symonds died in 2006 at the age of ninety-two. The general historical consensus is that Crowley blundered badly by appointing the initially enthusiastic but eventually unsympathetic Symonds his literary executor, although it may in fact be that Symonds was the best candidate to keep Crowley's name from disappearing entirely from the public radar, by emphasizing his notoriety. The 1951 edition of *The Great Beast* avoided discussion of matters like sex magick, owing to the times; a revised paperback version including such matters appeared in 1973, and the book was re-issued again in 1989 with a new title *The King of the Shadow Realm*. Israel Regardie referred to Symond's *The Great Beast* as 'a disgusting book...a malicious, contemptible piece of work crammed with deliberate misinterpretation and ignorant misunderstanding of what Crowley stood for.' (*The Legend of Aleister Crowley*, p. vi). Regardie's sentiments aside, most Crowley scholars or committed Thelemites recognize the importance of Symonds' work.

Aleister Crowley: The Man, the Mage, the Poet, by Charles R. Cammell, 1951, reprinted in 1962. The book was issued again in 1969 with a new lurid title, *Aleister Crowley: The Black Magician*.

The Magick of Aleister Crowley, by John Symonds (Muller, 1958). This was Symonds' attempt at conveying some of Crowley's ideas related to the inner work, in particular sex magick, drawing on Crowley's private diaries and letters.

The Beast, by Daniel P. Mannix (Ballantine Books, 1959). A lurid and tabloid-esque biography. The blurb on the front cover of Mannix's 1959 original edition makes no bones about where the author stands: 'The scandalous life of Aleister Crowley, who practiced sex-magick and worshipped Satan, founded a religion based on drugs and debauchery, and branded his wives and drove them insane.' Scott Michaelson aptly called this book 'stupid fun.'

The Eye in the Triangle: An Interpretation of Aleister Crowley, by Israel Regardie (New Falcon, 1970, most recent reprint 1993). This is probably the most interesting of all the biographies of Crowley (although it does not cover his whole life), mostly because of Regardie's personal experience with the man, but also because of Regardie's useful psychological insights. Robert Anton Wilson's Introduction to the book is great fun. Regardie begins the book with an assault on John Symonds and Daniel Mannix, Crowley's two most hostile biographers. It was Regardie's book that stemmed the tide of negative Crowley commentaries on his life and began the trend toward a deeper and more sympathetic view of the Beast.

The Magical World of Aleister Crowley, by Francis King (Coward, McCann & Geoghegan (1978). A shorter and much more sympathetic take on the Beast compared to Symonds' work, and the second one up to that point to attempt a biography of his entire life. King, like Regardie, was also a practitioner of the inner work.

Portable Darkness: An Aleister Crowley Reader, edited by Scott Michaelson (Harmony Books, 1987; reprinted by Solar Books, 2007). Not a biographical work, but rather a collection of key Crowley writings (including the full text of *The Book of the Law*) with insightful and witty commentaries by Michaelson, including an introduction by Robert Anton Wilson.

Aleister Crowley: The Nature of the Beast, by Colin Wilson (Aquarian Press, 1987; reprinted by Aeon Books in 2005). A short biography, written with Wilson's idiosyncratic blend of scepticism and genuine mystical interest. The book has been found wanting by those truly interested in Crowley's life and ideas, but in Wilson's defense he has always written for the general intelligent reader—the armchair mystic—not the actual practitioner of transformational pathways. Writing for the armchair mystic should not be automatically disparaged, as many make such books their leaping off point onto a genuine search.

The Legacy of the Beast: The Life, Work, and Influence of Aleister Crowley, by Gerald Suster (W.G. Allen, 1988; reprinted by Weiser in 1990). Suster's was arguably the first of the full length appraisals of Crowley's life that was reasonably fair and balanced (Regardie's writings did not cover all of Crowley's life). This book has been criticized as being *too* sympathetic, but something like this was clearly needed after decades of exaggerated vilification of the Beast.

The Magick of Aleister Crowley: A Handbook of Rituals of Thelema, by Lon Milo DuQuette (originally published in 1993 by Weiser Books, reprinted with a slight change to the title in 2003). DuQuette is that rare beast, an occultist who is also an excellent writer. He has great affection for Crowley and an outstanding ability to render difficult ideas into simple form. Crowley wrote over the head of the average reader—DuQuette 'downsteps' the magus in such a way as to make him digestible. What Ouspensky did for Gurdjieff, DuQuette has done for Crowley.

The Beast 666: The Life of Aleister Crowley, by John Symonds, 1997. I'm guessing this release was designed to capitalize on the turn-of-the-millennium hype that many in the new age subcultures were caught up in during the late 1990s. Symonds was not a supporter of Crowley's work, to put it mildly.

Aleister Crowley: The Great Beast Demystified, Roger Hutchinson, 1998. This book is largely an indictment of Crowley, and like most such treatments, the research is lazy, geared more toward confirming the author's previously made up mind about his subject. Nevertheless, it is worth mentioning for two reasons—one, for someone sufficiently unattached to the matter and with a connoisseur's appreciation of the Theatre of the Absurd elements of Crowley's life, the book can be a source of amusement, and two, it is always good to confront one's attachments. On occasion, reading writings that seem to be gratuitously critical can be a good opportunity to examine one's reaction and see how much of it is sourcing from an emotional attachment to one's object of hero-worship. In the end, one aspiring to be inwardly free has to free themselves of that as well, and criticism (in whatever direction it is sent) can be invaluable in that regard.

Do What Thou Wilt: A Life of Aleister Crowley, by Lawrence Sutin (St. Martin's Griffin, 2000). The author claims that he spent a decade researching and writing this book, and it shows. This is probably the most comprehensive of all biographies on the Beast (along with Richard Kaszynski's), written with a nice balance of objectivity and sympathy. A necessary basic volume for any serious student of Crowley's life.

A Magick Life, by Martin Booth (Hodder and Stoughton, 2000). A sound biography. Like Sutin, Booth was a writer, not a mystic or occultist, but his approach is sympathetic and his distance from his subject allows for a pleasing objectivity.

Perdurabo, by Richard Kaczynski, (New Falcon, 2002). As far as I know, this is the second biography of Crowley by an actual practitioner of his teachings (after Gerald Suster's), and the first full-length effort. Kaczynski is also a first rate scholar, always a rare and welcome bonus. For any interested in actually practicing some of Crowley's teachings and related disciplines, this is the biography of choice. (The book is being issued in a revised edition by North Atlantic Books in 2010).

Understanding Aleister Crowley's Thoth Tarot Deck, by Lon Milo DuQuette, 2003. Another excellent work by DuQuette. The title is somewhat understated, as the book covers more ground than just Crowley's famous tarot deck.

Secret Agent 666: Aleister Crowley, British Intelligence, and the Occult, by Richard Spense (Feral Publishing, 2008). An interesting attempt to shed light on the long speculated espionage activities of Crowley. Unfortunately despite extensive and sincere research, the book ultimately relies mostly on inference and speculation, as the author was unable to secure any substantial documentation that would have truly confirmed Crowley's activities in this area. Additionally I have to opine that any work that emphasizes Crowley's secondary activities (confirmed or not) misses the point of what his life and work was about.

The Weiser Concise Guide to Aleister Crowley, by Richard Kaczynski (Weiser Books, 2009). This is the Coles Notes version of Kaczynski's *Perdurabo*. The best short primer for anyone curious to find out more about the Beast and his ideas.

Initiation in the Aeon of the Child: The Inward Journey, by J. Daniel Gunther (Ibis Books, 2009). Not a biographical work but deserves to be mentioned all the same for the intelligent assessment of Crowley's ideas it provides, along with many original insights by the author. The material is advanced but Gunther writes with elegant skill that makes it digestible.

Aleister Crowley and Dion Fortune: The Logos of the Aeon and the Shakti of the Age, by Alan Richardson (Llewellyn Publications, 2009). A short comparative study of Crowley and Fortune, written with style and wit, although as the author freely admits, he prefers the 'Shakti of the Age'.

Gurdjieff:

In Gurdjieff's case, a number of books have appeared over the years written by students or observers of his life but most do not qualify as truly biographical, being instead commentaries on aspects of his teaching, or personal memories of specific times spent with him.

651

Below are some of the better works on the man and his life:

In Search of the Miraculous: Fragments of an Unknown Teaching, by P.D. Ouspensky, (Harcourt, Brace, Javonovich, 1949). Not a biography but requires mention anyway, by virtue of it being the best overall summary of Gurdjieff's ideas from the earlier stages of his teaching. Although Gurdjieff is quoted extensively throughout the book, the wording is in a style that is Ouspensky's and the book is more properly a reconstruction of Gurdjieff's ideas by Ouspensky. Ouspensky is a lucid writer and his description of his meeting in a Moscow café in 1915 on a 'noisy but not central street' with a man 'of an oriental type, no longer young, with a black mustache and piercing eyes,' is a classic of spiritual literature.

Teachings of Gurdjieff: A Pupil's Journal, by C. S. Nott (Arkana, 1961). One of the first and best accounts of life with Gurdjieff by a direct student of the master. The writing is honest, straightforward, and engrossing.

The Unknowable Gurdjieff, by Margaret Anderson (Arkana, 1962). A small book but an honest and captivating memoir of the author's days with Gurdjieff in the latter part of his teaching career.

Gurdjieff: A Very Great Enigma, by John Bennett (1963; revised edition published in 1984 by Samuel Weiser): This is only marginally a biography, a slim volume of 90 pages, being a collection of three lectures given by Bennett in England in 1963. At the time of these lectures, Bennett was in his mid-sixties and was passing on his knowledge of Gurdjieff's earlier years. Of all of Gurdjieff's first generation students, he was without question the most meticulous analyst of both Gurdjieff the man, and his teachings.

Our Life With Mr. Gurdjieff, by Thomas and Olga de Hartmann (Penguin Books, 1964): This is a slim volume but an important work, documenting the close relationship between a master and two of his most devoted students. Of all the accounts on Gurdjieff's life, this one probably has the most heart.

Boyhood With Gurdjieff, by Fritz Peters (Dutton, 1964; most recent reprint by Arete Communications, 2006). A classic, with the author reminiscing affectionately about his boyhood growing up at Gurdjieff's commune in Fontainebleau.

Gurdjieff Remembered, by Fritz Peters (Gollancz, 1965). A further memoir by Peters. This is the one where he recounts an outlandish (and almost certainly hugely distorted) account of the meeting between Gurdjieff and Crowley in 1926.

Journey Throughout This World: Meetings With Gurdjieff, Orage, and Ouspensky, by C.S. Nott (Weiser Books, 1969). Nott's continuing reflections on his time in the Work. The book was reprinted in 1984 by Red Wheel/Weiser with the new title *Further Teachings of Gurdjieff: Journey Through This World Including an Account of Meetings With G. I. Gurdjieff, A. R. Orage and P. D. Ouspensky*. Nott's books are to be particularly commended for their sincere concern with the matter of personal transformation above all else.

Gurdjieff: Making a New World, by John Bennett (Harper and Row, 1973): An excellent and comprehensive overview of Gurdjieff's life and teachings. For a man who according to his wife 'wrote with difficulty', Bennett was as prolific as Crowley, which says a great deal.

The Harmonious Circle: The Lives and Work of G.I. Gurdjieff, P.D. Ouspensky and Their Followers, by James Webb (G.P. Putnam, 1980; reprinted by Shambhala Publications in 1987): A substantial work, over six-hundred pages. Webb labored on it for a long time then committed suicide the year it was released at thirty-four years of age. The book is diligently researched and intelligently written, but the citations are sporadic; in many cases, Webb provides no sources for controversial information that he reports. The writing is at times insightful, at other times meanders and contains a bit too much speculation. All the same it is a valuable work, probably the greatest single attempt by a scholar outside of the Gurdjieff tradition to analyze the phenomenon of the master, his associates, and his work.

Gurdjieff: A Master in Life, by Tcheslaw Tchekhovitch (Dolman, 1990, reprinted in 2006). The author was one of Gurdjieff's original Russian students; he died in 1958.

Idiots in Paris: Diaries of J.G. Bennett and Elizabeth Bennett, 1949, by J.G. Bennett and Elizabeth Bennett (Weiser Books, 1991). A fascinating account of Gurdjieff's last days in Paris in 1949 and of the ritual feasts and Idiot toasts that were a unique part of his teaching toward the end.

Gurdjieff: Anatomy of a Myth, by James Moore (Element Books, 1991): Alongside Bennett's and Patterson's work, this is without doubt the most comprehensive and accurate of the Gurdjieff biographies, and the best one by a writer who was not a first generation student of Gurdjieff. It is very well researched with an extensive notes section. As with Webb's work, this is a substantial book, not a one-nighter.

Struggle of the Magicians: Why Uspenskii Left Gurdjieff (William Patrick Patterson, Arete Communications, 1996). An excellent account of the interplay between Gurdjieff and his most famous student between the years 1914-1949. Patterson is a committed second generation Gurdjieff student and has written several interesting books on his root-master. This book is written in a linear fashion in which pivotal global events of the first half of the 20th century are interspersed within the narrative about Gurdjieff and 'Uspenskii' (the spelling Patterson uses). The book also has an interesting final chapter on

Uspenskii, Orage, and Bennett, and an excellent notes section.

Gurdjieff and Orage: Brothers in Elysium, by Paul Beekman Taylor (Weiser Books, 2001). An engrossing study of the relationship between Gurdjieff and his important student A. R. Orage, drawing on numerous private letters written by Orage and his mate Jesse Dwight. The author was present at Gurdjieff's apartment in the late 1940s.

Gurdjieff: The Key Concepts, by Sophie Wellbeloved (Routledge, 2003). A highly useful reference work, basically an extended glossary of all important ideas taught by Gurdjieff. A concluding section gives a helpful biographical synopsis of many of Gurdjieff's key students.

Gurdjieff: An Introduction to His Life and Ideas, by John Shirley (Tarcher/Penguin, 2004): A somewhat more popularized treatment of Gurdjieff's life. Shirley is a polished writer. This is a worthy companion to Moore's, Patterson's, and Bennett's books, and probably the best of the lot for anyone looking for a basic primer.

Self-Observation: The Awakening of Conscience, by Red Hawk (Hohm Press, 2009). This book does for Gurdjieff's practical ideas and methods what J. Daniel Gunther's book did for Crowley's ideas: an excellent and up to date interpretation and useful application that if studied closely can yield powerful insights.

Osho

The situation with biographies on Osho is, quite frankly, on more precarious footing than it is with either Gurdjieff or Crowley. This is because the Osho biographies have, thus far, tended to be heavily polarized—written either by disgruntled ex-followers with axes to grind and journalists incapable of seeing Osho in anything but an essentially sinister light—or by devoted disciples who naturally viewed Osho as fundamentally irreproachable in terms of his ideas and words and actions. In the case of the latter, it is usually Osho vs.

Big Governments, Rotten Religions, and the World; a type of latter day passion play. One book penned in the late-1980s by Juliet Forman, a close disciple of Osho, was titled: *Bhagwan: One Man Against the Whole Ugly Past of Humanity*. By now the title may seem rather over the top, but at the time it was a very accurate rendition of how the majority of his committed followers regarded him. One work that did come close to providing a truly objective look at Osho and his movement was *The Way of the Heart* by the anthropologists Judith Thompson and Paul Heelas, published in 1988 (see below), but it was too short and written too soon to be anything like a comprehensive biography.

The simple truth is that a detached, balanced, and comprehensive biography of Osho and his work—along the lines of James Moore's *Gurdjieff: Anatomy of a Myth*, James Webb's *The Harmonious Circle*, or Lawrence Sutin's *Do What Thou Wilt: A Life of Aleister Crowley*—has not yet been written. Doubtless such biographies will come in the future; Osho's stature as one of the most important spiritual teachers of the 20th century clearly warrants it. Devoted followers of Osho may rue the day when the scholars begin to reinterpret Osho through the cooler and broader lens of history, but in some cases distance is indeed needed for greater clarity. The true seeker of trans-formation will always have to go beyond mere scholarly appraisal, but many cannot *reach* this jumping off point without first having that clear and unbiased study. The intelligent scholar thus functions as an important medium for many who are close to embarking on the path of inner Work.

Most of the works below are no longer in print, but most can be obtained in second hand form from Amazon.

The Mystic of Feeling: A Study in Rajneesh's Religion of Experience, by Dr. Ram Chandra Prasad (Motilal Banarsidass, 1970). One of the first, if not *the* first, assessment of Osho's work by a non-disciple. From my travels in India, I still have my yellowing copy of *The Mysteries of Life and Death*, by Acharya Rajneesh, first published in 1971; on the back of that book it mentions Dr. Prasad's book with the following summation that is interesting to read: 'This book offers in reasonable compass an enlightening analysis of the teachings of Bhagvan (sic) Rajneesh. It shows that while some of his great teachings are essentially the same as those found in Zen Buddhism and Krishnamurti, it goes beyond them in his keen awareness of the new and not-so-new problems of Sex and Indian Politics...'

Lead Kindly Light: Some Enlightened Moments with Bhagwan Shree Rajneesh by Ma Yoga Kranti (Jeevan Jagruti Kendra, 1972). One of the first books published about Osho by a disciple, written during his days in the Mumbai apartment in the early 1970s. Jeevan Jagruti Kendra ('Life/Soul Awakening Center') was the name of Osho's first spiritual organization formed in the 1960s when he went by Acharya Rajneesh; it was mostly dedicated to organizing his talks and meditation camps in numerous Indian cities, and publishing his lectures in small booklets. (In 1974, the name was changed to Rajneesh Foundation).

I Am the Gate, by Osho (first published by Ishwarlal N. Shah in 1973, with numerous reprints). I read this book sometime around 1980 as a young university student and it was for me at the time (along with Ouspensky and Castaneda) the proverbial 'mind-blower'. Osho's early works were his esoteric ones. In this one, in addition to incisive descriptions of the enlightened condition, Osho delved into wild matters like the occult links between the Tibetan Buddhists and the Nazis. The very title of the book 'I Am the Gate' is reminiscent of Jesus' 'I am the Way' and reflects the guru-centric approach (*surrender* to me) Osho took in his early years of teaching—an approach he decisively rejected in the last few years of his life.

Dimensions beyond the Known, by Osho (Rajneesh Foundation, 1975). An interesting collection of talks Osho gave in the late 1960s and early 70s. This, along with his book *I Am the Gate*, is the most esoteric of all his publications, delving heavily into such topics as his (claimed) last incarnation in Tibet in the 13th century AD, secret occult forces, the tasks of spiritual masters, the true nature of enlightenment, and so on. It all makes for heady reading and has the scent of innocence and youthful exuberance about it, reflecting a time in Osho's meteoric career that came before the deep disappointments and sufferings he passed through in the mid-1980s, after which he famously pronounced, 'esoteric is *bool-sit.*'

Dying for Enlightenment: Living with Bhagwan Shree Rajneesh, by Bernard Gunther (Harper & Row, 1979). A rather ironic title in retrospect. Most of the books written on Osho did not come until after the Oregon commune demise; during the late 1970s, the atmosphere of his movement was full of promise and excitement about the future. This book was written by a disciple and describes in detail some of the deep transformational work going on in the Pune ashram at that time.

Drunk on the Divine: An Account of Life in the Ashram of Bhagwan Shree Rajneesh, by Ma Satya Bharti (Grove Press, 1980). A devoted account by a close disciple at the time; the title is self-explanatory. (This book was published by Wildwood House in England with the title *The Ultimate Risk*.)

Death Comes Dancing: Celebrating Life With Bhagwan Shree Rajneesh, by Ma Satya Bharti (Routledge, 1981). Another work by Satya Bharti. The same author, going by Satya Bharti Franklin, would write a much more objective and critical account a decade later (see below).

The Awakened One: the Life and Work of Bhagwan Shree Rajneesh, by Vasant Joshi (Harper & Row, 1982). This book was, to my knowledge, the first attempt at a complete biography of Osho's life up to that point. It was written prior to the Oregon years, so is naturally missing the highly dramatic final decade of Osho's life. The author is a *devotee*, a term usually given to the most loyal and committed disciple of a guru. The book is out of print and I long ago lost my copy but as I recall it was certainly written in devotee fashion: in this case, intelligent, well crafted, and deeply supportive throughout.

Life as Laughter: Following Bhagwan Shree Rajneesh, by Bob Mullan (Routledge & Kegan Paul, 1983). The best and certainly the funniest of the many 1980s accounts of Osho and his work by a non-disciple. True to the title of the book, the author writes with great humor (granted, that could be easily done in the more innocent times prior to the '85 commune debacle). A couple of amusing examples:

> *Lady Zara, 33, travelled to India and joined the free love ashram of…*
> *Bhagwan…Lady Zara informs me that she now wishes to be known as*
> *Ma Preem [sic] Pratiti, which sounds like number 38 on a Tandoori*
> *menu…*
> *In 1979 I met my first rajneeshee, in Cambridge. 'I've even got orange*
> *underwear,' he boasted proudly. His name was unpronounceable. 'What*
> *do you believe in?' I asked him innocently. 'Nothing, man, it's a gas.'*

Glimpses of a Golden Childhood, Tao Publishing, 1985. Based on a series of informal talks Osho gave in the early 1980s documenting events from his early life. This is the only book in which Osho talks in depth about his childhood and early adulthood. Especially interesting are the sections in which he speaks of some of the spiritual mentors he had, a topic that he otherwise rarely spoke of. A number of excerpts from this are reprinted in *Autobiography of a Spiritually Incorrect Mystic*.

Rajneeshpuram and The Abuse of Power, by T.L. Schay (Scout Creek Press, 1985). I do not recall reading this book back in the '80s but the title is presumably self-explanatory as to its content.

Bhagwan: The God that Failed, by Hugh Milne, Caliban Books, 1986. This book was, to my knowledge, the first of the semi-autobio-graphical accounts of life before, with, and after Osho, by an erstwhile close follower. It is also by the far the most critical. Milne was a former disciple who turned against his master in a manner somewhat reminiscent of Andrew Cohen's falling out with his guru Harilal Poonja. Milne's work was of course castigated by most Osho disciples when it first came out, a time in the late 1980s when Osho was still alive. I did not like the book either when I read it back then. However, re-reading it with the benefit of two decades of hindsight, I think it's probable that Milne was unfairly maligned to some degree. He wrote it too soon after his bitter disappointments in Oregon and this shows in the axe-grinding feel of much of the book, yet parts of it at least are written with a certain common sense intel-ligence and make more sense now than they did a quarter of a century ago. The major weakness of the book is that it almost completely ignores the transformational element of being with a guru—which is, after all, the main point of being a disciple in the first place. Unquestionably, the title of the book is absurd, as Osho certainly never claimed to be a 'God'.

The Rajneesh Story: The Bhagwan's Garden, by Dell Murphy (Lindwood Press, 1986). A sympathetic account of Osho's Oregon days by a non-disciple. (The annoying habit journalists had of referring to Osho as 'the' Bhagwan, rather than simply 'Bhagwan,' is repeated in the title of the book—sure a sign as any that the author was not a disciple).

The Golden Guru: The Strange Journey of Bhagwan Shree Rajneesh, by James S. Gordon (Stephen Green Press, 1987). Generally considered to be one of the best 'objective' books written by a non-disciple. It is arguable of most gurus that their work cannot really be *deeply* under-stood by an outsider (that is, by one who has not been formally initiated as a disciple), owing to the importance of the connecting link between master and disciple. That idea has, of course, been wildly abused at times, but it still carries merit, much as it does in any domain of life (and, of course, it is also true that one too close to their subject suffers visual distortions as well). Gordon was a psychiatrist and observer of Osho's life and work (although also very sympathetic) and so naturally his view is from some distance, a fact that helps in some ways, and hinders in others.

Bhagwan: The Most Godless Yet The Most Godly Man, by George Meredith (Rebel Publishing, 1987). Another in the slew of books published in 1987. Meredith was Osho's personal doctor and one of his most loyal disciples. He was present with Osho when the master died in 1990. In 1991, he published an excellent summary of some of Osho's core ideas (see below).

The Ultimate Game: The Rise and Fall of Bhagwan Shree Rajneesh, by Kate Strelley (HarperCollins 1987). This book is comparable to Hugh Milne's, being written by a disaffected former disciple.

Bhagwan Shree Rajneesh: The Most Dangerous Man Since Jesus Christ (Rebel Publishing, 1987) and *Was Bhagwan Shree Rajneesh Poisoned by Ronald Reagan's America?* (Rebel Publishing, 1988), both by Sue Appleton. The titles of the books say it all—devotional accounts written by a close disciple during the intense and traumatic times following the collapse of the Oregon commune and Osho's bizarre 'world tour'.

The Way of the Heart: The Rajneesh Movement, by Judith Thompson and Paul Heelas (Borgo Press, 1988). This little book is largely an undiscovered gem. Written by two intelligent anthropologists who were remarkably sympathetic to Osho, it is a scholarly appraisal of his ideas and work. The concluding chapter, in which the authors provide the pros and cons of the matter of the Oregon commune, is worth the price of the book alone. It would have been interesting to have seen Thompson and Heelas wait a few years longer and write a larger work, but what they did put together is still valuable, even if not written from the point of actual participants in transformational work.

Bhagwan: the Buddha for the Future; Bhagwan: Twelve Days That Shook the World; and *Bhagwan: One Man Against the Whole Ugly Past of Humanity;* all by Juliet Forman (Rebel Publishing House, 1988-1990): Of all the books written by disciples and ex-disciples describing Osho's life and work, these three books are the most ambitious. Taken together, they amount to 1,500 pages and half a million words—longer than Gurdjieff's monument *Beelzebub*. Juliet Forman, who went by the name Maneesha, was a close disciple of Osho's and one of his most faithful. That said, she was no mindless follower but an intelligent woman and dedicated chronicler and her books are worth reading for one willing to invest the time. She, in all likelihood, gives the most technically accurate account concerning the 'who did what' of the highly controversial days leading up to the collapse of the Oregon commune in 1985 and its immediate aftermath. That said, she may have been too close and too attached to her master to be able to write in a purely objective fashion. Nevertheless, I recommend her books if for no other reason than the fascinating account they give of a life in the immediate inner circle of a profound and deeply controversial figure. No comparable work exists on the lives of Gurdjieff or Crowley by close students. In Gurdjieff's case in particular, all accounts written by his students usually only cover small slices of his life; Forman captured a very large chunk of Osho's story.

The Choice is Ours: The Key to the Future, by George Meredith (Rebel Publishing, 1991). Written by Osho's personal physician, this small book is an intelligent and lucid presentation of some of Osho's core ideas. What Ouspensky did for Gurdjieff and DuQuette for Crowley, Meredith does for Osho—with the only fault being, in my opinion, that the book is far too short.

The Promise of Paradise: A Woman's Intimate Story of the Perils of Life with Rajneesh, by Satya Bharti Franklin (Station Hill, 1993): A long and involving read, it is more properly the author's autobiography than a biography of Osho, but because she was a close disciple of his during some of the most dramatic years of his work, the book also amounts to a good summary of the last half of Osho's life. This book is probably the most absorbing of the various accounts written by former Osho disciples, and in some ways the most honest.

Diamond Days with Osho: The New Diamond Sutra, by Ma Prem Shunyo (Motilal Banarsidass, 1993): This one reads in a tone similar to Forman's books, although is less a work of history and more a personal memoir. Her book probably gives the most interesting account of Osho's last days.

A Passage to America: a Radically New Look at Bhagwan Shree Rajneesh and a Controversial American Commune, by Max Brecher (Book Quest, 1993). This is an interesting work and unfortunately no longer in print. Brecher did extensive research and interviewed many people, ultimately concluding that a deep conspiracy existed at high levels of government and organized religion to persecute Osho.

The Rajneesh Papers: Studies in a New Religious Movement, by Susan J. Palmer and Arvind Sharma (Motilal Banarsidass, 1993). An academic appraisal, dry but informative in places.

One Hundred Tales for Ten Thousand Buddhas, by Ma Dharma Jyoti (Shamsunder Singh, 1994). A devotionally oriented book written by one of Osho's very earliest disciples who had been initiated by him in 1970. It's a recounting of memories with her master told in present tense. If there could be said to be one book written about Osho that is polar opposite in tone to Hugh Milne's work it would probably be this one.

Life of Osho, by Sam, 1997, Sannyas Press: This is my personal favorite of the biographies written about Osho by his 'first-wave' disciples, those that were with him in Pune during the heady days of the 1970s. 'Sam' was the pen-name of Swami Paritosh, an English disciple of Osho who passed away in 2009. Paritosh did not accompany the Osho caravan from Pune to Oregon in the early 1980s and so he lacked first-hand experience of the American phase of the experiment. However, he more than makes up for that with his excellent account of the Pune ashram in the 1970s, and his commentaries on Osho's last days. He wrote his account in a very informal style as if chatting with the reader in a coffee house (which is part of its effectiveness). The book is full of good insights and has a balanced feel to it. His small book is, in my estimation, the best single attempt to see Osho in a truly human and balanced light. As of this writing, the book is available for free online, at
www.lofo.connectfree.co.uk/info.html

Hellbent for Enlightenment, 1998, White Cloud Press, by Rosemary Hamilton: A cogent and faithful rendering of a disciple's years with her master. Rosemary Hamilton had been Osho's private cook for several years, a trusted position, and she had direct access to many of the intimate goings-on in the organization. Compared to most of the other disciples who wrote accounts of their years with Osho, Hamilton was older, already past sixty when the dramatic Oregon events unfolded; add to that, she waited longer before writing her account. This extra life experience shows as hers is, in my opinion, the best of the 'I was there' accounts by one of Osho's inner circle. She is introspective and does not merely portray everything with 'us vs. them' duality, and yet neither does she show any signs of resentment. She never loses sight of the deeper reality that Osho's communes were, first and last, mystery schools in which to confront one's own mind, to 'know thyself'.

Autobiography of a Spiritually Incorrect Mystic, by Osho (St. Martin's

Press, 2000). Despite Osho's voracious reading, he famously never wrote a single book—all of his (as of this writing) over six-hundred and fifty books in print were faithfully transcribed by disciples, based on his numerous lectures spanning two decades. This book is no exception; despite the title of 'autobiography', it was not compiled by Osho, having been published ten years after he died. That said, it is a meticulously constructed book by nameless devoted disciples, accurately documenting much of Osho's life based largely on his own words. An indispensible resource for those wanting a fleshed-out, reasonably objective perspective of his life, and especially one that is chronologically in order.

Bibliography

Anderson, Margaret, *The Unknowable Gurdjieff* (Penguin Arkana, 1991).

Avabhasa, Da, *The Heart's Shout: The Liberating Wisdom of Da Avabhasa* (Sri Love-Anandashram, 1993).

Bakan, David, *Sigmund Freud and the Jewish Mystical Tradition* (Schocken Books, 1965).

Batchelor, Stephen, *The Awakening of the West* (Parallax Press, 1994).

Beck, Charlotte Joko, *Everyday Zen: Love and Work* (Harper and Row, 1989).

Bennett, J.G., *The Masters of Wisdom* (Turnstone Press, 1982).

Bennett, J.G., *Witness: The Story of a Search* (Turnstone Press, 1983).

Bennett, J.G., *Gurdjieff: A Very Great Enigma* (Samuel Weiser, 1984).

Bennett, J.G., *Gurdjieff: Making a New World* (Bennett Books, 1992).

Bennett, J.G. and Bennett, Elizabeth, *Idiots in Paris: Diaries of J.G. Bennett and Elizabeth Bennett, 1949* (Samuel Weiser, 1991).

Booth, Martin, *A Magick Life* (Hodder and Stoughton, 2001).

Brecher, Max, *A Passage to America* (Book Quest, 1993).

Brunschwig, Jacques and Lloyd, Geoffrey E.R., *A Guide to Greek Thought* (Harvard University Press, 2003).

Butterfield, Stephen T., *The Double Mirror: A Skeptical Journey into Buddhist Tantra* (North Atlantic Books, 1994).

Carswell, John, *Lives and Letters* (New Directions Books, 1978).

Cicero, Chic, and Cicero, Sandra Tabatha, *The Essential Golden Dawn: An Introduction to High Magic* (Llewellyn Publications, 2003).

Cohen, Andrew, *My Master is Myself: The Birth of a Spiritual Teacher* (Moksha Press, 1989).

Cohen, Andrew, *Autobiography of an Awakening* (Moksha Foundation, 1992).

Cohen, Andrew, *An Unconditional Relationship to Life* (Moksha Press, 1995).

Conger, John P., *Jung and Reich: The Body as Shadow* (North Atlantic Books, 1988).

Cooper, Rabbi David, *God is a Verb: Kabbalah and the Practice of Mystical Judaism* (Riverhead Books, 1997).

Crowley, Aleister, *The Confessions of Aleister Crowley* (Penguin Arkana, 1979).

Crowley, Aleister, *Diary of a Drug Fiend* (Weiser, 1996).

Crowley, Aleister, *The Book of Lies* (Weiser, 1986).

Crowley, Aleister, *Magick Without Tears* (New Falcon Publications, 1994).

Crowley, Aleister, *Magick: Book Four, Liber ABA* (Weiser Books, 1998).

Crowley, Aleister, *Book 4* (Weiser Books, 1980).

Crowley, Aleister, *777 and other Qabalistic Writings of Aleister Crowley* (Weiser Books, 1986).

Crowley, Aleister, *The Book of Thoth* (Samuel Weiser, 1992).

Crowley, Aleister, *The Law is For All* (Thelema Media, 1996).

Crowley, Aleister, with Neuberg, Victor B., and Desti, Mary, *The Vision and the Voice* (Red Wheel/Weister, 1998).

de Hartmann, Thomas and Olga, *Our Life with Mr. Gurdjieff* (Penguin Books, 1972).

Del Campo, Gerald, *The Heretic's Guide to Thelema* (Megalithica Books, 2008).

Deida, David, *The Way of the Superior Man* (Sounds True, 1997).

DuQuette, Lon Milo, *The Magick of Aleister Crowley: A Handbook of Rituals of Thelema* (Weiser Books, 2003).

DuQuette, Lon Milo, *Understanding Aleister Crowley's Thoth Tarot* (Weiser Books, 2003).

Fairfield, Richard, *Communes USA: A Personal Tour* (Penguin Books, 1972).

Fontana, David, *Is There an Afterlife? A Comprehensive Overview of the*

Evidence (O-Books, 2005).

Forman, Juliet, *Bhagwan: The Buddha for the Future* (Rebel Publishing, 1990).

Forman, Juliet, *Bhagwan: One Man Against the Whole Ugly Past of Humanity* (Rebel Publishing, 1990).

Fortune, Dion, *Psychic Self-Defence* (Samuel Weiser, 1997).

Fortune, Dion, *The Mystical Qabalah* (Weiser Books, 1998).

Franck, Frederick, *Zen and Zen Classics* (Vintage Books, 1978).

Franklin, Satya Bharti, *The Promise of Paradise* (Station Hill Press, 1992).

Freke, Timothy, and Gandy, Peter, *The Hermetica: The Lost Wisdom of the Pharaohs* (Piatkus Publishers, 1997).

French, Peter, *John Dee: The World of an Elizabethan Magus* (Ark Paperbacks, 1987).

Feuerstein, Georg, *The Encyclopedic Dictionary of Yoga* (Paragon House, 1990).

Feuerstein, Georg, *Wholeness or Transcendence? Ancient Lessons for the Emerging Global Civilization* (Larson Publications, 1992).

Feuerstein, Georg, *Holy Madness: Spirituality, Crazy-Wise Teachers, and Enlightenment* (Hohm Press, 2006).

Feuerstein, Georg, *Tantra: The Path of Ecstasy* (Shambhala Publications, 1998).

Greer, John Michael, *The Long Descent* (New Society Publishers, 2008).

Grof, Christina, and Grof, Stanislav, *The Stormy Search for the Self* (Jeremy P. Tarcher, 1990).

Gunther, J. Daniel, *Initiation in the Aeon of the Child: The Inward Journey* (Ibis Books, 2009).

Gurdjieff, G.I., *The Herald of Coming Good* (The Book Studio, 2008).

Gurdjieff, G.I., *Beelzebub's Tales to His Grandson* (Viking Arcana, 1992).

Gurdjieff, G.I., *Meetings with Remarkable Men* (Penguin Compass, 2002).

Gurdjieff, G.I., *Life Is Real Only Then, When I Am* (Penguin Arkana,

1999).

Gurdjieff, G.I., *Views from the Real World* (Penguin Arkana, 1984).

Hamilton, Rosemary, *Hellbent For Enlightenment* (White Cloud Press, 1998).

Hixon, Lex, *Coming Home: The Experience of Enlightenment in Sacred Traditions* (The Putnam Publishing Group, 1989).

Hogue, John, *Nostradamus: The Complete Prophecies* (Element Books, 1999).

Horney, Karen, *Neurosis and Human Growth* (W.W. Norton and Company, Inc., 1991).

Hutchinson, Roger, *Aleister Crowley: The Beast Demystified* (Mainstream Publishing, 1998).

Hutton, Ronald, *The Triumph of the Moon: A History of Modern Pagan Witchcraft* (Oxford University Press, 2001).

James, William, *The Varieties of Religious Experience* (Barnes and Noble Classics, 2004).

Jensen, Ferne, ed., *C.G. Jung, Emma Jung and Toni Wolff, A Collection of Remembrances* (The Analytical Club of San Francisco, 1982).

Jung, C.G., *Man and His Symbols* (Dell Publishing, 1962).

Jung, C.G., *Aion* (Princeton University Press, 1978).

Jung, C.G., *Mysterium Coniunctionis* (Princeton University Press, 1989).

Kaczynski, Richard, *Perdurabo* (New Falcon Books, 2002).

Kaczynski, Richard, *The Weiser Concise Guide to Aleister Crowley* (Red Wheel/Weiser, 2009).

Kapleau, Roshi Philip, *The Three Pillars of Zen* (Anchor Books, 2000).

Kaufman, Walter, *The Portable Nietzsche* (Penguin Books, 1982).

Kripal, Jeffrey J., *Esalen: America and the Religion of No Religion* (The University of Chicago Press, 2007).

Krishna, Gopi, *Kundalini: The Evolutionary Energy in Man* (Shambhala Publications, 1970).

Layton, Bentley, *The Gnostic Scriptures* (Doubleday, 1995).

Lisiewski, PhD, Joseph C., *Ceremonial Magic and the Power of Evocation* (New Falcon Publications, 2006).

Maharshi, Ramana,*Talks With Sri Ramana Maharshi* (Inner Directions, 2000).

Martin, Benjamin F., *France in 1938* (Louisiana State University Press, 2005).

Masters, Robert Augustus, *The Way of the Lover* (Xanthyros Foundation, 1989).

Mathers, S.L. MacGregor, editor, *The Key of Solomon the King,* (Dover Publications, 2009).

Mathers, S.L. MacGregor, translator, Crowley, Aleister, editor and introduction by, *The Goetia: The Lesser Key of Solomon the King,* (Ordo Templi Orientis, 1997).

Mathers, S.L. MacGregor, translator, *The Book of the Sacred Magic of Abramelin the Mage,* (Dover Publications, 1975).

Maxwell-Stuart, P.G. , *The Chemical Choir: A History of Alchemy* (Continuum Books, 2008).

Messadié, Gerard, *A History of the Devil* (Kodansha International, 1996).

Milne, Hugh, *Bhagwan: The God That Failed* (Caliban Books, 1986).

Mitchell, Stephen, translator, *Tao Te Ching* (HarperPerennial, 1988).

Moore, James, *Gurdjieff: Anatomy of a Myth* (Element Books, 1991).

Moore, Robert (Red Hawk), *Self Observation: The Awakening of Conscience* (Hohm Press, 2009).

Naydler, Jeremy, *Shamanic Wisdom in the Pyramid Texts: The Mystical Tradition of Ancient Egypt* (Inner Traditions, 2005).

Needleman, Jacob (editor), *The Sword of Gnosis: Metaphysics, Cosmology, Tradition, Symbolism* (Arkana, 1986).

Nott, C.S., *Teachings of Gurdjieff: A Pupil's Journal* (Penguin Arkana, 1990).

Nydahl, Lama Ole, *Riding the Tiger: Twenty Years on the Road: The Risks and Joys of Bringing Tibetan Buddhism to the West* (Blue Dolphin Publishing, 1992).

Osho, *Autobiography of a Spiritually Incorrect Mystic* (St. Martin's Griffin, 2000).

Osho, *From Sex to Superconsciousness* (Full Circle Publishing, 2008).

Osho, *I Am the Gate* (Harper and Row, 1977).

Osho, *Meditation: The First and Last Freedom* (St. Martin's Griffin, 2004).

Osho (Bhagwan Shree Rajneesh), *Notes of a Madman* (Rajneesh Foundation International,1985).

Osho, *Communism and Zen Fire, Zen Wind* (Rebel Publishing House, 1989).

Osho, *The Book of Understanding* (Harmony Books, 2006).

Osho, *The Book of Woman* (Penguin Books, 2002).

Osho, *Meditation: The Art of Ecstasy* (Tao Publishing, 2006).

Osho, *Tao: The Three Treasures, Volume I* (Rajneesh Foundation International, 1983).

Osho, *Books I have Loved* (Tao Publishing, 2005).

Osho, *Tantra: The Supreme Understanding* (Rebel Publishing, 1991).

Osho (Bhagwan Shree Rajneesh), *I Teach Religiousness not Religion* (Rebel Publishing House).

Ouspensky, P.D. , *In Search of the Miraculous: Fragments of an Unknown Teaching* (Harcourt Brace Jovanovich, Inc., 1949).

Ouspensky, P.D., *Tertium Organum: A Key to the Enigmas of the World* (The Book Tree, 2004).

Palmer, Susan J., and Sharma, Arvind, *The Rajneesh Papers: Studies in a New Religious Movement* (Motilal Banarsidass, 1993).

Patterson, William Patrick, *Eating the 'I'* (Arete Communications, 1992).

Patterson, William Patrick, *Struggle of the Magicians: Why Uspenskii Left Gurdjieff* (Arete Communications, 1996).

Patterson, William Patrick, *Taking With the Left Hand: Enneagram Craze, People of the Bookmark, and the Mouravieff Phenomenon* (Arete Communications, 1998).

Patterson, William Patrick, *Voices in the Dark: Esoteric, Occult, and Secular Voices in Nazi-Occupied Paris 1940-1944* (Arete Communications, 2000).

Patterson, William Patrick, *The Life and Teachings of Carlos Castaneda* (Arete Communications, 2008).

Peters, Fritz, *Gurdjieff Remembered* (Samuel Weiser, 1971).

Peters, Fritz, *Boyhood with Gurdjieff* (Arete Communications, 2006).

Plato, *The Republic* (Dover Publications, 2000).

Plato, *The Last Days of Socrates* (Penguin Books, 2003).

Plotinus, *The Enneads* (Penguin Classics, 1991).

Rabelais, Francois, *The Five Books of Gargantua and Pantagruel* (Random House, 1944).

Rawlinson, Andrew, *The Book of Enlightened Masters: Western Teachers in Eastern Traditions* (Carus Publishing, 1997).

Regardie, Israel, and Stephenson, P.R., *The Legend of Aleister Crowley* (New Falcon Publications, 1990).

Regardie, Israel, *The Eye In The Triangle: An Interpretation of Aleister Crowley* (New Falcon Books, 1993).

Reich, Wilhelm, *Character Analysis* (Farrar, Straus, and Giroux, 1990).

Rinpoche, Dzogchen Ponlop, *Wild Awakening: The Heart of Mahamudra and Dzogchen* (Shambhala Publications, 2003).

Robbins, Rossell, *The Encyclopedia of Witchcraft and Demonology* (Crown Publishers, 1959).

Sam, *Life of Osho* (Sannyas Press, 1997).

Schoch, Robert, *Voices of the Rocks* (Harmony Books, 1999).

Scholem, Gersholm, *Kabbalah* (Penguin Books, 1978).

Segal, Suzanne, *Collision with the Infinite: A Life Beyond the Personal Self* (Blue Dove Press, 1996).

Seldes, George, *The Great Thoughts* (Ballantine Books, 1996).

Shah, Idries, *A Perfumed Scorpion*, (Octagon Press, 1978).

Sheldrake, Rupert, *The Sense of Being Stared At and Other Aspects of the Extended Mind* (Hutchinson, 2003).

Shirer, William L., *The Rise and Fall of the Third Reich: A History of Nazi Germany* (Ballantine Books, 1983).

Shunyo, Ma Prem, *Diamond Days with Osho* (Motilal Banarsidass, 1993).

Sitchin, Zecharia, *The 12th Planet* (Avon Books, 1978)

Sitchin, Zecharia, *Genesis Revisited* (Avon Books, 1990).

Smoley, Richard, *Forbidden Faith: The Gnostic Legacy from the Gospels* to *The DaVinci Code* (HarperSanFrancisco, 2006).

Storr, Anthony, *Feet of Clay: A Study of Gurus* (HarperCollins, 1997).

Suster, Gerald, *The Legacy of the Beast: The Life, Work, and Influence of Aleister Crowley* (Samuel Weiser, 1990).

Sutin, Lawrence, *Do What Thou Wilt: A Life of Aleister Crowley* (St. Martin's Griffin, 2000).

Sutin, Lawrence, *All Is Change: The Two-Thousand Year Journey of Buddhism to the West* (Little, Brown, and Company, 2006).

Swimme, Brian, and Berry, Thomas, *The Universe Story* (HarperCollins, 1994).

Taylor, Paul Beekman, *Gurdjieff and Orage: Brothers in Elysium* (Weiser Books, 2001).

Thring, M. W., *Quotations from G.I. Gurdjieff's Teaching* (Luzac Oriental, 2002).

Thomson, Garrett, *On Gurdjieff* (Wadworth, 2003).

Thompson, Judith and Heelas, Paul, *The Way of the Heart: The Rajneesh Movement* (The Borgo Press, 1988).

Tracol, Henri, *The Search for Things that are True* (Element Books, 1994).

Trungpa, Chogyam, *Crazy Wisdom* (Shambhala Publications, 1991).

Trungpa, Chogyam, *The Lion's Roar: An Introduction to Tantra,* (Shambhala Publications, 1992).

Vaughn-Lee, Llewellyn, *The Face Before I was Born* (The Golden Sufi Center, 1998).

Vivekananda, Swami, *Raja Yoga* (Ramakrishna-Vivekananda Center, 1982).

Yates, Francis, *The Rosicrucian Enlightenment* (Routledge & Kegan Paul, 1972).

Yates, Francis, *Giordano Bruno and the Hermetic Tradition* (University of Chicago Press, 1991).

Yukteswar, Swami Sri, *The Holy Science* (Self-Realization Fellowship, 1990).

Waggoner, Robert, *Lucid Dreaming: Gateway to the Inner Self* (Moment Point Press, 2009).

Waite, Dennis, *The Book of One* (O Books, 2004).

Waite, Dennis, *Back to the Truth: 5000 Years of Advaita* (O Books, 2007).

Walker, Kenneth, *A Study of Gurdjieff's Teaching* (Award Books, 1969).

Wapnick, Kenneth, *Love Does Not Condemn: The World, the Flesh, and the Devil According to Platonism, Christianity, Gnosticism, and A Course In Miracles* (Foundation for *A Course In Miracles*, 1989).

Webb, James, *The Harmonious Circle: The Lives and Work of G.I. Gurdjieff, P.D. Ouspensky, and Their Followers* (G.P. Putnam's Sons, 1980).

Wellbeloved, Sophie, *Gurdjieff: The Key Concepts* (Routledge, 2003).

West, John Anthony, *The Serpent in the Sky: The High Wisdom of Ancient Egypt* (Quest Books, 1993).

Wilkinson, Toby, *Thames and Hudson Dictionary of Ancient Egypt* (Thames and Hudson Ltd., 2008).

Wilson, Colin, *The Outsider* (Jeremy P. Tarcher, 1982).

Wilson, Colin, *The Occult* (Grafton Books, 1972).

Wilson, Robert Anton, *Cosmic Trigger, Volume I* (New Falcon Publications, 1995).

Wilson, Robert Anton, *Sex, Drugs & Magick* (New Falcon Publications, 2008).

Woolly, Benjamin, *The Queen's Conjurer: The Science and Magic of Dr. John Dee, Advisor to Queen Elizabeth I* (Henry Holt and Co., 2001).

Notes

Chapter 1: Aleister Crowley: Wicked Magus

1. Aleister Crowley, *Diary of a Drug Fiend* (London: Samuel Weiser, 1996), p. 364. King Lamus is a character in the book based largely on Crowley himself. As for a physical description of Crowley as an adult, this extract from the British MI5 'black book' files is probably as good as any: 'Crowley, Aleister...height 5 ft. 11 in., age about 40, bald except for erect lock of hair on forehead; black eyes; athletic-looking, but air of effeminacy; plump soft hands; wears many rings.' (Richard Spense, *Agent 666: Aleister Crowley, British Intelligence, and the Occult*, Feral Publishing, 2008, illustration plate #14).

2. Israel Regardie, *The Eye In The Triangle: An Interpretation of Aleister Crowley* (Pheonix: New Falcon Books, 1993), p. XXIII.

3. Ibid, pp. X-XI.

4. Roger Hutchinson, *Aleister Crowley: The Beast Demystified* (Edinburgh: Mainstream Publishing, 1998), p. 5.

5. Israel Regardie and P.R. Stephenson, *The Legend of Aleister Crowley* (Las Vegas: New Falcon Publications, 1990), p. xi.

6. A good and thorough debunking of these can be found in Lon Milo DuQuette's *The Magick of Aleister Crowley: A Handbook of Rituals of Thelema* (San Francisco: Weiser Books, 2003), pp. 2-10.

7. As quoted by Robert Anton Wilson in his Introduction to Regardie's *The Eye In the Triangle*, p. XIII.

8. Aleister Crowley, *The Confessions of Aleister Crowley* (London: Penguin Arkana, 1979), pp. 42-43.

9. Crowley, *Confessions*, p. 172.

10. Lawrence Sutin, *Do What Thou Wilt: A Life of Aleister Crowley* (New York: St. Martin's Griffin, 2000), p. 4.

11. Yeats, from a letter to Thomas Sturge-Moore, 1925.

12. The best scholarly treatment of the period of intense Rosicrucian activity around the year 1600 is found in the works of Francis Yates, especially her *The Rosicrucian Enlightenment* (London & New York: Routledge & Kegan Paul, 1972).

13. Crowley, *Confessions*, p. 440.

14. Richard Kaczynski, *The Weiser Concise Guide to Aleister Crowley* (San Francisco, Red Wheel/Weiser, 2009) p. 23.

15. Sutin, *Do What Thou Wilt*, p. 157.

16. Crowley, *Confessions*, pp. 427-444.

17. Regardie and Stephenson, *The Legend of Aleister Crowley*, p. 91.

18. See
   http://web.archive.org/web/20040409082405/www.redflame93. com/Gardner.html, or Alan Richardson, *Aleister Crowley and Dion Fortune: The Logos of the Aeon and the Shakti of the Age* (Woodbury: Llewellyn Publications, 2009), pp. 177-184.

19. Gerald Suster, *The Legacy of the Beast: The Life, Work, and Influence of Aleister Crowley* (York Beach: Samuel Weiser, 1990), pp. 75-79.

20. Regardie and Stephenson, *The Legend of Aleister Crowley*, p. xii.

Chapter 2: G.I. Gurdjieff: Black Devil of Ashkhabad

1. William Patrick Patterson, *Eating the 'I'* (San Anselmo: Arete Communications, 1992, p. 36).

2. Colin Wilson, *The Occult* (London: Grafton Books, 1972, reprinted many times).

3. P.D. Ouspensky, *In Search of the Miraculous: Fragments of an Unknown Teaching* (Orlando: Harcourt Brace Jovanovich, Inc., 1949).

4. Gurdjieff had different passports over the years that gave different birth dates. The most common years given for his birth are 1872 and 1877. James Moore, in his comprehensive biography (*Gurdjieff: Anatomy of a Myth*) argued for 1866, and since the

publication of Moore's book in 1991, this date seems to have overtaken others, based on Moore's following points:

A. Gurdjieff claimed to be 78 years old in 1943, and 83 years old in 1949 (the year of his death).

B. The photos of him taken shortly before his death (in 1949) seem (to Moore) more like a man in his early 80s, rather than a man in his mid or early 70s.

C. Gurdjieff claimed that when he was a seven year old boy his father's cattle herd was wiped out by a plague. There was in fact a disastrous outbreak of cattle disease (rinderpest) in 1872-73 in Asia Minor.

D. Gurdjieff and his family arrived in the Turkish city of Kars not long after a Tsarist military victory in 1877, at a time when Gurdjieff already had four younger siblings.

E. This point is not mentioned by Moore, but it is worth listing: when Ouspensky first met Gurdjieff in 1915 in Moscow, he described Gurdjieff as a man appearing 'no longer young'. If Gurdjieff was born in 1877, he would have been 38 at the time of meeting Ouspensky; if born in 1872, then 43; and if born in 1866, he would have been 49. I think it safe to assume that 'no longer young' fits more closely with 43 or 49 rather than 38. Ouspensky himself was 37 at the time of this meeting; it is unlikely he would describe someone around his own age as 'no longer young'.

Gurdjieff did have a passport that gave his birth year as 1877, but as mentioned he had several passports, some with different dates—one indicated as early as 1864—and all of them he burned in 1930 before one of his trips to America. (see Patterson, *Struggle of the Magicians*, p. 216). While Moore's points are interesting, they are not foolproof, and he does appear to make one mistake. The counter-views are as follows:

A. The fact that Gurdjieff claimed a certain age for himself means little, as he was commonly known to have no fear of saying whatever he felt like saying at any given time, regardless if it was based in fact or not. Moore's first argument, that Gurdjieff claimed to be 78 in 1943, does not add up arithmetically—78 in 1943 would mean he was born in either 1864 or 1865, not 1866. And this appears to be Moore's mistake, because he states that one passport of Gurdjieff's listed his year of birth as the 'wildly discrepant 1864'—when Gurdjieff himself apparently stipulated this year (or 1865) when describing his age in 1943. Further, according to J.G. Bennett in his autobiography, he reports that Gurdjieff in January of 1949 claimed that he was now 80 years old. That would make his birth year 1869, not 1866. Bennett indicates that he believed Gurdjieff was not telling the truth, that in fact he was 'a good deal younger.' (See J.G. Bennett, *Witness: The Autobiography of John Bennett* (Wellingborough: Turnstone Press, 1983), p. 251.

B. The photos of Gurdjieff supposedly looking 83 years old could easily be pictures of a 72 or 77 year old man who had lived a very rugged life (which was certainly true in Gurdjieff's case). This was further suggested by the doctor who performed the autopsy on Gurdjieff's body, declaring that he should have died years before as most of his organs were in very poor shape.

C. Some video of Gurdjieff surfaced in the early 2000s on the Internet—mostly short silent clips of him interacting with students in public places during the last years of his life (1947-49). Examining those videos it is surprising to think that the short, portly man (as he was at the time) is in his early 80s. Very few overweight people live into their 80s. He moves around in a fairly nimble fashion that seems a bit quick for an 82 or 83 year old. (But he was, after all, a 'teacher of dance' as he liked to describe himself, and was clearly a very rugged man, so it is not impossible.)

J.G. Bennett favored 1872. In his book *Gurdjieff: A Very Great Enigma*, he wrote:

So far as I myself can make out from various sources, from what he himself and his family have told us, it does seem probable that he was born in 1872, in Alexandropol, and that his father moved to Kars soon after it was taken by the Russians, that is to say, somewhere about 1878, when he was six or so years old. (Bennett, 1963).

About ten years after that, Bennett wrote his loose biography of Gurdjieff (*Gurdjieff: Making a New World*) and had this to say:

The date of Gurdjieff's birth, as shown on his passport, was December 28th, 1877. He himself said he was much older and also claimed that he was born on January 1st old style. I have found it hard to reconcile the chronology of his life with the date of 1877, but his family asserts that this is correct. If this is so, he began his search at the early age of eleven, because he refers to the year 1888 as a time when new vistas opened up to him. He first went to Constantinople in 1891. He says he was a 'lad' at the time of this journey, so the dating is not obviously inconsistent. Nevertheless it does seem strange that, if he was born in 1877, he should not have mentioned that this occurred during the Russo-Turkish war. (Bennett, 1973).

Despite these misgivings, Bennett goes on to state:

In October of 1877, the city [of Kars] was in its last throes, and the tsar sent his brother, Grand Duke Nicholas, to lead the final assault. With an overwhelming superiority in numbers and armaments, the defenses were overrun on the night of November 17-18. Six weeks later, Gurdjieff was born in Gumru, already renamed Alexandropol in honor of the tsar's father. (Bennett, 1973).

So apparently Bennett either forgot that a decade before he'd declared Gurdjieff's probable year of birth as 1872, or he changed his view. Jeanne de Salzmann, Gurdjieff's chief administrator and designated leader of the world-wide Gurdjieff community, at his death in 1949, held to 1877.

All this is contradicted yet again in another of Bennett's books, his 1961 autobiography (*Witness: The Autobiography of John Bennett*), where he writes of his first meeting with Gurdjieff in 1920:

> It was only when he removed his kalpak after the meal that I saw his head was shaved. He was short but very powerfully built. I guessed that he was about fifty, but Mrs. Beaumont was sure that he was older. He told me later that he was born in 1866, but his own sister disputed this and affirmed that he was born in 1877. His age was as much as an enigma as everything else about him. (Bennett, 1961, p. 55).

That particular anecdote does not bode well for the 1866 date, as a man's sister would generally have little incentive for lying about such a thing, nor would she be likely to make such a large error as *eleven years* when estimating her older brother's age. (Although it is conceivable, if she was incompetent with arith-metic—i.e., an honest mistake.)

Finally, it bears mentioning here that one of the better more recent chroniclers of Gurdjieff and his Work, William Patrick Patterson (who has written several books and produced three good videos on the matter), weighs in with his vote for 1872. In the notes section of his *Struggle of the Magicians*, he remarks:

> I believe that Gurdjieff was born—not in 1877 nor in 1866—but in 1872. This is based on dates Gurdjieff gives in *Meetings with Remarkable Men*. (Patterson, 1996).

He then goes on to provide a series of arguments based on events in *Meetings* that easily counter Moore's arguments for 1866. Amusingly, he also notes that Olga de Hartmann, a close student of Gurdjieff's, always believed that he was older than the 1877 date, but was unable to prove it—despite the fact that her own passport listed her year of birth as 1896 when in fact she was born in 1885. At any rate, to me, the most logical date does indeed seem to be something closer to 1872, particularly judging from the video clips taken of Gurdjieff's last years. Bennett, though originally promoting this year, gives no real argument for it. Patterson (for 1872) and Moore (for 1866) seem to be the only researchers who provide reasonable arguments for their dates.

5. G.I. Gurdjieff, *Meetings with Remarkable Men* (London: Routledge Kegan Paul, 1963). Most recent reprint is by Penguin Compass, 2002.

6. For an interesting take on a possible connection between Gurdjieff's ideas and Castaneda's, see William Patrick Patterson, *The Life and Teachings of Carlos Castaneda* (Fairfax: Arete Communications, 2008).

7. Gurdjieff, *Meetings*, pp. 89-91.

8. Ibid., p. 99.

9. Ibid., p. 119.

10. Ouspensky, *In Search of the Miraculous*, p. 302.

11. James Moore, *Gurdjieff: Anatomy of a Myth* (Rockport: Element Books, 1991), p. 216.

12. P.D. Ouspensky, *Tertium Organum: A Key to the Enigmas of the World* (London: Kegan Paul, Trench and Trubner & Co., 1922). Most recent reprint is by The Book Tree, 2004.

13. William Patrick Patterson, *Struggle of the Magicians: Why Uspenskii Left Gurdjieff* (Fairfax, Arete Communications, 1996), p. 94.

14. G.I. Gurdjieff, *Beelzebub's Tales to His Grandson* (New York: Viking Arcana, 1992).

15. I myself can attest to the power of his idea of Objective Art, remembering my visits to sites such as the Taj Mahal, the Great Pyramid, the Sphinx, the Dome of the Rock in Jerusalem, Petra

in Jordan, and the Gothic Cathedral of Palma de Mallorca. The sheer power of these architectural forms is obvious, and the response I had to them seemed in accordance with Gurdjieff's teachings about the 'higher emotional body'. I found this especially so with the Dome of the Rock; Islamic mosques seemed to be originally designed with the intention to draw one's attention *up* toward the upper *chakras* of the subtle body.

16. www.gurdjieff.org/wright1.htm

17. John Carswell, *Lives and Letters* (New York: New Directions Books, 1978), p. 185.

Chapter 3: Osho: The Most Dangerous Man Since Jesus Christ

1. Sam, *Life of Osho* (London: Sannyas Press, 1997), p. 60.

2. According to High Milne, there is uncertainty about this. He claims that no one, not even his mother, really remembered the exact day or even year that Osho was born. See High Milne, *Bhagwan: The God that Failed* (Caliban Books, 1986), p. 110.

3. Anthony Storr, *Feet of Clay: A Study of Gurus* (London: HarperCollins 1997), p. xiii.

4. Osho, *Autobiography of a Spiritually Incorrect Mystic* (New York: St. Martin's Griffin, 2000), p. 25.

5. Vasant Joshi, *The Awakened One* (New York: Harper & Row, 1982), p. 27.

6. Bhagwan Shree Rajneesh, *I Teach Religiousness, not Religion* (Pune: Rebel Publishing House, 1988), p. 128.

7. A *koan* is a rationally insoluble statement or question—such as, 'Show me your face before your parents were born.' The idea is that when contemplating such a question one will eventually reach a point where the logical part of the mind 'gives up' and an epiphany follows, a deep intuition into the interconnectedness (or 'Oneness') of all things. This kind of breakthrough, if sufficiently profound, is called a *satori*, meaning 'sudden illumination'.

8. Suzanne Segal, *Collision with the Infinite: A Life Beyond the Personal Self* (San Diego: Blue Dove Press, 1996).

9. Osho, *Autobiography of a Spiritually Incorrect Mystic*, p. 63.

10. The entire description of Osho's enlightenment experience can be read in *Autobiography of a Spiritually Incorrect Mystic*, pp. 68-76.

11. Storr, *Feet of Clay*, pp. 49-50.

12. Osho, *Autobiography of a Spiritually Incorrect Mystic*, p. 62.

13. Roshi Philip Kapleau, *The Three Pillars of Zen* (New York: Anchor Books, 2000), p. 231.

14. Ibid., p. 254.

15. Lex Hixon, *Coming Home: The Experience of Enlightenment in Sacred Traditions* (New York: The Putnam Publishing Group, 1989), p. xi.

16. Osho, *Autobiography of a Spiritually Incorrect Mystic*, p. 89.

17. Ibid., p. 136.

18. Osho, *From Sex to Superconsciousness* (New Delhi: Full Circle Publishing, most recent printing 2008).

19. Ouspensky, *In Search of the Miraculous*, p. 227.

20. Juliet Forman, *Bhagwan: The Buddha for the Future* (Cologne: Rebel Publishing, 1990), p. 270.

21. Milne, *Bhagwan: The God That Failed*, p. 179.

22. Osho, *Autobiography of a Spiritually Incorrect Mystic*, p. 157.

23. Sam, *Life of Osho*, p. 134.

24. Osho, *I Am the Gate* (New York: Harper and Row, 1977), pg 2.

Chapter 4: Crowley's Magick and Thelema

1. Aleister Crowley, *Magick Without Tears* (Tempe: New Falcon Publications, 1994), p. 244.

2. Aleister Crowley, *Magick: Book Four, Liber ABA* (Weiser Books, revised edition 1998 is the most recent), Introduction.

3. Ibid., Introduction.

4. Ibid., Introduction.

5. Ibid., Introduction.

6. From Hitler's defense of himself during his 1924 trial for high

treason following the failed Beer Hall Putsch. See William L. Shirer, *The Rise and Fall of the Third Reich: A History of Nazi Germany* (New York: Ballantine Books, 1983), p. 116.

7. Crowley, *Magick: Book 4*, Introduction.

8. P.D. Ouspensky, *In Search of the Miraculous: Fragments of an Unknown Teaching* (Orlando: Harcourt Brace Jovanovich, Inc., 1949), p. 14.

9. Francois Rabelais, *The Five Books of Gargantua and Pantagruel* (New York, Random House 1944), p. 154

10. For a good overview of these aeons, see Lon Milo DuQuette's *The Magick of Aleister Crowley: A Handbook of Rituals of Thelema* (San Francisco: Weiser Books, 2003), pp. 16-21.

11. See J. Daniel Gunther, *Initiation in the Aeon of the Child: The Inward Journey* (Lake Worth: Ibis Books, 2009), pp. 159-190.

12. Aleister Crowley, *Magick Without Tears* (Tempe: New Falcon Productions, 1994), p. 302.

13. Aleister Crowley, *The Confessions of Aleister Crowley* (London: Penguin Arkana, 1979), p. 398.

14. Crowley, *Magick Without Tears*, p. 95.

15. Ibid., p. 303.

16. Ibid., pp. 281-282.

17. Ibid., p. 282.

18. Aleister Crowley (editor) and Samuel Liddell MacGregor Mathers (translator), *The Goetia: The Lesser Key of Solomon the King* (San Francisco: Weiser Books, 1997), p. 17.

19. J.G. Bennett, *The Masters of Wisdom* (Wellingborough: Turnstone Press, 1982).

20. Crowley, *Magick Without Tears*, pp. 77-78.

21. Ibid., p. 78.

Chapter 5: The Gurdjieff Work

1. G.I. Gurdjieff, *Views from the Real World* (London: Penguin Arkana, 1984), p. 42.

2. James Moore, *Gurdjieff: Anatomy of a Myth* (Rockport, Element

Books, 1991), p. 318.

3. P.D. Ouspensky, *In Search of the Miraculous: Fragments of an Unknown Teaching* (Orlando: Harcourt Brace Jovanovich, Inc., 1949), p. 21.

4. Kenneth Walker, *A Study of Gurdjieff's Teaching* (New York: Award Books, 1969), pp. 149-150.

5. Ouspensky, *In Search of the Miraculous*, p. 123.

6. Ibid., pp. 82-86.

7. Ibid., pp. 294-295 and 376-378.

8. A good example of some of the Movements can be seen in Peter Brook's 1979 film, *Meetings with Remarkable Men*, which covers the first part of Gurdjieff's life before he began teaching. Of interest about this film is that the role of one of Gurdjieff's early mentors, Prince Yuri Lubovedsky, is played by the well known English actor, Terence Stamp, who was himself a disciple of Osho in the late 1970s.

Chapter 6: Osho's Teachings

1. Osho, *Autobiography of a Spiritually Incorrect Mystic* (New York: St. Martin's Griffin, 2000), 171.

2. Excerpt from an interview with Howard Sattler, 6PR Radio, Australia, at Rajneeshpuram in 1985.
   www.youtube.com/watch?v=5ocbZhRQS9I

3. Osho, *Socrates Poisoned Again After 25 Centuries* (Cologne: Rebel Publishing House, 1986), Chapter 10.

4. Alan Watts, *Psychotherapy East and West*, (New York: Vintage Books, 1975), pp. 2-3.

5. Gopi Krishna, *Kundalini: The Evolutionary Energy in Man* (Berkeley: Shambhala Publications, 1970).

6. Grof specialized, amongst other things, in working with disturbing states brought about by zealous spiritual practice. See Christina Grof and Stanislav Grof, *The Stormy Search for the Self* (Los Angeles: Jeremy P. Tarcher, 1990).

7. See Wilhelm Reich, *Character Analysis* (New York: Farrar, Straus,

and Giroux, 1990).

8. Osho, *Autobiography of a Spiritually Incorrect Mystic*, pp. 196-197.

9. Jeffrey J. Kripal, *Esalen: America and the Religion of No Religion* (Chicago: The University of Chicago Press, 2007), pp. 364-365.

10. Osho, *From Sex to Superconsciousness* (New Delhi: Full Circle, latest reprint 2008).

11. Bhagwan Shree Rajneesh, *The Rajneesh Bible, Volume III* (Rajneeshpuram: Rajneesh Foundation International, 1985), p. 770.

12. Osho, *Meditation: The First and Last Freedom* (New York: St. Martin's Griffin, 2004), p. 4.

13. Osho, *Meditation: The First and Last Freedom*, p. 53.

14. Osho, *Communism and Zen Fire, Zen Wind* (Cologne: Rebel Publishing House, 1989), p. 256.

15. A good account of the 'chosen enlightened ones' selected by Osho can be found in Juliet Forman's *Bhagwan: The Buddha for the Future* (Pune: The Rebel Publishing House, 1991) pp. 345-358. For the Gurdjieff anecdote see Fritz Peters, *Gurdjieff Remembered* (New York: Samuel Weiser, 1971), pp. 112-113.

Chapter 7: Kings of the Night

1. From John Symonds' Introduction to *The Confessions of Aleister Crowley* (London: Penguin Arkana, 1979), p. 25.

2. From George Meredith's Introduction to Juliet Forman's *Bhagwan: The Buddha for the Future* (Pune: The Rebel Publishing House, 1991), p. xix.

3. Israel Regardie and P.R. Stephenson, *The Legend of Aleister Crowley* (Las Vegas: New Falcon Publications, 1990), p. xiii

4. G.I. Gurdjieff, *Beelzebub's Tales to His Grandson* (New York: Viking Arkana, 1992).

5. See www.youtube.com/watch?v=Gq7IUM4lCrs. Tom Robbins was the rare case of an established popular author coming out openly in eloquent defense of Osho. Shown a transcript of Robbins' remarks about him, Osho once commented 'he is my

sannyasin (disciple).' Of course Robbins wasn't, at least not formally, but Osho made the remark to express his view that Robbins was attuned to his understanding.

6. Georg Feuerstein, *Tantra: The Path of Ecstasy* (Boston: Shambhala Publications, 1998), p. 4.

7. This view has been disputed by some, most notably by Paramahansa Yogananda's guru Sri Yukteswar as well as by the contemporary Vedic scholar David Frawley. Yukteswar argued in his book *The Holy Science* that we left the Kali Yuga and entered the Dwaparu Yuga around the year 1700 AD, which, interestingly, corresponds to the advent of the European Age of Reason. However, even in this interpretation of the *yugas*, we are still in a dark time, roughly equivalent to the cusp of dawn. Light is coming, but it is still very murky.

8. For a good discussion of this, especially as it applies to the coming energy crisis, see John Michael Greer, *The Long Descent* (Gabriola Island: New Society Publishers, 2008).

9. For an in depth explanation of evolutionary forces, see Brian Swimme and Thomas Berry, *The Universe Story* (New York: HarperCollins, 1994) pp. 118-130.

10. Osho, *The Book of Understanding* (New York: Harmony Books, 2006).

11. Steele, James & Mays, Simon (1995). http://web.archive.org/web/20021208040702/http://www.soton.ac .uk/~tjms/handed.html

12. For a good study of this, see Gerard Messadié, *A History of the Devil* (New York: Kodansha International, 1996). Messadié's brief remark in the book on Crowley can, however, be safely ignored—or alternately, studied as a good example of typical scholarly misinformation about Crowley.

13. Aleister Crowley, *Magick: Book Four, Liber ABA* (Weiser Books, revised edition 1998 is the most recent), Chapter 21.

14. Ibid., Chapter 21.

15. Aleister Crowley, *The Book of Thoth* (York Beach: Samuel Weiser,

1992), p. 106.

16. John P. Conger, *Jung and Reich: The Body as Shadow* (Berkeley: North Atlantic Books, 1988), p.85.

17. C.G. Jung, *Man and His Symbols* (New York: Dell Publishing, 1962), p. 72.

18. C.S. Nott, *Teachings of Gurdjieff* (London: Routledge & Kegan Paul, 1961), p. 86.

19. For Gurdjieff's threat to Jesse Orage, see William Patrick Patterson, *Struggle of the Magicians* (Fairfax: Arete Communications, 1996), p. 123. Although Osho spoke respectfully of Jesus as an enlightened master in most of his 1970s discourses by the mid-1980s he was skewering Christianity and Jesus more and more. This seemed to coincide with his years in Oregon and particularly toward the end just prior to the destruction of the commune. For a good example, see *The Rajneesh Bible, Volume III* (Rajneeshpuram: Rajneesh Foundation International, 1985), pp. 308-317.

20. C.G. Jung, *Aion: Researches into the Phenomenology of the Self* (Princeton: Princeton University Press, 1978), p. 42.

21. For an excellent discussion of this from the point of view of a committed Thelemic scholar, see J. Daniel Gunther, *Initiation in the Aeon of the Child: The Inward Journey* (Lake Worth: Ibis Books, 2009), pp. 159-191.

22. From a letter to Gerald Kelly. See Lawrence Sutin, *Do What Thou Wilt: A Life of Aleister Crowley* (New York: St. Martin's Griffin, 2000), p. 160

23. Benjamin F. Martin, *France in 1938* (Louisiana State University Press, 2005), p. 128.

24. Aleister Crowley, *Magick Without Tears* (Tempe: New Falcon Productions, 1994), p. 277.

25. Ibid., p. 278.

26. This was how he signed off one of his letters to his close student A.R. Orage. See Paul Beekman Taylor, *Gurdjieff and Orage: Brothers in Elysium* (York Beach: Weiser Books, 2001) p. 159.

27. Osho, *Autobiography of a Spiritually Incorrect Mystic* (New York: St. Martin's Griffin, 2000), p. 18.

28. M. W. Thring, *Quotations from G.I. Gurdjieff's Teaching* (Oxford: Luzac Oriental, 2002), p. 188.

Chapter 8: Self-Perfection and the Myth of the Infallible Guru

1. P.D. Ouspensky, *In Search of the Miraculous: Fragments of an Unknown Teaching* (Orlando: Harcourt Brace Jovanovich, Inc., 1949), pp. 71-73.

2. G.I. Gurdjieff, *Views from the Real World* (London: Penguin Arkana, 1984), p. 78.

3. Adi Da Samraj, a controversial American guru and contemporary of Osho's. He changed his name several times over the years (Bubba Free John, Da Free John, Da Avabhasa, etc., finally ending with Adi Da Samraj). He was another provocative crazy-wisdom magus, along with Chogyam Trungpa. His spiritual autobiography, titled *The Knee of Listening*, is excellent and more lucid than Crowley's *Confessions* or Gurdjieff's *Meetings with Remarkable Men*. During the late 1970s and 1980s, Adi Da was generally considered Osho's main 'rival guru'. However, in the last two decades or so of his life, he drifted off the radar, choosing to live on a remote south Pacific island surrounded by a small coterie of followers. He also began communicating strangely, writing tracts declaring his spiritual supremacy, capitalizing every word in a sentence, and in general making himself more and more inaccessible. His body of writings is, nevertheless, worthy of study by any serious seeker. His book on death and dying, called *Easy Death*, is, in my opinion, the best ever written on the topic.

4. For the following discussion of Adi Da's levels of consciousness scheme, see *The Heart's Shout: The Liberating Wisdom of Da Avabhasa* (Naitauba: Sri Love-Anandashram, 1993), pp. 74-86, as well as www.adidam.org/teaching/seven-stages.aspx

5. Ouspensky, *In Search of the Miraculous*, p. 66.

6. Karen Horney, *Neurosis and Human Growth* (New York: W.W. Norton and Company, Inc., 1991) p. 111.

7. Ibid., p. 110.

8. The Tibetan masters are hard to beat when it comes to precise, comprehensive explanations of the nature of reality and the mind. For a good treatment of the 'Relative' vs. 'Absolute' levels of reality, see Dzogchen Ponlop, *Wild Awakening: The Heart of Mahamudra and Dzogchen* (Boston: Shambhala Publications, 2003), pp. 232-235.

9. Georg Feuerstein, *Holy Madness: Spirituality, Crazy-Wise Teachers, and Enlightenment* (Prescott: Hohm Press, 2006), p. 396.

Chapter 9: The Spiritual Commune I: Paradiso and Inferno

1. Richard Fairfield, *Communes USA: A Personal Tour* (Baltimore: Penguin Books, 1972), p. 3.

2. Ibid., pp. 12-13.

3. Aleister Crowley, *The Confessions of Aleister Crowley* (London: Penguin Arkana, 1979), pp. 864-865.

4. Lawrence Sutin, *Do What Thou Wilt: A Life of Aleister Crowley* (New York: St. Martin's Griffin, 2000), p. 289.

5. Martin Booth, *A Magick Life* (Great Britain: Hodder and Stoughton, 2001), pp. 366-367.

6. Crowley, *Confessions*, p. 881.

7. Booth, *A Magick Life*, p. 376.

8. This particular attraction appears to have been free of Crowley's libido urges: there is no evidence that his interest in Loveday was anything but spiritual-magickal. See Sutin, *Do What Thou Wilt*, p. 302.

9. Gerald Suster, *The Legacy of the Beast: The Life, Work, and Influence of Aleister Crowley* (York Beach: Samuel Weiser, 1990), p. 67.

10. Richard Kaczynski, *The Weiser Concise Guide to Aleister Crowley* (San Francisco, Weiser Books, 2009), p. 29.

11. Sutin, *Do What Thou Wilt*, pp. 303-304.

12. Booth, *A Magick Life*, pp. 389-390.

13. Crowley, *Confessions*, pp. 917-919.

14. Roger Hutchinson, *Aleister Crowley: The Beast Demystified* (Edinburgh: Mainstream Publishing, 1998), p. 181

15. Israel Regardie and P.R. Stephenson, *The Legend of Aleister Crowley* (Las Vegas: New Falcon Publications, 1990), pp. 146-148. (Originally published by Mandrake in 1930).

16. www.gurdjieff.org/sharpe.htm

17. www.gurdjieff.org/roberts.htm

18. *G.I. Gurdjieff's Institute for the Harmonious Development of Man: Prospectus No. 1, p. 3* (private printing 1922).

19. James Moore, *Gurdjieff: Anatomy of a Myth* (Great Britain: Element Books, 1991, p. 178).

20. John Carswell, *Lives and Letters* (London: Faber, 1978), p. 213.

21. William Patrick Patterson, *Struggle of the Magicians: Why Uspenskii Left Gurdjieff* (Fairfax: Arete Communications, 1996), pp. 89-90.

22. Thomas and Olga de Hartmann, *Our Life with Mr. Gurdjieff* (Baltimore: Penguin Books, 1972), p. 121.

23. Ibid., p. 121.

24. G.I. Gurdjieff, *Life Is Real Only Then, When I Am* (London: Penguin Arkana, 1999), pp. 80-81.

Chapter 10: The Spiritual Commune II: Paradiso and Inferno

1. Rosemary Hamilton, *Hellbent For Enlightenment* (Ashland: White Cloud Press, 1998) p. 87.

2. The Sanskrit term *satsang* is a compound of the words *sat* ('truth') and *sangha* ('company'), thus meaning literally 'the company of truth' or more precisely, 'gathering together in the name of spiritual truth'.

3. There are many versions of these facts in print. A good, unbiased summary can be found at www.lang.nagoya-

u.ac.jp/proj/genbunronshu/29-2/potter.pdf. See also, Max Brecher, *A Passage to America* (Mumbai: Book Quest Publishers, 1993). A further good general overview can be found in Osho, *Autobiography of a Spiritually Incorrect Mystic* (New York: St. Martin's Griffin, 2000), pp. 246-259. For the casual reader, this may seem a dubious source for accuracy on this matter but the book was actually written by others ten years after Osho's passing and it gets its facts right. Another source that documents the same facts, equally accurately but with a more critical attitude toward Osho, is Satya Bharti Franklin, *The Promise of Paradise* (New York: Station Hill Press, 1992), pp. 291-309.

4. There are a number of sources for these further events, but probably the most thorough is Juliet Forman's *Bhagwan: The Buddha for the Future* (Cologne: Rebel Publishing, 1990).

5. Brecher, *A Passage to America*, p. 206-207.

6. Ma Prem Shunyo, *Diamond Days with Osho* (Delhi: Motilal Banarsidass, 1993), p. 86.

7. www.justice.gov/opa/pr/2005/September/05_crm_502.html

8. Franklin, *The Promise of Paradise*, pp. 193-194.

9.   www.iosho.com/oBook/The%20Life%20Of%20Osho/08-25-sheela.htm

10.   www.iosho.com/oBook/The%20Life%20Of%20Osho/10-42-jealousy.htm

11. William Golding, *Lord of the Flies* (first published by Pedigree Books in 1953). A classic novel about a group of young boys shipwrecked on an island, all of whom gradually form into two competing factions, one 'good', the other 'bad'.

12. Sam, *Life of Osho* (London: Sannyas Press, 1997), p. 147.

13. Hamilton, *Hellbent for Enlightenment*, p. 95.

14. Ibid., p. 63.

15. Christopher Calder, *Osho, Bhagwan Rajneesh, and The Lost Truth*, (http://home.att.net/~meditation/Osho.html).

16.   The   Oregon   History   Project

(www.ohs.org/education/oregonhistory/historical_records/dsp Document.cfm?doc_ID=452B9942-1C23-B9D3-68ABFC4C434B91C1)

17. Lawrence Sutin, *All Is Change: The Two-Thousand Year Journey of Buddhism to the West* (New York: Little, Brown, and Company, 2006, p. 315).

18. Ibid., p. 315.

19. Stephen T. Butterfield, *The Double Mirror: A Skeptical Journey into Buddhist Tantra* (Berkeley: North Atlantic Books, 1994) p. 183.

20. Judith Thompson and Paul Heelas, *The Way of the Heart: The Rajneesh Movement* (San Bernardino: The Borgo Press, 1988), p. 123.

21. Osho, *Autobiography of a Spiritually Incorrect Mystic* (New York: St. Martin's Griffin, 2000) p. 254.

22. Ibid., p. 255.

23. Henri Tracol, *The Search for Things that are True* (London: Element Books, 1994), p. 114.

24. Robert Augustus Masters, *The Way of the Lover* (West Vancouver: Xanthyros Foundation, 1989), p. 148.

25. Robert Anton Wilson, *Cosmic Trigger Volume I* (Tempe: New Falcon Publications, 1995), p. 163.

Chapter 11: Of Women and Sex

1. Aleister Crowley, *The Confessions of Aleister Crowley* (London: Penguin Arkana, 1989), p. 48.

2. Lawrence Sutin, *Do What Thou Wilt: A Life of Aleister Crowley* (New York: St. Martin's Griffin, 2000), p. 263.

3. Lon Milo DuQuette, *Understanding Aleister Crowley's Thoth Tarot* (San Francisco: Weiser Books, 2003), p. 127.

4. Dion Fortune, *The Mystical Qabalah* (San Francisco: Weiser Books, 1998), p. 132.

5. Rabbi David Cooper, *God is a Verb: Kabbalah and the Practice of Mystical Judaism* (New York: Riverhead Books, 1997), p. 214.

6. Georg Feuerstein, *Tantra: The Path of Ecstasy* (Boston: Shambhala

Publications, 1998), p. 135.

7. Ibid., pp. 224-225.

8. Israel Regardie, *The Eye In the Triangle: An Interpretation of Aleister Crowley* (Phoenix: New Falcon Publications, 1993), pp. 274-280.

9. Crowley's quoted comments for each woman are taken from www.hermetic.com/220/crowley-comments.html

10. Sutin, *Do What Thou Wilt*, p. 360.

11. Deida is not technically of the 'men's movement', being more of a teacher of tantric-style relationship, but some of his books address ideas that are frequently talked about in men's personal growth groups.

12. David Deida, *The Way of the Superior Man* (Boulder: Sounds True, 1997), p. 27.

13. Aleister Crowley, *The Confessions of Aleister Crowley* (London: Penguin Arkana, 1979), p. 96.

14. Ibid., p. 96.

15. Deida, *The Way of the Superior Man*, p. 116.

16. Crowley, *The Confessions of Aleister Crowley*, pp. 96-97.

17. Deida, *The Way of the Superior Man*, p. 178.

18. Ferne Jensen ed., *C.G. Jung, Emma Jung and Toni Wolff, A Collection of Remembrances* (San Francisco: The Analytical Club of San Francisco, 1982), p. 53.

19. Llewellyn Vaughn-Lee, *The Face Before I was Born* (Inverness: The Golden Sufi Center, 1998), p. 102.

20. Aleister Crowley, *The Law is For All* (New York: Thelema Media, 1996), Introductory comments.

21. Ibid., Introductory comments.

22. Fritz Peters, *Boyhood with Gurdjieff* (Fairfax: Arete Communications, 2006), pp. 136-137.

23. Bentley Layton, *The Gnostic Scriptures* (New York: Doubleday, 1995), p. 399.

24. www.gurdjieff-legacy.org/40articles/vitvitskaia.htm

25. G.I. Gurdjieff, *Meetings with Remarkable Men* (New York: Penguin Compass, 2002), p. 127.

26. J.G. Bennett, *Witness: The Story of a Search* (Wellingborough: Turnstone Press, 1983), p. 250.

27. James Webb, *The Harmonious Circle: The Lives and Work of G.I. Gurdjieff, P.D. Ouspensky, and Their Followers* (New York: G.P. Putnam's Sons, 1980), p. 384.

28. Sutin, *Do What Thou Wilt*, p. 230.

29. Webb, *The Harmonious Circle*, p. 245.

30. Ibid., p. 247.

31. Ibid., p. 251.

32. Ibid., p. 253.

33. The best source of information on the complex triangle between these three is Paul Beekman Taylor's *Gurdjieff and Orage: Brothers In Elysium* (York Beach: Weiser Books, 2001).

34. G.I. Gurdjieff, *Views From the Real World* (London: Penguin Arkana, 1984), pp. 126-127.

35. J.G. Bennett, *Gurdjieff: Making a New World* (Santa Fe: Bennett Books, 1992), pp. 179-180.

36. Ibid., p. 179.

37. The best description of Vivek's last days—she had changed her name to Nirvano at that point—can be found in Ma Prem Shunyo's *Diamond Days With Osho* (Delhi: Motilal Banarsidass, 1993), pp 243-247. The author was one of Vivek's closest friends and she corroborated Osho's statement about Vivek's depression. According to Shunyo, Vivek struggled for many years with what appears to have been a chemical imbalance. Ironically, she held something in common with Sheela in that she "never meditated" and was a "very difficult person," although she was also capable of moments of startling clarity, warmth, and wisdom. Based on Shunyo's descriptions of Vivek's mood swings one does wonder what simple antidepressants might have done for her, the quality and general social acceptance of these drugs increasing markedly only in the 1990s, after Vivek's passing.

38. Hugh Milne, *Bhagwan: The God That Failed* (New York: St.

Martin's Press, 1986), pp. 115-116.

39. Ibid., p. 118.

40. Juliet Forman, *Bhagwan: The Buddha for the Future* (Cologne, Rebel Publishing, 1990), p. 275.

41. Georg Feuerstein, *Wholeness or Transcendence? Ancient Lessons for the Emerging Global Civilization* (Burdett: Larson Publications, 1992), pp. 114-115.

42. Osho, *The Book of Woman* (New Delhi: Penguin Books, 2002), pp. 25-26.

43. Osho, *From Sex to Superconsciousness* (New Delhi: Full Circle Publishing, 2008), p. 108.

44. Crowley, *The Confessions of Aleister Crowley*, p. 851.

45. Osho, *From Sex to Superconsciousness*, pp. 43-44.

46. Osho, *The Book of Woman*, p. 214.

47. Ibid., p. 214.

Chapter 12: Of Drugged Sages, Drunken Idiots, and Mysterious Deaths

1. For a good overview of all this in the context of inner work and related matters, see Robert Anton Wilson, *Sex, Drugs & Magick* (Reno: New Falcon Publications, 2008).

2. Martin Booth, *A Magick Life* (Great Britain: Hodder and Stoughton, 2001), p. 477.

3. Hubbard had, however, as a young man, been a member of Crowley's OTO chapter in Los Angeles and thus was, at least for a while, technically his student. The expression 'very good friend' was doubtless his way of saying that he admired Crowley's ideas.

4. Grant, a prolific and brilliant writer, was, at one time, considered to be Crowley's heir apparent. He eventually left the OTO and founded his own organization after a dispute with Crowley's OTO heir, Karl Germer.

5. See www.beyondcommunion.com/path/020819jour.html

6. Israel Regardie, *The Eye In the Triangle: An Interpretation of Aleister*

Crowley (Phoenix: New Falcon, 1993), pp. 114-117.

7. P.D. Ouspensky, *In Search of the Miraculous* (Orlando: Brace, Harcourt, Jovanovich, 1949), p. 271.

8. Ibid., p. 8.

9. William Patrick Patterson, *Voices in the Dark: Esoteric, Occult, and Secular Voices in Nazi-Occupied Paris 1940-1944* (Fairfax: Arete Communications, 2000), p. 22.

10. J.G. Bennett, *Gurdjieff: Making a New World* (Santa Fe: Bennett Books, 1992), p. 120.

11. Ibid., p. 71.

12. William James, *The Varieties of Religious Experience* (New York: Barnes and Noble Classics, 2004), p. 334.

13. Bennett, *Gurdjieff: Making a New World*, p. 121.

14. *Idiots in Paris: Diaries of J.G. Bennett and Elizabeth Bennett, 1949* (York Beach: Samuel Weiser, 1991), pp. ix-x.

15. Ibid., p. x.

16. James Moore, *Gurdjieff: Anatomy of a Myth* (Rockport: Element Books, 1991) p. 354.

17. Sam, *Life of Osho* (London: Sannyas Press, 1997), p. 158.

18. Satya Bharti Franklin, *The Promise of Paradise* (New York: Station Hill Press, 1992) p. 324.

19. www.home.att.net/~meditation/Weaver.html

20. Bhagwan Shree Rajneesh, *Notes of a Madman* (Rajneeshpuram: Rajneesh Foundation International, 1985), pp. 15-16.

21. Aleister Crowley, *Magick Without Tears* (Tempe: New Falcon Publications, 1994) p. 476.

22. William James, *The Varieties of Religious Experience* (New York: Barnes and Noble, 2004), p. 335.

23. Juliet Forman, *Bhagwan: One Man Against the Whole Ugly Past of Humanity* (Cologne: Rebel Publishing, 1990), p. 418.

24. Franklin, *The Promise of Paradise,*, p. 295.

25. http://emedicine.medscape.com/article/204930-overview

26. http://emedicine.medscape.com/article/821465-overview

27. www.sannyasnews.com/Articles/OshoDentalChair.html

28. Forman, *Bhagwan: One Man Against the Whole Ugly Past of Humanity*, p. 145.

29. Osho, *Meditation: The Art of Ecstasy* (Pune: Tao Publishing, 2006), p. 87.

30. Ibid., pp. 87-88.

31. Ma Prem Shunyo, *Diamond Days with Osho* (Dehli: Motilal Banarsidass, 1993), pp. 252-253.

32. Osho, *Tantra: The Supreme Understanding* (Cologne: Rebel Publishing, 1984), pp. 33-34.

33. See Rupert Sheldrake, *The Sense of Being Stared At and Other Aspects of the Extended Mind* (London: Hutchinson, 2003), or David Fontana, *Is There an Afterlife? A Comprehensive Overview of the Evidence* (Ropley: O-Books, 2005), pp. 22-23.

34. Dion Fortune, *Psychic Self-Defense* (York Beach: Samuel Weiser, 1997), p. 5.

Chapter 13: Magical Warfare

1. From *Thus Spoke Zarathustra*. Walter Kaufman, *The Portable Nietzsche* (New York: Penguin Books, 1982) p. 321.

2. C.S. Nott, *Teachings of Gurdjieff: A Pupil's Journal* (London: Penguin Arkana, 1990), pp. 121-122.

3. Crowley used standard 'Solomonic' ceremonial magick. This generally involves a magician sitting in a circle that is fortified with holy names (usually Hebrew). Outside the circle is the 'triangle of art', in which is usually a piece of glass that is painted flat black, and functions as a device to gaze upon. Various magical formulae are spoken or chanted, placing the seer or magician into an altered state of consciousness. What follows then may variously be understood as shamanic journeying, communication with discarnate intelligences, or what Jung called active imagination, that is, direct communication with elements of one's own subconscious mind. However understood, the point is to gain mastery over aspects of one's own self as one encounters whatever experience may unfold in

the ceremony. Lower forms of this type of magic involve evoking entities to gain power over situations in one's life, or even over others. Crowley did, on occasion, explore this type of 'low magick', but overwhelmingly he was concerned with the invocation of the Holy Guardian Angel, or Higher Self—i.e., High Magick. The classic grimoires dealing with Solomonic Magic are generally recognized to be *The Key of Solomon the King*, edited by S.L. MacGregor Mathers (Mineola, Dover Publications, 2009); *The Goetia: The Lesser Key of Solomon the King*, translated by S.L. MacGregor Mathers and edited and introduced by Aleister Crowley (Austin: Ordo Templi Orientis, 1997); and *The Book of the Sacred Magic of Abramelin the Mage*, translated by S.L. MacGregor Mathers (New York: Dover Publications, 1975).

4. Aleister Crowley, *Magick: Book Four, Liber ABA* (Weiser Books, revised edition 1998 is the most recent), Chapter 21.

5. P.D. Ouspensky, *In Search of the Miraculous: Fragments of an Unknown Teaching* (Orlando: Harcourt Brace Jovanovich, Inc., 1949), pp. 226-227. Gurdjieff was also accused of being a black magician by some. Rom Landau compared him to Rasputin. See www.gurdjieff.org/munson1.htm

6. C.S. Nott, *Teachings of Gurdjieff: A Pupil's Journal*, p.122.

7. James Moore, *Gurdjieff: Anatomy of a Myth* (Rockport: Element Books, 1991), p. 204.

8. Lawrence Sutin, *Do What Thou Wilt: A Life of Aleister Crowley* (New York: St. Martin's Griffin, 2000) p. 317.

9. James Webb, *The Harmonious Circle: The Lives and Work of G.I. Gurdjieff, P.D. Ouspensky and Their Followers* (New York: G.P. Putnam's Sons, 1980), p. 315.

10. Sutin, *Do What Thou Wilt*, p. 318. In a brief exchange I had with another established author who said he had spent twenty years in the Gurdjieff Work, he reported that he had knowledge of Webb's sources but was 'not free to reveal them'. He believed that Webb's version was in fact what happened. As he charac-

terized it, 'Crowley was not ill-treated by Gurdjieff—he was appropriately treated by Gurdjieff. Gurdjieff rightly sent him away.'

11. J.G. Bennett, *Gurdjieff: Making a New World* (Santa Fe: Bennett Books, 1992), p. 168.

12. Reading Webb's *The Harmonious Circle*, that becomes clear. It is a monumental work on a scholarly level, particularly the latter section of the book where he unearths some of Gurdjieff's likely sources for the theory of his System. And yet the intense intellectuality of the work suggests a person out of balance, one longing to penetrate the teachings but unable to make the move from scholarly observer to actual participant. This has long been the key point that differentiates the mystic from the scholar. The former participates directly in the transformational work (regardless of 'success'), the latter watches and takes notes (although, it goes without saying, that it is entirely possible to be both mystic and scholar).

13. Fritz Peters, *Gurdjieff Remembered* (New York: Samuel Weiser, 1971), pp. 67-68.

14. Gerald Suster, *The Legacy of the Beast: The Life, Work, and Influence of Aleister Crowley* (York Beach: Samuel Weiser, 1990), pp. 92-93. Especially amusing is the 'sniffing' reference, being naturally associated with dogs. Gurdjieff used the dog as a symbol of a man dying before he 'makes a soul'. In many cultures, the dog is often symbolically associated with death.

15. For Crowley's suicidal thoughts, see Sutin, *Do What Thou Wilt*, p. 311; For Gurdjieff's, see G.I. Gurdjieff, *Life Is Real Only Then, When I Am* (London: Penguin Arkana, 1999), pp. 33-34; or Moore, *Gurdjieff: Anatomy of a Myth*, p. 222.

16. It was published in 1933 but later repudiated by Gurdjieff and withdrawn from circulation. It is now available again from Book Studio, most recent edition 2008. Webb (1980) suggested that the book revealed Gurdjieff's shadow side, namely, his capacity to manipulate. For an interesting short essay on the book, see

Sophie Wellbeloved, *Gurdjieff: The Key Concepts* (London: Routledge, 2003), pp. 92-94.

17. Andrew Cohen, *My Master is Myself: The Birth of a Spiritual Teacher* (Larkspur: Moksha Press, 1989).

18. Andrew Cohen, *Autobiography of an Awakening* (Corte Madera: Moksha Foundation, 1992).

19. www.oshoworld.com/biography/innercontent.asp? FileName=biography9/09-09-krishnamurti.txt

Chapter 14: Transmission and Legacy

1. Aleister Crowley, *The Confessions of Aleister Crowley* (London: Arkana Penguin Books, 1979), p. 399.

2. Aleister Crowley, with Victor B. Neuberg and Mary Desti, *The Vision and the Voice* (Boston, Red Wheel/Weister, 1998), pp. 12-13.

3. See James Moore, *Neo-Sufism: The Case of Idries Shah* at www.gurdjieff-legacy.org/40articles/neosufism.htm; also J.G. Bennett, *Gurdjieff: Making a New World* (Santa Fe: Bennett Books, 1992), pp. 61-62.

4. Bennett, *Gurdjieff: Making a New World* pp. 39-82.

5. The word *sadhu*, according to Feuerstein (1990), means 'virtuous'; Waite (2007) provides a more explicit definition: 'A saint, sage, holy man, literally leading straight to the goal, hitting the mark.' That is, interestingly, the opposite of the meaning of 'sin', which means 'missing the mark',

6. For Osho's comments on the three masters mentioned in this section, see Osho, *Glimpses of a Golden Childhood* (Rebel Publishing House, 1998).

7. Sam, *Life of Osho* (London: Sannyas, 1997), p. 31.

8. For more on all this, see Robert Schoch, *Voices of the Rocks* (New York: Harmony Books, 1999), or John Anthony West, *The Serpent in the Sky: The High Wisdom of Ancient Egypt* (New York: Harper and Row, 1979; reprinted by Wheaton: Quest Books, 1993).

9. For a comprehensive discussion of this, see Jeremy Naydler, *Shamanic Wisdom in the Pyramid Texts: The Mystical Tradition of*

Ancient Egypt (Rochester: Inner Traditions, 2005).

10. Rene Guenon's essay on Hermes can be found in *The Sword of Gnosis: Metaphysics, Cosmology, Tradition, Symbolism*, edited by Jacob Needleman (London: Arkana, 1986), pp. 370-375.

11. Andrew Rawlinson, *The Book of Enlightened Masters: Western Teachers in Eastern Traditions* (London: Carus Publishing, 1997), p. 159.

12. See John Hogue, *Nostradamus: The Complete Prophecies* (Shaftesbury: Element Books, 1999), pp. 145-150.

13. Ibid., p. 145.

14. Lon Milo DuQuette, *The Magick of Aleister Crowley: A Handbook of Rituals of Thelema* (San Francisco: Weiser Books, 2003), p. 9.

15. Charlotte Joko Beck, *Everyday Zen: Love and Work* (San Francisco: Harper and Row, 1989), p. 93.

16. J. Daniel Gunther, *Initiation in the Aeon of the Child: The Inward Journey* (Lake Worth: Ibis Books, 2009), p. 124.

17. For an interesting look at the issue of gurus who present themselves in a manner that does not tally with how they live their lives, and whether or not any of their students are actually growing, see Andrew Cohen, *An Unconditional Relationship to Life* (Larkspur: Moksha Press, 1995).

18. Joseph C. Lisiewski, PhD, *Ceremonial Magic and the Power of Evocation* (Tempe: New Falcon Publications, 2006), p. 18.

19. For a full analysis of all this, see William Patrick Patterson, *Taking With the Left Hand: Enneagram Craze, People of the Bookmark, and the Mouravieff Phenomenon* (Fairfax: Arete Communications, 1998), pp. 47-61.

20. See Needleman's excellent summary at www.gurdjieff.org/needleman2.htm. It should be borne in mind, however, that the article was written in 1992.

21. Osho, *Notes of a Madman* (Rajneeshpuram: Rajneesh Foundation International, 1985), p. 8.

22. The office of the Karmapa has been marred by dispute since the late 1980s, and currently two men are recognized as the 17th

Karmapa by competing factions, although one of these has a majority backing.

23. Swami Siddharth's account can be found at www.sannyasnews.com/Articles/Lama%20Karmapa.html

24. Lama Ole Nydahl, *Riding the Tiger: Twenty Years on the Road: The Risks and Joys of Bringing Tibetan Buddhism to the West* (Nevada City: Blue Dolphin Publishing, 1992), p. 127.

25. Hogue, *Nostradamus: The Complete Prophecies*, p. 180.

26. Susan J. Palmer and Arvind Sharma, *The Rajneesh Papers: Studies in a New Religious Movement* (Delhi: Motilal Banarsidass, 1993), pp. 155-156.

27. Juliet Forman, *Bhagwan: One Man Against the Whole Ugly Past of Humanity* (Cologne: Rebel Publishing, 1990), p. 148.

28. The usual assumed reason is that many do not want to be associated with the Oregon debacle of 1985, but just as often it is because the former disciple seeks to come out entirely from under the shadow of the master, and thinks that they can only truly do this by not associating with the master's name again. This was never better illustrated than in the case of Ouspensky, who, after leaving Gurdjieff, forbade his own students to ever mention Gurdjieff's name again.

Chapter 15: Return of the Magi: Of Prophets and Prophecies

1. J.G. Bennett, *The Masters of Wisdom* (Wellingborough: Turnstone Press, 1982), p. 11.

2. Margaret Anderson, *The Unknowable Gurdjieff* (London: Penguin Arkana, 1991), p. 133.

3. Bennett: *The Masters of Wisdom*, p. 25.

4. Lama Ole Nydahl, *Riding the Tiger* (Nevada City: Blue Dolphin Publishing, 1992), p. 202.

Chapter 16: The Importance of Practice

1. J.G. Bennett, *Witness: The Autobiography of John Bennett* (London:

Turnstone Press Limited, 1974), pp. 57-58.

2. See Dennis Waite, *Back to the Truth: 5000 Years of Advaita* (Winchester: O Books, 2007); or Dennis Waite, *The Book of One* (Winchester: O Books, 2004).

Chapter 17: Practical Exercises from Osho's Work

1. These and many more are given in Osho's *Meditation: The First and Last Freedom* (St. Martin's Griffin, 2004—the earlier, less comprehensive version of this book was called *The Orange Book*). For a couple of decades after his death, these meditations were trademarked (by Osho International Foundation, the official representative of Osho's work), but in early 2009 this trademark was cancelled by the Trials and Appeals board of the United States Patent and Trademark Office. This was brought about by a decade long effort by an alternate Osho group called Osho Friends International. For more information on the Osho trademark issue, see www.sannyasnews.org/latest/archives/341

2. See Sam's *Life of Osho*, pp. 20-23 and pp. 30-32 for an interesting account of Dynamic Meditation in the early 1970s.

Chapter 18: Practical Exercises from Gurdjieff's Work

1. For a good, up to date work on lucid dreaming, see Robert Waggoner, *Lucid Dreaming: Gateway to the Inner Self* (Needham: Moment Point Press, 2009).

Chapter 19: Practical Exercises from Crowley's Work

1. Aleister Crowley, *Book 4* (San Francisco: Weiser Books, 1980), p. 23.
2. Swami Vivekananda, *Raja Yoga* (New York: Ramakrishna-Vivekananda Center, 1982), p. 34.
3. Crowley, *Book 4*, p. 22.
4. George Feuerstein, *The Encyclopedic Dictionary of Yoga* (New York: Paragon House, 1990), pp. 409-410.
5. Crowley, *Book 4*, p. 23.
6. See Dennis Waite: *Back to the Truth: 5000 Years of Advaita*

(Winchester: O-Books, 2007), p. 570. ; or Feuerstein, *The Encyclopedic Dictionary of Yoga*, p. 14.

7. Crowley, *Book 4*, p. 24.

8. Dzogchen Ponlop Rinpoche, *Wild Awakening: The Heart of Mahamudra and Dzogchen* (Boston: Shambhala Publications, 2003), p. 84.

9. Crowley, *Book 4*, p. 38.

10. Changes in consciousness do not result in *wholesale* changes in one's outer reality, except in all but the most theoretical sense. A product of the new age fundamentalism that grew out of the 1980s was the inevitable exaggeration and distortion of the idea that 'you create your reality' and that, therefore, you should be able to transform your reality totally by changing your mind. This view neglects the fact that there are several levels of cause and effect (karma), some of which are entirely invisible and unrelated to personal reality—obvious examples being natural disasters, sweeping political changes, inherited genetic predispositions, and so forth. This does not mean that we cannot cause changes in our reality via conscious intention—we certainly can, and indeed this idea is the basis of magick and techniques of manifestation. The point being stressed here is that such changes are most often of a quiet and gradual sort, and on occasion are completely overridden by large scale factors.

Chapter 20: Historical Influences on Crowley's Magick and Thelema

1. Rossell Robbins, *The Encyclopaedia of Witchcraft and Demonology* (New York: Crown Publishers, 1959), p. 4.

2. See Plotinus, *The Enneads* (London: Penguin Classics, 1991).

3. For an interesting discussion of Gnosticism in contrast to several other traditions, see Kenneth Wapnick, *Love Does Not Condemn: The World, the Flesh, and the Devil According to Platonism, Christianity, Gnosticism, and* A Course In Miracles (Roscoe:

Foundation for *A Course In Miracles*, 1989).

4. A good recent treatment of Hermetic principles can be found in Timothy Freke and Peter Gandy, *The Hermetica: The Lost Wisdom of the Pharaohs* (London: Piatkus Publishers, 1997).

5. There are many quality books on Jewish mysticism. A classic one is by the noted scholar Gersholm Scholem, *Kabbalah* (New York: Penguin Books, 1978). For an excellent work on the Hermetic version, see Dion Fortune, *The Mystical Qabalah* (Weiser Books, 1998). Regarding the spelling of the word, there are three main forms: *Kabbalah* within traditional Judaism, *Cabala* for the Christian version, and *Qabalah* for the Hermetic version. It is the latter spelling (which Crowley used) that is most commonplace in modern esoteric teachings.

6. David Bakan, *Sigmund Freud and the Jewish Mystical Tradition* (New York: Schocken Books, 1965), pp. 248-270.

7. Stephen Mitchell, *Tao Te Ching* (New York: HarperPerennial, 1988).

8. *The Key of Solomon the King*, edited by S.L. MacGregor Mathers (Mineola, Dover Publications, 2009), and *The Book of the Sacred Magic of Abramelin the Mage*, translated by S.L. MacGregor Mathers (New York: Dover Publications, 1975).

9. Jeffrey J. Kripal, *Esalen: America and the Religion of No Religion* (Chicago: University of Chicago Press, 2007), p. 481.

10. For a good study of Dee, see Peter French, *John Dee: The World of an Elizabethan Magus* (London: Ark Paperbacks, 1987). A more recent effort is Benjamin Woolly, *The Queen's Conjurer: The Science and Magic of Dr. John Dee, Advisor to Queen Elizabeth I* (New York: Henry Holt and Co., 2001).

11. For more on Bruno, see Francis Yates, *Giordano Bruno and the Hermetic Tradition* (London: University of Chicago Press, 1991).

12. Stephen Batchelor, *The Awakening of the West* (Berkeley: Parallax Press, 1994), pp. 40-41.

13. Aleister Crowley, *The Confessions of Aleister Crowley* (London: Penguin Arkana, 1979) p. 403.

14. Aleister Crowley, *Magick Without Tears* (Tempe: New Falcon

Publications, 1994) p. 198.

15. Aleister Crowley, *Book Four* (San Francisco: Weiser Books 1980), Part One: Mysticism, pg 7.

16. Ibid., p. 7.

17. Ibid., p. 10.

18. Ibid., p. 10.

19. Osho, *Tao: The Three Treasures, Volume I* (Rajneeshpuram: Rajneesh Foundation International, 1983).

20. Crowley, *Magick Without Tears*, p. 69.

21. Ibid., pp. 227-228.

Chapter 21: Historical Influences on the Gurdjieff Work

1. This was Gurdjieff's curt response to the skeptical Boris Mouravieff's question as to where he got his teaching from. For an interesting perspective on Mouravieff vis a vis Gurdjieff, see William Patrick Patterson's *Taking with the Left Hand* (Fairfax: Arete Communications, 1998), pp. 63-95.

2. P.D. Ouspensky, *In Search of the Miraculous: Fragments of an Unknown Teaching* (Orlando: Harcourt Brace Jovanovich, Inc., 1949), p. 36.

3. Plato, *The Republic* (Mineola, Dover Publications, 2000).

4. Ibid., p. 173.

5. P.D. Ouspensky, *In Search of the Miraculous*, p. 30.

6. Ibid., p. 102.

7. Ibid., p. 302.

8. www.aquarian-age.org.ua/en/Hesychasm/hesychasm-2.html

9. G.I. Gurdjieff, *Views from the Real World*, (London: Penguin Arkana, 1984), pg 273.

10. Ibid., p. 275.

11. Jeremy Naydler, *Shamanic Wisdom in the Pyramid Texts*, (Rochester: Inner Traditions, 2005), p. 7; *Thames and Hudson Dictionary of Ancient Egypt* (London: Thames and Hudson Ltd., 2008), p. 16.

12. J.G. Bennett, *Gurdjieff: A Very Great Enigma* (York Beach: Samuel

Weiser, 1984), pp. 28-29.

13. Idries Shah, *A Perfumed Scorpion*, (London: Octagon Press, 1978), p. 86.

14. James Moore, *Gurdjieff: Anatomy of a Myth* (Rockport: Element Books, 1991), p. 31.

15. www.minnesotabuddhistvihara.org/PDF/newsletters/ Newsletter2.pdf

16. Gurdjieff, *Views From the Real Word*, p. 275.

17. Ibid., p. 275.

18. William Patrick Patterson, *Eating the 'I'* (San Anselmo: Arete Communications, 1992), p. 62. Trungpa himself was much in the category of a 'dangerous magus' or 'crazy wisdom master'. Considered to be both brilliant and controversial, he passed away in 1987 at the age of forty-eight due mostly to damage to his liver brought on by years of heavy drinking.

19. Ouspensky, *In Search of the Miraculous*, p. 302. See also William Patrick Patterson's video documentary, *Gurdjieff in Egypt: The Origin of Esoteric Knowledge* (Fairfax: Arete Communications).

Chapter 22: Historical Influences on Osho's Teachings

1. Osho, *Books I have Loved* (London: Tao Publishing, 2005).

2. Ibid., p. 4.

3. Walter Kaufman, *The Portable Nietzsche* (New York: Penguin Books, 1982), pp. 115-116.

4. Jacques Brunschwig and Geoffrey E.R. Lloyd, *A Guide to Greek Thought* (Cambridge: Harvard University Press, 2003), p. 227.

5. Plato, *The Last Days of Socrates* (London: Penguin Books, 2003), p. 56.

6. Ibid., p. 60.

7. Osho, *Autobiography of a Spiritually Incorrect Mystic* (New York: St. Martin's Griffin, 2000), p. 105.

8. For an accurate and thorough scholarly overview of Tantra, see Georg Feuerstein, *Tantra: The Path of Ecstasy* (Boston: Shambhala Publications, 1998).

9. Tantra was a major theme of Osho's teachings—more than anything, the generally informed public tends to think of him as a 'Tantric master' and this is probably as good a label as any. For a good overview of some of his clearest thoughts on the matter see Osho, *Tantra: The Supreme Understanding* (Cologne: Rebel Publishing, 1991), pp. 94-149. This book was originally titled *Only One Sky*.

10. Feuerstein, *Tantra: The Path of Ecstasy*, p. 243.

11. Stephen Mitchell, *Tao Te Ching* (New York: HarperPerennial, 1988).

12. Frederick Franck, *Zen and Zen Classics* (New York: Vintage Books, 1978), p. 217.

13. Osho, *Autobiography of a Spiritually Incorrect Mystic*, pp. 274-275.

14. Chogyam Trungpa, *The Lion's Roar: An Introduction to Tantra*, (Boston: Shambhala Publications, 1992), p. 21.

15. Chogyam Trungpa, *Crazy Wisdom* (Boston: Shambhala Publications, 1991), p. 3.

16. Osho, *Meditation: The First and Last Freedom* (New York: St. Martin's Griffin, 2004), p. 20.

17. See *Talks With Sri Ramana Maharshi* (Carlsbad: Inner Directions, 2000). For an in depth and comprehensive overview of Advaita, see Dennis Waite, *Back to the Truth: 5000 Years of Advaita* (Winchester: O Books, 2007).

Notes to Appendix I

1. Aleister Crowley, *Magick Without Tears* (Tempe: New Falcon Publications, 1994), p. 303.

2. Osho, *Books I have Loved* (Tao Publishing, 2005).

3. See Sam's *Life Of Osho* (Sannyas Press, 1997) for more.

4. Satya Bharti Franklin, *The Promise of Paradise* (New York: Station Hill Press, 1992), pp. 38-39.

5. Israel Regardie and P.R. Stephenson, *The Legend of Aleister Crowley* (Las Vegas: New Falcon Publications, 1990), p. 111.

6. Osho, *Autobiography of a Spiritually Incorrect Mystic* (New York, St.

Martin's Griffin, 2000), p. 157. The number was not static; new cars were being bought for him regularly. It just so happened that the commune self-destructed when he had reached the tally of 93 Rolls Royces.

Notes to Appendix II

1. Aleister Crowley, *The Confessions of Aleister Crowley* (London: Arkana Penguin Books, 1979), p. 140.
2. Israel Regardie, *The Eye in the Triangle* (Phoenix: New Falcon Publications, 1993), p. 14.
3. P.G. Maxwell-Stuart, *The Chemical Choir: A History of Alchemy* (London: Continuum Books, 2008), p. 1.

Notes to Appendix III

1. G.I. Gurdjieff, *Beelzebub's Tales to His Grandson* (New York: Viking Arkana, 1992).
2. For the best summary of his ideas, see Zecharia Sitchin, *The 12th Planet* (New York: Avon Books, 1978), or *Genesis Revisited* (New York: Avon Books, 1990).

Notes to Appendix IV

1. Pierre Evald's is the only serious attempt at a scholarly study of Osho's library that I am aware of. His excellent paper can be viewed at www.pierreevald.dk/osho.php
2. The largest library in the world is the Library of Congress in Washington, D.C. As of 2008 it holds around thirty-two million books.
3. Peter French, *John Dee: The World of an Elizabethan Magus* (New York: Routledge & Kegan Paul, 1987), pp. 43-44.
4. Ibid., p. 44.
5. That would suggest that either Queen Elizabeth was unusually open-minded for a head of state, or that John Dee was a tame fellow compared to Osho. Somehow, I more suspect the latter. Although, granted, Osho did not have to worry about being

roasted at the stake (at least, not that type of stake). Dee was considered fortunate to escape the Inquisition.

6. www.oshoworld.com/biography/innercontent.asp?
   FileName=biography6/06-10-library.txt

7. www.docstoc.com/docs/10454192/Speed-Reading-Study

8. Sam, *Life Of Osho* (London: Sannyas, 1997), p. 37.

Acknowledgements

A work of this nature depends on the efforts of earlier biographers, scholars of the perennial wisdom traditions, and students of the lives of these three teachers, and for that I am indebted to Georg Feuerstein, Israel Regardie, P.R. Stephenson, Gerald Suster, Martin Booth, Lawrence Sutin, Richard Kaczynski, Lon Milo DuQuette, John Symonds, Kenneth Grant, Roger Hutchinson, Robert Anton Wilson, James Moore, William Patrick Patterson, James Webb, Sophie Wellbeloved, Margaret Anderson, C.S. Nott, P.D. Ouspensky, J.G. Bennett, Maurice Nicoll, Fritz Peters, John Shirley, Garrett Thomson, Gary Lachman, Rosemary Hamilton, Satya Bharti Franklin, Juliet Forman, Ma Prem Shunyo, George Meredith, Paritosh (Sam), Satya Vedant, Max Brecher, Pierre Evald, Judith Thompson, Paul Heelas, James Gordon, Hugh Milne, and the nameless disciples who compiled Osho's *Autobiography of a Spiritually Incorrect Mystic*. My thanks to the following for commenting on the manuscript or otherwise providing assistance: Dennis Waite, John Hunt and the good people at O-Books, John Anthony West, Donald Michael Kraig, Satyen Raja, Shivam Skipper, Sharon Bloedorn, Amy Ash, Karen Epp, Yona Bar-Sever, Prem Pramod, Tatiana Nemchin, and last but not least, the staff at Waves, J.J. Bean, Saltspring, and Solley's coffee shops on Main where much of this book was written... fuelled by caffeine and the spirit of the night. All errors or inaccuracies in this book are of course solely mine.

About the Author

P.T. Mistlberger is a transpersonal therapist, meditation teacher, writer, and lifelong student of the perennial wisdom traditions, who has been closely involved in the work and ideas of Osho, Gurdjieff, Crowley, and other controversial spiritual teachers since the 1970s. He is the author of a previous work, *A Natural Awakening: Realizing the True Self in Everyday Life*. Since the late 1980s he has run personal growth trainings in North America, Europe, and Israel, and is currently based in Vancouver, Canada. He can be contacted via www.ptmistlberger.com

18/6/11

BOOKS

O is a symbol of the world, of oneness and unity. In different cultures it also means the "eye," symbolizing knowledge and insight. We aim to publish books that are accessible, constructive and that challenge accepted opinion, both that of academia and the "moral majority."

Our books are available in all good English language bookstores worldwide. If you don't see the book on the shelves ask the bookstore to order it for you, quoting the ISBN number and title. Alternatively you can order online (all major online retail sites carry our titles) or contact the distributor in the relevant country, listed on the copyright page.

See our website **www.o-books.net** for a full list of over 500 titles, growing by 100 a year.

And tune in to myspiritradio.com for our book review radio show, hosted by June-Elleni Laine, where you can listen to the authors discussing their books.

MySpiritRadio